MW00528222

Japan Emerging

Japan Emerging

Premodern History to 1850

EDITED BY

Karl F. Friday

IES Abroad Tokyo Center

WESTVIEW
PRESS

A MEMBER OF THE PERSEUS BOOKS GROUP

Westview Press was founded in 1975 in Boulder, Colorado, by notable publisher and intellectual Fred Praeger. Westview Press continues to publish scholarly titles and high-quality undergraduate- and graduate-level textbooks in core social science disciplines. With books developed, written, and edited with the needs of serious nonfiction readers, professors, and students in mind, Westview Press honors its long history of publishing books that matter.

Copyright © 2012 by Westview Press

Published by Westview Press,
A Member of the Perseus Books Group

All rights reserved. Printed in the United States of America. No part of this book may be reproduced in any manner whatsoever without written permission except in the case of brief quotations embodied in critical articles and reviews. For information, address Westview Press, 2465 Central Avenue, Boulder, CO 80301.

Find us on the World Wide Web at www.westviewpress.com.

Every effort has been made to secure required permissions for all text, images, maps, and other art reprinted in this volume.

Westview Press books are available at special discounts for bulk purchases in the United States by corporations, institutions, and other organizations. For more information, please contact the Special Markets Department at the Perseus Books Group, 2300 Chestnut Street, Suite 200, Philadelphia, PA 19103, or call (800) 810-4145, ext. 5000, or e-mail special.markets@perseusbooks.com.

Library of Congress Cataloging-in-Publication Data
Japan emerging : premodern history to 1850 / edited by Karl F. Friday.
p. cm.
Includes bibliographical references and index.
ISBN 978-0-8133-4483-6 (pbk. : alk. paper)—ISBN 978-0-8133-4561-1 (e-book) 1. Japan—History—To 1868. 2. Japan—History—To 1868—Historiography. 3. Japan—Civilization—To 1868. 4. Japan—Civilization—To 1868—Historiography. I. Friday, Karl F.
DS850.J37 2012
952—dc23

2011037797

For G. Cameron ("Cappy") Hurst, III
A pioneer in the field, and
Our mentor, colleague and friend

Contents

List of Illustrations

FIGURES

TABLE

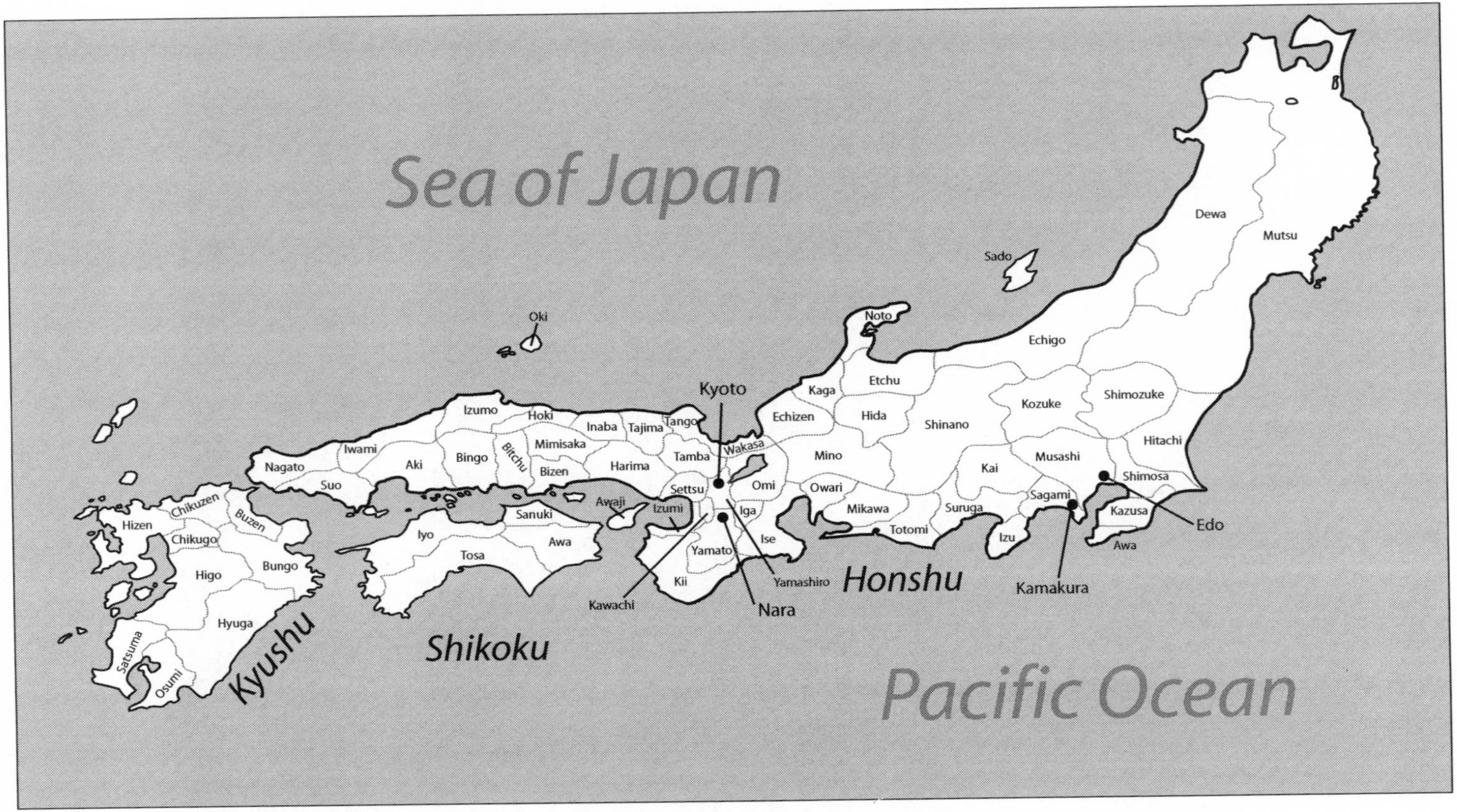

Figure 0.1. The provinces of premodern Japan

Preface

Scholarship on traditional Japan has grown spectacularly over the past four decades in both sophistication and volume. Historians in Japan have continued to be prolific, while in the West an unprecedented number of researchers specializing in the premodern (pre–seventeenth century) and early modern (seventeenth to nineteenth century) periods have entered the field. The new scholarship is marked by a shift in methodology from dependence on literary and narrative sources to reliance on documents, archeology, artwork, and other physical evidence of the past; by a shift in focus from the political and cultural history of elites to a broader examination of social structures; and by a reexamination—and rejection—tenet-by-tenet of what was once the received wisdom. As a result, the picture of the Japanese past now taught by specialists differs radically from the one current in the 1960s and early 1970s, when most of the textbooks still currently in use were written.

For early generations of historians, the story of premodern Japan was a quaint, romantic, but mostly inconsequential prelude to the appearance—as the result of thoroughgoing national reinvention in the Western image—of the twentieth-century military and economic superpower that more appropriately commanded scholarly attention. And in this version, the landscape of Japan's past was littered with failed regimes and radical breaks with what had gone before.

An emergent tribal confederation was transformed—very nearly at a stroke, in the wake of a spectacular coup d'état in 645—into a centralized imperial regime slavishly copied and shaped by reformers in awe of the splendor of Tang China. But this overly ambitious attempt to force Japanese square pegs into Chinese round holes was doomed from the start. Within decades of their inception, the organs and procedures of the system were abandoned as the ruling class became preoccupied with cultural affairs and divorced itself from concerns of governance, particularly outside the capital city. The imperial state was soon naught but a hollow shell: the effete, idyllic court aristocracy lost control over the political and economic life of the nation, while a stalwart and practical warrior class arose and took over the countryside.

In the mid-twelfth century (to continue this scenario), a series of events in the capital at last awakened provincial warriors to the fact that they, not the court nobility, had become the real figures of power in Japan. This discovery culminated in a great civil war and the founding of a new military government (the Kamakura Shogunate), which signaled the demise of the classical age and the onset of the medieval era and a "feudal" world ruled by warriors. Once loosed, however, the dogs of war were not easily restrained, and, like its European namesake, Japan's medieval period was a dark age of chaos and struggle as scores of regional warrior barons contested with one another for power. At last, in 1600, one of these warlords (Tokugawa Ieyasu) triumphed over his rivals and imposed a new countrywide order—but only by freezing society, stifling change, and hermetically sealing Japan off from contact with the outside world—that endured until the arrival of American gunboats brought it down in the late nineteenth century.

Despite the curious persistence of this view of things in popular accounts, however, historians have long since come to embrace premodern Japan on its own terms and, in so doing, have discovered a world of topics and developments incontestably linked to questions of contemporary concern. In twelfth-century Japan, students find, for example, a government dominated by private interest groups, as well as a culture that accorded women a fuller degree of legal and economic equality than do many modern societies.

In place of the sharp breaks and paradigm shifts that dominated earlier accounts, scholars today conceptualize Japanese history in terms of gradual—often surprisingly conservative—evolution within enduring continuities. These continuities begin, of course, with the island nation's geographic and political boundaries, which have remained largely—though not wholly—the same for most of the past millennium and a half. But they also include institutional continuities, such as the imperial state structure (which remained the anchor of political power and authority from the mid-seventh to the late nineteenth century), as well as enduring political dynamics: the interplay between *authority* (the right to rule) and *power* (the ability to rule), between civil and military power, between centralized (top-down) and locally based (bottom-up) models of authority, between rural and urban elites, and between centrifugal and centripetal forces.

The remarkable career of G. Cameron Hurst, III, to whom this volume is dedicated, looms large in the reinvigoration and reconsideration of premodern Japanese history. Hurst received his B.A. from Stanford in 1963 and his M.A. from the University of Hawai'i in 1966—the same year that John W. Hall published his landmark *Government and Local Power in Japan, 500–1700*, and ignited the revolution in methodology for studying premodern Japan that inspired the next generation of historians. From there, Hurst went on to study at Keio University in Tokyo, the University of Kyoto, and the University of Tokyo, before completing his Ph.D. at Columbia in 1972.

A prolific scholar, Hurst has written, co-authored, or edited five books and dozens of chapters and articles on Japanese history. He is also Japanology's foremost media star, contributing extensively to television programs, magazines, and newspapers. But it is in his contributions to teaching and program development that Cappy, as he is best known, has most deeply left his mark.

In 1969 he joined the faculty of the University of Kansas, where he served for two decades as professor of history and East Asian studies, director of the university's Center for East Asian Studies, and as chair of the Department of East Asian Languages and Cultures. Between then and 2010, when he retired as professor of Japanese and Korean studies and director of the Center for East Asian Studies at the University of Pennsylvania, Cappy was a charismatic and tireless champion of the study of premodern Japan. Along the way, he taught or administered programs at Doshisha University in Kyoto, CUNY Lehman Hiroshima College, Ewha Woman's University in Seoul, the University of Hong Kong, and the University of Washington; organized dozens of symposia and conference panels; delivered scores of guest lectures at institutions all over the globe; and inspired and mentored hundreds of undergraduates, graduate students, and junior colleagues. It would be no exaggeration to say that there are very few students or scholars of Japan whose lives and work have not been touched by Cappy's efforts.

This volume, then, is offered by his students, colleagues, and friends in appreciation of those labors, to commemorate his retirement. The other contributors and I would like to offer special thanks to Toby Wahl, Annie Lenth, and Steven Baker, at Westview Press, for shepherding the project through to completion; and to Gordon Berger and Lorraine Harrington, for advice, assistance, and support throughout the process of writing and publishing.

The history that follows comprises thirty-eight chapters penned by twenty-nine of the leading authorities in the field, introducing readers to the broad core topics commonly addressed in undergraduate survey courses. Collectively, they outline and explore the main developments in Japanese life from ancient times to the nineteenth century, focusing on turning points and developing social trends and structures and on the whys and hows (rather than the whos, whats, and whens) of Japanese political, social, economic, and intellectual evolution.

The chapters, which can be read or assigned in almost any order that readers or instructors see fit, are grouped into five thematic parts, each preceded by a timeline designed to assist readers in keeping events and developments in perspective. Part I, "Landmarks, Eras, and Appellation in Japanese History," focuses on the physical setting, the most efficient and helpful ways to subdivide the Japanese past, and the labels applied to periods of Japanese history. Part II, "Immigrants, Chieftains, and Kings in Ancient Times," addresses the key questions of when Japanese history began and just how ancient "ancient Japan" really was. Part III, "Court, Capital, and Countryside in the Classical Age," explores the emergence of the imperial (*ritsuryō*) state; the similarities and differences between the early (seventh- and eighth-century) and later (ninth-to-thirteenth-century) polities; and the dynamics that held the classical world together. Part IV, "Demesne, Dominion, and Diffusion in the Medieval Age," describes the decentralization and political fragmentation, social mobility and transformation, and institutional and cultural innovation that characterized the thirteenth to sixteenth centuries. And Part V, "Bureaucrats, Burghers, and Bailiwicks in the Early Modern Age," takes up the questions of how "reunified" seventeenth-to-nineteenth-century Japan really was and whether the brave new world of Tokugawa Japan is best understood as a postscript to the medieval era or a preface to the modern age.

NOTES ON NAMES, PRONUNCIATION, AND SPELLING

Western students of Japan are often startled to learn that, in spite of the complexity of its grammar and writing system, Japanese is actually a very simple language to pronounce. In its modern version, there are only five vowels and eighteen consonants, grouped into forty-eight possible syllables, most of which consist of a vowel, or a consonant plus a vowel. All of the vowels and all but two of the consonants can be found in English.

Vowels are always pronounced the same way. Long vowels, marked in transliteration with a macron (for example, ū), are simply longer in duration (actually two syllables); the sound does not change:

a as in f*a*ther
i as in t*i*er
u as in s*u*per
e as in *e*nd
o as in Ohi*o*

The consonant sounds include:

k as in *k*ick
g as in *g*ood
s as in *S*usan
sh as in *sh*ip

- **z** as in *z*oo
- **j** as in *j*ump
- **t** as in *t*op
- **ts** as in ca*ts*
- **ch** as in *ch*arm
- **n** as in *n*ew
- **h** as in *h*ouse
- **f** one of the three sounds not found in English; a cross between the English "h" and "f" sounds, pronounced like an *f* but with the lips together, rather than with the bottom lip against the teeth
- **b** as in *b*oy
- **p** as in *p*arty
- **m** as in *m*other
- **y** as in *y*es
- **r** not like the American English *r* (which is actually a semivowel), the Japanese *r* is flapped like a *d,* as in some British dialects ("Ve*r*y good, madam")
- **w** as in *w*onder

Japanese also utilizes a second "n" sound that is actually a syllable in itself. *N*s preceding vowels (na, ni, nu, ne, or no) are pronounced almost identically to their English counterpart. Those that precede consonants, come at the end of a word, or are marked with an apostrophe (n') are pronounced at the back of the mouth, very much like the English "ng" sound (as in ri*ng*), but without the harder "g" ending (as in shoppi*n'* or sitti*n'*).

Sometimes syllables consist of a combination of a consonant and a semivowel plus a vowel (ya, yu, or yo)—as in Tō*kyō* or *Kyō*to. Resist the temptation to pronounce these as "Tokiyo" or "Kiyoto"; the consonant plus semivowel sound should be a single syllable, as in the English word *cute.*

Syllables almost always divide after a vowel. The only exceptions are the special form of *n* described above, and some words in which consonants are doubled (for example, *kekkon, teppō, pittari,* and *bessō*), which actually represents two syllables with a glottal stop between them. The easiest way for Anglophones to approximate this is to pronounce the consonant twice, at the end of the first syllable and then again at the start of the following syllable (kek + kon).

Japanese names, in the text as in real life, are given surname first, in the reverse of the Western order. Thus Taira Shigemori is Mr. Taira, with the given or personal name of Shigemori. While publications aimed at popular audiences sometimes reverse the traditional order, such Westernization is déclassé and unsuitable for academic usage. After all, teachers and students in Japan do not turn "George Washington" into "Washington George"; we owe them the same courtesy.

And finally, a few special conventions apply to historical names: First, until modern times, individuals were often known by different names at different times of their lives. Many also carried titles of various sorts that functioned almost like part of their names. Because of this, scholars by convention usually refer to historical figures by the most famous of these names, irrespective of what he or she might have been called at the moment in time to which the writer is referring. Second, historical figures are by convention usually referred to by their given names, rather than their surnames. Thus shorthand references to Tokugawa Ieyasu become "Ieyasu," rather than "Tokugawa." This is in part a means of minimizing confusion between multiple (sometimes dozens of) people who share the same surname.

PART I

Landmarks, Eras, and Appellation in Japanese History

1

Japan's Natural Setting

Gina L. Barnes

A COUNTRY OF MOUNTAINS

Arriving in Japan at Narita or Kansai airport, one would hardly guess that mountains are the dominant topography of Japan. Far in the distance, a thin purple undulation of skyline tells differently. Satellite photos reveal an archipelago of steep, solid-green mountains and precipitous valleys across the four main islands: Hokkaido in the north, then Honshu, leading to Kyushu, with Shikoku nestled between (see figure 1.1).

Tectonic History

This archipelago is of relatively recent formation: it detached from the edge of the Eurasian continent only about 15 million years ago upon the opening of the Japan Sea. Surprisingly, the Japanese landmass was relatively flat when it detached.

The current mountains are products of tremendous tectonic stress, as the archipelago sits at the edge of the continental Eurasian Plate, facing two offshore oceanic plates—the Pacific Plate in the north and the Philippine Plate in the southwest. The continental plate is moving eastward, while the oceanic plates head westward, causing the islands in between to buckle and uplift into folded mountains. The landmass is still rising and the mountains are becoming higher, leading to one of the greatest rates of erosion in the world. Short rivers cut down steeply from the mountainous backbones of the islands, dumping their heavy sedimentary loads into the seas.

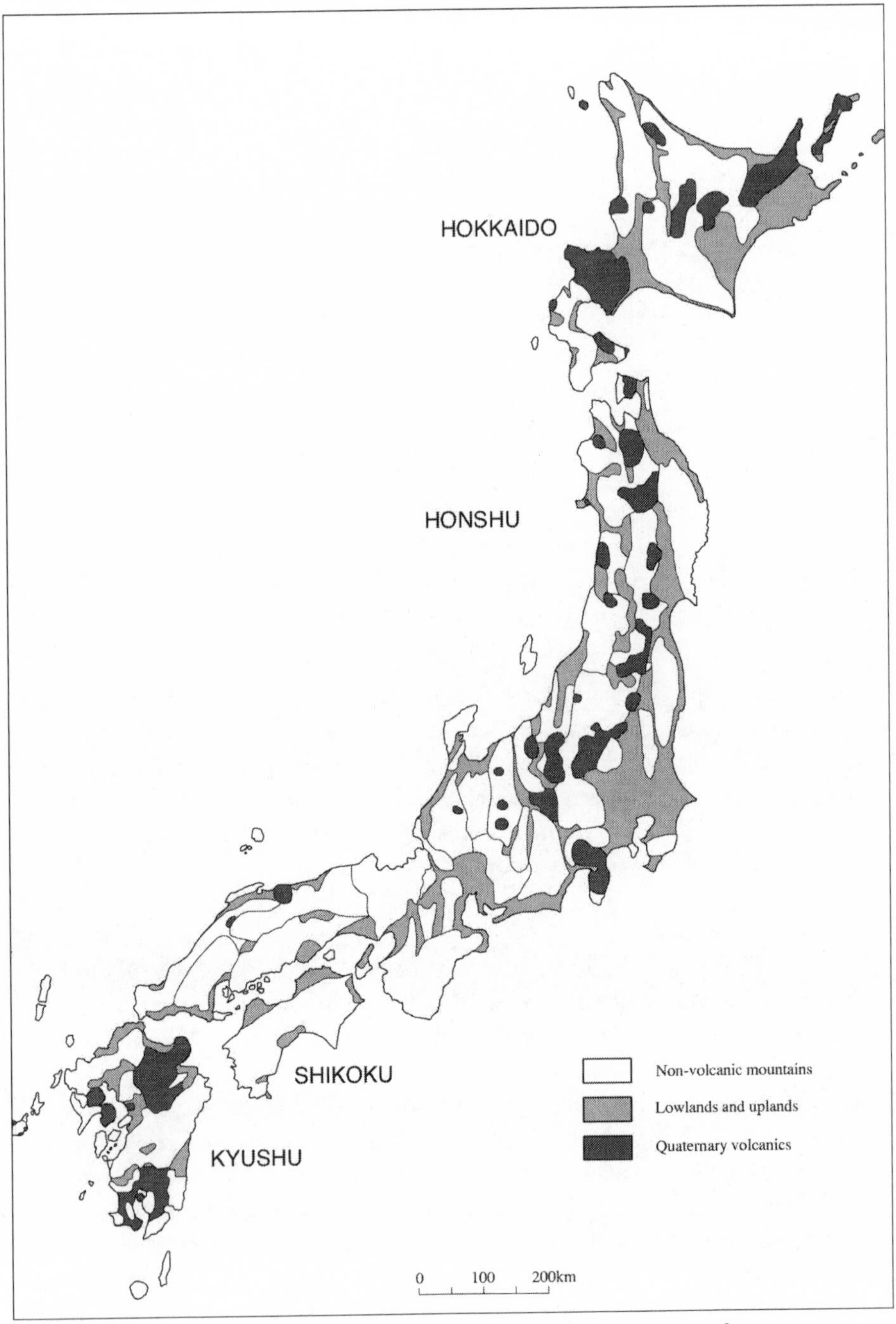

Figure 1.1. Japan and its mountains, most of which are folded along the axis of compression. The coasts and rivers are bordered by flat alluvial lands, but the uplands consist mainly of sloped or hilly volcanic deposits. (Prepared by Durham Archaeological Services after Yonekura et al., *Nihon no chikei 1,* fig. 1.3.2.)

This meeting of the plates also creates a subduction zone, where the oceanic plates are being drawn down (subducted) underneath the edge of the continental plate. Volcanoes and earthquakes are the result—constant menaces to life in the Japanese islands. The earliest volcanoes in the newly formed archipelago erupted around 14 million years ago, ranging across the Inland Sea area in western Honshu. About 2 million years ago, great volcanic explosions occurred in the Tōhoku region of northern Honshu; these left great collapsed calderas in the landscape, more than twenty kilometers in diameter, that now form some of the favorite crater lake tourist destinations, such as Lake Towada.

The current series of volcanic eruptions began around 700,000 years ago in three distinct areas: from Hokkaido through Tōhoku to central Honshu, from Tokyo south through the Izu Islands including Mt. Fuji, and north-south through Kyushu. Today, Japan claims about 10 percent (one hundred or so) of the world's active volcanoes, including Sakura-jima at the southern end of Kyushu. Nevertheless, volcanoes actually form a small proportion of all the mountains in Japan (see figure 1.1)—most of which are tectonically folded mountains.

New Coastal Plains

The contrast between mountains and plains is abrupt: the change in slope is often steep (35–40 degrees), wooded mountainsides meeting gently sloping (1–2 degrees) flatlands. Statistics vary: some say Japan is 86 percent mountains and 14 percent plains, while others measure 65 percent mountains and 35 percent plains. The difference lies in what is considered a plain (*heiya*). The coastal fringing plains are relatively flat, but the great Kantō Plain around Tokyo is actually a rolling dissected volcanic terrace landscape, while Hokkaido, northern Kantō, and southern Kyushu are characterized by broad volcanic slopes and plateaus. Add these volcanic uplands to the alluvial plains, and the percentage of "flat" land goes up. Thus, as a rule of thumb, everything but steep mountains fits in the category of 35 percent plains, and we can distinguish uplands, terraces, levees, and alluvial flats within that category.

The coastal plains that fringe the islands are relatively recent, emerging only when the high sea levels of the postglacial Climatic Optimum (6,000–4,000 years ago) receded. Groups of hunter-gatherers, the Jōmon, exploited the mountains (for hunting and gathering and some horticulture) and seashores (for shellfish collecting and coastal and deep-sea fishing). Soon thereafter, however, in the early first millennium BCE, rice agriculture was adopted from the continent. From that point onward, the plains became the focus of settlement, agricultural exploitation, and urban development.

Figures for today's Japan make it the fifth most densely populated country in the world, at an average of 343 persons per square kilometer. Nevertheless,

Figure 1.2. The city of Nagoya spreads over coastal plains and lower slopes, but the virtually uninhabited mountains behind rise abruptly. Remnants of the previous border between plains and mountain slopes can be seen in a series of isolated woods along the terrace paralleling the greenbelt line. (Author's photo, November 2008.)

this average is taken across virtually uninhabited deep mountains and solidly residential plains (figure 1.2). The density for Tokyo is 5,751 persons per square kilometer, seventeen times the "average" but indicative of the imbalance between mountains and plains. With so much population concentrated in the lowlands, mountain areas have been relegated to places of leisure: skiing, soaking in hot springs, viewing cherry blossoms. For the majority of the Japanese population, living in their national heartland is an unknown experience (figure 1.3).

A COUNTRY OF PADDIES AND DRY FIELDS

Historically, agriculture in Japan has been divided into upland crops and lowland rice paddies. Both uplands and lowlands are ecological areas subsumed under the term "plains," but their constituents are radically different. Uplands do not include steep mountain slopes, but in general the term refers to the rolling, eroded surface of volcanic terraces, riverine levees and terraces, and basin flanks. "Lowlands" generally refers to alluvial bottomlands and coastal flatlands. Over time, paddy fields have encroached on the uplands, but this is a trend now in reversal.

Rice Paddy Landscapes

Once wet rice agriculture was initiated in Japan, paddy field construction greatly modified the natural topography of lowland Japan. The nature of the soil was less important than the control of water: Rice paddies need to be leveled in order to maintain an even water depth for nourishing the rice during the three growing months. Thus, coastal plains of gley soils having small slope gradients were the first to be exploited from the beginning of the Yayoi period, in the early first millennium BCE. Rice paddies were initially carved out of river bottomlands, near sources of irrigation water, but these were often subject to

Figure 1.3. An isolated residence in the Yoshino River Valley, Nara Prefecture, located on a steep slope hosting a Japanese cedar (*sugi*) plantation. (Author's photo, August 2008.)

floods. With the advent of iron digging tools in the early first millennium CE, coarse sediments of lower basin flanks could be cultivated and irrigation canals built to supply them with water.

The first large-scale transformation of the lowland landscape, however, occurred in the seventh to eighth centuries, when the Yamato court adopted Chinese-style ruling technologies from Tang China. One of the innovations was the surveying and laying out of both agricultural land and cities on a grid framework, the *jōri* system. The gridded paddy fields, about one hectare in size, could then be subdivided into smaller units and allocated to individuals for rice tax purposes. The *jōri* layout can still be seen in the ever disappearing fields of the Nara Basin and in other areas of the Kinai, a regional designation for the "home provinces" of old Yamato now subsumed in Osaka, Kyoto, and Nara Prefectures.

Terracing of lower slopes and river valleys (of 5 to 6 percent slope) began in the seventh century. Only in the medieval period, however, as irrigation technology advanced, did terracing begin in steeper river valleys, with a gradual extension onto hillslopes (up to 16 percent gradient). This, in effect, pushed the forests farther up the mountains and increased the amount of arable land near the lowlands. In the Edo period, rice-growing was also extended onto volcanic soils in the Kantō region around Tokyo, a development facilitated by the digging of irrigation canals to supply both water and nutrients. In the nineteenth century, marginal lands including tidal flats, estuaries, lagoons, and some inland lakes were reclaimed for rice cultivation. For instance, Kyoto basin used to have a large lake near the juncture of the Yodo and Uji rivers that was eventually reclaimed for use as paddies.

The maximum extent of paddy land in Japan was reached in the early 1930s. Thereafter, the area devoted to rice production decreased with changing food preferences, including imported rice. In the inland mountain valleys, abandoned paddy fields are being recolonized by forest, while former paddies on valuable coastal plains have been consumed by urban expansion. Some of the large conurbations that now characterize many coastal areas have entirely obliterated the natural plains (Osaka, Kobe), and mountain basins are filling in fast with urban sprawl (Kyoto, Nara). Some municipalities have enforced greenbelt areas along the foot of the mountains, protecting the forests on the slopes, while others have encroached on lower foothills, blurring the distinction between plains and mountains. So the traditional landscape once demarcated between forest and paddy is now recast between forest, paddy, and conurbation.

Between Paddy and Forest

In contrast to lowland paddy fields, lands beyond the plains were highly diverse in the premodern period. Forests were traditionally distinguished by proximity to settlements: *Okuyama* (inner mountains) were places for hunting and collecting—rich in animal and plant (often nut) resources—while *satoyama* (village mountains) were forested areas near settlements and heavily exploited for wood for fires and tools; these trees were often chopped down and burned to provide more field space for dry crops. This latter pattern, referred to as slash-and-burn or swidden agriculture, lasted into the 1970s but is rarely seen today.

The deep mountain forests are discussed in a later section. Here let's look at the various forms of uplands within the plains that sustain dry-field crops, orchards, and vegetables. These plantings are often found around settlements, which were traditionally sited on high ground to avoid flooding. Even on alluvial flats, villages sat on natural river levees, and these natural levees also supported vegetable gardens. The difference in height between a paddy field and a vegetable garden could be as little as half a meter—reflecting the difficulty of lifting irrigation water up onto the levee.

A specific sector of Japanese plains is the volcanic terrace as seen in the Kantō Plain. The entire Kantō region, where Tokyo is sited, is such a terrace, comprising thick layers (some three hundred meters deep) of volcanic ash deposited in the Pleistocene period more than 10,000 years ago. Large rivers such as the Tone, Arakawa, and Sumida have washed out great portions of these layers. At the Nippori station on the Yamanote train line in Tokyo, one may see bluffs carved out by the Arakawa River towering above the tracks. Situated on these bluffs are Edo-period temples and their cemeteries, Tokyo University, and the

Ueno Park complex, including several national museums. When the Tokugawa established Edo as its capital, the bluffs were virtually unoccupied, with most activity carried out by fishing villages along the shore of Tokyo Bay. Thus developed the social distinction between the aristocratic occupation of the upper terraces now served by the Yamanote (hill-fingers) circle line and the commoner habitation of the coastal lowlands of *shitamachi* (lower town). But why were the bluffs previously unoccupied?

Volcanic soils in areas of high precipitation like Japan are notoriously poor in nutrients. The rain leaches out the calcium, magnesium, and potassium, and an unusual colloidal fixing of phosphate in volcanic soils also makes this element unavailable for plant growth. The absence of these vital nutrients from the Kantō Plain, plus their being too high above the streambeds for irrigation, made them poor for agriculture. Many volcanic soils around Japan, particularly on the flanks of volcanoes, are virtually unused for crops. They are often colonized by bracken, sasa bamboo, and pampas grass, as seen on the northern flanks of Mt. Fuji—used for filming galloping-samurai movies. Only with irrigation and fertilization have they been brought into production. Vegetables, particularly root crops such as radishes, carrots, and sweet potatoes, grow well in the fine-grained volcanic soils; orchards are another good investment, as in the thick deposits of white pumice of southern Kyushu.

Despite the image of Japan as a country of rice agriculture, in the nineteenth century before urbanization and industrialization, rice paddy accounted for 58.5 percent of the arable land, while dry fields amounted to a full 41.5 percent. To ignore the prominent role of dry crops in Japan's agricultural history is to misunderstand the life of the peasants, who were often barred from eating the rice they grew and were forced to subsist on dry crops such as barley and millet, and vegetables from their gardens.

A COUNTRY OF CLIMATIC EXTREMES

The Japanese archipelago, including the Ryūkyū Islands in the south, forms an arc that stretches from 45°30" to 20°24" north latitude. In North American terms, this is from Augusta, Maine, to Nassau in the Bahamas; in European terms, from Bordeaux, France, to the Aswan Dam on the Nile; and in Australian terms, from Brisbane in the north to Tasmania in the south. The archipelago thus stretches between cold temperate and subtropical regimes, so it is no surprise that Hokkaido is cool in summer and snowed over in winter, while Okinawa basks in mild temperatures year-round.

Japan, however, also has clear east-west differences in climate. It is a monsoonal country with seasonal influences of oceanic and continental regimes. In the summer, onshore winds from the Pacific Ocean bring heavy rain in June and typhoons from July through September; in winter, offshore winds from the continent bring cold air down from Siberia. These wintertime winds, however, are moderated by both the sea and high mountains. The dry, cold winds pick up moisture crossing the Japan Sea; then, as they are forced upward over the backbone of the mountain ranges, they drop their precipitation as snow. Thus, the northwestern flanks of Honshu and the high mountains suffer under heavy snowfall, while the eastern seaboard enjoys a maritime winter with relatively mild temperatures. The now dry winds, however, signal a deprivation of moisture, making winter in the eastern mountain flanks a time of forest fires.

The western snowbound regions are known traditionally as Snow Country, also the title of a novel by Kawabata Yasunari. The protagonist views a winter escape to the Snow Country as an antidote to city living. Not only did time slow down relative to other regions, because deep snow made getting about extremely difficult, but people living in these regions developed distinct customs to accommodate the snow. The children's snow "igloos" of Akita Prefecture are famous, and the Niigata Prefectural Museum gives an adult view of living with ten feet of snowpack in winter.

Average annual precipitation in Japan ranges from 944 to 4,060 millimeters, but usually exceeds 1,020 millimeters. This rate puts Japan on a par with South China, the Congo, and Brazil but is not as high as Indonesia's. One result of all this precipitation is a high rate of erosion of the land surface, as mentioned above; another is the acidification of volcanic soils as alkali and alkaline elements are leached away. A third is high humidity. In the dry winters, humidity can drop as low as 50 percent in Tokyo, but in summer, the humidity throughout the lower islands is often 98 percent even when it is not raining—all the more reason to escape to Karuizawa in summer, a famous mountain resort in central Honshu, or to Hokkaido for a cooler, drier summer.

A COUNTRY OF FORESTS

High precipitation also contributes to a lush growing season. The *okuyama* forests of Japan are dense, but their composition has changed over the centuries. Because of the north-south range of the islands, the climax forests in the northeast are cool temperate deciduous forests harboring familiar nut tree varieties such as chestnut, walnut, and deciduous oak. In the southwest, the climax forest was, until the arrival of agriculture, a laurelignosa forest similar to that in South China. This forest, largely unfamiliar to Westerners, consisted of evergreen oak, *hinoki* cypress (*Chamaecyparis* sp., used to build Ise Shrine and sushi bar counters), *kusunoki* (*Cinnamomum camphor*), and *sakaki* (*Cleyera japonica*, the sacred tree of Shintō), among others. This forest was decimated by the mid-first millennium CE because of agriculture, the iron and pottery industries, and urbanism. The majestic broad-leaved evergreens now survive only on shrine and temple lands, where they have been protected for the past fifteen hundred years; they can be seen in Meiji Shrine in Tokyo, around Miwa Shrine in Nara, and at Dazaifu in Kyushu, for example.

The changing state of Japanese forests throughout history has been perceptively and incisively documented by Conrad Totman. He identifies three periods of excessive forest degradation: in the Nara-Heian periods of court culture, affecting mainly the Kinai region; between 1570 and 1670, extending through the three main islands; and in the early twentieth century—the last period of destruction clearly apparent in photographs taken by visiting Westerners.

Anthropogenic destruction of upland woodlands is apparent from the very beginning of rice agriculture, in which Yayoi and Kofun farmers cut southwestern evergreens (both broad- and needle-leaved) for housing and fuel. With the beginning of stoneware production and iron forging in the Kofun period, vast areas were cleared to supply kilns and forges with fuel. This trend was accelerated with the intensification of shipbuilding and the introduction of monumental wooden architecture from China via Korea—the latter requiring kiln-fired roof tiles and large pillars to support the roofs. Construction of the Todaiji temple in Nara in 742 required eighty-four columns, each four feet in diameter and a hundred feet high, "900 hectares (2,200 acres) of first-quality forest" for post-and-beam buildings, and 163,200 cubic feet of charcoal for casting the large Buddha housed therein. By the end of this "Ancient Predation," as Totman terms it—between 2,000 and 1,500 years ago (0–500 CE)—the indigenous broad-leaved evergreen forest of southwestern Japan had mostly been replaced by secondary red pine growth.[1]

By 1550 CE, Totman notes, the forests of west-central Honshu were heavily exploited for green fertilizer and selected logging for elite construction until demand for monumental architecture and urban construction rose even higher after 1570. Competition for woodland products among elites, merchants, and commoners led to such devastation of the forest cover that upland erosion caused flooding and heavy sedimentation on the plains, disrupting the rice-growing tax base. Totman outlines two successive responses: an initial negative regulatory regime that closed forests to promote regeneration or prohibited the logging of certain tree sizes or species, and in the late Edo period, a positive afforestation movement that encouraged active intervention both governmentally and locally. The latter response was initially a grassroots phenomenon led by "itinerant scholars, village headmen, practicing farmers, minor officials," and others who wrote "agricultural treatises" or "farm manuals."[2] Their campaign sought to influence daimyo policies as well as villager activities.

Totman offers several reasons why afforestation was broadly successful: The natural succession patterns of forests suited human needs; cultural prohibitions against wheeled vehicles and crosscut saws prevented complete destruction of forests; an ideology of conserving resources and planning for the future made people sensitive to changes in their environment; the maintenance of peaceful relations discouraged outright competition; and the semiclosure of the country to outsiders precluded international sourcing of materials. It was eventually in the daimyos' interests to keep their forests well stocked not only to protect their tax base but to fulfill their feudal obligations, so afforestation efforts were permitted and encouraged on intimate local levels.

Totman cautions that the lush greenery seen today (as in the satellite photos referred to above) is a product of both eighteenth-century and postwar reforestation programs that have saved Japan from the fate of nations that have lost their forest cover. Unfortunately, much postwar forestry effort has been devoted to timber plantations, with the result that 41 percent of Japan's forests is now occupied by these monocultures with little biodiversity of plant and animal life.

A COUNTRY OF NATURAL DISASTERS

Because of its tectonic setting, Japan is subject to four major natural disruptions: earthquakes, volcanic eruptions, landslides, and tsunamis. A fifth disruption is caused by the islands' geographic positioning at the western edge of the Pacific, where typhoons (hurricanes) develop along the equator in the south and travel northwest toward land. Famine and disease can also be named as causes of considerable social disruption, having taken as much as a quarter of the population several times in the medieval period.

Perhaps living in a land of unpredictability has contributed to the Japanese reputation for stoic forbearance and a grain of fatalism. Nevertheless, the government has been working hard since the 1995 Kobe earthquake disaster to educate the public and provide resources for avoiding the worst of geohazard damages. The Japan Meteorological Agency (JMA) website provides key information on earthquakes, volcanic eruptions, and tsunami, in addition to weather reports including coverage of typhoon progressions.[3] These efforts are limited, however, as shown by the swiftness and severity of the tsunami accompanying the March 2011 Tōhoku-Oki earthquake. Buildings meeting earthquake standards survived the quake, but many were washed away in the tsunami. Moreover, the short time between the earthquake and tsunami, plus residential complacency, contributed to a great many deaths. One solution is not to build on coastal plains vulnerable to tsunami, as attested by stone markers showing historical tsunami heights. But human nature is territorially tenacious, and short-term economics override long-term safety.

The seismological network that monitors earthquakes throughout and around Japan is one of the world's most extensive and sophisticated. Informed by 4,400 monitoring sites, the JMA can, within three minutes of an earthquake, post on its website the location of the hypocenter (deep in the earth), magnitude, and seismic intensity. If the intensity of an earthquake is 3 or higher (on a scale of ten divisions), local "disaster prevention authorities" are notified within one and a half minutes, and reports are sent to the media. Since 2007, an Earthquake Early Warning service detects initial tremors and is able to issue warnings of an impending earthquake. The JMA issues a Tsunami Warning/Advisory within three and a half minutes of an earthquake in Japan, and it is linked into the Pacific Tsunami Warning Center in Hawai'i.

The tsunamis that often accompany earthquakes may be propagated by fault movement on the ocean floor or by landslides. These waves move out from the earthquake epicenter (location on the surface above a hypocenter) or the landslide entry point like the concentric waves caused by a pebble thrown in the water. In deep water, the waves are typically only one meter high and a kilometer apart, but they can move at seven hundred kilometers per hour. As they approach shallow water, the waves heighten and compact and can flow far inland at altitude. Waves twenty-five to thirty-five meters high are known in Japan to have flowed eleven kilometers inland, wiping out coastal fishing villages. The 2011 tsunami, however, was the first to destroy infrastructure to such an extent that it affected the global economy. As population densities increase in hazardous areas such as low-lying coasts or volcanic flanks, the world can expect to see more such disasters.

Volcano activity is also monitored by the JMA. Of 108 currently active volcanoes, 30 have seismic monitoring equipment in place, while the rest are under periodic observation. When magma moves in a volcanic chamber or neck, it causes earth tremors or small earthquakes. These are monitored seismologically just like those caused by subduction or active faults. Also in 2007, the JMA began its Volcanic Warning and Volcanic Forecast service. Volcanic ash warnings are also in place—as of this writing, for Sakura-jima and Suwanose-jima, both in southern Kagoshima Prefecture.

Volcanoes pose other hazards that can affect nearby communities. Pyroclastic flows and lahars are extremely dangerous. The former consist of hot ash, hot air, and rocks that can race down a mountainside at more than one hundred kilometers per hour. About a quarter of volcano-related deaths result from pyroclastic flows, as was the case for the volcanologists killed by the dome collapse on Mount Unzen in 1991. Once the ash settles from a pyroclastic flow or airfall, it can turn into a lahar (mud flow) if sodden with rain. Thus volcanic slopes can become highly unstable in a regime of high precipitation or further volcanic tremors or both. Given the steep-sided mountains with villages tucked at their feet, Japanese communities fear landslides more than they do other hazards because they are more frequent and can happen any time without warning.

Although "science" is not usually a part of Japanese studies, understanding the composition and natural environment of the Japanese islands is important to understanding life and events throughout Japan's history. The historical record is littered with natural disasters the likes of which modern society is struggling to prevent, mitigate, or avoid altogether in the future. The linking of scientific monitoring with local government is crucial for eliminating human-caused disasters such as the one bred of inaction after the Kobe earthquake. Living in Japan, one should be aware of the programs for protection and evacuation that this partnership offers.

A COUNTRY OF GREAT NATURAL BEAUTY AND COMPRESSED HUMANITY

In sum, Japan well deserves its tourist poster image, once one gets beyond the large cities, at least. Most human activity, however, occurs on the coastal plains. In particular, the urban corridor from north Kyushu through the Inland Sea to Tokyo is the focus of modern life. Iain Stewart, the BBC's geologist guide in the *Journeys into the Ring of Fire* series, made the outsider's observation that much of Japan's economic success is due to the compression of human resources on these coastal plains, allowing the development of efficient rail transport for commuting and for moving goods to and from deepwater ports. No other country in the world has population densities that can support such technologically advanced communication and transportation systems.

If one ventures into the countryside, on the other hand, it can be a long time getting there. One of the most interesting hot springs in Tōhoku (Geto, in Iwate Prefecture) is accessible only by a two-and-a-half-hour public bus ride over narrow mountain roads from the nearest train station. Getting from Matsumoto City in Nagano Prefecture across the border to the Kusatsu hot springs in Gunma takes more than three hours by bus. And traveling by train from Nagoya City to Lake Kawaguchi to see Mt. Fuji can take an entire twelve-hour day. All these places are worth the wait once gotten to.

Japan is a vast country with a rich history, a volatile but beautiful nature, and a welcoming population. Studying Japan within its natural setting is greatly enjoyable and ever intriguing.

Sources and Suggestions for Further Reading

See the bibliography for complete publication data.

Barnes, Gina L. "The Making of the Japan Sea and the Japanese Mountains: Understanding Japan's Volcanism in Structural Context" (2008).

———. "Landscape and Subsistence in Japanese History" (2010).

———. "Earthquake Archaeology in Japan: An Overview" (2010).
Bird, Winifred. "In Japan's Managed Landscape, a Struggle to Save the Bears" (2009).
Farris, William Wayne. *Population, Disease, and Land in Early Japan, 645–900* (1995).
———. *Japan's Medieval Population* (2009).
Minato, Masao. *Japan and its Nature* (1977).
Rothery, David A. *Volcanoes, Earthquakes, and Tsunamis* (2007).
Totman, Conrad. *The Green Archipelago: Forestry in Preindustrial Japan* (1989).
Trewartha, Glenn T. *Japan: A Geography* (1978).
Tsukada, Matsuo. "Vegetation in Prehistoric Japan: The Last 20,000 Years" (1986).
Yoshikawa Torao, Kaizuka Sohei, and Ota Yoko. *The Landforms of Japan* (1981).

Notes

1. Totman, *The Green Archipelago*, 17–18, 22.

2. Ibid., 116.

3. Japan Meteorological Agency (JMA), http://www.jma.go.jp/jma/indexe.html (accessed 24 August 2010).

2

Sorting the Past

Karl F. Friday

In the fall of 1999, as the world braced in panic over the utility shutdowns, bank crashes, and other horrors said to be awaiting us when computers (many of which kept track of years in two digits only) confronted the change from the 1900s to the 2000s, a clever piece of satire began popping up in email inboxes all over the United States. Purporting to be a translation from a Latin scroll dated "2 BC," a letter from someone named Plutonius to his friend Cassius, the text ranted over the pending "Y zero K" problem, lamenting the headaches that were sure to result from the transition from BC to AD and the need to begin counting years forward, after millennia of counting downward.

The punch line here is obvious, of course, but the joke also points us toward a number of important truths about labels like "premodern." First and foremost, they are all ex post facto—not merely unknown but also unknowable by the people living during the eras to which they are applied. The populations of "ancient" or "medieval" times could not have used these terms for their own eras, any more than citizens of the Roman Republic could have been counting backward toward the year zero. All peoples—everywhere and everywhen—live in contemporary times.

Second, labels like "BC" or "premodern" are teleological, in essence, if not necessarily in conscious application. That is, they do not simply point, in a value-neutral manner, toward later events or periods—the AD era or modern times—but also imply a developmental progression of some kind toward our own epoch.

And third, all historical labels are capricious, meaningful only in hindsight and as analytical tools. While societies with acute levels of historical consciousness—such as our own—can frequently become convinced that they have just witnessed an epoch-changing development, they are rarely, if ever, correct in this perception. For historians, "epoch-making" events and developments can be identified only in retrospect—usually the retrospection of decades or even centuries.

None of these observations should, however, lead us to the conclusion that periodization and era labeling are pernicious activities that would be best cast aside. They merely serve, rather, to caution us that all era labels are virtual, relative, and of finite utility. At the same time, periodization is essential to what historians do. It is to historians what categorization into species is to biologists. Without periodization, there can be no *history*—the critical reconstruction and analysis of the past—only random statements about *the past*—an undifferentiated and virtually infinite sequence of moments in time.

At a minimum, era labels provide us with an essential shorthand, without which any statements about the past become awkward and impossibly—not to mention artificially—precise. Labels enable us to generalize, and they assign an intuitively grasped identity to the periods to which we apply them. The rationale behind the construction of a university course titled "Premodern Japan" is, for example, more readily apparent than for one called "Japan between 500 and 1600."

If we cannot, then, dispense with periodization and era labels entirely, can we at least make certain that we are using precisely the *right* periodization scheme? Sadly, not so much. Unlike biological species, historical periods are imprecise and entirely relative constructs—they are pointers, not fixed delimitations. As world historian Jerry Bentley reminds us, identifying coherent periods of history is not a simple matter of discovering metaphysical or self-evident boundaries and defining moments; it is an abstracting process that turns on the issues and questions at the forefront of the researcher's own mind. Sorting out the past "requires the establishment of criteria or principles that enable historians to sort through masses of information and recognize patterns of continuity and change," while "changes in perspective can call the coherence of conventionally recognized periods into question."[1] Thus, evaluations of periodization schemes turn on utility, not Truth, and there is always more than one way to sort out the past.

While traditional Chinese historiography divided the country's history into dynastic periods and explained the divisions by reference to a dynastic cycle, Japan's political foundation myths postulated a single enduring imperial dynasty. Historians writing during the eras covered by this volume, therefore, typically broke the past down imperial reign by imperial reign, or cast it in Buddhist cosmological ages. But the latter is an impossibly broad division—embracing millennia—and the former an impossibly narrow one that imposes no conceptual order at all: There were 122 monarchs before the twentieth century, some reigning for only two or three years. Modern historians have, for that reason,

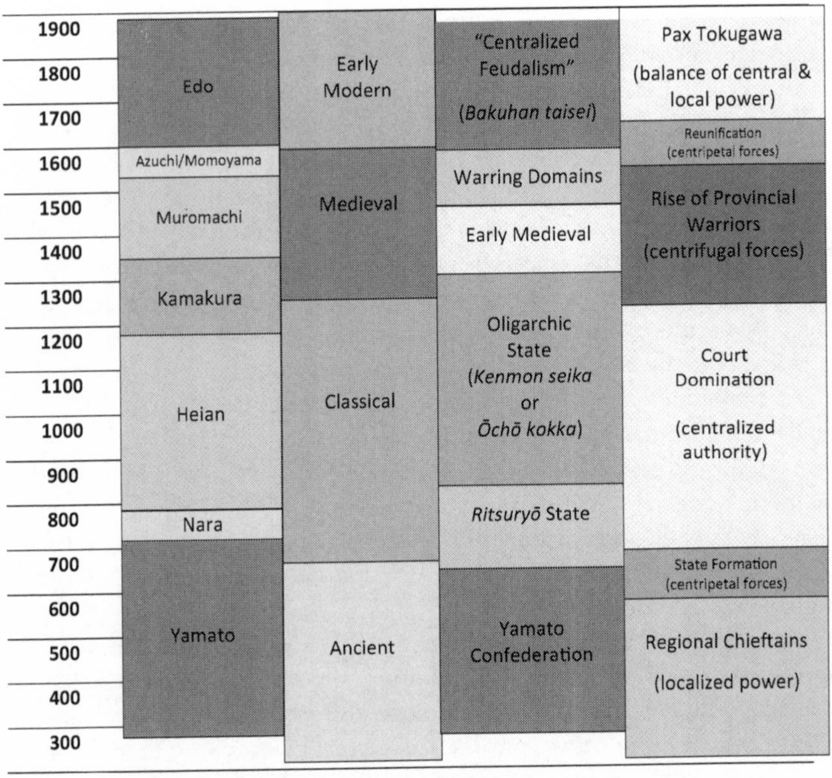

Figure 2.1. Periodization schemes for Japanese history.

devised a number of overlapping systems for conceptualizing Japanese history (see figure 2.1).

The most widely used and longest-standing periodization schema for Japan divides the past into "prehistoric" and "historic" epochs and sorts the latter (prior to the late nineteenth century, anyway) into eras defined by the geographic seat of power. There is some variation in this system among the various subfields of history, and individual scholars sometimes disagree over the precise boundaries of some periods, but by and large, this conceptualization identifies seven major epochs: the Yamato period, beginning around 400 CE and lasting until the turn of the eighth century; the Nara period (710 to 794); the Heian period (794 to 1185); the Kamakura period (1185 to 1333); the Muromachi period (1333 to 1568), subdivided into the Nanbokuchō (1336 to 1392) and Sengoku (1477 to 1573) periods; the Azuchi-Momoyama period (1568 to 1600); and the Edo period (1600 to 1868).

This system is useful for shorthand references ("the early Heian period" is less awkward than "the eighth, ninth, and tenth centuries," particularly in repetition), but many of the key cultural, social, economic, and political changes (and continuities) that interest historians did not coincide neatly with shifts in the location of the capital. A second common schema (and the one loosely employed for the organization of this volume), therefore, identifies four broad-stroke epochs: an ancient period ending in the mid-seventh century; a classical era, from the late seventh to the late twelfth century; a medieval period, from the late twelfth to the late sixteenth century; and an early modern period, from the late sixteenth to the nineteenth century. The ancient period is often divided into the protohistoric Asuka period (592–710) and three overlapping archeological epochs: the Jōmon (beginning around 14,000 BCE), Yayoi (from around 900 BCE), and Kofun (beginning around 250 CE) ages.

In recent decades, however, some historians have become uncomfortable with these labels, arguing first that they have been borrowed from European historiography (and therefore impose on Japanese history an outline of historical development originally developed for western Europe), and second that they, too, obscure important changes and imply differences that are not there. Among the numerous alternatives that have been proposed, at least two are worth mentioning here.

The first focuses on the nature of the sociopolitical power structure, identifying a Yamato Confederation era (from the fifth through the late seventh century); a *ritsuryō*, or imperial state, from the mid-600s until the late 800s; an oligarchic (*ōchō kokka* or *kenmon seika*) state from the mid-ninth through the mid-fourteenth century; an early (from the mid-1300s through the mid-1400s) and a late (fifteenth- and sixteenth-century) medieval polity; and a partially recentralized, warrior-led polity from the late sixteenth to the late nineteenth century, styled the *bakuhan taisei* in Japanese or (somewhat oxymoronically) "centralized feudalism" in English.

The second schema focuses on the dynamics of local versus centralized power and authority. This conceptualization gives us an age of locally based power under regional chieftains; a state-formation period beginning in the mid-500s during which centripetal forces dominated; an era of court domination lasting until the thirteenth century during which centralized authority persisted; an epoch characterized by the rise of provincial warriors and dominated by centrifugal forces, spanning the thirteenth to the sixteenth centuries; a reunification period during the late sixteenth and early seventeenth centuries when centripetal forces once again prevailed; and an era of balance between local power and centralized authority, lasting until the late nineteenth century.

There are, then, a variety of ways to conceptualize and divide Japan's past, and selecting the "best" method from among these is as futile and meaningless an effort as attempting to identify the "best" style of music. "Best," in both cases, is a function of context and purpose—best for *what*, and in *what sense*?

A periodization scheme that is helpful to legal historians may not be particularly useful to historians of technology, or to undergraduates enrolled in an introductory survey course. Thus, while era labels can easily take on lives of their own and can lure the unwary into conceptual traps, it is important that we never lose sight of the fact that periodization is nothing more than a tool for historical analysis. The key is not finding the right tool, but simply finding the right tool for a particular job, and not to confuse the tool with the material it is used to work.

Note

1. Bentley, "Cross-Cultural Interaction and Periodization in World History," 750.

3

Defining "Ancient" and "Classical"

Joan R. Piggott

Any historical narrative requires attention to time, and especially to the periods through which the story is told. Moreover, periodizing schemes change as different questions are investigated, different sorts of evidence are examined, and contexts shift. Historians of religion, art, literature, or music focus on different key moments, trajectories, and transitions than do researchers concerned with demographics, economics, or political structures. In the process, such researchers highlight different events, continuities, ruptures, and watersheds. Those who look at military history, gender relations, or technological developments create different timelines for their narratives. Those who focus on Japan's history tell their stories differently from those who look at the archipelago in the broader contexts of the Buddhist world, East Asia, or world history.

There are also different views as to the objectives of periodizing schemes. The master historian of the Mediterranean world Fernand Braudel (1902–1985) urged historians to get beyond events to study such long-term social realities as states, societies, economies, and civilizations.[1] Peter Burke says that we need to "make a narrative thick enough to deal not only with the sequence of events and the conscious intentions of the actors in these events, but also with structures—institutions, modes of thought, and so on—whether these structures act as a brake on events or as an accelerator."[2] Meanwhile the cultural historian Inoue Shōichi urges colleagues to reconsider the periodization of Japanese history in a broader Eurasian context. He explains his views:

> Since the Meiji era (1868–1912), the beginning of Japan's medieval age has been associated with warriors taking power [in the later twelfth century]. But at the same time, the medieval epoch in China is seen to have begun centuries earlier, and there are countries in the West that lack an ancient age (*kodai*). Should not our archipelago, located at the very eastern edge of Eurasia, be viewed in the context of world history?[3]

In his call, Inoue echoes a historian of Southeast Asia, Victor Lieberman, who has studied the historical commonalities of the Eurasian rimlands over the long term in an effort to transcend what he calls the East-West historical divide and a skewed European metanarrative of the modern nation-state.[4]

Here I want to consider how a few historians have periodized their narratives of Japan's earliest recorded epoch, while also examining how they name their periods and the historical trajectories that characterized those periods. To date, there has never been such a discussion in English, so the process will provide critical perspective on present practices, assumptions, and debates.

In textbooks and general overviews, one frequently finds periods named after the venue of the monarch's court and capital: there are the Asuka (592–710), Nara (710–794), and Heian (794–1185) periods. Another periodization system utilizes the family name of key power holders: the Soga period in the sixth and seventh centuries and the Fujiwara Regency period, from the later ninth through the early twelfth centuries.

But much of the postwar historiography written in Japanese divides history into four epochs: *kodai* (ancient age); *chūsei* (middle age); *kinsei* (early modern age); and *kindai* (modern age). This scheme is generally paired with a Marxist model of socioeconomic development that sees society developing from the primitive communalism of kin groups in prehistory, into a slave-based society in the ancient age, into a serf-based society in the medieval age, and then into a capitalist society in the modern age. Historians adopted this system of epochs because it was originally used in Europe and thus aligned Japan's history with global history. In their textbooks and overviews, however, Japanese historians have frequently divided each epoch into subperiods employing the names of palace location or power holders.

A difficulty associated with this epochal system is that there is little consensus as to when each of the four epochs began and ended, or the major historical trajectories characterizing each epoch. And in the case of *kodai*, our focus here, there are even alternative English translations, including "age of antiquity," "ancient age," or "classical age." I prefer the last, because it spotlights *kodai* as the foundational epoch of Japan's civilization, when its key elements were imported, adapted, and put in place. These elements include the Chinese-style monarchy of the *tennō* (literally, "heavenly sovereign"), together with its court and law; the use of Chinese language and learning as the basis of literacy and learning; the official religious system, including realm-protecting Buddhism and a realmwide system of shrines patronized by the throne; and the capital-to-provinces administrative system. However transformed through time, these elements endured for centuries, and some of them continue today as legacies of the classical age. Most scholars see this formative age beginning in the later seventh century. But its transition to the medieval age (*chūsei*) is the subject of debate. Its resolution requires agreement on the key historical trajectories and the identification of major changes and watersheds. To gain a sense of the thinking on these matters, I offer a sampling of how ten historians have characterized the major flows of classical history, and describe how and when they have marked the transition from classical to medieval within them.

A good place to begin is the work of Sir George Sansom (1883–1965), arguably the best-read historian of Japan in the twentieth-century West. In his three-volume *History of Japan,* published in the 1950s, he called the epoch during which Japanese civilization developed—from the fifth to the twelfth century—"antiquity." Concerning his views on trajectories and the significance of antiquity, Sansom explained how by the fifth century the early Yamato polity was receiving Chinese ways through contacts with Korean kingdoms. After the adoption of realm-protecting Buddhism by the mid-seventh century, the stage was set for "the full impact of Chinese institutions" at the eighth-century capital of Heijō (Nara).

But dynastic problems, the failure of laws regulating landholding and provincial taxation, and the rise of great private estates (*shōen*) signaled the failure of these systems by later Nara times. The Northern Fujiwara regent-led court, with its "rule of taste," presided over the realm from the later ninth century onward, and it terminated diplomatic contacts with the continent, even if commercial relations continued. A native script (*kana*) also enabled vernacular literature. Sansom specifically saw the aristocratic rule of taste as a reaction to Chinese influence.

Sovereign powers passed to the aristocracy by the turn of the eleventh century; and later in that century, by the time retired monarchs (*in*) led the court, warrior commanders were becoming increasingly important along with private estates, and both decreased the authority of court government. The result was emergence of the medieval "feudal" state by 1200, characterized by decentralized administration of the provinces in the hands of the provincial landed gentry.

John Whitney Hall (1916–1997) is another important historian of Japan writing in English. Inspired by Max Weber's historical sociology, Hall traced the development and transformation of authority systems in the capital and countryside over the long term in his *Government and Local Power in Japan, 500–1700* (1966). He began by describing a protohistorical society based on a kin system of segmenting conical clans (*uji*). This was followed by a confederacy of regional chieftains led by Yamato kings during the Tomb Age (300–600 CE), and then by a Chinese-style monarchy and state system that emerged around the turn of the eighth century. But after the move of the capital to Heian in 794, a return to reliance on kin structures and "abandonment of the concept of the state," as well as the rise of warrior bands and landed estates, advanced patrimonial and private authority from the early tenth century onward.

Despite Hall's employment of Weber's ideas, he was anxious that Japan's history be studied on its own terms. That is why he dug deeply into archives for documents that detailed local developments, which he then abstracted and wove into his narrative. In his textbook *Japan, from Prehistory to Modern Times,* Hall divided Japan's premodern history into an "aristocratic age" and a "feudal age," and he located the roots of the latter in the tenth century, with the rising influence of warrior commanders and their followings. This culminated still later in the formation of Kamakura warrior government in the late twelfth century. While Sansom and Hall came from different generations and used different methodologies and sources, they generally agreed on periodization and the main trajectories of change from the classical to the medieval age.

A third historian writing in English, Conrad Totman (1934–), brought a strong interest in environmental history to his survey history, *A History of Japan* (2000). Therein Totman traces human historical roles in Japan from top predator in pre–Agricultural Revolution times to manager of the human-centered biological community in classical and medieval times. He identifies two early epochs, based on changing technologies and modes of production, that look very different from those postulated by Sansom and Hall: up to 1000 BCE, "from origins to agriculture"; and from 400 BCE to 1200 CE, the "age of dispersed agriculturalists." In his narrative outlining developments during the second of these epochs, Totman describes the early *ritsuryō* polity as "classical" and traces a process of adaptation and change therein from mid-Nara times (c. 750). First regents and then retired monarchs presided as court leaders from the ninth century onward, and their eras saw the development of "classical higher culture." A transitional "diarchy," comprising joint rule by courtier and warrior centers, led the realm from the late twelfth to the later fourteenth century, until it was finally replaced by the medieval multicentered *kenmon* polity presided over by the Ashikaga shogun, Yoshimitsu (1358–1408; ruled 1368–1394).

A major influence on Totman's system of periodization was the historiography of Kuroda Toshio (1926–1993). Kuroda argued that traditional descriptions of the medieval polity focusing on the leading role of warrior organizations, the shogunates, is not sufficient. He insisted that we consider the effect of powerful households from various orders of society—aristocratic, military, and religious—that headed up realmwide chains of cliency relations and that he called "the gates of power" (*kenmon*). By later Heian times these alliances—others have called them factions—competed for power while cooperating with the throne to manage the realm. Each of the four types of *kenmon* had its own distinctive organization, but all looked to the monarch as their sacral liege, and the court remained the major ritual center as well as a place of mediation for quarrels between *kenmon*. In addition, all *kenmon* depended on the estate system presided over by the monarch for their livelihoods. Meanwhile a doctrine of the interdependence of the King's Law and the Buddha's Law supported this system ideologically, and the monarch's capital at Kyoto functioned as the political, economic, and cultural center.

Kuroda's timeline tracing the history of these cliency chains had three stages: First, in classical times the Northern Fujiwara regents and retired monarchs utilized their household offices to exercise political leadership at court; second, in the thirteenth and early fourteenth centuries, aristocrats resisted efforts by Kamakura's warrior government to suppress other *kenmon*; and third, in the later fourteenth century, the Ashikaga shogun Yoshimitsu successfully asserted leadership over other *kenmon*. Notably, Totman's periodization modifies that of Kuroda. Totman denotes only Kuroda's third stage as the "medieval *kenmon* polity," while he sees Kuroda's first two stages as the continuation of the long period of transition that bridged the classical and medieval ages. Totman therefore lessens the significance of the first warrior government at Kamakura.

William Wayne Farris's survey history, *Japan to 1600* (2009), adopts a demographic approach, in a move away from political and elite history. For the bones of his story, Farris proposes five demographic phases spanning the years 600 to 1600, with three that span the period from 600 to 1180: 600 to 800, "an end to growth"; 800 to 1050, the "age of depopulation"; and 1050 to 1180, the "epoch of minimal growth." As this scheme indicates, Farris thinks that population growth and the resource base turned static about 730 and remained so until 1300, due to poor harvests, adverse climatic developments, primitive agrarian technology, disease, and ecological degradation. Other trajectories described by Farris include the development of greater social complexity, the unraveling of the Chinese-style *ritsuryō* polity, the emergence of an aristocratic state, and rising levels of violence that resulted in militarization.

By 1050, he contends, specialization resulted in a trifunctional elite with aristocratic, clerical, and military members, and with each group having its own special relationship with the monarch. This growing complexity caused increasing competition and quarrels. Although Farris dates a modest economic recovery from the twelfth century, only after 1300 does he see signs of dynamic growth, along with still greater social specialization; tighter corporate organization of village, city, market, and family; and transformations in gender relations.

In addition to his demographic periods, Farris uses epochal designations such as "ancient" and "medieval," and he accepts that the medieval age began in the later twelfth century, when warrior commanders rose to become leaders of the realm. But those warriors and their institutions serve only as the subplot for Farris's main demographic story, and he reminds us that people from all orders of society considered the age one of millennial decline, the "Latter Days of the Buddhist Law" (*mappō*).

Kuroita Katsumi (1874–1946), whom many consider the founder of the formal study of documentary sources (diplomatics) in Japan, conceptualized Japanese history as divisible between an earlier age in which monarchs dominated the court and a later age in which warriors became increasingly influential as governors of the realm. Specifically, he proposed a four-part sociopolitical periodization that included an early age of conical clans (*uji*) that lasted through Nara times, followed by an age of aristocratic houses (*kuge*) that lasted through Heian times, followed by an age of military houses (*buke*) that lasted through 1868, and then the modern age. This basic schema has influenced historians writing in Japanese since Kuroita's time.

Another early contributor to the discussion was Hara Katsurō (1871–1924), who began using the term "medieval" to denote the intermediary and decentralized stage that bridged two more stable societies, the classical *ritsuryō* polity and the early modern Tokugawa shogunate. Hara was particularly interested in establishing parallels between Japanese and Western history; for instance, he drew a parallel between the fall of Rome caused by German invaders and the menacing of the Heian court by eastern warriors before the founding of the Kamakura shogunate in the 1180s.

In the same year when Kuroita died, Ishimoda Shō (1912–1986) wrote his magisterial *Chūseiteki sekai no keisei* (The Formation of the Medieval World). Still widely read today, it provides one of the most articulate discussions of the transition from the classical to the medieval age in Japan yet to be written. Therein Ishimoda describes the waxing and waning of the classical world based on Chinese-style monarchy and law and realm-protecting Buddhism. Following the Marxist model of social development, he saw Japan's state formation as an "Asian despotic polity" in which subjects were slaves because they lacked any claim to the land they cultivated. Deepening contradictions in this system fueled an epic struggle between "classical" and emerging "medieval" forces that eventually resulted in the decline of the former and the birth of the medieval world by the thirteenth and fourteenth centuries. In Ishimoda's view, the medieval was a synthesis between the world of kin relations in rural hamlets and the urban ways of the classical Heian capital based on Chinese-style law.

Through a case study of a well-documented estate (Kuroda no shō in Iga province, southeast of Nara), Ishimoda traced how deepening "contradictions" (i.e., threats to their livelihood) led local landholders to form dependent bonds—political, economic, and cultural—between themselves and patrons in the capital region who could protect their interests. Such bonds also allowed writing, law, and the prerogatives of office-holding to diffuse into the countryside. In this way the earlier social structure of rural hamlets was rearranged by the tenth century, a process that also saw the immanence of local deities replaced by the new idea of "reason" (*dōri*), whereby human relations should be organized according to law and human pragmatism. Over time, these same local landholders were being recruited as resident officials (*zaichō kanjin*) to serve at the headquarters of their provinces. Such service under provincial governors drew them more closely into the affairs of the capital.

Ishimoda identified the rebellion led by Taira Masakado (?–940), a local notable in eastern Japan, as "the dawn of a new age" in 939. Ishimoda portrayed Masakado and his peers as "feudal land holders" whose desire to protect privately opened fields led them to resist the authority of the distant Kyoto court. At the same time, Masakado and his peers prided themselves on being "men of the horse and bow," members of the military order. As authorities at the provincial headquarters responded aggressively and violently against Masakado and his ilk, these local elites sought stronger connections with noble or religious patrons in the capital, and so by the early eleventh century they were commending newly cleared lands to those patrons. According to Ishimoda, such contestations—which later involved warriors loyal to Kamakura's new shogunate in the thirteenth century—led to negotiation and significant changes in landholding practices, leading to conditions that Ishimoda saw as more serflike than slavelike. In this process, the earlier *ritsuryō*-based despotic polity, with its slave subjects, was transformed into a feudal polity in which commoner subjects held limited rights in land.

Ishimoda also argued that vectors and trajectories advanced at different speeds in the various spheres of politics, economics, and culture. For instance, in the cultural realm he saw the medieval age beginning during Heian times. He was particularly interested in the role played by Buddhist thought in loosening bonds of solidarity between aristocrats at court. He pointed to intellectuals like Yoshishige Yasutane (d. 1002) who were enthusiastic believers in Pure Land Buddhism (see chapter 21) as well as critics of government in their day. Ishimoda also pointed to the composition of prose tales (*monogatari*), the writing of military chronicles, and the compilation of short tales by courtier-intellectuals who were visibly conscious of being aristocrats at a time when Japan's classical world was breaking down.

He identified three pillars of the emergent medieval world in the thirteenth and fourteenth centuries, representing in turn the development of law, vernacular literature, and religion. Ishimoda saw all three as evidencing a heightened self-consciousness among commoners, and thus as signs of the opening of Japan's "first medieval age."

Ishimoda's grand narrative remains of significant interest, the more so because specialization has divided researchers studying the classical and medieval periods and the different spheres of politics, society, and culture whether urban or rural. Current researchers focus on particular trajectories outlined in Ishimoda's story, such as the development of urban kingship, the development of landholding in the countryside, and the emergence of what some researchers have called protonationalist sentiment by marginalized midranking courtier intellectuals.

Dynamic and abundant research on the tenth and eleventh centuries, which Ishimoda highlighted as an important transitional era, is of particular interest. Researchers have described a post-*ritsuryō* "court-centered polity" (*ōchō kokka*) that bridged the earlier monarch-centered polity and the regime presided over by retired sovereigns (*in*) at the turn of the twelfth century. Key components of this transitional polity included great noble households at the apex of long cliency chains—in English they have been called vertical factions—that transmitted the authority and influence of court leaders far into the countryside and then transported provincial treasures back to the capital. Many scholars consider the court and realm led by retired monarchs to be sufficiently different in organization to be pronounced "medieval," in contrast to their classical predecessor. To others, the twelfth-century court simply reflects the ongoing transition from classical to medieval, as Ishimoda argued.

Toda Yoshimi (1929–1991) and Irumada Nobuo (1942–) have clarified trajectories and structures of this "court-centered polity." Both see the transition from classical to medieval taking place from the eleventh to the twelfth centuries. They have studied new power arrangements that linked the capital and the provinces by way of the estate (*shōen*) system, which they see developing between the tenth and thirteenth centuries in response to the lack of a unified government. The system legitimated claims to private land in the hands of hierarchies (chains, factions) of holders with hereditary posts and perquisites (*shiki*) that gave them income from the land. At the apex of each hierarchy was a leading royal, court noble, or official religious institution with overlord rights, while management rights at the local level were held by resident manager-proprietors (*ryōshu*) supervising cultivators. The hereditary posts and perquisites of the latter represented a medieval form of older *ritsuryō* posts. Irumada's research adds the importance of regional differences between eastern and western Japan. The east was dominated by military men of the horse and bow (most commonly known as samurai in English) who shaped the characteristic institutions of Japan's medieval age. Those institutions, according to Irumada, glorified martial prowess, bravery, and violence. This same eastern Japan, Irumada argues, was the womb of the proprietor system, for it was there that land openers made huge plots available, organized themselves as a class, and created the shogunate. By contrast, the west was dominated by small landholders who had very different lifestyles and values and organized their communities in very different ways.

Cultural historians have also articulated the process by which intellectuals became increasingly conscious of Japan's distinctiveness from continental realms. Kimura Shigemitsu (1946–), for example, has described signs of changes in the *ritsuryō*-based administration of the capital city, the emergence of specialist producers, new links between center and periphery, and disregard of old status rules due to new problems with hygiene, infrastructure, and law and order. All show up frequently in the tenth-century record, as does popular enthusiasm for new religious cults. Moreover, diplomatic competition between Japan and the kingdom of Silla on the Korean peninsula, in addition to pirate attacks in the 830s and 860s, strengthened exclusionist sentiment at court, even as private trade relations with greater Asia grew stronger. The fall of the Tang dynasty in 907, together with the end of diplomacy with China, led to the decline of the earlier royal strategy of "ruling the realm through the literary arts" (*monjō keikoku*), a classical Chinese ideal. That development weakened the royal university while lessening the role of middle-ranking intellectuals whose functions at court and in diplomacy had been substantial. The result was a weakened monarchy whose projects and advisers were more limited, while aristocratic minister-affines were aggressively asserting their leadership.

Specifically, Kimura argues that Northern Fujiwara regents concentrated on developing court ritual. Rites increasingly replaced law as the courtiers' main concern, and poetry written in Japanese (*waka*), along with the arts of divination (*onmyōdō*), gained favor. To the extent that regents made clients of some intellectuals, they also contributed to increasing factionalization. This was precisely the context, Kimura posits, when "home realm" (*kokufū*) consciousness emerged among middling intellectuals, who were increasingly marginalized. This replaced the earlier sentiment favoring the replication of Tang ways, which had united court leaders and intellectuals from mid-Nara into early Heian times.

In light of this new home-realm consciousness, members of the intelligentsia became more interested in their surroundings. For instance, Minamoto Shitagō (911–983) compiled his *Wamyōruijūshō* dictionary of things Yamato in 930, to serve as a textbook for a princess. Similarly Minamoto Tamenori (?–1011) wrote his Buddhist handbook, the *Sanbōekotoba,* for another princess in 984. The scholar-monk Genshin (942–1017) produced his compendium of Pure Land texts, the *Ōjōyōshū,* in 985. And Yoshishige Yasutane's accounts of countrymen who had gained salvation in Amida Buddha's paradise, the *Ōjōden*, appeared around 1000. The trend culminated in the mid-eleventh century, when Fujiwara Akihira (?–1066) compiled his *Literary Essence of Our Court* (*Honchō monzui*) to preserve what he considered to be the finest writing in Chinese by Japanese literati up to his day. He also authored "*The New Monkey Music*" (*Shinsarugakuki*) as an encyclopedia of urban arts, specialties, and vocabulary for his time. As Kimura points out, Akihira's knowledge of China enabled his home-realm consciousness and the ability to articulate it.

The foregoing survey of various periodizing schemes and the debates they prompt highlights two key points. First, that we can refer to the period from the sixth or seventh century through the late twelfth (the epoch Japanese historians call the *kodai* era) as Japan's classical age, because that was when the foundations of Japanese civilization were set. And second, that the boundaries of this era are defined by how different historians envision aspects of the transition between the classical and medieval ages. We need not be bothered by the fact that some scholars think that the medieval age began in the twelfth century, while others date it from the fourteenth or fifteenth century. As long as we know what their reasoning is, we can recognize and learn from them, while integrating new information, arguments, and insights.

Sources and Suggestions for Further Reading

See bibliography for complete publication data.

Batten, Bruce. "Provincial Administration in Early Japan" (1993).
———. "Climatic Change in the Japanese Islands: A Comparative Overview" (2008).
Burke, Peter. *New Perspectives on Historical Writing* (1992).
Farris, William Wayne. *Heavenly Warriors: The Evolution of Japan's Military, 500–1300* (1995).
———. *Japan to 1600: A Social and Economic History* (2009).
Friday, Karl. *The First Samurai: The Life & Legend of the Warrior Rebel Taira Masakado* (2008).
Hall, John W. *Japan, from Prehistory to Modern Times* (1970).
Kiley, Cornelius J. "Estate and Property in the Late Heian Age" (1974).
Lieberman, Victor. *Beyond Binary History: Reimagining Eurasia to c. 1830* (1997).
———. *Strange Parallels: Southeast Asia in Global Context, c. 800–1830* (2009).
Mass, Jeffrey, ed. *The Origins of Japan's Medieval World: Courtiers, Clerics, Warriors, and Peasants in the Fourteenth Century* (1997).
Piggott, Joan R., ed. *Capital and Countryside in Japan, 300–1180: Japanese Historians Interpreted in English* (2006).
Piggott, Joan R., et al., eds. *Dictionary of Sources of Classical Japan* (2006).
Revel, Jacques, and Lynn Hunt, eds. "Braudel's Emphasis on the Long Term" (1995).
Sansom, George. *A History of Japan* (1958).
Sasaki Muneo. "The Court-Centered Polity" (2006).
Wickham, Chris. "Historical Transitions: A Comparative Approach" (2010).

Notes

1. Revel and Hunt, "Braudel's Emphasis on the Long Term."

2. Burke, *New Perspectives on Historical Writing*, 240.

3. Inoue Shōichi, *Nihon ni kodai ha atta no ka,* back cover statement.

4. Lieberman, *Beyond Binary History,* 1–21. Lieberman wants to get beyond comparison, but Chris Wickham says that historians need to look for and understand transitions and the causation than leads to breakdown.

4

Defining "Medieval"

Andrew Edmund Goble

This essay examines four key questions: When was the medieval period? Why do we refer to a medieval Japan? Was the medieval age an undifferentiated period? And what distinguishes the medieval from other periods of premodern Japanese history?

THE MEDIEVAL TIME FRAME: WHEN WAS JAPAN MEDIEVAL?

We may usefully understand Japan's medieval period as the approximately four hundred years from the late twelfth to late sixteenth centuries. As the term is commonly employed, the "medieval era" embraces at least seven overlapping subdivisions: the Kamakura age (named after a city) of 1180–1333; the Kenmu period (named for a calendar era) of 1333–1336, or 1336–1339; the Muromachi (named after a location in Kyoto) or Ashikaga (named after a ruling family) period of 1336–1573; the Northern and Southern Courts era of 1336–1392; the Ōnin period (named for a calendar era) of 1467–1477; the Warring States period (the name drawn from classical Chinese usage, but an apposite thematic descriptor for endemic warfare) of 1477–1573; and the Azuchi-Momoyama era (named after the location of warlord castles) of 1573–1598.

Scholars do not uniformly agree on precise starting and ending points for the medieval era. Moreover, the transitions between classical and medieval and between medieval and early modern are inextricably tied to questions of beginnings and endings. Thus we have a variety of possible dates and rough time frames for the start of the medieval period—the 1150s, 1180s, or 1330s—and for its ending—variously between the 1580s and the 1630s. These dates also reflect differences over the rhythms of the medieval age and over whether the medieval period was one era or an era with multiple stages.

THE GENESIS AND APPLICATION OF THE IDEA OF MEDIEVAL JAPAN

Why do we refer to a medieval Japan? The idea of a medieval period is an appropriation from European historiography. It was introduced into Japanese historiography in the early twentieth century by the historian Hara Katsurō, who, after extensive study of European history, concluded that Japan, too, had had a period in which medieval characteristics were prominent and thus that the idea that Japan had experienced a medieval era had explanatory utility. It has since become a central organizing element in the conceptualization of Japanese history. What prompted the appropriation of the term "medieval"?

The appropriation occurred in the context of the emergence of a new international and epistemological structure that privileged the achievements of the West and was associated with industrialization, imperialism, colonialism, and the onset of "modernity." Although the West was not internally monolithic, and certainly not a unified entity, as an overall package of Christian civilization creatively linked to a classical and biblical heritage and to the discoveries of the Enlightenment, it was represented as the supervening culmination of human progress. Its ability to conquer was the clearest proof, though tautological, of that superiority. A natural corollary of this ability was that other civilizations ranked below the West and that there was a hierarchy (not precisely delineated) into which societies, nations, or cultures might be placed. Japan was part of the world, and its level of civilization required clarification.

Arguably the most familiar part of the effort to demonstrate that Japan deserved to be evaluated highly is the program of industrialization and modernization pursued under the guidance of the Meiji leadership after 1868. Success was marked by such things as victory in war, the creation of a constitution and a constitutional monarchy, and the establishment of representative government. The 1899 abolition of the privileges of extraterritoriality enjoyed by Western nations was perhaps the most explicit symbolic recognition that Japan was civilized.

The modernization process also included studying new Western knowledge. As a corollary, existing Japanese knowledge in most fields was denigrated when not explicitly discarded. Historiography was one of the new areas, for an essential element in claiming to have a civilization was to be able to solidly document its past. This need lay behind the establishment of a historical compilation bureau, the gathering of primary sources from around the country, and an effort to bring new historical interpretations to the Japanese past. While the collecting of sources built upon a strong tradition of preserving and classifying primary materials, "scientific methodology" was a new element in interpreting the past. Exposure to Western history made it possible to examine Japan's past from entirely new intellectual (historiographical) perspectives. Japanese historians (a new professional category) trained in Western methods and theories appear, like their counterparts in fields such as medicine or philosophy, to have eagerly imbibed Western knowledge.

The notion of stages of historical progress, and of phases in the development of civilization, was integral to the new historiographical knowledge. The available Western divisions were "ancient," "medieval," and "modern"; the terms "antiquity," "classical," and "feudal" were also in use. Conveniently, Japanese words existed for most of these. For example, in his discussions of medicine and medical writings, the Buddhist physician Kajiwara Shōzen (1265–1337) uses the terms "former age" (*zendai*), "recent era" (*kinsei*), and "modern age" (*kindai*). Emperor Hanazono (1297–1348), in his discussions of history and human events, also uses *zendai*, *kinsei*, and *kindai*, as well as such terms as "the past" (*mukashi*), "antiquity" (*ko*), "previous ages" (*sendai*), "middle past" (*chūko*), "recent past" (*kinko*), "the contemporary present" (*tōji*), and "the future era" (*kōsei*).

A fuller study of how Japanese thinkers organized the past in the many centuries prior to the late 1800s might well reveal additional terms and, perhaps, might also demonstrate that thinkers living in different eras may have applied the same vocabulary for different periods of time. But the basic point here is that the modern classifiers of the past had readily available to them a vocabulary and a set of organizing concepts that could be appropriated and deployed. Scholars today use the standard progression of *kodai* (ancient), *chūsei* (middle, medieval), *kinsei* (recent, i.e., early modern), and *kindai* (modern), as well as *posuto modan* (postmodern).

Of these terms, "medieval" represents the most intriguing (and successful) effort to reconceptualize the past. While we have noted the prior existence of a "middle past," the term appears only to have been a fuzzy indicator of temporal distance and was not invested with any particular explanatory significance or connotation of an "age." The notion of antiquity was positively associated with a laudable and venerable earlier time. The idea of recent or modern was likewise a useful organizing category, although it was used in more than one sense: sometimes to imply an era that represented some form of decline from antiquity, but at other times with reference to specific areas of endeavor (such as medicine) to connote "recent" and "better." Thus the discovery of the medieval in Japan was an intellectually profound development.

Two main and complementary components informed the discovery of the Japanese medieval. The first was the realization that the concept of feudalism could readily be applied to Japanese history. The idea of feudalism has had its own history, and its usefulness as a construct has come under increased scrutiny. Nonetheless, it was a dominant historiographical concept in the late nineteenth and much of the twentieth century. Among the elements of feudalism, or that make a feudal society, non-Marxist historians identified such things as the absence of a strong centralized state; a mounted warrior class that dominated society; ties between leaders and followers in the warrior class based on the notions of service and reward, characterized as a system of lordship and vassalage; and an economic foundation in which wealth was not generated from money, commerce, or industry, but was based upon ownership or control of agricultural land and those who worked it.

These elements were all present in Japan. The relationship between central and local power shifted over time in Japan, but overall we may note decentralization and a hegemonic, rather than dictatorial, central authority. From the 1200s through the 1600s, local authority, in the form of increasingly autonomous warlords who ruled what were in effect their own principalities, held sway, and thus these centuries may be accurately characterized as decentralized. The samurai warrior class—mounted, proficient with bows and swords, supported by rights in land, expecting rewards in return for service, and at least professing a concern to loyal service (though it was a highly conditional, almost contractual matter)—was easily identifiable as an equivalent to European knighthood. The fact that a similar warrior society had not been identified elsewhere outside Europe apart from Japan, only strengthened the sense that Japan too had had a feudal stage in its history and thus could be seen as medieval.

The second component informing the discovery of the Japanese medieval was that turning points that might delineate a distinct period and distinguish it from what preceded and what succeeded it were also readily identifiable. In fact, they had been well known in Japan for some time. Those turning points were associated with the rise of the warrior class to political prominence, whereby the warriors became the single most important group in the shaping of Japanese history for some seven centuries. Two examples of such turning points serve also as a prelude to the varied perspectives on the medieval that exist in the present: the first from a Japanese Buddhist thinker writing in 1219, and the second from a Portuguese Jesuit writing in 1620.

Gukanshō ("Miscellany of an Ignorant Fool"; also translated as "The Future and the Past"), by the Buddhist priest Jien, is sometimes taken as Japan's first interpretive history, written from a Buddhist perspective. But while Jien's conceptualization of stages of Japanese history owes much to Buddhist notions of stages in the unfolding and influence of Buddhist truth in the world, he was prompted to write by an entirely secular phenomenon: the rise of the warrior class, as embodied in an autonomous warrior administration in the city of Kamakura (the regime we call the Kamakura shogunate). Jien could not predict the future, and so was unaware of the later history of the shogunate, or that warriors would dominate and be prominent for another 650 years, but he harbored no doubt that the emergence of the warriors (which had commenced more than sixty years earlier, in the 1150s, and was one of the verities of his life) was a significant turning point in Japanese history. It was this fact that he wanted to explain. Even though it was evident to many contemporaries that something significant had occurred in the late 1100s and that the imperial court aristocracy was being eclipsed, Jien's work was the first to treat the emergence of the warriors as a development of historical significance. As it happens, we also note the emergence of the warriors as a historical turning point.

The second example, provided by author Joao Rodrigues, offered a different date for a historical turning point catalyzed by warriors. Rodrigues lived in Japan from 1580 to 1610 and wrote his account in Macao a decade after being expelled. Nonetheless, he was fluent in Japanese, had interacted with learned people, and had witnessed the end of endemic civil war and the foundation of the Tokugawa shogunate. We may thus safely assume that his views are a reliable guide to contemporaneous Japanese understanding of the past.

Rodrigues divided Japanese history into three periods. The first, the "true and proper" period, lasted 1,960 years from the time of the first "king," Jinmu, until 1340. In this first era, "kings" (i.e., emperors) ruled, rites were performed, taxes were collected, and civil nobles served the court and also enjoyed revenues from lands. In addition, a military nobility was commanded by a shogun, who resided in Kamakura and who did not usurp the king's authority. The second period, lasting from 1340 to 1585, commenced with the rebellion of Ashikaga Takauji, who became shogun. In consequence the country fell into warfare, the realm was left without a central government, and the country was split up into "diverse kingdoms." Robbery, banditry, and piracy were rife; dwellings of the old nobility were burned down and destroyed; peasants lived a wretched existence. Trust was non-existent; treachery was commonplace. The "only authority was military might." The third period began in 1585, with the commencement of Hideyoshi's eventual subjugation of the country, but Rodrigues also acknowledged that this period "partly began" during the lifetime of Hideyoshi's lord, Nobunaga. After Hideyoshi's conquest of Kyushu in 1588, peace reigned; culture, trade, and laws were restored; and the old elite was completely replaced by a new, upwardly mobile one. It was eminently clear that the end of warfare and the restoration of civil rule, even though under the aegis of a shogun, was the hallmark of the new era. The failure to mention Ieyasu or the Tokugawa no doubt reflects an animus held against them by Rodrigues, but the overall schema remains intact.[1]

These two examples provide food for thought about pivotal turning points and historical rhythms. But it is clear that the emergence of warriors and the attendant introduction of violence into political life were seen as a major historical turning point. And Rodrigues is clear that the elimination of warfare also marked a defining moment.

To return to the discovery of the medieval, it would have been strikingly obvious to historians in the early twentieth century that there was much in the Japanese record, and in indigenous Japanese understanding of that record, to support the idea that Japan had in fact experienced a medieval period.

MEDIEVAL BEGINNINGS AND PIVOTAL TURNING POINTS

Was the medieval an undifferentiated period? The rise of the warrior class is inseparable from the dating of the medieval era; in essence these are the two elements around which debate about medieval chronology revolves. If the medieval period commenced with the emergence of the warriors in the late 1100s, it would make sense that it ended with the decline of the warriors in 1868. Since, however, there is clear consensus that the medieval era ended somewhere around 1600 and that warriors continued to be dominant after that, might it be possible that the emergence of the warriors did not mark the beginning of the medieval? But if that is the case, is the emergence and century-and-a-half-long existence of the first warrior government (the Kamakura shogunate) *not* medieval? That seems counterintuitive.

The issue of when the medieval period began is thus not a spurious one, and has wider implications for our understanding of the premodern era as a whole. Intriguingly, some of the understandings that have been offered reflect perspectives that we have already identified with earlier observers (Jien and Rodrigues) and involve crossroads in the 1180s and the 1330s.

The pivotal moment of the 1180s is based on the establishment of the first warrior government, the Kamakura shogunate. Its historical significance, understood then as well as now, lay in the fact that for the first time the traditional ruling elite had lost its ability to control both substantial portions of the country and a significant social group—the warrior class of eastern Japan. A much older narrative, that the rise of the warrior class was inevitable, is no longer regarded as meaningful and has been superseded by the realization that the rise of the warriors was facilitated by particular circumstances and was not predictable. This perspective of contingency, which also argues against any notion that warriors had identifiable longer-term goals, is strengthened by the fact that the first shogunate acted in concert with the old polity (centered in the imperial capital of Kyoto) to maintain, rather than eliminate, structures of authority, despite the shogunate's military dominance. That said, over time the shogunate did become the senior partner in this so-called dual polity.

Evidence for designating the 1330s as a turning point suggests a rupture rather than a transition. In this view, the first shogunate was the result more of an evolution than of a sharp break. The change initiated in the 1330s is highlighted by three points. First, the Kamakura shogunate was totally extirpated; this was a qualitative change from the past practices that had effected political change through institutional restructuring rather than elimination. Second, sharp ideological divisions emerged in the 1330s. The conflict, although often mistaken as one between warriors and civil authority, was over competing visions of the future—the past was not the issue. Third, violence emerged as an accepted political tool, and warfare became a new element in Japanese society. As a result, warriors became the driving force of political and institutional change, thereby eclipsing an order of civil aristocrats that had held sway since the mid-600s.

The factual basis for calling either the 1180s or the 1330s a turning point is not in dispute. Accordingly (and while my personal inclination is to see the 1330s as the more powerful catalyst for a churning medieval era), there is much merit in considering the medieval era, like others, a dynamic one and discerning several stages within it. As the chronological-named periods noted at the beginning of this chapter suggest, the number of possibilities for slicing and dicing the medieval is virtually limitless. Here, however, I modestly divide the medieval era into two broad phases, which we may label early and late medieval. The early medieval encompasses the emergence of warrior political power in the late 1100s and the demise of the first warrior political institution, the Kamakura shogunate, which was distinguished by its governing ethos of adjudication and negotiation. The late medieval commenced with an explosion of violence and came to an end when warfare was brought under control two and a half centuries later. Warrior institutions of this age were distinguished by the fact that overt military power provided their legitimacy.

I now identify specific aspects of the early and the late medieval, along with broader characteristics that distinguish the medieval from other eras.

SOME CHARACTERISTICS OF THE MEDIEVAL AGE

What distinguishes the medieval period? Three characteristics differentiate it from the preceding classical (Heian) period and the succeeding early modern (Tokugawa) period: warfare, social mobility, and active engagement with the overseas world.

The extent of military violence was different in the early medieval than in the late medieval. While limited during the early medieval epoch, such violence was a newly important element in Japanese politics from the 1150s. The Kamakura shogunate was established as a result of battles that occurred throughout the country; internecine violence punctuated the tenure of the shogunate, and there were two foreign invasions of Japan. Yet in every case, the fighting was of limited duration and intensity.

The military violence of the late medieval era was qualitatively different, introducing warfare into Japanese society. The fighting involved virtually all social classes, and campaigns extended across distance and time. Warfare could persist over decades. This was the only period in Japanese history when warriors could expect warfare to be a permanent part of their lives. The organization of warfare became progressively complex and specialized, and by the mid-1550s warlord domains (or principalities) were placed on a permanent war footing in order to achieve the twin goals of supporting an effective army and protecting the domain's productive capacity.

A second characteristic of the medieval age was social mobility. Much of this social mobility was a by-product of warfare, which transformed the composition of the warrior order. During the Kamakura period, warrior-landholders represented a largely closed hereditary elite with a virtual monopoly on fighting skills, and warriors and warrior families did not actually base their claims to martial talent on regular demonstrations. After the 1330s, and particularly after the 1460s, not only did the demands of warfare require recruitment of fighters not born into warrior families, but warfare also proved to be a ruthless winnowing process in which claims to martial prowess reflected only actual battle success. As a result, the composition of warrior society changed radically. The most spectacular example of this was the warlord Toyotomi Hideyoshi, who was born into a peasant family and died as the most powerful individual of his day.

Social mobility was accompanied by economic changes, among them the ongoing transfer of ownership of agricultural land from proprietors to cultivators and the development of farming for the market, noticeable by the end of the Kamakura period; the increasing monetization of the economy from the mid-1200s; the emergence of trade guilds as significant economic and social forces by the late 1300s; and the development of the money-lending industry as a key component of commercial activity by the early 1400s. All these changes offered new possibilities for bypassing the structures and assumptions that had made wealth largely a by-product of elevated social and political status. Instead, it now became possible for agriculturalists and merchants to create their own wealth and to gain influence through the use of financial resources rather than depending on political or social prerogatives.

Social mobility is also readily seen in the development of new artistic forms. Part of the impetus for this change came from powerful warriors who demanded and patronized modes of artistic expression not primarily associated with the traditions and arbiters of the classical age. Ready examples include the Noh theater, the standards of aesthetic appreciation emanating from Zen models of painting and ceramics, and the creation of what we have come to describe as the culture of tea. We might perhaps describe these new forms as upwardly mobile arts, but they contributed to social mobility by enabling individuals of diverse social backgrounds (including the very humble) to develop creative talents that, when recognized, could translate into positive economic and social benefits.

The third characteristic of the medieval era was extensive overseas contact, particularly with the mercantile, religious, and artistic milieu of South China. In medieval times, Japan was an integral part of an East Asian macro-culture. The rhythms of engagement stand out on their own terms, but given the limited nature of late classical interactions and the conscious and enduring restrictions on overseas contact that marked the succeeding Tokugawa era, the medieval experience is arresting.

This contact incorporates a second major wave of Chinese influence on Japanese civilization, an influence perhaps best known in the form of the appropriation and development of a multifaceted and cosmopolitan Zen culture encompassing poetry, literature, painting, landscaping, ceramics, architecture, and cuisine—now recognized as a quintessential component of the Japanese cultural tradition. But the contact also included such things as new medical knowledge transmitted via printed Song, Yuan, and Ming medical texts, which in turn opened up a new world of pharmaceuticals and medical formulas whose ingredients included such items as frankincense imported from the Middle East and whose compounding techniques owed much to Islamic medicine. And, because of the trade routes, or the knowledge that Japan was a destination point in a trade network stretching from Africa, the Portuguese and other Europeans for the first time made their way to Japan, bringing new knowledge, including cartographic evidence that Japan was part of a world larger than its inhabitants had previously imagined. Of note also is the fact that the monetization of the Japanese economy was made possible only because of the importation of hundreds of millions of Chinese coins, which compensated for the absence of currency issued by any Japanese political authority.

The overseas contact was facilitated by a maritime network run by Chinese merchants whose activities propelled the growth of Hakata in Kyushu into an international trading center. Many of these merchants took up residence there and established a substantial, long-term community that, through trade and through intermarriage, fashioned a cosmopolitan milieu. Throughout the medieval era, people and goods transited Hakata in a two-way exchange, and for many Japanese, overseas study and sojourn were, while memorable, a familiar and unexceptional, rather than strange or extraordinary, experience. The ubiquity of overseas contact is additional testimony to the importance of the medieval as a historical era and enriches our understanding of it beyond the more familiar images of a feudal society or an age of warriors.

How then do we define the medieval era? Chronologically, we fruitfully locate it between the late twelfth and the late sixteenth centuries. Conceptually, while the notion of medieval is an appropriation from European historiography, it can be meaningfully applied to the events and rhythms of Japanese history, and its use has enhanced our understanding of the Japanese past. The medieval age also had distinct characteristics—including military violence, social mobility, and overseas contact—that set it apart from other eras of Japanese history (with the possible exception of the modern era, which in good humor we might dub the post-medieval).

Sources and Suggestions for Further Reading

See the bibliography for complete publication data.

Adolphson, Mikael S. "Social Change and Contained Transformations: Warriors and Merchants in Japan, 1000–1300" (2004).

Cooper, Michael. *They Came to Japan: An Anthology of European Reports on Japan, 1543–1640* (1965).

Duus, Peter. *Feudalism in Japan.* 3rd edition (1993).

Friday, Karl F. "The Futile Paradigm: The Quest for Feudalism in Early Medieval Japan" (2010).

———. *Samurai, Warfare and the State in Early Medieval Japan* (2004).

Goble, Andrew Edmund. *Confluences of Medicine in Medieval Japan: Buddhist Healing, Chinese Knowledge, Islamic Formulas, and Wounds of War* (2011).

———. "Medieval Japan" (2007).

Goble, Andrew Edmund, Kenneth R. Robinson, and Haruko Wakabayashi, eds. *Tools of Culture: Japan's Cultural, Intellectual, Medical, and Technological Contacts in East Asia, 1000s–1500s* (2009).

Hall, John Whitney. *Government and Local Power in Japan, 500 to 1700: A Study Based on Bizen Province* (1966).

Keirstead, Thomas. "Inventing Medieval Japan: The History and Politics of National Identity" (1998).

Mass, Jeffrey P., ed. *The Origins of Japan's Medieval World: Courtiers, Clerics, Warriors, and Peasants in the Fourteenth Century* (1997).

Note

1. Rodrigues, "Three Periods of Japanese History," in Cooper, *They Came to Japan*, 28–32.

5

Defining "Early Modern"

Mary Elizabeth Berry

"Early modern" is a general temporal label used by historians to describe many societies scattered across the globe. Unlike particular labels, such as "Tokugawa Japan" or "Stuart England," which evoke singular local conditions, the general term insists on a comparative framework. The comparison can be internal—as, for example, the phrase "early modern Japan" implies differences from both an earlier "medieval Japan" and a later "modern Japan." The comparison can also be external—as, for example, the phrase "early modern Japan" implies similarities with "early modern England" (or America or China or any number of other places).

This chapter explores two major developments in early modern Japan that mark both a break with the medieval Japanese experience and a connection with the early modern experience elsewhere in the world: the emergence of a strong state and the penetration of a market economy. These developments occasioned additional changes that, collectively, historians tend to take as defining features of early modernity: urbanization; the specialization and integration of labor; the redistribution of income to a nascent middle class; the growth of popular consumption; the spread of schooling, literacy, and commercial printing; and the improvement in standards of well-being, from nutrition to life expectancy.

Implicit in the "early modern" label is the useful suggestion that these features provided a common foundation for the "modern" experience. Even so, the label erases distinctions neither with modernity proper (which brought such stunning changes as industrial production and world war) nor between early modern societies themselves. No two were alike. Early modern Japan stood apart from early modern Europe, for example, in the trajectory of the state. Strong by many measures, the Japanese state was not highly centralized.

More important, it used its authority to enforce a pacification agenda that precluded the aggressive foreign expansion, both in trade and in war, emblematic of early modernity elsewhere. So, too, the penetration of the market economy did not encourage the forms of democratic liberalism critical to civil society in the West.

Why? Here we come to the power of comparison. Like all labels, the term "early modern" is a blunt tool for detecting shared properties without leveling its subjects into uniformity. But insofar as it draws into relief the differences as well as the similarities in those subjects, the term abets the goal of historical analysis: understanding the reasons for convergence and divergence by examining the particularities of local experience. Early modern change across the globe derived from variable sources and effected variable outcomes. Below, I consider them in the Japanese context.

A useful beginning date for the early modern period is 1573, when the last Ashikaga shogun fled into exile in the face of escalating conquests by Oda Nobunaga. A useful ending date is 1868, when the last Tokugawa shogun resigned his office in the face of ascendant demands for imperial restoration. Although dates are no more than signposts, these choices foreground the importance of political power in shaping change. It was the laws of several generations of victorious generals that created the framework for the early modern transformation. So, too, it would be the laws of several generations of governing oligarchs that dismantled that framework to establish the contours of modern rule in the late nineteenth century.

The prelude to the early modern experience was a civil war so long, pervasive, and hungry for combatants that most men over the age of fifteen were recruited for battle. Fighting began in 1467, with quarrels over succession in the Ashikaga shogunate, and continued for over a century as scores of martial houses exploited the chaos to build bases for local dominance. The indeterminate contests among these houses shifted course with the rise of Oda Nobunaga. Conquering a third of the country, Nobunaga inaugurated the climactic campaigns of "unification" that delivered centralized control over Japan to his successors: first Toyotomi Hideyoshi, later Tokugawa Ieyasu.

Unification entailed war making of unprecedented scale, bloodletting, and devastation to martial houses (even, in the end, the Oda and Toyotomi themselves). But it also entailed peacemaking of astonishing virtuosity; for the mounting consequences of the late campaigns indicated that no victory could be conclusive, and no victor safe, without a break in the cycle of violence. Policies of domestic pacification became, then, the core agenda of Toyotomi Hideyoshi (in power 1582–1598). They were sufficiently expanded by Tokugawa Ieyasu to undergird a durable regime that would govern Japan for fifteen generations under the title of shogun.

One critical instrument of peace was alliance between warlords. Although long an opportunistic strategy of combat, alliance served Hideyoshi and Ieyasu as a precept of state building. Both men disavowed visions of absolutist power concentrated in a single hegemon to conceive the polity as a coalition, or confederation, of daimyo lords. In effect, they chose to build on wartime legacies of strong local rule. Hence, even as they launched their final campaigns, Hideyoshi and Ieyasu shared power with numerous allies (including former rivals and enemies) by formally vesting them with domainal lands and conceding substantial autonomy in domainal governance. Significantly, the daimyo retained control over their own armies and their own land taxes. They varied in number (reaching a rough total of 260 during the mature stage of the Tokugawa regime), in the size of their holdings (lurching from vast to petty), and in origin (crossing the spectrum of old and new, trusted and dubious, kindred and nonrelated houses). The daimyo role in rule was nonetheless so elemental that the early modern state has come to be called the *baku-han* system: a union of the central authority of the shogun (*baku*) and the local authority of the daimyo (*han*).

Central authority took most aggressive form in a series of laws that, once daimyo alliances emerged as the path to peace, aimed at cutting the very roots of violence. Farmers were to be stripped of all weapons and registered in villages as full-time cultivators responsible for paying land taxes. Samurai were to be withdrawn from villages to the castle towns of their individual daimyo lords and supported there on rice stipends (the equivalent of salaries). By separating the classes and forbidding movement between them, early modern leaders sought to deny warriors the direct access to human and material resources that had long fueled combat. They also constrained the freedom of daimyo, notably with the system of "alternate attendance" perfected by the Tokugawa: each lord was required to spend half of each year in the shogunal capital of Edo and to leave permanently there his principal consort and his heir.

Backing up these flamboyant initiatives were many quieter but far-reaching policies, which confirmed central authority over both the daimyo and vital public interests. The Toyotomi and the Tokugawa compelled the daimyo to reduce their fortifications; to renounce private pacts; to provide military service and corvée labor for their overlords; to transfer domains on command; and, most important, to submit to central discipline for maladministration. The Toyotomi and Tokugawa heads emerged as public rulers with an equally formidable program of national regulation. Their administrations assumed control over religious institutions, major ports and cities, the system of highways, most mining resources, the minting of coins, and the standardization of measures. They came to serve as the nation's ultimate courts of appeal. They effectively managed, and financed, the imperial court.

To discharge these responsibilities, the Tokugawa shogunate developed an increasingly refined bureaucracy—staffed by daimyo and samurai—that would eventually embrace over two hundred offices and many thousands of officials. To enable rational land administration, the shogunate spearheaded the cadastral and cartographic surveys that underlay the systematic distribution and taxation of resources throughout the country. And to project the rightful character of its authority, the regime amplified the prestige of shogunal title by elaborating a sacred cult of the founder, Tokugawa Ieyasu. Over time, scholars in service to the regime would formulate a Confucian philosophy of governance. They projected the shogun as the guardian of peace whose benevolent rule secured harmony among the four status groups, each separate in function but bound together by reciprocal obligations: The samurai administered the realm through wise oversight and virtuous example; the farmers generated the harvests of a bountiful nature; the craftspeople fabricated the goods essential to society; and the merchants circulated those harvests and goods throughout the integral social body.

What is striking in these policies and practices of the early modern state is an ambition unrivaled since the formation of the classical state. If the local prerogatives of the daimyo remained substantial, central authorities nonetheless assumed powers comprehensive enough to engineer a social revolution. Remarkably, they succeeded. The Pax Tokugawa lasted for almost 250 years: between 1615 (when the Tokugawa prevailed over Toyotomi partisans) and 1853 (when international pressure fractured the unity of the polity), only one major armed uprising disturbed the peace: the Shimabara rebellion of 1637–1638.

These circumstances help explain a seeming paradox: The strong state created to secure order stalled in growth once order prevailed. The Tokugawa state did not continue to expand its powers in new directions; nor, indeed, did it continue to exercise existing powers with vigor. Notably, shogunal controls on the daimyo eased dramatically after about 1650. This change sometimes puzzles historians, who marvel that the regime did not build on strength to approach some version of the centralized absolutism emerging in early modern Europe. One factor militating against such a development was a persisting commitment, both structural and ideological, to confederation, which took form in the appointment of daimyo to the highest shogunal offices at the center and the reliance on daimyo to enforce shogunal policy in the locale. While surely in tension, the concerns of center and locale were ultimately imagined as complementary. But another factor was the achievement of peace itself. Without the demands of war—for men, material, capital, infrastructure, information—the incentives to concentrate power waned.

International circumstances also contributed to the relaxation of state power, although not before tumultuous changes that converted the expansionist policy of the Toyotomi to the containment policy of the Tokugawa. In an act of foreign aggression unprecedented in Japan's history, Toyotomi Hideyoshi launched two invasions of Korea in the 1590s. Aimed at rebuking Korea for perceived diplomatic insults and subduing China for personal aggrandizement, the invasions ended in disaster for all parties. Japanese commanders withdrew their troops upon Hideyoshi's death. The Tokugawa shogun abjured belligerence abroad thereafter.

So, too, the Tokugawa regime increasingly regulated and curtailed a once extensive foreign trade. New global connections had opened for Japan with the arrival from the 1540s of European merchant ships. Subsequently, Japanese merchants, licensed by Toyotomi and early Tokugawa authorities, traveled as far as Manila, Macao, and Tonkin. Trade was dominated in volume by the exchange of Chinese silk for Japanese silver. But it also brought to Japan an enormous range of goods and technologies (including woolen textiles, tobacco, sweet potatoes, musketry, lens crafting, and advanced mining techniques). Crucially, moreover, it brought deepening cultural contacts as European missionaries took up residence in Japan and began to combine evangelism with serious study of Japanese language and literature, history and civilization. For their part, Japanese students pursued knowledge of European arts and sciences—intimating the sort of cosmopolitan encounter with Western society that had long developed with China. The very missionary presence that enabled close meetings with the West would become, however, the source of rupture and, finally, Japanese withdrawal from open contact.

Alarmed by the religious zealotry of the missionaries, as well as their compromising entanglements in economic and political activity, Japanese authorities assailed what they saw as a Christian threat to state power. They issued a sequence of edicts, dating from 1587 until 1640, that eventuated in the expulsion of missionaries; the prohibition of Christian faith; the persecution of converts who refused to recant; and the routine interrogation of Japanese subjects, who were compelled to identify as non-Christians by registering with Buddhist temples. Despite intense interest in foreign trade, the Tokugawa regime also narrowed opportunities for most forms of presumptively dangerous foreign encounters. By the early 1640s, European trade was confined to an island in Nagasaki harbor and Japanese trade abroad was terminated.

We return, then, to the paradoxes of pacification. During the opening stage of unification, Japan appeared to share with early modern states in Europe an expansionist ambition in both foreign war and foreign trade. Yet reversals in Korea, together with wariness over mounting Manchu power in China, turned the Tokugawa away from armed aggression abroad to the consolidation of authority at home. Trade, too, brought trials: not only the episodic conflicts over economic advantage and political jurisdiction that sparked threats of martial reprisals among trading partners, but the foundational challenges to culture and ideology that confronted all parties to foreign encounter. Tellingly, the final Tokugawa controls on contact were put in place following the Shimabara rebellion. Although provoked by economic immiseration and local misrule, the uprising included Christian sympathizers who could be projected as doctrinally inspired traitors to the state. Seizing that rationale, Tokugawa rulers shifted conclusively from expansion to seclusion under the mandate of pacification. And a regime that had assumed the genuinely exceptional powers required to achieve domestic peace and foreign containment found itself, once successful on both fronts, without inducements to grow.

Seclusion did not mean the closing of Japan to contact. Exchange with the Dutch continued, as did official relations with Korea and unofficial trade with China. Tributary relations were established with the Kingdom of Ryūkyū and the Ainu of Hokkaido. Piracy and other forms of "informal" trade by opportunists and adventurers never ceased. Nor did the traffic in ideas, which remained at least as important as the traffic in goods. Ideas traveled with people—through the Dutch trade representatives and Korean ambassadors who were interviewed periodically in Edo, and through the Japanese scholars and students who went to Nagasaki in search of overseas learning. Ideas also traveled through Chinese and European books, which were imported and translated in increasing numbers from the mid-eighteenth century, inspiring enlarging circles of "Dutch" or "foreign" studies in medicine, the sciences, and other subjects. Even so, the frames of containment established in the early generations of Tokugawa rule remained in place. They were rattled from the late eighteenth century, when international activity in Northeast Asia (by whalers, naval fleets, and imperialist powers) escalated and pressure to open Japanese ports intensified. But not until Matthew Perry led an American fleet into Uraga Bay in 1853, demanding access to port facilities and assent to a commercial treaty, did those frames face collapse.

During the centuries between the Shimabara uprising and Perry's challenge, we find a second major development in early modern history: the penetration of a market economy. This development was related to the first, the emergence of the strong state, since economic change was set in motion by the pacification policies of the unifiers: in particular, the removal of most samurai from agrarian villages to the castle towns of their daimyo and the requirement that those daimyo reside for half the year in the shogunal capital of Edo. The consequence was a process of urbanization unmatched in scope and speed anywhere in the early modern world. At the outset of the unification era, perhaps 3 to 4 percent of the Japanese population lived in large towns or cities. By 1700, the figure was 12 percent and growing. Here, in urban migration, was the prime source of an economic transformation unintended by the unifiers but driven by their decisions.

Samurai and their families—an uncommonly vast elite constituting 6 to 7 percent of the total population—formed the magnetic core of urban movement. In their wake came equally large numbers of merchants, craftspeople, and providers of disparate services who shifted from agrarian to commercial employment to meet the needs of these privileged consumers. Remarkable in dimension, this urban migration was the more remarkable in its dispersal. Like other early modern nations, Japan had a monster city—the shogunal capital of Edo, propelled by great daimyo entourages to roughly one million people by around 1700. Unlike other early modern nations, Japan had two additional monsters (the commodity exchange center of Osaka and the luxury craft center of Kyoto, both with well over 300,000 people in 1700) as well as many score castle towns, twenty of them numbering 70,000 and more.

Implicit in these figures is the replacement by the market of the manorial economy that, even in the late medieval period, had sustained the comparatively small elites based in cities. Although in decreasing measure, those elites had relied for foodstuffs and other commodities on bundles of tax goods provided in kind from individual proprietary holdings, and for processed and finished products on clients attached to their households. The very size of the samurai core precluded such arrangements in the Tokugawa period. So, too, did an impersonal tax system predicated on payments in the single medium of rice and subsequent distributions to samurai of rice salaries. Those salaries (converted to cash by brokers) had to be exchanged for whatever was needed and desired. And to supply what was needed and desired, there developed around the samurai a large and intricate market network.

In mature form, Japan's early modern market was made up of highly differentiated but integrated sectors organized for profit from specialized work. The market relied, in the first instance, on the intense production of both agrarian and nonagrarian commodities, which often went through basic processing in rural areas as off-season enterprise. Beyond the realm of production, the market relied on the delivery of commodities to urban centers through specialized chains of purchasing agents, transporters, warehousers, and wholesalers. Thereafter, it relied on elaborate urban craft operations for the final processing and fabrication of goods. In typically stratified stages of expertise, craftspeople built buildings, processed food and drink, and manufactured all manner of goods ranging from textiles (the leading urban product) to household furnishings and personal accessories. The retail operations of urban merchants crossed the full spectrum of commodities and manufactures. And the service operations of other urban professionals included banking, teaching, medicine, entertainment, and any number of mundane ventures (from hairdressing to gardening). Backing up most urban enterprises, finally, were large numbers of apprentices, day laborers, and household servants.

This abbreviated litany of the employments that grew up to sustain urban samurai suggests not only the complexity of the early modern market but its implication over time of virtually all members of early modern society. If elite consumers depended on the market for provisions, so did all nonagrarian workers engaged in everything from transport to fine embroidery. Soon enough, moreover, the market entangled the agrarian producers who focused on cash crops, pursued cottage industries, and sent their sons and daughters to town for seasonal labor and service. Subsistence agriculture and self-sufficient villages all but disappeared as the reliance of individual farmers on the market extended from discretionary purchases (such as commercial fertilizer and paper) to the food staples their own specialized harvests no longer included. Everyone became a consumer. In the process, commoner consumption displaced elite consumption as the lead mover of the market.

Like the achievement of peace, the successful conversion to an urbanized, market-centered economy is surprising. The unifiers may have mandated the samurai exodus from villages, but in 1600 Japan hardly seemed ready for the ensuing transformation. Apart from the dangers posed by demobilized soldiers crowded into rudimentary castle towns, the structures for economic transformation were weak: a reliable network of roads, waterways, and ports remained incipient; systematic registration and taxation of resources was only beginning; no stable monetary, banking, or measurement systems united even regional economies; large transport and storage operations were geared solely to Kyoto and the largest daimyo armies; commercial agriculture thrived only in the home provinces around Kyoto. How, then, did the economic conversion occur?

Continuing initiatives by the state were important. These included efforts to standardize the currency and measurement systems. They also included critical efforts, joined by the daimyo, to develop transport networks as well as infrastructure—streets, canals, water supply—in the major cities. Most significant were the combined investments by rulers and private developers in the irrigation and reclamation projects that, by the end of the seventeenth century, doubled the amount of cultivated rice paddy.

Throughout the economic conversion, however, the diverse contributions of commoners proved paramount. Hard labor joined with *smart* labor enabled what historians call Japan's "industrious revolution"—not a machine-powered development of factory industry but a brain-powered commitment to maximum productivity. In the background of this revolution was dramatic population increase (from 12 to 30 million between 1600 and 1700), which was a source as well as a peril of growth. On the one hand, population increase sustained both mass urban migration and expanding demand for public works and farm labor. On the other, it threatened the food supply in a mountainous country where only about 12 percent of the land is arable. Farmers addressed the threat with more intense and experimental methods (touching everything from hybrid plant selection to pest control) that multiplied their productivity, even permitting triple cropping in some areas. Workers in other sectors joined the industrious revolution with an ethic focused on punishing hours, iron thrift, and constant improvement (based on rigorous accounting and strict business standards).

Still, hard and smart work, typically involving real risks, required incentives. Taxation practices helped provide them. The rates originally imposed on agriculture appeared all but confiscatory, but official laxity in registering gains in productivity meant that farmers effectively kept the proceeds from improved methods. Taxes on commerce and urban land were never prohibitive: Largely suspended in the early Tokugawa years (to lure migrants with "freedom" in entrepreneurship), they later concentrated on fees from trade associations and "gifts" from neighborhood associations. There was, then, potential *profit* to be made from enterprise—a word more and more conspicuous in the advice manuals that mushroomed to instruct commoners in the new creed of business-first-ism.

The trend across the early modern period was toward greater commoner wealth, both agrarian and nonagrarian, although distribution was so jagged that poverty remained aggressive throughout sectors. Even after agrarian development neared its limit in the eighteenth century, wealth continued to increase selectively, since population control (often through infanticide) and proto-industrial manufacture protected a degree of economic growth. The martial elite, however, tended to diminish in prosperity. The shogunate responded to swelling debt with lunging programs of currency debasement, price controls, loan management, and frugality ordinances, but only rarely, and temporarily, with aggressive tax reform. While certain daimyo did profit from commercial monopolies in particular domains, the Tokugawa retained a largely hands-off policy toward market resources, continuing to entrust even state enterprises (such as mining, minting, and control over foreign imports) to the privileged merchants who primarily profited from them. Among the chief losers were samurai retainers with modest and inflation-ridden stipends.

This disparity between rich commoners and poor samurai intimates changes that rippled far beyond the economic sphere to reconfigure many aspects of society and culture. Much of the profit pursued by industrious commoners was reserved for the savings and cautious business investments that helped ensure the security of the family, the heart of the Confucian value system. But much was channeled into material improvement—from small luxuries that became commonplace (such as cotton bedding and oil lamps) to showier expenditures that stirred envy (such as precious fabrics and tea ceremony wares). And much was channeled into education, from basic schooling to higher learning. Training became pervasive, too, in the disparate forms of civility—calligraphy, poetry, and music, for example. Literate and cultivated commoners with discretionary income emerged, in turn, as both audience and subject of a burgeoning print and performance culture. Indeed, commoner patrons and tastes were the target of all the defining art forms of early modernity: *kabuki* and *bunraku* drama, haiku poetry, popular fiction, and woodblock prints. Although historical heroics had an important place on the stage, the focus of art was the everyday—the domestic and social experience of recognizable characters in mundane settings: love and money mattered most.

In sum, market penetration brought complex departures from the medieval world: general gains in such standards of well-being as nutrition, longevity, literacy, and material comfort; particular gains in social and cultural capital to what we might broadly conceive as a nascent middle class. This was the group of specialists and professionals who owned land and led enterprises that generated most of the nation's surplus wealth. This was also the group that displaced the values of hereditary aristocrats with an ethic of striving, mobility, and professional expertise. Crucially, moreover, the group cut across status lines. If it was built on urban and rural commoners, it included the many superfluous samurai who fashioned independent lives as writers, physicians, scientists, and teachers. Far too large and disparate to function as any sort of cohesive elite, the samurai made up an anxious, underemployed body riddled with mavericks.

In the market-driven changes described here, the arc of early modernity in Japan conforms to the arc of early modernity in Europe. Urbanization, the specialization of labor, national economic integration, high levels of popular consumption, the social and cultural climb of a nascent middle class—all such developments belong to both stories. The political stories, however, are different. They differ in the character of the state, which was strong in Japan but neither absolutist in authority nor expansive in foreign relations. They differ, too, at the level of popular politics. Certainly Japan saw extensive political protest in the form of rural and urban uprising, scholarly criticism of rulers, angry graffiti, and literary mockery. Still, the agitation for representative government that was the hallmark of European civil society remained absent. Economic transformation did not provoke stirrings of political revolution in Japan. Why not? We circle once more to the anomalous character of the state. While extraordinarily powerful in the work of pacification, the regime ruled indirectly through legions of daimyo and samurai officials, who left considerable autonomy in local governance to the neighborhood and village associations of commoners. It retained a light hand on domestic commerce and a cautious approach to taxation, enabling general growth and selective prosperity. And it kept the peace. The most disaffected group under these circumstances was the samurai. When rebellion against the regime finally did come, it rose not from populist progressives but their own reactionary retainers.

Sources and Suggestions for Further Reading

See bibliography for complete publication data.

Hayami Akira, Osamu Saito, and Ronald Toby. *The Economic History of Japan, Volume 1: Emergence of Economic Society in Japan, 1600–1859* (2004).

Smith, Thomas C. *Native Sources of Japanese Industrialization, 1750–1920* (1989).

Totman, Conrad. *Early Modern Japan* (1995).

PART II

Immigrants, Chieftains, and Kings in Ancient Times

C. 30,000 BCE	Oldest known evidence of humans in Japan
C. 14,000 BCE	Oldest know pottery in Japan; beginnings of Jōmon culture
1700–1027 BCE	Shang dynasty in China
1027–771 BCE	Western Zhou dynasty in China
C. 900 BCE	Beginnings of Yayoi culture
770–221 BCE	Eastern Zhou dynasty in China
660 BCE	Ascension of first (mythical) emperor, Jinmu
C. 300 BCE	Old Chosŏn kingdom in Korea
221–207 BCE	Qin dynasty in China
206 BCE–9 CE	Western Han dynasty in China
9–24 CE	Wang Mang interregnum (aka Xin dynasty) in China
25–220 CE	Eastern Han dynasty in China
239 CE	Himiko (Pimiko) receives seal of investiture as Queen of Yamatai from Wei Emperor
248 CE	Himiko dies
220–280 CE	Three Kingdoms/Six Dynasties period in China
C. 250 CE	Construction of first mounded tombs (*kofun*), according to Chinese records
300–668 CE	Three Kingdoms period in Korea
420–588 CE	Northern and Southern Dynasties period in China
438 CE	King Zhen receives titles "King of Wa" and "General Who Maintains Peace in the East" from Liu Song kingdom
507 CE	King Buretsu overthrown; new royal line established by Keitai
538 CE	Paekche presents Yamato court with Buddhist statuary
552 CE	Buddhism arrives in Japan, according to *Nihon shoki*
581–617 CE	China reunified under Sui dynasty

587 CE	Soga family annihilate the Mononobe
592 CE	Suiko becomes the first monarch to use the title of "Emperor" (*tenshi*, literally "Child of Heaven")
604 CE	Promulgation of Shōtoku Taishi's "Seventeen Article Constitution"
618–907 CE	Tang dynasty in China
645 CE	Taika Coup d'État
668 CE	Fall of Koguryŏ Kingdom, beginning of United Silla Kingdom in Korea
668 CE	Naka no Ōe takes throne as Emperor Tenji
670 CE	Tenji sends embassy to Tang court requesting Japan be called Nippon, rather than Wa
671 CE	Ōmi *ritsuryō* codes promulgated
672 CE	Jinshin Rebellion; Tenmu becomes emperor
681 CE	Tenmu orders compilation of royal histories (origins of *Kojiki* and *Nihon shoki*)
C. 690 CE	Adoption of Daoist term *tennō* ("Heavenly Sovereign"; usually translated as "emperor") for Japanese monarch
694 CE	Capital established at Fujiwara–kyō
701 CE	Taihō *ritsuryō* codes promulgated

6

Origins of the Japanese People

C. Melvin Aikens

The cultural and ethnic character of the Japan we know today can be seen emerging most definitively in the Yayoi and Kofun periods, an era marked by immigration and strong new continental influences entering from the adjacent Korean peninsula. The deeper roots of Japanese population, ecological adaptation, and cultural tradition are much older, however—on current evidence reaching back to the Upper Paleolithic, about 35,000 years ago. This chapter begins with these antecedent people and traditions, describing how their hunting-fishing-gathering lifeways persisted over thousands of years. It then focuses on the story of how the unique people and culture we know today came into being on Japanese soil in fairly recent times.

I show that this long historical sequence was not a succession of cultural breaks and replacements, as long-term archaeological histories are often simplistically portrayed, but rather a set of *continuities*, *interconnections*, *mergings*, and *becomings*. From Late Paleolithic times onward, highly similar hunting-fishing-gathering traditions were established on climatically and environmentally similar landscapes all around the Sea of Japan: in the Russian Far East, adjacent Manchuria, the Korean peninsula, and the Japanese archipelago. These traditions descended from Upper Paleolithic cultures that came originally from the west, and continued to be shaped in Northeast Asia by shared environmental factors that fostered highly similar diets, stone tool inventories, pottery types, and architectural forms over a vast area. Tools and behaviors that emerged in one or another part of this "Japan Sea Oikumene" were often broadly applicable and widely shared among locally anchored foraging communities whose warm-season plant harvesting, fishing, and hunting circuits inevitably touched with those of others all around the edges of their respective home ranges. As we know from comparative ethnography, other normal concomitants of life that encourage cultural sharing include intermarriage and trade between regional groups.

Although much that is new appears over time in any cultural setting, it is important in thinking about Japanese (or any people's) origins to stress that much ancient human practice and knowledge—most obviously those elements entailed in discovering, hunting, catching, collecting, and preparing the many wild foods and industrial materials endemic to a region—has been passed down and renewed in every succeeding human generation living on that ground through the agency of intrafamilial experience and instruction. In this sense all those ancient and later occupants of Japan who passed down their accumulating knowledge and tradition to subsequent generations living on the same landscape are properly seen as cultural ancestors of the "modern" Japanese we know today.

PALEOLITHIC JAPAN

Currently the oldest known human bones and teeth found in Japan are those of anatomically modern *Homo sapiens*, radiocarbon-dated to between 34,000 and 28,000 years ago at cave sites in the Ryūkyū Islands at the southern end of the Japanese archipelago. Of similar date are large, bifacially flaked and often partially edge-ground choppers or hand axes, along with smaller flaked stone knives and scrapers. These are dated to about 28,000 years ago in Tokyo area sites, while in Kyushu comparable specimens were uncovered beneath tephra from massive volcanic explosions dated to about 32,000 years ago.

Following this earliest known period, new artifact types—notably bladelike side-blow flakes, parallel-sided end-blow blades, and the prepared cores they were struck from—become increasingly numerous throughout the Japanese archipelago, from northern Hokkaido to southern Kyushu. After about 20,000 years ago large parallel-sided blades and much smaller microblades struck from distinctive wedge-shaped and conical cores succeeded earlier types at many sites, and bifacially flaked stone points were also part of such assemblages. These blades and microblades are clearly related to Upper Paleolithic artifacts made all across Eurasia, from the Atlantic to the Pacific.

During this era people became quite numerous in the highly varied and biotically rich environment of seashores, bays, rivers, plains, and mountains that the Japanese archipelago provided. Sites in the western Tokyo area offer good examples of their encampments, and many more are known. Interestingly, broad-scale excavations around a number of such sites have turned up many small, deep pit traps of a size appropriate for catching the native wild boars and small deer that are numerous in the Japanese islands even today. The earliest such traps have come from locations buried under volcanic tephra erupted in

Kyushu about 28,000 years ago, which fell to earth across much of Japan, Korea, and the Russian Far East, and they are known to have persisted into much later times, even down to the Jōmon and Yayoi periods.

JŌMON JAPAN

The Jōmon cultural pattern emerged over a long period of climatic and biotic change brought on by terminal Pleistocene and postglacial warming, and its ecological context is key to defining its essential character. Sediment cores from lakes and bogs along the length of the Japanese archipelago have yielded pollen records that show dramatically how temperate forests of broad-leaved deciduous oak, beech, and other species—limited to the far south during the time of glacial cold—spread northward over thousands of years as the global climate warmed. Oak woodland present in southern Kyushu before 20,000 years ago spread into southern Honshu by about 14,500 years ago and reached Hokkaido by about 8,000 years ago. The spread of beech and other trees is similarly documented. These temperate woodlands, which remain characteristic of Japan today, provided foods of all kinds much more abundantly than did the conifer-dominated cold-climate forests they replaced. Rich in edible (and storable) acorns, beechnuts, walnuts, chestnuts, and roots, the mixed broad-leaved forests also provided a great variety of fruits and greens in season and were well populated by game animals, including bear, boar, deer, raccoon, hare, otter, wolf, fox, and many kinds of birds and freshwater fishes. There were also abundant seasonal runs of anadromous salmon swarming up rivers from the sea to spawn in freshwater, and catadromous lamprey eels that swam down the same rivers to spawn in the ocean.

Within this increasingly productive biotic context—emergent not only in the Japanese archipelago, by the way, but also throughout adjacent continental Asia around the Sea of Japan—some of the world's oldest pottery appeared in the form of small cooking pots. Regional differences in early vessels show that experimentation and development were going on over a broad geographical front. Much farther afield, pottery was also being invented during the same period in comparable environments at the European end of Eurasia, in response to the same basic ecological forces.

Pottery was no accidental discovery. People of northerly Eurasian latitudes were by the Late Paleolithic creative and skilled artificers long accustomed to tailoring clothing, footwear, and house covers out of animal skin and fashioning practical equipment and containers out of hide, bark, willows, and woven fibers. They were also ancient users of fire who surely knew as a fact of everyday life that a campfire built on wet earth of a certain kind would harden it, and who quite early used that knowledge in making fired clay ceremonial figurines.

Learning to fashion pottery vessels was not a big step for them, and easily made containers that could be heated directly in a fire were called forth in ecological contexts across Eurasia where the warming late Pleistocene and postglacial environment encouraged a florescence of both plant and animal foodstuffs. An apt picture of the cultural context is offered by the nineteenth-century Ainu of far northern Japan, among whom a great many different plant, animal, terrestrial, and littoral foods were part of the diet. In the typical Ainu household, whatever items were obtained or on hand on any given day would be simply added to household cooking pots kept simmering more or less all the time. By mid-Holocene times, ceramic containers had also become very important for storing large amounts of durable acorns, chestnuts, berries, and other such foodstuffs, capacious vessels being producible quickly and in quantity from clays available within practical distance of a well-chosen village site.

This kind of highly productive forest and littoral harvesting economy was characteristic of Japan's post-Paleolithic and long-lived Jōmon cultural tradition. The oldest Japanese pottery currently known has been dated to about 16,000 years ago at the far northern end of Honshu. A long Incipient Jōmon phase, between 16,000 and 10,000 years ago, is characterized by pottery that was not marked before firing with the cord impressions that later became definitive of the tradition. These Incipient Jōmon wares were variously plain, scratched, nail-marked, shell-impressed, or decorated by appliqué strips on their surfaces, while subsequent Jōmon types all exhibited cord-marking in a variety of styles and patterns.

Given the high productive potential realized in the Japanese archipelago under postglacial climatic conditions, it is no surprise that Japan's human occupants early on became quite numerous by settling themselves in well-chosen locations where the harvesting of surrounding natural resources could feed a stable community reliably on a year-round basis. Pithouses with excavated floors and perishable superstructures mark established residential sites by Initial Jōmon times (10,000–6,000 years ago), and significant communities of such houses were everywhere by the Early Jōmon period (6,000–5,000 years ago). In the impressively large Early/Middle Jōmon communities (6,000–4,000 years ago) of northern Honshu, people built large communal longhouses and stored community food resources in capacious pottery vessels on a major scale. Communities of this time range across northern and central Honshu left behind highly elaborated and specialized pottery vessels, anthropomorphic figurines, and other items—impressive evidence of high levels of sociocultural and ceremonial complexity. The region around Tokyo Bay also flourished in Early and Middle Jōmon times, with many large communities and strong evidence of trade and interaction. The high biotic productivity of vast Tokyo Bay, its surrounding wetlands, and its wooded uplands, made the Kanto—then as now—the most densely populated space in Japan.

In Late and Final Jōmon times (4,000–3,000 and 3,000–2,000 years ago), the Jōmon communities of northern Japan persisted and continued to elaborate their ceramic, artistic, social, and ceremonial productions in distinctive ways. Some of their cultural luxury items—for example, burnished pottery wares and spouted and handled ceramic teapots—reflect a growing awareness of distant continental cultures and practices. Other artifacts, especially beautifully made serving vessels and pottery drums, are obviously the furnishings of grand feasting events that would have been important in maintaining community solidarity and strengthening the growing social influence and leadership of prosperous elite households within the community. The Jōmon tradition also persisted in southern Honshu, Kyushu, and Shikoku. Although not as numerous or richly elaborated as in the north, the Jōmon people and culture were nevertheless well represented in the south, with concentrations in the Kyoto-Osaka, Okayama, and southern Honshu–northern Kyushu regions.

During southern Japan's Final Jōmon period, new cultural influences emanating from Korea were beginning to be felt in Kyushu. For thousands of years previously, fishermen and traders had made contacts back and forth across the Korea Strait, as shown by finds of Jōmon pottery in the great shell mound of Tongsam-dong at modern Busan and the occurrence of Chulmun pottery—a Korean counterpart of Jōmon—at Jōmon sites near Fukuoka in northwestern Kyushu. Japanese obsidian was one valuable commodity being traded into obsidian-deficient southern Korea, while Korean artisans produced *Glycymeris* clamshell bracelets highly valued in southern Japan. During Late and Final Jōmon times far-reaching new productive and social processes were developing in Korea, and the high civilization of China was in an expansive phase. Together these forces portended great cultural and historical changes for a Japan that Koreans had long been in touch with but had not taken a major interest in.

YAYOI-KOFUN–PERIOD JAPANESE CULTURE AND ITS KOREAN ANTECEDENTS

The Yayoi period, and the Kofun period that grew out of it, is inseparably linked to an earlier emergence of agriculture and Bronze Age society in Korea; thus a brief excursion into peninsular archaeology is needed here to elucidate the historical processes by which these new elements arose. The Middle Neolithic Chulmun culture of the Seoul region, which was strikingly similar in its fundamentals (and even the cord-marking of its pottery) to the hunting-fishing-gathering Jōmon tradition of Japan, began about 5,500 years ago to incorporate the cultivation of millet and other continental plants into its local version of the broad-spectrum hunting-fishing-collecting harvest economies that grew up in parallel all around the Sea of Japan.

By 3,500 years ago, the Korean population was growing vigorously. Chulmun community groups had over time added one cultivated plant after another to their initially very Jōmon-like woodland hunting-fishing-gathering economic base, and as this was happening, the distinctive cord-marking that decorated their Chulmun pots and jars gradually became less and less common until finally by about 1500 BCE the characteristic pottery was effectively *mumun* (without cord-marking). Archaeologists recognize at this point of transition a Mumun tradition of plain coarse pottery, by which they define the fully emergent early agricultural society.

As prosperity and population grew with the gradual addition of cultivated crops to traditional harvesting activities, some larger transitional Mumun households with strong internal leadership and community influence turned to the intensive collective labor of building the dams, ditches, and paddy fields needed to move into much more productive paddy rice cultivation. Rice cultivation was then already ancient in neighboring China, where it is well attested in the lower reaches of the Yangtze River by at least 7,000 years ago; and contemporary examples of how to do it were widely present in Shandong and the lower Liao River Valley, bordering Korea. Rice of the cool climate–adapted *Oryza japonica* type, along with irrigated paddy fields, appeared at a number of Mumun sites that also contained the earlier-adopted set of Chulmun cultigens named above.

As Mumun settlements became increasingly large and numerous, local communities became more differentiated internally and more competitive with their neighbors. These stresses are evident in the well-known example of Songguk-ni, a large community where a moated precinct separated the residential and cemetery area of a community elite from the majority of the populace. Another definitive characteristic of the site is a series of large raised-floor storage buildings that consolidated the community's mixed-crop harvest (including rice) in one area of the site, no doubt to facilitate its management by the local leaders. Elite stone cist graves displayed bronze and polished stone daggers, spear points, and arrowheads, while the graves of ordinary folk were as a rule wholly unfurnished. Conspicuously, the weaponry found in elite graves, in addition to moats, fortifications, and a notable incidence of violent fires known from a number of other Mumun settlements like Songguk-ni, show the prevalence of stress and competition among and perhaps within communities.

When such communities exceeded the practical capacity of locally available lands, they hived off new settlements into space still available farther afield. By at least 400 BCE this process was bringing a growing number of Korean emigrants across the Korea Strait into northwest Kyushu and southern Honshu, then populated by Late Jōmon hunter-fisher-gatherers at a comparatively low density that afforded space into which emigrant cultivators could insert themselves. The distance between modern Busan in southernmost Korea and Fukuoka City on the northwest coast of Kyushu is about 130 kilometers, with a midcourse stop on the island of Tsūshima—not an insignificant journey but one well within the means of the time.

The conspicuous archaeological markers of Korean arrival in Japan include plain coarse Mumun pottery, Liaoning bronze daggers, Korean slender bronze daggers, polished stone daggers, spear points, and arrowheads; stone cist elite graves or dolmens containing such items, and commoner jar burials with few or no grave goods; and rice paddy fields, along with evidence of millet and other typical Korean crops. The human skeletons from emigrant Yayoi period graves in Japan are also readily recognizable as those of Koreans, quite different in skull morphology, stature, and other characteristics from the native Jōmon people.

The skeletal features of Kyushu natives found in Late Jōmon graves are most similar to those of the contemporary Ainu of northern Japan and Ryūkyūans of far southern Japan, who are clearly descended from the native Jōmon population. The modern Japanese population is recognizably different from both the Jōmon and Korean populations, and unmistakably the product of intermarriage between Korean emigrants and Jōmon Japanese natives. These biological relationships have been documented over many decades in a substantial literature based on various forms of morphological analysis, and more recently confirmed by genetically based research on a set of contemporary populations that compared twenty different genetically determined blood group, red cell enzyme, and serum protein systems.

The new way of life that arose in Japan from this flowing together of emigrant Korean and in situ Japanese peoples and cultures is called Yayoi (so named because the distinctive plain coarse pottery type, so different from Jōmon and so like Korean Mumun ware, was first described archaeologically from a site in Yayoi-chō, Tokyo). The premier Late Jōmon–Early Yayoi site of Itatsuke in modern Fukuoka City looks very Mumun in its basic character and gives evidence of irrigation channels, water ponds, and ridged paddy fields divided into small sections. There were also carbonized specimens of Japonica rice and wooden hoes preserved in the waterlogged soils, along with polished stone reaping knives and daggers of types definitive of the Korean Mumun culture. Near the agricultural area is an Early Yayoi settlement with both inner and outer moats, evoking the Songguk-ni settlement type. The long-known Arita, Imakawa, and Magarita sites, not far from Itatsuke in northern Kyushu, are of similar character and a somewhat later age, and they, now along with many others, give a very substantial record of Yayoi cultural growth in northern Kyushu over centuries.

Dating of the Jōmon-Yayoi transition has for a long time seemed problematic because it appeared to happen very fast, with final Jōmon and earliest Yayoi evidence conflated into a single time period. Subsequent reanalysis of transitional Jōmon and Yayoi pottery assemblages in northern Kyushu clarified matters somewhat, as did the finding of paddy field systems in which overlapping rice fields spanned a considerable period. This work led to the recognition of an Initial (or "Earliest") Yayoi period interposed between Final Jōmon and Early Yayoi times, which affords a more reasonable time perspective on the transition. Dating ambiguities remain, however, as some quite recently obtained and still very controversial C-14 dates suggest that the previously established date of about 400 BCE for Early Yayoi might be pushed back to 800–900 BCE, or perhaps even further.

Whatever the ultimate resolution of this issue, the rapidity with which Yayoi culture spread throughout Japan was impressive. Continuing research has shown that pioneering Early Yayoi sites are scattered all along the Japan Sea coast, from Kyushu in the south to the northernmost end of Honshu. Also rapid, and much more intense, was the spread of Yayoi cultural patterns up the Inland Sea region into the Osaka-Kyoto-Nara area. Farther north the rate of cultural transformation slowed; in Kanto and beyond, the well-established Jōmon foragers' reluctance to fully assimilate to the new agricultural way of life is seen in the emergence of a distinctive pottery tradition that suggests Yayoi influence but preserves important Jōmon elements of vessel form and decoration. Indeed, both biotic remains from archaeological sites and subsequent written histories confirm that ancient hunting—and especially fishing—practices persisted into Yayoi and later historic times in northern Japan. Even in the modern world fishing remains everywhere a fundamental leg of the Japanese economy.

Returning to the main theater of Yayoi cultural growth in southern Japan, we see that population and societal complexity grew rapidly throughout the Early, Middle, and Late Yayoi periods. Many sites give evidence of this process, but the grandest exemplar is the site of Yoshinogari, now a national historical park. It is located about thirty kilometers south of Fukuoka City, just across the Sefuri Mountains at the high edge of a broad plain that slopes down to Kyushu's inland Ariake Sea. This extensive site spans the Yayoi period and continued to be occupied into the medieval Nara and Heian periods as well. Yoshinogari is remarkably like large Korean sites of the Songguk-ni type in its scale, layout, and cultural contents, and many of its inhabitants were surely emigrant Koreans who maintained trading and other contacts with their homeland. The archaeological traces found there include many bronze and iron tools of Korean make, as well as bronze mirrors and other items brought all the way from the Han Chinese border garrisons at Lelang and Taifeng in the Liaoning region, just beyond the northwest Korean frontier.

Yoshinogari gives evidence of moated southern and northern inner enclosures, a large northern mound containing multiple elite burials, a Late Yayoi period outer moat bounding a large area, a concentrated zone of raised-floor granaries, and other features that set it off as a major center dominated by an elite class of leaders. Some Japanese archaeologists have suggested it may have been the very capital of Himiko, queen of Yamatai, a small Japanese principality or "country" described in the Chinese history of the Wei Kingdom (221–265 CE). The weight of archaeological (as opposed to media) opinion, however, is that the capital of Queen Himiko was most likely in the Nara region to the north, where the kingdom of Yamato, Japan's first historic state, was later established. In any event, the historical dates place Yamatai within Middle and Late Yayoi times, which fits both the archaeological record of Yoshinogari and the evidence of Chinese bronze mirrors and other artifacts found there. The Wei chronicles mention many little "countries" in the land of Wa (a Chinese name for Japan), and Yoshinogari was probably the capital of one of them. Additional large moated Yayoi sites now known throughout the southern half of Japan no doubt represent other such "capitals," the seats of power of emerging Yayoi elite houses that preceded those of the Kofun, or Mounded Tomb, period.

Like their Songguk-ni–like predecessors in Korea, the Yayoi communities that were rapidly established in Kyushu, along the Inland Sea, and in the Nara region beyond were hierarchically organized groups within which a few dominant households organized and managed communal productive labors and in so doing increasingly set themselves apart as a prosperous aristocratic class. In addition to farmers these communities employed bronze-casters, ironworkers, potters, and other specialists whose small local workshops made everyday tools for ordinary householders, as well as weaponry and luxury items for the aristocrats who were their leaders and increasingly their masters. Agricultural settlements with substantial populations, a labor-intensive infrastructure of dams, ditches, and paddy fields for rice cultivation—and often moated internal precincts that guarded ruling elites and the community granaries against internal as well as external stresses—spread rapidly as the Yayoi population boomed and the power and economic control of local elite houses grew.

As the Yayoi period became the Kofun period after about 300 CE, the same basic agrarian and artisan economy continued to function. A substantial Korean influx continued over time, as aristocratic Korean houses and their retainers fled periodic defeats in the almost incessant wars prosecuted over centuries among the kingdoms of Koguryŏ, Paekche, the Kaya states, and Silla in the Korean peninsula. Japanese warlords who had involved themselves in some of these conflicts accepted such refugees as allies, and the educated elites, along with the ironworkers, potters, and scholars in their retinues, contributed massively to economic, political, and religious life in Kofun and later times.

The Japanese population continued to expand, and regionally dominant aristocratic houses came to control enough wealth and peasant labor to ceremoniously inter their leaders in large burial mounds. Thousands of these *kofun* tumuli in various sizes and forms dot the Japanese countryside, from their center of gravity in the Osaka-Nara-Kyoto region south into Okayama and Kyushu and north into the Tokyo area. Their simple existence shows that effectively all of central and southern Japan then supported and was dominated by strong aristocratic ruling houses. The distinctive "keyhole-shaped" *kofun* burial mound has long been thought the signature type of early Japan's Yamato house and its allies, but rounded and square forms are also common. Built over about four centuries between 300 and 700 CE, *kofun* typically were large, the construction of each one consuming thousands of man-days of peasant labor. The largest, attributed to the Emperor Nintoku, is an astounding 486 meters long. Others are much smaller, but even a relatively modest *kofun* 50 or 60 meters in diameter required major investment. The pervasive physical presence and sheer number of Japan's *kofun*-period mounded tombs, and not least their often rich contents, impressively demonstrate the wealth and power enjoyed by the aristocratic families that buried their leaders in them.

The goods buried with local rulers in early Kofun times tended to be Chinese bronze mirrors; bronze spears and daggers of Korean type but in exaggerated forms that imply display rather than combat use; polished-stone curved beads (*magatama*); and other symbolic items. These suggest an initial peaceful phase when emerging elite houses focused mainly on acquiring rich goods demonstrative of their wealth and social status through trade and courtly exchanges and relied mainly on ritual and symbolic reinforcement of their dominant status vis-à-vis the peasant farming and artisan classes.

About 500 CE, however, the goods placed in *kofun* burial troves began to take on a much more warlike cast, indicating the transition to an age devoted to competition and combat among aristocratic houses that had turned to aggressively seeking greater wealth and dominance at the expense of one another. Typical items were trappings for warhorses, suits of armor, swords, and daggers for elite mounted warriors; bows, spears, and halberds for conscripted peasant infantrymen; and caches of iron ingots as a form of wealth that could be fashioned into tools and weapons as needed. The instruments of war were conspicuously of imported Korean types, and ingots of Korean iron continued to be imported for the use of local smiths until eventually the iron sands of Japan were discovered and developed.

Japanese scholars suggest that at least a million Koreans poured into the Kinki region during the fifth and sixth centuries along with these items, to the degree that, according to *Shoku Nihongi*, eight or nine out of ten residents in the Nara basin claimed to have descended from Paekche. Korean scholars, priests, scribes, and skilled bureaucratic functionaries were assimilated into the upper levels of Yamato society. Missions sent to China in the 600s by Yamato leaders with the good offices and support of west-central Korea's Paekche royal house returned to Japan in due course with Chinese concepts of a court hierarchy defined by official ranks and prerogatives, provincial governors, road systems, population registers, and the all-important collecting of taxes, among other elements. In 646 CE, a Yamato court edict laid out a social and political system inspired by the Chinese example; it necessarily continued to evolve in the ferment of the times, but nevertheless established the historical basis for a centralized imperial state in Japan. In 710 CE, the state of Nihon was officially declared, ushering in the Nara-period crystallization of the Japanese society and culture we know today.

Sources and Suggestions for Further Reading

See the bibliography for complete publication data.

Aikens, C. Melvin, Irina S. Zhushchikhovskaya, and Song Nai Rhee. "Environment, Adaptation, and Interaction in Japan, Korea, and the Russian Far East: The Millennial History of a Japan Sea Oikumene" (2009).

Aikens, C. Melvin, and Takeru Akazawa. "The Pleistocene/Holocene Transition in Japan and Adjacent Northeast Asia" (1996).

Habu, Junko. *Ancient Jōmon of Japan*. Cambridge: Cambridge University Press, 2004.

———. *Subsistence-Settlement Systems and Intersite Variability in the Moroiso Phase of the Early Jōmon Period of Japan* (2001).

Ikawa-Smith, Fumiko. "Humans Along the Pacific Margin of Northeast Asia Before the Last Glacial Maximum: Evidence for Their Presence and Adaptations" (2004).

Imamura, Keiji. *Prehistoric Japan: New Perspectives on Insular East Asia* (1996).

Kidder, J. Edward. *Prehistoric Japanese Arts: Jōmon Pottery* (1968).

Koike, Hiroko. "Prehistoric Hunting Pressure and Paleobiomass: An Environmental Reconstruction and Archaeozoological Analysis of a Jōmon Shellmound Area" (1986).

Omoto, Keiichi, and Naruya Saitou. "Genetic Origins of the Japanese: A Partial Support for the Dual Structure Hypothesis" (1997).

Pearson, Richard J., Gina Lee Barnes, and Karl L. Hutterer, eds. *Windows on the Japanese Past: Studies in Archaeology and Prehistory* (1986).

Rhee, Song Nai, C. Melvin Aikens, Sung Rak Choi, and Hyuk-jin Ro. "Korean Contributions to Agriculture, Technology, and State Formation in Japan: Archaeology and History of an Epochal Thousand Years, 400 BCE–600 CE" (2007).

Zhushchikhovskaya, Irina S. *Prehistoric Pottery-Making of the Russian Far East* (2005).

7

What Used to Be Called Shinto

The Question of Japan's Indigenous Religion

Mark Teeuwen

Modern Shinto theology posits that Shinto is rooted in the indigenous or native religion of the Japanese islands. Like most dogmas, this is both true and untrue. There are indeed continuities between the ancient past and the present. Quite a number of today's Shinto shrines have histories that go back to the seventh century at least, and some of the deities they enshrine figure in eighth-century sources. Yet the Shinto vision of its own past differs radically from historical understandings of early Japanese society.

Shinto's conception of its ancient origins revolves around the idea that Japanese antiquity was an age of indigenous authenticity that had not yet been corrupted by foreign influences. In that distant age, Shinto exegesis maintains, emperors descended from powerful deities (*kami*) were able to extend their rule over the islands because the people and their rulers were united in their wholehearted worship of those same deities.[1] In other words, the Japanese were bound together by a shared faith in the native *kami*, and this indigenous creed was called Shinto.

In fact, this notion of a nation united by a single indigenous religion first emerged in early modern times. Shinto as we know it today was molded out of classical sources and new ideas in the nineteenth century, and modern Shinto's teachings are of no help if we want to reconstruct the multifarious religious traditions of ancient Japan. This is why recent scholarship tends to avoid using the term "Shinto" with reference to the ancient period, resorting instead to phrases like the one that forms the title of this essay.

In Shinto's vision of a pure past, ancient Japan has been imagined as a place of stability and unity. Such a view is, however, hardly in line even with the selected classical sources that Shinto thinkers have relied upon—the two earliest court chronicles, *Kojiki* (completed in 712) and *Nihon shoki* (completed in 720). Neither conveys an image of peaceful harmony or unity; rather, both describe the inconclusive struggles of a "heavenly" dynasty against powerful "earthly" enemies.

These works begin with the separation of heaven and earth and the birth of the Japanese islands. The *kami* of heaven then decide to impose celestial rule on the "Central Land of Reed Plains" below, and after a number of failed attempts, the *kami* of the earth are finally forced to relinquish the land. The leading *kami* of heaven—the sun-goddess Amaterasu in *Kojiki*, the male Takami-musuhi in the main variant in *Nihon shoki*—orders the "heavenly grandson," Ninigi, to establish an everlasting heavenly dynasty on earth.[2] Yet even this heavenly mandate does not result in peaceful rule. The first human emperor, Ninigi's great-grandson, Jinmu, wins the Yamato heartland only after a long and hard-fought battle. Many generations later, the warrior-hero Yamato-takeru faces an endless list of both human and divine enemies in western and eastern Japan, until he is finally killed by the *kami* of Mt. Ibuki in Owari, a typical "earthly deity" who attacks him in the guise of a wild boar. Even when peace is won, it never lasts long.

The Japan depicted in *Kojiki* and *Nihon shoki* is, moreover, not an isolated place of unstained indigenous culture. Quite the contrary, both works record countless links with Korea and China and strive to relate their tale about the origins of Japan and its ruling dynasty to established continental principles. While this is more evident in *Nihon shoki* than in the slightly earlier *Kojiki*, even *Kojiki* includes an introduction that describes the "great beginning" in terms of yin and yang—Chinese, not Japanese, concepts—and compares Emperor Tenmu, who gave orders for *Kojiki*'s compilation, to the Yellow Emperor and the kings of Zhou. Both chronicles record the arrival of immigrant groups, mostly from the Korean kingdoms of Paekche and Silla, and describe their close links to the Yamato court. They even tell of Korean deities who crossed the sea to Japan and settled there. *Nihon shoki* gives a detailed account of the advent of Buddhism in the sixth century and records how Yamato rulers used Buddhist and non-Buddhist rites in conjunction, both as regular performances and as special measures in times of crisis.

It is in the archeological record, however, that the full weight of Japan's connections to Korea comes to light. In the centuries that preceded the compilation of the court histories, known as the Tomb age (c. 250–700 CE), life in the Japanese islands was utterly transformed by techniques, beliefs, and practices transmitted from Korea. Ironworking, large-scale irrigation, new methods of producing stoneware, stonemasonry, bronze-casting, silk-weaving, writing, and many aspects of statecraft were introduced from the mainland. Some of these innovations spread rapidly across most of the islands, while others took centuries to reach eastern Japan. Continental technologies entered different local contexts at different times and produced different outcomes. Long after advanced regions such as northern Kyushu and Yamato had adopted sophisticated techniques—including greatly improved agricultural methods and the art of writing—in order to manage coherent political units based on the large-scale growing of rice, large parts of eastern and northern Japan still depended largely on hunting and fishing.

It is unthinkable that "the Japanese," to use an anachronism, could have shared a single religion at any time during this period. Arguably, there was never a period in Japan's history with so much regional diversity, and therefore any attempt to pin down "what the ancient Japanese believed" is doomed to fail.

The tombs that gave their name to this age are a good illustration of the mixing of local and continental impulses in this period. The idea of building monumental grave mounds derived ultimately from China. Continental influences are obvious in tombs of the early, mid-, and late Tomb periods alike.[3] Yet Japanese tombs remained very different from their Korean or northern Chinese counterparts. Some prominent indigenous elements include the keyhole-shaped (*zenpō kōen*) design that is among the more common tomb types in Japan, and tombs' adornment with clay figures called *haniwa*. In the late period, wall paintings inside the grave chambers of tombs ranged from obvious copies of models from northern Korea or China (e.g., the deities of the four directions) to more local motifs such as ships, horses, fish, and spirals. All in all, then, these greatest monuments of ancient Japan display a complicated interplay between influences from the Asian mainland and elements of local culture.

The late Tomb period saw both the introduction of Buddhism and the development of a new court cult of *kami*, the so-called *jingi* cult, named after a Chinese term meaning "deities of heaven [*jin*] and earth [*gi*]." Buddhism arrived in the sixth century, and temples gradually replaced tombs in the course of the seventh. The *jingi* cult, which Shintoists consider the earliest mature form of their religion, emerged more than a century after the appearance of Buddhism in Japan, in the last decades of the seventh century. *Kojiki* and *Nihon shoki*, with their narrative about the dynasty's roots in the *Kami* age, were finished not much later, in the early eighth century, though their accounts clearly are the result of a long formative history. With such a wide variety of impulses, agendas, and ongoing experiments, sifting the "native" from the "foreign" in retrospect is neither possible nor productive, and constructing a straightforward narrative of development is a tall order indeed.

THE COURT'S *KAMI* CULT AND THE ARCHAEOLOGICAL RECORD

The court cult of *kami* and the myths about the *Kami* age have often been isolated from the religious landscape and presented as the indigenous roots of Shinto. But even if we leave aside the question of defining "Shinto," we are left with the problem of how to relate the *kami* myths and rituals of the late seventh and eighth centuries to the archaeological record. To what extent can these myths and practices shed light on the material culture of the Tomb period excavated by archeologists?

Here it is hard not to be disappointed. The tombs themselves, those impressive monuments that symbolize the age, hardly figure in the myths at all, nor do we learn much about the rituals that must have been staged on or around them. There is certainly no explanation to be found anywhere for their idiosyncratic design. Those who try to decode the symbolism of the *haniwa* find little of substance in *Kojiki* or *Nihon shoki* to guide them. Female figures wearing curved jewels and sashes are often identified as shamanic priestesses (*miko*) devoted to the *kami,* but jewels and sashes were commonly worn and there is no reason to identify these figures as more religious in nature than others. *Haniwa* house models are often interpreted as dwellings for the spirits of the dead, lines of human figures and animals as funeral processions, and replicas of weapons as protection against evil spirits, but neither the *kami* myths nor recorded *kami* rituals are of any help here, and we can only speculate.

The case of the *haniwa* symbolizes the way older practices were reimagined and reframed when the court compiled its chronicles around the year 700. *Nihon shoki* includes a rather grisly legend about the *haniwa.* As part of the burial ceremonies of one of Emperor Suinin's brothers, we are told, his personal attendants were buried alive with him, standing upright on top of the tomb. They took a long time to die and ended up being eaten by dogs and ravens. Some years later, when one of Suinin's wives died, it was therefore decided that clay images would be set up instead.[4]

Archaeology, however, reveals this tale to be pure fiction. Not only is there no evidence to suggest that human sacrifice ever took place at Japanese tombs, but *haniwa* depicting humans are a late development from more abstract prototypes that archaeologists interpret as offering vessels. By the time the *Nihon shoki* was compiled, then, earlier significations had either been forgotten or rejected, and a new meaning was adopted that presented the *haniwa* as tokens of imperial benevolence.

Of course there are also continuities. One such is the use of mirrors, which are ubiquitous both in early tombs and in the *kami* myths and rituals of the seventh and eighth centuries. But this does not mean that the large caches of mirrors buried in tombs as early as the third century conveyed the same meanings as the single mirrors that feature in the *kami* myths and that were enshrined in *kami* sanctuaries. Like the *haniwa*, mirrors may well have taken on radically different functions and significations in the intervening centuries.

The *haniwa* mystery illustrates the problems that adhere to *Kojiki* and *Nihon shoki* as sources on earlier periods. These works contain many references to ancient practices, but present them in a very selective manner and reframe them in a narrative that bears little relation to their older functions and meanings. The same goes for the *kami* and their rituals. The selection of *kami* who found their way into the court chronicles was never representative of Japanese "indigenous religion," whatever that may be, and we cannot assume that those *kami* who *were* included in the chronicles were part of popular religion at any time.

AMATERASU AND ISE

The most famous *kami* of all, and the undisputed star of *kami* myth, is the sun-goddess and imperial ancestor, Amaterasu. From medieval times onward, Shinto was largely construed around the cult of Amaterasu and her shrine in Ise. A closer look at Amaterasu's ancient roots allows us to gauge the degree to which ancient religion "lived on" in later Shinto. Since the early eighth century, Amaterasu's Ise shrine has been honored by the court above all others, and in the chronicles compiled at that same time (especially in *Kojiki*), Amaterasu was given supreme status as the leader of the heavenly deities. Was this Amaterasu a truly ancient Japanese *kami*, or was she an eighth-century invention? Are the myths about this deity representative of Japan's indigenous religion, or do they reflect new developments within the narrow confines of the court? Was Amaterasu a purely "native" figure, or was her conception the result of continental influences?

The chapters on the *Kami* age in *Kojiki* and *Nihon shoki* contain two main myths about Amaterasu. The first relates how Amaterasu was visited in her heavenly domain by her brother, Susanowo, who defeated her in a contest and celebrated his victory by committing all kinds of defiling acts. When he threw a flayed horse into Amaterasu's weaving hall, she wounded herself with her weaving shuttle and withdrew into a cave, leaving the world in utter darkness.[5] The *kami* of heaven then gathered in front of the cave and decorated a tree with cloth, jewels, and a mirror; materials for this ritual were collected from a Yamato mountain called Ame no Kaguyama. The goddess Ame no Uzume performed a lewd dance, pulling out her nipples and pushing down her skirt band. When Amaterasu heard the gods laugh, she opened the cave door to see what was going on. Confused by her own reflection in the mirror, she allowed herself to be pulled out of the cave, and light was once more restored to the world.

The second myth deals with the descent of the heavenly grandson, Ninigi. After the earthly *kami* had been pacified and forced to hand over the land to the *kami* of heaven, Ninigi descended to a mountain in Kyushu with a following of *kami*. His train included the same *kami* who had led the proceedings in front of Amaterasu's cave; these same *kami* are further identified as ancestors of prominent court lineages. In *Kojiki*, it was Amaterasu who granted Ninigi eternal rule over the "Central Land of Reed Plains"; in the main variant in *Nihon shoki*, it was another sun-deity called Takami-musuhi. Amaterasu is presented as Ninigi's paternal grandmother, and Takami-musuhi as his maternal grandfather.

A few generations after Ninigi, the *Kami* age ended and rule passed to a dynasty of human "emperors." Amaterasu makes a few rare appearances in this part of the chronicles; three are important here.

First, the first human emperor Jinmu left Kyushu to conquer Yamato. He ran into trouble when he attacked Yamato from the west, and concluded that since he was a "descendent of the sun *kami*," he must strike from the east so that his troops will have the sun at their backs.[6]

Second, generations later, when Emperor Chūai was in Kyushu for a military campaign, his consort Jingū Kōgō was possessed by Amaterasu, who told the emperor that he should invade Korea. When Chūai disobeyed, he soon died, and Jingū Kōgō led the expedition in his stead. With Amaterasu's help Korea was easily reduced to a Japanese tribute state.

And third, a rather complicated sequence explains Amaterasu's enshrinement at Ise. During the reign of Emperor Sujin, the land was struck by an epidemic that killed "more than half the people," triggering a wave of "vagabondage" and a violent rebellion. In response the emperor "asked that he be punished by the gods of heaven and earth" for any failures on his part. He especially feared the presence of two *kami* in his palace: Amaterasu and Yamato Ōkunitama, the "Great Spirit of the land of Yamato." He entrusted these *kami* to two of his daughters; one of them took Amaterasu to the village of Kasanui to be worshipped there. Still the pestilence showed no sign of abating, and Sujin assembled the "eighty myriad *kami*" on an open plain near his palace to gauge their will through divination. There, yet another *kami*, Ōmononushi of nearby Mt. Miwa, took possession of yet another maiden, who revealed that the emperor's failure to offer Ōmononushi proper worship was the cause of the country's calamities. Not much later, Ōmononushi appeared to Sujin himself, saying that he would stop his mischief if only he was worshipped by a named man who was his own descendant. Sujin transferred the worship of both Ōmononushi and Yamato Ōkunitama to the right "*kami* masters"; with this, he deemed that it was now propitious for him to worship the eighty myriad *kami*. He "decided which were to be heavenly shrines and which earthly shrines" and allotted land and service households to them. With that the epidemic finally gave way, peace was regained, and the five grains yielded abundant harvests once again. Amaterasu reached her final destination a generation later, when another maiden led Amaterasu to the site in Ise where her shrine is still to be found today.[7]

What are we to make of these myths and the practices implied in them? First of all, it is worth noting that the cult of Amaterasu appears to have been closely associated with important technologies of continental origin. One of these is weaving; another is metallurgy.

Weaving has a long history in Japan; even silk was produced in the islands well before the Tomb period began. Throughout East Asia, woven cloth served as a medium of economic exchange. Tribute and taxes were to a large degree paid in cloth, and cloth was offered to the gods in considerable quantities. Japanese weaving techniques were revolutionized by impulses from China and Korea, and important immigrant lineages at the court (particularly the Hata) identified themselves with weaving.

These technologies included much that we would today regard as cultic information. Many elements of Chinese folk religion appear in the cult of Amaterasu, and it has even been suggested that the myth of the cave depicts Amaterasu as a cocooning silkworm. In Chinese lore, the mysterious silkworm was not just a producer of precious silk but also a symbol of longevity or even immortality. *Nihon shoki* documents the occurrence in Japan of a cult dedicated to the "insect of the Eternal World" (*tokoyo no mushi*), which was believed to confer wealth on worshippers; Ise, too, was associated with this Eternal World.[8] At Ise, miniature looms were among the numerous objects deposited in Amaterasu's shrine, and silk thread figured prominently among seasonal offerings; in fact, the main priest of Amaterasu's shrine was obliged to keep silkworms in his own residence. This web of associations shows that the figure of Amaterasu reflects a shared East Asian complex of ideas and practices in which weaving, wealth, and immortality were closely intertwined.

Amaterasu was also associated with metalworking techniques and weapons. A tenth-century list of shrines (*Jinmyōchō*) shows that there were ten "Amaterasu" shrines in addition to Ise. At nine of these shrines, the title "Amaterasu" (heaven-shining) referred to the *kami* Ame no Hoakari of the Owari lineage. This lineage traced its descent to Ame no Hoakari through his son Ame no Kaguyama, whose name is identical to that of the mountain that supplied the materials used to lure Amaterasu from the cave. Among those materials was the ore from which the mirror was made.

The Owari ancestor Ame no Kaguyama was also known as Taguri-hiko; *taguri* (vomit) was a technical term for the melted metal flowing from the heated ore. Elsewhere in *Nihon shoki* it is said that the *kami* of the "ore mountains" were born when their mother, Izanami, was burnt by the *kami* of fire and vomited in pain.

In Jinmu's time, Amaterasu ordered Ame no Kaguyama (under yet another name) to give Jinmu a heavenly sword that won him victory in his conquest of Yamato. This loose web of *kami*, lineages, iron, treasures, and weapons suggests that a body of blacksmiths' lore is also reflected in the Amaterasu cult.

Of course, such webs did not emerge out of thin air. Encoded in them are political and military struggles between competing lineages and kin groups, some quite old at the time the chronicles were compiled, others more recent. As long as the myths were truly alive, new developments were constantly being worked into them, sometimes leaving in place traces of earlier events, and at other times cutting large holes in the overlapping webs of *kami*, lineages, places, objects, and practices.

One major set of events that must have brought great changes to the cult of Amaterasu occurred in the late seventh century. This was the Jinshin War of 672–673, in which Emperor Tenmu defeated his nephew and took the throne. *Nihon shoki* relates that at an early phase in his campaign, Tenmu worshipped Amaterasu in the field; soon after his enthronement he sent one of his daughters to "the shrine of Amaterasu in Ise," where she was to serve that *kami* as an "abstinence priestess."[9] No such priestesses had been sent to Ise for a long time, and for five generations Tenmu's predecessors had shown no interest whatsoever in Ise. Many have interpreted these events as a sign that Tenmu attributed his victory to Amaterasu and raised that *kami*'s cult in Ise to a new, higher status early during his reign. It is worth noting that in real life, Tenmu had been fostered as a child by the Owari, those keepers of many Amaterasu shrines, and that the Owari were among the main supporters of his coup.

What kind of a figure was "Amaterasu" in Tenmu's time? If the worship of Amaterasu at Ise was initiated (or, at least, transformed) by Tenmu after 673, it seems logical to regard the legends of Ise's origins, chronicled as events from the reigns of Sujin and Suinin, as products of Tenmu's age. In those legends Amaterasu shows two faces: one as a wrathful *kami*, spreading disease and disorder and even threatening the emperor's life; the other as a powerful figure who stands at the apex of a hierarchy of "earthly and heavenly deities" (*jingi*).

Like Yamato Ōkunitama and Ōmononushi, Amaterasu was entrusted to a maiden of jealously guarded virginity. This fact alone suggests that Amaterasu was at some point a male *kami* who behaved much like those two "earthly *kami*" of the Yamato area; indeed, Ame no Hoakari, who dwelt in the Amaterasu shrines of the Owari, was male, too. As soon as Amaterasu settled in Ise, however, this *kami's* status changed. *Nihon shoki* tells that Emperor Suinin was visited in a dream by Amaterasu's old companion, Yamato Ōkunitama, soon after Amaterasu had reached Ise. This *kami* revealed that Amaterasu had always governed heaven; now, her imperial descendants had assumed absolute authority over the "eighty [myriad] spirits and *kami*." Ōkunitama therefore announced that his tenure as the ruler of the land had come to an end.[10] In other words, now that Amaterasu had been installed in her (his?) proper place, it was time for Ōkunitama, the old master of the land, to retire. The spirits and *kami* of the land were henceforth subject to Amaterasu's heavenly rule. Amaterasu's transfer to Ise signaled that this *kami* had now become the supreme *kami* of heaven whose descendants ruled on earth.

Yamato Ōkunitama's oracle echoes a passage we encountered above in the sequence about Sujin's quelling of *kami*-caused calamities: after the three *kami* Amaterasu, Ōkunitama, and Ōmononushi had been pacified, the emperor categorized the eighty myriad *kami* as "heavenly and earthly shrines" and allotted land and service households to them. This legend marked the beginning of the court cult of *kami* as *jingi* (heavenly and earthly deities).

The central idea of this cult was that the emperor, as the descendant of the heavenly deities, presented offerings to the *kami* of the earth in all corners of the realm, and in that way ensured peace and prosperity. Tenmu was the first to design the court's *kami* worship around this categorization, and the first to conceive of the idea that the emperor should be sending offerings to all the (deserving) *kami* of the realm. When the term *jingi* appears in earlier chapters, it is always in connection with the Amaterasu myths summarized above. This suggests that the term was included in those chapters to supply Tenmu's newly conceived *jingi* cult with ancient precedents.

One more twist was added to the story of Amaterasu after Tenmu's death, during the reign of his formidable widow, Jitō. Jitō fought a long battle to pass the throne first to her own son, Prince Kusakabe, and, when he died young, to Kusakabe's young son, Monmu. Jitō granted rule over Japan to her grandson Monmu, just as Amaterasu did to her grandson, Ninigi. Many scholars think that these events shaped the figure of Amaterasu as this deity appears in the chronicles. Herman Ooms, for example, argues that Amaterasu was "a transparent double of the female *tennō* Jitō."[11] There are two convincing arguments for such a thesis: textual studies reveal that Amaterasu was inserted into the Ninigi myth at a late date, replacing Takami-musuhi; and Jitō showed an ardent interest in Ise. She visited Ise personally in 692, staffed the shrines with new priests, and likely initiated the Ise practice of renewing the shrines and their treasures every twentieth year. If Amaterasu was ever male, only Jitō would have had the motivation and power to change this *kami*'s gender. All the evidence is circumstantial, but in my view, the notion of tracing the imperial lineage to a female deity of the sun (which is obviously yang and therefore male) in a patrilineal society is an anomaly that could only have occurred under special historical circumstances. Only Jitō's reign offers clues that can explain why the myths turned out as they did.

Reflected in the figure of Amaterasu, that most famous of all *kami*, are (1) at least partly continental lore associated with specialist techniques of great economic and military value, such as weaving and metallurgy; and (2) political events of the decades around the year 700. What is true for Amaterasu applies also to other *kami*. The myths in *Kojiki* and *Nihon shoki* cannot be read as a simple account of Japan's indigenous beliefs. Likewise, the *kami* rituals that the court adopted in the late seventh century (the *jingi* cult) were not a straightforward continuation of Japan's ancient traditions. Rather, they represented an innovative selection and adaptation of both Japanese and continental practices.

This chapter emphasizes the fact that the Shinto vision of a purely indigenous Japanese antiquity is a myth. Yet it is equally obvious that both the myths of *Kojiki* and *Nihon shoki* and the rituals of the *jingi* cult represented a striking deviation from Chinese examples. Neither Tenmu nor Jitō made any attempt to copy the largest ritual undertakings of the Tang court, and the notion of the emperor making offerings to all deities in the realm is very un-Chinese. The *jingi* cult, and the Ise cult more specifically, represented radical departures from the example set by the Tang. Rather than allowing ourselves to become obsessed with a search for "non-Japanese" ingredients in what has been misrepresented as indigenous religion, we should perhaps begin to address the more interesting question of why the Japanese court chose a ritual format so different from continental models, in spite of the pervading influence of China and Korea. It appears to me that we have hardly even begun to explore that issue.

Sources and Suggestions for Further Reading

See the bibliography for complete publication data.

Aston, W. G. *Nihongi: Chronicles of Japan from the Earliest Times to A.D. 697* (1972).

Breen, John, and Mark Teeuwen. *A New History of Shinto* (2010).

Como, Michael. *Weaving and Binding: Immigrant Gods and Female Immortals in Ancient Japan* (2009).

Farris, William Wayne. *Sacred Texts and Buried Treasures: Issues in the Historical Archaeology of Ancient Japan* (1998).

Kōnoshi Takamitsu. "Constructing Imperial Mythology: Kojiki and Nihon shoki" (2000).

Naumann, Nelly. *Die Mythen des Alten Japan* (1996).

Ooms, Herman. *Imperial Politics and Symbolics in Ancient Japan: The Tenmu Dynasty* (2008).
Philippi, Donald L., trans. *Kojiki* (1969).
Teeuwen, Mark. "Comparative Perspectives on the Emergence of Jindō and Shinto" (2007).

Notes

1. The term *kami* refers to a diverse array of beings, spirits, and forces that were objects of worship, in both prehistoric and historic times. These include the pantheon of anthropomorphic deities described in texts such as *Nihon shoki* and *Kojiki* (discussed below), as well as a wide range of infinitely numerous, omnipresent spirits that inhabit and activate the universe—the sun, moon, stars, clouds, wind, rain, mountains, rivers, and oceans, and also animals, trees, stones, and objects such as mirrors and swords.

2. *Nihon shoki* lists various versions of the myths, presenting one version as the main narrative and others as variants from other sources.

3. According to the most common periodization, the early Tomb period covered roughly the third and fourth centuries, the mid-Tomb period the fifth, and the late period the sixth and seventh centuries.

4. *Nihon shoki*, Suinin 28 and 32.

5. In the *Kojiki* version of this tale, Amaterasu's weaving maiden pierces her genitals with her shuttle and dies, whereupon Amaterasu locks herself into the cave in shock.

6. *Nihon shoki*, Jinmu, the year *tsuchinoe muma*.

7. *Nihon shoki*, Sujin 4–11 and Suinin 25.

8. *Nihon shoki*, Kōgyoku 3 (644); Suinin 25.

9. *Nihon shoki*, 672 6/26 and 673 4/14.

10. *Nihon shoki*, Suinin 25 3/10.

11. Ooms, *Imperial Politics and Symbolics in Ancient Japan*, 32.

8

The Emergence of Political Rulership and the State in Early Japan

Gina L. Barnes

Among the world's nations, the Japanese state is one of the most ancient, tracing its roots back to the third century CE when an emerging elite defined itself through shared aristocratic burial customs and an ideology that celebrated political rulership. These customs constitute the archaeological "Mounded Tomb Culture" of the Kofun period (250–710 CE), characterized particularly by keyhole-shaped tombs (figures 8.1, 8.2) provisioned with precious grave goods indicating access to valuable raw materials, the availability of specialist craftsmanship, and command of labor. In anthropological terms, mounded tomb burial signifies the stratification of early Japanese society into two classes: the rulers and the ruled.

Social stratification, in social evolutionary thinking, is considered the threshold for state formation. The preceding Yayoi societies had chiefs ruling regional polities. The crucial aspect of the Mounded Tomb Culture, however, is that it integrated many rulers of small polities in western Japan into a wide network across the archipelago from southern Tōhoku to Kyushu. The elite sharing of common values, aspirations, beliefs, and ideology in the Early Kofun period was the springboard for the emergence of an actual organization that could be called a state. Although scholars differ as to precisely when, the centralized state of early historic Japan emerged between the fourth and seventh centuries.

Figure 8.1. The green profile of the Hōraisan keyhole tomb, attributed to the Early Kofun ruler Suinin, rises near the Heijo (Nara) Palace Site, Nara City. The tomb mound consists of a round rear mound on the right, with a triangular front mound projecting at a lower level to the left (length 227 m, height 74 m). (Photograph by the author.)

This chapter traces the development of the Mounded Tomb Culture; the Early Kofun political ideology; the formation of overseas links with political leaders on both the Korean peninsula and mainland China; the transformation of Kofun-period culture through aristocrats and craftspeople newly immigrated from the continent; and the emergence of Yamato as the ancient Japanese state. Foremost in these discussions is political rulership in early Japan, which had a surprising female component that later disappeared.

The Kofun period is known through written documents as well as archaeology; the documents, however, are either contemporaneous foreign accounts (Chinese court histories) or native accounts written several centuries after the events recorded (Japanese court chronicles). The latter must be used cautiously due to political manipulation of their contents. The most important Chinese history for our purposes is what the Japanese call the *Gishi Wajinden*, or *Records of Wa in the* Weizhi, part of the *History of the Three Kingdoms* (*Sanguozhi*), written in the late third century. "Wa" is the Japanese pronunciation of Wo, the name by which the Chinese designated the archipelago and its inhabitants. The most important Japanese record is the *Nihon shoki*, or *Nihongi*, which was compiled and submitted to the Nara court in 720, soon after the end of the Kofun period. These two texts give very different views of early Japanese rulership, which remain unresolved despite centuries of investigation.

CHIEFTAINS UNITE UNDER THE MOUNDED TOMB CULTURE

Mounded burials became known in Japan probably through interaction with the Lelang Commandery, the center of the Chinese Han-dynasty military oc-

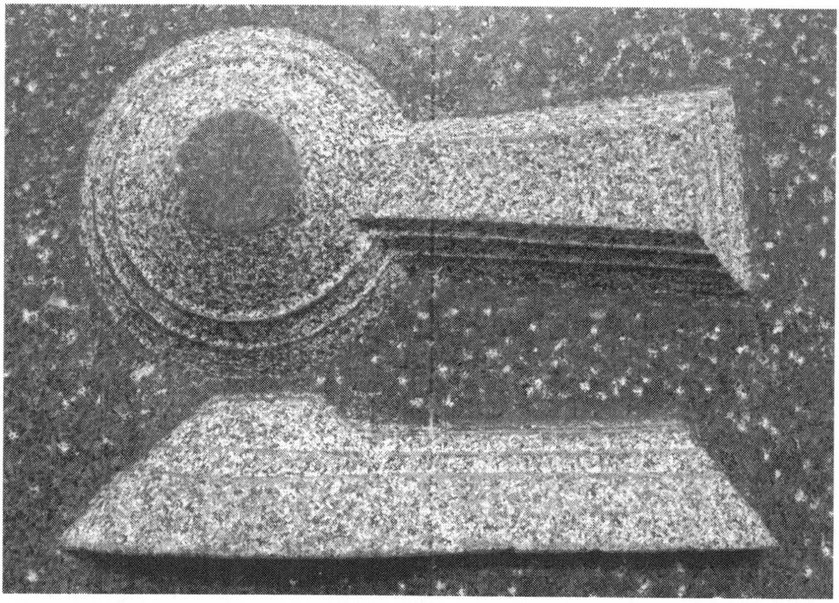

Figure 8.2. A model of a keyhole-shaped tomb carved in granite at the Goshikizuka Tomb in Kobe. The profile shows the round rear mound and front projection, thought to be a stage for burial rituals. The plan view illustrates the tiered construction of standardized mounds. (Photograph by the author.)

cupation of the northern Korean peninsula, from Middle Yayoi onward. The first large mounded burial was constructed at Yoshinogari in Kyushu in the first century BCE, though it contained eight jar burials rather than one exalted ruler. Even so, the grave goods in two of the jars testify to trade relations with Bronze Age chieftains on the Korean peninsula, and imported goods such as a bronze dagger and glass beads marked the status of the interred. Nevertheless, this burial did not set a trend, and no other mounded tomb was built in Japan for another two centuries until, in the Late Yayoi period, regional chiefs began to construct burial mounds, in different shapes, approximately ten meters square or ten meters in diameter.

The variation in Late Yayoi mound shape between regions seems to have been a cultural preference, signifying differences between regional groupings of polities. And none of these burials were lavishly supplied with grave goods—maybe one iron sword. The prevalence of swords in these mound-burials, together with the variation in shape, probably indicates competition between chiefs of different regions. This archaeological view is compatible with the Chinese records of disturbances in Wa throughout western Japan between 147 and 189 CE. At this time, then, political leadership involved regional competition underwritten by access to iron swords of continental style.

In the early third century, after the end of the Wa hostilities, keyhole-shaped tombs appear in the Miwa region of Nara Prefecture—around ninety meters long, far larger than the Late Yayoi mound-burials. These mark the birth of the Mounded Tomb Culture, which then spread rapidly from Nara throughout southwestern Japan. Why did regional chieftains adopt these new burial customs, which integrated them in a network of elites, rather than resist the imposition of a nonlocal burial ritual?

As far as archaeologists can ascertain, the rapid spread of the Mounded Tomb Culture was accomplished without military operations, and it resulted in a peaceful Early Kofun period, despite the implied subjugation of a newly defined commoner population. There were nonparticipants, however: The chiefs in the Izumo area (now Shimane Prefecture) opted out of the Mounded Tomb Culture until the fifth century, but without incurring the wrath of the other polities. Again, seemingly peaceful interaction characterized trade and exchange with this area.

It is at this point that we may speak of an emerging sense of countrywide identity among the elite, but not yet of state organization. Whereas scholars in the 1960s viewed the extension of Kofun rituals across the landscape as reflecting the imposition of state authority, recent theories propose a "keyhole-tomb state." All such theories assume a central authority able to "impose" certain practices, peacefully, and imply that all rulers buried in keyhole tombs fit into regional hierarchies under this central authority. In fact, there is no evidence of any sort of administrative organization beyond the burial rituals themselves, and the minute variations within this homogeneous elite burial culture reveal that there was no imposed standardization of mass-produced objects traceable to a central authority.

The grave goods assemblage changed through time: Most Early Kofun objects appear to have a ritualistic purpose, while the Middle Kofun assemblage is dominated by armor and weaponry. This has been interpreted as a shift from a ceremonial form of rulership to one based on military might. Although some Japanese scholars have speculated that Early Kofun ritual contained an element of Daoism, no specific evidence has been identified. As a case study in how archaeological interpretation proceeds, I describe the probable content of the rituals and suggest why and how they facilitated the adoption of the Mounded Tomb Culture across so broad a landscape so rapidly.

EARLY KOFUN BURIAL RITUAL AS POLITICAL IDEOLOGY

To understand why the Mounded Tomb Culture was so attractive to regional rulers, we must look at the burial facilities and funerary goods and consider what they might have signified within the East Asian worldview of the third century. Moreover, we have to take into account the Chinese records that describe the elevation of a shamaness to political prominence after the end of Wa hostilities. The *Gishi Wajinden* refers to this woman as Himiko (Pimiko), queen of Wa. She is described as living in a secluded compound accessed only by her younger brother but attended by a thousand servants. Between 238 and 247 she sent two embassies and a memorial to China's newly formed Wei court with tribute; in return for her allegiance, she received a gold seal and many fine gifts from that court, including at least one hundred bronze mirrors.

The most prominent type of bronze mirror found in Early Kofun tombs has a rim with triangular cross-section and is decorated with deity-beast images of a Chinese folk goddess, the Queen Mother of the West, her deity husband the King Father of the East, and her tiger and dragon companions. Triangular-rim mirrors are hypothesized by Japanese scholars to have been the ones received by Himiko and used by the Nara political leaders in gifting regional leaders to solidify relations, much as the Chinese used them to ensure Himiko's political alliance. But not all Early Kofun tombs have triangular-rim mirrors, not all can be traced back to Nara, and not all mirrors bearing the deity-beast motif have triangular rims. Given these problems in postulating a strictly hierarchical distribution system, is it possible that the illustrative content of the deity-beast mirrors was more important than the act of their distribution?

The Queen Mother of the West, who from 100 CE enjoyed great popularity in northeastern China as a cult figure, is a Daoist deity with a long list of attributes known through two millennia of written works and iconographic representations. She began as a ferocious and predatory deity but was later domesticated by the addition of a husband. She is known to have been

- Situated at the "center of the universe, whence she may control the rhythm of the cosmos"[1]
- Associated with Mt. Kunlun and a cosmic tree or pillar
- Able to bestow immortality
- Able to favor earthly rulers
- Resident in a cave or stone chamber
- Associated with leopards (especially the tail), tigers (especially the teeth), and dragons
- Associated with jade, carrying a jade staff
- Decorated with a headdress called a *sheng,* composed of disks at each side of the head
- Fond of holding banquets and receiving supplicants

Were these mythological elements transmitted to Japan in conjunction with the deity-beast mirrors themselves? Reviewing the contents and structure of the Mounded Tomb Culture, one finds convincing evidence that they were. The most telling aspect is the sudden formation of the Mounded Tomb Culture and its coherence, involving many elements unknown, or nearly so, in the Late Yayoi period.

Surprisingly, the tangible attributes mentioned above can be seen in the Early Kofun ritual repertoire. If the Queen Mother was associated with mountains, the sudden monumentalization of mounded burial might signify the provision of artificial mountains to the rulers. Many tombs contain stone burial chambers of monumental size, unknown in Yayoi, serving as "caves" or stone residences for the deceased. Green stones resembling and including jade suddenly became the favored material for making precious objects: Bracelets, staffs, and beads—formerly made of shell, wood, or glass in Yayoi—were reproduced in jade or in green beadstone substitutes for jade (jasper and green tuff). The curved beads (*magatama*) known from Jōmon times onward suddenly became immensely popular at this time and eventually formed one of the three components of imperial regalia—mirror, sword, and bead. Often thought to have derived from an animal tooth or claw, could these *magatama* have been reinterpreted as tigers' teeth? Although the cosmic tree does not appear in the burial assemblage, tree branches are often depicted in Kofun-period art, and *sasaki* branches are mentioned in the *Nihon shoki* as being hung with mirror and jewels to show elite identification. The sacred tree of Shintō is the *sasaki* (*Cleyera japonica*). Could it have derived its importance from Queen Mother mythology?

Such are the tangible aspects of the Queen Mother myth represented in the Mounded Tomb Culture, but the intangible aspects are much more important. The Queen Mother was able to confer immortality. What more would an earthly ruler wish? Interment of deity-beast mirrors in the grave would allow the Queen Mother to guide the deceased to immortal life. She was also the ultimate authority, able to dispense favors on earthly rulers—again, what more could a local ruler desire? These tangible and intangible aspects of Queen Mother mythology lead me to propose a hypothesis that the shamaness Queen Himiko, recognized by the Chinese as an early Yamato ruler, perhaps acted as the earthly analog of the Queen Mother of the West, forming the center of a burial cult that both legitimized rulership and elevated leaders who possessed the cult talismans to exalted status within their local polities. By subscribing to the cult, not only did they join an elite group of shared status, they could encourage others through marriage alliances, for example, to join while distributing the talismans further through the network. Such a scenario would account for both the nonimposed, voluntary aspects of Mounded Tomb Culture membership and the variation in both grave good assemblages (few possessed all attributes) and artifact construction (made by numerous craftspeople, but not standardized or mass-produced).

The interpretation of Early Kofun material culture as relating to the Chinese Queen Mother mythology is entirely my own; it is not history, but a hypothesis. It is offered here to illustrate the nature of archaeological research and interpretation; other views abound. For example, the official list of Japanese emperors begun in the *Nihon shoki* does not include a woman ruler named Himiko for the mid-third century. Japanese scholars have, however, identified two female seers in the Sujin line of kings (ruled late third to mid-fourth centuries) who may correlate with the Chinese identification of Queen Himiko. The first is the seeress aunt of the first historical sovereign, Sujin, while the second seeress is daughter to the sovereign Suinin and sister to the sovereign Keikō. While the Japanese chronicles emphasized the male sovereigns, the Chinese were impressed with the female seers.

A second possible objection is that Japanese mythology makes no direct references to the Queen Mother. It would seem likely, however, that the Queen Mother *does* feature prominently in early myths—in the form of Amaterasu Omikami, the heavenly ancestor of the current imperial line, elevated by otherwise staunchly Confucian eighth-century society above other, male gods. We do not know how the third-century Japanese referred to the Chinese deity, but the records that cover the Early Kofun period already have Amaterasu (literally, "Heaven shines") in place. Could this not be how the early Japanese conceived of the deity, given that a mirror is a reflector of light and that virtually every Shintō shrine has a mirror as deity substitute? The chronicles even state that Amaterasu withdrew into a cave, causing darkness to descend on the land until dance and laughter drew her out again (often interpreted as a solar eclipse). In any case, the Japanese do have as their ultimate being a female deity that legitimizes earthly rule and governs the cosmos. The last word in this debate has yet to be written.

Another aspect of the Queen Mother mythology is also important to early Japanese rulership. The *Nihon shoki* is replete with examples of brother-sister and male-female ruling pairs, often referred to as *hime* (princess)–*hiko* (prince) pairs. Himiko and her younger brother fit this pattern of "dual gender rulership," as do the two princesses mentioned above. The *Nihon shoki* records many male-female ruling pairs in the peripheral regions and contains myriad stories of the mystical capabilities of women. In time, however, belief in the seeress capacities of early Japanese womanhood diminished or was channeled into formalized religions: in Buddhism as nuns and in the emerging Shintō beliefs as *miko* (shrine attendants). The Nara period saw several women succeeding male relatives to the throne, but by this time their rule was rational rather than mystical and fully acknowledged by their male peers and successors.

MILITARIZATION OF JAPANESE RULERSHIP

In the mid-fourth century, Wa rulers were drawn into relations with similar emerging states on the Korean peninsula. As attention shifted from China to Korea, the Early Kofun mirror cult waned, especially with wars and political transition limiting access to authentic triangular-rimmed bronze mirrors. The mounded tomb burials of the late fourth and fifth centuries are filled with armor, weaponry, and, from the late fifth century, horse trappings, indicating the adoption of continental forms of elite equestrian status.

Both archaeological and documentary evidence allows us to see increasing interaction between elites of the Korean peninsula and Yamato. Paekche, an emerging state in the western peninsula, gifted a seven-branched sword forged in 369 CE to Yamato, which was preserved in the Isonokami Shrine in Nara until moved to the Tokyo National Museum. This gift is interpreted as the beginning of several centuries of alliance between Yamato and Paekche. According to a stela erected in 414 CE in the capital of the northernmost Korean state, Koguryŏ, Yamato troops fought on Paekche's turf in the wars with Koguryŏ in the late fourth century. Protection of the source of imported iron was one of the likely reasons that Yamato became involved in peninsular disputes. Whereas the southernmost Kaya area of the peninsula had initially been the center for manufacturing iron armor, Yamato quickly expanded its imports of iron ingots from this area to support local armor production. It is thought that Kaya blacksmiths helped start the local industry in Yamato, as Chinese bronze-casters had done for mirror production in the preceding century. The largest tombs of the Middle Kofun period often have accessory chambers or even accessory mounds in which large amounts of armor and weaponry were deposited.

Yamato rulership in the late fourth century, however, is difficult to discern. The adjusted dates for the chronicles attribute this time period to Empress Jingu's reign, but given that she is judged a fictitious insert (to account for the earlier Chinese records of Himiko), who *did* exert Yamato leadership during the peninsular wars? This was probably a time of some competition between the various local rulers in Yamato after the decline of the Miwa burial cult. The formation of new tomb groups in the Kawachi area of Osaka, the Saki area of Nara, and in Kazuraki in western Nara suggests the emergence of more nuclei of local rulers. The *Nihon shoki* is clear that local uprisings occurred in Nara at this time and that the Kazuraki leader disobeyed imperial orders.

Rather than featuring a coordinated territorial hierarchy across the Kinai, then, the late fourth century seems to have been an era of still-developing regional polities more involved in continental warfare than in state building. As to whether Saki exerted overall authority or whether new rulers in Kawachi and Osaka challenged the established order, archaeologists are divided, especially given the new rulers' peninsular contacts as known from grave goods imported from Paekche and Kaya. The late fourth century began to see immigration of craftspeople from these peninsular areas who established their crafts in Japan to serve the Yamato elite. First were potters who built stoneware kilns in southern Osaka to make the new Sué ware. These ceramics were the focus of the sixth-century grave goods repertoire that provided food for the deceased, but they eventually became the serving ceramics of the Nara court.

FIFTH-CENTURY FORMATION OF THE YAMATO STATE

The *Nihon shoki* list of sovereigns contains a break in dynasties in the late fourth century: The Sujin line of kings of the Early Kofun period is succeeded by the Ōjin line, thought by many historians to represent a foreign dynasty. There is no evidence that Yamato was conquered by peninsular troops (as proposed by the "Horserider Theory" most closely associated with Egami Namio). Paekche was rather busy defending its northern border against Koguryŏ with Yamato's help; and although Koguryŏ horsemen apparently swept down to the southern coast in 400 CE, destroying the coastal Kaya polities, there is no evidence that they crossed the straits to the archipelago. Still, there is no disputing the influx of all kinds of craftspeople and court nobles to the archipelago during the extended wars on the peninsula. The fact that the ninth-century *Shinsen Shōjiroku* lists one-third of aristocratic families as having non-Japanese origins attests to the great capacity of Yamato to absorb and use the skills and knowledge of the refugees. Yamato court scribes of the late fifth century were Paekche immigrants, facilitating the beginning of the aristocratic household records that would eventually be collected into the *Nihon shoki*.

The fifth century is marked by the construction of extremely large tombs on the Osaka coastal terraces. Daisen Tomb, attributed to the sovereign Nintoku—480 meters long and dated to the mid-fifth century—suggests both the emergence of a dominant power and a desire to advertise this to the continent. By analyzing tomb clusters in the Kyoto basin, archeologists have discovered that local power shifted from one ruling lineage to another, a transfer coordinated with changes in rulership at the center. Such shifts have been documented from other areas of Kyoto and Okayama Prefectures, indicating discontinuities in leadership at both the central and local levels. Archaeologists postulate shifts in rulership several times: with the fall of the Miwa court, the establishment of the Kawachi court, and successively with the downfall of the Katsuragi clan in the late fifth century and of the Otomo clan in the mid-sixth century, the routing of the Mononobe clan at the turn of the seventh century, and the collapse of the Soga clan in the mid-seventh century. It can thus be inferred that the central court clans favored particular ruling lineages in the provinces that rose and fell in concert, and one wonders if these clans weren't more powerful at court than the nominal kings.

Yamato kings applied to the Chinese courts several times in the fifth century for titles to bolster their ruling status. King Zhen (as the name appears in the Chinese records), for example, applied for the title "Generalissimo Who Maintains

Peace in the East Commanding with Battle-Ax All Military Affairs in the Six Countries of Wa, Paekche, Silla, Imna, Chin-han, and Mok-han." In return he was simply acknowledged as "King of Wa" and granted the title "General Who Maintains Peace in the East."[2]

This appeal by a Japanese king for Chinese legitimization of his reign reveals a felt need for external support, while also evidencing continued Wa involvement in southern peninsular affairs. Recently several keyhole-shaped tombs discovered in the Mok-han area of southwestern Korea have been identified as Japanese-style, while it is clear that Imna and Chin-han remained a source of iron for the archipelago until the early sixth century. Nevertheless, direct Yamato power was limited to the Kinai region, with much of the archipelago under the control of regional rulers. Under the late fifth-century king Yūryaku, swords were gifted to outlying chieftains to cement alliances—as occurred earlier between Paekche and Yamato. Swords with bestowal inscriptions have been excavated from tombs in Saitama (in Kantō) and Kumamoto (in Kyushu) Prefectures.

In addition to turning to Paekche for scribes, the Yamato court of the late fifth century also adopted a new system of economic organization derived from Paekche's territorial administrative pattern but applied in Yamato to groups of craftspeople and payers of taxes in kind. This was the *be* system (pronounced "bay"), whose institution marks the development of a true administrative organization with managers and other bureaucrats. The *be* managers were termed *muraji*; for example, Haji no muraji was overseer of the provision of native earthenware (*haji*) to the court. Other *muraji* were in charge of the saddlers' *be*, the brocade-weavers' *be*, the painters' *be*, and so forth—each comprising foreign craftspeople now serving the Yamato court. Managerial control extended to the collection of natural products as well; *be* of fishermen and of mountain wardens were also established.

The new managers served as the foci for the development of clans, called *uji*. With the introduction of Buddhism in the mid-sixth century, clan heads began to construct temples instead of tombs to celebrate their leadership, and Shintō shrines to local deities were built, their design stimulated by the new temple architecture imported from the continent. The shrines became the focus of the *uji*, along with *ujigami* (clan gods) and *ujinoko* (clan shrine members), the last term applying to local shrine parishioners even today even though the "clans" are extinct.

The administrative aspect of the *be* crucial for state formation is that these managers represented the central Yamato court in extracting goods directly from commoner producers, bypassing local rulers and laying the foundations for the manipulation of individuals within a state organization. In time, the *muraji* managers became powerful clan chiefs, and under the Keitai line of kings, which took control at the beginning of the sixth century, the accession of a new ruler was accompanied by the appointment of two or three men to bear the enhanced titles (*kabane*) of *ō-muraji* and *ō-omi* (*ō* meaning "great") and serve the paramount directly.

The introduction of Buddhism in the sixth century caused the diversion of elite resources from tomb building to temple building. Acceptance of the religion was initially contentious, as two of the clans, the Soga and Mononobe, fought each other for and against Buddhism, respectively. The former won, with the head of the Soga clan being the sole appointee to the paramount as *ō-omi* in what one scholar has termed a "dyarchy [between one clan head and the emperor] that was to characterize Japanese rulership for centuries to come."[3]

In summary, the Kofun period saw the emergence of a countrywide elite that shared a ritual burial system reinforcing the status systems of local rulership. This burial cult may link with the beginnings of Shintō religious beliefs in that female gods and female shamans were both politically important. The distraction of peninsular warfare in the late fourth century may have delayed political centralization, but it resulted in the inflow of fresh talent in crafts and courtly skills from the Peninsula. A clear organizational structure, the Yamato court, combining territorial hierarchies, economic production, kingly status, and aristocratic titles, emerged in the late fifth century, only to be superseded within a century and a half with the adoption between 645 and 702 of the *ritsuryō* system from Tang China.

Sources and Suggestions for Further Reading

See the bibliography for complete publication data.

Anazawa, W., and J. Manome. "Two Inscribed Swords from Japanese Tumuli: Discoveries and Research on Finds from the Sakitama-Inariyama and Eta-Funayama Tumuli" (1986).

Aston, W. G. *Nihongi: Chronicles of Japan from the Earliest Times to A. D. 697* (1972).

Barnes, Gina L. "The Role of the *Be* in the Formation of the Yamato State" (1987).

———. *State Formation in Japan: Emergence of a 4th-Century Ruling Elite* (2006).

Cahill, Suzanne. *Transcendence and Divine Passion* (1993).

Egami, Namio. "The Formation of the People and the Origin of the State in Japan" (1964).

Farris, William Wayne. *Sacred Texts and Buried Treasures: Issues in the Historical Archaeology of Ancient Japan* (1998).

Kleeman, Terry. *Great Perfection* (1998).

Loewe, Michael. *Ways to Paradise: The Chinese Quest for Immortality* (1979).

Miller, Richard J. *Ancient Japanese Nobility: The Kabane Ranking System* (1973).

Onoyama Setsu. "The Sumptuary Restrictions on Tomb Mounds in the 5th Century AD" (1970).

Piggott, Joan R. "Chieftain Pairs and Co-rulers" (1999).
———. *The Emergence of Japanese Kingship* (1997).
———. Review of Barnes, *State Formation in Japan* (2009).
Tsude, Hiroshi. "Chiefly Lineages in Kofun-Period Japan: Political Relations Between Centre and Region" (1990).
Tsunoda, Ryūsaku, and L. Carrington Goodrich. *Japan in the Chinese Dynastic Histories: Later Han Through Ming Dynasties* (1952).

Notes

1. Loewe, *Ways to Paradise*, 103.
2. Tsunoda and Goodrich, *Japan in the Chinese Dynastic Histories*, 22.
3. Miller, *Ancient Japanese Nobility*, 5.

9

Early Japan and the Continent

Bruce L. Batten

Japan is an island country, but its history is far from insular. From earliest times, residents of the archipelago placed considerable importance on contacts with continental Asia. Objectively, too, such contacts played a significant, and at times crucial, role in the development of Japanese society and civilization.

In premodern times, travel among the Japanese islands and between them and the continent was necessarily by sea. Travel within the archipelago was facilitated by the Seto Inland Sea between Honshu, Shikoku, and Kyushu. The archipelago was linked to the continent by three natural corridors: the Ryūkyū Islands stretching between Kyushu and Taiwan, the Korea Strait between Kyushu and Korea, and the route connecting Hokkaido, Sakhalin, and Siberia to the north. Adventurous travelers might also set sail across open ocean in the East China Sea or the Sea of Japan.

As has frequently been noted, Japan's physical location had positive consequences for the development of a distinctive, independent society. In what might be called a Goldilocks effect of physical geography, Japan was "just the right" distance from Korea and China: close enough to permit small-scale contacts and selective cultural borrowing, but far enough to prevent Japanese society from being overwhelmed by foreign influence, either cultural or political.

Japan was on the eastern periphery of what is sometimes called the East Asian world. This was an interaction sphere centered on China, the oldest, most populous, and most advanced civilization in the region. It also included the Korean peninsula, which, partly because of its proximity to China, developed somewhat earlier than Japan.

Over the course of history, interactions among China, Japan, and Korea varied in both nature and intensity. The nature of the interaction was influenced largely by political events and trends: the emergence of strong states or empires, particularly in China, naturally encouraged political or military interaction; while, conversely, periods of weak leadership were associated more with trade and piracy. The intensity of interaction was affected by numerous factors. One of them, of course, was distance (or accessibility), but of equal or greater importance was the participants' degree of motivation. This was a function of their subjective assessment of the costs versus the benefits—not just material but also symbolic or psychological—of foreign intercourse. That said, as a general rule interactions tended to intensify over time, partly because population growth meant there were more potential travelers, and partly because cumulative advances in geographic knowledge and transportation technology reduced some of the barriers to overseas travel.[1]

With this brief introduction, let us embark on a brief chronological survey of Japanese contact with the Asian mainland from earliest times through the end of the twelfth century CE. Roughly speaking, early Japanese foreign relations developed in five overlapping phases. These were characterized respectively by (1) immigration from the continent to Japan; (2) tributary relations with China; (3) peer-polity interactions with Korea; (4) the attempted creation of a Japan-centered international order; and (5) a shift from diplomatic relations to largely commercial ones, with a smattering of piracy.

Population movements from the continent to the islands began with the first settlers and continued through the eighth or ninth century CE. Immigration occurred in several "waves," the first beginning around 35,000 BCE and consisting largely, but by no means exclusively, of settlers from the south. These Paleolithic hunter-gatherers were the original inhabitants of the Japanese islands and the ancestors of the Jōmon people.

A second wave of immigrants began to arrive in Kyushu from the Korean peninsula in the final millennium BCE. Most Japanese living today are descended from these Yayoi settlers, who spoke a language ancestral to modern Japanese. They also introduced wet rice farming, which remained the mainstay of the Japanese economy through the early twentieth century CE. Over a period of centuries, the Yayoi people spread throughout the archipelago, intermarrying with or displacing the aboriginal Jōmon population except in northeastern Honshu and Hokkaido. (The Ainu people of Hokkaido trace much of their genetic heritage to the Jōmon.)

A final wave of immigrants, from both China and Korea, began to arrive in the mid-first millennium CE. It peaked with an influx of political refugees from Korea in the 660s (see below), diminished during the eighth and ninth centuries, and then came to a virtual stop. These later immigrants brought with them skills, knowledge, and cultural attributes that played a crucial role in the development of the early Japanese state and civilization. They were responsible for introducing (or at least diffusing knowledge of) the Chinese ideographs (*kanji*) that made written language possible, legal systems (e.g., the *ritsuryō*), political philosophy (Confucianism), religion (Buddhism), and numerous aspects of art and architecture.

One question worth asking is why these people came to Japan in the first place. Here it is useful to distinguish between *push* and *pull* factors. Push factors are circumstances that encourage people to leave their homelands—for example, overcrowding, warfare, famine, or environmental degradation (including climate change). Of these, warfare certainly played an important part in early migrations to Japan, the aforementioned Korean refugees being a case in point. Climatic cooling may also have played a role in some early migrations, especially during the last millennium BCE and the first few centuries CE. Pull factors, or circumstances that made the site of relocation particularly attractive, are not very relevant to discussions of early Japan, because potential immigrants would have had little knowledge about living conditions there. Many immigrants probably settled in Japan almost by default, because it was relatively accessible from their homelands and once there they saw no particular reason to leave. Finally, we should note that some people came to Japan against their will. Castaways from foreign vessels, who make frequent appearances in the Japanese historical records, are one clear-cut example. It is, however, also possible that some people arrived as prisoners of war captured during Japanese military operations in Korea (discussed below) or as the result of human trafficking by pirates.

The second phase of interaction, roughly from the first to fifth centuries CE, was characterized by intermittent "tributary" relations in which Japanese leaders played the role of political subordinates to the Chinese emperor. Chinese dynastic histories record the arrival of envoys from "Wa" (Japan) during the Later Han dynasty in 57 and 107 CE. Almost miraculously, the gold seal of investiture bestowed upon the former envoy, bearing the inscription "King of Na in Wa of Han," was rediscovered in a field in Fukuoka Prefecture in 1784. In 239, an embassy sent by "Queen Himiko of the land of Yamatai in Wa" to the Chinese (Northern Wei) outpost of Daifang in Korea received another gold seal and one hundred mirrors. Some scholars believe that the latter correspond to the "triangular-rimmed deity-beast mirrors" recovered by archaeologists from tumuli throughout western Japan. In the fifth century, a succession of Japanese rulers known to historians as the Five Kings of Wa sent tribute missions to the Chinese Southern Dynasties. The Five Kings asked for, and generally received, titles granting them authority over the Japanese islands and, more surprisingly, parts of Korea.

What was the purpose of these early diplomatic contacts? It seems reasonable to take the Chinese records at face value and conclude that political leaders in the Japanese islands sought material goods and titles; but we must still ask why acquiring them was important enough to merit arduous overseas voyages. The most likely answer is that what the Japanese leaders were really after was the official Chinese recognition such gifts implied, which reinforced their legitimacy at home and helped them consolidate their rule. Political leadership in Japan at this time was fluid and unstable; under such conditions, Chinese certification of one's status as King (or Queen) of Wa was certainly an important political asset, despite (or perhaps because of) the political subordination it implied. On the Chinese side, of course, tributary relations were welcome because they reinforced the Chinese view of that country as the "Middle Kingdom."

Another focus of interaction was the Korean peninsula, which was occupied from early times by the three kingdoms of Silla in the east, Paekche in the west, and Koguryŏ in the north. Japan's relations with Korea developed in tandem with the above-described diplomacy vis-à-vis China. Unlike Sino-Japanese relations, however, these became more intense over time, peaking in the sixth and seventh centuries CE—the third phase of early Japanese contact with the continent.

Relations with the Korean kingdoms, which are perhaps best described as peer-polity interactions, involved complex, constantly shifting political-military alliances and rivalries. On balance, Japan's relations were friendliest with Paekche and Koguryŏ, and least friendly with Silla. This was unfortunate, since over time Silla gained strength at the expense of the other kingdoms, eventually unifying the peninsula in 668 with the aid of Tang China. In the prolonged fighting that led up to that event, Japan allied itself with Paekche, going so far as to send large numbers of troops to the aid of its ally. These were ingloriously defeated in 663 in a naval battle at the mouth of the Kŭm River near the Paekche capital. Surviving Japanese troops, together with numerous refugees from Paekche, fled to Kyushu, and Japanese leaders spent several years building defenses in that island to stave off a feared Silla-Tang invasion. Fears of an invasion—which never materialized—also contributed significantly to Japanese political development around this time by imparting a sense of urgency to state-strengthening reforms.

Once again, it is important to consider motivations. One basis for Japanese-Korean relations was clearly material. Japanese leaders desired Korean goods ranging from gold jewelry (from Silla) to, more prosaically but also probably more importantly, iron ingots (particularly from Kaya, an originally independent region at the southernmost tip of the peninsula). Flows of goods in the other direction seem to have been less important (although it is difficult to be certain, given the fragmentary nature of the historical record); at least part of the "exchange balance" was probably paid in the currency of Japanese political backing or military assistance, not only in the late seventh century but in earlier times as well. Leaders in Japan and Korea were also motivated by nonmaterial, symbolic factors such as the desire for prestige and legitimacy. They competed amongst themselves on the diplomatic stage and occasionally on the battlefield, in an ongoing game of political one-upmanship. Success in foreign relations conferred political legitimacy at home, while greater power at home conferred higher status abroad. Tensions escalated as the competition ratcheted to ever higher levels, with the results described above.

One important backdrop to this peer-polity competition was the unification of China by the Sui (581–618) and Tang (618–907) dynasties. Chinese expansion caused the international environment to become tenser and more competitive; at the same time, Chinese culture and institutions were widely admired and imitated by other states in the region, not least because China, as the preeminent state and civilization in the region, provided the only obvious model of development—"if you can't beat them, join them." Japan was quick to jump on the bandwagon of what historians call Sinification, and in 600 it renewed its diplomatic ties with the Middle Kingdom, which had lain dormant since the time of the Five Kings. Although Japan deliberately gave China a wide berth for several decades after the wars of the 660s, diplomatic relations were restored in 702 with Japan's dispatch of a party of *kentōshi* (envoys to Tang).

During the eighth and ninth centuries—the fourth phase of Japan's interaction with the continent—Japan was an integral part of a Tang-centered international order that also included former enemy Silla and the Manchurian state of Parhae, a Koguryŏ offshoot founded in 698. This interaction sphere was held together—strongly at first, then more tenuously—by shared high culture (e.g., Buddhism, the use of Chinese writing) and by diplomatic exchanges among the parties concerned.

From the Chinese point of view, Japan was as before a tributary, subordinate state, but in contrast to the time of Himiko or the Five Kings, this was not how the relationship was construed in Japan. A mission sent to China in 607 famously offended the Sui emperor by presenting a letter from the "the Child of Heaven in the land where the sun rises" to "the Child of Heaven in the land where the sun sets."[2] Later Japanese missions avoided such bald assertions of equality; the letters they carried used deliberately ambiguous language that meant one thing to the Chinese and another to the people back home in Japan. One important conclusion to be drawn from this is that the imperial institution in Japan was now sufficiently well developed that an overt relationship of subordination to the Chinese emperor was no longer a political asset.

At the same time, Japanese rulers must have still valued diplomatic ties with Tang, or they would not have continued to send *kentōshi*. To the extent that relations could be portrayed at home as taking place between equals, they redounded to the prestige of the Japanese emperor. And, of course, diplomatic relations also ensured access to valuable information and luxury goods. Cultural exchanges may also have been valued in their own right; certainly many cases are known of Japanese students or monks traveling to China with *kentōshi*. Some of these stayed for years or decades in the Middle Kingdom before returning to Japan with knowledge and experience that greatly contributed to the "internationalization" of Japanese high society. (There are also cases of Chinese monks coming to Japan with returning *kentōshi*; for example, Jianzhen [in Japanese, Ganjin; 688–763] arrived in 753 after five failed attempts and went on to found the temple Tōshōdaiji in Nara.) In any case, *kentōshi* were generally dispatched once per reign of each Japanese emperor during the Nara and early Heian periods. A plan to send one more mission after a hiatus of half a century was scuttled in 894 by ambassador-designate Sugawara no Michizane, who cited dangerous travel conditions and political unrest in Tang. This turned out to be prescient; Tang collapsed in 907, initiating a period of fragmentation and turmoil (the Five Dynasties era) that lasted until the emergence of the Northern Song dynasty in 960.

A corollary of Japan's changing relationship with China was its attempt to re-create itself in the image of the Middle Kingdom, not just culturally but in geopolitical terms as well. During the Nara period, embassies to Japan from Silla and Parhae were generally treated as tribute missions from subordinate states. Japan, in other words, now viewed itself as an empire in its own right, one that could command the respect and fealty of lesser kingdoms on its periphery. Nevertheless, just as Japan no longer subscribed to China's view of the world, Silla and Parhae did not necessarily subscribe to Japan's. In the case of Silla, the disconnect in worldviews led to rancorous diplomatic exchanges, military tensions, and eventually, a complete rupture of formal ties by the end of the eighth century. Relations with Parhae were more amicable from the start, possibly because Parhae, which bordered Silla and Tang, needed all the friends it could get. Japan continued to receive embassies from Parhae until the latter was overrun by a Khitan tribal invasion in 926.

In all of these cases, states exchanged diplomatic envoys just so long as both parties were willing and able. In general, political actors had ideological goals (e.g., to create relationships that added to their own legitimacy) as well as more concrete, material ones (e.g., to obtain luxury goods unavailable from domestic sources). Sometimes their goals were mutually incompatible, as when both parties wished to portray themselves as superior. This in itself did not necessarily preclude intercourse if the contradictions could be papered over or fudged by envoys, as by using ambiguous language or by acting one way in the host country while putting a different spin on events back home. But when the costs or difficulties began to outweigh the benefits for one or both parties, the relationship inevitably came to an end, as in the case of Japan and Silla in the late eighth century. Relationships also came to an end, of course, when one or both parties lost the political or economic capability to send embassies—or in the extreme case, ceased to exist as a state. By the early tenth century, Tang, Parhae, and Silla were all gone.

The fifth phase of early Japanese relations with the continent began in the early tenth century and lasted through the twelfth. Despite various opportunities, Japan's leaders made no effort to establish formal relations with any of the successors to its former diplomatic partners, not even the long-lived Northern Song dynasty (960–1279) in China or Koryŏ (918–1392) on the Korean Peninsula. Building on the discussion thus far, we may conclude that the court was no longer capable of or interested in conducting diplomacy. Regarding capability, from the tenth century the Japanese government began to experience severe fiscal problems, so it is possible that the cost of dispatching or receiving diplomatic delegations became prohibitive (or, at least, served as a disincentive). Regarding motivation, there was less need for external legitimation than in prior centuries, since the authority of the emperor and his court were now well established. More important, perhaps, information and material goods from the continent—as well as actual passage to China for intrepid Japanese monks such as Jōjin (1011–1081)—could now be obtained without recourse to diplomacy, through purely commercial channels.

It is difficult to date the origins of commercial exchange with the continent. Diplomatic missions had always involved the exchange of material goods in the form of presents from one sovereign to the other. In many cases envoys also brought along goods to sell, or exchange, on their own. The first clear examples of foreign trade outside the context of diplomacy, however, come from the early ninth century, when Korean and Chinese merchant vessels began calling at Hakata Bay, Japan's designated "gateway" for foreign visitors and Japanese traveling abroad. The goods imported by these merchants included many of the same items formerly brought by diplomats, notably spices, medicines, and precious woods from Southeast Asia, along with textiles, books, and objets d'art, mostly manufactured in China. The merchants also brought large quantities of Chinese porcelain and, later, copper coins. All of these items were sold under official supervision at the Kōrokan, a guesthouse located on the shore of Hakata Bay. Japanese buyers, generally limited to court officials and representatives of aristocrat families from the capital, paid for their purchases with Japanese silk floss and, later, gold. The foreign merchants either took these materials back home or traded them in Kyushu for other desirable Japanese goods, including raw materials such as sulfur and, later, high-end manufactures such as lacquerware, armor, and swords.

These exchanges are sometimes characterized as "private trade," but private they most definitely were not, at least through the eleventh century. They took place under official supervision and benefited the powers-that-be at court, who naturally wished to retain their monopolistic access to foreign goods and knowledge. Over time, however, the court's power to control trade waned. Chinese merchants began to settle along the shores of Hakata Bay, and the locus of trade gradually shifted from the Kōrokan to the merchant community. Eventually, toward the very end of the Heian period, merchants began to call at ports other than Hakata, and trade became, for the first time, relatively unregulated. An effort was made by Taira Kiyomori to bring the China trade under his control in the late twelfth century, but this was as short-lived as the Taira regime itself.

The fifth stage of early Japanese contact with the continent was also notable for piracy. As a general rule, pirate activity is a consequence (or in some cases, a cause) of weak governmental authority in border regions. During the period of Silla's decline in the ninth century, northern Kyushu suffered various attacks by Korean pirates. The most famous of these occurred in 869, when a fleet of Japanese ships containing tax goods bound for Kyoto was plundered at anchor in Hakata Bay. Piracy remained an occasional problem during the tenth and eleventh centuries. A series of attacks on Kyushu in the 990s were ascribed to "southern barbarians" from Amami in the Ryūkyū Islands. Although some of these were extremely damaging, with hundreds of Kyushu residents being abducted, their historical background is completely obscure. Also of some consequence was a large-scale attack on northern Kyushu, incongruously by Jurchen tribesmen from Manchuria, in 1019. This so-called Toi Invasion resulted in the murder or abduction of more than fifteen hundred individuals and the slaughter of hundreds of livestock on the islands of Tsūshima and Iki and in the area around Hakata Bay. The Japanese defense effort was valiantly led by officials at Dazaifu (the Kyushu Government General) with essentially no help from the court. Travel from Hakata to Kyoto took about a week one way, which meant that the central administrators were unable to learn of, much less control, events on the frontier in anything like real time—an important fact of life throughout the premodern era in Japan.

This brief survey merely touches upon some of the many facets of early Japanese relations with the Asian continent. In particular, it fails to do justice to the cultural aspects of international exchange—for example, in art, architecture, philosophy, and religion. Fortunately, those topics are covered in detail elsewhere in this volume. The sketch presented here will at least arm the reader with sufficient historical background to understand the important material contained in those sections.

Sources and Suggestions for Further Reading

See the bibliography for complete publication data.

Barnes, Gina L. *The Rise of Civilization in East Asia: Archaeology of China, Korea, and Japan* (1999).

Batten, Bruce L. *Gateway to Japan: Hakata in War and Peace, 500–1300* (2006).

———. *To the Ends of Japan: Premodern Frontiers, Boundaries, and Interactions* (2003).

Borgen, Robert. *Sugawara no Michizane and the Early Heian Court* (1994).

———. "Jōjin's Travels from Center to Center (with Some Periphery in between)" (2007).

De Bary, Wm. Theodore, Donald Keene, George Tanabe, and Paul Varley, eds. *Sources of Japanese Tradition, Volume One: From Earliest Times to 1600* (2001).

Farris, William Wayne. *Sacred Texts and Buried Treasures: Issues in the Historical Archaeology of Ancient Japan* (1998).

Holcombe, Charles. *The Genesis of East Asia: 221 B.C.–A.D. 907* (2001).

Reischauer, Edwin O. *The Japanese Today: Change and Continuity* (1980).

Verschuer, Charlotte von. *Across the Perilous Sea: Japanese Trade with China and Korea from the Seventh to the Sixteenth Centuries* (2006).

———. "Looking from Within and Without: Ancient and Medieval External Relations" (2000).

Wang Zhenping. *Ambassadors from the Islands of the Immortals: China-Japan Relations in the Han-Tang Period* (2005).

Notes

1. Even so, in premodern times a regime that wished to limit foreign contacts was sometimes capable of doing so, as occurred in Japan during the Tokugawa period.

2. From the *Sui History*, quoted in De Bary et al., *Sources of Japanese Tradition,* 1:11.

10

Centralization and State Formation in Sixth- and Seventh-Century Japan

Douglas Fuqua

This chapter examines the process of centralization and state formation in Japan during the sixth and seventh centuries, a span of time incorporating the conclusion of Japan's final archaeological era, the Kofun period (250–600 CE), and the start of Japan's first historical period, the Age of Reform (c. 552–710 CE). These two centuries mark a formative era when the Kofun-period culture evolved into what we recognize as "Japanese" and when the Yamato confederacy developed into the first centralized Japanese state, one configured with Chinese-style laws known in Japanese as *ritsuryō*.

A number of key events accelerated the political reform process, including (1) the adoption of Buddhism in the mid-sixth century and the related political upheaval that led to the prominence of the Soga clan; (2) court restructuring during the reign of the monarch Suiko and the regency of Prince Shōtoku; (3) the Taika coup d'état of 645 and the subsequent Taika Reforms, which brought an end to Soga influence and served as a catalyst for further reforms based on Chinese paradigms; (4) a military threat from the continent that led to efforts to strengthen the state; and lastly, (5) the Jinshin War, a civil conflict that brought forth a "heavenly sovereign," situated at the apex of a centralized Chinese-style state.

REFORM IN THE YAMATO CONFEDERATION

Japan's sixth-century confederacy, led by the Yamato *uji* (clan), extended from central Honshu to Kyushu and comprised territories dominated by aristocratic *uji*. The Yamato leader, referred to as *ōkimi* (great king), served as a hegemonic leader within the central Kinai region. In contrast, Yamato influence in the periphery was nominal, based for the most part upon Yamato control of diplomacy and trade with the continent in essential commodities such as iron.

As the Yamato court tried to extend its influence into the provinces, the *ōkimi* met resistance from local *uji* chieftains. These chieftains challenged the authority of the Yamato *uji* over land, resources, and manpower, and during the first half of the sixth century, the court faced rebellions from both the east and west. At the same time, the Yamato court was confronted with social and economic complexities accompanying new agricultural developments and technologies adopted from China and the Korean peninsula.

Political reform thus arose out of necessity. While certain reform measures were indigenous, continental models of statecraft were increasingly embraced by Yamato leaders. Emigrants, mostly from the Korean peninsula, accounted for the initial transfer to Japan of continental ideas, technologies, and skills (e.g., writing, metalworking), but from the early sixth century, diplomatic intercourse between the Yamato and the Korean courts of Paekche, Silla, and Koguryŏ encouraged further transfer of knowledge. The Paekche court, for instance, sent Confucian scholars, musicians, diviners, specialists in Chinese calendars, and physicians to Yamato from as early as 513. This infusion of continental knowledge encouraged Japan's cultural and political development.

One of the earliest examples of Yamato reform inspired by continental modes of governance was the implementation of the *kabane* system. Prior to the sixth century, the Yamato monarch used this system of ranks, likely modeled after Korean practices, to issue titles of nobility to individuals who demonstrated loyalty to the Yamato confederacy. Individuals who received *kabane* titles gained recognition for their families as royally acknowledged *uji*.

In the early sixth century, the monarch Keitai (reigned 507–531) embraced a Paekche model of succession whereby an "elder prince" of the queen consort was designated to ascend to the throne. Keitai's first two sons died after brief reigns, but his third son and long-term successor, Kinmei (reigned 539–571), adopted aspects of Chinese imperial rule, including court rituals based on the Chinese classics, and Chinese protocols for receiving envoys from the mainland. Kinmei's efforts to redefine the Yamato monarchy in Confucian terms began a trend continued by subsequent Yamato leaders throughout the sixth and seventh centuries.

THE ADOPTION OF BUDDHISM AND PROMINENCE OF THE SOGA

The adoption of reform measures such as these strengthened the prestige of the Yamato monarchs within the confederation, but did not necessarily increase their power. Keitai and Kinmei were dominant political figures, but the political fortunes of powerful *uji* leaders also improved. In the latter half of the sixth century, the leadership of one *uji* in particular—the Soga—threatened to usurp power and render the Yamato monarch a figurehead. The Soga *uji* had achieved prominence by collecting revenue for the court and by acting as intermediary for immigrant craftsmen and scholars. Clan members married into the royal family and provided Kinmei with at least two consorts.

The inherent weakness of the sixth-century monarchy in relation to court clans was made apparent with the official introduction of Buddhism to Japan, which reportedly occurred in 552, when a Paekche diplomatic mission presented a statue of the Buddha and several sutras to the Yamato court.[1] Kinmei asked his court what to do with these items. A faction led by the Soga advised Kinmei to worship the gifts, while an opposing faction warned him that prayers to the new religion would incur the wrath of the islands' gods. This latter group viewed Buddhism as a threat to the indigenous belief system, which upheld the political and social order by legitimizing the *uji* chieftain's role as the representative priest for the clan's guardian spirits (*ujigami*). The adoption of Buddhism was thus seen as an affront to the legitimacy of these *uji* heads. Those leading the opposition to Buddhism included the Nakatomi *uji*, members of which served as hereditary ritualists for the shrines associated with the Yamato rulers.

Kinmei tried to bring about a compromise between the court factions by allowing the Soga family to worship the religious objects without embracing Buddhism himself, but his decision did not avert an eventual court struggle. The court was torn by the issue of Buddhism for several decades until a military conflict broke out in the 580s. After the Soga proved victorious in 587, the court officially recognized Buddhism.

The adoption of Buddhism foreshadowed a willingness to incorporate foreign ideas and systems that had great social and political ramifications in Japan. Construction of large burial mounds, on the decline since Kinmei's reign, ceased as Buddhist temples co-opted the funeral rites of the indigenous religion. Buddhist monks bore Chinese culture to Japan, transmitting texts and knowledge unrelated to religion, such as treatises on astronomy, geomancy, and calendar making. Japan's monarchs even brought Buddhist monks to court as healers and diviners and appointed many to serve as advisers, scribes, and ambassadors. Sovereigns also began to sponsor Buddhist religious rites in order to secure peace and prosperity in the realm.

With its enemies defeated in 587, the Soga became the primary power behind the throne until 645. Soga influence was most evident in 592, when its head, Umako, orchestrated the assassination of his nephew, the Yamato monarch Sujun, and replaced him with his niece, Suiko, who was also Kinmei's daughter. The Soga also set up Prince Shōtoku (573–621), son of the monarch Yōmei and also of Soga descent, to serve as regent and coruler for Suiko.

THE REIGN OF SUIKO AND REGENCY OF PRINCE SHŌTOKU

The Suiko reign (592–628) became an era of great social and political development in Japan. It began during the time of the powerful Sui dynasty (581–618), the centralized Chinese state that united northern and southern China after centuries of disunion. One cannot underestimate the influence the Sui had on state formation in Japan. Sui China utilized Buddhist, Confucian, and Daoist ideology to establish an empire with a strong centralized military, an effective legal code based on local traditions, and a new state bureaucracy that curtailed the authority of local officials to enable greater central control. The Sui moved to limit hereditary privilege and create a civil administration based on meritocracy. The Sui state became the model for its successor, the Tang (618–907), and it served as the prototype for political reform on the Korean peninsula. The Korean kingdoms, having already adopted Buddhism and other important aspects of sixth-century Chinese culture, now embraced this newly restructured Chinese governmental system to strengthen their positions vis-à-vis their neighbors.

Like the leaders of the Korean states, the court in Japan was intrigued by reports of Sui China and its bureaucratic institutions, which were directing large-scale public works projects such as the Grand Canal and repair of the Great Wall. Not surprisingly, the Yamato court tried to redefine its own political structure based on Sui practices of rulership. From the early seventh century, the Japanese court sent students directly to Sui China as a part of official diplomatic missions (*kenzuishi*) to bring back elements of Chinese civilization, including books, religious writings, and Buddhist images. Some of these students remained in China for decades before returning with expertise regarding Chinese legal systems and administrative institutions. Four missions were sent to Sui China, with at least five more dispatched to Tang China (*kentōshi*) before the end of the seventh century. They delivered and retrieved individuals who contributed to the structuring of Japan's first centralized state. The returnees' efforts led to such watershed events in early Japanese institutional history as the Taika Reforms and the *Taihō Code* of 701.

Prince Shōtoku was the force behind the dispatch of the Sui missions and is credited with major political reform, such as implementation of the first merit-based court ranks in 603, known as the cap-rank system, and authorship of the *Seventeen Articles* in 604, a document written to promote a Chinese-style state system in Japan under a reigning Chinese-style sovereign. Prince Shōtoku embraced the Confucian model for his reform ideas, but he was also a devout Buddhist who convinced the Yamato court of the usefulness of Buddhism as an additional tool for governance. Suiko was also likely receptive to Buddhism, which, unlike Confucianism, gave support to female rulership.

Cap Rank

In contrast to the *kabane* system, which allowed the titles of *uji* chiefs to pass to descendants, Shōtoku's twelve-grade cap-rank system of 603 awarded court status according to ability. Based on Paekche and Koguryŏ models, the cap-rank system helped strengthen the state by recognizing individuals for administrative talents rather than for ancestry. Recipients of the new ranks were those who excelled in service to the court, including returnees from successful diplomatic or study missions to China. The cap-rank system transformed officials into Chinese-style courtiers outfitted in Confucian dress. The twelve ranks were denoted by cap color and named after junior and senior levels for each of six Confucian values (namely, virtue, benevolence, propriety, sincerity, justice, and knowledge). With the exception of the highest court officials (*ō-omi* and *ō-muraji*), who still received hereditary ranks, court appointments were, in theory at least, no longer based on hereditary ties to one's *uji*; posts were to be awarded to those with the experience and ability to perform the required tasks. Cap rank represented an important advancement toward establishing a Japanese meritocracy.

The Seventeen Articles

Prince Shōtoku's *Seventeen Articles* of 604 spelled out a set of governing principles, deeply rooted in Confucian values, that called for ethical governance. It rationalized the relationship between ruler and subject, likening it to that between heaven and earth. The first article emphasized the Confucian principle of peace and harmony—most likely a cautionary plea to the Soga leaders who were preeminent in the court and were threatening the decision-making authority of the royal family. The second of the *Seventeen Articles* promoted Buddhism as a tool for the state—only adherence to the teachings of the Buddha would lead to social harmony within the state. The third article, like the first, reflected Confucian teachings, equating the monarch with heaven and his subjects with earth and affirming the maxim "When heaven speaks, the earth must obey." The remainder of the *Seventeen Articles* advocated propriety, caution, impartiality, meritorious service, and other traits in keeping with the teachings of both Confucianism and Buddhism.

Some scholars doubt Shōtoku's authorship of the *Seventeen Articles*. The text uses anachronistic phrasing, and questions persist whether the ideal of supreme imperial rule could have been set forth so early in Japan's history. Nevertheless, evidence suggests that Shōtoku, or at least scholars working under him, did try to implement a political hierarchy based on Confucian ideals that placed the Yamato sovereign at the pinnacle of a centralized Chinese-style state and that vested him with authority analogous to that of the Sui emperor. Rules were adopted regarding court etiquette, and regulations for a civil bureaucracy were promulgated. The court of Suiko and Shōtoku began to reflect refinements suggestive of a Chinese-style court.

Shōtoku's reform attempts had limited success, however, as the clans were still able to exercise independent control over their lands and resources. It became apparent to many that the Soga was the greatest roadblock to any significant change.

THE TAIKA COUP AND REFORMS

Soga interference in the affairs of the ruling family was never greater than in the late 620s, following the death of Suiko. One of the contenders for the throne was Prince Shōtoku's son, Prince Yamashiro, but the Soga leader at that time, Emishi, arranged the enthronement of the monarch Jomei (reigned 629–641). This led to a falling out between Prince Yamashiro and the Soga, a relationship that further deteriorated after another contentious succession debate following Jomei's death in 641, when Yamashiro was once again passed over for enthronement. The greatest Soga blow to the prestige of the monarchy came in 643, when Emishi's son, Iruka, forced Yamashiro and twenty-two other Shōtoku descendants to commit suicide.

Angered by the elimination of Prince Yamashiro, a faction at court decided to strike against Soga domination. Nakatomi Kamatari, who later became the founder of the Fujiwara clan, approached Prince Karu (the future monarch Kōtoku), Prince Naka Ōe (the future monarch Tenji), and others, including some who had returned from studies in China. In 645 Kamatari and Prince Naka orchestrated an attack on Iruka in front of the reigning monarch Kōgyoku (reigned 642–645) during a ceremony for Korean diplomats. Iruka was killed, ending the preeminence of the Soga. Kōgyoku then abdicated, and Prince Karu, who was Kōgyoku's younger brother, succeeded to the throne becoming the monarch Kōtoku. In an effort to give Prince Naka a voice in state affairs, he was named crown prince in emulation of Prince Shōtoku's role decades earlier. Kamatari was appointed "inner minister" (*naidaijin*) and became an important adviser to the monarch and crown prince. This move against the Soga is referred to as the Taika (great change) coup d'état. "Taika" was chosen as the first Chinese-style *nengō*, or era name in Japan, and refers to the first half of the reign of the monarch Kōtoku (645–654).

Prince Naka and the other victors of the coup called for a far-reaching governmental reform movement, collectively referred to as the Taika Reforms. State scholars (*kuni no hakase*), who had studied in China, were tasked with contributing to government restructuring. Imperial decrees were promulgated to curb the authority of *uji* chiefs and create a more centralized state under a powerful monarch. Initial edicts included a call for court officials to swear oaths of allegiance to the new monarch, Kōtoku, and Crown Prince Naka; for weapons to be confiscated, save in eastern regions threatened by frontier fighting; for private land sales to be banned; and for government officials to reduce the number of commoners used for construction projects.

The key components of the Taika Reforms were proclaimed in a four-article edict supposedly issued on the first day of the New Year, 646. The first of these articles shared the concern of Prince Shōtoku's *Seventeen Articles* for direct imperial rule. It called for imperial control of resources by announcing an end to *uji* possession of land and people. All agricultural land was to be turned over to the state and direct servitude to the clans disallowed. People and communities were now subject to the throne, signaling a transition from an indigenous clan-ordered government system toward a sinicized state administered by a bureaucracy answerable to a sovereign. The move to nationalize land began with a symbolic move by Prince Naka, who gave his own property to the state. The success of other land handovers is unclear, as Japan did not yet possess the administrative capability to enforce compliance.

The remaining New Year's Day articles called for (1) establishment of a geographical hierarchy of officials to administer the capital, regions in close proximity to the capital, and outlying provinces; (2) implementation of land surveys and a population census in an attempt to institute land reform in line with the equal-field system of Tang China; and (3) the institution of a systemized tax system that would allow payment in rice, cloth, or other locally produced commodities.

Additional edicts were issued shortly thereafter, some of which clarified aspects of the New Year's Day four-article document. These dealt with Prince Naka's transfer of his agricultural estate to government control, the assumption of Yamato lands under government management, the establishment of new departments for central government administration, the institution of new ranking systems in 647 and 649, community contribution of conscript laborers, and the completion of the first land surveys and tax censuses. Overall, the reforms changed the status of local officials, who were now to be appointed as agents of the central government and bound to a code of systematic laws.

Historians once viewed the Taika Reforms as marking a great transition to a new centralized *ritsuryō* state fashioned after the Chinese model. More recent scholarship, however, emphasizes that the reforms of the Taika did not take place overnight and were not entirely successful. The court at this time still lacked the power to fully implement these new measures. Like the efforts of the Suiko and Shōtoku court some four decades earlier, the Taika reform effort was one of several steps in a long process of centralization spanning the sixth and seventh centuries. The Taika Reforms did, however, reinvigorate the long process of bureaucratic state building that continued through the end of the century.

RESPONSE TO THE TANG SILLA MILITARY ALLIANCE

Within a few years of the Taika coup d'état, events on the Korean peninsula provided additional impetus in Japan for reform. By 650, Tang China and the Korean kingdom of Silla had established an alliance that alarmed Japan and Silla's peninsular neighbors, Paekche and Koguryŏ. Prince Naka tried to maintain good relations with the Tang and sent missions in 653 and 654, but he also transferred the capital from the port city of Naniwa to an inland location in preparation for a possible invasion.

Japan's fears were partially realized in 660 as Tang and Silla combined their forces to defeat Paekche. Japan sent generals and troops to try to restore the Paekche kingdom between 661 and 663, but in late 663 the Japanese were defeated by Tang forces in a naval battle at the mouth of the Paekch'ŏn River. By 668 Silla defeated Koguryŏ as well and took control of the Korean peninsula as that region's first united state.

Japan's defeat impelled Prince Naka, who eventually took the throne as Tenji (reigned 668–671), to strengthen defenses and prepare for a possible Tang attack on Japan. Tenji expanded the authority of the Japanese ruler. He ordered his brother, Prince Ōama (the future Emperor Tenmu), to restructure and expand the court ranking system, resulting in a more elaborate hierarchy—a twenty-six-grade ranking system that integrated additional lineages from the provinces. Tenji also made the sovereign's approval necessary for confirmation of new *uji* chieftains, who were now allotted state subsidies. He also ordered the compilation of ceremonial regulations and, supposedly, an early version of an administrative law code, known as the *Ōmi Code,* which may have been compiled circa 668. In 671 Tenji appointed his son, Prince Ōtomo, as prime minister, to preside over a new council of state (*daijōkan*) tasked with executing the monarch's orders. These measures, some of which were modeled on Tang and Silla systems, advanced the move toward a more centralized state under a more powerful monarch. The fear of a Tang invasion and the impetus it produced for reform did not subside until Tang withdrew from the Korean peninsula in 676.

THE JINSHIN WAR AND REFORMS UNDER TENMU AND JITŌ

Upon Tenji's death in 671, a civil conflict of succession known as the Jinshin War ensued between Tenji's younger brother, Prince Ōama, and Tenji's son, Prince Ōtomo. Within a year Ōama defeated his nephew to become the monarch Tenmu (673–686). Tenmu and his consort-successor, Jitō (reigned 690–697), were crucial to the further centralization of the state.

Tenmu, whose name translates as "heavenly warrior," channeled his power and prestige from victory in the Jinshin War into bolstering the authority of the monarchy. He reconfigured the court by placing his supporters at the top, asserted his right to serve as chief judge within the realm, and augmented ties with the periphery by incorporating local elites into his court. Tenmu also ordered the compilation of the *Kiyomihara Code,* which contained legal and administrative regulations affirming the prerogatives of the monarch. Although no longer extant, the *Kiyomihara Code* was the precursor to the *Taihō Code* of 701, Japan's first comprehensive set of Chinese-style *ritsuryō* laws. After Tenmu's death, state development continued during the reign of his consort, Jitō. Under Jitō, Japan's first "permanent" Chinese-style capital, Fujiwara-kyō, was completed. Jitō also moved to ensure the stability of the ruling dynasty by choosing her successor and retiring. Precedents for this move existed in China, but her decision was a first for Japan.

Under Tenmu and Jitō, the monarchy was transformed. The *Seventeen Articles* of nearly a century earlier had used the Confucian lexicon to define the Japanese sovereign as an ideal Chinese ruler. It made no claims of royal divinity. By Jitō's reign, however, Tenmu, Jitō, and their offspring were being described as "living gods," with a divine right of perpetual rule based on their ancestral link to the sun goddess, Amaterasu. Accordingly, the Japanese rejected the Chinese-style relationship between emperor and heaven whereby heaven periodically bestows and retracts the right to rule (the Mandate of Heaven); they turned instead to Chinese classical texts describing heavenly or "bright" deities to whom the Chinese emperors prayed on behalf of the Chinese state. The Japanese made Amaterasu one of these deities, thereby attributing divinity to her progeny, now referred to as *akitsukami*, or "shining deities." Royal divinity was also asserted in the eighth-century Japanese histories *Kojiki* and *Nihon shoki*, likely commissioned by Tenmu or Jitō, that chronicled the Yamato dynasty's genealogy. Interestingly, Jitō also began to refer to herself by the aptly chosen term *tennō* (heavenly sovereign). The eighth-century genealogies retroactively applied *tennō*, usually rendered as "emperor" or "empress" in English, to all prior monarchs. The term eventually fell out of use for a number of centuries, but is now used in modern Japanese to refer to the imperial personage.

In addition to redefining the nature of Japanese sovereignty, Tenmu and Jitō helped unite their realm under a shared culture of literacy and Buddhism. They required literacy of all courtiers and ordered the compilation of the first character dictionary in Japan. They sent literate officials into the periphery who helped disseminate the written language to local elites. Tenmu and Jitō also went further than prior monarchs in adopting Buddhism, making it an inextricable part of the Japanese state and society. Tenmu, in particular, was a strong adherent of the "Sutra of the Golden Light." This sutra, or Buddhist scripture, promised rulers a Buddhist divine right to rule—conveniently complementing the ancestral divine right discussed above—based on religious merit earned by promulgating Buddhist teachings throughout the realm. Accordingly, Tenmu sponsored the composition and recitation of sutras and encouraged the building of chapels in the provinces. Indeed, more new temples were constructed during the last two decades of the seventh century than ever before. Tenmu and Jitō's efforts cemented the government's close association with Buddhism—a connection that continued until the nineteenth century.

By the end of Jitō's reign in 697, a more centralized Chinese-style state had evolved, but the process was not complete, as largely autonomous chiefs remained in the outlying regions. Before long, another *uji*, the Fujiwara—descendant of Kamatari, who had engineered the coup against the Soga—came to assert itself in a manner similar to that of the Soga *uji* half a century earlier.

At the turn of the sixth century, "Japan" was largely a confederation of loosely connected territories headed by a Yamato king whose power was nominal. As Yamato leaders adopted methods of continental statecraft, the confederation evolved, coalescing by the turn of the eighth century into the *ritsuryō* state, an indigenous Japanese rendering of a centralized Sui/Tang-style state with penal laws, an administrative code, and a "divine ruler" at its apex. The events addressed in this chapter were seminal to Japan's political evolution and set the stage for the promulgation of the *Taihō Code* in 701.

Sources and Suggestions for Further Reading

See bibliography for complete publication data.

Aston, W. G. *Nihongi: Chronicles of Japan from the Earliest Times to A. D. 697* (1972).

Batten, Bruce L. "Foreign Threat and Domestic Reform: The Emergence of the Ritsuryō State" (1986).

———. *Gateway to Japan: Hakata in War and Peace, 500–1300* (2006).

Bowring, Richard. *The Religious Traditions of Japan, 500–1600* (2005).

Como, Michael. *Shōtoku: Ethnicity, Ritual, and Violence in the Japanese Buddhist Tradition* (2008).

Farris, William Wayne. *Heavenly Warriors: The Evolution of Japan's Military, 500–1300* (1995).

Hall, John Whitney. *Government and Local Power in Japan, 500 to 1700* (1966).

Inoue Mitsusada. "The Century of Reform" (1993).

Inoue Tatsuo and Michiko Aoki. "The Hitachi Fudoki and the Fujiwara" (2006).

Kidder, J. Edward. *The Lucky Seventh: Early Horyu-ji and Its Time* (1999).

Ooms, Herman. *Imperial Politics and Symbolics in Ancient Japan: The Tenmu Dynasty* (2009).

Piggott, Joan R. *The Emergence of Japanese Kingship* (1997).

———, ed., *Capital and Countryside in Japan, 300–1180* (2006).

Seeley, Christopher. *A History of Writing in Japan* (2000).

Takahashi Tomio and Karl Friday. "The Classical Polity and Its Frontier" (2006).

Tsude Hiroshi and Walter Edwards. "Early State Formation in Japan" (2006).

Wang Zhenping. *Ambassadors from the Islands of the Immortals: China-Japan Relations in the Han-Tang Period* (2005).

Note

1. The *Nihon shoki (Chronicles of Japan)*, compiled in 720, dates this event to 552. An alternative document dates the introduction of Buddhism to 538.

PART III

Court, Capital, and Countryside in the Classical Age

C. 690	Adoption of Daoist term *tennō* ("heavenly sovereign"; usually translated as "emperor") for Japanese monarch
694	Capital established at Fujiwara-kyō
701	Taihō *ritsuryō* codes promulgated
710	Capital established at Heijō-kyō (Nara)
712	*Kojiki* published
718	Yōrō *ritsuryō* codes written
720	*Nihon shoki* published
729	Prince Nagaya incident
735–737	Smallpox epidemic
740	Fujiwara Hirotsugu Rebellion
741	Court orders creation of provincial temple (*kokubunji*) network, centered on Tōdaiji monastery
749	Completion of Tōdaiji
751	*Kaifusō,* Chinese-style poetry collection, published
752	Dedication ceremony for Tōdaiji and giant Buddha statue
755	An Lu-shan rebellion in China
757	Yōrō *ritsuryō* codes promulgated
757	Tachibana Naramaro conspiracy
C. 760	*Man'yōshū* compiled
764	Fujiwara Nakamaro rebellion
769	Dōkyō Incident
774–811	"Pacification Campaigns" against *emishi* inhabitants of the northeast
784	Capital moved to Nagaoka
788	Saichō establishes Enryakuji (officially named in 823) on Mt. Hiei
792	Provincial regiments (*gundan*) abolished in most of the country
794	Capital moved to Heian-kyō (Kyoto)
797	*Shoku Nihongi* published
816	Kūkai establishes Kongōbuji on Mt. Kōya
838	Last official embassy to Tang China

858	Fujiwara Yoshifusa appointed regent (*sesshō*) for Emperor Seiwa
887	Fujiwara Mototsune appointed chancellor (*kampaku*) for Emperor Kōkō
907–960	Five Dynasties period in China
907–979	Ten Kingdoms period in China
918–1388	Koryŏ Kingdom in Korea
927	Promulgation of *Engishiki* (*Regulations of the Engi Era*)
939–940	Taira Masakado insurrection
916–1125	Liao dynasty in China
960–1279	Song dynasty in China
C. 1008	Murasaki Shikibu completes *Genji monogatari* (*The Tale of Genji*)
1016	Fujiwara Michinaga becomes regent (*sesshō*) for Emperor Go-Ichijō
1028–1031	Taira Tadatsune insurrection
1038–1227	Western Xia dynasty in China
1051–1062	Former Nine Years' War
1069	Anna Incident
1083–1087	Latter Three Years' War
1086	Emperor Shirakawa retires; beginning of Insei era of court politics
1115–1234	Jin dynasty in China
1156	Hōgen Incident
1160	Heiji Incident
1167	Taira Kiyomori becomes prime minister (*daijō daijin*)
C. 1175	Hōnen founds the Jōdo shū (Pure Land School) sect of Buddhism
1179	Taira Kiyomori places ex-emperor Go-Shirakawa under house arrest
1180	Prince Mochihito calls for overthrow of Taira Kiyomori
1180–1185	Genpei Wars
1181	Taira Kiyomori dies
1183	Minamoto Yoshiie captures capital
1184	Battle of Ichinotani
1185	Battle of Dannoura
1191	Eisai returns to Japan from China; beginnings of Rinzai school of Zen Buddhism
1192	Minamoto Yoritomo takes title of Seii taishōgun
1199	Minamoto Yoritomo dies; is succeeded by son Yoriie
1205	Hōjō Yoshitoki becomes first shogunal regent (*shikken*)
1212	Kamo no Chōmei composes *Hōjōki* ("A Tale of a Ten Foot Square Hut")
1219	Minamoto Sanetomo assassinated
1221	Jōkyū War
1224	Shinran completes the *Kyōgyō shinshō*; beginning of Jōdo Shinshū (True Pure Land School) sect of Buddhism
1232	Hōjō Yasutoki promulgates *Jōei shikimoku* (*Goseibai shikimoku*)
1233	Dōgen founds Kōshōji; beginning of Sōtō Zen sect in Japan
1238	Great Buddha at Kamakura completed
1253	Nichiren begins lecturing on *Lotus Sutra*; beginning of Nichiren sect of Buddhism
1268	Mongol envoys visit Japan to demand tribute
1274	First Mongol invasion
1279–1368	Yuan dynasty in China
1281	Second Mongol invasion; ended with *kamikaze* (divine winds)
1299	Shogunate establishes Gozan (Five Mountain) network of Zen temples
C. 1332	Yoshida Kenkō completes *Tsurezure-gusa* (*Essays in Idleness*)
1333	Kamakura Shogunate destroyed

11

Emperor, Aristocracy, and the *Ritsuryō* State

Court Politics in Nara

Ross Bender

The eighth century represents a critical period for later Japanese culture, an era whose institutions and ways of thinking helped shape the rest of Japanese history. This chapter focuses on the dynamics of court life in a time when the influence of Chinese institutions and Buddhist thought rushed into the islands. These foreign stimuli created a synthesis with native ways that would determine the future of Japan.

Present-day Nara is the site of the ancient capital of Heijō-kyō, the Chinese-style city established in 710. Although the capital was moved to Nagaoka in 784 and then to Kyoto in 794, the eighth century is generally known as the Nara period. Archaeological surveys have determined the boundaries of the emperor's palace, and in 2010 a reconstruction of some of its ancient buildings was unveiled. The Nara Tōdaiji (Great Eastern Temple), housing the giant Great Buddha statue, is a UNESCO World Heritage Site and is said to be the largest wooden structure in the world. Visitors to Nara can walk through temples founded thirteen hundred years ago, view archaic sculptures, and imagine the period's ancient cultural glories. Near the train station stands a statue of Gyōki, a popular and powerful Buddhist priest of the time.

But while the eighth century was indeed a time of flourishing Japanese culture, it was also a period of political instability, notable for the intrigues of great families, Buddhist monks, and powerful empresses. With the close of the century a distinctive phase of Japanese culture ended, and yet Nara patterns of politics, religion, and literature have influenced Japanese history up to the present.

CHANGING THE CAPITAL

At the dawn of the eighth century, the capital of Japan was Fujiwara-kyō (*kyō* meaning "capital"), south of present-day Nara. Archaeologists do not agree on its precise layout, but it was evidently a Chinese-style city with a checkerboard design, built on a north-south axis similar to that of Changan, the capital of Tang China.

Founded in 694 by Empress Jitō (reigned 690–697), Fujiwara-kyō was unusual in that it was the seat of three rulers—Jitō; her grandson, Monmu (reigned 697–707); and his mother, Genmei (reigned 707–715). Previously the location of the court had shifted after the death of each ruler. Perhaps this was because the king's death was thought to have polluted the old palace. Another reason may have been that the home of the crown prince, who usually lived elsewhere with his mother's family, was designated as the new palace. Fujiwara, then, marks a change in the residential patterns of Japanese rulers: it was not only a Chinese-style city but also home to three emperors.

NARA

Nara (Heijō-kyō) was the primary capital from 710 to 784. Like Fujiwara-kyō, it was laid out on a north-south axis in a checkerboard pattern, with the palace enclosure located in the central area at the city's north end. From the throne, the ruler faced south toward his subjects. At the center of the southern end of the palace lay a great gate, the Suzakumon, or "Red Bird Gate," and the main boulevard, the "Red Bird Avenue," ran south, bisecting the city into the left and right sectors. A wall enclosed the palace complex, but unlike Tang Changan, the city itself was not surrounded by a wall. Although Nara was home to several major Buddhist institutions, no Daoist temples or great Shinto shrines were erected inside the new capital—even the Kasuga Shrine, housing the ancestral deities of the powerful Fujiwara family, lay on the city's eastern fringe.

The government established two large official markets in the southern part of Nara, one in the eastern sector and one in the west. Here the aristocrats obtained necessities and luxury goods transported in from the provinces. The court minted coins, and the new cash economy experienced inflation, counterfeiting, and attempts to control the value of money. Taxes, however, were largely collected in rice, and other products in kind from land and sea. Estimates are that the population of Nara approached 100,000 by the mid-eighth century, when the total population of Japan may have been about six million.

Our knowledge of the Chinese-style law codes (*ritsuryō*) proclaimed during this period is uncertain. The *Taihō Code* of 701 and the *Yōrō Code* of 718 have been reconstructed from evidence in ninth-century legal compilations, but there are still questions as to how closely these sets of laws were actually followed. A major factor complicating our understanding here is that the *Yōrō Code,* although apparently written in 718, was not actually promulgated until 757. Fundamentally, these laws instituted a census, a system of land distribution and taxation, and a bureaucracy. In theory, all people and all land belonged to the centralized state. The emperor and a council of high officials designated as the Daijōkan, or Council of State, presided over a bureaucracy divided into eight sections. The court sent governors from the capital to approximately sixty provinces to build and oversee local headquarters. A system of about thirty court ranks classified officials from first (highest) to eighth, with all but the top three each subdivided into Senior and Junior, and Upper and Lower, categories.

From the beginning the government revised the Chinese-style laws to accommodate to Japanese realities. An obvious example is the establishment of the Jingikan, or Council of Divinities, charged with oversight of native (Shintō) institutions and clergy. Theoretically an equal counterpart to the Council of State, this institution had no parallel in the Chinese bureaucratic structure. Another example of Japanese adaptation is that while the central government appointed governors to fixed terms of about four years, officials at the lower district levels were frequently chosen from the local aristocracies. The government in Nara could, and frequently did, change provincial governors, but the lower-level positions tended to become hereditary in local families.

IMPERIAL WANDERINGS

Although Nara is often said to be Japan's first permanent capital, it is obvious that the archaic pattern of shifting imperial palace sites was still in practice through most of the eighth century. In 740 a disgruntled official named Fujiwara Hirotsugu raised a rebellion in Kyushu. Although quickly subdued, this affair disturbed Emperor Shōmu (reigned 724–749) sufficiently that he left Nara and founded a new capital at Kuni to the northeast. Three years later he pulled up stakes again and established another capital at nearby Shigaraki, only to return to Nara in 745. Palace buildings were moved and recycled for use in the new capitals. In addition to starting two new cities, Shōmu also rebuilt an ancient palace at Naniwa (present-day Osaka), which had burned in the late

600s. Then, in 758, Junnin (reigned 758–764) built yet another palace at Hora, near Lake Biwa. In the year 770, just before her death, Empress Shōtoku (reigned 764–770) attempted to establish a new palace at Yugi-no-miya in Kawachi province. In 784 the imperial capital was moved to Nagaoka-kyō for a mere ten years, then shifted again to Heian-kyō, or Kyoto, which remained the home of the emperors until 1868.

Various theories have been advanced as to why the capital cities changed so frequently in the eighth century. Some hypothesize that the move from Fujiwara due north to Nara was inspired by geomantic considerations, the situation of the capital among mountains in Nara being thought superior to that in Fujiwara. It is suggested that the move from Nara to Nagaoka-kyō to the north was due to the end of the Tenmu dynasty and the reversion to the dynastic line of Emperor Tenji, whose capital had been at Ōtsu on the shores of Lake Biwa. Nagaoka was abandoned after ten years, it is surmised, because the landholdings of the most powerful families were in the Kyoto region, because of flooding, or even because of a vengeful ghost!

Why, then, did the imperial capital finally come to rest in Kyoto and remain there for the next thousand years? Certainly this question invites further research and debate. One hypothesis is that Emperor Kanmu, who moved the capital to Kyoto, lacked the political influence to make yet another move, even though the southwest quadrant of the new capital was soon subject to periodic flooding. Another possible answer is that the government, which had once possessed the financial wherewithal to move and recycle the palace and other official buildings, finally ran out of resources. By the mid-ninth century the drop in population growth and other economic factors had apparently put a stop to the archaic impulse to move the imperial palace at the emperor's whim.

CULTURAL GROWTH

Perhaps the most momentous cultural change of the eighth century was the beginning of the official use of writing on a large scale in a country that had previously known no writing system. Throughout the Nara period the first great monuments of Japanese history and literature were produced by order of the emperor and court. These include works in classical Chinese—two histories (*Nihon shoki*, 720; *Shoku Nihongi*, 797) and a poetry collection (*Kaifūsō*, 751)—and a history (*Kojiki*, 712) and poetry collection (*Man'yōshū*, c. 759) in Old Japanese. The works in Old Japanese used Chinese characters in a complex mixed style expressing both meaning and pronunciation.

The histories were political documents. Court nobles who edited *Kojiki* and *Nihon Shoki* merged the ancient myths and traditions of the powerful families constituting the court at Nara. They emphasized that the sun goddess, Amaterasu, was the ancestor of the imperial family, which she had sent down from heaven to rule Japan. Other major deities were depicted as ancestral gods of less powerful lineages that had supported the imperial conquest of the Japanese islands. Some of the later material in *Nihon shoki* is considered a more accurate historical record, particularly for the sixth and seventh centuries. *Shoku Nihongi* is the fundamental documentary source for the history of the eighth century. Essentially free of the mythic quality of the earlier histories, it is judged by Japanese and Western scholars to be a largely factual record of court activities. Even the poetry collections had a political function in establishing the authoritative canons of taste. Only the works of poets sanctioned by the court were included. Some of the major poets were deeply involved in court politics; in fact, even emperors wrote poetry.

Along with hundreds of thousands of wooden tablets (*mokkan*) displaying fragments of official documents, and other primary sources, such as population registers preserved in the government storehouse Shōsōin, the formal written sources published during the period are voluminous and still provide untapped resources for scholars. In addition, Buddhist sculpture, temple architecture, and archaeological finds such as roof tiles provide visual proof of the magnificent cultural flowering.

POLITICAL INTRIGUE

At the same time that Japan was experiencing an influx of cultural influence from China and the Korean peninsula and beginning to produce its own great works of art and literature, the Japanese centralized government system was also expanding. The newly formed bureaucratic state experienced tremendous instability along with this growth. Competitors for power at court included the imperial family, powerful old native lineages, immigrant groups from Korea, Buddhist monks, and specialists in Chinese learning.

These struggles may be characterized generally as succession disputes. Power centered in the figure of the emperor, who had the authority to grant high rank in the bureaucracy and the economic benefits that went with it. Those who controlled the throne had supreme power, and the rebellions, conspiracies, and outright coup attempts that mark the time centered on the question of who should rule.

A listing of the major crises and rebellions helps to clarify the overall pattern of political struggle during the Nara period. In table 11.1 one can readily see that one crisis involved an imperial prince and another a Buddhist priest. The Fujiwara family, which was battling for influence during this era, was responsible for the two overt rebellions. Tachibana Naramaro, scion of another powerful clan, plotted a conspiracy that was easily suppressed.

YEAR	MAIN CHARACTER	INCIDENT
729	Imperial Prince Nagaya	Forced to commit suicide with family
740	Fujiwara Hirotsugu	Armed rebellion
757	Tachibana Naramaro	Conspiracy to overthrow government
764	Fujiwara Nakamaro	Armed rebellion
769	Buddhist Priest Dōkyō	Hachiman oracle naming him Emperor

Table 11.1. Major crises and rebellions during the Nara period

The two Fujiwara were grandsons of Fujiwara Fuhito (658–720), whose powerful father, Nakatomi Kamatari (614–669), was awarded the surname "Fujiwara" toward the end of his life, in recognition of his support for the future Emperor Tenji in the Taika coup d'état of 645. Fuhito's four sons, all high-ranking bureaucrats, perished in a smallpox epidemic that ravaged Japan from 735 to 737. His daughter Kōmyō, however, became Emperor Shōmu's empress, and many of his grandsons eventually held high rank and office in the later Nara period. Nevertheless, Hirotsugu and Nakamaro were not content to rise through the bureaucratic route.

As mentioned earlier, in 740 Hirotsugu raised a rebellion in Kyushu. His chief enemies at court were a Buddhist priest, Genbō, who had established a Buddhist chapel within the palace, and Kibi Makibi, a scholar who had studied in China. Genbō and Makibi represented a sort of brain trust for the Emperor Shōmu; they were intellectuals steeped in the latest Buddhist and Confucian thought, political science, and military tactics. The court sent an army to subdue Hirotsugu and, within several months, defeated his forces and beheaded him.

Fujiwara Nakamaro actually gained great influence at court by rising through the bureaucracy thanks to support from his aunt, the Empress Kōmyō. From about the year 757, he instituted reforms and updated the titles of officialdom to Chinese designations, changing his own name to the Chinese-style "Emi Oshikatsu." At the time of his rebellion, in 764, he was the most powerful man in Japan, since the current emperor, Junnin, was something of a puppet. Nevertheless, the retired sovereign, Kōken, on the advice of the Buddhist priest Dōkyō, resisted his claim to absolute power, and thus Nakamaro eventually revolted. As in the case of Hirotsugu, the court's armies defeated him within a short time.

Tachibana Naramaro was the scion of another great family. His powerful father, the Minister of the Left, died in early 757. Naramaro conspired to overthrow Empress Kōken in the seventh month of that year, but spies betrayed his plans and his conspiracy was nipped in the bud by the court's armies and the forces of Fujiwara Nakamaro.

The circumstances of the death of Prince Nagaya, whose mansion was surrounded by the court's troops in 729, and who was forced to commit suicide along with his family, are still mysterious, although obviously the result of factional struggles at court. However, partly because archaeologists have found the location of his luxurious home south of the palace and discovered tens of thousands of *mokkan* on the site, the incident attracts continued interest.

POWERFUL WOMEN IN NARA

Even from this short summary the extreme complexity of Nara government is obvious. Some of the complications stem from the fact that Emperor Shōmu abdicated in 749 and his daughter Kōken took the throne. When Shōmu died in 756, he left a will designating an imperial prince to be Kōken's successor. Within a year this will was overturned, and a different prince appointed. This succession dispute was partly responsible for the Tachibana Naramaro conspiracy of 757. After Naramaro was executed, Kōken herself abdicated and gave the throne to the puppet emperor Junnin.

In 764, after Fujiwara Nakamaro's revolt, his supporter Junnin was exiled and then assassinated. At that point, Kōken reascended the throne as Empress Shōtoku, with the support of the Buddhist priest Dōkyō. In 769 an oracle from the shrine priestess of Hachiman, a native deity in Kyushu, was reported to the court. It said that if Dōkyō were named emperor, even though he was not of royal blood, there would be peace in the realm. When Shōtoku sent her own messenger to the shrine to confirm the prophecy, a different oracle was given pronouncing that only a descendant of the imperial lineage could be made emperor. The priest was exiled and Shōtoku died in 770. She never married and left no descendants.

THE ERA OF FEMALE SOVEREIGNS

From 592, when the first female sovereign, Suiko, took the throne, until the death of Shōtoku in 770, six women reigned as supreme rulers of Japan, interspersed among male rulers. In the official histories they were all named *tennō* (heavenly sovereign). Although usually translated as "emperor," the Japanese word does not distinguish between male and female. One of the difficulties in writing about ancient Japanese history in English is the ambiguity of the term "empress," which is used for both reigning female monarchs and the consorts of reigning monarchs. We speak, for example, of "Empress Jitō," who was both the spouse of Emperor Tenmu but also *tennō* in her own right after his death.

But the female *tennō* Genmei, Genshō, and Kōken were never the consorts of male rulers, and the latter two never married. One solution would be to simply call the female *tennō* "emperor," but at present the convention is either to term them all "empress" or to use some circumlocution such as "female sovereign."

At any rate, this pattern of ancient female sovereigns is quite remarkable, especially in contrast to ancient China, which only had one female "emperor"—Wu Zetian, who reigned from 690 to 705. There has been considerable debate recently concerning the political significance of female rule. Some historians look back to the example of Himiko, the mysterious Japanese woman ruler mentioned in Chinese histories of the third century, and see rule by women as a remnant of shamanistic female charisma. Other scholars believe that these monarchs functioned as regents or place-holders, ruling until a male successor was old enough to take the throne. Still others think that the female sovereigns actually performed in much the same way as their male counterparts.

In the eighth century it was a female ruler, Genmei, who founded the capital at Nara. She handed the throne to her daughter Genshō, who in turn abdicated in favor of her nephew Shōmu. Shōmu reigned from 724 to 749, when he also abdicated, became a Buddhist monk, and gave the throne to his daughter Kōken. As we have seen, Kōken abdicated and Junnin ascended the throne. Junnin is known in history as the "Deposed Emperor." In fact, he was never acknowledged in the official line of emperors until modern times. There are many indications that he was no more than a puppet. Kōken, as retired *tennō*, had him exiled and then reascended the throne in 765. She ruled as Shōtoku until her death in 770.

THE "LAST EMPRESS"

Kōken/Shōtoku is a fascinating figure in Japanese history. Traditionally she has been condemned as the lover of the scheming priest Dōkyō, regarded as having used her to advance his own political career and his quest to become emperor. More recent scholars, however, have viewed her as a canny political actor in her own right, and seen Dōkyō as just another politically influential Buddhist priest, like Gyōki and Genbō before him. Seen in this light, she appears as a powerful woman who managed to fight off continual challenges to her authority, from Tachibana Naramaro, Fujiwara Nakamaro, and eventually Dōkyō.

In fact Kōken/Shōtoku, Naramaro, and Nakamaro were all cousins of a sort. The three had either Fujiwara Fuhito or his consort, Lady Tachibana, in common as their grandparents. Lady Agata Inukai Tachibana was another remarkable woman of the era. In her first marriage, to an imperial prince, she gave birth to Tachibana Moroe, the father of Naramaro. In a second liaison, with Fuhito, she gave birth to Fujiwara Kōmyō, who became Shōmu's empress. She was the step-grandmother of Fujiwara Nakamaro. Thus the conspiracies and rebellions of the 750s and 760s can be viewed to some extent as intrafamily feuds in a very complex and inbred household.

Empress Kōmyō is yet another fascinating great woman of the Nara period. Not only was she a devout Buddhist and remarkable patron of the arts, responsible for donating many of the treasures of the Shōsōin, the great imperial storehouse in Nara, but she was an astute politician as well. It was largely due to her influence that her nephew Nakamaro ascended to power in the official bureaucracy. It was only several years after her death in 760 that Nakamaro rebelled against her daughter Kōken.

Kōken may be viewed as inheriting the strong character of both her father, Emperor Shōmu, and her mother, Fujiwara Kōmyō. She also inherited their Buddhist piety, and in fact she herself took holy orders. It is evident that, when she reascended the throne, she gave profound thought to the issues of reconciling Buddhist doctrine of divine protection of the state with the native political tradition. In several of her imperial edicts, she explicitly considers the contradictions inherent in uniting the two streams of royal ideology.

After Kōken/Shōtoku's death in 770, there were no more female *tennō* until a thousand years later, when political power had long passed to the military rulers, the shoguns. Traditional histories have attributed the end of the rule of women to Shōtoku's supposedly wicked relationship with the priest Dōkyō and to his attempt to seize the throne. In fact, however, the particulars of their relationship are not known. Also, it was her caution in the matter of the Hachiman oracles that helped reinforce the principle that only a candidate of imperial blood could inherit the throne. It may be that the rise of Confucian political thought during the eighth century, which denied supreme power to women, was responsible for ending the era of female rule in ancient Japan.

THE NARA SYNTHESIS

In retrospect, we can see that by the close of the eighth century, several key patterns of institutional structure and political thought had been established in Japan. These include (1) the establishment of a major capital city on the Chinese model; (2) an imperial institution at the apex of a ranked bureaucracy; (3) an aristocracy grounded in law and based on wealth in landholding; and (4) an emerging syncretic royal political ideology. This political ideology incorporated elements of Buddhist protection of the emperor, Chinese philosophical and practical ideas about the conduct of an ideal state, and native ideas concerning the divine ancestry of the nation and its leaders.

With the benefit of centuries of hindsight, we can see that certain issues had been definitively settled, though these were by no means self-evident to the people of the time. It was, for example, by no means certain that the capital city would remain in Kyoto, or that other new imperial capitals would not be established as they had been earlier in the eighth century. From our vantage point in the twenty-first century, it seems obvious that the pattern of female emperorship was finished, though that was not necessarily clear at the time. We can observe that the nascent principle that only one of royal ancestry could occupy the throne was firmly established. Again, although the idea had been heralded in the case of Hachiman and Dōkyō, it, too, might have been subject to change.

Perhaps the most profound change during this period was the adoption of the Chinese written language by the elite and the beginning of its adaptation for the expression of Japanese. Obviously, our evidence for most of the history of this period depends on the production and survival of written texts. Once more in retrospect, we can now see how the evolution of the Japanese script began and how it developed in counterpoint to writing in Chinese.

The fact that over the centuries these elements of political structure and ideology proved to be enduring enables us to speak of a "Nara synthesis." This foundational epoch produced fundamental elements of Japanese civilization and a scaffolding upon which Japanese institutions and culture have developed down to the present.

Sources and Suggestions for Further Reading

See bibliography for complete publication data.

Aston, W. G., trans. *Nihongi: Chronicles of Japan from the Earliest Times to A. D. 697* (1972).

Bender, Ross. "Changing the Calendar: Royal Political Theology and the Suppression of the Tachibana Naramaro Conspiracy of 757" (2010).

———. "The Hachiman Cult and the Dōkyō Incident" (1979).

———. "Performative Loci of the Imperial Edicts in Nara Japan, 749–70" (2009).

Como, Michael. "Horses, Dragons, and Disease in Nara Japan" (2007).

———. *Weaving and Binding: Immigrant Gods and Female Immortals in Ancient Japan* (2009).

Farris, William Wayne. *Population, Disease, and Land in Early Japan, 645–900* (1985).

———. "Trade, Money, and Merchants in Nara Japan" (1998).

Levy, Ian Hideo, trans. *The Ten Thousand Leaves: A Translation of the Man'yōshu, Japan's Premier Anthology of Classical Poetry* (1981).

Nippon Gakujutsu Shinkōkai, trans. *Manyōshū*. (1965).

Ooms, Herman. *Imperial Politics and Symbolics in Ancient Japan: The Tenmu Dynasty* (2008).

Philippi, Donald L., trans. *Kojiki* (1969).

Piggott, Joan R. "The Last Classical Female Sovereign: Kōken-Shōtoku Tennō" (2003).

———. "Mokkan: Wooden Documents from the Nara Period" (1990).

Toby, Ronald P. "Why Leave Nara?" (1985).

Van Goethem, Ellen. *Nagaoka: Japan's Forgotten Capital* (1990).

Vovin, Alexander, trans. *Man'yōshū: Book 15* (2009).

Yoshie, Akiko. "Gender in Early Classical Japan: Marriage, Leadership, and Political Status in Village and Palace" (2005).

12

Oligarchy, Shared Rulership, and Power Blocs

Mikael S. Adolphson

From its inception, Japan's imperial court was, despite the emperor's supreme position, more inclusive than exclusive. Rather than eliminating noble competitors, the imperial family surrounded itself with and relied on ranking families to support its rule as long as it was not challenged, though this was something that had already by the early ninth century become all but unthinkable. The drawback with this arrangement was that it also bred competition and factionalism among these same nobles for positions and offices close to the throne.

Perhaps no period in Japanese history is more characterized by such factionalism than the Heian age, and its intensification in the late twelfth century came to have a profound effect on the ruling structures. Leading up to this competitive society were three major developments that began in preceding centuries: a modification of the Chinese political system, privatization of government, and the emergence of blocs of power known as *kenmon* (influential houses; literally, "gates of power").

These changes were gradual and cannot be pinpointed easily, but from a political perspective, two transitions can be identified with some precision. The first occurred in the mid-ninth century when the Fujiwara became the dominating family at the imperial court, signaling the beginning of the privatization process. The second took place around the turn of the twelfth century as the imperial family made a dramatic comeback, beginning an age of shared rulership among elite blocs that also included the leading religious centers.

MODIFICATION OF THE CHINESE BUREAUCRATIC SYSTEM OF RULE

When Emperor Kanmu (737–806; reigned 781–806) moved the imperial palace, and thus the capital, to the Heian plain in 794, he was in every sense a sovereign who ruled as well as reigned. The departure from the old capital of Nara was motivated by a desire not only to utilize the social and proprietary foundation of the Tenji line (of which Kanmu was a descendant) in the Heian basin but also to establish firmer control of the Buddhist establishment, which was perceived as a threat to unimpeded imperial rule. This strengthening was further consolidated in 810, when Emperor Saga (786–842; reigned 809–823) eliminated unwanted imperial descendants by "granting" them a surname (members of the imperial family do not to this day have a surname); most commonly "Taira" or "Minamoto." In the process, Saga's foremost supporters, the Northern Branch of the Fujiwara, similarly managed to eliminate competitors from other branches to become the second family in the realm.

The family progenitor, Nakatomi Kamatari, had acquired the surname Fujiwara as a reward for his role in the Taika coup d'état of 645, and his son Fuhito was a leading player in the creation and promulgation of the *ritsuryō* codes. In the third generation, the clan split into four main houses—the Northern, Southern, Ceremonial, and Capital branches—each descended from one of Fuhito's sons. While all four branches were important during the eighth century, by the Heian period, the Northern branch came to overshadow the others and emerged as the dominant house at court.

The Northern Fujiwara gained access to the imperial family through private means rather than their official position at court. That is to say that the key to their success lay in their daughters, who were made consorts of emperors and princes, and in turn gave birth to the next generation of emperors. Fujiwara marital ties to the imperial house began with Fuhito's daughter, Kōmyōshi (701–760), who became a consort to Emperor Shōmu, an arrangement that continued well into the medieval era. By imperial decree, Fujiwara women were the only consorts not of royal blood eligible for the title of principal imperial consort (*kōgō*), and men of the Northern Fujiwara were the only courtiers permitted to marry daughters of emperors—men of other houses could wed no closer to the throne than royal granddaughters.

In the mid-ninth century, Fujiwara fortunes reached a new plateau under Yoshifusa (804–872). Husband to a daughter of Emperor Saga (785–842; reigned 809–823) and father-in-law to Saga's grandson Emperor Montoku (827–858; reigned 850–858), Yoshifusa became chancellor (*daijō daijin*, the highest government post defined under the *ritsuryō* codes) in 857. Montoku died the following year and was succeeded by his infant son, Emperor Seiwa (850–881; reigned 858–876). Eight years later, Yoshifusa was appointed regent (*sesshō*) for his nine-year-old grandson, the first time someone outside the imperial family had been honored with that title.[1]

Yoshifusa's son, Mototsune (836–891), was equally, if not more, ambitious. Like his father, he became *sesshō* (in 876), but he felt threatened by Emperor Kōkō (830–887; reigned 884–887), who was an adult at the time of his accession. Skillfully using his influence and the power of his own faction, Mototsune managed to retain his regency position by creating a new title, *kanpaku* (regent for an adult emperor), loosely based on a Chinese precedent. While his control was challenged by the next emperor, Uda (867–931; reigned 887–897), and although in a confrontation in 887 other courtiers remained committed to the older system of promotion by merit and experience, Mototsune prevailed, thus making the adult regency a new tradition. From this time forward, imperial regents—styled either *sesshō* or *kanpaku*, depending on the age of the monarch at the time—became a permanent fixture of the court hierarchy, and a permanent possession of the Northern Branch of the Fujiwara house, which became known as the Regents' House (*sekkanke*, a term derived from *SESshō* + *KANpaku*).

Few events mark the ascendancy of the Fujiwara and the privatization of government more than these developments, which allowed the Fujiwara to dominate the court for two centuries, while their opponents found it all but impossible to assert their own interests. Perhaps the most tragic example was Sugawara Michizane (845–903), a scholar who was promoted by Uda in an attempt to weaken the Fujiwara, but who died in exile in Kyushu. Based, then, on their personal connections with the emperor and the imperial family as a whole, the Fujiwara managed to dominate court politics for the following two centuries.

The regental offices were central to this process, but functioned more as an indicator of their power than the reason for it. Curiously, regency appointments remained ad hoc, without a legal basis in the *ritsuryō* codes or any formal amendments to them, and subject to renewal or replacement at each change of monarch—unlike regular government posts, which carried fixed terms of office, irrespective of imperial reigns.

This notion is further strengthened by those circumstances in which the Fujiwara chieftains dominated the court even without these offices, as in the case of the most famous of them all, Michinaga (966–1027). Michinaga was never appointed regent but maintained an official recognition of his power as an internal examiner of documents (*nairan*), which allowed him to check on edicts and verdicts and be consulted before they were issued. Where he writes that "When I reflect, this world is indeed mine" in a poem at the celebration of his daughter's appointment as principal consort of the reigning emperor, one gets the sense that he was not boasting, but just describing the world as he and everyone around him saw it.

But how could the Fujiwara chieftain exert such influence on the imperial family even if he was the grandfather of reigning and future emperors? The answer is to be found in the marriage customs of the time. As we have seen, there was no primogeniture, by which the oldest son (or child) would automatically become the successor to the throne. Rather, the imperial family—and indeed Heian nobles in general—kept the choice open for parents to make, in effect ensuring that the strongest candidate be chosen, based not just on health and intelligence but also on the support he had. For the imperial family, this meant that the prince with the highest-ranking mother would most frequently ascend the throne—and daughters of the Fujiwara Regents House were rarely outranked. Moreover, in the context of competition and factionalism at court, it became natural for the prince with the strongest backing to become the consensus choice, thus giving the already favored Fujiwara an indirect link to and control of the imperial throne.

In addition, marriages among the Heian nobility were largely matrilocal, whereby the male figure would normally move to or visit the home of the consort and residences accordingly were kept separate. Consorts spent time in the imperial compound as well, of course, but the key was the offspring, who were usually brought up under the roof of their maternal grandfather, ensuring that the Fujiwara chieftain had all but complete control of future rulers.

Because of the openness of the inheritance structures, the competition for chieftainship, and control of the court that followed in its wake, success depended on the private assets of each faction. In fact, private means—in terms not just of social status but also of wealth, military retainers, religious support, and cultural capital—came to be the all-encompassing keys to success in Heian Japan.

PRIVATIZATION OF GOVERNMENT

The Fujiwara Regents House spearheaded what has often been called the privatization of government by controlling the imperial court, not through official offices, but through their private connections.[2] Nevertheless, while the Fujiwara were the *most* successful at using such assets, these venues were open also to other court nobles, some of whom were relatives, and so the more private assets in their portfolio the better. It should come as no surprise that in this environment land, religious ceremonies, and military retainers became increasingly used by individual nobles to support their careers at court. Accordingly, from the early Heian period onward, we find a gradual but consistent process of privatization in different arenas of society, mirroring what had happened behind the imperial throne.

The most obvious, and also complex, aspect of this trend was the drawn-out process of privatization of governance and landholding in the countryside, through which land was removed from provincial taxation and made into private estates known as *shōen* (described in chapter 16). The ranking nobles, especially the Fujiwara, together with a handful of influential temples, had the necessary status to protect these creations as patrons and thus promoted the spread of *shōen,* although they were at the same time part of the imperial court that was now seeing a decline of tax revenues. In short, the removing of land from provincial taxation and administration benefited the ranking elites more financially than it threatened the imperial court itself. Still, as crucial as landed wealth was to the lifestyles of the noble elites and their ability to jockey for power, it was not enough to ensure a prominent position at the court.

Access to military power became increasingly important as well—and, by the late Heian period, indispensable to the capital elites, either for show of force and support in capital factionalism or protection of assets in the capital or the countryside. These armed men, headed by lesser nobles, who in turn employed military land-managers from local estates and villages, played an important role already in the so-called Anna Incident of 969, when the Fujiwara military retainer Minamoto Mitsunaka (912–997) staged a coup to implicate competing families in Kyoto.

Noble elites, moreover, depended on the spiritual and political powers of Buddhism as well as local beliefs (Shintō) to reinforce and augment the status of their secular positions in the competition for power. Whereas religious rituals, especially Buddhist ones, had been generally promoted by the imperial court in the Nara age, by the Heian period, it was the individual patrons and sponsors who received credit for them. Thus, ceremonies for the welfare of the state, the health of the emperor, or the safe birth of a prince or princess all reflected and enhanced the status of the participants and the patrons, even down to the seating order (which reflected the status of those who participated) specified during such rituals. Ties to and patronage of monks who performed rituals for the state and the imperial family served the same purposes. The rituals served, in other words, as a way to define and reinforce power, in a manner reminiscent of what Clifford Geertz has called the "theater-state," in which the ritual represents and constructs the ruling configuration itself.[3]

Another important asset in the competition for power was cultural capital, which can be described as knowledge or familiarity with those cultural practices that defined the nobility. The production of literary works, poetry competitions, and parties, as well as the writing of diaries, was, in other words, among the activities not just expected of ranking courtiers but also serving to define their social status—as indicated in the famous "Yugao" chapter in *The Tale of Genji*, in which the protagonist determines that a court lady down on her luck was an appropriate target for a romance based on her poetry skills. The same was true for the collection and display of cultural products, including luxury goods from China, which appear with some frequency in contemporary records. Such cultural capital accordingly served to distinguish those with the proper education and upbringing from lower-ranking courtiers and ambitious warriors, who could otherwise easily dress up as, and receive appointments corresponding to, higher-ranking officers.

THE EMPIRE STRIKES BACK

Factionalism had always been part of court politics, but the Fujiwara brought the competition to a new level by relying heavily on extragovernmental assets, eventually ushering Japan into a new era of rulership in which elites from various sectors of society both competed and cooperated to rule through their private means. Other noble families, including lesser Fujiwara and the Ōtomo, attempted to keep pace with the Regents House but were considerably less successful. In contrast, the major Buddhist centers, such as Enryakuji, Onjōji (both of the Tendai School), Kōfukuji, and Tōdaiji, became increasingly wealthy through land donations and judicial immunity, gaining a considerable level of independence. In essence, the monastic homesteads were areas beyond the jurisdiction of provincial and government officials; so rowdy clerics and other figures associated with the religious community could in effect evade punishments by hiding out in the monasteries, even though the leading monks were expected to hand criminals over to the authorities if asked to do so. The special privileges enjoyed by the likes of the Fujiwara, Enryakuji, Kōfukuji, and Tōdaiji were recognized in contemporary records with the term *kenmon*, which began to appear in documents and diaries by the mid-Heian period. By the late eleventh century, another powerful faction emerged to challenge both the Fujiwara's power and the major temples' independence: a resurgent imperial family.

It has often been supposed that, at least in the early decades of the *ritsuryō* state, emperors ruled with transcendent power and authority, while the great noble houses of the court served them as obedient bureaucrats. Yet while there can be no disputing the political *authority* of the emperor, his political *power* was closely circumscribed by the very codes and customs that rendered his status unique and unchallengeable. Among the most important practical checks the *ritsuryō* codes placed on the monarch's ability to exercise power arbitrarily was the provision that imperial edicts be drafted and promulgated by the Council of State (Daijōkan). Coupled with the custom that emperors preside over the debates of their ministers from behind semitransparent curtains of state, thus not participating directly in the discussions, this stipulation effectively ensured that the "imperial will" could be enacted only after obtaining not merely advice, but also some measure of consent, from the rest of the ruling oligarchy.

In or about 810, Emperor Saga created a new organ of government, styled the Chamberlain Office (Kurōdo dokoro), charged with handling imperial documents and intended to tip the balance of power within the court back toward imperial hands. Located within his private residence and staffed by men with close personal ties to him, the new office offered the emperor an alternative means of communicating with his bureaucracy—a way to bypass the Council of State and issue orders directly to the ministries and bureaus that carried them out.

For a time, the Chamberlain Office did increase the power of the throne and serve as a check on Fujiwara power. But because it also served to blur the lines between the imperial person and the imperial position, and to further focus the exercise of power away from the formal mechanisms of the *ritsuryō* state and toward a simpler, more privatized model of governing, in the longer run, the Kurōdo dokoro also served the interests of the Fujiwara, whose familial ties to emperors soon enabled them to dominate this new office as well.

It has often been said that Fujiwara chieftains were in a better position to exploit the authority of the throne than were reigning emperors themselves. This was because the Fujiwara's enormous wealth (derived through official rank and office stipends, revenues from private estates, and—not inconsequentially—from gifts and bribes received from provincial and other officials seeking appointments to office or other political favors), high court rank, and unique relationship with the imperial house gave them a footing in each of the three key political arenas of the day: the Council of State, the behind-the-scenes trading of political favors and influence, and the Chamberlain Office.

No other noble house could roam as freely or operate as effectively across all three spheres. And reigning emperors found themselves ironically hamstrung, on the one hand by their lofty status and identity as the embodiment of the public sphere (which forestalled efforts to acquire wealth through private lands and impeded backstage political wheeling and dealing), and on the other by their familial obligations to Fujiwara grandfathers and fathers-in-law. Eventually, however, the imperial family discovered a way to reassert itself by exploiting the stature and the freedom of *retired* sovereigns (*in*).[4]

The absence of clear-cut rules for imperial succession meant that there was always an ample number of potential crown princes around to contend for the throne. In the seventh and eighth centuries, this often led to bloody interregnum conflicts following the death of a monarch. But by the Heian period, emperors had learned to avoid this problem by abdicating in favor of their chosen heirs rather than postponing the transfer of power until death. Succession by abdication very quickly became the norm. The Fujiwara, in fact, often exploited this practice to their own advantage, pressuring emperors to abdicate in favor of Fujiwara grandsons, and sometimes engineering the succession of children or even infants, who would be particularly malleable to grandfatherly influence.

Abdication, however, also introduced a new figure to court politics, in the form of retired sovereigns who, though now having formally reverted to the status of common subjects, in practice retained a substantial aura of royal authority—and therefore considerable potential for political influence. While the *ritsuryō* codes made no provisions for retired monarchs, in practice ex-emperors were provided with retirement palaces and income-producing lands, and continued to enjoy much of the prestige, as well as many of the prerogatives, of their former status. Retired sovereigns were, moreover, recognized as the effective heads of the imperial house, and exercised substantial familial authority over their sons and grandsons on the throne.

Thus there were, in effect, two kinds of regency competing for control of the court during the early and mid-Heian periods: the Fujiwara *sesshō* and *kanpaku* and the *in*. The Fujiwara retained the upper hand for most of the ninth, tenth, and eleventh centuries, but their dependence on marriage and maternal connections to the throne made their position inherently fragile.

During the regency of Fujiwara Yorimichi (997–1074), which lasted for an amazing fifty-two years, there were no signs that the Northern Branch would relinquish its grip on capital politics any time soon, but his own daughters somehow failed to produce male heirs (he was regent for his nephews). As a result, Yorimichi was forced to allow the accession of an emperor whose mother was not a Fujiwara in 1068, when Go-Sanjō (1034–1073; reigned 1068–1072) became emperor. Not only was Go-Sanjō anti-Fujiwara, but he was also an adult, and so he proceeded to take steps to reassert the imperial family's position. Besides endeavoring to stop the further spread of private estates, his most important action was to appoint a successor who was, like himself, not under the thumbnail of the Fujiwara.

That successor ascended the throne as Shirakawa (1053–1129; reigned 1072–1086) and became the most successful and innovative ruler of the entire Heian age after Kanmu. Although he proceeded cautiously as a reigning emperor, Shirakawa became much more aggressive in reasserting the imperial family's power following his abdication in 1086 and the subsequent weakening of the Fujiwara owing to the timely deaths of two chieftains in 1099 and 1101. In addition, as a retired sovereign, Shirakawa could act more freely, without the ritual and procedural constraints of emperorship, to establish new procedures and precedents to take more direct control of matters of governance.

First and foremost, Shirakawa made sure to control imperial succession so that he controlled the following three emperors (Horikawa, Toba, and Sutoku—his son, grandson, and great-grandson), rather than the Fujiwara. But this strategy was not just about succession; it was also about controlling court politics as Shirakawa continued to wield power behind the throne, thus in essence replacing the Fujiwara as puppet masters. Second, he continued his father's policies of restricting the spread of private estates; but at the same time, he made the unprecedented move of creating *shōen* for the imperial family, often in the name of consorts and princes, since in principle the emperor himself could not own land. In addition, to assure for himself a loyal retainer corps, he assigned public land as "proprietary provinces" to his commanders. Third, he implemented new religious policies in an attempt to control important rituals, both by creating new ones to counter Fujiwara control of existing rituals and by placing members of the imperial family in powerful monasteries.

Shirakawa was thus transforming the imperial family into a privatized elite, based on the strategies of the Fujiwara. The period beginning with Shirakawa's retirement until the end of the Heian age (1086–1185) is therefore commonly known as the age of rule by retired emperors (*insei jidai*). The retired emperor did not, however, control the capital region or all spheres of society entirely; rather, rulership was effectively shared among factions, but also divided up between blocs depending on their functions, in a configuration wherein the retired emperor had emerged as the dominating force in the twelfth century.

THE *KENMON* SYSTEM OF SHARED RULERSHIP

Once Shirakawa had given the imperial family private powers, rulership no longer depended on control of high government offices, since rulers typically retired to be able to exert their power. In effect, bureaucratic titles mattered little in the twelfth century either to the imperial family or the Fujiwara leaders. To be sure, mid-ranking nobles and ambitious warriors still coveted and competed for various appointments, but less for the status that they might accrue than for the income that they might yield. Direct control of estates, provinces, and manpower was more important than government titles for exercising influence or dominating the government. Although the term *kenmon* (influential house) was initially reserved for noble elites and, by the twelfth century, members of the imperial family, it came to include members of religious institutions such as Enryakuji, Kōfukuji, and Tōdaiji. To this group of new members can also be added warrior-aristocrats, who in the late twelfth century came to establish their own branch of the government (the Kamakura Shogunate; see chapter 18) and acquired enough independence and power to assume the characteristics of *kenmon*.

According to Kuroda Toshio, the Japanese scholar who first identified these elites as corulers of the realm, the *kenmon* shared several characteristics that defined their elite status. First, they had their own private headquarters, where they handled administrative and economic matters. The Fujiwara and many religious institutions developed such organizations early in the Heian period; the retired emperor and the warrior elites followed in the eleventh and twelfth centuries with their own versions during their rise to national prominence.

Second, these headquarters issued orders from the head of the group, thereby controlling matters pertaining to land, as well as adjudicating in internal disputes. Such orders did not replace government edicts, but even though they used different formats and wording, they became indistinguishable from those issued by official organs.

Third, each *kenmon* had loyal retainers or followers under the jurisdiction of its head. These retainers included both armed and nonmilitary personnel, but while they were privately employed, they were also used to perform tasks in the name of the imperial court. For example, military retainers were frequently asked to pursue and arrest criminals and rebels, especially in cases that threatened the peace of entire provinces.

Fourth, the head of each elite had complete rights to self-rule, including judicial rights, over his own family and lineage. Promotions within the Fujiwara family or within a temple were thus an internal issue, even if the imperial court and the emperor held a nominal right to confirm or (as rarely occurred) deny it. For example, the Fujiwara chieftain normally appointed the head abbot at Kōfukuji, based on the recommendation and approval of the clergy.

Fifth, the *kenmon* had exclusive control and jurisdiction (another aspect of self-rule) over their assets, which came to include a large number of *shōen*. This privilege was equivalent to extraterritoriality, since the authority of government officials did not extend into private estates or temple compounds, which could thus serve as refuges for criminals, though, as mentioned earlier, the proprietors were expected to extradite them. It should also be remembered that the *shōen* embraced a vertical division of rights (*shiki*) that was an integral part of the *kenmon* system (see chapter 16). In fact, the *kenmon* constituted the political elite of a socioeconomic system based on *shiki* and *shōen*, making the two terms inseparable. Moreover, the term *shiki* itself first appears in *shōen* documents of the mid-Heian period.

The elites formed three larger power blocs that performed administrative, military, and religious duties, respectively, in a codependent arrangement of shared rulership. The court nobility (*kōke* or *kuge*), consisting of the imperial family and the capital aristocracy, held the administrative and ceremonial responsibilities of the state. Supported by their private assets, these nobles maintained their privileged hold on government offices and remained the state's formal leaders.

The emperorship remained above the system as the untouchable symbol of the state, ensuring its survival through ages of both peace and turmoil. Accordingly, the emperor made all central appointments, including the shogun (from the Kamakura period onward) and monks to lead important Buddhist ceremonies at the imperial court, even though such rights were at times in name only and the imperial power per se may have been limited. In other words, all three power blocs needed this figurehead in whose name they ruled and maintained financial and judicial privileges.

The main responsibility of the warrior aristocracy (*buke*) was keeping the peace and physically protecting the state. From the late eleventh century, these duties were entrusted increasingly to prominent warrior leaders from the Minamoto, Taira, and other central warrior houses (see chapter 17). This division of responsibilities was formalized with the establishment in the east of the Kamakura Shogunate by Minamoto Yoritomo (1147–1199) in the 1180s. Although the shogunate could overpower the court and its supporters in the capital area (which actually happened in the Jōkyū War of 1221), it could not eliminate or supersede the court and rule on its own, since it lacked the administrative and bureaucratic apparatus to extend its rule over all classes in thirteenth-century Japan. Its main responsibility was confined, rather, to maintaining peace and controlling the warrior class. The court and the shogunate consequently complemented one another in an overlapping rulership that has aptly been termed a dual polity.

The third member of the ruling triumvirate supplied the state and its members with spiritual protection through a panoply of religious services and rituals. These ceremonies were also important as status markers since they supported a vertical differentiation between rulers and ruled through participation in and sponsorship of magical and expensive rituals. In contrast to the other two blocs, however, the religious establishment had no clear apex, but consisted instead of a handful of elite temples supported and patronized by various factions in the capital.

Thus, for example, Kōfukuji and its affiliates worked closely with the regent as the family temple of the Fujiwara. Tōdaiji, still the main imperial temple, was supported by individual members of that family. Enryakuji, perhaps the most powerful of all monastic complexes during the late Heian and Kamakura ages, received funding from and performed ceremonies for members of both the Fujiwara and imperial factions, which allowed it a measure of independence that made it all the more powerful. Other *kenmon* temples included Kōyasan and Onjōji.

The establishment of the Ashikaga Shogunate in the 1330s spelled the beginning of the end of this system of cooperative rulership. The new regime gradually asserted itself as the sole ruler of the realm, and under the third shogun, Ashikaga Yoshimitsu, the shogunate's authority trumped all the old rights and jurisdiction formerly held by the religious and noble elites. The shogunate began to tax activities, such as those of merchant guilds, that had previously been exempt thanks to the privileges and protection of the *kenmon*. In addition, it denied or ignored the pressure applied by the elite temples on the capital through their time-proven religious protests. To show who was master of the religious sphere in late-fourteenth-century Kyoto, Yoshimitsu even appointed temple magistrates to maintain order within and keep an eye on the monastic complexes.

This did not mean that the nobles and religious elites disappeared from the political scene. On the contrary, they continued to wield power and even regained some of their former strength as the Ashikaga Shogunate's power declined from the middle of the fifteenth century. But cooperative rulership with shared responsibilities and privileges was no more.

MULTIPLE ELITES AND SHARED RULERSHIP

The system of governance that was in place in Japan from the late eleventh to the mid-fourteenth century can best be understood as an inclusive system in which elites from three sectors of society—noble, military, and religious—coruled under a common understanding of judicial and financial privileges in return for services rendered in their respective areas of expertise. Broad at the top yet centralized over several elites, the *kenmon* system was thus highly integrated vertically, but poorly connected horizontally.

When the early Ashikaga shoguns challenged this system, the vertical ties broke down in favor of new solidarities based on similar occupational or social foundations. Many of the *kenmon* remained influential, but they were not afforded the same privileges or rights to participate in governing. Enryakuji, for example, regained much of its strength following Yoshimitsu's death, but instead of taking an active role in court politics, it became increasingly independent, focusing mainly on strengthening its own fiscal and military foundations.

Not all temples fared so well, however; Kōfukuji was effectively eliminated as a force, while others, such as Kōyasan and Negoroji in Kii province, used the vacuum created by the gradual weakening of the Ashikaga Shogunate in the fifteenth century to aggrandize themselves in the local arenas. At times, these elites were still called *kenmon,* and contemporary documents and diaries occasionally refer to their old privileges, but the notion of cooperative rulership effectively died in the late fourteenth century.

Sources and Suggestions for Further Reading

See bibliography for complete publication data.

Adolphson, Mikael. *The Gates of Power: Monks, Courtiers, and Warriors in Premodern Japan* (2000).

Adolphson, Mikael, Edward Kamens, and Stacie Matsumoto, eds. *Heian Japan: Centers and Peripheries* (2007).

Borgen, Robert. *Sugawara no Michizane and the Early Heian Court* (1994).

Hurst, G. Cameron, III. *Insei: Abdicated Sovereigns in the Politics of Late Heian Japan, 1086–1185* (1973).

McCullough, William. "The Heian Court, 794–1070" (1999).

———. "Japanese Marriage Institutions in the Heian Period" (1967).

Nickerson, Peter. "The Meaning of Matrilocality: Kinship, Property, and Politics in Mid-Heian" (1993).

Toby, Ronald. "Why Leave Nara? Kammu and the Transfer of the Capital" (1985).

Notes

1. The best-known regent until that point was undoubtedly Prince Shōtoku. See chapter 10.

2. The notion of privatization in the Heian period is largely a scholarly interpretation of the developments during that age, but it should be noted that the term is used in various Heian sources to describe people who privately take Buddhist vows or take control of land.

3. Geertz, *Negara.*

4. Abdicated emperors received the title "great abdicated emperor" (*dajō tennō*), but they were more often called by the shorter—and more revealing—title "elevated monarch" (*jōkō*). Many took Buddhist vows in retirement, after which they were styled as "great priestly sovereign" (*dajō hōō,* often abbreviated to *hōō*). But in courtier diaries of the time and in later history texts, former emperors were most commonly referred to as *in* ("cloister," after the institutions to which they retired).

13

Aristocratic Buddhism

Mikael S. Adolphson

According to the *Nihon shoki*, Buddhism was introduced in Japan in the year 552, when the king of the Korean kingdom of Paekche sent Buddhist scriptures (sutras) to the Japanese ruler. The penchant in such texts for assigning distinct beginnings and giving kings sole credit for such accomplishments alone makes it difficult to believe such claims, but there is no doubt that Buddhism did indeed come to Japan around that time, though it was more likely brought over by educated Korean immigrants. That this foreign religion was attractive to many Japanese aristocrats is hardly surprising, since it came with comprehensive rhetoric about an afterlife, and other aspects of the spiritual world, of greater sophistication than previously available in the local cults (Shintō). But it also included a writing system, advanced architecture and art forms, and tools for a centralized state, all associated with the most advanced culture in the known world—China.

Yet there was some resistance as well, and in 587 a war broke out between the pro-Buddhist Soga, of Korean descent, and pro-Shintō families such as the Mononobe. Although the conflict has come down to later generations as a war between the two faiths, it was in reality a conflict between aristocrats who wished to create a centralized state, much with the help of Buddhism, and local clans that wished to maintain greater independence, a stance that could be supported by beliefs in local *kami* (Shintō deities). The Soga won, and Buddhist complexes were constructed in central Japan, often adjacent to local shrines, which indicates a lack of doctrinal opposition between Buddhism and local deities.

The most famous of these early temples was Hōryūji, just southwest of Nara, the home of Japan's first national hero, Prince Shōtoku (574–622), who promoted Buddhism and sent several missions to China, and also favored

Confucian ideals among aristocrats serving as loyal ministers. By the mid-eighth century, Buddhism had become the main religion of the imperial state, as evidenced by the completion in 749 of Tōdaiji, the centerpiece of the state temple network, just outside the Nara capital. Although smaller than the original, Tōdaiji is still considered one of the largest wooden buildings in the world, and houses a fifty-two-foot statue of the Sun Buddha—a clear reference to the temple's protective powers over the state and the imperial family.

From the outset, Buddhism was thus both highly political and elitist, and while there were certainly some genuine aristocratic believers, it was also widely used by these elites as a tool for state building. As a result, little if any of Buddhist ideology reached common people in early Japan, despite the evangelizing efforts of mendicants such as Gyōki (668–749) in the mid-eighth century. In part, this elitist approach was conditioned by a form of Buddhism that was in reality closer to the Hinayana (Lesser Vehicle) branch, according to which nirvana could be attained only by improving one's karma after numerous rebirths, than to the Mahayana (Greater Vehicle) teachings, which taught that all living beings had Buddha potential. Commoners were thus hopelessly removed from any chances of achieving enlightenment after this life, whereas monks and nobles who patronized Buddhist temples and rituals appeared to have a distinct advantage. More important, many of the rituals of early Buddhism focused on the state and its main patrons, which naturally helps explain the elites' attraction to this foreign ideology.

There were, however, actors in this equation beyond the noble elites. The monks themselves were agents of elitism, as many found it advantageous to cater to the ruling class. This predilection also meant that they could be caught in the factional struggles of the court, as seems to have been the case with the infamous Dōkyō (700–772). Dōkyō became a confidant of Empress Kōken (reigned 749–758) and was even instrumental in her rise to power when she reascended the throne as Empress Shōtoku (reigned 764–770), much to the dismay of her main group of opponents, the Fujiwara. In the end, the Fujiwara came out victorious in this short-lived struggle, as they managed to exile Dōkyō shortly after the empress died in 770.

Dōkyō has frequently been seen as a usurper who attempted to unseat the imperial family and ascend the throne himself, but given that the historical records were sponsored by the Fujiwara, they may not be wholly reliable. The more important point, however, is that Buddhist monks and institutions were becoming more powerful in the Nara state, a development that, whether real or perceived, bothered some courtiers and rulers. Above all, Emperor Kanmu (reigned 781–806) took measures to limit the tax exemptions of temples and enforce more strictly the rules of ordination. Moreover, he decided to move the imperial palace to Nagaoka in 784, only to relocate it farther north to Heian-kyō (Kyoto) ten years later, distancing the court from the Nara temples.[1]

This is not to say that Kanmu or the imperial court in general was anti-Buddhist. On the contrary, few members of the court at this point could have envisioned a state without the spiritual protection and endorsement of the Buddhas. But the court was ripe for new ideas and schools that could broaden the scope of Buddhism itself. Such alternatives were indeed introduced not long after the move to the Heian plain by monks who explored teachings that opened up Buddhism to a larger contingent of believers. Two monks were crucial to this new development: Saichō (767–823) and Kūkai (774–835).

THE TENDAI AND SHINGON SCHOOLS

Saichō was born in the province of Ōmi, but traveled to Nara to become a monk at a young age. There, he became interested in Tendai Buddhism, a Mahayana school that preached that all human beings had the potential for enlightenment and that held a syncretic view of Buddhist practices. After becoming a monk at Tōdaiji in 785, Saichō returned to his home province, building a small temple on Mt. Hiei on the western shore of Lake Biwa. This location was fortuitous beyond what anyone could possibly have imagined, as the mountain overlooked the Heian plain, where Emperor Kanmu moved the capital a few years later, in 794. As if that was not enough, Mt. Hiei was also located to the northeast of the new capital, thus protecting the latter from the evil spirits believed to come from that direction. Because of this coincidence and his focus on teachings seen as an alternative to the established Nara sects, Saichō caught the attention of the court, earning him an appointment as imperial court monk in 797.

Subsequently, Saichō concentrated on collecting texts and lecturing, and after a successful performance in a debate on the Tendai teachings in 802, he began to separate himself from the Nara sects more openly. Saichō maintained that the Buddha's own words, most explicitly expressed in the *Lotus Sutra,* needed more attention than the commentaries that many Nara sects relied on, and so he petitioned the emperor to have original texts obtained directly from Buddhist masters in China. In the twelfth month of 802, Emperor Kanmu granted Saichō permission and the funds to go to China.

It was another two years before the pilgrimage took place, but Saichō finally arrived in southern China after an arduous journey, travelling straight to the Chinese center of Tendai teachings, Mt. Tiantai. He stayed for a little more than six months before heading back to the coast. While waiting for a ship to arrive, Saichō decided to study esoteric rites, which had become increasingly popular in Tang China as they were believed to earn benefactors more immediate benefits. Once back in the capital, Saichō set out to promote the Tendai teachings more vigorously, but he soon discovered that the esoteric rites and their magical powers were more in demand at the new court in Kyoto. Unfortunately for Saichō, he had received only limited training on such matters, and even though the Tendai teachings were eclectic, he felt rather inadequate in his knowledge. And so when the monk Kūkai returned from China with more substantial knowledge of these rituals, he, rather than Saichō, eventually became the rage in the capital.

Born on the island of Shikoku to a provincial noble family with central connections, Kūkai was sent to live with a relative in the then-capital of Nagaoka at the age of fourteen to study Confucianism. He was not, however, particularly enamored with the reigning ideology of rule, which was in any case not then as prominent or as promising for his career as the alternative that caught his attention: Buddhism. Kūkai first appears to have taken private Buddhist vows; when the capital was moved to the Heian plain, he set out to spread the word of Buddha by himself. At some point, he must have caught the attention of the court of Kyoto, for he was added to the mission to China in 804 for which Saichō had already been selected. It is unknown exactly why he was chosen, but like Saichō, Kūkai preached Mahayana Buddhism, and he may thus have provided an attractive alternative to the Nara sects for Emperor Kanmu and his supporters.

The circumstances behind the selection of Saichō and Kūkai may thus have been similar, but their agendas in China illustrate fundamental differences in their approaches. Kūkai, who landed first in the southern Chinese province of Fukien, was more politically astute and went straight to the Tang capital of Changan, where he arrived in the twelfth month of 804. After a three-month stay at a residence supplied by the Tang court, Kūkai moved to the famous temple of Ximingsi, where he eventually met the great master Huiguo (746–805), who became his teacher. Huiguo was the transmitter of popular esoteric teachings based on the *Mahāvairochana Sutra* (J. Dainichi-kyō) that had been introduced in China almost a century earlier. Following his teacher's death in 805, Kūkai left China with a large number of Buddhist texts, mandalas (cosmic paintings used in esoteric Buddhist meditation), and books of poetry. Arriving on the coast of Kyushu, Kūkai sent a memorandum to the court in Kyoto accounting for his achievements while asking for support to start a new esoteric school. He waited almost three years for a response, but the imperial court eventually allowed him to take up residence at Takaosanji, just northwest of Kyoto, though the reigning emperor (Heizei) showed little interest in the monk's teachings.

The accession of Emperor Saga in 810 changed Kūkai's fortunes dramatically. Saga appreciated artworks, which were an integral part of Kūkai's teachings, as well as the poetry skills of the erudite monk. With the new emperor's support, Kūkai was allowed to gather a group of students and disciples to study esoteric Buddhism at Takaosanji, and he was appointed head abbot of Tōdaiji, a position that eventually enabled him to incorporate esoteric rites in Nara by establishing a subcloister called the Shingon'in (822) within the imperial temple.

Kūkai's knowledge of esoteric rites and his artistic skills won him a favorable reputation and a network of supporters among the court elites. Saichō, on the other hand, continued to have incomplete knowledge of esoteric rituals; when his relationship with Kūkai broke down after the Tōdaiji abbot refused to lend him important scriptures, the future looked bleak for the Tendai temple on Mt. Hiei. In fact, Saichō had serious difficulties retaining his own monks, and he encountered resistance from the Nara schools in his attempt to persuade them to acknowledge Tendai as a separate school. Saichō died on the 4th day of the sixth month of 822 without having achieved full recognition for Tendai's independence, but only seven days later his requests were granted posthumously.

Tendai's independence was thus recognized, and the temple on Mt. Hiei was officially named Enryakuji in 823. This concession was an important step toward independence from the Office of Monastic Affairs, which was dominated by Kōfukuji monks, and other temples soon followed suit. It was thus now possible for temples in general to manage their own affairs and to establish more direct ties with their patrons, marking the beginning of independent monasteries and eventually leading to the development of religious institutions as powerful elites (see chapter 12).

Although Kūkai encountered less resistance from other temples than Saichō, he wished to separate his school from the influence of the monastic office, and he eventually received permission to build a temple on Mt. Kōya (Kōyasan), located several days' walk from Kyoto south on the Kii peninsula. Given Kūkai's success in the capital, one might wonder why he chose such a remote location. He may have been concerned with keeping his own doctrines separate from other schools and ideas in the capital, where monks often became multisectarian. Kūkai named the temple Kongōbuji (Diamond Peak Temple), thereby using the surrounding peaks to evoke a worldly map of the Buddhist cosmos with his monastery at its center.

In 823, the same year that Saichō died and Tendai was recognized, Kūkai's own school, Shingon (True Word), received official recognition as well. Kūkai seems to have outdone his rival again, for he also received an imperial decree stating that only Shingon monks could reside at Tōji (one of the two temples marking the southern entrance to Kyoto), where he had been abbot. This was undoubtedly an important moment for Kūkai. It not only marked the official recognition of the Shingon School but also gave it the unusual distinction of exclusivity from other schools, contrary to the general practice then current of studying several different doctrines within one and the same monastery. To those who became his disciples, Kūkai offered a unique three-pronged approach: the secret transmission of specific mantras (prayers), meditative hand postures (mudras), and cosmic diagrams (mandalas).

By the time of his death on Mt. Kōya in 835, Kūkai had managed to gain further privileges for his school. First, he established a Buddhist hall within the imperial palace where annual Shingon rituals would be performed for one week in the first month of every year. This series of rituals, known as the Mishiho, became one of the prestigious services performed annually for the welfare of the imperial court and the state in the Heian era. Second, Kūkai was granted the ordination of three new state-supported Shingon monks every year. As in the case of Saichō and the ordination of Tendai monks, this meant important recognition of Shingon as one of the state-sponsored Buddhist schools.

Shingon Buddhism was now, just like Tendai and Hossō, a recognized part of the Buddhist establishment, marking the early form of a multidoctrinal system that incorporated competing schools within the framework of the imperial state. What the addition of two new schools did not accomplish, despite the founders' intentions, was a general proliferation of Buddhist beliefs among the general population. Rather, Buddhism remained an aristocratic affair, albeit with an expanded presence in the economic and political arenas of society.

ARISTOCRATIC BUDDHISM

Saichō and Kūkai were undoubtedly central figures in their own age, but their importance increased posthumously as their schools became more and more successful. Yet despite the founders' accomplishments, Tendai and Shingon were at some point in the early Heian age in real danger of decline with diminishing funding, while Hossō monks and Kōfukuji, the Fujiwara temple in Nara, continued to dominate and control many of the most important rituals well into the twelfth century. Moreover, because of the new schools' independence, Tendai and Shingon both had to rely on direct ties with and patronage from the capital elites, which in turn meant that they needed to ensure demand for their religious services from the nobles. It was here that the esoteric rituals—believed to carry benefits both in this and the next life—became the crucial bond between court society and the Tendai and Shingon institutions.

Two Enryakuji monks, Ennin (793/794–864) and Enchin (814–891), were particularly successful in this regard. Both embarked on protracted travels to China, in 838–847 and 853–858, respectively, to learn about the latest currents from the Chinese esoteric schools. By the tenth century, Tendai monks had not only caught up with those from Shingon in terms of popularity, but had perhaps even eclipsed them as the main competitors to the Hossō School, which still benefited from the patronage of the Fujiwara.

Accordingly, by the mid-Heian period, Buddhism was integral to the Japanese state, to the imperial court in general, and to its individual members. The relationship between the various Buddhist schools and the secular leaders was complex, but a certain grasp of it is essential in understanding both Heian rulership and society. First, as noted by Neil McMullin, the patrons and sponsors of Buddhism were more pragmatic than dogmatic. In fact, their main interest lay in the ceremonies and the benefits that these offered patrons, as evidenced by the innumerable esoteric and other Buddhist rituals performed for individual nobles and their families, for the imperial family, and for the Heian state. The underlying doctrines were less important in the selection of ceremonies than the rituals themselves and the monks performing them.

The second consideration in choosing rituals and monks was that of the institution. Because direct links were established between the secular elites and specific temples or cloisters, the choice of master of ceremonies naturally fell on an ally within the monastic complexes that were close to the patron. Doctrine, according to McMullin, ranked as the third consideration for the secular leaders—a notion supported by evidence of a tendency to include in the training of novices a variety of schools of thought.[2] Perhaps the best evidence of these priorities and of the development of close ties between the noble elites and the monastic leaders is provided by the monk credited with making Enryakuji into the most powerful complex in premodern Japan: Ryōgen (912–985).

After having received training on Mt. Hiei in various doctrines of the Tendai tradition, Ryōgen was appointed to serve at Kōfukuji's central ceremony, the Yuima'e, in 937. That the court thus appointed an Enryakuji monk to this Fujiwara-controlled ceremony indicates its preference for ceremony, institution, and doctrine in that order, and even the protest raised by Kōfukuji monks was based on institutional rather than doctrinal grounds. Ryōgen also distinguished himself at a debate held between Hossō and Tendai monks in 963, which gained him enough attention to become head abbot of Tendai shortly thereafter. Prior to Ryōgen's tenure, the monastic complex on Mt. Hiei had experienced a decline as some buildings had been destroyed by fire and others suffered from lack of maintenance. Now Enryakuji was revived and soon expanded, so that by the late tenth century, the Mt. Hiei monastery is said to have reached a population of 3,000 monks, acolytes, and clerical staff.

The key to Ryōgen's success lay in his connection to the Fujiwara chieftain Morosuke (908–960), who saw in the monk a vehicle for promoting his own line against other members of the Fujiwara. Ryōgen not only received financial support but was also entrusted with one of Morosuke's sons, who came to succeed Ryōgen as the Tendai head abbot in 985. Besides confirming the close ties between Ryōgen and Morosuke's line, the chieftain's act also marked the beginning of a new trend of sons of ranking nobles entering monasteries as privileged monks on a fast track to abbotships, which in the following century became attractive careers for young nobles as well as a means to controlling religious ceremonies and resources for noble factions.

HEIAN MONASTERIES AND HIERARCHIES

In theory, the monastic world was open to anyone, and with the proper training and seniority, a monk of humble origins could also become abbot. With the influx of nobles, however, a dual hierarchy was established in which key posts were monopolized by sons of ranking nobles, who frequently lived in separate cloisters, called *monzeki*, at some distance from the monastery. The religious order thus became an integral part of court factionalism, resulting in an aristocratization of the temple hierarchies. Noble monks competed with the help of their court relatives against monastics associated with other noble factions. Religious training became a less relevant qualification for monastic appointments, and while noble monks were certainly highly educated, their knowledge of Buddhist tenets was not as advanced as one might expect from religious leaders.

The monastic complexes of Heian Japan were accordingly worlds of men ordered by hereditary rank. Women were rarely, if ever, allowed to visit, much less take vows at these temples—in sharp contrast to the Nara period, when hundreds of nuns participated in ceremonies alongside monks. From the late eighth century, the number of ordained women declined (disappearing completely in 828), as did the number of provincial nunneries that had been established the previous century. At the same time, the most prestigious monastic complexes, such as Enryakuji, Kōyasan, and Tōdaiji, even prohibited women from their precincts. It is not clear exactly why these changes occurred, but it is worth noting that women lost most of the public functions at the imperial court at the same time, in favor of more informal, supporting roles behind their male counterparts.

As in court society, noble women were active members in the Buddhist world, though in less public roles than previously. Their devotion and religious practices became instead matters of personal choice based on their particular circumstances, irrespective of how the imperial court viewed their status. Thus women, especially of the nobility, could become "private nuns," without official vows or recognition, by simply cutting their hair—and in some cases receiving precepts from individual monks. These acts were most commonly precipitated by events—such as the death of a husband, personal misfortune, or severe illness—that affected the woman's social standing. The act of becoming a lay nun, then, was the act of removing oneself from the political, social, and sexual worlds of the Heian court.

Since there were no ordained nuns, men necessarily served as the spiritual teachers of women seeking to retreat from this society. The aforementioned Ryōgen, for example, helped his own mother by establishing a Buddhist hall close to the capital that she was allowed to visit, and by also moving off Mt. Hiei an important relic festival believed to accrue merit for attendees. Other high-ranking court ladies established their own cloisters for their retirement, marking a distinct boundary between the courtly world and their renunciation of it. Another well-known expression of male guidance is the *Sanbōe* (*Illustrations of the Three Jewels*), written in 984 by the courtier Minamoto Tamenori for the nineteen-year-old Princess Sonshi for her retirement from the court. Tamenori offered the princess advice on her path to enlightenment through good deeds by providing stories and examples from other texts along with images. The reasons for Sonshi's retirement are unclear, but it is worth noting that Tamenori would have accrued merit for himself as well by providing this service for a young court lady.

Not only was the monastic world aristocratized during the Heian period, but, as the above account suggests, this process was preceded by genderization as well, a trend paralleled within the imperial court. The removal of public roles for women in court and religious ceremonies was, in other words, another expression of the privatization that characterized the Heian age. Playing a less important public role did not necessarily mean a loss of power for women, as influence in politics became increasingly based on private assets; but women undeniably became less prominent in the Buddhist world. Whatever engagement they had with that world resulted from their status as nobles, since temples, monks, and Buddhist rituals were absolutely integral to the courtly state, where women did play a significant role throughout the Heian period.

In fact, the distance between secular and religious leaders narrowed so much that by the second half of the era, the persons in charge in the two spheres were more often than not relatives. For example, Jien (1155–1225), the author of the well-known chronicle *Gukanshō* ("A Miscellany of Ignorant Views," or "Foolish Comments"), was the head abbot of Tendai and also the brother of the Fujiwara chieftain Kanezane (1149–1207). The secular and Buddhist worlds were codependent, and indeed it was so conceived in the Heian state as well.

The main ideology driving this coexistence appears in various documents as *ōbō buppō sōi*, or "the mutual dependence of the Imperial and Buddhist Laws." One appeal from 1053 makes an explicit allusion to this codependence: "the Buddhist and the Imperial laws are like the two wings of a bird or the two wheels of a cart."[3] Such ideas were based on and supported by the Buddhist notion of historical cycles of religious consciousness, according to which 1052 was the final year of the final age of the Buddhist Law. While the world did not, in fact, decline into complete chaos that year, it was common rhetoric among monks and courtiers to refer to this notion of decline whenever they encountered changes in or threats to their own worlds.

THE BEGINNINGS OF POPULIST BUDDHISM

Because Buddhist rituals and institutions were controlled by and catered to the elites during the Heian and Kamakura eras, Buddhist ideas did not reach many members of the lower classes or outside the capital area. Nevertheless, some trickling down took place via *kami* worship, as most shrines served as affiliates of temples, and their deities served as protectors of their Buddhist counterparts. More important, regardless of the elitism of Buddhism in the Heian period, ideas that opened the path to enlightenment to a broader segment of society began to gain ground as well. Central to these beliefs was the idea Saichō and Kūkai had emphasized that anyone with the right training or guidance could achieve enlightenment after this life.

As an extension of these ideas, faith in the savior Amida began to spread among noble patrons from the mid-Heian age. According to this belief, simply proclaiming one's faith in Amida would ensure one's rebirth in the Western Paradise. Since no temptations existed in this paradise, no sins would be committed, and a continuation to nirvana would thus be guaranteed. Early evidence of such beliefs can be seen at the Phoenix Hall at the Byōdōin, a temple devoted to Amida with numerous wall paintings depicting scenes from the Western Paradise. Constructed in Uji just south of Kyoto by the Fujiwara chieftain in the mid-eleventh century, the temple is today a UNESCO World Heritage Site and the most visited tourist attraction in the area.

While the Amida faith was originally supported by nobles who may have been attracted by its shortcut to enlightenment, some monks also began to proselytize among the general population. Kūya (903–972), a monk trained at Enryakuji, preached in the streets of the capital that anyone chanting the name of Amida (*Namu Amida Butsu*) would be saved. The immediate impact of Kūya's preaching was limited, but he did receive enough support to found a temple in Kyoto, though it was not devoted exclusively to Amida worship. Another important promoter of Amida beliefs was Genshin (942–1017), whose treatise *Essentials of Salvation*, was said to have reached and become popular in China. While little evidence supports this claim, Genshin's graphic depictions of paradise and hell left an impression for generations to come. By the twelfth century, two monks, Hōnen (1133–1212) and Shinran (1173–1263), took the next logical step in proclaiming praise of Amida as the superior method for reaching enlightenment, which together with other monks' efforts to promote the exclusivity of Zen (Dōgen and Eisai) or the *Lotus Sutra* (Nichiren), set the foundation for new directions in Buddhism that were to bloom in the medieval age.

Sources and Suggestions for Further Reading

See the bibliography for complete publication data.

Abé, Ryūichi. *Weaving the Mantra: Kukai and the Construction of Buddhist Esoteric Discourse* (2000).

Adolphson, Mikael. *The Gates of Power: Monks, Courtiers, and Warriors in Premodern Japan* (2000).

Bowring, Richard. *The Religious Traditions of Japan, 500–1600* (2008).

Fukutō Sanae, with Takeshi Watanabe. "From Female Sovereign to Mother of the Nation: Women and Government in the Heian Period" (2007).

Groner, Paul. *Saicho: The Establishment of the Japanese Tendai School* (2000).

———. *Ryogen and Mt. Hiei: Japanese Tendai in the Tenth Century* (2002).

Kamens, Edward. *Three Jewels: A Study and Translation of Minamoto Tamenori's* Sanboe (1988).

McMullin, Neil. "Historical and Historiographical Issues in the Study of Pre-modern Japanese Religions" (1989).

Ruppert, Brian. *Jewel in the Ashes: Buddha Relics and Power in Early Medieval Japan* (2000).

Stone, Jacqueline. *Original Enlightenment and the Transformation of Medieval Japanese Buddhism* (2003).

Notes

1. The reasons for these moves have been debated, but two carry the most weight: Kanmu's desire to move closer to his own power base in Ōtsu, close to Lake Biwa; and a need to establish more distance, geographical and political, between the palace and the by now very powerful Buddhist centers in Nara.

2. McMullin, "Historical and Historiographical Issues in the Study of Premodern Japanese Religions," 10–12.

3. Adolphson, *The Gates of Power*, 272.

14

The Canons of Courtly Taste

Robert Borgen and Joseph T. Sorensen

During Japan's classical age, a small civilian aristocracy produced a body of literature that would inspire later generations. Moreover, many of these aristocrats actively participated in the visual and performing arts and patronized the calligraphers, painters, sculptors, and many others with specialized skills needed to construct and decorate the buildings that served as the stage upon which the nobility conducted their lives, private and public, secular and religious. These works of art are also seminal elements in Japan's artistic heritage. In modern times, the most notable literary classics have been translated into many languages, and some are now counted among the masterpieces of world literature. The visual art also has found an international audience, and examples can be viewed in major Western museums. These works, both the literary and the visual, can be characterized as courtly because they were associated with an elite society, centered on Japan's imperial court, that prized elegance. Looking at the products of this courtly taste, one is apt to be struck at first glance by their apparent uniformity and the continuities that persisted over many centuries, in some cases down to the present day. Closer examination, however, reveals both diversity and change over time.

This essay covers the roughly five hundred years that constitute the Nara and Heian periods, with some attention to the following Kamakura period. During these centuries, Japan's culture went through many changes. The literature of the Nara period incorporated elements from earlier times that, by the refined standards of the Heian court, seemed primitive. By the Kamakura, elements of medieval Japan's warrior culture were blended into the aristocratic arts.

The Nara period began with a burst of enthusiasm for the cultures of continental Asia. Chinese culture may have dominated, but Buddhism, an Indian religion, and Central Asian elements such as music and dance had already been absorbed by the cosmopolitan Chinese of the Tang dynasty (618–907). Koreans, who helped convey this culture to Japan, added elements of their own to the blend. Borrowing high culture from the Asian continent predates the Nara period by at least a century, as Hōryūji, the great Buddhist temple about ten kilometers from Nara, reveals. The temple, first constructed in 607 on Chinese models, burnt in 670 and was soon rebuilt. Objects from the original compound survive, and the reconstructions are among the oldest wooden buildings in the world. Today, the most familiar monument in Nara, the Great Buddha of Tōdaiji temple, may be a later reconstruction; but nearby stands the Shōsōin, a storehouse built in 756 to preserve the personal treasures of Emperor Shōmu, who had sponsored the temple's construction. The objects in the Shōsōin come from many lands, including even Roman-style glass from the eastern Mediterranean, but most are distinctly Chinese and vividly convey a sense of the elegant, cosmopolitan tastes of the Nara aristocracy.

At first, written literature, too, was Chinese in appearance. Japan's earliest works that might be classified as literature were two histories, *Kojiki* (*A Record of Ancient Matters*) and *Nihon shoki* (or *Nihongi*; *Chronicles of Japan*), compiled in 712 and 720, respectively, both written exclusively in Chinese characters. Like most of the world's peoples, the Japanese adopted the writing system of a nearby culture. Since Chinese script does not easily lend itself to writing other languages, the Japanese often wrote in Chinese. This choice also reflects the great prestige attached to the Chinese language as a mark of civilization in East Asia. Although these two early works may have used Chinese script, certainly parts of both, and perhaps all of the first, were meant to be read in Japanese. Both begin with stories of Japan's creation by its native deities and the establishment of its imperial line by one of their descendants. Although these may appear to be ancient myths and were even taught as history in pre–World War II Japan, modern scholars assume they were specifically designed to legitimate the imperial family, which had sponsored their writing, and to establish the status of other aristocratic families, whose ancestors appear as lesser deities. *Nihon shoki* goes on to recount Japan's history down to 697 and appears to offer a reasonably accurate version of events from later centuries. In form, it is modeled closely on the "basic annals" sections of China's dynastic histories, which offer chronological accounts of events.

The system the Japanese used when writing their own language in Chinese characters was clumsy, but it allowed the Japanese to compile their first unambiguously literary work, *Man'yōshū* (*Myriad Leaves* [or possibly *Generations*] *Anthology*), a collection of approximately 4,500 poems compiled around 760. Although most of the poems (roughly 4,200) were in the *waka* form, consisting of only thirty-one syllables in five "lines" (or, more accurately, "phrases"), some of *Man'yōshū*'s most admired poems are *chōka*, which could have as many as 149 "lines." After *Man'yōshū*, long poems became rare in Japanese literature until modern times. The content of *Man'yōshū*'s poetry, too, seems remarkably diverse, at least compared to that in the canonical anthologies of later times. Some *Man'yōshū* poems appear to be ancient songs in simple language that someone chose to write down. Others were written by commoners; for example:

To frontier guard duty,
at the dawn I set off,
but as I left the gate,
she would not let go my hand:
my beloved in tears.

In some respects, this poem anticipates later courtly literary taste, for love—particularly unhappy, tearful love—would remain a central concern of classical literature. On the other hand, in later times, the more courtly literary genres avoided even mild suggestions of physical love, such as holding hands, and major anthologies did not preserve poetry by such commoners as mere guardsmen. Even poems by members of the elite showed distinctive features. One poem ponders the fate of a corpse spotted on a lonely seashore. Although life's uncertainties would remain a persistent theme in Japanese literature, corpses were avoided as the subject of poetry.

At one time, nationalists admired *Man'yōshū* for preserving a pure Japanese spirit unsullied by foreign influences, but in fact Confucian, Daoist, and Buddhist ideas are conspicuous in some of the poetry. If *Man'yōshū* may not be as "pure" as Japanese enthusiasts once believed, it does reveal distinctive Japanese tastes. For example, love was, at best, a secondary theme in Chinese literature. Furthermore, *Man'yōshū* included notable compositions by women, and women would remain important participants in literary life at court. They were far less conspicuous in the literature of traditional China. Another pattern begun by *Man'yōshū* was that anthologies would come to define key periods and styles in the history of court poetry. *Man'yōshū* is a remarkable collection of poetry. It includes some of the most cherished Japanese poems; here is but one:

The world of ours,
to what might it be compared?
Like the dawn departing
of a boat, rowed away,
without a trace.

This poem by the monk Mansei uses natural imagery to convey the idea that our world is one of impermanence, a key teaching of Buddhism that would

Figure 14.1. Byōdōin, a Buddhist monastery not far from Kyoto, built in 1052 as a retreat for a high-ranking courtier. Consisting of buildings connected by corridors and facing a garden with a pond, its layout hints at that of Heian aristocratic mansions such as those depicted in a version of *The Tale of Genji*. (Photograph by Robert Borgen.)

become central to classical Japanese literature. In some ways *Man'yōshū* may be idiosyncratic, but in others it set significant patterns for later court taste.

If the Nara period tends to be seen, not quite accurately, as an age that valued foreign culture, the conventional view is that, in the Heian period, aristocrats assimilated continental elements to produce a distinctively Japanese culture. Again, the situation is more complicated. The start of the Heian period was followed by a few decades in which esteem for things Chinese, notably its literature, reached a peak. Between 814 and 827, Japan's emperors sponsored the compilation of the three anthologies of literature, written in classical Chinese, by Japanese authors. Although these anthologies are no longer widely read, they set an important precedent for imperial sponsorship of literary activity. Particularly after imperial sponsorship turned to poetry in Japanese at the start of the tenth century, enthusiasm for literature in Chinese waned, but Japanese court men (not women) continued to compose official documents and other works in Chinese, and educated women, too, were familiar with at least some of the Chinese classics.

Literary composition in Chinese declined, in part because the Japanese developed a convenient phonetic script for writing their own language based on simplified forms of Chinese characters. Very little writing in Japanese survives from the years between the compilation of *Man'yōshū* and the middle decades of the ninth century when a generation of noteworthy poets established a style that would come to be associated with *Kokinshū* (*Anthology of Poems, Ancient and Modern*), the first imperially sponsored collection of poetry in Japanese, compiled around 905. By this time, the short *waka* form was predominant, and poems tended to focus on certain elegant themes, notably the beauties of nature and the unhappiness of love. Poems often seem to present an aesthetically logical argument, as in the following example:

In this world of ours,
if cherry blossoms absolutely
did not exist,
our feelings in the springtime
would be tranquil.

Japanese admired their cherry blossoms, at least in part because they bloom spectacularly but for only a short time and then scatter—another sad metaphor, like the disappearing boat in Mansei's poem, for the uncertainties of our world. Here, the poet is arguing that if only we did not have the blossoms, we would not be reminded of our unhappy fate. This poem is by Ariwara Narihira (825–880), one of the pioneers of this new style of poetry and also the hero of *Tales of Ise* (*Ise monogatari*) a collection of anecdotes, largely centered on his poems—and his love affairs—that was compiled later in the Heian period. *Tales of Ise* was long admired particularly as a guide to poetic practice, and it is still counted among the masterpieces of Heian literature.

Kokinshū offers insights into Heian courtly taste. Unlike the haiku of a much later time, *waka* in the *Kokinshū* manner have not found a wide audience outside Japan. This may in part be due to their verbal complexity. The best haiku display great subtlety but are apt to be linguistically uncomplicated and hence relatively easy to appreciate, even in translation. Composers of *waka*, particularly in the *Kokinshū* style, delighted in complex wordplay. For example, words with double meanings—puns for serious rather than comic effect—allowed poets to squeeze an extraordinary amount of meaning into a mere thirty-one syllables. Such effects are apt to be lost, not only in translation but even in the original to readers unfamiliar with the art.

This was poetry for an educated elite. Heian aristocrats may not all have been great poets, but most, both men and women, were capable of producing a competent poem when needed, since exchanges of poetry were a standard form of social interaction, notably courtship. Inept poets risked ridicule or, in the case of courtship, rejection. The best poets aspired to have their work included in one of the imperially sponsored anthologies, of which twenty-one were compiled, the last in 1439. They may be said to define an age in which courtly tastes, as displayed in elegant *waka* poetry, held a preeminent place in the culture of Japan's literate elite.

In the Heian period, this was a civilian aristocracy, but at least some warriors, too, acquired a taste for poetry and the values associated with it. A famous episode from *The Tale of the Heike* (*Heike monogatari*), the story of the wars that led to the establishment of the Kamakura Shogunate, tells of a warrior who, after first fleeing the capital, sneaks back to deliver a scroll of his best poems, hoping one will be included in the next imperial anthology once peace is restored. The compiler does select one for the anthology, although the name of the warrior, who has died in battle, cannot be used as he has been declared an enemy of the court. The story underscores the importance of poetic reputation, even to a warrior.

In Western literature, poetry and prose are typically distinct genres. In Japanese court literature, the two are difficult to keep apart. Perhaps to clarify ambiguities that result from their brevity, *waka* sometimes appeared in anthologies with short prose passages explaining their context. Today, *Tales of Ise* is classified as prose, but some of its episodes consist of little more than such introductory notes followed by poems. In fact, poems were a conspicuous element in most literary prose, which, like the poetry, was apt to focus on love. But, in contrast to the concision of the poems, works of prose could be quite long. The most important work of Heian fiction, *The Tale of Genji* (*Genji monogatari*), is about eleven hundred pages in English translation. Men and women wrote both prose and poetry, but major poets were apt to be men. The greatest prose authors, however, were all women. Poems tell us much about courtly ideas and aesthetics. To that, prose works add extraordinarily detailed accounts of aristocratic life, or at least certain aspects of it. We learn many details regarding courtship and marriage, for example, but little about household kitchens and budgets. Love was a literary topic; food and finance were not.

Classical prose can be divided into different genres, though the distinctions were blurred, as were those between prose and poetry. The boundary between fiction and nonfiction was not always clear, either, as the following examples, each from a key genre, will reveal. "Diaries" were an important part of classical Japanese literature, "diaries" being in quotation marks because the literary ones do not meet the modern definition of that word. The only one that, in form, is a daily record of events, *A Tosa Journal* (*Tosa nikki*), was obviously fictionalized for artistic effect. A more interesting diary is *Kagerō nikki* (in English translations, *The Gossamer Years* or *Kagerō Diary*), by an aristocratic woman from the Fujiwara family whose given name is unknown, as are the given names of all the major women writers of the day. She begins by explaining that the numerous old tales she has read are fantasy, so she wants to offer a more realistic picture of the life of a woman married to an important nobleman. Her husband would become the most powerful man at court. As was the custom, he had many "wives," a term that is problematic when applied to Heian marriage practices. A man would have one principal, formally recognized wife, and ties, some long-standing and openly acknowledged, with other women whose relationship with him seems to have been only loosely defined.

The diarist was one of these secondary wives. Around 971, as relations with her "husband" were deteriorating, she started a memoir, beginning with their courtship seventeen years earlier. Courtship, as recounted in the memoir, consisted largely of exchanging poems. Poetry is found throughout the text, which contains 119 *waka* and two long poems. Aside from the long poems, this pattern is typical of Heian "prose." As the author writes, she completes her memoir and her text becomes more diary-like, describing recent events. It can be read as an indictment of Heian marriage practices, in which secondary wives remained in their own residences and waited for their husbands to come visit. The author was devoted to her husband and was distraught when his visits became infrequent. By the end of her diary, the marriage has fallen apart. As she promises at the start of her text, she demonstrates that real life is not always the stuff of romantic fantasy, a conclusion unlikely to surprise modern readers. Perhaps more remarkable is the focus on her personal thoughts and feelings, not always pretty ones. She offers little in the way of plot or action. The resulting psychological realism, to use an anachronistic term, would become characteristic of much court prose.

A prime example of this is *The Tale of Genji,* surely the most admired work of classical Japanese literature, both in Japan and throughout the world. *Genji* was written at the start of the eleventh century by a woman we know as Murasaki Shikibu—her actual name, again, unknown. In the manner of the tales that had displeased the earlier diarist, it starts out by recounting the birth of its splendid hero, who comes to be known as Genji, the Shining Prince, to an emperor and one of his lesser concubines. Great things are foretold of him. Soon, however, Genji's life gets complicated, as Murasaki, in her fictional narrative, presents complexities beyond the predictably self-centered view of a diary. Again, the focus is often on romantic attachments, but now we are shown a variety of them, for Genji is a womanizer. The women in Genji's life are presented with recognizable, individual personalities, as are his male friends and a few of his enemies, too. Although the story may center on Genji's romantic liaisons, political intrigue often lurks in the background. The tale consists of fifty-four chapters. Chapter 42 begins by announcing that Genji has died, and afterwards two of his descendants, one actual, the other putative, become the central figures. Despite repeated assertions that Genji is all but flawless, time and again he reveals his very human failings. Most scandalously, he has an illicit affair with one of his father the emperor's concubines, a woman who is said to resemble his own mother. She not only becomes pregnant, but her son later becomes emperor. Buddhist teachings underlie much of *Genji*, which illustrates the fundamental Buddhist idea that life is suffering. As if to demonstrate the workings of karma—in this case, the concept that people will be punished for their misdeeds—a princess whom Genji was asked to take as his wife, though he has little interest in her, ends up being seduced by the son of his best friend. She has a son that Genji realizes cannot be his own. Although the emperor has treated as his own the son Genji in fact fathered, Genji realizes that the emperor too may well have known the truth. Genji may be flawed, but he matures and learns as he—and the author who created him—grows older.

As these examples suggest, Heian courtly taste in literature tended toward the lachrymose—with one notable exception. *The Pillow Book* (*Makura no sōshi*) by a woman we know as Sei Shōnagon, a contemporary of Murasaki, consists of more than three hundred short sections. Where other women wrote of difficult human relationships, Sei described the pleasures of life at court as a lady-in-waiting to an imperial consort. Some of her sections are amusing lists of things she liked or disliked. Others are brief descriptions of incidents in the daily life of a court lady: a nocturnal visit by a lover, a pet dog and cat, a contest to guess how long a pile of snow will last. Literary works such as these, mostly written by women—some fiction, some nonfiction, and others somewhere in between—leave modern readers with a remarkably vivid sense of Heian aristocratic life. Nonliterary sources, mostly written by men in Chinese, fill in further details, and actual objects extant from the period reveal the exact appearances of many things. Surviving artifacts include examples of calligraphy on beautifully colored paper, elegantly lacquered household items such as small boxes or low tables, elaborately decorated swords, Buddhist ritual objects, and scroll paintings.

The scrolls came in two forms. Some were hung on walls in the manner of Western paintings. Surviving examples are all religious. Others could be over thirty feet long and were meant to be slowly unrolled and viewed horizontally one scene at a time. Typically they tell a story, combining text and illustration. The earliest extant examples, several fragments of a Buddhist work, have the text on the bottom with pictures illustrating it above. These works, dating from the Nara period, appear to be copies of Chinese originals. In the Heian period, scroll paintings evolved into distinctly Japanese styles. References in literary works reveal that they were already popular in the tenth century, but the earliest extant examples are from the twelfth. Many continued the tradition of illustrating Buddhist stories, but now some told of Japanese holy men, portrayed in distinctly Japanese style.

Perhaps the most famous of these Late Heian scrolls is an illustrated version of *Genji*. Unfortunately, it survives only in fragments, but they are glorious fragments indeed. By this time, the Japanese had adopted the format of alternating sections of text with sections of illustrations. The text is written in a delicate hand that seems to flow down the pasted-together sheets of paper, each in slightly different brown tones and decorated with patterns of gold and silver foil. Although Heian courtiers prized a good calligraphic hand, modern readers not acquainted with the art may have trouble appreciating it. That is less true of the pictures. They offer detailed images of aristocratic mansions, with their roofs removed so the interiors are visible. Inside one sees, for example, a nobleman coming to visit a friend who is lying in bed, ill. The picture shows various types of screens that were used to partition interior space, some adorned with landscape paintings and framed with brocade. Discretely screened off from the men are a group of ladies. All the costumes are elaborate, particularly those of the ladies. In the next scene a man tenderly holds an infant, ladies attending by his side. The pictures are touching, even if one does not realize that the bedridden man is suffering from guilt because he has fathered a child by the wife of another man, Genji. It is Genji who is looking at that infant, knowing full well that he is not the true father. Although much of the pigment has fallen away from the pictures, enough remains to show that they once were brightly colored. Whereas Heian literature was often dark in tone, the story here being a case in point, court taste in the visual arts and crafts tended toward the vibrant and colorful.[1]

At one time, scholars writing in English noted the great emphasis Heian courtiers placed on aesthetic values and argued that success both in courtship and in court careers might depend on one's skills as a poet. In fact, a clever poem may have helped win a woman's hand, but it was unlikely to earn one a good position in the government. The best poets held only modest official posts; the most powerful politicians were not known for their literary skills. The once common view that Heian courtiers devoted most of their attention to love of the arts and of the opposite sex resulted from selective reading of the sources; that is, from looking only at works in Japanese that have been admired through the centuries, which do give the impression that romance and poetry were all-important. Other sources leave a different impression. Court histories, of only limited interest as literature, detail unseemly struggles for political power. In the imperially sponsored anthologies of poetry, love consists mostly of longing for a person whom one almost never actually sees. Other literary sources, in both Chinese and Japanese, depict a more robust form of love, as may be seen in the following:

Wine cups and
Fish that cormorants eat and
Women:
One never tires of them.
Let's sleep together, the two of us!

That is an *imayō* (literally "modern style"), the lyric to a type of song that had originated among women entertainers similar to modern geisha. Despite that somewhat disreputable provenance, these songs found an audience among aristocrats. Both Murasaki Shikibu and Sei Shōnagon mention them. Surviving examples come from *Ryōjin hishō*, freely translated as *Songs to Make the Dust Dance*, a work compiled in 1179 by the retired emperor Go-Shirakawa consisting of song lyrics and essays on the form. Despite their plebeian origins and unrefined language, these songs appealed to the same people who admired the more elevated poetry of *Kokinshū*. Go-Shirakawa demonstrates this. In addition to compiling *Ryōjin hishō*, he also sponsored an important anthology of *waka* even as he collected these popular songs. Despite this imperial patronage, *imayō* did not share the prestige of *waka*, and *Ryōjin hishō* disappeared from view in the fourteenth century. The few fragments rediscovered in 1911 provide an important counterbalance to the imperial anthologies of *waka* by presenting a glimpse into the lyrics of common people and the less refined side of court taste.

Today, Go-Shirakawa is remembered less for his artistic interests than his involvement in the civil wars that led to the establishment of Japan's first warrior government in 1185. The political power of the aristocratic court may have been diminished, but the prestige of its culture remained high. Emperors continued to sponsor anthologies of poetry. One of the most important imperial anthologies, *Shin Kokinshū* (*New Anthology of Poems, Ancient and Modern*), dates from the early decades of the thirteenth century. The title of the collection and the poems it contains show a blend of continuity and innovation, as well as a consciousness of a classical past upon which the poets deliberately drew. Styles evolved, but poets continued to compose *waka* that are still admired. Court ladies maintained the tradition of literary diaries describing their private lives. They also continued to enjoy narrative tales that described affairs at court and beyond. Artists produced picture scrolls illustrating episodes from court life and literature. In other words, the end of the Heian period was not the end of courtly tastes associated with the age. As in the political realm, the ancient culture survived for centuries in parallel with new cultural elements more closely associated with the new warrior society.

Sources and Suggestions for Further Reading

See the bibliography for complete publication data.

Bowring, Richard, trans. *The Diary of Murasaki Shikibu* (1993).
Carter, Steven D. *Traditional Japanese Poetry: An Anthology* (1991).
Hempel, Rose. *The Golden Age of Japan, 794–1192* (1983).
Keene, Donald. *Seeds in the Heart* (1993).
Nippon Gakujutsu Shinkokai, trans. *Manyoshū* (1940; reprinted 1965 and 2005).
Kim, Young-Hee. *Songs to Make the Dust Dance* (1994).

Mason, Penelope. *History of Japanese Art* (1993).
McCullough, Helen C. *Classical Japanese Prose: An Anthology* (1990).
———. trans. *Kokin Wakashū: The First Imperial Anthology of Japanese Poetry, with Tosa Nikki and Shinsen Waka* (1985).
McKinney, Meredith, trans. *The Pillow Book* (2007).
Rabinovitch, Judith N., and Timothy R. Bradstock. *Dance of the Butterflies* (2006).
Rodd, Laurel Rasplica, and Mary Catherine Henkenius, trans. *Kokinshū: A Collection of Poems Ancient and Modern* (1984).
Seidensticker, Edward G., trans. *The Gossamer Years* (1989).
———, trans. *The Tale of Genji* (1978).
Shirane, Haruo, ed. *Traditional Japanese Literature: An Anthology; Beginnings to 1600* (2007).
Tyler, Royall, trans. *The Tale of Genji* (2001).

Note

1. Many examples of Heian art can be found online by searching for images. Searching for "Tale of Genji Scroll," "Heian period art," or "Heian period clothing," for example, you will find many authentic Heian works of art or, in the case of clothing, accurate modern recreations. Unfortunately searches will also yield items that uninformed bloggers or mistaken links will identify as examples of Heian art. Be sure to check the actual website to determine the reliability of sources.

15

The Provinces and the Public Economy, 700–1100

Charlotte von Verschuer

The imperial state's provisions for ruling and taxing the countryside were designed, above all, to establish centralized control and to produce revenue for the sovereign and the court elite. This fundamental conception of the proper order of things changed little between the seventh century, when the *ritsuryō* state was created, and the late Heian period, but the mechanisms of control and exploitation—of resource collection—did change dramatically, particularly from the late eighth century onward.

Under the system borrowed from China and formalized in the Taihō *ritsuryō* codes of 701, land on the Japanese archipelago was viewed as state property to be exploited for the benefit of the court nobility. The Yamato kings-cum-emperors carried out population and land censuses and assigned rice-producing farmlands as "household fields" (*kubunden*) to cultivators across the realm. The household fields, distributed at rates that varied with the recipient's age, gender, and status—about one-fourth hectare per adult male and one-sixth hectare per adult female, with lesser allocations for slaves and elderly people—remained public property and, as such, could not be sold, exchanged, or used as security for loans. But the tenants held lifelong cultivation rights, as long as the land was tilled and not wasted. In return, the cultivators paid a variety of land, product, and labor taxes.

Arable lands in excess of those needed for the household field allotments were classed as public fields (*kōden*), some of which were distributed as grants to provide income to court nobles and provincial office holders. The rest were managed by the provincial and district governments, with the produce thereof supporting various local public services—including horse breeding and the maintenance of roads, bridges, post stations, and the militia—and other costs of governance. In both cases, public fields were either farmed by corvée labor or leased to farmers at a rent (*jishi*) set at one-fifth of the assessed yield of each plot.

A third category of lands was added in the early eighth century in the form of reclaimed fields (*konden*), which were intended to stimulate the opening of new farmland by recognizing ownership of newly created paddies for the holder's lifetime. When this proved insufficient incentive, possession of reclaimed fields was extended in 723 to three generations, and then made permanent in 743 for the developer and his heirs.

The introduction of reclaimed fields, which could be bought and sold at the discretion of the owner, revived the institution of private property and thereby undermined the concept of state ownership of all arable land. In 749 the state took one more step when Emperor Shōmu's (reigned 724–749) will called for the founding of provincial temples throughout the realm, granting reclaiming rights for thousands of hectares to the Tōdaiji and other temples around the Nara capital. From that time on, land was reclaimed by anyone who could afford the labor force, and thus the first landed estates (*shōen*) were born.

FROM BUREAUCRATIC ADMINISTRATION TO AUTHORITARIAN RULE

By the late eighth century, the various types of farmland—household fields, reclaimed fields, public fields, and private estates—were undergoing changes in structure and management. Two changes, in particular, define the transformation of the *ritsuryō* land and tax systems to those of the Heian period: the cessation of distribution of household fields, and the reorganization of farmland to meet the change in tax requirements.

Under the allotment system, household fields were adjusted every six years to fit changes in household size and composition. This system, although elegant in principle, depended on periodic population and land acreage surveys that proved difficult to carry out in practice. Land distributions accordingly became rare from the end of the eighth century, around the time when the capital moved to Heian, and ended altogether in many provinces during the ninth century. After 902, household fields simply remained in the hands of the families tilling them. Around the same time, private estates began to proliferate, surpassing public domain land in acreage by the early twelfth century. Cultivators on estate lands paid rents to aristocratic proprietors in the capital, but all farmland other than private estates continued to be regarded as public land under public authority, and subject to taxation as before.

Under the new system, public farmland was divided into parcels or tax units, called *myō*, controlled by wealthy landholders selected by the governor and designated as "unit controllers" (*fumyō*). Each unit comprised a varying number of individual plots, each of which was granted to one or more subscribers who acted as field contractors (*tato*) or local tax agents. The field contractors, who had to renew their tax levy rights every year, could farm, lease, or assign cultivation rights on the plots, but paid a fixed rent to the public authorities.

In Heian society, the balance between rights of possession and cultivation was unclear and floating. It depended on the duration of land control and occupation, various rights pertaining to tax collection, the leverage of political and military power, and the personal authority of various agents within the local community; and it was shaped by a chain of concessions and personal agreements. Thus land management in Heian Japan bore scarce resemblance to the bureaucratic farmland administration of the Nara period; yet central control persisted as before. Only from the twelfth century did changes in provincial management begin to effect a shift in power from the center to the provinces.

Changes in land distribution went hand in hand with changes in land management and regional administration, as court priorities shifted from a strident assertion of direct central oversight to an emphasis on maintaining centralized authority while delegating responsibility to locals for many of the workaday functions of government in the provinces.

The *ritsuryō* codes defined a four-layered system of administration and supervision, establishing fifty-eight (later increased to sixty-six) provinces (*kuni*) gathered into seven circuits (*dō*) and a capital region (*kinai*) and subdivided into districts (*gun*), which were further divided into townships (*sato* or *gō*). Provincial officers—the governor (*kami*), assistant governor (*suke*), secretaries (*jō*), and inspectors (*sakan*)—were all central nobles dispatched from the capital. They served four-year terms after which they moved on to new positions in other provinces or in the central government. As representatives of the emperor, governors and other provincial officials had jurisdiction over almost everything that went on in their provinces, including the maintenance of census registers, promotion of agriculture, maintenance of law and order, oversight of military affairs and training, oversight of religious ceremonies, and collection of taxes. Their authority was restricted only from above, ensuring that the power of the central government, justified by the authority of the emperor, checked and overrode the role of provincial elites in local and regional governance.

Under the original *ritsuryō* law, the four senior provincial officers shared authority for most functions of government. During the ninth century, however, this arrangement began to unravel as the census and land redistribution systems broke down and direct control of the farming population and land acreage weakened. In response, the court began to concentrate rights, powers, and responsibilities in the hands of the governor, rendering the positions of assistant governor, secretary, and inspector largely superfluous. Governors were recast as "custodial governors" (*zuryō*), charged primarily with the duty of forwarding fixed amounts of tax proceeds to the Heian court, and afforded unprecedented discretion as to the means by which the revenues were collected, in order to both secure tax incomes and counter the increasing influence of district chieftains, who were re-emerging as local magnates and dominating village affairs.

Although in principle the imperial state subordinated provincial residents to governing officers dispatched from the capital, one must be careful not to equate principle too closely with practice; in reality, elite local families were never far removed from power. To begin with, they monopolized the positions of district governments and staffed the dozens of lower-level offices that performed the day-to-day chores of provincial government administration. By the Heian period, they also began to acquire higher titles in the provincial bureaucracy as the court retrenched its position in the countryside.

Their position at the grassroots end of the government's chain of command and their permanent presence on the land gave provincial elites a familiarity with neighborhood affairs that no officer dispatched from the capital could match. Provincial governors therefore found themselves dependent on local figures for many key functions of government. From the eleventh century, lower-level functionaries in the provincial government, called *zaichō kanjin* (literally, "on-site officers"), were appointed by the governor and, in principle, served at his pleasure. In practice, however, they were usually selected from a fairly small group of families with hereditary ties to the provincial office and, because they provided an essential—but otherwise missing—element of continuity and stability, tended to retain their positions from administration to administration.

From the late tenth century, high court officials handpicked personal favorites for provincial governor assignments and thus promoted patron-client ties between the court elite and the provincial tax collectors. The custodial governors were also allowed to bring their own staff from the capital to the province. Such retainers, most often referred to as personal attendants (*rōtō*), included warriors whom the governors sent into the villages to seize local produce by force.

On the strength of these developments, governors and their families soon discovered that they could use the power and perquisites of their offices, and the strength of their court connections, to establish landed bases in their provinces of appointment and to continue to exploit the resources of these provinces even after their terms of office expired. As former officials settled in the countryside, they quickly became powers to contend with, competing with subsequent governors, district magistrates, and other gentry houses for resources and influence.

At the same time, governors who "settled down" in the countryside were careful to maintain their ties to the capital. They needed to, for cutting themselves off completely from the court would have meant severing themselves from the source of official appointments and from critical personal connections, and would thereby have ended all hope of maintaining the family's social and political position—even in provincial society. Typically, the carpetbaggers built homes and held bundles of income-producing lands scattered about the countryside, as well as homes in the capital, to which they shipped most of the profits from their rural enterprises.

Indeed, from the eleventh century, it became common for *zuryō* to administer their provinces largely or even entirely in absentia. Governors, who sometimes held appointments in more than one province at the same time, established absentee offices (*rusudokoro*) staffed by *zaichō kanjin* and overseen by deputies (*mokudai*) dispatched from the governor's personal staff, and visited their provinces only infrequently—if at all.

RICE AS AN ACCOUNTING DEVICE IN THE PUBLIC ECONOMY

From the ninth century, the tax system met with new developments that paralleled the new land system. Fiscal levies underwent changes in rates, assessment, and management.

The *ritsuryō* codes stipulated three types of taxes: a land tax, per capita taxes in kind, and labor services. The basic land tax (*so*) was assessed pro rata by acreage, at one and a half sheaves of rice per *tan* (0.3 acres). This was a somewhat abstract figure in that it ignored the yield, the quality of the soil, the natural conditions at harvesttime, and the location and size of each field. In addition to the land tax, which consumed between 5 and 25 percent of the harvest, cultivators were also subjected to an additional rice tax in the form of a system of compulsory loans, called *suiko*, under which peasants were compelled to borrow seed rice in the spring and repay it, with interest at rates ranging from 30 to 50 percent, after the autumn harvest. From early on, however, the government ceased bothering to recover the loan capital and collected only the annual interest, turning the loan system into an annual tax. The two kinds of rice levy provided annual income for local governments and were utilized, on the one hand, for operational costs of both the province and the district administrations—including the stipends for district chieftains—and, on the other, as an accumulated capital reserve for future rice loans.

The *ritsuryō* codes also prescribed three types of per capita taxes in kind payable in craft or food products sent to the capital: regular tribute (*chō*); a products tax or tax in kind (*soemono* or *chūnan sakumotsu*; literally, "additional tax" or "young people's tax," respectively), comprising a wide range of handcraft items; and a commuted labor tax (*yō*), paid in cloth, rice, or salt in lieu of the ten days of yearly labor service owed by all adult men to the central government. In addition, taxpayers were liable for sixty days of corvée labor (*zōyō*) on public construction projects, owed to the province governments. Such service was originally uncompensated, but was later supported by subsistence wages. In the mid-ninth century the required period was reduced to twenty days.

The Taihō *ritsuryō* codes included a long list of products to be rendered in order to supply the court with the textiles and other manufactured goods it needed. But this procedure proved no less cumbersome than the provisions for land redistribution, and so in the course of the ninth century the system was simplified. Thereafter, handicraft imposts were levied collectively, with fixed annual quotas for provinces and districts. The lists can be found in the *Engishiki* (*Protocols of the Engi Era*), promulgated in 927.

To comply with the requirements, taxpayers' resources were pooled by district authorities, and the tax products were manufactured in district workshops or by hired specialists. As the craftsmen were paid in rice for their labors, the officials in charge collected tax payments in rice to support this manufacturing. Taxes in kind thus came to be actually paid in rice; taxpayers rendered fewer actual products, but higher rice payments; and tax calculations shifted from per capita to per acre levies. By the tenth century, all taxes fell into two basic categories: tax products (*kanmotsu*) and the corvée services (*rinji zōyaku*, or "various occasional services"); and from the eleventh century, even the labor services were assessed in rice and based on acreage, rather than per capita labor by individuals. In some provinces this merging of assessments also resulted in the merging of tax accounts, and the *kanmotsu* category came to include the corvée labor taxes as well.

Such merging of taxes led to an inflation of rice levies and to overcharging by the contract governors. In a matter of decades, the new tax structure turned everyone involved—except peasant cultivators—into tax farmers collecting revenues beyond their assigned quotas and pocketing the surplus. Gubernatorial posts became more lucrative than ever, while the officials themselves demonstrated a less-than-noble inclination to regard their provinces chiefly as revenue-producing resources, and became increasingly indifferent to the needs and welfare of residents.

By the eleventh century, the situation had become so egregious that the court—ostensibly the principal beneficiary of tax collection—moved to curb abuse and rapacious levies. The *Kōden kanmotsu rippō* (*Regulations for Standard*

Assessment Rates on the Public Domain), published by the court in the 1040s, stipulated that tax levies in kind had to follow local precedents and limited rice taxes to a standard of about three *to* (three sheaves) of rice per *tan* of land. Notably, this standard is very close to the volume of rice levies obtained through the land and loan taxes during the eighth century. In all cases, rice came to be the main currency for public accounts.

AGRICULTURAL PRODUCTION AND FOOD

The Nara and Heian states were built on rice. The "agriculture" that formed the base for public income consisted only of rice paddy fields. Public prices for goods and services were calculated in rice, all provincial expenditures of the provinces were underwritten in terms of rice, provincial annual accounts were expressed in volumes of rice, and from the tenth century, all taxes—even manufactured goods—were computed and levied in rice. Crops other than rice were not subject to any regulations and were free from public control and taxes. Only from the seventeenth century did other crops such as wheat come fully under the public tax system, but even then, taxes were levied in rice and not in the crop itself. Rice remained the main accounting device in the public economy until the Meiji period (1868–1912).

The preeminence of the rice economy throughout Japanese history has led to a scarcity of written sources on grains other than rice. For this reason, rice has long been believed by historians—both Japanese and non-Japanese—to have been the main, or even the only, crop and the primary staple food in Japan from early times until the twentieth century. More recently, however, some scholars have challenged this view, citing both written and archaeological evidence for dry-field and slash-and-burn cultivation throughout the premodern era of millets (*awa* and *kibi*), wheat and barley (*mugi*), buckwheat (*soba*), barnyard grass (*hie*), and beans including soybeans (*daizu*) and red beans (*azuki*). Indeed, it is now argued that dry-field grains dominated the Japanese diet until at least the seventeenth century.

A more anthropological approach to history has enhanced new discoveries in ecohistory and biodiversity. Perhaps the first thing one notices when looking at a topographic map of Japan is that more than 70 percent of the archipelago (excluding Hokkaido) is covered by mountains. In the ancient and medieval periods, then, only about 10 percent of the country consisted of the flat and level surfaces convenient for wet rice agriculture: paddy fields, like swimming pools, cannot be constructed on hillsides without elaborate terracing, lest the water run off. On the other hand, the extensive mountain terrain formed an ideal natural environment for slash-and-burn cultivation, and the population of ancient and medieval Japan lived in surroundings with ample space available for dry crops. There can, moreover, be no doubt that, for their personal needs, premodern Japanese farmers privileged crops that were tax-free and did not demand expensive, backbreaking terracing and irrigation construction.

Nevertheless, it remains unclear how much of the rice harvests in ancient and medieval Japan remained with the cultivators' households after taxes. Scholars of medieval European history generally assert that proprietors or public authorities absorbed about half of agricultural earnings, leaving the other half for the producers' consumption. But rice production in eighth-century Japan appears sufficient to have covered less than half the staple food needs of average farming households after taxes, suggesting that millet, wheat, beans, and other grains must have accounted for more than half of the peasants' daily diet. Clearly, then, a gap must have existed between the public rice economy and the private nutritional practices of the general population during the Nara and Heian periods, a gap that persisted until the seventeenth century. During the entire medieval period, the lion's share of the rice produced was channeled to the elites in the cities of Nara, Kyoto, and Kamakura and formed the diet of court nobles and military leaders.

Historians' appraisals of agricultural output and farmland acreage have also changed in recent years. Whereas scholars formerly attributed the expansion of private estates between 1050 and 1150 to large-scale land clearance, most now agree that this expansion mainly involved the reopening of once productive, but then abandoned, land. Similarly, historians have recently revised a long-held assumption that total acreage under cultivation increased dramatically between the late tenth and early eighteenth centuries, recognizing that, while figures reported in historical encyclopedias and official censuses record only paddy fields for the eighth to sixteenth centuries, those for the early modern era include dry fields, which represented about 40 percent of the total farmland.

PRODUCTION FOR THE CAPITALS

Rice, other foodstuffs, textiles, raw materials, and craft wares were regarded by court elites, not as luxury goods, but as essential to sustaining their daily lives and official duties. Such goods were channeled from the provinces to the capital via tax levies and contract tributes and through patron-client relationships.

Although the imperial court directly managed some farmland and a number of craft shops, it relied heavily on deliveries of foodstuffs, raw materials, and manufactured goods from the provinces. The kinds of products transported from the provinces to the Nara and Heian capitals each year remained essentially the same for four or five centuries.

Provincial governments stored the bulk of the tax rice they collected in provincial granaries and sent only a small portion to the capital. The latter was then distributed to the court's bureaus and offices as food allowances for the officials on duty, served at all banquets accompanying the regular court ceremonies, or presented as offerings during various annual rituals. Other food products received at the Heian court included salt, seafood—fish, shells, and seaweed, which were either dried, cooked, salted, or marinated for preservation—and grains such as millet. Oil, pressed from sesame seeds, perilla seeds, hemp seeds, walnuts, viburnum, camellia, or other plants, was used both for cooking and for lamp fuel.

Furniture and equipment for the imperial household was manufactured in craft shops in the capital, but the court also requisitioned from the provinces wooden chests, bamboo boxes, wooden tubs, bamboo trellises, kegs, straw mats, and paper for use in its offices. Similarly, textiles were woven both in provincial and capital workshops.

Precious silk fabrics included highly sophisticated weavings such as brocades, damask, and twill silk fabrics. These were used for the formal garments of the imperial family, as well as for furniture such as screens, cushions, and tablecloths. Whereas these special fabrics were produced and consumed in relatively small amounts, thousands of bolts of plain woven taffeta silk reached the capital from the provinces—more than four thousand bolts for the sewing workshop for imperial garments alone, and many more bolts to dress the clerks, attendants, and guards. Taffeta was often distributed as a reward for services at court ceremonies and was in high demand because it served as a kind of currency in barter for rice at rates fixed by court protocols.

Linen and cotton were unknown in Japan until early modern times. The typical textile for daily clothes of court nobles off duty and for the entire Japanese population in general was hemp. Large amounts were distributed to court officials, who received regular semester stipends consisting of silk taffeta, silk thread, hemp cloth, and iron hoes.

Wood and plant substances served as the main primary materials for manufacturing the furnishings and equipment used in daily court life. Other raw materials delivered by the provinces to the royal craft shops included silver ore, gold, roebuck horn, and animal skins. Varnish, made from the resin of the Japanese sumac tree (*urushi*), was, and still is today, the basis of the Japanese lacquer craft. Heian craft shops manufactured lacquered dishes, chests, boxes, tables, frames for screens, and other equipment for court offices and royal residences.

Whatever the form of these goods, they converged in the capital and filled the needs of the aristocracy and the religious institutions there, giving rise at the same time to commercial activities in the capital region and the countryside. Heian nobles did not need to resort to trade, but official markets in the capital provided sites for selling off excess tribute goods and purchasing other needed items. In the provinces, local markets provided tax managers the means to procure for themselves some of the furnishings that were due the central elites.

Contrary to popular images and assumptions, not all peasants were farmers; some rural dwellers also engaged in other activities. Fishermen were active along the coasts. Shipping and packhorse services were available for transportation, and special products were offered locally for sale. Day laborers swarmed near the anchorages in Yamazaki south of Heian or at the port of Ōtsu on Lake Biwa. And craftsmen, including iron smiths and carpenters, produced manufactured goods.

Yet this commercial diversity did not affect the principal social order stipulated by the *ritsuryō* codes. Classical society knew only two main social classes: an aristocracy comprising a small minority exempted from taxes, and the commoners forming the bulk of the tax-paying population. Villagers were free to conduct activities of their choice, but all commoners, including fishermen, craftsmen, and merchants, were members of rice farm households attached to farmland and subjected to taxes based on land. Rural merchants did not make their livings solely from trade but were simply people who offered products for sale at local fairs held two or three times a month. Trade involving large quantities was still rare, and both the markets of the capitals and the provincial fairs were controlled or supervised by public authorities. Goods were mainly bartered, because coins were not yet in wide distribution and mintage of coins was halted in the tenth century. The principal media of exchange were rice, silk, and hemp fabric.

Throughout the Nara and Heian ages, Japan remained an agrarian society and a tax-based economy. Land was the source of power. Distributions of resources were commanded by fiscal channels, and wealth was produced not through market activities but through farmland.

Sources and Suggestions for Further Reading

See the bibliography for complete publication data.

Farris, William Wayne. *Population, Disease, and Land in Early Japan, 645–900* (1985).

Morris, Dana Robert. "Land and Society" (1999).

Piggott, Joan R., ed. *Capital and Countryside in Japan, 300–1180: Japanese Historians in English* (2006).

Verschuer, Charlotte von. *Across the Perilous Sea: Japanese Trade with China and Korea from the Seventh to Sixteenth Centuries* (2006).

———. "Demographic Estimates and the Issue of Staple Food in Early Japan" (2009).

———. "Life of Commoners in the Provinces: The Owari no gebumi of 988" (2007).

16

The *Shōen* System

Ethan Segal

As in most premodern societies, the early Japanese placed tremendous importance on the control of land and agricultural production. The land provided food and clothing to those who lived on it. Taxes collected in the form of rice and other goods from provincial landholdings were used to pay the salaries of government officials and allowed the nobility and religious houses to construct mansions and temples and enjoy extravagant lifestyles. Later, in the medieval period, warriors fought over land and rights to income (*shiki*, discussed below). They built power bases by drafting men, levying taxes, and rewarding their followers with fiefs. And, of course, the majority of the population during these centuries consisted of peasants who lived off the land in the countryside. It would be difficult to understand Japanese history without paying close attention to who controlled the land and how they administered it.

One of the most important land management institutions in pre-1600 Japan was the *shōen*. *Shōen* were provincial landed properties, homes to cultivators engaged in agricultural production and obligated to pay part of their produce to local managers and absentee proprietors. These properties are often referred to in English as "private estates" because they were exempt in part or whole from paying taxes to the central government. In most cases, the holders of *shōen* also had the right to deny entry to public officials. Although some scholars have drawn parallels between *shōen* and medieval European manors, there were significant differences. *Shōen* holdings were often scattered, for example, and the complex system of rights to income that emerged was quite distinct from the European manor system.

Shōen could be found in every region of Japan, from Iriki Estate in southwestern Satsuma province (modern Kagoshima prefecture) to Yoshima Estate in northeastern Mutsu province (modern Fukushima prefecture). The earliest estates were created in the eighth century, and a noticeable rise in their formation occurred from the eleventh century onward. Some lasted for only a few years, but others endured for centuries. Few survived the warfare and daimyo aggrandizement of the Warring States period (1467–1573), and the last remaining estates were eliminated by the warlord Hideyoshi in the late sixteenth century. As one might imagine, there was a tremendous amount of variation in how *shōen* were organized from region to region and over time. This makes it difficult to speak in general terms about *shōen*, but this chapter covers their most important features and explains how *shōen* evolved.

MANAGING LAND BEFORE THE *SHŌEN*

Given the government laid claim to all land back in the seventh century, it might seem strange that "private" estates could emerge at all. As earlier chapters in this volume explain, the imperial court drew upon Tang Chinese models to create a wide array of new legal and administrative institutions as part of the Taika Reforms. Among the reforms was the government's claim that all land belonged to the emperor. The government distributed the land to the people in allotments on the basis of a census conducted every six years. It also provided assistance by lending seed rice so that farmers could plant their crops. In return, the people had to pay taxes: a grain tax (usually rice), a tax on local goods (often cloth or silk), and corvée (manual labor).

Another of the seventh-century reforms was the division of the realm into provinces. The central government appointed officials to collect the taxes levied within their respective provinces. By the eighth century, most of the land under the control of the imperial court was subject to this system of land distribution, although there were a few notable exceptions. For example, an aristocrat might be awarded a certain number of commoner households (and their land) in keeping with his rank and office. Temples were also allowed to hold certain lands tax-free as a way of covering their operating expenses. But the vast bulk of the population lived on "public" lands subject to provincial taxation. These territories, and the provincial officials who administered them, are described in greater detail in chapter 15.

This system worked reasonably well as a way for the government to collect food and extract wealth from the countryside. Nevertheless, problems emerged within decades of its establishment. Provincial residents sometimes underreported the local population in order to avoid taxes or military conscription, making the census figures on which land was redistributed unreliable. In addition, cultivators had little incentive to develop and improve land that they might lose only six years later. Further complicating the government's attempts to manage land, people, and taxes were epidemic diseases that ravaged the population. The smallpox epidemic of the 730s, for example, may have killed 25 percent or more of the islands' six million people.

Perhaps because there were not enough cultivators to work the land, the government took steps to promote agricultural activities. In 723 the imperial court announced an incentive program to encourage the opening of new land, declaring that newly reclaimed territory could be held tax-free for three generations. It made the offer even more attractive in 743 by proclaiming that new lands could be held exempt from taxation in perpetuity. These reclaimed lands formed the basis of some of the earliest *shōen*.

EARLY *SHŌEN*

The government's incentives helped bring more land under cultivation. Of course, only those with significant resources, such as temples, local elites, or members of the nobility, could afford to invest in land reclamation. In many instances, an ambitious proprietor searched out land that seemed reclaimable and then hired nearby local labor to carry out the backbreaking work of cutting down trees, draining swamps, removing rocks, and the like. Geographic variability meant that not all of the new estate's land was contiguous; parcels might be scattered, though usually in close proximity to each other.

The challenges of bringing wild lands under cultivation were significant. Extreme weather, cold temperatures, insects, and other problems could undo months of work. The records of some estates show that they lost more land than they gained in many years. For example, documents concerning Kuwabara Estate in Echizen province, a Tōdaiji property founded in the mid-eighth century, show that natural disasters and disputes with neighbors frequently led to certain parts of the estate reverting to wasteland. Furthermore, provincial officials often contested estates' boundaries and even their tax-exempt status. If officials could get an estate declared part of the public domain, it would be subject to provincial taxation.

Estate managers turned to the central government for help in protecting their properties. Some procured documents from the Council of State (Daijōkan) or the Ministry of Popular Affairs (Minbushō) certifying that their lands were exempt from public taxation. These documents carried great weight and made it difficult for provincial officials to challenge a *shōen*'s exempt status. Scholars refer to such document-backed estates as *kanshōfu shōen* (literally, "council and ministry–certified estates"). One of the earliest examples was Ōyama Estate in Tanba province, a Tōji holding founded in 845. When disputes arose over who actually controlled the land, the temple appealed to the central government and received documents confirming (1) who owned the land, (2) that the fields were tax exempt, and (3) that its cultivators did not have to provide manual labor to the government. *Kanshōfu shōen* started to become more common in the tenth century.

Other estates in this period were created when proprietors exploited the tax-exempt status granted to temples and shrines. These religious institutions were expected to pray for the welfare of the state. In exchange, they did not have to pay taxes but instead could use the income from their landholdings to support themselves. Some estate managers forged close relationships with nearby religious institutions and took advantage of the tax exemption by successfully claiming that their holdings were shrine or temple lands.

MANAGERS AND CULTIVATORS

On most Heian period *shōen*, a resident estate manager (*shōkan, gesu,* or *azukari dokoro*) supervised the estate's daily operation. In some cases, this was the individual who had sponsored and led the land reclamation; on temple estates, it was often a priest appointed by and sent from the main temple. The estate manager had a number of officials, clerks, and other workers assisting him in running the estate.

Cultivators carried out the estate's agricultural activities, ranging from growing rice, vegetables, and other foodstuffs to producing goods such as cloth, incense, and tatami mats for the estate's proprietors. Cultivators had few rights in the early Heian period. Individuals known as *tato* contracted to work specific fields on a yearly basis. Their positions were tenuous, however, since estate administrators could choose not to renew their contracts, forcing *tato* to give up their lands. Even so, disease, poor harvests, and other problems kept the population from growing, so managers could rarely afford to dismiss laborers capriciously.

Over time, the *tato* gained stronger claims as cultivators of the land, with a few becoming relatively well-to-do. One eleventh-century source, the *Shinsarugakuki*, describes a prominent *tato* as owning several *chō* of land,[1] maintaining his own farm equipment, and hiring workers to help him dig ditches, repair waterways, and finish the busy planting season. According to this source, successful *tato* could plant any of a wide variety of crops, from rice and barley to buckwheat and millet. But it is unlikely that the typical cultivator enjoyed such prosperity. Work in the fields was extremely difficult, with few oxen, horses, or metal tools to help with the backbreaking manual labor.

GOVERNMENT EFFORTS TO REDUCE THE NUMBER OF *SHŌEN*

The *shōen* system worked effectively to provide income for temples such as Tōji and for aristocrats including the Fujiwara regents' family. But every parcel incorporated as a private estate meant less land was paying provincial taxes into governmental coffers. This led the imperial government to make several attempts to curtail the spread of *shōen*. In 902 the Daijōkan banned the creation of new *shōen*. Although this decree was adhered to in some instances, no provincial governor was able to challenge a *shōen* backed by a powerful proprietor such as a member of the Fujiwara. The government made similar efforts to rein in estates in 985, 1040, and 1056, but with little effect.

The most concerted attack on the proliferation of *shōen* was made by Emperor Go-Sanjō, who created the Records Office (Kirokujo) in 1069. He declared that all *shōen* established after 1045 were invalid and that estates from earlier times would need to provide documentation to prove their exempt status. This was likely an effort by Go-Sanjō, an emperor without a Fujiwara mother, to stem the power of that great family (see chapter 12). It met with resistance, and subsequent emperors chose to acquire *shōen* of their own rather than try to stop the process of estate creation. They competed for land quite successfully, and the imperial family soon came to hold rights to more *shōen* than did the Fujiwara.

COMMENDATION *SHŌEN*

One factor in the imperial family's success in gaining rights to *shōen* had to do with a new way of creating them: commendation. The original method of reclaiming land, popular in the ninth and tenth centuries, had become impractical by the eleventh century because it was difficult to find suitable available land. Meanwhile, provincial officials remained as eager as ever to claim that estate lands were actually public lands subject to taxation. In some cases, one provincial governor might recognize a particular estate as legitimate, but his replacement would deny the land's *shōen* status.

These kinds of troubles led estate managers to seek protection against government officials by "commending" their rights of proprietorship to more powerful individuals or institutions. The new proprietor (*ryōshū* or *ryōke*), usually a temple or an aristocrat, would provide protection and confirm the on-site estate manager in his post in exchange for a regular payment from the estate. Sometimes the new proprietor lacked enough political sway to fully guarantee the estate's status, so he might commend rights to income from the estate to someone even more powerful, such as a member of the Fujiwara or the imperial family. We refer to those individuals as patrons or guarantors (*honke*); and, like the *ryōke*, they received part of the estate's produce in exchange for providing protection.

One such commendation *shōen* was Kanokogi Estate, located in Higo province. A Buddhist acolyte named Jushō reclaimed the land in the early eleventh century, but his descendant Takakata must have felt that the holding was in danger, because he commended the property to Fujiwara Sanemasa in 1086. Sanemasa became the *ryōke*, protecting the estate from interference by public officials in exchange for four hundred *koku* of rice each year.[2] Later, Sanemasa's descendant could no longer provide sufficient protection, so he commended half of his share to imperial princess Kaya no In; her share was eventually given to Ninnaji, which became the *honke*.

Another commendation *shōen* was Yano Estate. In the late eleventh century, a provincial figure, Hata Tametoki, founded a private holding from reclaimed land in Harima province. He commended this estate to a provincial governor, Fujiwara Akisue, who confirmed Tametoki in his position as manager. In the early twelfth century, Akisue's son Nagazane commended the *honke* rights to Bifukumon'in, an imperial consort of Emperor Toba. At each commendation, the higher authority provided protection in exchange for a share of the estate's rent.

This process of commendation (*kishin*) was used not only to protect existing *shōen* but also to create new estates out of public lands. Influential connections within the government were crucial to the success of these transactions. Commendation led to a rapid increase in the number of estates, and by the late twelfth century, more than half of the territory in most provinces was *shōen* rather than public land.

EMERGENCE OF THE *SHIKI* AND THE *MYŌ*

The examples of commendation discussed above show how complex, multilayered, and hierarchical *shōen* property rights were. Key to the coexistence of different rights within the same estates were *shiki*, "rights-to-income" paid by the estate in exchange for some service. For example, *honke* and *ryōke* each held *shiki* that entitled them to a designated amount and type of income in exchange for the protection they provided. Estate managers had their own *shiki*, as did the various levels of cultivators. Because each *shiki* came with unique responsibilities and payment, they could overlap—that is, different people could hold different *shiki* arising from the same parcel of land. Over time, *shiki* came to be bought and sold like commodities.

Documents from the late Heian period also begin referencing a new unit of taxation, the *myō*, which continued on many estates until the fourteenth century or later. On many estates, the land was divided into a small number of large *myō*. Each *myō* was named, and a specific individual (*myōshū*)—usually a prominent cultivator—was responsible for supervising the territory within it, collecting taxes on the people and goods produced therein, and delivering them to the estate manager. Their positions seem to have been more secure than those of *tato* in earlier times.

In the 1250s, for example, land surveys conducted on Tara Estate, a Tōji holding in Wakasa province, revealed five *myō* of twenty-two *tan* each and two *myō* of eleven *tan* each (probably a full-sized *myō* that had been divided in half).[3] Altogether, some two-thirds of the entire estate's land under cultivation was designated as *myō* fields. The remaining one-third was divided up among twenty-seven "small peasants," who held much less secure claims to their properties. The sizes of these peasants' holdings varied, but on average they were less than three *tan* each.

Scholars have long debated the significance of the *myō*. During the late Heian and early Kamakura periods, *myō* were often uniform in size, as in Tara Estate. This uniformity has led some scholars to conclude that central proprietors played a part in constructing *myō* and that the *myōshū* were lower-level estate officials. Other historians, however, believe that the *myōshū* emerged as leading local cultivators gained stronger (though still limited) property rights. Regardless of which interpretation one accepts, it seems clear that the rise of *myō* paralleled a trend in which the central government was taking a more hands-off approach and increasingly leaving management of the countryside to provincial and local officials.

LANDHOLDING AND LAND MANAGEMENT IN THE LATE HEIAN PERIOD

The mature *shōen* system that emerged toward the end of the eleventh century was the product of a three-way competition for control of lands and the profits that could be derived from them among wealthy peasants and other elite provincial residents, provincial governors, and the great houses and religious institutions (*kenmon*; see chapter 12) of the court in Kyoto. This competition was characterized by shifting alliances among members of the three groups, resulting in a stable but uneasy balance between central and local power and interests.

The fundamental dynamic at play here is easily grasped. Provincial governors were responsible for collecting taxes for the public coffers and, more important, drew much of their personal income from overcollecting taxes and pocketing the difference. The more land that became incorporated into *shōen*, the less that was available for taxation (and skimming); governors, therefore, were naturally disposed to resist the growth of *shōen*. At the same time, however, governors depended on sponsorship and patronage from the very same high-ranking aristocrats and members of the imperial family who were serving as estate proprietors and guarantors for the appointments to office that made their careers as government officials possible. Governors were, therefore, vulnerable to pressure from *kenmon* to look the other way with regard to the creation or expansion of particular estates.

Accordingly, governors tended to squeeze provincial landholders for as much tax revenue as possible. They also confiscated lands from existing estates and blocked efforts to turn lands within their provinces into *shōen*. In the face of this, provincial landholders often commended their lands to powerful court figures who could use their influence to keep the governors at bay. But commendation also had its downside for the provincial elites, who went from independent landlords to contractual managers of estates that now belonged to someone else.

Before long, however, canny governors and provincial elites realized that they could be allies, as well as opponents, in this contest, and began to work out special arrangements under which the landholder agreed to keep his lands nominally public (not to commend them to a *shōen* proprietor). In exchange, the governor agreed to accept a fixed level of tax revenues from the land—at a rate usually lower than either the rents demanded by *shōen* proprietors or the normal public tax rates—and to guarantee the landholder's rights to manage the fields. Such arrangements were, of course, only as good as the provincial governor's word and, after the official who signed off on them left office, only as binding on his successors as the subsequent governors wished them to be.

The result of these developments over time was a seesawing game of shifting alliances, interests, and balances of power that transformed both public and private landholding. The standout feature throughout was the continued prominence of central authority and the continued dependence of provincial elites on the court and its officials for protection of their rights to income from the lands they administered.

By the end of the Heian period, somewhere between 40 and 60 percent of the agricultural land in Japan had been converted to *shōen*. The rest, which came to be known as *kokugaryō* (provincial government lands), remained under the control of provincial governors but in a form that bore little resemblance to the land and tax system described by the *ritsuryō* codes. In fact, *kokugaryō* are perhaps best understood as publically held *shōen*. The only real difference between "public" and "estate" lands under this system was that the former paid *taxes* collected by a local government official and submitted to the court through the provincial governor, while the latter paid *rent* collected by an estate manager and submitted to a court proprietor. For the peasants who actually worked the fields, and even for the managerial class, this was largely a distinction without a difference; for both, day-to-day life on *kokugaryō* and *shōen* lands was essentially the same.

WARRIORS AND ESTATES IN THE KAMAKURA PERIOD

The victory of Minamoto Yoritomo's forces in the Genpei Wars led to his creation of Japan's first warrior government, the Kamakura Shogunate (see chapter 18). In 1185 Yoritomo secured one of the most important powers of his new administration: authorization to appoint his followers as military land stewards (*jitō*) on *shōen*. Initially, the *jitō* were placed on estates that had supported the Taira (the family that lost the Genpei Wars). Later, *jitō* would come to be placed on other estates, such as those that had supported Retired Emperor Go-Toba's failed war against the shogunate in 1221.

On most *shōen*, the *jitō* held a position similar to that of the estate's on-site manager. *Jitō* were involved in tax collection, policing, and the overall supervision and management of the estate. For these services they were entitled to a certain amount of the estate's income (usually in keeping with what was paid to estate managers). The key difference, however, was that the *jitō* did not answer to higher authorities within the *shōen* hierarchy. While the estate's proprietor or patron could appoint or remove the traditional estate manager, only Kamakura could recall the *jitō*.

As one might expect, this system invited abuse. Few *shōen* managers and proprietors wanted warriors as *jitō* on their estates, since they interfered with estate management, were an added tax burden, and sometimes took more than their due. When *jitō* abused their positions, traditional authorities could do little but complain to Kamakura or take the *jitō* to court by filing a lawsuit. The shogunate tried to prevent *jitō* from overstepping their authority and often handed down judgments against them. Still, proprietors faced a difficult decision: a lawsuit could be expensive, often took years to resolve, and offered no guarantee that the verdict would be in the proprietor's favor.

Because of this uncertainty, some proprietors opted to reach compromise agreements (*wayo*) with the *jitō* on their estates. The *jitō* might be given free rein to manage the *shōen* as he saw fit in exchange for giving the proprietor a fixed amount of the estate's annual produce (such agreements were known as *jitō ukesho*), or the proprietor and the *jitō* might agree to divide the estate in half (*shitaji chūbun*). Finally, even when the proprietor managed to get a corrupt *jitō* removed from his position, some became bandits (*akutō*) who continued to plague the estate for years.

Not all *shōen* experienced such difficulties, however. Some estates had no *jitō*, while on others, the *jitō* coexisted peacefully with traditional authorities. We should also note that new *shōen* were still being created in the Kamakura period. But it became increasingly common for warriors to interfere with proprietor-estate relations and disrupt the flow of goods from the provinces to the nobles and religious houses.

THE LATE MEDIEVAL DECLINE OF THE *SHŌEN*

Estate proprietors faced even greater challenges after the destruction of the Kamakura Shogunate. From the mid-fourteenth to the late sixteenth centuries, the *shōen* declined for several reasons. First, warriors became ever bolder in appropriating provincial income and ignoring the concerns of traditional proprietors. Particularly damaging was the new, Muromachi period right of provincial military governors (*shugo*) to claim half of an estate's produce. This privilege, known as *hanzei,* was originally intended as a temporary emergency measure to cover wartime expenses, but it became permanent in 1368.

Second, cultivators took advantage of the growing economy to assert their independence. New agricultural techniques meant that cultivators could grow more than in earlier times, but absentee *shōen* proprietors were unable to capture the higher yields. Local residents, including warriors and well-to-do peasants, competed with traditional estate officers and proprietors in asserting control over the land and demanding income. As estate proprietors proved inept in defending their interests, peasants became more assertive. By the fifteenth century, some had formed villages that pooled their resources to purchase land and water rights and demand reductions in the tax owed to proprietors.

Third, proprietors began losing control of their estates because they fell into debt or simply found that they could not effectively manage properties from a distance. In some cases, they had to turn over management of their *shōen* to their creditors, an arrangement that may have temporarily helped them with financial difficulties but that also demonstrated their inability to effectively manage their landholdings.

Finally, the violence and chaos of the Warring States period (see chapter 22) meant that proprietors could no longer rely on the central government to support their traditional claims to income. The scattered holdings, absentee proprietorships, and multilayered *shiki* of the *shōen* system were impossible to maintain under such conditions. Instead, the emerging warlords, or daimyo, sought contiguous domains that they could better defend. They recruited local warriors and peasant leaders as their vassals and conducted cadastral surveys that redefined land rights with little regard for estates. Later, Toyotomi Hideyoshi's land surveys of the 1580s (see chapter 29) redefined everything from the units of measure to the means of tax assessment. He eliminated multilayered rights and made the village the lowest basic unit of taxation. Those policies brought the eight-hundred-year history of the *shōen* to an end.

Sources and Suggestions for Further Reading

See the bibliography for complete publication data.

Batten, Bruce. "Provincial Administration in Early Japan: From Ritsuryō kokka to Ōchō kokka" (1993).
Hurst, G. Cameron. "*Kugyo* and *Zuryo*: Center and Periphery in the Era of Fujiwara no Michinaga" (2007).
———. "The Reign of Go-Sanjo and the Revival of Imperial Power" (1972).
Keirstead, Thomas. "Fragmented Estates: The Break-up of the Myo and the Decline of the Shoen System" (1985).
———. *The Geography of Power in Medieval Japan* (1992).
Mass, Jeffrey P. "The Missing Minamoto in the Twelfth-Century Kanto" (1993).
Nagahara Keiji. "Landownership under the Shōen-Kokugaryō System" (1975).
Sato, Elizabeth. "The Early Development of the Shoen" (1974).
Segal, Ethan Isaac. *Coins, Trade, and the State: Economic Growth in Early Medieval Japan* (2011).
Yamamura Kozo, ed. *The Cambridge History of Japan*, Vol. 3: *Medieval Japan* (1990). Especially chapters by Ōyama and Nagahara.
Wintersteen, Prescott. "The Muromachi Shugo and Hanzei" (1974).

Notes

1. One *chō* was equal to approximately one hectare.
2. One *koku* equals approximately 180 liters.
3. One *tan* was equal to approximately one-tenth of a hectare.

17

The Dawn of the Samurai

Karl F. Friday

By the middle of the Heian period, the imperial court, outwardly at least, maintained neither an army nor a police force of its own, depending instead on private forces directed by private warriors for its martial dirty work. Such warriors—known as *bushi*, *tsuwamono*, *musha*, *mononofu*, and other terms at various times in their history, but most popularly as the samurai—began to dominate the political and economic landscape by the early 1200s, and ruled outright from the late fourteenth to the late nineteenth century.

The assumptions of earlier generations of historians were heavily conditioned by visions of the court portrayed in literary classics like Murasaki Shikibu's *Tale of Genji* and by expectations colored by the conditions that produced European knights and lords. To these scholars, the Heian period developments suggested an appalling short-sightedness or naïveté on the part of the emperor and the aristocracy, and were presumed to reflect a deep-set apathy to provincial administration and to military and police affairs.

According to this view, a warrior order was spontaneously generated during the middle years of the Heian period, just as one had been in Europe a few centuries earlier, to fill yawning holes in the military and administrative structures of the provinces caused by the collapse of early imperial military institutions and the rampant growth of private estates (*shōen*). The court's martial ineptitude and lapsing supervision of the provinces led to a breakdown of order in the countryside so severe that those who owned or administered the great estates were forced to develop private retinues of fighting men to protect their lives and property. But within decades of their inception, these bands of fighting men had undermined what little remained of centralized rule in the provinces, emerging as masters of the countryside.

More careful examination in recent decades, however, has made it clear that the court neither ignored the countryside nor abandoned provincial residents to fend for themselves in matters of general administration or defense and law enforcement. It simply delegated responsibility for the logistics and particulars of these functions to locals and private contractors, even as it carefully preserved its rights and powers to oversee them from the center. Indeed, the ties binding capital to countryside were growing stronger, not thinner, during the middle and late Heian periods.

Similarly, the samurai came into being during the ninth and tenth centuries to serve the imperial court and the noble houses that comprised it, as hired swords and contract bows—just one more by-product of the broad trend toward the privatization of government functions and delegation of administrative responsibility that distinguished the Heian polity from its Nara-era predecessor. This new order of private warriors saw the profession of arms not as a matter of self-defense, but as an avenue to career success and advancement in civil rank and office. The first significant steps toward warrior autonomy and political power came only in the 1180s, and real warrior rule was yet another two centuries in the making after that.

"The rise of the samurai" was, therefore, less a matter of revolution or collapse than of incremental evolution, occurring in fits and starts. It began with a shift in imperial court military policy in the middle decades of the eighth century that picked up momentum in the ninth.

THE *RITSURYŌ* MILITARY

The *ritsuryō* military system was designed in the face of internal challenges to the sovereignty of the court and the regime, and the growing might of Tang China, which had been engaged since the early 600s in one of the greatest military expansions in Chinese history. Fortuitously for the emerging Japanese imperial court, fear of the latter helped mute the former. Specters of Tang invasion fleets looming over the horizon promoted support for state-strengthening reforms, motivating central and provincial noble houses to set aside their differences in the face of a perceived common enemy.

Predictably, then, the centralization and restructuring of the military constituted a major element of the state reformation process. While "national armies" of the confederation era had been cobbled together from forces raised and commanded independently by the various noble houses, the post-Taika military structure placed the whole of the state's military resources—weapons, auxiliary equipment, horses, troops, and officers—under the direct control of the emperor and his court. Henceforth, centrally appointed officers and officials oversaw all military units and activities, and direct conscription—supervised by the court—replaced enlistment of troops through provincial chieftains. This transformation of the army paralleled the transformation of rule in the hinterlands into a centrally administered imperium.

The reformers designed the imperial military around two fundamental principles: central control and direction of all military affairs, and public conscription, whereby military service was viewed as a basic duty to the state incumbent on all subjects. The *ritsuryō* codes reserved control and direction of all but the most minor military and police affairs for the emperor and his court. Overall administration of the state's armed forces was conducted by the Ministry of Military Affairs (Hyōbushō) and the five offices under it, and was delegated at the provincial level to the governor and his staff (all of whom were central appointees). Mobilization of troops required an imperial edict, issued through—and with the concurrence of—the Council of State.

All free male subjects between the ages of twenty and fifty-nine, other than rank-holding nobles and individuals who "suffered from long-term illness or were otherwise unfit for military duty," were liable for induction as soldiers.[1] Conscripts were enrolled in provincial regiments (*gundan*), which were militia units, akin to modern national guards. Once assigned and registered as soldiers, most men returned to their homes and fields. Provincial governors maintained copies of regimental rosters that they used as master lists from which to select troops for training; for peacetime police, guard, and frontier garrison duties; and for service in wartime armies.

The new system was modeled on the institutions that inspired it—the military apparatus of Tang China. Contrary to the images that still dominate many popular histories, however, the *ritsuryō* armed forces, like most components of the imperial polity, represented a careful Japanese *adaptation*, not a wholesale adoption, of the Chinese system. And they were later abolished, not because they had been impractical from the start, but because the military and political demands of the late eighth century differed from those of a hundred years earlier.

One of the difficulties the government faced was enforcing its conscription laws. Under the *ritsuryō* polity, military conscription was simply one of many kinds of labor tax, and induction rosters were compiled from the same population registers used to levy all other forms of tax. For this reason, peasant efforts to evade any of these taxes also placed them beyond the reach of the conscription authorities. Military reforms during the eighth and subsequent centuries are therefore closely analogous to the government's reshaping of its general tax structure and tax-collection mechanisms during the same period.

Far more important than the reluctance of peasants to serve in the military, however, were the fundamental tactical limitations of the imperial armies. Like their Tang archetypes, the regiments that formed the backbone of *ritsuryō* armies were mixed-weapons system forces: predominantly infantry, but augmented by heavily armored archers on horseback. This infantry-heavy balance was the product of both design and necessity.

Large-scale, direct mobilization of the peasantry offered the imperial state planners part of the answer to both of the threats that concerned them (a Chinese invasion and regional insurrections led by the old provincial chieftains). The system they created enabled the court both to corner the market on military manpower—incorporating all or most of the bodies that could be drawn off to serve as soldiers into the state's armed forces—and to create loyalist armies of daunting size, thereby effectively closing the door on military challenges to court power or authority. An army of imposing numbers was also precisely what would have been needed to cope with a foreign invasion; while a militia structure made it possible for a tiny country like Japan to muster large-scale fighting forces when necessary without bankrupting its economic and agricultural base—as a large standing army would have. But the court had opted for size at the expense of the elite technology of the age, choosing a military force composed primarily of infantry, while the premier military technology of the day was mounted archery, not foot soldiers.

The government did try to create as large a cavalry force as it could, but efforts to that end ran afoul of major logistical difficulties. Foremost among these was the simple truth that fighting from horseback, particularly with bows and arrows, demanded complex skills that required years of training and practice to master. It was just not practical to attempt to develop cavalrymen from short-term peasant conscripts. The court addressed this problem through the straightforward expedient of staffing its cavalry units only with men who had acquired basic competence at mounted archery on their own.

This policy had far-reaching consequences for the shape of military things to come in Japan. It meant, first, that only a small portion of the imperial armies could be cavalry. It also meant that the cavalry would be drawn exclusively from the elite ranks of Japanese society—for if the prerequisite to becoming a cavalryman was skill with bow and horse prior to induction, cavalrymen could come only from families that kept horses, a practice that did not spread beyond the nobility and the very top tiers of the peasantry until the tenth century or later.

None of this mattered a great deal initially: the *ritsuryō* military structure was more than adequate to the tasks for which it was designed. But by the middle of the eighth century, the political climate—domestic and foreign—had changed enough to render the provincial regiments anachronistic and superfluous in most of the country.

The Chinese invasion the Japanese so feared simply never materialized. Whatever real peril there might have been ended by the late 670s, when the kingdom of Silla forced the Tang out of the Korean peninsula and checked its eastward expansion. Later, a rebellion (lasting from 756 to 763) by a Turkish general named An Lu-shan shook the Tang dynasty to its foundations, making it abundantly clear to the Japanese that the danger of Chinese warships approaching their shores was past. The likelihood of violent challenges to the central polity from the regional nobility had also dwindled rapidly, as former provincial chieftains came to accept the *ritsuryō* structure as the arena in which they would compete for wealth and power. The passing of these crises all but ended the need to field large armies and prompted the court to begin restructuring its armed forces.

In nearly all parts of the country, the principal need for troops was for dealing with bandits and other criminals. Unwieldy infantry units based on the provincial regiments were not well suited to this type of work, which called for small, highly mobile squads that could be assembled and sent out to pursue marauders with a minimum of delay.

In the meantime, diminishing military need for the regiments encouraged officers and provincial officials to misuse the conscripts who manned them. As early as 704 the court was admonishing governors that soldiers were "not to be used for purposes other than those specified by statute." A 753 Council of State edict complained that provincial officials regularly "violate that law and use troops for private labor; soldiers throw away the bow and arrow, and attend instead to the plow."[2]

The court responded to these challenges with a series of adjustments, amendments, and general reforms. The first major change came in 719, when the numbers of regiments, officers, and soldiers were reduced nationwide, and eliminated entirely in three of the smallest provinces. By the 780s the government was grumbling that most of its troops were unfit for service, and ordered that "those already conscripted who so desire should be released, and the weak returned to their farms"; that "wealthy subjects skilled with the bow and horse" were to be sought out and inducted; and that future conscription be centered on "the sons of those with court rank but without posts and the sons and younger brothers of the idle rich" with cavalry skills or combat experience.[3] Finally, in 792, the court declared that the regimental system had become more trouble than it was worth: "Our soldiers exist for emergencies, yet in recent years provincial officials and regimental officers have used them unreasonably, thus wasting public funds and revealing themselves to be evil officials. . . . Henceforth, the regiments shall be abolished."[4]

The pattern of edicts issued from the 730s onward, then, indicates that the government had concluded that it was more efficient to rely on privately trained and equipped elites than to continue attempting to draft and train the general population. Accordingly, troops mustered from the peasantry played ever smaller roles in state military planning, while the role of elites expanded steadily across the eighth century. The provincial regiments were first supplemented by new types of forces and then eliminated entirely. In their place the court created a series of new military posts and titles that legitimized the use of personal martial resources on behalf of the state. In essence, the court moved from a conscripted, publicly trained military force to one composed of privately equipped professionals.

WARRIORS AND WAR BANDS

The expansive social and political changes taking shape during the Heian period spawned intensifying competition among the premier noble houses of the court, which in turn led to a private market for military resources, arising in parallel to the one generated by evolving government military policies. State and private needs thus intersected to create widening avenues to personal success for ambitious young men with military talents, and provincial elites and lower-ranking court nobles increasingly turned to military service as a path to the entourages of powerful aristocrats and lucrative government posts. The result was the emergence of a new order of warriors in both the capital and the provinces. An early-eleventh-century text describes the archetypical member of this order:

> The greatest warrior in the land, he is highly skilled in the conduct of battles, night attacks, archery duels on horseback, and ambushes; in shining for deer,[5] and in all forms of mounted and standing archery. . . . He is, moreover, a heavenly gifted genius in the arts of donning armor, bearing bow and arrow, taking up his spear, and using a sword; in flying banners and setting up shields; and in directing companies and leading troops. A fierce and courageous man of great martial skill, he is known to emerge victorious from every battle site; he has yet to know the shame of submission to an enemy.[6]

Among the key players in early samurai development were the *zuryō*, the middle-ranked court nobles whose careers centered on appointments to provincial government offices. Compelled by the desire to maximize the profits that could be squeezed from taxpayers, and by a need to defend themselves and their prerogatives against outlawry and armed resistance, many governors began to include "warriors of ability" among the personal entourages that accompanied them to their provinces of appointment. A few also took up arms for themselves, established reputations as military troubleshooters, and curried the patronage of the higher nobility, and recognition by the state, by serving as bodyguards, police, and soldiers. By the tenth century, military service at court and service as a provincial official had become parallel and mutually supportive careers for many *zuryō* families, which were increasingly identified as warrior houses.

Two of the most illustrious warrior names of the Heian age, Taira and Minamoto, had their beginnings in efforts to prune the imperial family tree and dispose of extraneous princes and princesses. There were seventeen major lines of Minamoto and four of Taira, all descended from different emperors. Branches of two of these—the Seiwa Genji, deriving from Emperor Seiwa (reigned 858–876), and the Kanmu Heishi, descended from Emperor Kanmu (reigned 781–806)—became famous as warrior houses.

From the late tenth to the early twelfth century, warriors of Minamoto descent dominated the military world of the capital owing to a combination of martial prowess and a hereditary client relationship with the Fujiwara regents. But Genji preeminence peaked during the eleventh century with the careers of Yoriyoshi (995–1082) and his son Yoshiie (1041–1108), and then waned considerably over the next few generations. In the meantime, during the late 1090s, Taira Masamori managed to establish for himself and his family a patron-client relationship with successive retired emperors similar to the one that existed between the Minamoto and the Fujiwara Regents House. By the second decade of the twelfth century, the strength of this new alliance had brought the Taira to full parity of prestige with the Minamoto at court.

In the countryside, warriors emerged both from families that derived from the old provincial nobility or other longtime provincial elites, and from cadet branches of central court houses that had established bases in the provinces. The latter competed with longer-established provincial elites, but they also formed alliances and intermarried with them.

Heian marriages were polygamous or serially monogamous and usually involved not just separate bedrooms but separate residences. Children reckoned descent primarily from their father and took his surname. But they were usually raised in their mother's home and inherited much of their material property from her. Often, moreover, when the bride's family was of significantly higher station than the groom's, the children—and sometimes the new husband—adopted the surname of the bride's father. As a result, court-derived surnames like Taira, Minamoto, and Fujiwara gradually supplanted those of the older provincial noble families, and a large percentage of families that, strictly speaking, belong to the second group appear instead in the genealogies of the first.

As discussed in chapters 15 and 16, competition among provincial residents, governors, and court families, shrines, and temples for wealth and influence in the provinces gave rise to shifting alliances between members of these groups, as well as to the discovery that military force could be valuable in the game.

These developments, in turn, led warriors to arrange themselves into privately organized martial bands and networks.

Warriors began forming gangs by the middle of the ninth century—perhaps even earlier—and by the third decade of the tenth century, private military networks of substantial scale had begun to appear. Although the court initially opposed these developments, it soon realized that private military organizations could be useful as mechanisms for conscripting troops. By the mid-tenth century, the government had begun to co-opt private arrangements between warriors, transferring much of the responsibility for mustering and organizing the forces necessary for carrying out military assignments to warrior leaders, who could in turn delegate much of that responsibility to their own subordinates.

From the late eighth century onward, the court slowly groped and experimented its way toward a system that centered on commissioning professional warriors with new military titles legitimating their use of private martial resources on behalf of the state. Commissions such as *ōryōshi* ("envoy to subdue the territory"), *tsuibushi* ("envoy to pursue and capture"), *kebiishi* ("investigator of oddities"), and *tsuitōshi* ("envoy to pursue and strike down") held true to the spirit of the eighth-century military system in most respects. Appointments and compensation alike came from the center, following principles and procedures that closely paralleled those specified for comparable posts under the *ritsuryō* codes. These essential similarities enabled the court to retain exclusive authority over—and at least general control of—military affairs throughout the Heian period. But the new offices fundamentally differed from their *ritsuryō* antecedents on one critical point: They were premised not on the existence of a publicly conscripted pool of manpower over which the officer's commission gave charge, but on the appointee's ability to recruit troops for himself.

Curiously, the court established no statutory guidelines for drafting or otherwise raising troops immediately after it dismantled the provincial regiments in 792. For most of the ninth century, troop mobilizations remained grounded in public authority, but were conducted through ad hoc means. Responsibility for mustering fighting men as the need arose rested with provincial governors; the specific manner in which this was to be accomplished varied from case to case, but generally involved drafting the necessary manpower on the basis of the general corvée obligations required of all imperial subjects. This notion of public military service and induction based on public duties remained alive throughout the early medieval era, but by the middle of the tenth century, recruitment had become largely privatized, with "government" troops enlisted and mobilized through private chains of command.

Private military organizations during the Heian period tended to be patchwork assemblages of several types of forces. Leading warriors in both the provinces and the capital maintained relatively small, core bands of fighting men who were direct economic dependents of the warriors, lived in homes in or very near the warriors' compounds, and were at their more or less constant disposal. Manpower for these entourages came from a variety of sources. Some troops were sons or close relatives of the organization's leader; others were simply hired. For major campaigns, samurai also mobilized the cultivators, woodsmen, fishermen, and other residents of the lands in and around the estates and districts they administered. Such men were, strictly speaking, not under the warrior's control, but they often leased land from him, borrowed tools and seed from him, and conducted trade at his compound, making his residence an important economic center for them. By exploiting whatever political and economic leverage they could bring to bear on these semidependents, warriors could assemble armies numbering in the hundreds.

Larger armies had to be knit together through networks based on alliances of various sorts between samurai leaders of different sociopolitical status. This technique made it possible for warriors to assemble forces that involved thousands of troops.

Nevertheless, the standout feature of Heian-era warrior alliances was their fragility. Unlike the land commendation arrangements through which estates (*shōen*) were formed (see chapter 16), alliances between warriors were not supported by legal contracts, and the exchange of obligations that accompanied warrior partnerships was vague, tenuous, and in most cases short-lived. The larger the organization, the more ephemeral it tended to be because the integrity of Heian military networks was only as strong as the members' perceptions that affiliation worked to their advantage. Warrior leaders could count on the services of their followers only to the extent that they were able to offer suitably attractive compensation—or, conversely, to impose suitably daunting sanctions for refusal.

The ability to bestow rewards depended on a number of factors. Some of these factors, such as government posts or administrative positions on private estates, were relatively stable and could even be inherited. Others, such as personal military skills and reputation or connections at court, were more elusive. Similarly, the rewards offered could take many forms, including help in securing government posts or managerial positions on private estates, division of spoils from successful campaigns, and intercession with provincial governors or other higher authorities on behalf of one's followers.

Warrior allegiances were further circumscribed by the multitiered hierarchical structure of the military networks to which they belonged. Most of the provincial warriors in the organizations of prominent samurai had vassals of their own, and many of the members of those organizations, in turn, had followers. The loyalties of lower-ranking figures to those at the top of this complex hierarchy were tenuous at best, being buffered at each interceding level by the allegiances of their higher-ups.

And ethics and ideology were of suprisingly little help in holding early warrior alliances together. For the most part, early medieval warriors viewed loyalty as a commodity predicated on adequate remuneration, rather than an obligation transcending self-interest.

A warrior order organized into private military networks is visible in Japanese historical sources by the late ninth century. By the mid-tenth century, privately trained and equipped fighting men had been handed a near-monopoly over the country's martial resources. The evolution of military posts during the Heian period and the emergence of the samurai across the same span of time were, in fact, reciprocal processes: deputizing provincial elites and members of the middle and lower central aristocracy inevitably helped catalyze the development of private martial resources under these leaders, which in turn led to the introduction of new assignments and the modification of existing ones.

Nevertheless, although historians once equated the appearance of the samurai with the collapse of court rule, more recent scholarship makes it clear that military power in Japan became privatized and decentralized long before governing power did. In fact, court enfranchisement of private warriors from very early on worked, paradoxically, to keep connections between the military and political hierarchies thin for many centuries thereafter. The nascent warrior order of the Heian age—comprised mainly of lower-tier central nobles and elite residents of the provinces—was constrained from without by the same public (state) and private (court noble) political and economic policies that encouraged its development, and from within by the inability of its members to forge secure and enduring bonds with one another.

Heian warriors still looked to the center and the civil ladder for success, and viewed the profession of arms largely as a means to an end, identifying more strongly with their nonmilitary social peers than with warriors above or below them in the political hierarchy. Japan remained firmly under civil authority; there was no power vacuum into which incipient warlords could rush, and little warrior class-consciousness to incite a warrior revolution.

Sources and Suggestions for Further Reading

See the bibliography for complete publication data.

Adolphson, Mikael S. *The Teeth and Claws of the Buddha: Monastic Warriors and Sōhei in Japanese History* (2007).

Farris, William Wayne. *Heavenly Warriors: The Evolution of Japan's Military, 500–1300* (1992).

Friday, Karl. *The First Samurai: The Life and Legend of the Warrior Rebel Taira Masakado* (2008).

———. *Hired Swords: The Rise of Private Warrior Power in Early Japan* (1992).
———. "Pushing Beyond the Pale: The Yamato Conquest of the Emishi and Northern Japan" (1997).
———. *Samurai, Warfare, and the State in Early Medieval Japan* (2004).
Goble, Andrew Edmund. "War and Injury: The Emergence of Wound Medicine in Medieval Japan" (2005).
Ikegami, Eiko. *The Taming of the Samurai: Honorific Individualism and the Making of Modern Japan* (1995).
McCullough, Helen C. "A Tale of Mutsu" (1964).
Rabinovitch, Judith N. *Shōmonki: The Story of Masakado's Rebellion* (1986).
Varley, H. Paul. *Warriors of Japan as Portrayed in the War Tales* (1994).
Wilson, William R. "The Way of the Bow and Arrow: The Japanese Warrior in the Konjaku Monogatari" (1973).

Notes

1. *Ryō no gige,* p. 192.
2. *Shoku Nihongi,* 704 6/3; *Ruijū sandaikyaku,* 2:553 (753 10/21 *daijōkanpu*).
3. *Shoku Nihongi,* 780 3/16, 783 6/6, 788 3/3.
4. *Ruijū sandaikyaku,* 2:547–548 (792 6/7 *daijōkanpu*).
5. "Shining for deer" (*tomoshi*) is a style of hunting at night in which torches were used to locate deer. The eyes of a deer are highly reflective and appear to glow in the dark when struck by even small amounts of light (this same phenomenon can be observed today when driving at night past deer by the side of the road), making them easy targets for hunters equipped with torches, who need only shoot at the glowing eyes. Poachers today still use this technique, substituting flashlights for torches.
6. "Shin sarugakki," 138.

18

The Kamakura Shogunate and the Beginnings of Warrior Power

Andrew Edmund Goble

The Kamakura Shogunate (or Kamakura Bakufu) was founded by Minamoto Yoritomo and lasted for almost 150 years, from 1185 to 1333. It was the first of three successive warrior governments that held varying degrees of national political hegemony for some seven hundred years, until the Meiji Restoration of 1868. Kamakura leaders developed the foundations of administration, a legal culture, and an ethos of warrior rule that served as the models for warrior governance. In fact, the Kamakura regime is distinguished by its success in civil administration. Nevertheless, since warfare was responsible both for the creation and the destruction of the shogunate, the regime also highlights a significant cultural difference between the classical Heian period and the medieval era: from the Kamakura era on, violence became an accepted political tool.

THE 1150s AND THE TAIRA ASCENDENCY

The 1150s marked a significant turning point in Japanese history. During that decade the ruling oligarchy of the imperial family and civil aristocracy, which had ruled over an essentially peaceful country since the 670s, lost the ability to control the activities of a segment of the nation's warrior class. Concomitantly, some warriors now perceived new opportunities for carving out their own niche within the structure of government.

Until the 1150s, neither the rural elites—who served as civil functionaries, upholders of authority, land managers, landholders, leaders of local society, and men-at-arms—nor the Kyoto-based warrior aristocrats, who led military forces in the service of the oligarchy, opposed the ruling aristocracy. There was little sense of a national "warrior identity," and there were no national warrior leaders. But in 1156, and again in 1159, political developments in Kyoto altered some of these dynamics, to the benefit of warriors.

In the 1150s a complex set of rivalries emerged over the issue of succession to the imperial throne. Always of great interest, over the centuries, that issue served as the catalyst for significant changes in the power structure and access to resources. That someone from within the imperial family would succeed was not an issue, since only its members were eligible. The issue was *which* imperial would succeed, with the only reliable rule being that he had to be living. Most monarchs were sons or grandsons of previous emperors, but this was a convention and not an absolute requirement. The succession issue in the 1150s was further complicated by the fact that the reigning emperor was rarely the head of the imperial family. That role was performed by a retired emperor, who was usually the father or grandfather of the reigning emperor. It was possible for more than one former emperor to be alive at one time, and every retired emperor sought to ensure that future succession went through his own line.

While the details need not detain us here, in 1156 a succession dispute broke out between the reigning emperor, Go-Shirakawa, and his half-brother, the retired emperor Sutoku. Sutoku and his adviser, Fujiwara Yorinaga, mobilized troops commanded by Minamoto Tameyoshi that were met by forces loyal to Emperor Go-Shirakawa and led by Taira Kiyomori and Tameyoshi's son Yoshitomo. Following a brief but bloody round of fighting (later known as the Hōgen Incident, after the calendar era in which it occurred), Go-Shirakawa's side prevailed. In the aftermath, Kiyomori reaped the lion's share of the rewards, much to the chagrin of Yoshitomo, who had even been compelled to execute his father and most of his brothers, who were loyal to Sutoku. Yoshitomo's resentment festered, erupting three years later when he and Kiyomori once more used Kyoto as a battleground in what became known as the Heiji Incident (again after the calendar era). This time, however, warriors fought under their own authority, without the permission of their civil masters.

The Heiji Incident of 1159, then, had (for our purposes) two main legacies. First, it introduced a new culture of violence. In the course of the fighting, palaces were torched; unarmed courtiers were cut down; defenseless court women were trampled, drowned, and burnt to death; heads of defeated enemies were gruesomely displayed in public. This shocking assault on the nonviolent conventions of civility that had governed the court for centuries, a blow against which it had no physical or mental defense, left a lasting psychological scar on the aristocracy.

The second legacy was the realization by Taira Kiyomori that warriors now had a role in court politics and that he controlled those warriors. That said, he did not support greater authority for provincial warriors. Instead, he became a new stakeholder in the existing central aristocratic polity, and he built the same type of patronage and family networks familiar to Kyoto power brokers: He obtained provincial governorships for himself and supporters, acquired provincial land rights, built marriage ties to the imperial family (Emperor Antoku was his grandson), and seems to have seen new opportunities for wealth from overseas trade. The Taira prospered. But Kiyomori's success engendered resentment, which came to a head in the late 1170s. Kiyomori responded boldly to challenges to his influence—incarcerating or executing plotters in 1177, putting the emperor under house arrest in 1179, briefly relocating the capital and executing an imperial prince in 1180, and permitting the incineration of the religious center of Nara in 1181.

Because Kiyomori died in 1181 and his successors were destroyed in 1185, it is not clear what future direction this new "warrior power" might have taken had the Taira continued as a dominant force in the Kyoto oligarchy. Nevertheless, Kiyomori's regime did demonstrate that military force could be used to underpin political power. Ironically, that very demonstration proved to be his undoing.

THE 1180s: CIVIL WAR AND THE FOUNDING OF THE SHOGUNATE

In 1180 Imperial Prince Mochihito sent a message, randomly distributed around the country, calling on warriors to rise against the Taira—and was executed for his trouble. Moreover, his plea fell largely on deaf ears, because warrior society was not an organized entity and because warriors were deeply embedded in an administrative structure that largely secured rather than undermined their social and economic base.

One recipient of Mochihito's call to arms, however, was Minamoto Yoritomo, who had been sent into exile in eastern Japan in 1159 following the execution of his father, Yoshitomo. Separated from his surviving siblings and nursing a grudge against Kiyomori, prior to 1180 he had no realistic prospect of changing his circumstances. Still, he was of distinguished lineage, had spent two decades gaining an extensive knowledge of eastern warrior society, and had married Hōjō Masako, eldest daughter of his most recent warrior guardian. These turned out to be substantial assets.

Using the call to arms from Mochihito as a pretext for action, he spent months building support for what we can reconstruct now as a radical new vision, predicated on the assumption that a united eastern warrior society could protect itself from outside interference. The result was the establishment of an autonomous warrior regime, headed by Yoritomo, that guaranteed existing property rights and promised new awards for loyal service to warriors who backed his cause.

Given that all previous warrior-led challenges to central authority had ended in utter failure, it is perhaps no surprise that Yoritomo initially enjoyed only limited backing. Thus when he initiated military action in the eighth month of 1180, it was a high-stakes gamble. Defeated in his first major battle, he nonetheless managed to rally sufficient support over the next two months to establish a permanent base in the seaside village of Kamakura and to defeat a Taira army sent from Kyoto. This was to be the last direct external military challenge that he ever had to face, and his victory meant that until late 1183, he was able to devote his resources to consolidating his authority in the east.

The major factor ensuring Yoritomo's freedom from external threat was that his uprising inspired others. Following news of his successes, numerous local warriors, especially those descended from Minamoto forebears, rose against Taira authority. Yoritomo's cousin Kiso Yoshinaka began his own long-term and far more active campaign to unseat the Taira in Kyoto; and the Taira, previously able to rely on administrative mechanisms to exercise its power, was forced to devote attention and resources to strengthening its strategic base in central and western Japan. These activities were, in essence, pursued separately from Yoritomo's own eastern project.

Scholars have yet to explain with convincing nuance the underlying tensions that must have existed in this situation: a multistranded civil war, emerging seemingly out of nowhere, in which several actors simultaneously pursued disparate goals. There also seems to have been no consistent overarching goal, and it is difficult to argue that what we know to have been the outcome, the establishment by Yoritomo of the first shogunate, was a predictable result. What is clear, however, is that the Kyoto aristocracy had become something of a bystander to national events and that warriors had now fully arrived on the historical stage.

The civil war may be conceptualized as moving through three broad and somewhat overlapping phases. In phase one, lasting from 1180 to late 1184, Yoritomo endeavored to establish his authority firmly in eastern Japan. By the end of 1180 he had rebelled, established a headquarters at a highly defensible location that grew to become the city of Kamakura, and defeated a Taira punitive expedition. For the next few years he built up his administrative apparatus, recruiting civil officials to run it, creating a self-legitimating documentary regime that asserted his de facto supreme title to land enjoyed by eastern warriors, and developing Kamakura into Japan's first new, purposely built city in nearly four hundred years. He also asserted his authority through bloodshed. Warriors who killed their lords in the hopes of currying favor with him were executed; those who followed his orders might be killed on his command if the result of following those orders ignited controversy; those suspected of plotting against him were eliminated; and those who actually declared against him were hunted down to their deaths. By the end of 1184 Yoritomo had an iron grip on eastern warriors, many of whom benefited directly from the elimination of individuals and families that had been long-standing local rivals.

Phase two involved two broad elements. The first, from early 1181, involved Taira moves to gain control of the Inland Sea, and thus western Japan, between Kyoto and the trading port of Hakata. The Taira created new base areas and took military action against warrior families that, acting independently rather than in concert, declared against the Taira. The results were mixed, but overall the Taira maintained hegemony in the west until early 1185. The second element was a contest between the Taira and Yoritomo's cousin Kiso Yoshinaka over possession of Kyoto, a struggle that involved repeated efforts by both sides to gain strategic control of the Japan Sea coast to Kyoto's north. Allowing for hiatuses stemming from a shortage of supplies caused by successive years of crop failure and famine, the fighting between the two sides was the most identifiable sustained military activity through the end of 1183. That contest ended when Yoshinaka drove the Taira from Kyoto. Flush with victory and with physical control over the imperial family, he turned his strategic attention on Yoritomo, thus opening another phase of the civil war.

This third phase was initiated by Yoshinaka but driven by Yoritomo's perception that, while he had successfully established his authority in the east and made no moves beyond it, that authority would not remain permanent unless he eliminated every possible military threat. From late 1183 through early 1185 his expeditionary armies mounted campaigns first against Yoshinaka, then against the Taira, with the single aim of destroying both. Although this goal was ambitious, Yoritomo could rely on armies comprising warrior families bound to him as subordinates and beneficiaries, and unlike his enemies, he had not had to squander his resources during the preceding three years.

In the first few months of 1184, Yoritomo's brothers Yoshitsune and Noriyori killed Yoshinaka and destroyed his forces, routed the Taira decisively at the battle of Ichinotani (the first main-force encounter between them since 1180), and achieved total control of Kyoto. As a result Yoritomo became a new player in national politics and was in effect acknowledged by the court as its protector. The remainder of that year was given over to planning and political consolidation. In early 1185 Yoshitsune and Noriyori launched a two-pronged, land- and sea-based campaign along the shores of the Inland Sea. In the second month, Yoshitsune's forces destroyed the Yashima base on the island of Shikoku, and in the following month, Noriyori's forces destroyed the remaining Taira leadership in the sea battle of Dan-no-ura. With this victory, Yoritomo achieved national hegemony.

Thus the civil war that had been set off by Yoritomo's desire to set up an independent eastern regime had many strands, and developed a momentum of its own that progressively engulfed the entire country. In the end, Yoritomo emerged as military hegemon, and the shogunate as a new institution. But this could not have been predicted in 1180.

LEADERSHIP AND ITS CRISES

From 1185 until his death in 1199, Yoritomo ruled supreme. His administration based in Kamakura received the imprimatur of legitimacy from the court, enabling him to institutionalize his authority in a number of different ways. The court granted him authority to appoint provincial military constables (*shugo*) nationwide and conferred on him the title of shogun to acknowledge that he was the nation's preeminent warrior. There was de facto agreement that civil government in the east was under the aegis of the Kamakura administration, and it was tacitly acknowledged that any documents issued under his authority enjoyed full legal validity. These elements provided Yoritomo with a structural and legal framework that enabled him to oversee the primarily eastern warriors whose landholdings he had confirmed or to whom he distributed rewards for service.

Yoritomo died in 1199, having achieved unprecedented feats. His passing presented the shogunate with issues of leadership and institutional survival and continuity that were not resolved for a quarter of a century, after the founding generation had largely died off and a second generation of leaders had emerged.

The crisis of leadership had a number of elements. Apart from Yoritomo, there was no leader of the eastern warriors: The leading families saw themselves as equals and would not countenance one of their peers being made a Yoritomo replacement. Nevertheless, the shogunate had already become a valued institution that conferred many advantages on them. Yoritomo's two sons were thus natural candidates, and in succession inherited the mantle of organizational legitimacy, now symbolized by the title of shogun. But these youths had no experience or achievements of their own, and it was apparent that the longer-term survival of the shogunate would require additional guiding hands. Whose hands those would be was the most divisive political issue in the quarter-century after Yoritomo's death.

The story had many twists and turns, and it featured no little violence. In 1203, following the extirpation of his in-laws, the Hiki, by the Hōjō, the natal family of Yoritomo's widow, Masako, the second shogun, Yoriie, was ousted; he died suspiciously the following year. In 1205 the Hōjō patriarch was deposed by Masako and her younger brother, Yoshitoki, who became the new shogunal regent, retaining the position until his death in 1224. In 1213 an old-line warrior family, the Wada, was eliminated, which also enabled the Hōjō to expand its landholdings in key eastern provinces. In 1219 the second shogun, Sanetomo, was assassinated in broad daylight by his nephew, who was himself promptly killed.

With this the direct line of Yoritomo came to an end, ushering in a new crisis. In 1221 an ex-emperor attempted to rally warriors against the Hōjō, but met with complete failure. This fiasco, known as the Jōkyū War, confirmed both the authority of the shogunate and Hōjō hegemony over it. Using the position of shogunal regent as its institutional base, the Hōjō ruled as Japan's first warrior dynasty until 1333.

These events provide a schematic narrative for the emergence of Hōjō power, but not an adequate sense of who provided leadership after Yoritomo's death. While we may note the public prominence of males, periods of collective decision making involving leaders of several warrior families, and the important role of civil officials in keeping the shogunate running, the single most important figure appears to have been Hōjō Masako. Indeed, just as we credit Yoritomo for founding the shogunate, we may credit Masako with ensuring its survival. Important also is that between 1180 and her death in 1225, Masako was the only person we can identify who was continuously involved at the highest level of the Kamakura shogunate.

Masako was the eldest in a warrior family of fifteen siblings, and respectively seven and nineteen years older than her two brothers Yoshitoki and Tokifusa. Around 1177, against her father's wishes, she married Yoritomo. They had four children together. Entries in the *Mirror of the East* (*Azuma Kagami*) leave no doubt that Masako was considered a strong personality—by Yoritomo and everybody else. Having shared in Yoritomo's uprising from the outset—which meant accepting the possibility of death in the event of failure—she was almost certainly well apprised of the dynamics of eastern warrior society. And over the next two decades, her stature almost certainly increased. Upon Yoritomo's death she represented the foremost link with Yoritomo, his vision, and through her children, the future. She was the embodiment of the personal bonds forged between warrior leaders and Yoritomo, and at the very least, she enjoyed their respect as Yoritomo's long-term life partner. She was also the strongest-willed member of her natal family and the only reason it enjoyed prominence.

Few documents were issued under her name that hint that she possessed formal public powers, and we must necessarily be cautious in reading too much between the lines of events described in the *Mirror of the East*. Yet she seems to have been directly involved in all key events between 1199 and her death at age sixty-nine in 1225. In some instances she is known to have been the decisive voice, and it is difficult to imagine that she would not have been consulted on actions that might directly affect her immediate family. After taking holy orders (which among other things precluded remarriage and thus prevented any male figure from impinging on her stature), she was referred to as the "nun shogun," reflecting a contemporary perception of her significance.

BUREAUCRACY AND GOVERNING

Yoritomo's military and political actions were accompanied by a concerted effort to develop administrative organs through which he might rationalize and institutionalize his authority. Simply by virtue of establishing such organs, Yoritomo telegraphed his interest in stability and continuity of ruling structures. He sought to carve out a niche within existing structures of authority rather than replace or eliminate them. Like his contemporaries, Yoritomo was well aware that the issuing of administrative documents was one of the primary manifestations of authority.

Yoritomo had promised his followers that he would guarantee their land rights and had also held out the possibility that he would disburse further benefits. Thus we find him recognizing existing property rights; acknowledging bequests as legally valid documents; investing his new vassal corps, the Kamakura housemen (*gokenin*), with the title of land steward (*jitō*), which served as the supervening umbrella appointment for whatever existing property rights in a given location a warrior already possessed; and awarding additional property confiscated from his opponents. In most cases this meant that Yoritomo, while not overturning existing hierarchies of land ownership, inserted his own authority within those hierarchies, in effect creating multiple lines of legal jurisdiction wherever his housemen owned land. In time, this spurred the development of a new phenomenon within warrior society, that of legal culture.

As we might expect, the need to issue documents, and the number of documents issued, increased in tandem with Yoritomo's military and political successes. The most important documents were, naturally enough, those written and signed by himself; Yoritomo retained his discretionary right to issue any document at any time on any matter throughout his lifetime. But his authority was also institutionalized through the documents issued by his administrative organs, which obviously drew their initial authority from him. Over time (and particularly after Yoritomo's death) these offices came to enjoy their own institutional legitimacy.

The core administrative functions were defined by three offices established by 1185: the Samurai Office (Samurai dokoro), the Chancellery (Mandokoro), and the Judicial Office (Monchūjo). The Samurai Office was always headed by a warrior. The other two entities, more obviously bureaucratic, were at the outset staffed by highly educated civil officials, and the first generation of officials (most notably Ōe Hiromoto and Miyoshi Yasunobu) founded hereditary bureaucrat families that served the shogunate until its demise in 1333.

The Samurai Office, while the least documented of the three organs, was responsible for two main tasks. First, it kept registers of vassals based on province of origin, size of family, how frequently they performed required duties, and which current obligations were owed. Second, the office usually worked through the provincial military constable (*shugo*) for each province to summon vassals for periodic guard duty in Kamakura (later this service could also be performed in Kyoto), muster them for military or peacekeeping duty, and process claims for rewards.

The Chancellery and Judicial Office were the civil administrative heart of the shogunate. The Chancellery was responsible for issuing most of the shogunate's public documents, in the names of the shogun or the Hōjō regent. The Judicial Office was responsible for drafting various laws and regulations, but its most significant role was to provide the administrative and documentary framework by which the shogunate developed its core governing function as an arbitrator of civil disputes. The Judicial Office received documents from litigants, required defendants to reply to charges, collated the rejoinders between the parties, assembled case files to be heard by higher councils and courts, and wrote out in legal Chinese (which enjoyed a functional role akin to that of Latin in western Europe) the resulting decisions.

The hereditary bureaucrat families were also responsible for, or at least interpreted their charge as, maintaining the official records of the shogunate. Since so much seems to have been incinerated with the destruction of Kamakura in 1333, we have only an incomplete picture of what those records contained. But at a minimum they comprised anything relating to the family functions of the bureaucrats, as well as sufficient general information to have made possible the completion of the shogunate's own official history, the *Mirror of the East.*

KAMAKURA'S ETHOS OF GOVERNING

While founded on the basis of military force, Kamakura's institutional continuity owed a great deal to its successful transition from upstart center of power to familiar source of authority. One element that symbolized that transition was the conscious development of a governing ethos, reflected in the actions and written legacy of some members of the second generation of Hōjō leaders, who came to power in the mid-1220s. The two most prominent figures in this process were the half-brothers Yasutoki (1183–1242) and Shigetoki (1198–1261).

Between them, they occupied the most important leadership posts in the shogunate for almost thirty-five years, from 1221 to 1256. They also produced two landmark documents, Yasutoki's 1232 *Goseibai shikimoku*, and Shigetoki's *Gokurakuji Letter* of circa 1260, that articulated the intellectual basis of warrior governance. Here I comment on the former.

Yasutoki's *Goseibai shikimoku* is a fifty-one-article law code designed as a guide to adjudicating the many disputes involving warriors that had come to be channeled through the shogunate's legal system. As the first law code created by warriors, it reflected the common sense of warrior society. Although not systematically organized, and though including matters that would today be separately classed as civil or criminal law, it covers a range of topics: respect for divine authority, appointments at the imperial court, duties of officeholders, penalties for crimes, inheritance rights, and the circumstances under which family members may or may not be held jointly liable for crimes. The third of the document that deals with matters of property and inheritance reveals, among other things, the extensive legal prerogatives enjoyed by women in warrior society at this juncture.

The *Goseibai shikimoku* is informed by a general sense that actual decisions should be made, not by mechanical application of rules, but by a thorough understanding of the context in which an action occurred, with an eye to fairness and equity. That sense is reinforced through an oath, signed by all members of the Council of State, that Yasutoki had established at the beginning of his regency. The signatories promise to render judgment fairly and to avoid self-interest or conflict of interest. Lastly, two letters sent by Yasutoki to Shigetoki (then the shogunate representative in Kyoto) emphasize that laws and judgments must accord with the times and with social circumstances, and that in all matters, *dōri* (common sense and reasonableness) should prevail.

In sum, Japan's first warrior government emerged as the result of a series of events that could not have been predicted. Although the Kamakura Shogunate was founded as the result of military action, from the second generation of leaders its survival as an institution owed much to successful development of institutions and an ethos of civil administration. Yet, while the Kamakura shogunate was a successful administrative entity, its procedural mechanisms were unable to contain a perfect storm of social, economic, and political tensions that fused in the early fourteenth century, bringing about the violent demise of the shogunate.

Sources and Suggestions for Further Reading

See the bibliography for complete publication data.

Collcutt, Martin. "Nun Shogun: Politics and Religion in the Life of Hōjō Masako (1157–1225)" (2002).

Goble, Andrew Edmund. "The Kamakura *Bakufu* and Its Officials" (1985).

Mass, Jeffrey P. *The Development of Kamakura Rule, 1180–1250: A History with Documents* (1979).

———. *Yoritomo and the Founding of the First Bakufu* (1999).

Shinoda, Minoru. *The Founding of the Kamakura Shogunate, 1180–1185; with selected translations from the* Azuma Kagami (1960).

Varley, H. Paul. "The Hōjō Family and Succession to Power" (1982)

PART IV

Demesne, Dominion, and Diffusion in the Medieval Age

936–1388	Koryŏ kingdom in Korea
1115–1234	Jin dynasty in China
1175	Hōnen founds the Jōdo shū (Pure Land School) sect of Buddhism
1180–1185	Genpei Wars
1202	Eisai founds Kennin-ji; beginning of Rinzai Zen sect in Japan
1221	Jōkyū War
1224	Shinran completes the *Kyōgyō shinshō*; beginning of Jōdo Shinshū (True Pure Land School) sect of Buddhism
1233	Dōgen founds Kōshōji; beginning of Sōtō Zen sect in Japan
1238	Great Buddha at Kamakura completed
1253	Nichiren begins lecturing on *Lotus Sutra*; beginning of Nichiren sect of Buddhism
1274	First Mongol invasion
1279–1368	Yuan dynasty in China
1281	Second Mongol invasion
1299	Shogunate establishes Gozan ("Five Mountain") network of Zen temples
1317	Bunpō Compromise for alternate succession between competing branches of imperial house
1331	Emperor Go-Daigō exiled to Ōki island
C. 1332	Yoshida Kenkō completes *Tsurezure-gusa* (*Essays in Idleness*)
1333	Go-Daigō escapes from exile on Ōki
1333	Kamakura Shogunate destroyed
1334	Go-Daigō proclaims "Kenmu Revolution"
1336	Ashikaga Takauji deposes Go-Daigō; Go-Daigō establishes rival imperial court in Yoshino
1336–1392	Nanbokuchō Wars

1338	Ashikaga Takauji becomes Seii taishōgun; Muromachi (Ashikaga) Shogunate established
1343	Kitabatake Chikafusa completes *Jinnō shōtōki* (*A Chronicle of Gods and Sovereigns*)
1350–1352	Kannō Disturbance
C. 1363	Motokiyo Zeami, playwright and Noh actor, born
1368–1644	Ming dynasty in China
1369	Ashikaga Shogunate establishes trade relations with Ming China
1392	Southern Court defeated; end of Nanbokuchō era
1392–1897	Chosŏn kingdom in Korea
1397	Trade relations established with Chosŏn
1397	Ashikaga Yoshimitsu builds the Golden Pavilion
1402	Ashikaga Yoshimitsu invested by Ming emperor as King of Japan
1404	Tally trade with Ming begins
1423	Shō Hashi unifies the Kingdom of Ryūkyū
1467–1477	Ōnin War
1489	Ashikaga Yoshimasa builds the Silver Pavilion
1543	Arrival of first Portuguese; introduction of harquebus firearms
1549	Arrival of first Jesuit missionaries
1560	Battle of Okehazama
1568	Oda Nobunaga enters Kyoto as champion of Ashikaga Yoshiaki
1570	Battle of Anegawa
1571	Oda Nobunaga burns Enryakuji
1573	Last Ashikaga shogun deposed
1575	Battle of Nagashino
1582	Oda Nobunaga assassinated; Toyotomi Hideyoshi takes power
1585	Toyotomi Hideyashi named imperial regent (*kanpaku*)
1588	Ashikaga Shogunate formally dissolved
1588	Toyotomi Hideyoshi orders first nationwide sword hunts
1592	Toyotomi Hideyoshi orders invasion of Korea
1597	Toyotomi Hideyoshi orders second invasion of Korea
1598	Toyotomi Hideyoshi dies

19

Kamakura and the Challenges of Governance

Ethan Segal

In the late twelfth and early thirteenth centuries, warriors made some impressive accomplishments. They had, for the first time in centuries, created a viable, enduring government—the Kamakura Shogunate—that operated independently of the imperial capital at Kyoto. To lead that government, they transformed the position of shogun (formerly a temporary position) into a permanent, powerful office to be wielded by the nominal head of the regime. They gained the authority to place warriors on landed estates (*shōen*) and guarantee their positions. And they survived Retired Emperor Go-Toba's attempt to destroy them during the Jōkyū War of 1221, in the process garnering expanded powers to appoint retainers to estates and even select future emperors. It seems very unlikely that anyone living in the mid-twelfth century could have imagined how much stronger warriors' political positions would be merely one hundred years later.

Recognizing warriors' significant gains and their creation of a second capital in the eastern city of Kamakura, historians came to refer to the years of the first warrior government, from 1185 to 1333, as the Kamakura period. Today we concede that the term may be misleading: The old imperial government continued to function, and Kyoto and Kamakura made significant efforts to demarcate their respective realms. Kamakura was not the only seat of power, so most scholars now refer to government during this period as a diarchy. Still, warriors were very active in creating a host of new institutions that helped to define the period.

Among those was the shogunate's legal system, which made use of precedent, valued written documents, and helped keep many disputes in the courtroom and off the battlefield. Also established were administrative bodies such as the Board of Councilors (Hyōjōshū), created in 1225 to involve more warriors in governance. These institutions, and others described in the previous chapter, continued into the second half of the Kamakura period, providing some measure of stability. But significant challenges to effective rule also emerged in the late thirteenth century. Some of these challenges were external threats like the Mongols, who twice sent military expeditions to invade the Japanese islands. Others were domestic concerns that affected major segments of the population, such as the periodic famines that devastated peasant communities. Among warriors and nobles, the limited availability of land caused a decline in female property inheritance and forced men into conflict over their rights to landed income. These and other problems led to rising discontent focused on the Kamakura Shogunate by the early fourteenth century, and to its eventual destruction in 1333.

CHANGES IN LAND AND INHERITANCE

During the first half of the Kamakura period, the shogunate rewarded its retainers by giving them secure appointments to land. It is important to remember that in the twelfth and thirteenth centuries, there was no sharply delineated warrior "class." Rather, many of the men whom we identify as warriors also served as local officials, land managers, tax collectors, bureaucrats, and police. In the Heian period they were easily appointed to and removed from their positions by higher authorities, including the central government and the landowning nobility and religious houses. Thus, they were vulnerable and often lost their posts. Initially, Minamoto Yoritomo won adherents to his cause by promising to guarantee their job security. They could rely on him rather than worry that a noble or temple might suddenly deprive them of their positions. After Yoritomo's forces won the Genpei Wars (1180–1185), they secured authorization to appoint his followers to *jitō* posts on estates that had supported his defeated enemies.

This move started several decades of land redistribution as the Kamakura Shogunate followed Yoritomo's practice. The destruction of the Ōshū Fujiwara in 1189 and the Wada in 1213 and the defeat of Go-Toba's allies in 1221 were all followed by widespread redistribution of land rights from the losers to the victors. But as the thirteenth century progressed, fewer landholding families challenged the shogunate. Without rivals to vanquish (and their assets to confiscate), there were no lands for Kamakura to distribute as rewards. The last major warrior landholding family to challenge the Hōjō was the Miura. After its defeat in 1247, the shogunate had little opportunity to claim lands that it could give to faithful retainers. In addition, there was not much unclaimed land available except for tracts that would be difficult to bring under cultivation.

Matters were further complicated by warrior inheritance practices. Prior to the thirteenth century, warriors usually divided property equally among their children. This meant that, if a family had several children, each child's share would be only a fraction of the original family property. If a family's holding was divided equally among more than one or two children for several generations, the size of each parcel soon became too small to support its owner. Under these circumstances, warriors were bound to come into conflict with other landholders if they sought to increase the size of their holdings.

One response was a gradual change in inheritance practice. Families began choosing one primary heir, often the oldest son, to designate as the house head (*sōryō*). This individual might receive most or all of the family property and be instructed by his parents to provide for his siblings. In some cases, daughters were given "lifetime bequests"—property they could use to support themselves during their own lifetime but that would revert to the main family line when the woman died. These new inheritance practices emerged only slowly. Some families continued to follow the older practice of dividing property equally until as late as the fifteenth century. For those that switched, the new *sōryō* system had the advantage of concentrating land in the hands of one heir, thereby ensuring the economic viability of the main family line. But the daughters and sons not so chosen started losing the ability to own, manage, or pass on property to heirs of their choosing.

Another response to the shortage of available land was that warriors tried to take more than their designated share of income from private estates. Warriors appointed as *jitō* were paid a certain percentage of the estate's produce in exchange for their work as police and tax collectors. The amount they were paid was decided by estate custom or by the shogunate. But some *jitō* took advantage of their positions to appropriate more than their due. Because warriors' positions were guaranteed by Kamakura, they could not be disciplined or fired by the estate's authorities. If warriors began keeping too much of the rent, landholders' only option was to complain to Kamakura by taking the offenders to court. Many of the surviving documents from this period concern the legal battles between *jitō* and landholders. Because those judicial disputes often took years to settle and the outcomes were never certain, landowners began giving some of their rights to warriors in compromise agreements known as *wayo*. For example, in some cases a landowner would agree not to interfere with the *jitō*'s management of the estate in exchange for a guaranteed amount of income. In other compromise agreements, the *jitō* and the landowner might simply divide the estate in half, each asserting control over his share. Even in cases where the landowner won back control of his estate through the legal system, warriors could retaliate by becoming bandits, called *akutō,* who raided estates and challenged legal authorities for decades.

COMMONERS

The majority of the population did not consist of warriors, aristocrats, or priests. Instead, most people were peasants involved in agriculture, fishing, or other kinds of production. Many were involved in wet rice cultivation and had to hand over significant percentages of their crops to the various authorities that taxed them or charged them rent. Abuse of peasants by local warriors and other authorities was not uncommon, though since most peasants were illiterate, we have little evidence of what they thought about their lives. If they felt that taxes were too high or that estate managers or public officials were mistreating them, they could protest by absconding. This was an especially powerful weapon during planting and harvest times, since seeds could be planted only at certain times of the year and ripe crops left in the fields would spoil.

In a few instances, peasant communities petitioned higher authorities for relief. The most famous example is the 1275 petition of the Ategawa Estate peasants, who charged the local warrior with levying extra taxes, physically beating them, and mutilating their wives and children, among other abuses.

Peasant houses were rather crude, single-room dwellings with thatched-grass roofs, earthen floors, and little ability to control temperature. Diet was limited, especially during the winter months, and famine was a constant threat. The Kangi famine of 1229–1232, brought on by cold, wet weather, led to widespread starvation, banditry, and piracy. The stricken population in some areas took decades to recover to pre-famine levels. The Shōka famine of 1257–1260, probably triggered by volcanic activity, caused similar suffering as people died from malnutrition and disease. Yet by the late thirteenth century, some positive developments were beginning to take shape for the common people. Iron tools and farm animals such as oxen became more common, as did new, heartier varieties of rice. A few documents mention estates engaged in double-cropping—that is, collecting two harvests per year. These were small but positive steps that would eventually help the population grow from the fourteenth century onward.

Not all peasants worked in rice fields, of course. Some living along the coasts were involved in seafood or salt production. Others, where climate and geography permitted, raised silkworms, gathered nuts, made paper, or mined for metal ores. Small groups of artisans were located on various estates and in the cities, manufacturing goods from saddles and swords to furniture and works of art. A small number of traveling merchants, many of whom started out procuring goods for temples and shrines, facilitated trade. Their religious connections helped them to move more easily across political boundaries and offered them protection against competitors as well as greedy warriors. Trade was facilitated by the use of imported Chinese coins and the appearance of regional markets in the countryside, which allowed estate managers to sell some of their produce locally and start paying taxes in cash. Only a few estates took part in these activities, though, since even the most active markets opened just three times per month.

Finally, we must note that Buddhism made significant gains among the common folk during the Kamakura period. New sects such as Pure Land, True Pure Land, and Nichiren, as well as older sects including Tendai and Shingon, began successful efforts to appeal to the masses. These were due in part to doctrinal innovations that made it easier for common people to work toward enlightenment. For example, the Pure Land traditions taught that one did not need to become a professional monk or nun; instead, sincere expressions of faith in Amida could be sufficient to ensure one's rebirth in the Pure Land. Zen found support among the warrior class, and the new capital of Kamakura came to feature several important Zen temples. These critical economic and religious developments are addressed in other chapters of this volume, and so are only mentioned here in passing.

CONTENTIOUS POLITICS IN KYOTO AND KAMAKURA

By the mid-thirteenth century the Kamakura Shogunate had become an important political institution. It not only had authority over most of the country's warriors but had also begun to exercise power vis-à-vis Kyoto. Following the Jōkyū War of 1221, shogunate officials stationed a permanent ambassador in Kyoto (known as the Rokuhara *tandai*) with the job of monitoring the court. Kamakura also played a key role in determining who would be emperor. In 1242, when the previous emperor died without an heir, it selected Emperor Go-Saga over the preferred choice of the leading Kyoto aristocrats. Go-Saga, who reigned until 1246 and continued to wield influence as a retired sovereign until his death in 1272, was quite supportive of the shogunate. Some speculate that he may have been so amenable because he recognized that he owed his position to Kamakura. He even allowed one of his sons, Munetaka, to become the first imperial prince adopted by Kamakura to serve as shogun in 1252.

Yet it is important to remember that a dual polity ruled Japan during the Kamakura period: In addition to the warrior administration, the imperial court in Kyoto remained active. The imperial judicial system continued to function and handled all legal suits that did not involve Kamakura-affiliated warriors. The emperor and his nobles still issued laws, appointed governors to administer provincial public lands, and performed the important religious ceremonies intimately connected to Japanese notions of rulership. In theory, the emperor remained the highest authority in the land, and the shogun served him (though reality was quite different). Kyoto remained a major political center as well as the cultural and religious capital of the islands. It was also the country's largest city with an estimated population over 100,000. Kamakura was the second largest, probably home to 60,000 or more by the late thirteenth century.

Although Emperor Go-Saga appeared to be quite supportive of Kamakura during his lifetime, he left a conundrum for both capitals when he died in 1272 without clearly indicating which of his sons should succeed him as the dominant figure within the imperial family. Two of his sons had held the throne (Go-Fukakusa [reigned 1246–1259] and Kameyama [reigned 1259–1274]), and each believed that the imperial line should continue through him and his sons. Each faction had powerful supporters at court and came to be known by the major temples where later members of the lines resided: Go-Fukakusa's descendants were based at the Jimyō-in, whereas Kameyama's used Daikakuji as their headquarters. Their rivalry lasted for decades as members of each faction bickered over everything from political appointments and the distribution of landed estates to preferences for Chinese or Japanese artistic styles.

Ultimately, the shogunate decided on a compromise: The eldest son of each line would alternate, becoming emperor for ten years before giving the throne to his cousin. It is unclear why Kamakura favored this approach rather than simply choosing one line or the other. Perhaps shogunal leaders thought that a divided imperial family could pose no threat to Kamakura's dominance. Regardless of the reason, the imperial family remained divided in this way until the end of the Kamakura period. An interesting perspective on life at court and the fraught political climate of these years comes from a woman known as Lady Nijō, who served as an attendant to Retired Emperor Go-Fukakusa. Later she became an itinerant Buddhist nun and traveled much of the country, including to Kamakura. Her memoir reveals the personal sides of the most important leaders of the day.

Within Kamakura, it was not the shogun himself but rather the shogunal regent (*shikken*) who became the most important figure in the warrior capital. One reason the regent's office could dominate was that for most of these decades, the shogun was a young Fujiwara or imperial prince adopted from Kyoto. Although some shoguns tried to assert their authority, the regents were able to outmaneuver them. For example, when Hōjō Tokiyori became regent in 1246, he forced Shogun Yoritsune out of office when the latter tried to determine on his own who would hold certain offices. The office of shogunal regent was monopolized by members of the Hōjō family from its creation until the end of the period. Yet their rule was far from stable: Repeatedly they faced threats from other warriors who sought to claim the regency or even the shogun's title. These challenges led to violence and the destruction of many eastern warrior families, including the Miura, Nagoe, and Adachi, among others.

In the provinces, *jitō* and *shugo* remained important warrior posts. But there were divisions among warriors as well. Perhaps the most significant was between those who were shogunal retainers (known as *gokenin*) and those who lacked any formal connections to Kamakura. Only warriors who could prove that they (or their father or grandfather) had served the shogunate were able to utilize the Kamakura judicial system. Even among those who served the leading warrior clans, rivalries began to emerge between the *gokenin,* who owed their allegiance to the shogun, and others (*miuchibito*) who were private vassals of the head of the Hōjō family.

By the late 1270s, tensions between these groups were manifested in the hostility between two leading warriors, Adachi Yasumori and Taira Yoritsuna. Both men held prominent positions in government and were close to the shogunal regent, Hōjō Tokimune. Yasumori was the regent's father-in-law and a leading *gokenin,* while Yoritsuna was the regent's close confidant and the most influential *miuchibito.* Yoritsuna's forces attacked and killed Yasumori in 1285, claiming that Yasumori's heir had been plotting to claim the shogun's seat for himself. Many others close to the Adachi were killed, exiled, or chose to take their own lives out of loyalty to Yasumori. Yoritsuna briefly became the most influential figure in Kamakura, ruling autocratically, as the new shogunal regent (Tokimune had died in 1284), Hōjō Sadatoki, was still a teenager. But in 1293, a now mature Sadatoki ordered Yoritsuna killed. Ironically, the pretext was very similar to the one that Yoritsuna had used to eliminate Yasumori: that Yoritsuna plotted to make his son the next shogun. As these incidents suggest, politics was a dangerous game in the late Kamakura period.

THE MONGOL INVASIONS

In the midst of these complicated domestic political problems, a new concern arrived from overseas. Kublai Khan, who succeeded his grandfather Genghis Khan as leader of the Mongol Empire, had set his sights on ruling all of East Asia. His forces conquered Koryŏ (Korea) in 1259, but his primary goal was to conquer Song China. In 1266, he ordered Koryŏ representatives to accompany his envoy and convey a diplomatic letter to the Japanese. They arrived at Dazaifu, Japan's port on Kyushu for handling foreign merchants and diplomats, early in 1268. The letter proclaimed the greatness of the Mongol Empire, explained how the Koreans had "willingly" become subjects of the Mongols, and invited the Japanese to recognize the Mongols by sending a tribute mission. Although positive in tone for the most part, the letter ended by hinting that failure to comply might lead to military conflict.

Shogunal officials at Dazaifu forwarded the letter to Kamakura, which in turn sent it to the imperial court in Kyoto. Although the letter was addressed to the "king of Japan," which presumably meant the emperor, it was the shogunate that decided to ignore the missive. The Mongols sent several more diplomatic missions, but all were turned away without a formal reply from the Japanese. Meanwhile, the shogunate ordered *shugo* and *gokenin* with holdings in western Japan to begin preparing to defend against possible invasion. At the same time, Kublai Khan ordered the Koreans to start constructing a fleet of ships for his forces. After suppressing a short-lived Koryŏ uprising in 1271 and finding some success in their war against the Song in 1273, the Mongols began serious preparations for an attack on Japan.

The invasion force included both Mongol and Korean soldiers; it reached the Japanese archipelago in the late autumn of 1274. After conquering the small islands of Iki and Tsūshima, the invaders landed at Hakata Bay. The Japanese seem to have been hard-pressed to defeat them. Some sources suggest that Mongol tactics such as advancing in formation and using gongs and drums to signal advances and retreats proved difficult to counter for the Japanese, who favored individual combat. The Mongol forces withdrew after winning some skirmishes; legend claims that a storm forced them to retreat, though historians are dubious. Certainly neither side regarded the 1274 invasion as a Japanese victory. Kublai Khan sent another diplomatic mission to Dazaifu the following year, and the Japanese began preparing for an anticipated second invasion. They ordered the construction of a defensive wall around Hakata Bay, claimed the right to muster fighting men from all parts of the country, and even planned a preemptive strike on Korea in hopes of destroying the Mongol invasion fleet (though they did not carry this out).

The second invasion came in the summer of 1281. The Song dynasty had fallen to the Mongols two years earlier, so this new, larger invasion force included Chinese soldiers as well as Mongols and Koreans. Again the invaders landed at Hakata Bay, where the Japanese engaged them and a typhoon may have aided the defenders. Some primary sources mention rumors that the gods defended Japan from foreign invasion by sending "divine winds" (*kamikaze*), though other evidence suggests that the Japanese fought off the invasions without needing heavenly assistance. Regardless of the reason, the Mongol-led forces withdrew, though fears of a third invasion kept the Japanese in their defensive positions for decades to come.

Although the Japanese had prevented a Mongol victory, they were left with some significant problems in the wake of the invasions. The most pressing was that the shogunate had no new lands to distribute to those who fought on its behalf. Warriors expected to be rewarded for their service, but no lands were confiscated from the Mongols. This only added to the financial difficulties of many warriors, who had to bear on their own the costs of preparing for battle and traveling to Kyushu. A second problem was that the Hōjō took advantage of the crisis to place many of its own family members and close affiliates in key positions, such as the *shugo* posts for Kyushu's nine provinces. This move may have helped the Hōjō to monopolize important government plums, but it simultaneously alienated other warriors who were excluded from coveted shogunate posts.

THE KAMAKURA SHOGUNATE IN THE FOURTEENTH CENTURY

The position of the Kamakura shogunate as Japan's leading political institution must have appeared quite secure as it entered the 1300s. Its warriors had proven their staying power in the countryside as *jitō* positions were passed from parent to child. Kamakura warriors had devised their own legal institutions, fought off a foreign invasion, and ensured a certain measure of order and peace. The shogunate's greatest rival, the imperial court in Kyoto, was also active during these years, but many of its actions, such as judicial reform, seem to have been patterned after shogunal practices. Meanwhile, Kamakura retained the right to choose the emperor, and the imperial house was divided between the Daikakuji and Jimyō-in lines. Under such circumstances, it must have seemed unlikely that an emperor would succeed in any effort to bring about Kamakura's destruction.

But these signs of success must be tempered by recognition of the serious problems that left many dissatisfied with Kamakura's leadership. Members of the traditional landowning classes, including the nobility and the major religious houses, were unhappy with warriors' arrogance and their increasingly bold appropriation of land rights. Shogunal retainers were frustrated by the lack of rewards for their service against the Mongols. Some also found themselves in debt to moneylenders and could satisfy their creditors only by forfeiting their lands. In addition, politically ambitious warrior families were threatened by the dominance of the Hōjō faction in Kamakura. The troubled times led people to violate conventional norms. Documents from the shogunate's last decades attest, for example, to the selling of fractional shares of *jitō* positions and the holding of office by people without proper status—things that would have been considered unthinkable only a few years earlier.

In the end, Emperor Go-Daigō—a well-educated, savvy leader—capitalized on these frustrations and convinced some of the shogunate's leading warriors to turn against their own government in the 1330s. The resulting battles, the destruction of the Kamakura Shogunate, and the creation of a new imperial administration are topics for the following chapter.

Sources and Suggestions for Further Reading

See the bibliography for complete publication data.

Brazell, Karen, trans. *The Confessions of Lady Nijo* (1973).

Conlan, Thomas. *In Little Need of Divine Intervention: Takezaki Suenaga's Scrolls of the Mongol Invasions of Japan* (2001).

Farris, William Wayne. *Japan's Medieval Population: Famine, Fertility, and Warfare in a Transformative Age* (2006).

Goble, Andrew Edmund. *Kenmu: GoDaigo's Revolution* (1996).

Harrington, Lorraine. "Social Control and the Significance of the Akutō" (1988).

Hori, Kyotsu. "The Economic and Political Effects of the Mongol Wars" (1974).

Ishii Susumu. "The Decline of the Kamakura Bakufu" (1990).

Kondo Shigekazu. "1247 as a Turning Point for the Kamakura Bakufu" (2002).

Mass, Jeffrey P. "Jitō Land Possession in the Thirteenth Century: The Case of Shitaji Chūbun" (1974).

———. "The Kamakura Bakufu" (1990).

———. *Lordship and Inheritance in Early Medieval Japan: A Study of the Kamakura Soryo System* (1989).

———. "Of Hierarchy and Authority at the End of Kamakura" (1997).

Segal, Ethan. "Awash in Coins: The Spread of Money in Early Medieval Japan" (2009).

Tonomura, Hitomi. "Women and Inheritance in Japan's Early Warrior Society" (1990).

20

Go-Daigō, Takauji, and the Muromachi Shogunate

Andrew Edmund Goble

The fourteenth century was a time of wrenching transformation. The social structures that had informed what we may call the Heian system were reshaped as a range of actors—agriculturalists, merchants, warriors, and hegemons—responded to the attractions and challenges of a new phenomenon in Japanese history: social opportunity. Such opportunity emerged from a churning environment involving the growing monetization of the economy, greater control of production by agriculturalists, booming overseas trade, divisive inheritance disputes within both warrior and aristocratic families, and repudiation by some political actors of existing ideologies, assumptions, and practices of rule.

The fourteenth century is also notable for another broad phenomenon, one that also marks a significant turning point. During this period, Japan transitioned from a society governed by the force of authority to one governed by the authority of force. The first decades of the century witnessed a progressive inability of existing dispute-resolution structures to manage social frictions. Cultivator and taxation disputes were marked by increased violence and a new sense of proprietary territoriality; armed and mobile bandit groups (*akutō*) emerged, particularly in the economically advanced central region around the Inland Sea and the environs of the capital Kyoto; the labeling of people as bandits as a pretext for taking armed action against them was also noticeable; and from the 1310s, shogunal pacification expeditions, designed to deal forcibly with threats to public peace, added their own fuel to the fire. Against this background, the total destruction of the Kamakura Shogunate and its ruling Hōjō dynasty, an unprecedented action against a governing institution (previously they had been side-stepped or superseded, but not extirpated), appears as a natural culmination of the trend toward violence.

The extent of the multistranded changes during the fourteenth century makes a neat narrative tricky to construct. Yet the challenges to the historian are arguably less arduous than those faced by the fourteenth-century Japanese who confronted a world in which transition and instability were the norm and in which these dynamics had no predictable outcome.

Among all the myriad players of this dramatic era, two stand out as particularly responsible for shaping their times: Emperor Go-Daigō (1288–1339; reigned 1318–1339) and Ashikaga Takauji (1305–1358). I use them as our guides through the turmoil.

GO-DAIGŌ

Go-Daigō came to prominence in 1308, when, following the death of his half-brother Emperor Go-Nijō (1285–1308; reigned 1301–1308), he was selected as the crown prince to the new emperor, Hanazono. No one had anticipated that he would be eligible for the imperial succession. He was a relative outsider: He had not been educated for the throne, he had little emotional attachment to the rest of the family, and his mother enjoyed little favor from his father, Go-Uda (1267–1324; reigned 1274–1287). And, whereas crown princes and emperors normally became such while still minors, Go-Daigō was an independent-minded adult whose sense of self was well developed.

Go-Daigō became crown prince because his branch of the imperial family, which since 1272 had been bitterly divided into two lines of succession (see chapter 19), had no viable alternative. The division between the branches, the Daikakuji and Jimyō-in, was not healed until the 1390s, well after Go-Daigō's lifetime, but his efforts to end it drove much of his life. Go-Daigō was meant to be a stopgap, and by the time he became emperor in 1318, various agreements were in place to ensure that outcome. But few comprehended that he had no intention of living up to the agreements that the rest of political society imagined would preserve its interests.

Go-Daigō had a broad, revolutionary vision that included restructuring the line of succession (limiting it to his descendants only), reinvigorating the power personally available to the emperor, subordinating the hereditary aristocracy and the older generation to his will, finding alternative sources of revenue, attracting clients and supporters, and overcoming the autonomy and ending the interference of the Kamakura Shogunate. In short, far from being committed to the maintenance of existing political arrangements and structures, Go-Daigō was committed to a radical, unsentimental reshaping of them.

In the decade from 1318, Go-Daigō began remodeling the Kyoto world during a time when it was restructured, and left virtually leaderless, by the unexpected deaths of many senior political and social figures. He abrogated prior agreements regarding the imperial succession, actively asserted judicial and policing authority within Kyoto and its immediate vicinity (acting where possible to undercut aristocratic privileges), and placed his clients in key administrative positions. Motivated by the need to raise revenue, he also made a significant conceptual break: recognizing that the monetization of the economy, the growth of the merchant population, and Kyoto's position as a major economic hub made it feasible to raise revenue from taxes on commerce. Land and property ownership, in other words, were no longer the only sources of wealth, and Go-Daigō's understanding of that placed him with merchants and moneylenders at the cutting edge of economic change.

By 1324 Go-Daigō had concluded that the Kamakura Shogunate was the only real impediment to a reassertion of unitary imperial rule, and that it could be eliminated only through military force. Thus, unlike other members of the imperial family, but like all warrior leaders of his time, he embraced the reality that warriors were an essential component of political power. The problem, however, was that while only a fraction of the warriors nationwide were under the direction of the Kamakura Shogunate, these Kamakura vassals constituted the only organized military force in the country. The challenge, then, was to build an alternative military organization capable of opposing the shogunate and its eastern warrior clients.

Go-Daigō's planning seems not to have made much progress in 1324, limited as it was to approaching a few disaffected Kamakura vassals serving in Kyoto. Nevertheless, the shogunate got word of his intentions and moved against the alleged plotters. Shogunate leaders evidently believed Go-Daigō incapable of recruiting viable forces, and expecting him to soon complete his term as emperor, they took little action against him. Inaction proved a mistake, for Go-Daigō interpreted it as a sign of weakness that left him free to continue his preparations. From 1324 to 1331 he primarily built links with warriors in central Japan, irrespective of their affiliation with Kamakura; with merchants and traders who had extensive communication networks; and with some bandits. All of these groups saw the Kamakura Shogunate as an unwelcome presence.

In 1331, fearing imminent arrest by the shogunate, Go-Daigō fled Kyoto and declared war. Armed supporters led by his son Moriyoshi (1308–1335; also called Morinaga) and by the local warrior Kusunoki Masashige (1294–1336) established two mountain redoubts, which soon fell to shogunal troops. Go-Daigō was captured and sent into exile. Moriyoshi and Masashige, however, remained at large and waged an insurgent guerrilla campaign. In late

1332 Kamakura sent forces against them. Kamakura vassals incurred casualties and made little progress, and both morale and the shogunate's credibility began to suffer. The conflict moved to another level when, in the third month of 1333, Go-Daigō escaped from exile and rallied additional troops. In response, Kamakura dispatched more forces from the east, including an army raised and commanded by Ashikaga Takauji.

ASHIKAGA TAKAUJI

In 1333 Takauji was twenty-eight years old and had been head of his house since the death of his father in late 1331. The Ashikaga were already a prominent eastern family when Minamoto Yoritomo founded the Kamakura Shogunate in the 1180s. Although the family held military constable (*shugo*) appointments and other posts under the regime, and even formed marriage alliances with the shogunate's ruling Hōjō family, it had an uneasy relationship with shogunal leaders. The Hōjō and the Ashikaga basically represented opposite types of warrior families. The former owed their power to their position within the shogunate, but did not otherwise enjoy prestige in provincial warrior society, whereas the latter claimed Minamoto ancestry and retained considerable stature in warrior society, based primarily on their extensive landholdings.

When Takauji became family head in 1331, nothing compelled eastern warriors to support Go-Daigō. Nevertheless, the insurgency was being waged in his name, and the increasing demand for service from shogunate vassals—few of whom were rewarded for that service—was becoming an irritant. Takauji, for his part, also resented the fact that he had served well in 1331, but the Hōjō had not accorded him the public recognition it granted to others for similar service. A final element in the mix of factors was a purported family prophecy that the family leader in Takauji's generation (who was of course Takauji) would overthrow the Hōjō and rule the country. Thus, after the insurgency reignited in late 1332, and when Go-Daigō escaped from exile in the third month of 1333, warriors throughout western and central Japan moved to support his cause, and the Hōjō regime was faced with a sudden and unexpected level of military opposition.

The Hōjō were sufficiently disturbed that, to demonstrate their support among eastern vassals, they took the unprecedented step of granting sole authority to command an expeditionary army to someone who was not a family member. But instead of demonstrating stability, the Hōjō exposed the shogunate's greatest structural weakness. The selection of Takauji to recruit this army implied that he was the single most important figure in eastern warrior society, apart from the Hōjō themselves. Takauji took advantage of his new strength.

When he arrived in the Kyoto region late in the fourth month of 1333, he declared in favor of Go-Daigō, routed the shogunate army he had been sent to support, and took control of the capital. When word of these events reached eastern Japan, eastern warriors under the self-proclaimed leadership of Nitta Yoshisada (1301–1338) attacked the Hōjō, broke through Kamakura's defenses, and destroyed the warrior capital in the middle of the sixth month.

Takauji's actions marked a turning point. His success telegraphed to all concerned that the Hōjō were finished, and in response, warriors across the country declared against them. The shogunate's main constituency, the eastern warrior class, thus deliberately destroyed its own regime in the name of an imperial cause. Takauji's prestige was high, but so too was that of other generals, many of whom were neither easterners nor shogunal vassals. The warrior class nationally, not just in the east, was now involved in national politics. And Go-Daigō had become the only legitimate political authority in the nation.

GO-DAIGŌ'S KENMU REGIME AND REVOLUTION

The Kenmu regime (named for the calendar era), established by Go-Daigō in mid-1333, has challenged historians for the past seven hundred years or so. What are we to make of a unitary imperial government that claimed powers not exercised by emperors for many centuries? What, moreover, are we to make of a nonwarrior regime in the context of three successive warrior regimes that claimed national hegemony between 1185 and 1868?

These are unavoidable questions, but are premised on hindsight and known outcomes and therefore blind us to an appreciation of the dynamics at work at the time. If, however, we regard Go-Daigō and his polity as integral to the ferment of the fourteenth century, and if we acknowledge that Go-Daigō was in fact consciously breaking with the past, we get a fuller appreciation of his visions for the future.

Go-Daigō wished to start a new chapter in the history both of the imperial family and of Japanese governance. His actions toward the rest of the imperial house, his preference for his youngest cohort of children by a new partner, his choice of era name, his attraction to a Chinese ideal of strong emperorship over a Japanese ideal that stressed stability and continuity, and his self-image as the source of new precedents rather than as someone bound by past practice, all confirm that he saw himself as founding a new dynasty. He envisioned a unitary regime that would incorporate all social groups under the imperial banner, and an administrative structure that would reintegrate the jurisdictions of the court and shogunate. Among the many administrative and policy issues he articulated, the most critical were those concerning landownership and control over the nation's warriors.

Go-Daigō asserted the primacy of his authority most extensively over issues of land ownership (as, in fact, the Kamakura Shogunate had done), proclaiming that only property rights confirmed by his regime would be legally valid. This policy highlighted conflicting views of equity. Some landholders called for confiscation and redistribution of lands held by former Kamakura vassals, while former Kamakura vassals protested ex post facto dispossession of lands to which they held legal title. Others wanted Kamakura legal decisions retroactively declared invalid, while current owners wanted security of tenure. But all wanted valid legal documents, and all wanted fair hearings. Obviously these conflicting stances could not be easily reconciled.

While much criticism has been leveled at the Kenmu regime's land rights policies, and dissatisfaction with them has often been cited as a major reason warriors later turned against Go-Daigō, examination of judicial organization and processes, and of the actual documentary record, leads to a more positive assessment. The regime's signature organ, the Court of Miscellaneous Claims, was staffed by a combination of bureaucratic professionals, aristocrats, and warriors—representing all of the many constituencies within national warrior society, including the Ashikaga—and took cognizance of local circumstances in processing claims. Documentary evidence of title, irrespective of the previous issuing authority, was accorded greatest weight. Broadly speaking, warriors were given even greater security in their land rights under the Kenmu regime than they had been under Kamakura. Absentee proprietors seem to have fared less well, which confirms a general trend toward greater local control over land.

At the same time, the warrior class over which Go-Daigō claimed authority was not a monolithic entity. The most obvious division lay between former Kamakura vassals and those classed by the shogunate as nonvassals. The latter formed the majority of the warrior class and resented assertions of superior social status by the vassals. After mid-1333, new divisions emerged as a result of warrior contributions to the campaign against the shogunate—a phenomenon that might be viewed alternatively as the emergence of new stakeholders in warrior society. Classifications sometimes hinder rather than help our understanding of dynamic processes, but for the 1330s at least, they help us understand the complexities of warrior society. We may, therefore, identify the following: warriors-cum-guerrillas of central Japan who fought for Go-Daigō, former vassals not of eastern origin, nonvassals in western Japan, eastern vassals who had relocated to western Japan, warriors who were rewarded by Go-Daigō with appointments outside their home region, and eastern warriors (almost all of whom had been shogunal vassals).

After mid-1333, Go-Daigō claimed jurisdiction over *all* warriors irrespective of their origins or declared allegiances. While it would be unrealistic to assume that all warriors were happy with this subordination, the success of the new arrangements may be gauged by the fact that on those few occasions when anti-Kenmu or Hōjō remnant forces rose in arms, warriors obeyed the summons of the regime and successfully put down these threats. That is, the warriors' actions lead us to conclude that they were prepared to accept the authority of the new regime. Thus, the crucial issue for governing in this new post-Kamakura era was not who might head a regime (a civil head, such as an emperor, or a military head, such as a shogun) but whether the regime was capable of exercising meaningful control over the warrior class.

On the other hand, as we know from recent studies, warriors did not automatically acknowledge anyone as a national overlord. Self-interest was central to the warrior ethos, and romantic notions of unconditional loyalty to institutions and leaders came overtly into play only when there were alternative institutions from which warriors might seek benefits or alternative leaders under whose aegis efforts to improve their situation might be legitimately pursued. Nevertheless, in mid-1335, Ashikaga Takauji was forced to confront the issue of personal and family survival, and his response to that challenge, which effectively destroyed the notion of a single source of legitimacy, provided warriors with a prime opportunity to pursue their interests.

ASHIKAGA SELF-PRESERVATION AND CIVIL WAR, 1335–1392

It is impossible to overestimate the crucial role that Ashikaga Takauji played in the fall of the Kamakura Shogunate. Like any warrior, he expected rewards for his service, and his main desire was to be recognized as not just a remarkable general but also as successor to the mantle of leadership of eastern warrior society. In fact, it seems that most eastern warriors did regard Takauji in precisely this way. Takauji's ambitions were, however, stymied by two main factors. First and most important, Go-Daigō was actively opposed to any suggestion that the privileges enjoyed by the eastern warrior class should survive the destruction of the shogunate, and was reluctant to acknowledge any eastern warrior as preeminent. Second, the new group of national warrior leaders (which included at least one eastern rival of Takauji) did not view warrior society as a united bloc requiring the leadership of an eastern warrior with pretensions to Minamoto Yoritomo's heritage.

Takauji nonetheless maintained a special status and considerable autonomy. While he was not himself a formal member of the new regime, his top supporters were. After the fall of Kamakura, he chose Kyoto as his headquarters, maintained a highly visible presence, and kept in close touch with former Kamakura vassals. He accepted provincial appointments and honors from Go-Daigō, but he held effective sway over the eastern regional office of the regime and was not subordinate. But while this suggests a strong position, it also appears that he could not afford to physically absent himself from Kyoto. At the same time, his absence from the east carried its own dangers, highlighted in mid-1335, when Hōjō remnants swept down from a redoubt in the Japanese Alps and occupied Kamakura.

This 1335 revanchist effort presented Takauji with a dilemma. If he stayed in Kyoto, his stature as an eastern warrior leader would be diminished, and the Ashikaga risked being ejected from their homelands. If, on the other hand, he left Kyoto to avoid that outcome, he would lose the stature he held in the capital and provide easy opportunity for opponents there to move against him. When Go-Daigō rejected his request to raise an army to retake the east, Takauji was left on his own. His alternatives were unenviable, and whatever choice he made would be a gamble on his future.

Unsurprisingly, Takauji decided that his best chances lay with his proven strength, military action. He left Kyoto, recruited forces while *en marche*, retook Kamakura, and declared himself in charge of eastern Japan. He thereby demonstrated unequivocally that he was the only person in Japan, apart from Go-Daigō, who enjoyed autonomous freedom of action at the national level. Neither man was willing to compromise, and only a military outcome would resolve the issue between them.

For the next two years or so, intense battles—marked by heavy casualties, fighting in winter even in deep snow, and sieges that on occasion reduced defenders to cannibalism—were waged by main-force armies all across the country. Takauji himself had to fight his way back into Kyoto, was ejected by Go-Daigō's forces, fled to the southern island of Kyushu, and then had to mount another campaign to take Kyoto, which he occupied in mid-1336. He immediately supported Go-Daigō's imperial rivals (which became the "northern line") for the emperorship, and this move made it possible for him to claim that he was the only warrior with any form of national political legitimacy. He then set up his de facto new warrior administration (it was formalized in 1338) with its headquarters in Kyoto and issued a founding law code, the *Kenmu Formulary.* He also captured Go-Daigō and believed that all that remained was to establish some sort of military hegemony.

Unfortunately, Go-Daigō escaped at the end of 1336 and established an alternative capital at an impregnable redoubt at Yoshino in the mountains south of Kyoto. He died in 1339, with his legitimacy still intact and with a substantial number of generals and their armies still constituting a potent military force. Go-Daigō's successors in his "southern line" of emperors continued fighting, albeit with declining frequency and intensity, for the next several generations. Regional commanders occupied territory for extended periods in the 1340s, and at one point in the 1350s they briefly reoccupied Kyoto. From the 1360s to the 1380s one imperial prince effectively established his own statelet in Kyushu, complete with diplomatic relations with Ming China. Finally, in 1392, a political settlement brought the competition between the descendants of Go-Daigō and of Takauji to an end.

This Nanbokuchō (Northern and Southern Courts) conflict continued as long as it did because of four inseparable factors. First, the ongoing existence of two rival branches of the imperial family not only provided the opportunity to mask any action as being in accord with legitimate authority, but simultaneously also vitiated the notion of supreme and legitimate central authority. Second, the post-Kamakura warrior class, apart from the Ashikaga, was focused on carving out new regional power, and so what we call the civil war was in reality a decentralized, self-perpetuating conflict carried out under the rubric of support for either of the imperial lines. Third, while the Ashikaga claimed a national presence, it essentially depended on regional warriors for military resources and thus could really establish hegemony only through proxy. That proxy came at a considerable price: regional figures, appointing themselves as military constables, appropriated up to half of any tax or production formally destined for Kyoto proprietors, which of course strengthened their hands even more. Fourth, as an inevitable consequence of these factors, a military solution to the civil war was impossible.

The end of the civil war, however, marked the consolidation of a new regime, the Muromachi Shogunate, Japan's second warrior administration.

THE MUROMACHI SHOGUNATE

The Muromachi Shogunate (or Ashikaga Shogunate) made its headquarters the imperial capital of Kyoto. The choice was so counterintuitive for a warrior administration that the issue was even addressed in Takauji's foundational *Kenmu Formulary* law code. But despite the diminution of the authority of the old oligarchy resident there, the city remained the only recognizable national center. No national claim was possible without controlling it, and since the Ashikaga were making that claim, they had little option. In short, Go-Daigō's understanding of a national regime—ruling from Kyoto and tolerating no alternative power centers—was now the norm.

The Go-Daigō legacy—or, alternatively, the new, fourteenth-century understanding, shared by Go-Daigō and the Ashikaga—is visible in other areas as well. For its income the Muromachi Shogunate drew not on rural property, but on the revenue generated from the commerce that flowed through Kyoto. That commerce flowed from an increasingly monetized market economy most advanced in central Japan, where Kyoto was located, and the social morphology of that city was changing with the influx and generation of wealth by a new urban merchant and artisan population. Thus the Ashikaga drew revenue from licensing fees and from the functional equivalent of sales taxes and benefited particularly from flourishing activity in sake rice wine production and moneylending.

The Ashikaga also inherited the broader notion of the capital as a cultural metropolis reflecting the glory of its political ruler. While not a new concept, the idea had been flamboyantly resuscitated by Go-Daigō, who constructed palaces as architectural symbols of power, gave extravagant patronage to selected religious institutions, and interacted with a favored intellectual elite. The Ashikaga had to follow this example to establish its luster: constructing new palaces and new "power complexes," appropriating ritual and procession, and making verbal pronouncements of its authority and governing ethos. Perhaps the readiest example of this was the Zen monastic institution, which fused cosmopolitan architecture, aesthetic appreciation (landscapes, tea, ceramics), and Ashikaga patronage to create an overarching network that oversaw both a domestic Zen system and a multitiered diplomatic and cultural interaction with China.

Administratively, the Muromachi Shogunate hewed closely to the model of its Kamakura predecessor, which in part reflects the fact that surviving Kamakura bureaucrats played key roles in the new establishment. Jurisdiction was largely limited to Kyoto and its environs (as had been the case with Go-Daigō's early administration). But since it was backed by the Ashikaga retainer corps, which, though not vast, constituted the largest armed body in the capital, the shogunate provided an effective city government that exercised the full range of civil and criminal judicial functions. The Muromachi regime might not have had a national reach, but it controlled Kyoto, which is best seen as a unique urban hub that functioned as medieval Japan's wealthy city-state.

Politically, the Muromachi Shogunate was a complex hierarchy of stakeholders. The title of shogun was held by an Ashikaga. Below that, the post of deputy shogun, which had been created during the civil war to provide dynastic support, rotated, with some contention, among three hereditary retainer families. And national hegemony was maintained, or tolerated, through shifting quasi-alliances with various regional warlords, who formally drew authority from their appointments as provincial military constables. That is, many players benefited from an institution in which each had defined roles, but in which the exercise of authority came to depend on shifting perceptions of influence and exercise of that influence not infrequently entailed familial destabilization for competing stakeholders.

Accordingly, while scholars use the explanatory framework of the "Muromachi Shogunate" to make sense of the era's history, it is helpful to recognize that it was an evolving institution. It was established under Takauji, but then was nearly destroyed by internal infighting in the 1350s as nationwide civil war continued. By the 1390s, with the end of the Nanbokuchō wars, and then for another four decades, it was run by dynamic shoguns who benefited from a postwar efflorescence of economic and cultural activity. But by the 1440s, dynastic and regional authority and economic concerns (including commoner debt revolts) began to vitiate shogunal authority such that by the 1460s the hierarchy of interests represented in the shogunate had become incapable of containing or resolving competing interests. The resulting Ōnin War (1467–1477) was a watershed that reshaped the medieval era.

Sources and Suggestions for Further Reading

See the bibliography for complete publication data.

Conlan, Thomas. *State of War: The Violent Order of Fourteenth Century Japan* (2003).

Friday, Karl F. *Samurai, Warfare and the State in Early Medieval Japan* (2004).

Gay, Suzanne Marie. *The Moneylenders of Late Medieval Kyoto* (2001).

Goble, Andrew Edmund. *Kenmu: Go-Daigō's Revolution* (1996).

Grossberg, Kenneth. *Japan's Renaissance: The Politics of the Muromachi Bakufu* (1981).

———. *The Laws of the Muromachi Bakufu* (1981).

Mass, Jeffrey P., ed. *The Origins of Japan's Medieval World: Courtiers, Clerics, Warriors, and Peasants in the Fourteenth Century* (1997).

Varley, H. Paul. *Imperial Restoration in Medieval Japan* (1971).

Yamamura, Kozo, ed. *The Cambridge History of Japan,* Vol. 3: *Medieval Japan* (1990).

21

Medieval Religion

William M. Bodiford

Religion figured prominently in all the developments that characterized medieval Japanese society. The Kamakura and Muromachi Shogunates competed culturally with the aristocracy by donating lands to religious institutions formerly associated exclusively with the court (e.g., Ise, Mt. Hiei) and by sponsoring temple construction for new religious movements (Pure Land, Lotus, and Zen). Emerging rural warlords constructed new religious institutions of their own that cemented their local domains together, linked them to centers of culture, and displayed their new identities. Theatrical performances, storytelling, and recitation of verse and legends at religious festivals gave voice to the peasantry and merchants as they ritually invoked the presence of Buddhas and gods. Renewed contacts with the Chinese mainland fostered the growth of new forms of Zen monasticism and aesthetic sensibilities that found expression in Japanese adaptations of newly imported Chinese styles of painting, architecture, and ceramics. Non-Buddhist cosmologies appeared for the first time, both in home-grown forms (as the secret teachings of Watarai Shintō and Yoshida Shintō) and in forms from abroad (as the Christianity introduced by Portuguese and Spanish missionaries).

The people of medieval Japan thus experienced a greater range of religious diversity than during any other period of Japanese history prior to contemporary times. Within this complexity, three sets of developments stand out as especially noteworthy: (1) the birth of religious historiography; (2) the maturation and nationwide diffusion of the aristocratic Buddhist organizations of central Japan; and (3) the appearance of new Buddhist, Shintō, and Christian religious movements.

THE NEW HISTORICISM

Renewed cultural exchanges with the continent, the establishment of the Kamakura Shogunate, and the threat of foreign invasion seems to have awakened in medieval Japanese a need to explain their own unique historical circumstances. Numerous Buddhist monks composed religious annals to justify the changing relationships between the political realm and the divine power of the Buddhas and gods. Many of these texts are available in English translation, including *Gukanshō* (*Foolish Comments*, 1219), by the Buddhist monk Jien (1155–1225) of the Tendai monastery on Mt. Hiei, which attempts to explain the underlying logic (*dōri*) of the decline of Buddhist spirituality (*mappō*; i.e., decline of the dharma), a change that allowed warriors to supplant aristocrats as rulers. *Shasekishū* (*Sand and Pebbles,* 1283), by the Zen Buddhist monk Mujū Dōgyō (aka Ichien-bō; 1226–1312), explains how the local gods promote the teachings of the Buddhas in ways accessible to the people of Japan. *Jōdo hōmon genrushō* ("Origins of Pure Land Buddhism"; 1311), by the Buddhist monk Gyōnen (1240–1321) of Tōdaiji monastery, documents the religious basis for the new Pure Land movement, started by Hōnen (aka Genkū; 1133–1212). *Jinnō Shōtōki* (*Chronicle of Gods and Sovereigns,* 1339), by Kitabatake Chikafusa (1293–1354)—a general, Shingon Buddhist monk, and student of Watarai Shintō—provides religious justification for the attempt by Go-Daigō (1288–1339) to restore direct rule by the royal family.

The most important historical work of this period is *Genkō Shakusho* (*History of Japanese Buddhism,* 1322) by the Zen Buddhist monk Kokan Shiren (1278–1346) of Tōfukuji monastery. By combining biographies, chronological history, and gazetteers, *Genkō Shakusho* emulated the format of Chinese dynastic histories to produce the first comprehensive account of religion in Japan. Unlike Chinese Buddhist histories, which focus almost exclusively on the achievements of eminent monks, the biographies in *Genkō Shakusho* encompass all categories of Japanese society. The Buddhists of Japan thus include not just eminent monks (*kōsō*) and virtuous patriarchs (*kotoku*), but also kings and ministers (*ōshin*), aristocrats and commoners (*shisho*), nuns and women (*ninyo*), local gods and wizards (*jinsen*), and apparitions or ghosts (*ryōkei*). The lack of any clear distinction between the members of the clergy and laypeople is especially noteworthy. The *Genkō Shakusho* and the other texts mentioned above provide an especially rich account of the religious lives of medieval Japanese and to a large extent still shape the way that contemporary Japanese view their religious past.

INSTITUTIONAL AND DOCTRINAL ALIGNMENTS

The aristocratic Buddhist organizations of central Japan originally consisted of the mainline monasteries (Kōfukuji and Tōdaiji) in the old southern capital of

Nara, the Tōji monastery in the new northern capital of Kyoto, and the monastic complexes of Onjōji and Mt. Hiei, located just outside Kyoto. Today the Buddhism of Nara identifies itself with the Japanese Yogacara (Hossō) and Flower Garland (Kegon) traditions, while Tōji is seen as representative of Shingon esoteric traditions, and Onjōji and Mt. Hiei represent Tendai esoteric traditions. One should not, however, regard these sectarian identities as mutually exclusive. During the medieval period each of these monastic establishments housed specialists who taught and practiced all forms of Buddhist academic learning and religious devotion. Japanese scholars refer to this medieval form of combined Buddhism as the exoteric-esoteric teachings (*ken-mitsu hōmon*). During the medieval period this shared tradition of combined exoteric and esoteric teachings assumed its mature doctrinal characteristics.

The exoteric-esoteric Buddhism of medieval Japan generally advocated the one-vehicle (*ichijō*) doctrine of universal salvation and universal Buddha nature. This revealed (i.e., exoteric) doctrine was made concrete through the performance of secret (i.e., esoteric) rituals that promised immediate benefits in this world (*genze riyaku*) and the embodiment of Buddhahood in this lifetime (*sokushin jōbutsu*). Moreover, this Buddhism was said to be taught by all the gods of the cosmos and of Japan. These gods act within a vertical hierarchy consisting, from top to bottom, of timeless cosmic Buddhas who provide the vehicle of salvation: the god Brahmā (Bonten), who rules our world system; the god Śakra (Taishaku or Indra), who promotes Buddhism among humans; the four heavenly kings (*shi tennō*, gods of the four directions), who protect Buddhist kingdoms; the minor gods who control the fates of men; the gods of Japan's ruling houses; local Buddhas (enshrined in local temples), who grant blessings; and local gods (likewise enshrined in the local Buddhist temples and shrines) who protect the property of the local Buddhas and who punish wrongdoers. Buddhist doctrines explained the relationships between these different spiritual levels in terms of the fundamental spiritual ground of potentiality (*honji*), from which avatars (*suijaku*) appear as local gods, bodhisattvas, and Buddhas.

When warriors assumed control of new territory, they tended to consolidate their military and political authority by sponsoring the construction of new Buddhist temples and shrines that could be linked to those of central Japan. In this way they helped the aristocratic Buddhist organizations to develop regional networks of branch temples and shrines in rural areas. At the same time, the Buddhist monasteries of central Japan developed their own monastic militias (*sōhei*) to defend their institutional economic and political interests. Regardless of institutional affiliation, the local Buddhas and gods (enshrined in the branch temples and shrines) accepted the fruits of the land as offerings (i.e., taxes), promised blessings to local patrons, and threatened divine retribution for anyone who encroached on the land. This popularization of organized religion helped spread the cultural riches of central Japan, its arts, theater, literature, and learning, to the ordinary people across the country.

NEW BUDDHIST MOVEMENTS AND CURRENTS

Warriors also distinguished themselves from the old culture of central Japan by sponsoring new religious movements. Today the Pure Land, Lotus (Hokke), and Zen denominations of Buddhism that originated in medieval times constitute the religious mainstream of Japan, but initially all of them were regarded as heretical and were suppressed by the aristocrats of the capital. Without the support of local warrior leaders who stood against the aristocrats, they would never have survived.

The exclusive (*senshu*) Pure Land movement of the monk Hōnen (aka Genkū; 1133–1212) presented the most radical challenge to the religious establishment. Hōnen advocated the practice of *nenbutsu*—recollecting Amitābha Buddha (Amida Butsu) by chanting His Name in the formula "Namu Amida Butsu"—as a method of personal salvation open to anyone regardless of social status or gender. Hōnen transformed *nenbutsu* into a matter of personal choice (*senchaku*, or *senjaku*) in which any individual could practice religion without relying on the intermission of priests or local gods. This emphasis on individual choice threatened the very foundations of Japan's traditional social hierarchy. Shinran (1173–1263), one of the followers of Hōnen, further radicalized the Pure Land teachings by arguing that Amitābha Buddha had already saved the sinners of the world. One need merely to accept Amitābha's gift of deliverance (*ōjō*) to the Pure Land. A life of religious fulfillment becomes possible only by accepting the "other power" (*tariki*) that comes from Amitābha. According to this view, traditional displays of religious piety (e.g., worship of Buddhas, gods, art, etc.) are unnecessary. Hōnen's radical interpretation of Pure Land Buddhism was denounced by orthodox monks, such as Jōkei (aka Gedatsu-bō, 1155–1213) and Kōben (aka Myōe, 1173–1232), but no one condemned it more vehemently than did Nichiren.

Nichiren (1222–1282) agreed with Hōnen that only a new approach to religion could meet the needs of a new age. But while Hōnen opened the door to individual choice, Nichiren envisioned religion as a societal issue. If government leaders fail to promote the truth, he contended, the Buddhas and gods will no longer protect the realm. The result will be lawlessness, natural disasters, and ultimately the destruction of society by internal revolt and foreign invasion. Nichiren argued that the government must not promote the mixed exoteric-esoteric Buddhism of the mainline temples or permit the false Pure Land Buddhism of Hōnen. Instead it must promote the true Buddhism of the *Lotus Sutra*.

According to Nichiren, one could invoke the spiritual presence of the true Buddha, or the fundamental icon (*honzon*), by verbally invoking the title (*daimoku*) of the *Lotus Sutra* with the formula "Namu Myōhō Renge Kyō" ("Submission to the Lotus Blossom Scripture of Sublime Truth"). Chanting the title in this way not only saves individuals but also protects society as a whole. Nichiren's followers credited him with having saved Japan by correctly prophesying the Mongol invasion of 1274.

While radical clerics like Hōnen, Shinran, and Nichiren turned their backs on traditional forms of Buddhist monasticism, other reformers sought to reinvigorate Japan's monastic institutions by introducing new forms of Buddhist discipline. The Nara monk Eison (1201–1290) founded a new religious order at Saidaiji temple, where he and his followers revived strict adherence to the rules of training spelled out in the scriptures of the *Vinaya*, the Buddhist rules of monastic discipline. The Tendai monk Shunjō (1166–1227) of Mt. Hiei traveled to China, where he too studied the discipline of the *Vinaya*. Upon returning to Japan, he founded Sennyūji temple in Kyoto as a center for *Vinaya* studies.

Other Japanese clerics sought to introduce a full range of monastic practices based on contemporary Chinese norms. In China, the state-sponsored, elite monasteries received official designation as Meditation (Chinese, Chan; Japanese, Zen) cloisters. It is important to note that in China, the label *chan* (*zen*) referred to nonsectarian institutions open to all Buddhists. But once Buddhist practices based on this Chinese model found a home in Japan, they stood out as being distinctively Zen in ways that set them apart from other forms of Buddhism in Japan. Eisai (1141–1214) and Dōgen (1200–1253) were early Japanese advocates of Chinese-style (or Zen) Buddhism, but the adoption of this new Buddhism did not gain momentum until after the 1270s when the fall of the Song dynasty in China prompted many Chinese Buddhist teachers (who had been sponsored by the Song leadership) to flee to Japan. These Chinese Buddhist teachers found refuge in Kamakura and Kyoto, where they constructed Chinese-style (or Zen-style) monasteries.

THE GOZAN SYSTEM

When the Ashikaga Shogunate came to power in 1336, it assumed administrative control over these monasteries by establishing the Office of Meditation and *Vinaya* Temples (Zenritsugata). Over the next ten years or so the shogunate ordered its vassal warrior leaders to found similar Zen-style "Temples for Pacifying the Realm" (Ankokuji), which eventually were established in sixty-eight provinces. In 1379 the shogunate established a Samgha Registrar (Sōroku) to administer this nation-wide network of Zen temples. Today this network is known as the

"Five Mountain" (or Gozan) System, a name derived from the honorary title *gozan* that the shogun bestowed on the most important Zen temples in Kamakura and Kyoto. The establishment of this new network of temples failed to achieve its political objective of solidifying Ashikaga rule. Nonetheless, the Gozan exerted enormous cultural influence as centers for the diffusion of Chinese language and arts, especially printing, poetry, painting, tea, and Neo-Confucianism.

After the Ōnin War of 1467 the Gozan System declined along with the fortunes of the Ashikaga Shogunate. Other Zen groups, known as the Rinka (Beneath the Groves), rose to prominence. Monks in Rinka monasteries gained renown not through Chinese literary studies, but for their strict monastic discipline, long periods of sitting Zen (*zazen*) meditation, memorization of *kōan* dialogues, and Buddhist rituals. They performed simplified rites to bring worldly benefits, conducted lay initiation ceremonies, and exorcised evil spirits and ghosts. The distinction between Sōtō and Rinzai, the two main Zen denominations of modern Japan, was not significant during the medieval period. Both the Gozan and the Rinka included groups that today would be regarded as having Sōtō or Rinzai affiliation. It was, though, the Rinka monasteries of Daitokuji and Myōshinji that gave birth to modern Japanese Rinzai Zen, and the Rinka monasteries of Eiheiji and Sōjiji that gave birth to modern Japanese Sōtō Zen.

Both the aristocratic Buddhist establishments of central Japan and the new Buddhist denominations of Pure Land, Lotus, and Rinka Zen spread along pilgrimage routes that linked towns to mountains. Ordinary people regarded the mountains as dangerous spiritual realms where one could encounter visions of other worlds and hear the oracles of the Buddhas and gods. By the sixteenth century many Buddhist monasteries had organized associations of guides (called *sendatsu* or *ajari*) who trained selected groups of pilgrims to enter into the mountains. Eventually the practices of these organizations became known as Shugendō (after a term meaning "the cultivation of the miraculous") and the pilgrims came to be called *yamabushi* (those who sleep in the mountains). Although subsequent governments separated Shugendō from its Buddhist institutional foundations and even suppressed or outlawed its practice, its survival today serves as a reminder of an earlier time when Japanese saw no opposition between Buddhas and gods.

THE EMERGENCE OF NON-BUDDHIST SHINTŌ

The emergence of Shintō out of its original Buddhist context (as Buddhist Shintō or "*jindō*") and its development as a separate religion occurred after the end of the medieval period. Nonetheless, this process has medieval roots. The first non-Buddhist Shintō appeared at the Shrines of Ise, where the shrine celebrants were devout Buddhists. Two of these celebrants, Watarai Yukitada (1236–1305) and Watarai Ieyuki (1256–1362), helped give birth to Watarai Shintō (aka Ise Shintō) by compiling secret books of oracles, gazetteers, and precedents to justify use of the "imperial" (*kōtai*) title by the Watarai Shrine at Ise. The contents of these books were not in any sense anti-Buddhist, but they could be interpreted that way by later generations because they cited pseudo-histories (rather than the usual Buddhist scriptures) in support of the claims made by the Watarai family. Once the secret books of the Watarai became public, they helped promote the idea that local traditions matter more than the universal doctrines of Buddhism.

About two hundred years later, Yoshida Kanetomo (1435–1511) formulated secret Shintō teachings of a more explicitly non-Buddhist or anti-Buddhist character. Yoshida classified Shintō into three varieties. The most common form, which he called Honjaku Engi (Origins of Avatars), consists of the Buddhist Shintō that emphasizes the miraculous powers of the local gods who appear in this world as avatars of the Buddhas. A more sophisticated version, which he called Ryōbu Shūgō (Combinations of the Twofold Mandalas), consists of Buddhist doctrines that explain how the characteristics of local gods manifest the universal spiritual qualities of Buddhist awakening. Finally, there is Yoshida Shintō, which he called Yuiitsu Shintō (Only One Shintō) and explained through vocabulary that sounds more Daoist than Buddhist, though its overall structure still resembles Buddhism. Just as in mainstream Japanese Buddhism, for example, Yuiitsu Shinto consists of revealed, exoteric doctrines (*genro kyō*) that are made concrete through the performance of secret, esoteric rituals (*in'yū kyō*). These Yoshida Shintō rituals allow individuals to attain the divine within themselves just as Buddhist rituals (from which they were derived) allow individuals to embody Buddhahood.

Buddhism faced no real challenge to its spiritual hegemony until the second half of the sixteenth century when Christian missionaries came to Japan from Portugal and Spain. After a great deal of confusion—initially the Europeans interpreted Buddhism in Christian terms, while the Japanese interpreted Christianity in Buddhist terms—many warrior leaders in Kyushu converted to Christianity and gave free reign to Christian teachers. In 1576 a large Christian church (Our Lady of the Assumption; also known as the Nanbanji, or "Barbarian Temple") was dedicated in Kyoto. During this same decade, between 1571 and 1581, the warlord Oda Nobunaga (1534–1582) conducted a series of military campaigns against several major Buddhist monasteries and their armed militias. His attack on Mt. Hiei is especially noteworthy since it destroyed the heart of traditional aristocratic Buddhism. Subsequent hegemons, however, saw Christianity as the greater threat to their political power. First,

Toyotomi Hideyoshi (1536–1598) issued orders to expel the missionaries, and then the Tokugawa Shogunate enforced those orders by establishing a nationwide system of family registration at Buddhist temples. The establishment of temple registration marks the end not just of medieval religion but of the diversity and freedom that engendered it.

Sources and Suggestions for Further Reading

See the bibliography for complete publication data.

Adolphson, Mikael S. *The Gates of Power: Monks, Courtiers, and Warriors in Premodern Japan* (2000).

———. *The Teeth and Claws of the Buddha: Monastic Warriors and Sōhei in Japanese History* (2007).

Blum, Mark L. *The Origins and Development of Pure Land Buddhism: A Study and Translation of Gyōnen's* Jōdo Hōmon Genrushō (2002).

Bodiford, William, M. "The Medieval Period: Eleventh to Sixteenth Centuries" (2006).

———. *Sōtō Zen in Medieval Japan* (1993).

Bowring, Richard. *The Religious Traditions of Japan, 500–1600* (2005).

Collcutt, Martin. *Five Mountains: The Rinzai Zen Monastic Institution in Medieval Japan* (1981).

Dobbins, James C. *Jōdo Shinshū: Shin Buddhism in Medieval Japan* (1989; reprinted, 2002).

———. *Letters of the Nun Eshinni: Images of Pure Land Buddhism in Medieval Japan* (2004).

Elison, George. *Deus Destroyed: The Image of Christianity in Early Modern Japan* (1973).

Faure, Bernard. *Visions of Power: Imagining Medieval Japanese Buddhism* (1996).

Grapard, Allan G. *The Protocol of the Gods: A Study of the Kasuga Cult in Japanese History* (1992).

Groner, Paul. *Ryōgen: The Restoration and Transformation of the Tendai School* (2000).

LaFleur, William R. *The Karma of Words: Buddhism and the Literary Arts in Medieval Japan* (1983).

McCallum, Donald F. *Zenkōji and Its Icon: A Study in Medieval Japanese Religious Art* (1994).

McMullin, Neil. *Buddhism and the State in Sixteenth-Century Japan* (1984).

Morrell, Robert E., trans. *Sand and Pebbles (Shasekishū): The Tales of Mujū Ichien, A Voice for Pluralism in Kamakura Buddhism* (1985).

Rambelli, Fabio, and Mark Teeuwen, eds. *Buddhas and Kami in Japan: Honji Suijaku as a Combinatory Paradigm* (2003).

Ruppert, Brian D. *Jewel in the Ashes: Buddha Relics and Power in Early Medieval Japan* (2000).

Stone, Jacqueline. *Original Enlightenment and the Transformation of Medieval Japanese Buddhism* (1999).

Tanabe, George J., Jr. *Myōe the Dreamkeeper: Fantasy and Knowledge in Early Kamakura Buddhism* (1992).

22

Warriors, Warlords, and Domains

David Eason

"Because the realm consists of warring states (*sengoku*), it is of the utmost importance to keep one's military equipment at the ready."[1] This was one among the many directives issued by the warrior leader Takeda Shingen (1521–1573) to his followers as part of the *Fundamental Laws of Kai Province,* a legal code first crafted in the sixth month of 1547. The warning was not only pragmatic but also astute, for instability and violence were two of the features most common to the latter half of the medieval age. Indeed, by the middle decades of the sixteenth century, the larger administrative landscape was one of extreme fragmentation, with the country subdivided into a patchwork of rival domains. Battles were frequent. So too were bitter disputes over goods, revenues, and land. Within these shifting, conflict-ridden borders the influence and prestige formerly accorded to absentee noble and religious proprietors declined steadily, and the overarching authority once wielded by central institutions no longer held much, if any, sway. In place of these previously dominant outside interests arose new, local claimants to power as competing warrior houses attempted to establish their own regional regimes.

People of the time referred to the heads of these families using a specialized vocabulary indicative of respect. One term was *tono,* an honorific form of address initially assigned to the homes of the aristocracy, then to courtiers themselves, and finally to warriors. Another was *yakata,* an appellation with similar origins that, as of the mid-1300s, was limited in its application to a small and exclusive group of the shogun's most dedicated supporters. Starting in the fifteenth century, however, a widening circle of provincial commanders received permission to adopt this designation until, during the sixteenth century, it was ultimately taken up as a title irrespective of official rank. Observing the political realities before them, Jesuit missionaries who traveled throughout the Japanese islands during the latter half of the sixteenth century readily defined *tono* and *yakata* as "lords." European visitors further characterized these elites as sovereign rulers and likened them to the more familiar cast of "nobles," "princes," and "kings" found back home. To both domestic and foreign observers alike, local warrior leaders were viewed as largely autonomous figures well deserving of esteem.

Historians have come to call these men by another name: *daimyō*, or as the word has often been translated in recent years, "warlords." This choice, which conjures up an image of ruthless strongmen constantly engaged in armed struggle, does have a certain appeal. Some warriors did employ arguably less-than-reputable means to acquire, hold, and enlarge the areas under their control. For instance, Takeda Shingen came to power by engineering the forced exile of his own father as part of a coup d'état staged in 1541, a troubling fact that his enemies eagerly highlighted when seeking subsequent justification for the seizure of his lands.[2] Moreover, it is also true that most local leaders of the late fifteenth and sixteenth centuries maintained a strong focus on military affairs. Again in the case of Takeda Shingen, this meant summoning followers for repeated incursions into nearby Shinano province; once he conquered the region, he imposed even heavier levies on the local warrior families there. The result was a marked increase in the frequency and scope of warfare, an outcome no less familiar to inhabitants of the many other areas whose local leaders pursued near-identical approaches and goals.

Another of these leaders was Imagawa Yoshimoto (1519–1560), Shingen's ambitious neighbor to the south. Born to the daughter of a courtier and sent to train as an acolyte in various Buddhist temples throughout much of his youth, Yoshimoto was an unlikely candidate for succession who became ruler over the provinces of Suruga and Tōtōmi only when his elder brother died suddenly from illness in 1536. Yet, upon seizing control of this territory, he promptly resumed the unfinished campaigns of his forebears, occupying fortresses in adjoining Mikawa province and then using them as a springboard to advance into regions even farther west. Thus, by the final years of the 1550s it was not unusual for Yoshimoto and his lieutenants to lead armies numbering in the thousands—in some instances, tens of the thousands. Mobilization of so sizable a force was no simple undertaking, however, and the logistical difficulties inherent in supplying and maneuvering such a vast assembly of soldiers were correspondingly immense. In response Yoshimoto moved to enact an assortment of military laws. These regulations, designed to instill discipline among his subordinates, included prohibitions on an array of behaviors that ranged from unauthorized plundering to unrestrained arguments and fights.

Restrictions of this sort were very much in keeping with the tendency among local leaders of the time to impose sweeping limitations on violence. Except, of course, when they were the ones promoting and directing its use.

In this way Takeda Shingen and Imagawa Yoshimoto had far more in common with each other than just geographic proximity. Both deserve the label "warlord," albeit with a twist. As purveyors of organized violence, they possessed an impressive ability to marshal large numbers of warriors. Equally outstanding was their unwavering determination to defend and expand the boundaries of their respective domains.

Nonetheless, their authority was by no means absolute. So-called warlords developed innovative strategies for enhancing their military capacities, including the construction of permanent, well-defended castles, the implementation of extensive cadastral surveys, and the accompanying requirement that local warriors contribute military support in strict proportion to the assessed value of their lands. Yet they also confronted lingering questions regarding the underlying legitimacy of their rule. There was, after all, no "divine right of daimyo" to which they might conveniently appeal. Instead, even the most independent of warlords sought to enhance their governing credentials both by claiming ties to the Muromachi Shogunate and through acknowledging their continued indebtedness to earlier institutions and laws.

FROM *SHUGO* TO DAIMYO

The post of *shugo*, or military governor, served as the primary link between local leaders and the Ashikaga shoguns, though it was a connection rendered increasingly remote and abstract as time went on. This relationship began during the 1330s when those appointed to the post were called upon to play a central role in providing the shogun with essential military support. The main responsibility of these military governors was to crush the continuing armed resistance offered by forces aligned with the Southern Court. To that end, they were also expected to requisition men and materials sufficient for the task.

For this reason the Ashikaga selected military governors from among the members of two separate groups. The first consisted of families that traced their descent through the same lineage as the shogun, families such as the Imagawa that, though small and undistinguished at the start of the fourteenth century, were thought to be more dependably pro-Ashikaga than the rest of their peers. As an added benefit, their kinship with the shogun ensured the warriors who fought under their banner an inside track when petitioning for rewards. The second group, on the other hand, was comprised of unrelated warrior families with considerably larger landholdings. The Takeda, for example, belonged to this latter category, having held military governorships at multiple points throughout the preceding Kamakura period as well. Deemed less trustworthy but with greater resources at their disposal, the families in this group were often appointed to oversee those provinces where they held few hereditary properties of their own. The challenge was thus to balance reliability with potential utility and to create a system in which military governors would diligently serve the shogun without being able to accumulate the resources needed to mount a successful revolt.

The intent of Ashikaga leaders was clear. In 1338 shogunal officials had warned military governors not to overstep the limited authority entrusted to them during the Kamakura period, and counseled that "*shugo* who disobey the shogun's orders must be replaced."[3] It soon became apparent, however, that changes to this basic policy were necessary to ensure military governors the ability to keep their followers adequately supplied. Therefore, as fighting against the Southern Court—and, briefly, between rival factions within the Ashikaga leadership itself—intensified, military governors received permission to exact an annual "half tax" (*hanzei*) on the revenues collected from local estates. The measure was temporary and applicable to less than a dozen provinces when the first decrees were issued in 1352, yet military governors quickly transformed it into a regular impost. Moreover, around this same time military governors were also given additional responsibilities that included the investigation of lesser criminal complaints and the adjudication of certain types of property disputes. These developments enhanced the scope of their local jurisdiction. Even so, receiving such concessions did not release them from the larger framework of Ashikaga rule.

Far from it, for in the period that followed, the power wielded by shogunate leaders reached its brief but glorious peak. This was especially evident during the reign of the third shogun, Ashikaga Yoshimitsu (1358–1408), under whose authority a number of recalcitrant warriors were finally brought to heel. Significantly, the negotiated surrender of the Southern Court in 1392 finally removed the one unifying cause around which the Ashikaga's opponents had previously rallied. Thereafter, when the military governor who had helped to mediate this agreement launched his own, ill-conceived rebellion later that decade, he was swiftly defeated and his co-conspirators subsequently punished. Yoshimitsu continued to strengthen his position through carefully staged interactions with both the civil and the military elite. He provided lavish receptions for members of the nobility and acquired high court ranks that had not been held by warriors since the time of the Taira. To foster even greater stability, he also summoned military governors to the capital, creating an opportunity to both monitor their activities and impress upon them the splendor and permanence of his rule.

As the seat of the imperial court since the end of the eighth century and home to a host of leading temples and shrines, Kyoto had long functioned as the focal point within a complex network of offices, titles, and valuable ties of patronage that brought together the lives and fortunes of both capital and provincial elites. During the Kamakura period the Hōjō family had maintained a presence in the city with the establishment of an administrative outpost at Rokuhara. But it was not until after the Hōjō's defeat in the 1330s and a decision by the newly ascendant Ashikaga to relocate their own headquarters to Kyoto that the city became a true center for warrior rule. This was symbolized by the completion of two major building projects during Yoshimitsu's tenure: the Muromachi Palace (Muromachi-dono)—hence the alternate name for the Ashikaga government—and his retirement villa at Kitayama, which included the Kinkaku-ji (Golden Pavilion). Both of these structures amply demonstrated the affluence of the shogun, replete as they were with expensive materials and elaborate designs. What is more, they also suggested the degree to which cultural practices limited formerly to the aristocracy were now becoming available to a somewhat wider audience. For in addition to architecture and landscape design, subjects such as painting, poetry, and proper ceremonial etiquette soon joined the list of those interests and pursuits to which warrior leaders in the capital were increasingly drawn.

Military governors were some of the key participants in furthering this trend. Urged to move to Kyoto and construct elaborate, permanent residences within the city limits, they commissioned artists to apply a variety of classical motifs to the alcoves, walls, and sliding doors of their antechambers and reception rooms. Not limiting their patronage to painters, military governors also sponsored calligraphers, theater performers, and other "people of skill." They eagerly attended banquets, poetry gatherings, and courtier-led lectures on subjects as diverse as Heian period fiction, Buddhist metaphysics, and Confucian-inspired ethics. Many requested copies of the works under discussion and gradually amassed sizable collections of texts. Some became so well versed in the contents of these materials that they even produced glosses and commentaries of their own.

Such was the case with Imagawa Ryōshun (1325–1420), a figure renowned for his accomplishments in several different fields. Imagawa Yoshimoto's most illustrious ancestor, Ryōshun was not only an experienced commander but also a skilled poet and prolific man of letters who left detailed instructions for his heirs. These precepts, likely produced around the year 1400, were among the earliest to frame warrior conduct in decidedly "public" terms. Specifically, Ryōshun insisted that leaders study both military and literary arts, defer to legal precedents, and hold regular meetings with followers as a means to solicit their counsel and listen to their pleas. He indicated that a failure to follow these steps would invite disaster, and admonished that "one who aspires to protect his territory without the benefits of learning will prove unable to govern" and that "whether in charge of a district or a province, it will be exceedingly difficult for you to exercise your abilities to the fullest if you lack the people's sympathy and respect."[4] To instill fear was not enough. Rather, according to Ryōshun, an effective ruler inspired obedience through the proper and diligent performance of his official duties—a lofty ideal that resonated with later warriors as well.

At least as a theory, that is. For in practice few lived up to these aims, least of all the Ashikaga leaders of the early fifteenth century. The sixth shogun, Ashikaga Yoshinori (1394–1441), was notorious for his autocratic ways. Diarists living in and around Kyoto during the 1430s recorded that Yoshinori once ordered a follower to be placed under house arrest for having laughed during a ceremony. On another occasion he punished eight people for accidentally breaking the branch of a transplanted plum tree. And in the sixth month of 1433 he summarily banished all of the city's chickens, for a few days before a flock of the birds had dared to disrupt one of his processions. Unsurprisingly, these and other instances of excessive, seemingly impulsive punishments did little to endear Yoshinori to his subjects, while several military governors began to openly decry the shogun's stubborn unwillingness to heed their advice.

Yoshinori did consult with military governors on almost one hundred separate occasions throughout the 1430s. Unlike the consistently convened Board of Councilors (Hyōjōshū) of the Kamakura Shogunate, or the formal assemblies arranged by earlier Ashikaga leaders, however, these meetings were highly irregular affairs. Since the mid-fourteenth century a *kanrei*, or deputy shogun, had been selected from among the Ashikaga's most influential collateral families to both oversee a council of military governors and coordinate the workings of other offices and boards. Yet Yoshinori frequently bypassed this deputy and held private gatherings attended by no more than two or three of his most trusted confidants. He also relied on a cadre of mid-ranking magistrates to transmit petitions to him directly, once again undermining the established roles of both his deputy and the council. These tactics enabled the transfer of considerable power to the shogun and were met with open resistance. Opposition intensified to the point that the *kanrei* and five other military governors even threatened to burn down their residences and return to the provinces in protest if Yoshinori did not moderate his ways. He did not, and in 1441, with rumors swirling that Yoshinori intended to move against the Akamatsu family of military governors, the Akamatsu struck first, inviting him to a reception at their residence and killing him there.

THE ŌNIN WAR

The assassination of Ashikaga Yoshinori was a desperate act prompted by the harsh misrule of a single individual. Yet it also figured within a broader pattern of deepening factionalism and spreading unrest that stretched well beyond the confines of the capital. Kyushu, the northeast, and even the Kantō Plain were all areas where the influence of the Muromachi shogunate was inconsistent and often quite weak. The military governors from these regions rarely moved to Kyoto, and as a result the shogun held little direct leverage over their actions. For instance, following participation in a failed uprising in 1416, the Takeda were temporarily divested of their post as *shugo* until assistance from provincial warriors allowed them to regain their standing. Similarly, although the shogun endorsed an heir for the Imagawa family in early 1433, it was not until later that year, when the two competing claimants assembled their followers and attacked one another, that the matter was ultimately settled. By the middle of the fifteenth century most warrior leaders were far less preoccupied with securing the shogun's approval than with finding reliable sources of local support. At the same time, there also now arose an assortment of fierce and seemingly intractable quarrels that no amount of unilateral decision making could solve. These included succession disputes within two of the three families eligible to serve as *kanrei* and, beginning in the 1460s, another, even more serious inheritance struggle that involved members of the Ashikaga main line.

These crises culminated in the Ōnin War. Waged from 1467 until 1477, the long-running conflict was accompanied by destruction on a massive scale. The most severe damage was concentrated in Kyoto, where tens of thousands of warriors engaged in repeated raids and skirmishes that left over half of the capital reduced to ashes by the time they were through. Even so, other, less dramatic confrontations were equally instrumental in hastening the Ashikaga family's decline. For instance, the Takeda took advantage of these unsettled conditions to chastise local adversaries. Similarly, although summoned to join the fighting in Kyoto, Imagawa forces withdrew quickly in order to redirect their efforts toward the defeat of enemies much closer to home. They were not alone in abandoning the capital and concentrating on more immediate concerns. To the contrary, as hostilities continued to flare, military governors intensified their efforts to pacify the *kokujin*, or "men of the province," who collectively controlled the overwhelming majority of local lands. Military governors who succeeded in securing the services of these warrior families became warlords of their own well-organized domains, while those who did not were either overrun by aggressive neighbors or supplanted by ambitious subordinates who hailed from this very same *kokujin* class.

THE COUNTRY AT WAR

In the wake of the Ōnin War, the position of military governor withered and declined. To be sure, many of the most powerful warrior families of the late fifteenth and early sixteenth centuries continued to occupy positions as *shugo*—the Akamatsu, Hatakeyama, Hosokawa, Imagawa, Kitabatake, Ōtomo, Ōuchi,

Rokkaku, Shimazu, Takeda, Toki, Uesugi, and Yamana, to name but a few. Moreover, various new appointments were also arranged. In 1558, Takeda Shingen was formally recognized as military governor of Shinano province. And during the early 1560s the Mōri family, minor *kokujin* who quickly rose to prominence thanks to alliances with other local warriors, received *shugo* posts for three provinces they had recently seized. Nevertheless, the belated distribution of titles in cases such as these merely reaffirmed, rather than fundamentally enabled, the exercise of authority. The Takeda and Mōri had already invaded and occupied the regions over which they were ultimately granted official recognition as governors, and it was their adherence to certain norms of rule, rather than any direct endorsement from the Muromachi Shogunate, that permitted them to preside successfully over their domains.

This wholesale shift in the distribution of military and political power did not escape the notice of contemporaries. During the early sixteenth century even some courtiers began to refer to their present era as a period of *sengoku*, or "warring states."[5] By this point battles among rival warlords were routine. In addition, whereas earlier generations of military governors had possessed a vested interest in preserving the old order, most of these new warlords were perfectly content to stand by and watch as it collapsed. Local warriors unceremoniously ousted those military governors who did not rush back from Kyoto to defend their territories, and even ones who managed to return were often met by deputies who had grown strong in their absence and who now refused to relinquish control.

These restless circumstances lent a new level of relevance to another word: *gekokujō*, an expression in reference to the phenomenon of "the low overcoming the high." As a descriptive term for social upheaval, *gekokujō* had already come into use among playwrights and satirists as early as the fourteenth century. But it gained even greater immediacy in the decades following the Ōnin War when it became a standard phrase to emphasize the widespread disorder and uncertainty of the time.

Warlords did not require endorsements from the shogun to justify their status. Nevertheless, they remained heavily indebted to the Ashikaga for providing them with an enduring model of rule. Nowhere was this reliance more apparent than in the realm of shared jurisprudence and the compilation of *bunkoku-hō*, or "domain laws." Such codes bore a strong resemblance to those previously issued by the Kamakura and Muromachi Shogunates. Similarities in vocabulary and style undoubtedly stemmed from the fact that many of these laws came from warlords who were also military governors and thus already familiar with the language of legal texts. But it was surely no coincidence that these detailed regulations began to proliferate in the aftermath of the Ōnin War, when a growing number of nobles, artisans, and scholars fled Kyoto and sought refuge in the provinces. Neither was it an accident that both the Ōuchi and Imagawa, whose vibrant castle towns boasted populations comprising merchants, musicians, tea masters, and poets, were among the earliest warlord families to promulgate domain laws, in 1492 and 1526. Knowledge of legal norms was almost certainly one of the elements transmitted within this broader wave of cultural diffusion, a likelihood reinforced by the evidence of more than a dozen articles borrowed from Imagawa regulations and later included as part of Takeda Shingen's *Fundamental Laws of Kai Province.*

Both these and other domain laws were formulated in a manner that allowed warlords to pose as the practitioners of an impartial, "public" form of rule. As with the military governors who came before them, warlords continued to impose taxes and levies, compensate followers for their services, and oversee the transfer of land. In addition to these well-established prerogatives, however, they also assumed an expanded role as mediators. Just as the Muromachi Shogunate had banned battles among its military governors, warlords acted to similarly prohibit all fights and quarrels between the *kokujin* of their domains. Rather than participate in feuds now labeled as illegal and "private," local warriors were encouraged to turn to warlords for official adjudication. For as Imagawa Yoshimoto stated in a 1553 addenda to his family's code, although "there was once a period when *shugo* were appointed by the decree of the shogun," it was now time "to bring about tranquility through the use of laws based upon our own power."[6] No longer dependent on the Ashikaga, by the middle of the sixteenth century warlords claimed sole authority as the final arbiters in all matters of local dispute.

Warlords were bound to both enforce and uphold the laws of their domains. The *Fundamental Laws of Kai Province* stated this explicitly in the final article, where Takeda Shingen vowed to abide by the procedures for conducting investigations and punishments precisely enumerated throughout earlier sections of the code. Other warlords expressed a similar willingness to adhere to an integrated and consistent process for settling conflicts. For the Ōuchi this involved meeting with ten commissioners six times a month to review petitions. The Rokkaku, in contrast, relied on a council attended by the five most powerful local warriors in the domain. And in the case of the Imagawa, courts were held each month on the second, sixth, and eleventh days for suits filed by landholders in Suruga and Tōtōmi, while they were convened on the sixteenth, twenty-first, and twenty-sixth days for those originating in Mikawa.

There were limits to the jurisdiction of these courts. Children were not permitted to sue their parents, nor could subordinates lodge petitions against their superiors. Villagers, moreover, were required to bring cases before their local proprietors, who would then determine whether or not to pursue the matter. The preservation of hierarchical distinctions remained an overriding priority, and courts were not accessible to all. But they did provide eligible warriors with a promising method of dispute resolution that was in many ways preferable to the dangers of armed combat. It was so advantageous, in fact, that during the late 1550s the Mōri, lacking their own domain law, were beseeched by followers to appropriate the code of the recently defeated Ōuchi. Subsequent records suggest that the family ultimately complied with these requests.

Serious consequences awaited those who failed to follow these laws. Depending on the infraction, local warriors faced a range of punishments that included fines, banishment, and death. Yet there were also dire risks involved for those warlords who, whether because of overconfidence or simple ineptitude, dared to disregard the regulations that they had established within their own domains. Leaders of the Rokkaku family discovered this in 1567 when, having just endorsed a set of domain laws, they then proceeded to deviate from these very same rules. "As there is a code, how is it that you can break it?" wrote one dissatisfied follower, casting into doubt the legitimacy of Rokkaku rule.[7] Comments such as these echoed the thoughts and practices of warriors in ages past. Institutions could be modified but not eliminated. Laws could be reinterpreted but not ignored.

Views like these lingered well into the Warring States period. But they did not last. For just a few months later Oda Nobunaga (1534–1582) would complete his march on Kyoto, sweeping aside both warlords such as the Rokkaku and, eventually, the very last vestiges of the Muromachi Shogunate as a whole. The first of the "three unifiers," Nobunaga would acquire new sources for his authority. He, together with his successors, would transcend this old order and usher in a new and more stable age of warrior rule.

Sources and Suggestions for Further Reading

See the bibliography for complete publication data.

Arnesen, Peter Judd. *The Medieval Japanese Daimyo: The Ōuchi Family's Rule of Suō and Nagato* (1979).

Berry, Mary Elizabeth. *The Culture of Civil War in Kyoto* (1994).

Butler, Lee. *Emperor and Aristocracy in Japan, 1467–1680* (2002).

Elison, George, and Bardwell L. Smith, eds. *Warlords, Artists, and Commoners: Japan in the Sixteenth Century* (1981).

Grossberg, Kenneth A. *Japan's Renaissance: The Politics of the Muromachi Bakufu* (1981).

Hall, John Whitney, Nagahara Keiji, and Kozo Yamamura, eds. *Japan Before Tokugawa: Political Consolidation and Economic Growth, 1500 to 1650* (1981).

Hurst, G. Cameron III. "The Warrior as Ideal for a New Age" (1997).

Notes

1. From Article 15 of the "Kōshū hatto no shidai," reproduced in Satō Shin'ichi et al., *Chūsei hōsei shiryō-shū 3*, 197.

2. Uesugi Kenshin (1530–1578) was one such opponent who repeatedly chastised Shingen on this point, calling his actions both "unprecedented" and "shameful."

3. Grossberg, ed., *The Laws of the Muromachi Bakufu*, 26–28.

4. "Gusoku Nakaaki seishi jōjō," as reproduced in Ozawa, *Buke kakun, ikun shūsei*, 78.

5. The name "Warring States period" (Sengoku jidai, in Japanese) was borrowed from Chinese history, where it referred to the era of division (403–221 BCE) that followed the Spring and Autumn Period (770–403 BCE) of the Eastern Zhou dynasty. Because sixteenth-century Japan was not actually divided into separate kingdoms (as fifth- to third-century BCE China had been), historians today sometimes translate Sengoku jidai as "age of the country at war."

6. From Article 20 of the "Kanamokuroku tsuika," reproduced in Ishii Susumu et al., *Chūsei seiji shakai shisō 1*, 204–205.

7. "Mikumo Shigemochi shojō," reproduced in Murai Yūki, *Sengoku ibun: Sasaki Rokkaku-shi hen*, 307–308.

23

Medieval Warfare

Thomas D. Conlan

Military conflicts propelled historical change and punctuated most of the historical periods of premodern Japan. The end of the Heian period (794–1185) coincided with the Jishō and Jūei conflicts (collectively known as the Genpei Wars) of 1180–1181 and 1183–1185, respectively, and the sacking of the city of Kamakura in 1333 marks the end of its era. The Muromachi, or Ashikaga, age likewise began with the wars of the 1330s and functionally ended with the cataclysmic Ōnin War of 1467–1477, which ushered in the Warring States period (Sengoku jidai), as it is commonly known. Finally, the onset of the Tokugawa era generally coincided with the epic battle of Sekigahara in 1600.

"PUBLIC WARS"

The civil or "public" wars that so often demarcate eras of historical change were initiated by edicts of emperors or princes. Some of these documents, such as Prince Mochihito's 1180 demand that warriors should attack the Taira, constituted an explicit call to arms. Others were more cryptic, as in a message asking for warriors to travel to the capital, then explaining: "This is the beginning of upheaval in the realm."[1] Messengers transmitted declarations of war, the documents so small at times that they could be hidden in the messenger's topknot. Receiving such a call to action required time for warriors to respond. Minamoto Yoritomo received Mochihito's missive in the fourth month of 1180 but did not rebel until nearly four months later. An edict declaring one's rival to be an enemy of the court proved essential in making a conflict a "public war," and such wars were fought with great intensity, particularly at their onset.

By contrast, "private wars," which constituted acts of judicial violence designed to defend proprietary rights, were commonly waged over the course of the thirteenth and fourteenth centuries. These conflicts usually entailed plunder and arson, but resulted in few fatalities. Private wars, sometimes described as "outrages" (*rōzeki*) in times of peace, were subsumed under the more general violence as judicial opponents became rivals with the onset of civil war in the fourteenth century.

These public and private wars entailed damage to property and the injury and deaths of participants, but the need to supply armies constituted the greatest systemic demand on state and society. Surviving documents concerning the wars of the 1180s, for example, reveal very little about the conflict per se, save for warrior depredation of "commissariat rice" for provisions. Thirteenth-century conflicts were limited in span and duration, and thus supply shortages did not arise during the Jōkyū War of 1221, which lasted only a few weeks, or the Mongol invasions of 1274 and 1281, which likewise remained limited to northern Kyushu. Commanders sometimes provided ponies and spare supplies to their followers, but the burden remained on individual warriors to arm and provision themselves in the field.

BATTLE

From the eleventh through the mid-fifteenth century, Japanese wars were waged primarily by small units of skilled horse riders who relied on their prowess in archery to defeat their opponents. Japanese longbows were powerful, capable of piercing steel at short range. Most archers rode their slow and small, but rugged mounts to within tens of yards of their opponents, whereupon they unleashed arrows. The face proved particularly vulnerable in pre–fourteenth century armor, and was thus a primary target. Swords were rarely used in battle, because hand-to-hand combat proved so rare.

Japanese horses were small and, by today's standards, would be classified as ponies. They were not particularly fast, but they could easily scramble across rough terrain. And even on small ponies, a mounted squad armed with bows could mow down any opposition on foot by relying on its superior mobility to wheel around and pepper its enemies with arrows. These mounted archers sometimes chased down rivals, but this too required great skill. At times they relied on other weapons such as a *kumade* (bear claw) to unhorse opponents.

Japanese armor was designed for lightness and flexibility. Composed primarily of small leather plates covered in lacquer and sewn together with colorful braiding, the armor's style and artistry expressed the wearer's rank and identity. Some have argued that this armor was primarily for display, but it seems to have been quite functional and designed initially to protect an archer on horseback from stray arrows.

Prior to the mid-fifteenth century, warfare in Japan remained small in scale. Even the Mongol invasions of the late thirteenth century involved only a few Japanese defenders, and armies of the fourteenth century consisted of hundreds, rather than thousands, of troops. Military petitions submitted by warriors who fought from 1333 to 1392 reveal that for this span of two generations, a total of 8,634 individuals fought in the civil war, with 1,250 suffering wounds and 1,173 perishing in battle.

RECONSTRUCTING WAR

Surprisingly few reliable sources survive for the battles of the 1180s, commonly known as the Genpei Wars. The most important sources for the conflict consist of either court chronicles, such as the *Gyokuyō*, or compilations of sources such as the *Azuma Kagami* (*Mirror of the East*) that were completed roughly a century after the event and are replete with anachronisms. The Kakuichi text of 1371, the most famous version of *The Tale of the Heike*, which recounts the battles of 1180–1185, contains fabrications, such as the transformation of an aged warrior who in an earlier version of the text cannot flee fast enough, into a tragic figure who dyes his hair black so as to appear young and fights a ferocious rearguard action. Thus, the accurate reconstruction of these wars proves challenging. The Mongol invasions of 1274 and 1281 are the first Japanese wars that can be understood through contemporary documents.

THE MONGOL INVASIONS

The Mongol invasions of 1274, instigated by Kublai Khan in an attempt to expand his empire, witnessed a combined Korean and Mongol fleet landed on the shores of Kyushu's Hakata Bay. Japanese defenders resisted, but the Mongols held their beachhead. After the Japanese defenders retreated to distant fortifications at Mizuki, the Mongols burned the coasts at Hakata before they returned to the mainland.

A few thousand Japanese defenders managed to thwart the second Mongol attack of 1281. Japanese defenders, manning walls constructed after the first invasion, held the Mongols off for six weeks before a typhoon shattered the Mongol fleet, which inexplicably sought shelter in a harbor, instead of going out to sea, as was typical for most fleets during such a storm. These typhoons, known as the "divine winds," or *kamikaze*, have left such a strong memory that the real prowess of the Japanese defenders in the invasions has been overlooked.

Much of this invasion is knowable because one of Kamakura's men, Takezaki Suenaga, commissioned a remarkable illustrated account of the invasions, which describes how he charged the Mongol defenders, was shot from his horse, and later fought the Mongols on the high seas. Suenaga traveled to Kamakura and received lands and a horse for his actions, but thereupon the shogunate prohibited warriors from coming in person to request rewards.

The Kamakura *bakufu* established an elaborate system of verifying service. Upon reaching an encampment in response to a summons, warriors submitted reports of arrival. After fighting in battle, warriors submitted petitions for reward that recounted their verifiable actions. In some cases witnesses, who were not friends or family members—for their testimony was prohibited—submitted oaths verifying service. During the Mongol invasions, this process was inchoate, and Takezaki Suenaga successfully argued that his listing first on the roster meant that he was first to receive rewards. Nevertheless, proof of military service—the capture of a piece of an enemy's body or his armor or verifiable deaths, and wounds of warriors or their horses—proved the best avenue to secure rewards in future encounters.

THE DOCUMENTS OF WAR

The petition for reward, the document that Kamakura encouraged after the Mongol invasions, constitutes one of the most remarkable sources in Japanese history. These documents conferred prestige on the recipient, for they allowed him to assert status as a houseman (*gokenin*) of Kamakura. This explains why these documents were preserved.

Petitions for reward were requests for compensation, and they commonly recount the damages that a warrior had incurred. Wounds were rigorously inspected, and sometimes Kamakura officials added notations of "deep" or "shallow" to describe the injuries. Analysis of casualties registered in these documents reveals that from two-thirds to three-fourths of all wounds were caused by arrows, with the remainder caused by swords or the occasional pike or rock. Analysis of these sources allows for a reconstruction of the composition of armies and the nature of warfare.

Petitions also reveal that mobilization occurred in an ad hoc manner before 1350 as warriors arrived and departed from camps as they saw fit. The need to have one's service verified proved so significant that some warriors strove to leave a paper trail of their behavior, even they did not fight in battle. Some simply arrived at camp, submitted their documents, and then departed. In other cases, members of a single family fought for one side while they dispatched another member to fight on their behalf for an opposing force.

THE WARS OF THE FOURTEENTH CENTURY

The emperor Go-Daigō unleashed a civil war in 1331 and ultimately triumphed in 1333, destroying Kamakura and founding his Kenmu Regime. This government proved authoritarian and unpopular, leading Ashikaga Takauji, an ex-Kamakura general who had abandoned the *bakufu* in 1333, to once again rebel in 1335. For nearly a year, battles raged from Kamakura, to Kyoto, and to Northern Kyushu before Takauji ultimately gained control of the capital in the summer of 1336 and Go-Daigō established an alternate court at Yoshino, in the mountains south of Kyoto. The military campaigns involved high casualties. The armies of the 1330s also lacked cohesion, as men from a variety of provinces fought together in the same region, and joined and left the conflict as they saw fit.

The Ashikaga established a modicum of control over most of Japan after victories in 1338 against Go-Daigō's forces. Thereafter the wars of the fourteenth century devolved into a series of regional conflicts. Siege campaigns conducted in eastern Japan proved bloody and costly. Kitabatake Chikafusa, who directed Southern Court defenses in the east, tied down Ashikaga armies for five years before ultimately suffering defeat. A remarkable cache of letters written by Yamanouchi Tsuneyuki, who fought for the Northern Court, and only recently discovered in a Buddhist statue, reveal that warriors lacked adequate funds to remain fighting, and so had to borrow horses and provisions from their commanders.

Supply proved to be the limiting factor in military success, as plundering armies readily depleted local food sources. Instead, generals preferred to amass cash with which they could purchase supplies. Nevertheless, ad hoc measures became impossible to sustain with the onset of the Kannō Disturbance in 1350–1351. This incident developed out of a rift between Ashikaga Takauji and his brother Tadayoshi, which triggered a complex tripartite struggle between the two Ashikaga factions and the surviving forces of the Southern Court. A disproportionate number of commanders and leaders were killed in the struggle, including Tadayoshi himself. Takauji triumphed because he instigated the "half tax," or *hanzei*, system, which allowed provincial commanders to amass considerable public revenue and contributed to their rise as incipient regional magnates. The endemic conflicts of the fourteenth, fifteenth, and sixteenth centuries were sustained by this delegation of central authority to regional constables (*shugo*).

HANZEI AND REGIONAL MILITARY ORGANIZATION

The *hanzei* system earmarked half of a province's public revenue for military provisions. This edict suddenly elevated the post of *shugo* (constable) from a policing office with little prestige to a highly desirable prize, for state revenue could be used to build fortifications and amass supplies. After 1350 the most powerful warriors competed for this position, which constituted the basis of regional power in Japan. *Hanzei* caused the profound decentralization of the state, and the wealth it produced allowed those appointed to the post of *shugo* to undermine the autonomy of warriors in their provinces, forcing the latter to serve in a *shugo*'s army without promises of compensation. This process became more pronounced after the 1392 surrender of the Southern Court.

Once warriors became subsumed into a *shugo*'s organization, they no longer submitted petitions for reward, and with the disappearance of these sources, it becomes much more difficult to reconstruct the wars of the fifteenth century. Nevertheless, the few surviving documents that do exist reveal that mounted archers continued to command the battlefield for most of the 1400s. The wars of the fourteenth century had not led to dramatic tactical changes, but they did allow for improvements in organization and supply.

THE ŌNIN WAR

Shugo offices became the foundation for a regional organization of society, but conflict over the inheritance of this desirable post caused instability. A notable dispute arose between members of the Hatakeyama family in 1454 when two rivals, Yasaburō and Yoshinari, continued to fight over inheritance in the provinces. Yasaburō triumphed by using a well-organized force of pikemen in Kii province in 1454. His victory stemmed from the first organized use of pike-wielding infantry in Japan, units that required warriors to train together for some time. The ability to supply an army thus led to an organizational change, as well as a tactical one in the form of massed units of pikemen, who later proved capable of defeating cavalry on the open battlefield.

The Hatakeyama inheritance dispute also proved to be the catalyst for the Ōnin War, for neither faction of the Hatakeyama would accept mediation. Finally, the hapless shogun Ashikaga Yoshimasa permitted the Hatakeyama to fight on the grounds of the Gōryō Shrine, in order to determine who would be the legitimate heir. The inconclusive outcome of this encounter, however, sparked a larger war, as the two competing factions of the Hatakeyama were aided by other *shugo* and these opposing forces ultimately coalesced into the Eastern and Western Armies. Ultimately, Hosokawa Katsumoto commanded the former army, and Yamana Sōzen the latter. The court and Ashikaga Yoshimasa deemed the war a private dispute and remained neutral.

The conflict began as members of each army burned areas of the capital to make room for their troops to maneuver but Hatakeyama formations of pike-wielding soldiers defeated Rokkaku cavalry forces on the open battlefield.

Thereupon, infantry formations soon dominated the battlefield, and *shugo* mobilized additional foot soldiers known as *ashigaru* to occupy contested ground.

The Ōnin War devolved into a tactical stalemate. With the advent of pike formations, horse riders could no longer dominate the battlefield. Defensive tactics predominated instead, as pike-wielding infantry occupied territory, dug trenches, and manned watchtowers. *Shugo* skill in supplying their forces meant that each army could entrench in the capital and remain there for a decade.

Some new weapons were used during this conflict, as well. From Okinawa, the first primitive firearms, known as *tebiya*—smoothbore and three-barreled—were introduced to the capital and used sporadically, though they did not noticeably influence the battlefield. Some catapults, too, were used in the conflict, but none of these weapons proved capable of breaking the stalemate.

Ōuchi Masahiro, a major *shugo* from western Japan, joined the Western Army and forced the Eastern Army led by the Hosokawa to retain a defensive posture. Unable to secure a victory in the capital itself, the Western Army relied on cavalry to blockade the city, managing to gain control of six of the seven roads into the capital. But the eastern army clung to this last road and could not be defeated. A cavalry raid forced scattered settlements in the vicinity of the capital to become cohesive villages. Nevertheless, Ōnin commanders strove to undermine the authority of their rivals by encouraging their deputies to rebel, and proved profoundly destabilizing. In 1477, each *shugo* returned home, leaving the capital decimated and all authority fragile. *Shugo* organizational prowess made it possible for the Ōnin War to last for a decade, but the burdens of waging this war ultimately undermined *shugo* authority.

WARRING STATES

Commonly the end of the Ōnin War has been thought to coincide with the start of the Warring States period, but in fact Ashikaga Yoshimasa continued to reside in Kyoto and rule over the ruins of the capital until 1490, outliving his son Yoshihisa, who died of alcohol poisoning while fighting the Rokkaku, a *shugo* of Ōmi province. After Yoshimasa's death, his nephew Yoshitane became shogun. His succession proved intolerable to eastern partisans such as Hosokawa Masamoto, the son of Katsumoto, who revolted because Yoshitane's father had earlier supported the Western Army. This event, the Mei'ō coup d'état, marks an important example of *gekokujō* (lower attacking the higher), for Hosokawa launched an attack against the Ashikaga shogun, something that had not been countenanced by the opposing generals in the Ōnin War. At the same time, this coup d'état revealed the limits of *gekokujō* as well, because the Hosokawa likewise had to install another Ashikaga as shogun instead of seizing power directly.

Hosokawa Masamoto was killed in his bath by a follower (a manifest example of *gekokujō*), whereupon, in 1508, Ōuchi Yoshioki returned to Kyoto with Ashikaga Yoshitane and helped restore Ashikaga fortunes. For a decade Yoshioki supported Ashikaga rule, but he could not adequately control his extensive domains and so returned to the provinces, forcing Yoshitane to once again flee.

Central Japan remained in the greatest turmoil during the early sixteenth century, for the Hosokawa were largely supplanted by a deputy family, the Miyoshi, whose warriors were good fighters but ruthless and disdainful of earlier modes of legitimacy. The Miyoshi eventually attacked and killed their Hosokawa overlord and, in addition, expelled a later hapless Ashikaga successor, the shogun Yoshiteru, from the capital in 1549.

Military innovations arose in the provinces, and *shugo*, increasingly referred to as *daimyō,* or regional lords, engaged in new methods of mobilizing their troops. For example, the Hōjō of eastern Japan were effective at mobilizing larger armies from the population they ruled, so that forces of originally a few hundred in the 1490s expanded to the tens of thousands of able-bodied individuals. The Hōjō were most effective at surveying their lands and at linking military service to income, for their levies were directly based on the productivity of domains.

With the increasing size of armies, changes occurred in weapons and armor as well. Pikes became the favored and dominant weapon of the battlefield, and as units of pikemen came to dominate, gradually longer pikes came to be preferred, with the Hōjō having pikes of nineteen feet in length, while Oda Nobunaga utilized pikes over twenty-nine feet. So effective were these units that in 1549, Miyoshi Nagayoshi defeated Ashikaga Yoshiteru and expelled him from the capital with a force of nine hundred pikemen.

During the sixteenth century, a new style of armor of simplified construction appeared, consisting of more metal panels and less lacquered leather than previous armor had. Known as *tōsei gusoku*, the armor used chain to link metal panels together, and its style of braiding changed to *sugake*, or "simple hanging," although in some instances, rectangular plates of armor and chain were sewed onto fabric, thereby dispensing with lacing altogether.

These new styles of armor in some cases bore a uniform crest of the wearers' *daimyō.* The Hōjō, in particular, clothed their followers in uniforms and supplied armor for their troops. In contrast to this trend toward uniformity, helmets exhibited great variation. Once plates of metal could be shaped and welded together (an innovation of the early sixteenth century) into the "head-shaped" (*zunari*) helmet, the heavier steel could support elaborate decorations, giving rise to "strange" or "novel" helmets (*kawaribachi*).

The Hōjō were perhaps the earliest to mobilize a large army, but the successive heads of this family did not organize units by weapon. Over the course of the sixteenth century, daimyo became better at amassing armies in the tens of thousands and assessing levies of food so as to better mobilize a large force. Ultimately, when Toyotomi Hideyoshi sought to "unify" Japan, he amassed an army, cobbled together from the forces of multiple daimyo, that exceeded a hundred thousand men. The ability to mobilize an army of such unparalleled size allowed Hideyoshi to launch a costly invasion of Korea and also, in 1640, allowed the Japanese to muster a military force sufficient to expel the Portuguese from Japan's shores.

THE INTRODUCTION OF PORTUGUESE GUNS

It is well known that the Portuguese introduced firearms shortly after their arrival in Japan in 1542, and significant tactical changes have been ascribed to the introduction of these weapons. Nevertheless, the change from cavalry to massed-infantry tactics had occurred well before the Portuguese arrival, as too had the expansion in the size of armies. Although use of these weapons in Japan was not unprecedented—Okinawan guns had arrived first in 1466—the Portuguese harquebuses represented an improvement over the earlier weapons. They were disseminated widely: The daimyō of Tanegashima gave one to the Ashikaga shogun, while the priests of Negoroji gained control of another and quickly learned how to manufacture these weapons.

Equally important to making the weapons themselves was possession of a good recipe for gunpowder. Ashikaga Yoshiteru received such a recipe from the Portuguese, via the Tanegashima daimyo, and he notified an ally, Uesugi Kenshin, about these new weapons. Uesugi Kenshin was not an administrative innovator, but he fought well. Armed with these new weapons, Kenshin proceeded to attack and defeat his Hōjō rivals.

Although guns did not cause a transformation in tactics, they did incrementally lengthen the battlefield. This proved noteworthy in the famous battle of Nagashino in 1575, in which the forces of Oda Nobunaga and Tokugawa Ieyasu decisively defeated Takeda Katsuyori. This battle has often been cited as a milestone in firearms tactics, with the Oda forces purportedly firing in volleys of three, but no proof exists that this actually happened. Nevertheless, guns did prove effective at killing Takeda commanders, who were not used to the weapons' range. Trickery, however, was the main reason for the Takeda defeat, for an Oda ally used an offer to defect to entice the Takeda to try to encircle the Tokugawa forces. Expecting the defection of half the opposing army, one wing of the Takeda became overextended and entrapped, and this accounted for the high Takeda casualties.

Trickery also figured in the battle of Sekigahara in 1600, in which forces allied with Toyotomi Hideyoshi's loyal administrator Ishida Mitsunari fought

Tokugawa Ieyasu's eastern army. The treachery of Kobayakawa Hideaki, who was on the right wing of Ishida's forces, proved decisive, for instead of attacking the Tokugawa, Hideaki turned on his erstwhile allies and rolled up the Ishida lines. Despite their commanding position in the hills overlooking Sekigahara, Ishida Mitsunari's forces suffered a crushing defeat. Shimazu Yoshihiro, standing in the center of the Ishida lines, alone escaped by cutting his way through the Tokugawa armies and then fleeing to southern Kyushu. Pikes were the dominant shock weapon of this encounter, causing seventy-five out of seventy-six documented wounds, the sole exception being a sword, revealing the limited use these weapons had in hand-to-hand combat. Guns also were the dominant projectile weapon, with bullets inflicting 80 percent of missile wounds at Sekigahara, while arrows inflicted the remaining 20 percent, demonstrating that the bow had not been entirely supplanted.

Cannon, obtained from the Europeans, were also prized, and proved more transformational than hand-held firearms in that they led to changes in military architecture, as stone walls became favored over earlier earthen works, a trend that began in earnest in central Japan in the 1560s. Ōtomo Sōrin converted to Christianity so that he could acquire some Portuguese cannon, known as "country destroyers" (*kuni kuzushi*), and Tokugawa Ieyasu, who ultimately unified Japan, amassed a large store of cannon so that he could defeat his rival Toyotomi Hideyori in 1615. The fierce battles of 1600 and 1615 provided Japan with a modicum of stability and the enforced peace of the Tokugawa era.

Sources and Suggestions for Further Reading

See the bibliography for complete publication data.

Conlan, Thomas D. "Instruments of Change" (2010).

———. *In Little Need of Divine Intervention: Takezaki Suenaga's Scrolls of the Mongol Invasions of Japan* (2001).

———. *State of War: The Violent Order of Fourteenth Century Japan* (2003).

———. "Traces of the Past: Documents, Literacy, and Liturgy in Medieval Japan" (2009).

———. *Weapons and Fighting Techniques of the Samurai Warrior* (2008).

Friday, Karl F. *Samurai, Warfare and the State in Early Medieval Japan* (2004).

Note

1. Conlan, "Traces of the Past," 32.

24

Medieval Arts and Aesthetics

Linda H. Chance

Medieval times in Japan were marked, in the arts and aesthetics, by some of the most powerful developments to emerge in any tradition. Ikebana, the martial arts, and the tea ceremony have become global phenomena. Theater practitioners worldwide recognize the name of Zeami (1363–1443), theorist of Noh stage and actor training. Even the haiku, now taught in grade schools internationally, evolved from the medieval practice of linked verse. We can (and do) argue about which era's products were most formative of typical Japanese sensibilities—the classical courtly taste epitomized by the delicate layers in *The Tale of Genji*, the solemn dream-inflected aura of the Noh, or the early modern bravura of kabuki dance and song. Regardless of the choice, without the membrane centered in the fourteenth to sixteenth centuries, nothing we hail as "Japanese" would look as it does. This era shaped the canon of earlier classics through recuperative scholarship and variations on inherited themes, while creating innovations that underlie later urban modes. In that sense, these are indeed medieval centuries.

It follows that the middle ranges of Japan's artistic history are in no way "dark ages"—anti-humanist, depressing, negative, or colorless (although these last two were among the highest ideals of the time). In the wake of social change, elites suffered reduced expectations. They faced challenges to their power, and countrywide unrest. Yet out of these unpromising conditions, they created tranquil oases of poetry, gardens, and music. The age was expansive in important ways. Beyond the triumvirate of nobility, clergy, and military, commoners participated in the rise and proliferation of cultural forms in and outside the central capital. Buddhist philosophies permeated both the practice and content of many arts, but in spite of the founding assumption that all life is unsatisfactory (*ku,*

Figure 24.1. Tōgudō, the private chapel (1486) that contains Dōjinsai, the first extant small tatami mat room of the type that became typical for drinking powdered tea. Part of the "Silver Pavilion" in the eastern hills of the capital, it was built for Ashikaga Yoshimasa. (Photograph by Frank L. Chance.)

also described as "suffering"), the effect was not overwhelmingly dismal. The austere images that we associate with this period—the single blossom hung in a dusky tea room, or "snow mounded in a silver bowl" (Zeami's evocation)—did not preclude extravagant displays of finery or ample doses of broad humor and irreverence—say, servants filching sugar from their master in comic *kyōgen* plays, or poems about gross bodily noises. In fact, as this chapter shows, one of the main characteristics of literary, performance, and plastic productions was the coexistence of seemingly paradoxical elements in a fruitful balance.

To appreciate the culture of medieval Japan as it was, and not as it has reached us through later interpretations, it would be best to try seated meditation (*zazen*), to experience the mind-emptying pain of sitting and counting our breaths. We must prepare to strip away preconceptions and convenient handles. The still-useful studies from half a century ago tell us that Japanese poetry is lyric and expressive. This does not mean, however, that poems merely express the emotions of their creators or passively reflect what they thought about the world—literature creates possibilities for that world as well. Some scholars go so far as to shun such terms as "art" and "aesthetics," since equivalents do not exist in premodern Japanese practices. Instead there was a strong concern with, for example, rhetoric and style in writing, with bodily behaviors in theater, and with brush movements in calligraphy. Verse was frequently composed on celebratory occasions, or even before battle, to ensure success. Difficult as it is to do, our best commentators avoid locating persistent "traditions" across time. Traditions were dynamic, with the most conservative poets or potters simultaneously crafting a relationship to existing schools or monuments that could legitimate their work, and innovating whenever possible.

Such were the aims of the poets who assembled the *Shinkokinshū* (*New Anthology of Poems, Ancient and Modern*) in about 1205. Among them was Fujiwara Teika (aka Sadaie; 1162–1241), a prickly radical whose early poems struck his contemporaries as the spawn of Daruma, China's Bodhidharma, transmitter of the Zen way.

Gazing all around,
blossoms, maple leaves
nowhere.
The bay, a reed hut,
autumn's dusk

miwataseba
hana mo momiji mo
nakarikeri
ura no tomaya no
aki no yūgure[1]

"Daruma Poem" was an insult, criticizing the young Teika for posing a question (What do I see when I look about?) but ignoring the normal answer (spring flowers or autumn foliage) in favor of a third phrase signifying negative space. His choice was similar to the technique of the Zen *kōan*, which breaks our everyday relationship to language and logic. This poem is now regarded as one of the "three [read: great] autumn evenings" in *Shinkokinshū*, set in an atmosphere drained of color. Teika worked with many of the styles that grabbed contemporary minds, while also keeping a journal in classical Chinese and collating editions of native classics, including *The Tale of Genji*. Teika's father, Fujiwara Shunzei (1114–1204), insisted that every poet had to know *Genji* and that composition of poetry was fundamentally not different from the practice of Buddhism.

But wait—Buddhism is religion and, furthermore, religion that warns people away from the folly of words (so prone to creating deception and ignorance), not to mention from attachments, those investments in desire that block us from awakening to the true nature of existence. The impasse between the demands of Buddhism and the seductions of belles lettres presented a deep problem to medieval thinkers. They "solved" it by realizing that intentions determine the quality of one's actions, thus approaching secular behaviors with the same attitude as religious discipline. Holding these opposites in tension to pursue a middle path, however, was not easy, as the monk-poet Saigyō (1118–1190) discovered:

> *I thought I was free*
> *of passions, so this melancholy*
> *comes as a surprise:*
> *a woodcock shoots up from marsh*
> *where autumn's twilight falls.*[2]
>
> *kokoro naki*
> *mi ni mo aware wa*
> *shirarekeri*
> *shigi tatsu sawa no*
> *aki no yūgure*

The body (*mi*) that has let go of the heart-mind (*kokoro*, also a term in poetics for "emotion") through concentration on external objects or internal disturbances should be perfectly still, so that awakening can flash through it. Instead a bird recalls the wandering poet to the world at the break of night.

Recent studies find that firm dualities are not that helpful in describing the mindsets of medieval Japan. We speak of "religio-aesthetic" or "aesthetico-moral" principles. *Shinkokinshū* was orchestrated by a meddling editor who was also a retired sovereign, Go-Toba (1180–1239), offering what we might call a "politico-artistic" collaboration. "Literature" itself can be a misleading term for the multisensory union of words, music, and image. Poems were memorized and sung. In *The Tale of Genji*, skill with stringed or wind instruments is an index to the worthiness of characters. Similarly, in the war narrative *Tale of the Heike* (*Heike monogatari*), Atsumori, a young warrior on the losing, Taira, side, is recognized in death by the storied flute at his waistband. The eastern fighter who slices off Atsumori's powdered head sheds tears as he remembers his enemy's playing.

The *Heike* evolved over time, from terse records in Chinese compiled in the immediate aftermath of the intermittent battles that shocked society in the 1180s, to the 1371 symphonic version best known today. Each of its two hundred or so episodes was recited by blind performers accompanying themselves on *biwa* lute. *Heike* segments range from martial tales that take half an hour to pound out on the strings, to lyrical laments that (in modern performance, and surely when *biwa*-strumming lay priests traveled the country singing on request) need three times as long to perform. Nor are all the lyrics lyrical: They sometimes quote documents in sinicized prose and enumerate Chinese precedents in formal language. The musical styles of the *Heike*—unsurprisingly, inasmuch as they memorialize fallen soldiers—derive from Buddhist chant and funeral music. This is a literature of placation, as much as of history. Memorials aided the audience, stroking memory and warding off danger, the twanging of bowstrings a prophylactic against angry spirits cut down in their prime. At the same time, they comforted those spirits, functioning as prayers for their release from the karmic torment of lives, on earth and in the hereafter, that were steeped in death.

One of the beautifully observed principles of medieval literature is impermanence. The music of the *Heike*'s opening passage (which chanters could not learn until they had mastered much of the rest) mimics the echoing toll of a bell that proclaims "all phenomena do not last." The powerful are destined to fall, as a spring night's dream. Kiyomori, the leader of the *Heike*, who successfully modeled himself on politicians of the past, manipulating wealth and numerous daughters to forge ties to the nobility, is portrayed as ultimately dying in a bathtub, boiling from his own intense fever. The unfolding of other conflicts in the intervening centuries no doubt shaped the tale's trajectory of decline and sympathy for the defeated members of the family who were victimized, as the tale has it, by Kiyomori's lack of leaderly virtue. Older treatments of Japanese culture suggest that this was a time of darkness and pessimism. Indeed, the tale laments the current degenerate age in which salvation was not readily possible. But it is also filled with striking action, and with female figures who pray for their fallen relatives to gain spiritual liberation and transfer it to others as well. The accomplishment of the *Heike*, and of many other works in the medieval age, was to fashion the most human responses to grief and confusion, loss and terror. The only unchanging thing is change, they tell us, and real acceptance of that condition brings solace.

Vanishing courtly values appear everywhere, but they are not simply the object of nostalgia and mourning. A pragmatic realization that what is gone is gone, and the need to make the best of it, animates thinkers. Kamo no Chōmei (c. 1155–1216) wrote his *Hōjōki* (*Record of a Hut Ten Feet Square*) in 1212, borrowing images of transience from the Buddhist sutras: "The flow of a river without cease goes on, and yet the waters are not as they were. The bubbles floating on slow whirls disappear, then come together, in no instance stopping for a while."[3] Chōmei chose the tonsure evidently because Go-Toba did not appoint him to a shrine post, but his observations are no less gripping for that. As Chōmei watches quakes, fires, floods, winds, and resultant famines and devastation wreck the capital, his response is wholly comprehensible—he craves a cocoon of smaller lodgings. By the time he outlines the joys of his cunningly designed quarters, both reader and author sense the distracting appeal of the hermit life. Chastened, Chōmei dissolves the end of his text into prayers.

Writing perhaps shortly after Go-Daigō's revolution of the early fourteenth century, Kenkō (c. 1283–c. 1352) delivers impermanence in its most positive guise. Death, or anything that reminds us of it, is crucial—even the markers and funeral pyres of two of the capital's main graveyards: "Were it the way of this world for the dews at Adashino never to disappear, or the smoke of Mt. Toribe never to trail off, imagine how little we would feel things. Its very unfixedness makes life dear."[4] Although he is not lacking in firm opinions on the ills of his day, Kenkō crystallizes the value of change. A monk who fled time-consuming entanglements with inferior companions, he remained near the city and his fellow poets. His *Tsurezuregusa* (*Essays in Idleness*) is the single piece of medieval prose most read by later generations, who often imitate its loose style, akin to a blog. It teaches little about poetics, but much about whatever else came to Kenkō's open ears.

Gossip is a mainstay of medieval writing, even in collections of unabashedly didactic, yet fun anecdotes (*setsuwa*), many of them centered on religious belief. Narratives that commemorate the founding of temples and shrines spring from a similar motive to describe the world, and some of the best, such as the illustrated biography of Saint Ippen (1239–1288; *Ippen hijiri-e*), offer an excellent window into commoner life, while demonstrating once again the union of word and picture.

In Japan, the line between crafts and arts is not necessarily distinct. Any inventory of high points in medieval material culture would include metalwork, ranging from mighty swords to fine tracery, pottery, textiles, and lacquer, each of which saw advances, including those catalyzed by imports from the continent. Expertise in these areas was fostered by guild organization. The umbrella term for devotion to technique, as well as to disciplines like poetry-as-Buddhist-way, was *michi*, or "path." Kenkō esteems the special knowledge of waterwheel makers, tree climbers, and equestrians, just as he cautions that one must not take up a path too late in life, or bore people with disquisitions on specialties you know nothing about. Japanese were aware that the indiscriminate honoring of artistic and knowledge production as *michi* could be silly: see *Fukutomi chōja monogatari* (*The King of Farts*). In this illustrated tale, a wife browbeats her husband into begging the secrets of the art of farting from a neighbor who has gotten rich off his talent. The plan backfires horribly when the wealthy man provides a laxative to his disciple.

In Japanese medieval high aesthetics, attenuation merits praise. Linked verse (*renga*) operated by focusing on the pared essence of poetic subjects. Participants in a linking session (often three) had to fit phrases together with other poets, and their mutual mastery of the canon of existing verse, combined with shared notions of complementary items, enabled them to do so on the spot. Ink painting, second only to calligraphy in the hierarchy of coveted lines on paper or silk, made a virtue of suggestion. The most famous examples, such as those by Sesshū (1420–1506), feature bold lines of varying thickness and saturation playing off against areas of negative space. Whether the format is a scroll, a hanging, or an album, one has to look intently to be sure that the lines do not simply describe an abstraction (which of course they do, while also portraying figures from nature). Tea culture made much of *sabi*, the kind of loneliness experienced by *Shinkokinshū* poets on twilight evenings, which evolved into a feeling of rusticity. *Wabi*, a distinct term for simplicity in surroundings, found its embodiment in small rooms dedicated to serving a guest or two with only a charcoal brazier, a simple flower from the fields, a scroll with ink calligraphy, and the hot water for tea (*chanoyu*) itself. Bowls, tea caddies, water jars, scoops, and shelves to display them on were at first imported in richly decorated sets, which gave way to *wabi* taste, or a judicious combination of both. The harmony of materials in tea rooms is intensely elegant, but never showy.

This is not to say that elaboration has no place in medieval schemes. The sumptuous costumes of the Noh theater, precious furnishings of sandalwood, and the decorative programs of palaces and temples such as Toyotomi Hideyoshi's memorial hall to his son who died in infancy, preserved on the island of Chikubushima, all deny any preference for plainness. (This memorial also illustrates how salvation for the son and political legitimation for the father could fuse in one monument.) Although poverty and restraint were forged into ideals in the tea ritual, and Kenkō called for the exclusion of intricate Chinese crafts and useless ornamental plants from gardens, exuberance infected those who could afford it. Temples, palaces, and later, castles housed screen and sliding-door paintings that reflected both the wealth of their owners and the dim light of interiors via gold-leaf backgrounds. Magnificent screen pairs that lavishly detail the sights of the capital around the mid-sixteenth century activate specific representations to mold a vision of power through place.

What kind of painting was most present in the lives of people in these centuries? The answer must be religious icons of various types. From the mandala that represent the universe, or that portion of it associated with a particular shrine-temple complex, as at Kasuga, to decorations on sutras, especially the prized *Lotus Sutra*, with its heavy use of metaphor and imagery, these were the subject of sumptuous production. Preachers and fund-raisers, female (*Kumano bikuni*) and male, used pictures in various formats to make points about the rewards and punishments attendant upon certain behaviors and beliefs.

Much medieval sculpture is, of course, religious. The contribution of recent scholars to our appreciation of this body of work is nothing more or less than taking the ritual contexts and belief in icons seriously. Art historians will continue to debate dates and authenticity through connoisseurship—development of a good eye that can judge, based on a comprehensive grasp of stylistic factors, when pieces might have been produced—but we now focus equal attention on the setting and uses of objects. Some of these sculptures frustrate the simplest apprehension or definition of "art," such as the Zenkōji Amida Triad, housed in an important temple in Shinano but never available for viewing. The power of the three statues comes from the secrecy in which they are held, but also, fortunately, from the propagation of the icon around the country. Some four hundred copies indicate the desire for salvation and presumed efficacy of the images of the "Living Buddha" and attendants.

How were women involved in medieval arts—only as objects of male authority or as cross-dressing usurpers, as we see in dance? Flower arranging and tea, which are now associated with female training in etiquette, were the preserve of men. Women patronized the plastic arts, but were seldom producers. A number of popular tale types denigrate women, recasting reportedly beautiful poets of the past such as Komachi or Izumi Shikibu as hags who earned rejection on account of seducing men. Noh plays attribute ultimate spiritual benefit to Komachi's fall, but other roles show women going mad. As women's status in society declined, the portrayal of female entertainers as prostitutes appears to have become more frequent. Yet by Buddhist logic, one function of the prostitute is to show compassion to men, allowing her to transcend defilement and participate in salvation, albeit as a neutralized facilitator.

Older literary histories make it appear that premodern women's roles in literature disappeared after the classical period. This is not entirely true (and in any case, as time went on, women's literate activities simply moved to posts in the royal bureaucracy). The *Mumyōzōshi* (1196–1202), an account of women commenting on tales by "Shunzei's Daughter" (his adopted granddaughter), shows them debating the paramours of the eponymous hero of *The Tale of Genji*. *Towazugatari* (*A Tale Unbidden*), is Lady Nijō's (1258–after 1307) own story of abandoning the sexual entanglements of the court for pilgrimage. In the course of imitating her hero Saigyō, she encounters women of other classes.

Women writers of the past are acknowledged as the wellspring of the vernacular in this period. Even Kenkō, who often seems to reject women as hindrances to male serenity, credits Murasaki Shikibu and Sei Shōnagon for beating him to his own views. Courtiers such as Ichijō Kaneyoshi (aka Kanera; 1402–1481) devoted much effort to explicating *The Tale of Genji*, whose text had been collated by Teika.

Medieval prose narratives (*otogi zōshi*) were once viewed as entertainment for women and children, with the nuance that they did not merit consideration. Women and children were no doubt entertained by visions of love or of inverted social and gender hierarchies or tales of demons and animals. The wide range of these stories nonetheless defies easy characterization and blanket dismissal.

Noh theater, or *sarugaku* (monkey music), as it was known, represents a pinnacle, uniting poetry, music, and philosophy. Emerging from commoner theatrics closely tied to expression of sacral concerns (an "emergence" that involved suppressing a variety of competitors), with the introduction of written texts, Noh was transformed to appeal to an elite audience whose patronage would be vital. Zeami's twenty-one treatises, filled with everything from practical hints to cryptic terminology, have drawn the most attention, but revealing the existence of secret texts bolstered Noh's authority. Among the most spectacular plays are those that feature a dream in which a warrior from *The Tale of the Heike*, disguised as a reed cutter in the case of Atsumori, tells his story to a bystander. In the second half of the performance, the warrior appears in his true form to relive his defeat in dance and song, seeking an end to the bonds that tie him to the world, with the accompaniment of eerie flute and irregular percussion. Zeami held that female roles expressed the highest principle, *yūgen* ("mystery and depth" when applied to poetry; "grace" in the Noh context).

Kyōgen, considered the comic counterpart to Noh, appears in the historical record in an early form in the middle of the fourteenth century, but libretti do not materialize for another two hundred years. A *kyōgen* play might stand normal values on their head, as with *The Beard Fortress,* in which a warrior has to defend his hair from his wife and her halberd-wielding friends by means of a beard-sized portable castle-enclosure.

The strong appeal of Zen in the West has led to interpretive controversies surrounding the medieval arts. Best-selling books claim that ink painting, archery, tea, and Noh all have Zen as their essence. One garden at the Ryōanji temple in northern Kyoto has catapulted, some say thanks to Western scholarship, from relative obscurity to shorthand for the universe in fifteen rocks, despite a lack of textual evidence that it was built as an apotheosis of Zen symbolism. Later scholars have found that where there is a claim of Zen influence, there are usually other religious traditions, reflecting the syncretic tendencies of Japanese thought and practice. Amidist salvation imbues Noh plays, whereas the meditation (the original meaning of *zen*) regimes of esoteric Buddhism inflect vernacular poetry at least from the time of Shunzei forward. Some true Zen poetry, such as that designated as Five Mountain (Gozan), however, has been neglected by literary critics. The mere fact that it is written in Chinese should not disqualify this achievement from inclusion in the legacy of medieval Japanese literature. A phrase from Gidō Shūshin (1325–1388) shows that he joined discourses on hiding in plain sight to those on seeking liberation through the collapse of distinctions.

> *White clouds and cinnabar canyons, abode of the man of the Way;*
> *Forested mountains are not always far from the world of man.*
> *Going and stopping like the clouds, originally without ties;*
> *Body and mind like the canyons, naturally empty.*[5]

As presented by the major interpreter D. T. Suzuki (1870–1966), Zen captivated an audience used to sweeping pronouncements on the peculiarities of Japan. In North American popular culture, "Zen" has come to mean "relaxation," describing mellow attitudes or, for example, spa treatments. A backlash against Suzuki's apparent obfuscations has produced much scholarship that points out the hierarchical workings of Zen institutions (and has criticized the role of aesthetics in Japan's claims to a unique role in Asia). For a religion that speaks of a special transmission outside scripture and the emptiness of forms, Zen poets and clerics have written vast numbers of pages. It is undeniable, nonetheless, that Zen approaches, and medieval habits of thought engendered by Buddhism more generally, are qualitatively different from so-called Western thinking. The world looks different when one believes that nonattachment is an obtainable goal, and certainly when one argues that nothing can be obtained and goals are only contingent means. One of the sticking points in the field is how to define and describe that irreducible difference without implying that medieval Japanese were less rational, moral, or garrulous (not to mention less stupid, wicked, or poorly spoken, in some cases) than any other people.

One Zen poet who exemplifies the disdain for pieties in Buddhist thought is Ikkyū (1394–1481). A shocking figure who did not hesitate to invoke excrement as an equalizer, he drew the admiration of his followers for the purity of his Zen. His teaching is encapsulated by a verse such as "On a Brothel":

> *A beautiful woman, cloud-rain, love's deep river.*
> *Up in the pavilion, the pavilion girl and the old monk sing.*
> *I find inspiration in embraces and kisses;*
> *I don't feel that I'm casting my body into flames.*[6]

Buddhism taught men to revile women as obstacles to practice; Ikkyū viewed rigid attitudes as the obstacle.

Not everyone who caroused on the margins of society had pure intentions. Going back to the war narrative *Taiheiki* (*Chronicle of Great Peace*)—completed by 1372, shortly after the events it describes—we find critiques of *basara*, wanton, excessive behavior. Competitions in verse had a long pedigree, but parvenus

Figure 24.2. The reconstructed Golden Pavilion (1397) represents fourteenth-century sumptuous taste. It was built in the hills north of Kyoto for the patron of the Noh theater, shogun Ashikaga Yoshimitsu, in the latest Chinese style. (Photograph by Frank L. Chance.)

bet on guessing types of tea, and engaged in other amusements, including linked verse. This last was always closely allied with Buddhist notions of transience, however, and would spread poetic knowledge around the country as its teachers fled the war-torn capital.

Warrior elites were much aware of the power of symbols. The Ashikaga Shogunate's move to the environs of the capital facilitated its acquisition of cultural capital. Kenkō provided advice to Kō Moronao (d. 1351), a violent warrior, on proper dress for appearances at court. *Taiheiki* claims that Moronao had Kenkō brush a love letter in his stead, attempting a seduction of a married woman that became a base for the play *Chūshingura*. Some of the greatest collectors of Chinese objects were the shoguns Yoshimitsu and Yoshimasa, who relied on monks from China and lay monks known as *dōbōshū* to manage their treasures. They also built retreats in the latest styles, the Golden (1397) and Silver (1483) Pavilions, respectively, features of which remain in domestic architecture today.[7]

Theater was particularly useful to rulers, since they could gather an audience and impress them on several levels at once. Toyotomi Hideyoshi (1536–

1598) commissioned Noh plays about his own conquests, real and desired, and even acted in some of them. Such performances were part of an arsenal of cultural appropriations that have not endeared him to history, including forcibly importing potters from Korea, constructing a solid gold teahouse, and bringing the Living Buddha of Shinano's Zenkōji to the capital. Hideyoshi was only the last of four powerful warrior leaders to capture the icon, a sign of what conflict—and in Hideyoshi's case, an earthquake in 1596—could bring men to.

A caveat, then, about Japanese medieval arts and aesthetics is: "It's not all Zen." Zen was an insult to Teika. Neither Saigyō nor Kenkō were adherents of the Zen sect. The meditative orientation may be as much a product of the habits of reverence toward nature also expressed in Shintō, of the longing for tranquility seen in Daoism and eremitism, of a response to a world in political turmoil and efforts to control it. Human needs to shape and comprehend the most terrible losses were well served by an acceptance and even celebration of paradoxical complementary opposites, and by an aesthetics that preferred the imagination of perfection to actual physical completion, recognizing the inevitability of ends and beginnings.

Sources and Suggestions for Further Reading

See the bibliography for complete publication data.

Brazell, Karen, trans. *The Confessions of Lady Nijō* (1973).

Brown, Steven T. *Theatricalities of Power: The Cultural Politics of Noh* (2001).

Butler, Lee. *Emperor and Aristocracy in Japan, 1467–1680: Resilience and Renewal* (2002).

Carter, Steven D. *Regent Redux: A Life of the Statesman-Scholar Ichijō Kaneyoshi* (1996).

Huey, Robert N. *The Making of Shinkokinshū* (2002).

Kimbrough, R. Keller. *Preachers, Poets, Women, and the Way: Izumi Shikibu and the Buddhist Literature of Medieval Japan* (2008).

Komine Kazuaki. *Setsuwa no gensetsu: Chūsei no hyōgen to rekishi jujutsu* (2002).

LaFleur, William R. *The Karma of Words: Buddhism and the Literary Arts in Medieval Japan* (1983).

Marra, Michele. *Representations of Power: The Literary Politics of Medieval Japan* (1993).

McCallum, Donald F. *Zenkōji and Its Icon: A Study in Medieval Japanese Religious Art* (1994).

McCullough, Helen Craig, trans. *The Tale of the Heike* (1988).

McKelway, Matthew Philip. *Capitalscapes: Folding Screens and Political Imagination in Late Medieval Kyoto* (2006).

Rath, Eric C. *The Ethos of Noh: Actors and Their Art* (2004).
Skord, Virginia, trans. *Tales of Tears and Laughter: Short Fiction of Medieval Japan* (1991).
Ury, Marian. *Poems of the Five Mountains: An Introduction to the Literature of the Zen Monasteries* (1992).
Watsky, Andrew M. *Chikubushima: Deploying the Sacred Arts in Momoyama Japan* (2004).
Yamada, Shōji. *Shots in the Dark: Japan, Zen, and the West* (2009).

Notes

1. Kubota and Kawamura, *Gappon Hachidaishū*, 457.
2. LaFleur, *Awesome Nightfall*, 68.
3. Yanase, *Hōjōki kaishaku taisei*, 9.
4. Yasuraoka, *Tsurezuregusa zenchūshaku*, 1:42.
5. Parker, *Zen Buddhist Landscape Arts of Early Muromachi Japan*, 151.
6. Arntzen, *Ikkyū and the Crazy Cloud Anthology*, 117.
7. University of Pennsylvania student Ken Winterbottom IV assisted with the graphics for this and chapter 34.

25

Gender Relations in the Age of Violence

Hitomi Tonomura

In the mid-fourteenth through the sixteenth century, evolving social, economic, and military conditions and emerging ideas and ideals shaped gender relations in ways that differed significantly from those of earlier centuries. Historical investigation is made difficult by the contemporaneous decline in writing by and about women, a factor that reflects the highly decentralized and increasingly violent conditions that tended to obscure women's activities behind masculine endeavors. The evidence we do find typically appears in scattered fragments and challenges us to decipher meanings and weave them together into perceivable patterns of changing gender relations. This chapter considers the broad trends for three groups: warriors (*buke*), courtiers (*kuge*), and commoners.

WARRIORS

The historical sources produced by warriors after the fourteenth century loudly announce that this was becoming a masculine age. Women-related sources were eclipsed, and while women continued to play significant roles in warrior affairs, they increasingly worked behind the scenes, supporting the goals and strategies of their houses to survive and thrive in turbulent times. This contrasts with the Kamakura period, when women had property, taxation, and military duties just like men. How did this change occur? The answer highlights the effects of war-prone conditions and the impact of violence on gender relations.

Transformation in Landed Rights

During the Kamakura period, women wrote and received documents because they held titles, especially the *jitō-shiki* (see chapter 18), which they could inherit, transmit to their heirs, or make the subject of disputes. Historians call this the Golden Age of Women, a unique time in Japanese history when the warrior government granted a military and landholding title (*jitō*), which vested in its holder the privilege to extract profits from the land and the requirement to serve in the shogunate's guard and pay land fees. Initially granted to meritorious vassals or their kin, the *jitō* title was transmitted to the next generation in accordance with the custom of divided inheritance. Importantly, the *jitō* title was ungendered. Husbands and wives, who held property separately, conferred their property—secured in the form of titles such as *jitō*—to sons and daughters. In some cases husbands left land and titles to widows.

Attached to most wills that conveyed property was the prescription, "For the service duty levied by the Kamakura Shogunate, follow the leadership of the main heir (*sōryō*), and fulfill it in accordance with the land portion received," which articulates the nongendered nature of the military and economic obligations that *jitō* titleholders owed to the shogunate. One owed service commensurate with the size of one's landholdings for as long as one held them, and the responsibilities attached to the land were to be carried out, either in person or by proxy, regardless of the holder's gender. We have evidence of women serving guard and routine sentinel duty. But the Kamakura period was mostly peaceful, with no major battles until the Mongol invasions of 1274 and 1281. This first ferocious military exigency from outside Japan tested the balance between rights and responsibilities in a gendered way.

How did the *jitō* fight in this war? While many fought bravely and some lost their lives, others, men and women alike, sent their children, husbands, or other—paid—proxies. But the shogunate condemned women for not fighting in person—targeting *only* women in this regard. In 1286 it issued an edict prohibiting the future conveyance of *jitō* property to daughters of warriors living in Kyushu, where the invasions took place, as long as the threat continued. Families without sons were to adopt one from a kinsman or kinswoman. Because Kamakura law was not strictly enforced and often served largely as guidance, warrior families for the most part ignored the edict, continuing to ensure the transmission of property to children of both genders. Nevertheless, this legal measure fueled the certain, albeit gradual, transformation that was already under way. Divided inheritance over generations was shrinking each landholder's income and, by the end of the thirteenth century, families were attempting to consolidate all of their lands under a single, male heir. The subsequent political instability accompanying the fall of the Kamakura regime, and the increase in population due to rising productivity, compounded the difficulty each warrior family faced.[1] Not only women but also secondary sons experienced the diminution or loss of land rights. But sons and daughters were different; the subsequent opportunities life offered would not be the same for men as for women.[2]

Land and Male Honor

The consolidation of family resources under one man was both a defensive and a potentially aggressive measure. The form of landholding also began to change, from the *shōen* system, under which multiple holders enjoyed segmented rights (including *jitō*) over the same land unit, to a territorial system under which a single lord controlled the entire unit.

The main heir was responsible for keeping or promoting the strength of the corporate family unit associated with its ancestral territory. For him, the land itself was both real and symbolic in the power it authorized. The family's *name*—its history, honor, prestige, and strength—was closely tied to the land it possessed, and the heir was charged with the defense and promotion of the economic and human resources that defined the land's military capacity. If the heir lacked strength, he could subordinate himself and his resources to a more powerful lord. Secondary sons, who held little or no land independently, had little choice but to become vassals of the heir or of another territorial lord. And female family members, like younger sons, were subordinated to the authority of the main heir—although daughters were different from sons because they could not be integrated into the vassal corps. This does not mean that women never wielded weapons; rather, women were not part of the regular army, which was part of the multilayered, two-way exchange of service and reward in the personalized relationship between lord and vassal.

Service under the Kamakura Shogunate, a formal government with a countrywide network of retainers, had been more bureaucratic than personal, and therefore open to women *jitō*. In the new age, the name of the reward land, an embodiment of masculine pride, was linked to a man's lineage, which followed patrilineal descent. War tales, beginning with the fourteenth-century *Taiheiki* (*Record of the Grand Pacification*) and followed by many others, glorified masculine courage in killing and dying, often expressed in phrases such as "Let us embellish our *name* by being the first to charge into the enemy." Women were outside this rhetoric. The exigencies of the war-prone society, restructured military units, and an evolving consciousness of masculinity left women no opportunity to hold land with military value.

Battles and Women

As wars escalated in the fifteenth and sixteenth centuries, women received no rewards for meritorious deeds. Or rather, if they did, we have no reliable records of it. One court diary mentions a "female cavalry" with no further explanation, but this could be more metaphor than real, meant to degrade the army by feminizing it. Nevertheless, women did fight, but outside the context of documented action that led to rewards. Women were fully embedded in the violence of the time, as they typically stayed in the fortresses or castle towns with their husbands. Oda Nobunaga even punished vassals who refused to move their entire families to a castle area. Sengoku battles often took the form of sieges wherein the entire family would fight to defend the castle. In 1589 the Jesuit missionary Louis Frois observed that women defended Amakusa Hondo Castle against Konishi Yukinaga's attack so bravely that "they filled the moat with the bodies they slew."[3]

"The Memoir of Oan" is a unique, secondhand recollection of a woman's experience during the battle of Sekigahara (1600).[4] In it we read of women supporting the army by casting bullets for muskets. They also enhanced the appearance of severed enemy heads brought back as trophies, blackening the teeth and restyling the hair to elevate the apparent rank of the enemy and increase the reward their men would receive from their lord for capturing it. Nights spent in a room with a pile of bloody heads apparently left a strong impression on Oan.

MARRIAGE, ADOPTION, AND SEX

Warlords (daimyo) of the Warring States period were innovative, implementing increasingly sophisticated techniques for gaining strategic advantage. Their methods touched on every aspect of life, from deciphering weather, refining weapons, and constructing fortresses to extracting taxes and enhancing ritual and cultural capital such as tea wares, Noh dances, and poetic accomplishments. Consolidation of alliances through marriage ties was another such technique.

Marriage in late medieval Japan was thoroughly patrilocal (in contrast to the matrilocal practice more typical of classical times), and the typical husband had one primary wife, identified as such, as well as a number of concubines. Under this arrangement, the wife distanced herself from the network of support she had had in her natal house and thoroughly integrated herself in her new home. She took on the administrative requirements of the military household, including arranging ceremonies and rituals, hosting visitors, managing vassalage relationships and her husband's concubines—in addition, of course, to bearing and educating children. There was little division between what we might call public and domestic; the entire household was devoted to the promotion of its business. The wife had her tasks to perform, and the husband his. Many women came to be known as powerful wives or mothers, well informed and well enough versed in military affairs to counsel vassals on strategic matters.[5] Even so, wives were ultimately outsiders, whose ties to their natal families never broke completely. They did not change their names to those of their husbands, and according to some daimyo laws, their trousseau land was to be administered according to testaments written by their natal families. A wife's position, moreover, did not necessarily assure a peaceful relationship between the two families. She also could become a target of suspicion from her husband and his retinue.

Marriage also had a symbolic meaning. For major warlords, the splendid procession that carried the woman's body, trousseau, and entourage to the man's house visually and symbolically declared the military might of the two houses. In general, brides were some warlord's daughter or sister but, given the limited supply of those women, daimyo also adopted girls from other families, called them daughters, and married them to vassals to assure allegiance.

By far the most famous "trafficked woman" is Oda Nobunaga's sister Oichi (1547?–1583). Nobunaga wedded her first to Azai Nagamasa, whom he destroyed in 1573, whereupon Oichi and her children were released. Then Nobunaga's successor, Toyotomi Hideyoshi, forced her to marry Shibata Katsuie. The following year, Hideyoshi destroyed Shibata Katsuie, and this time Oichi chose death over yet another forced marriage. From her first marriage, Oichi had three daughters, who survived her. Hideyoshi took one as his concubine, and the two other sisters each became the wife of an important lord, Kyōgoku Tametsugu and Tokugawa Hidetada (the second Tokugawa shogun). Oichi's main son was killed and another took the tonsure. Trafficked women were victims and lacked the freedom to choose their mates. On the other hand, so did most husbands, upon whom wives were often imposed for potentially dangerous political purposes.

Warrior society maintained a pragmatic and flexible concept of kinship, adjusting nomenclature as needed. Warrior families often adopted boys and even adult men to carry on the family line. Adoptees, male or female, were socially recognized as members of the adopting line. One extraordinary warlord, Uesugi Kenshin (1530–1578), who himself had two adopted fathers, never had a wife or biological sons, but adopted four sons, one his older sister's son and another a son of the Hōjō, a rival house. Although adoption was as viable a method for obtaining an heir as impregnating wives, neither option completely preempted a dispute over control after the lord's death, as exemplified by the war Kenshin's two adopted sons started after his demise.

The institution of marriage operated as a part of a larger organizational unit, the family, lineage, and the army corps, with the goal of promoting their human and material resources. For reproduction, marriage predicated sexual relationships between the man and the woman, but love and sexual desire only partially defined a family. To be sure, affection underpinned some husband-wife relationships, such as the one between Hideyoshi and Oné, who married in 1561, long before Hideyoshi's rise to prominence. But male sexual desire was wide-ranging.

Polygamy being the norm for warlords, and a husband's desire for his main wife was easily diverted to concubines. Hideyoshi's passion for his mistress Yodo, one of Oichi's daughters, is also legendary. It was the male seed that counted, though the mother's identity also mattered.

In addition, a husband's sexuality was often directed toward other males, especially boys. All sexual relationships, male or female, influenced the strength and well-being of the fighting unit. Common among warriors and priests, male-male sex horrified the Jesuits who visited Japan in the sixteenth century. Alessandro Valignano lamented: "They are much addicted to sensual vices and sins, a thing which has always been true of pagans, . . . [and] their great dissipation in the sin that does not bear mentioning [is] regarded so lightly that both the boys and the men who consort with them brag and talk about it openly without trying to cover the matter up."[6] Yet this was a society and a time with no classificatory categories for sexual choice; desire ran across a continuum, without the participants making moral judgments. The culture of the time freely applied the vocabulary of aesthetics, especially to young men. Oda Nobunaga's younger brother, "who was no more than fifteen or sixteen years old," for example, is described as having possessed "skin white as powder, exquisite lips red as a peony," while "his countenance so surpassed any beauty's that no metaphor could express it."[7]

ARISTOCRATS AND THE IMPERIAL FAMILY

Gender relations in aristocratic society changed greatly between classical and medieval times, but the shape of that transformation was not the same as that experienced by the warrior class, except for one feature: Female aristocrats received less and less inheritance after the fourteenth century. Nevertheless, among aristocrats, the reduced economic prerogatives of women occurred as part of the broader dissolution of the courtiers' landed wealth into the hands of the rising warriors—a major loss that affected the entire class.

Penury was not the only hardship courtiers experienced. As a class, they had lived for centuries rooted in one location, Kyoto, but the Ōnin War (1467–1477) destroyed many of their residences, forcing them to move elsewhere. In the late fifteenth century, many returned to Kyoto, but during the Sengoku period, the court had to make ends meet with much-reduced human and economic resources. The poverty of this class determined the course many of its members took.

Women Around the Emperors

Whereas the Heian and Kamakura periods produced abundant literary masterpieces written by aristocratic women, changing circumstances in the fourteenth century and thereafter gave educated women fewer reasons to write—and little of what they did write survives. A gendered comparison is useful. From the period between 1350 and 1600 more than one hundred journals by aristocratic men have survived, but the last journal we have by an aristocratic woman dates from the mid-fourteenth century.[8] Instead of writing diaries, female administrators served as personal scribes for emperors and transmitted imperial messages. They also maintained a remarkable record, the *Oyudono no ue no nikki* (*Imperial Housekeeping Record*; literally, "Journal from the [room called] Oyudono no ue"), which logs continuously from 1477 to 1826 the emperors' personal and ceremonial affairs, including sutra reading; visitors and gifts received; attendance at Noh, dance, and music performances; food and sake consumed; and bathing and hair grooming, along with select incidents, such as the theft of clothes in the palace. As this record reveals, women filled indispensable functions in managing the details of imperial affairs.

In considering changes in gender relations, we must also remember that between 592 and 770, eight out of sixteen emperors were female.[9] Yet between the reigns of Emperor Go-Daigō (1318–1339) and Emperor Go-Mizunoo (1618–1629), the court produced no prominent female figures, or even women holding the title of imperial wife. For nearly three hundred years—until Hidetada (ruled 1605–1623), the second Tokugawa shogun, married his fifth daughter, Masako (1607–1678), to Emperor Go-Mizunoo in 1620—Japan's male emperors remained formally unmarried and had sex with the women around them.[10] The major reason for this astounding state of affairs was the lack of funds to support the formal Office of Empress and its requisite architectural space, officials, serving personnel, and ceremonies.

The regent and ministerial families having sufficient rank to supply imperial wives also were too poor to contribute to the upkeep of the empress's quarters. Court women thus became mothers of crown princes without being wives of emperors. These women came from the third or fourth tier of the aristocratic hierarchy and were too low in rank to take the title of imperial wife. As functionaries, female officials sustained the weakened imperial office with their crucial, multitasking contributions, both administrative and sexual. But, in contrast to the Heian period, when wives' natal families put enormous pressure on the behavior of emperors, the late medieval era provided few opportunities for a woman's male kin to exert influence.

Courtier Families

Precise divisions marked the strict hierarchy of prestige among aristocratic families. Bureaucratic ranks and titles, held across generations, roughly coincided with the family's social status. At the top were the regent families, followed by those that rose to the positions of Minister of the Left and Minister of the

Right. Marriage for these elites was complicated in the Sengoku period. In the past, regent families had married daughters to princes and emperors and never married down. Now that emperors were not marrying, their family members intermarried within their peer group and leftover sons and daughters were sent to monasteries and nunneries. Some daughters became wives of the Ashikaga shoguns.

As with warriors, marriage became a more public affair than ever before, made visible by formalized ceremonies. In contrast to the imperial family, in aristocratic households the position of primary wife grew in importance. Each aristocratic family in the Sengoku period became identified with a house-specific profession or talent: shrine affairs for the Yoshida; poetry for the Nijō, Reizei, Asukai, and Sanjōnishi; *biwa* lute for the Fushimi, Saionji, Imadegawa, Ayanokōji, and Sono; yin-yang divination for the Tsuchimikado; and so on. With this development, the primary wife became responsible for promoting these family professions, and the practical techniques for guarding them passed from senior to junior wives. The new patrilocal residential arrangements, wherein two (or more) generations increasingly lived together, facilitated this mode of transmission. Another change, and a tell-tale sign of the significance of the male line, was that primary wives were buried in the cemeteries of their husbands, in contrast to the Heian period, when a wife's tombstone was separate from that of her husband's family. This signaled the consolidation of the patrilineal structure and a more complete transfer of married women into the husbands' line, but it did not necessarily mean that the authority of the individual female as wife and mother was weakened within the household.

COMMONERS

Sources for understanding gender relations among commoners are scarce for all periods. But compared to earlier times, improved productivity and increasing commercialization, on the one side, and the warfare, rebellions, and other hardships, on the other, generated written and pictorial materials that allow us to imagine medieval commoners' lives in cities and villages.

In highly commercialized cities, especially Kyoto, artisans and merchants from near and far set up shops and congregated at markets. Women headed a number of merchant guilds. The most renowned were guilds for indigo dye, salt, fans, and brocade sashes made of Nishijin silk, some of which were important export items to Ming China. These guild proprietors' names appeared in disputes over trade or when the Muromachi Shogunate confirmed rights to it. The *Shokunin uta awase* (*Pictorial and Poetic Representations of Artisans and Merchants*), from 1500, mentions 142 artisans and traders. Although the figures represented are imagined caricatures by artists and not necessarily precise portrayals of real commoners, they suggest a general range of gendered ideal job types. Of the 142, 108 are male and 34 female. Interestingly, female-gendered jobs are of the sort modern society associates with the domestic sphere, female aesthetics, and sexuality: weaving textiles and sewing; making dye and cosmetics; brewing and selling sake; selling cotton, *tatami* mat paper, fans, *obi* sashes, and food; and performing as blind female singers, stand-up solicitors for prostitution, dancers, and various types of priestesses and shamans. In contrast, the male-gendered trades include a wider array of tasks: making and selling clothing for men; making bows, arrows, rafts, and Buddha statues; making pots; making papers; and crafting gold and silver items. Yin-yang artists, Zen and Ritsu Buddhists, mountain ascetics, doctors, *biwa* players, *sarugaku* dancers, *renga* poets, and kitchen knife wielders were also professions portrayed as male.

Among female professions, the category of stand-up solicitors helps us to consider the way in which certain females lost independent agency over the centuries. In early medieval times, female entertainers (*yūjo*) who sang, danced, and also engaged in sex managed their own profession and enjoyed the patronage of emperors and aristocrats. By 1500, with the rise of the money economy, sex, too, became a commodity. In 1589, Toyotomi Hideyoshi authorized the establishment of a brothel quarter in Kyoto to place these women under the eyes of male political authority. Similarly, the depiction of female sake brewers and sellers in 1500 commands our attention. Until the mid-fifteenth century, sake brewing was a woman's profession. Then warrior and temple authorities began formally taxing sake. They created formal registers that listed names responsible for the tax, following an age-old convention of listing men's names regardless of who did the labor or who had actual authority over the trade. A temple register of 347 sake makers compiled in 1426 shows only three female names. In the sixteenth and seventeenth centuries, the sake-brewing profession was gendered male both on paper and in practice, and by the mid-Tokugawa period, women were barred even from entering the brewery, because of a developing notion, closely tied to religious rituals, of female-specific pollution that was, by then, believed to defile the sake. Prostitution and sake brewing came to be controlled by male authority in different ways and for different reasons, but those who took control were in a position to gain economically, and women's autonomy was, in turn, limited.

The late medieval period was, nonetheless, a vibrant time for women's creative expression. Female entertainers, shamans, priestesses, picture-explainers, and yin-yang specialists traversed the archipelago, narrated popular stories of hell and salvation, and collected payment from the audience. Some of these women became famous. A nineteen-year-old female *kusemai* dancer from Mino province, for example, was "so splendid as to defy speech," and more than four thousand people watched as she performed in Kyoto in 1466. Female dancers flourished, but male entertainers such as the Noh performer Zeami who had the patronage of shogunal officials disparaged the art of itinerant female entertainers.

In rural areas self-governing villages (*sō*), such as Imabori and Sugaura in the Kinai provinces, emerged to protect community interests. Village records show the workings of a sophisticated, self-ruled community that imposed its will on authorities. When these villages had violent altercations with neighboring communities, both women and men picked up available tools and fought. But the formal decision-making process rested mostly with men, who were the formal members of the shrine organization that administered rituals and community affairs. Men in some villages, especially in the east, were conscripted by warlords to fight in battles. In the absence of men, women took over their tasks in the fields, and in this sense as well, women's undocumented labor helped to sustain the late medieval machinery of war and economy.

VICTIMIZATION

The news of approaching battles must have been ominous to villagers. Typically the enemy warlords' foot soldiers (*ashigaru*) stole horses and food, destroyed harvests, and abducted people. The abductees were overwhelmingly women and young boys and girls, and according to Frois, they endured "cruelty that cannot be stated"—that is, rape. Some were also sold into prostitution or slavery and sent to Macao, Manila, and Europe on Portuguese and Spanish ships. Apparently, female slaves had a higher cash value than males. The law code of the Date daimyo house, *Jinkaishū,* stated that if an escaped slave were found, the rightful owner had to pay three hundred *hiki* cash for a male slave and five hundred *hiki* cash for a female slave.

An economy in transformation, dispersed political authority, and the stress from perpetual violence affected how men and women allocated resources and related to one another. These centuries saw attempts to stabilize family, lineage, and community through masculine principles, including marriage practice, village organization, and business operations. In this process the gendered allocation of power shifted, without necessarily benefiting men. Among aristocrats, the power of men grew precarious, while women solidified their personal authority within the masculinized framework. Warriors, the seeming guardians of masculine principles, developed those tenets to the point of self-suffocation and forced much suffering on others and themselves. The most vivacious group may have been the itinerant women who, outside that framework, relied on their own resources and built the foundation of an imaginative popular culture.

Sources and Suggestions for Further Reading

See the bibliography for complete publication data.

Cooper, Michael, ed. *They Came to Japan: An Anthology of European Reports on Japan* (1965).

Farris, William Wayne. *Japan's Medieval Population: Famine, Fertility, and Warfare in a Transformative Age* (2006).

Kurushima Noriko. "Marriage and Female Inheritance in Medieval Japan" (2004).

Tonomura, Hitomi. "Re-envisioning Women in the Post-Kamakura Age" (1997).

———. "Women and Sexuality in Premodern Japan" (2007).

Tonomura, Hitomi, Anne Walthall, and Wakita Haruko, eds. *Women and Class in Japanese History* (1999).

Wakita Haruko. *Women in Medieval Japan: Motherhood, Household, Management, and Sexuality* (2006).

Notes

1. The population doubled during that period, and famine and disease were less lethal.

2. The shogunate also prohibited women from adopting heirs of their own, previously a legal practice that had been common.

3. Fujiki Hisashi, *Kiga to sensō no sengoku o iku*, 201–202.

4. Oan died at the age of more than eighty sometime between 1661 and 1673, and the story, originally told to a child of nine, was in print by 1730.

5. Famous examples include Toyotomi Hideyoshi's wife, Oné (or Nene), and Uesugi Kenshin's sister Sentōin.

6. Cooper, *They Came to Japan,* 46. Valignano (1539–1606) was in Japan in 1579–1582, 1590–1592, and 1598–1603.

7. Okuno Takahiro and Iwasawa Yasuhiko, *Shinchō kōki*, 39.

8. *Writing in View of the Bamboo (Takemukigaki),* by Hino Meishi (d. 1358), described in Tonomura, "Re-envisioning Women in the Post-Kamakura Age," 139–153.

9. More precisely six of fourteen imperial personages were women, because two women reigned twice.

10. Following the fashion of Heian and Kamakura times, Masako entered the palace in 1620 but did not receive the title of wife (*chūgū*) until 1624. She gave birth to two sons, both of whom died young, and five daughters. The second daughter succeeded to the throne as Emperor Meishō (ruled 1629–1643) and became the first woman to reign in eight and a half centuries.

26

The Rise of the Peasantry

Thomas Keirstead

Marx famously likened them to potatoes in a "sack of potatoes": individual, yet indistinguishable from one another; comprising a "vast mass," but unable because of the nature of their relationships to land and property to act as anything other than atomized units. "Small-holding peasants," he wrote in *The 18th Brumaire of Louis Bonaparte,*

> live in similar conditions but without entering into manifold relations with one another. Their mode of production isolates them from one another instead of bringing them into mutual intercourse. . . . Each individual peasant family is almost self-sufficient, directly produces most of its consumer needs, and thus acquires its means of life more through an exchange with nature than in intercourse with society. A small holding, the peasant and his family; beside it another small holding, another peasant and another family. A few score of these constitute a village, and a few score villages constitute a department.[1]

As a result, peasants are isolated, politically inert, reactionary in defense of their smallholdings, and thus susceptible to being "rescued . . . from the idiocy of rural life" by the bourgeoisie.[2]

Decades of scholarship and successful peasant-led insurgencies in China and Southeast Asia have disputed Marx's characterization of the political possibilities of the peasantry. Yet other parts of the formulation, which is by no means restricted to Marx, remain influential, perhaps because they seem so commonsensical. By definition, it seems, peasants are farmers, they work small plots of land—enough to support a family, sometimes a bit more, but never a lot more—and they live in isolated rural villages. They are largely self-sufficient; premodern rural life is marked by little of the differentiation of labor or specialized production that distinguishes towns (or modern agriculture). Derived no doubt from the state of rural life in eighteenth- and nineteenth-century Europe, these ideas conjure up an image that is hard to shake. Yet as this chapter shows, the three key elements of the definition of a peasant—self-sufficiency, agriculture, and the village—merit further examination. In the case of medieval Japan, while it may be true that the bulk of the population did not live in cities and that agriculture was an essential occupation, there is sufficient variance to suggest that the standard definition needs to be extensively qualified.

THE PROBLEMATIC NATURE OF THE SOURCES

Anyone trying to write about the medieval Japanese peasantry faces some seemingly intractable difficulties. One significant problem arises from the character and quality of the sources one must use. Since the vast majority of the peasant population was illiterate, historians depend on people of other social orders for information about the peasantry. And the elites who possessed the literacy and means to record events showed little interest in the everyday lives of common folk. While elites kept meticulous records of their lands and the revenues they derived therefrom (documents from which we can infer a good deal about certain aspects of rural life), hardly any sources comment directly on the peasantry. The same is true of the few documents generated by peasants themselves. They overwhelmingly concern legal proceedings: land disputes, contested inheritances, complaints about rents and taxes, remonstrances against the misdeeds of government officials—situations, that is, unusual enough to warrant documenting. The records in which peasants appear are therefore doubly exceptional: few in number and likely to stress unusual situations. Peasants show up in the documentary record when behaving atypically—refusing to pay their rents and taxes, complaining about damage to their crops, rebelling against estate owners or managers. The written record, while loquacious on certain topics, is far more reticent on everyday concerns. Our picture of the lives of commoners is skewed toward disputes, confrontation, and uprisings.

Since neutral descriptions of rural life are exceptionally rare, historians have turned to materials such as picture scrolls for less biased portraits. Some scrolls do feature scenes of rural life. One illustrating the life of the monk Ippen (1234–1289), for example, shows peasants tilling the fields and paying rents; one famous scene depicts a rural market, affording us a chance to see peasants bringing goods to market and a sense of the variety of goods produced in the countryside. The focal point of these scrolls is the holy man passing by or the miracle being performed by the patron saint of a shrine—the peasants provide background color. Precisely because they are not the center of attention, it might be supposed that such images offer a glimpse into "normal" peasant life. And that could be the case; the oft-cited scene of rice transplanting in the picture scroll depicting the life of the monk Hōnen (*Hōnen shōnin eden*) might well be a faithful rendition of a ritual carried out innumerable times across the centuries. Men prepare the rice paddy (one guides a harrow pulled by a horse through the muddy field, another follows smoothing the surface with a wide rake), while women transplant the seedlings; a pair of drummers and a man with a kind of rattle provide rhythmic accompaniment. The scene has become iconic (it is quoted at the close of Kurosawa's *Seven Samurai*, for instance) as a representation of the close-knit character of village life. We see peasants working together at one of the pivotal events of the agricultural calendar. We also catch sight of the gendered division of labor, something that land surveys, tax registers, and legal proceedings do not comment on. There is no doubt that the image is rich and that it allows us to "see" rural life in a compelling way. Yet simply because an image offers a seemingly realistic portrait of a scene from daily life does not mean that it can be taken at face value. The images of rural tranquility to be found in picture scrolls may also be ideologically charged.

One of the few images in which a peasant features front and center is also a good example of the difficulties that even simple depictions can present. The picture is found in an unusual source: an illustrated scroll depicting a poetry contest between pairs of craftsmen. A number of such scrolls survive for the medieval period, the earliest dating to the thirteenth century, the last to about 1600. Poetry contests were a fashionable elite pursuit. Groups competed in pairs to see who could produce the better poem on a set topic; frequently a judge was named whose duty it was to decide the winner in each pair and explain why the winning poem was superior. The poetry contests featuring tradespeople form a distinct subgenre. In these contests, the competing poets take on the persona of craftsmen and -women, and the goal is to exemplify the character of the artisan or laborer being performed. While these contests could be simple party games, they might on occasion be much more elaborate affairs, one worth recording for posterity in, for example, an illustrated scroll.

In one such scroll, produced at the close of the fifteenth century, we find the figure of a peasant—in the company of a painter, lion-dance performer, monkey trainer, vegetable seller, stonemason, Zen monk, and Pure Land priest, and another twenty-odd tradespeople. He is exchanging poems on "reminiscence" with a gardener. The image shows a man, in a walking pose, with a hoe against his right shoulder. He is dressed extremely simply—a single robe held shut with a nondescript sash. His hair is tied up in a rudimentary topknot. Other images in the scroll are more complex: figures shown with companions or surrounded by tools or wares that identify their trades. Clothing and headgear, too, can be important markers, distinguishing, for example, a Zen monk from a follower of the Pure Land sect. The peasant, by contrast, is simplicity itself—no distinguishing garments, no special wares. Only the hoe and the label *nōjin*, "farmer" or "cultivator," identify the figure as a peasant. In fact, the lack of specific features seems to be what identifies the peasant most: he is a simple farmer, someone whose life and livelihood are tied to the land and to agriculture.

In this respect, however, the figure in the scroll is misleading. Even a cursory survey of the rent rolls in which major landowners recorded the goods collected from their holdings reveals that "farmers" produced a stunning variety of goods—including many manifestly nonagricultural goods. Rice, wheat, millet, buckwheat, hemp, soybeans, and other crops are common, but so are agricultural goods that have undergone varying degrees of processing, such as sake, vinegar, miso, and lamp oil (pressed from sesame or rapeseed). Lumber and wood products, including charcoal, were regularly assessed as rents from some parts of the country, while extensively manufactured goods such as lacquerware, silk, and tools, are also commonplace. Some villages appear to have specialized in the manufacture of salt or iron. In short, the image in the scroll misrepresents the great variety of enterprise engaged in by the figure it labels an "agriculturalist."

Reading the accompanying poem also casts the "farmer" in a rather different light. The cultivator remarks somewhat wistfully, "Gathering, grumbling menacingly about restitution for damaged crops—that's what farmers are known for now."[3] The judge's commentary elaborates: "Farmers protest to local authorities demanding redress for lost crops, . . . then they make trouble." The hoe the peasant shoulders, then, is not as we might suppose on first glance simply a tool for tilling the soil; it is also a weapon. The farmer is not a simple cultivator, but a political actor, known for his threatening, rebellious attitude toward those in authority. The message seems clear. The poem and its commentary show that the picture is deceptive, that peasants can be duplicitous. While they should be simple cultivators, respectful and submissive toward their betters, they are in fact prone to challenging authority.

This picture of peasants and the threat they pose reflects the political situation at the time of the scroll's composition. Over the course of the fifteenth century, the capital region was beset by a series of large-scale uprisings involving leagues of local warriors, cultivators, and others. In 1428, for example, an uprising by cart drivers (*bashaku*) who transported rice and other goods within the capital region was joined by peasants and local warriors, who flooded into the capital breaking into pawnshops and wrecking warehouses. Again in 1441, a league of peasants and warriors seized upon the turmoil occasioned by the assassination of the shogun Yoshinori to demand that the shogunate issue a decree canceling debts. The largest of the uprisings broke out in 1485 in the region just south of the capital. The area had been plagued for years by the armies of two warlords, who battled back and forth across the region as they tried to gain control of a vital road connecting Kyoto to Nara. These marauding armies incited local landholders and warriors to join together in opposition to the two warlords. A string of uprisings broke out in the summer of 1485, with peasants demonstrating in the capital calling for the cancelation of their debts, and cart drivers in Nara protesting for the abolition of tolls on the roads. Pierre-Francois Souyri describes the scene:

> On the eleventh day of the twelfth lunar month, the local barons and warriors of the southern districts of Yamashiro formed a council with thirty-six members and went solemnly, bearing torches, to the nearby Iwashimizu Hachiman shrine, where they exchanged bowls of sacred water and held talks. Their curiosity piqued, the peasants of the area went running to the shrine. Soon, a crowd surrounded the sacred site where the council was meeting. It was decided to mobilize the entire population of southern Yamashiro in an ikki [league]. An ultimatum was sent to the two armies, demanding their immediate and unconditional withdrawal from the province, and the league threatened violence against those who did not comply. . . . After that, assemblies of low-ranking warriors and peasants were held all over southern Yamashiro province.[4]

The leagues went on to promulgate a set of *Rules and Laws of the Province*, to charge taxes, and to dispense justice—all prerogatives usually reserved for the governor of a province.

DEFINING "PEASANTS"

The events of the time point to another fundamental difficulty that arises when we try to discuss the medieval peasantry: the difficulty of determining who was or was not a peasant. In the context of the Yamashiro Uprising and its league, it is difficult to tell who exactly is a peasant or a warrior or to say who is ruler and who ruled. An armed peasant who joins a league that asserts political authority is not so easily pigeonholed as a simple cultivator. To be sure, these were extraordinary events, but even in normal times, the "peasantry" is not easily defined.

This is a common problem facing historians of the peasantry in many societies: status terms like "peasant" are notoriously difficult to define, and the boundaries of status groups tend to be porous. In Japan, the problem is compounded by nomenclature. Since perhaps the end of the sixteenth century, *hyakushō* has been the generic term for peasant; nowadays, the term means "farmer." The word also appears regularly in documents from earlier eras. In the middle ages, for example, petitions calling for rent relief or complaining about the misdeeds of a local official are invariably signed by the "*hyakushō*" of such-and-such a village. When landowners sent orders—to cooperate with surveyors or rent collectors, for example—they invariably addressed them to the "*hyakushō*" of the estate. Because the same term is used, we might be tempted to assume that modern ideas about the peasantry can be transferred to earlier eras. We might conjecture that medieval *hyakushō*, like their early modern and modern namesakes, were farmers who raised crops—especially rice—in order to provide for themselves and their families, that they lived in rural villages, that their lives were tied to the land and the rhythms of agriculture. We might also reason that they were recognized as a broad group or class by those in authority.

The continuity in terminology, however, masks fundamental differences in meaning. In medieval usage, *hyakushō* were not simple farmers. Rather, they were members of a rural elite, one that, as the available documentation attests, had its hand in any number of enterprises, not just agriculture.

Prior to the Tokugawa period, Japan had no generic term for "peasant." It had instead a welter of terms, some very local, some in widespread use, for various types of cultivators or local landholders. Invariably, the terms do not describe occupational categories, but indicate different kinds of status within the systems that defined medieval landholding and taxation. Although many *hyakushō* may have been farmers or what we might recognize as peasants, the term also encompassed people whom we would think of as warriors or officials or craftsmen. It took centuries and a revolution in governing structures for a peasant class to emerge. Thus when historians speak of a medieval Japanese peasantry, they are importing a category that did not exist at the time; we should be careful to regard it as a heuristic device, not a simple description of medieval reality. "Peasant" or *hyakushō* signifies a "vast mass," but not a uniform group. The terms identify, instead, a heterogeneous nonurban non-elite—a group that included, but was not at all confined to, self-sufficient, smallholding farmers.

THE HISTORICAL DEVELOPMENT OF A PEASANTRY

Several institutional developments shaped this "vast mass." Transformations in the state and its institutions that governed landholding and revenue collection were among the most important. The first imperial state, as it came into being in the seventh and eighth centuries, created an elaborate bureaucracy and a hierarchy of rank and office tied to that bureaucracy. But below a certain threshold, it was remarkably evenhanded, preferring to regard everyone equally as subjects of the emperor. *Hyakushō* meant something close to its literal meaning—the "hundred surnames." Since "hundred" here indicates "myriad" or "countless," the term encompassed the entirety of society, save for the nobility, the imperial house, and some outcast groups. In this, the early Japanese state followed Chinese usage, established in the *Analects* and other classical texts, in which the term refers to everyone who possessed a surname. *Hyakushō* indicated, in effect, the broad public. The state's population registers did not differentiate by occupation or location, thus regarding farmers and merchants, city dwellers and villagers alike as commoners. Each commoner was allotted a certain portion of rice paddy, which was to return to the state after his or her death. In return, commoners owed the state various labor services and taxes assessed on their portion of land. Only rice paddy was deemed taxable, although other types of land—from vegetable plots to woodlots—might be subject to miscellaneous levies.

Within a couple of centuries, this system foundered. The cumbersome nature of the land distribution system; the fact that land was not inheritable (providing little incentive to individuals to improve their holdings); lack of cooperation from elites, who were the major beneficiaries of the tax revenues—these and other developments brought an end to the imperial state's disinterested treatment of the populace. The land distributions ceased as did, somewhat later, the direct collection of taxes and other levies from ordinary commoners. In place of direct, centralized rule, an indirect approach to governing and revenues emerged, and the central elites turned increasingly to middlemen to manage their affairs. A significant portion of public land was removed from the state's authority and reconstituted as private estates (see chapter 16), while even public lands came to be governed in ways that closely resembled those of private estates. As a result, by the mid-eleventh and early twelfth centuries, what historians refer to as the system of estates and public lands had taken shape. In this system, successful elite groups, often temples or aristocratic families, recruited clients at different levels of the social hierarchy, offering them patronage (including appointment to office, for which influential sponsorship could be decisive) in return for secure revenues. Empowered by the rank and office bestowed on them, these clients became in effect tax farmers for the central elites, collecting the annual land rents and miscellaneous levies, forwarding an agreed-upon portion up the chain, and siphoning off the rest for themselves. The sharp rise in protests against provincial governors and their agents that begins at the very close of the tenth century and continues through the eleventh offers an index of the changes occurring. As central elites turned over management of the countryside to new agents, the system underwent a period of adjustment, with the middlemen testing just how independent (i.e., rapacious) they could be before drawing fire from either side.

These transformations in governance, landholding, and revenue collection introduced changes that reordered the landscape, with profound consequences for the inhabitants. For example, in Echizen province from about the middle of the eleventh century, new units of governance proliferated—within a century upwards of one hundred new estates, hamlets, and other units had been created, each constituting part of the asset base of a vertically aligned structure of patronage. As these structures took over work that a couple of centuries earlier had been performed by the state and its legal and bureaucratic apparatus, old terms assumed new meanings. Notably, *hyakushō*, which had indicated nearly the entire commoner populace, came to identify those who occupied the lowest tier in these structures. On estates and public lands, *hyakushō* were responsible for the land rent and other levies, and their holdings were the basic units for assessing and collecting these levies. In return, they were confirmed as local elites and gained standing to remonstrate with authorities and pursue legal cases in the proprietor's courts. As noted earlier, though historians commonly refer to *hyakushō* as peasants, these were not peasants in the modern sense of the term, but a mixed group that included warriors, landlords (many *hyakushō* possessed land far in excess of what could be farmed by a single family), and craftsmen, as well as farmers.

Still, we can note a pair of developments that prefigure later shifts in the meaning of the term. First, seen from above, from the perspective of the central elites, *hyakushō* came to resemble what we know as peasants. A pervasive agrarianism infects documents relating to land. Surveys, rent rolls, and similar documents—and these are among the most common types of sources from the premodern era—all tend to treat nonagrarian production as if it were agrarian. On many estates, salt or iron production was accounted for as if it, like rice, grew out of the ground. As a result, landholders counted as "farmers" many whose livelihoods depended on trade or manufactures and not agriculture; *hyakushō*, whatever their actual means of livelihood, tend to appear in documents of the era as if they were peasant farmers.

Second, the devolution of revenue collection and other aspects of land management to middlemen and local elites reinforced a growing separation between the central aristocracy, firmly ensconced in the capital city of Heian, and the provinces—thus firmly identifying *hyakushō* with the countryside. Again, documents produced on behalf of the great landowners tend to paint a picture of rural, agrarian uniformity that obscures the real diversity. An example comes from the fourteenth century and an estate held by Tōji, the great Shingon temple in Kyoto.

In 1334 a monk named Jinson, sent the previous year to survey the Niimi Estate (in western Japan, not far from present-day Okayama) and assess its rents, sent his accounts to the temple. The resulting document is a detailed accounting of the rents due from the estate. The result of a painstaking field survey, the scroll summarizes the rents due from each unit of the estate. For each holding, it lists first the amount of rice paddy and the overall annual rent (this is calculated in bushels of rice—a bit of subterfuge for much of the estate, which was a major center of iron production), then the extent of "damaged fields" (fields not in cultivation for a variety of reasons), and deducts the latter amount to arrive at the total taxable paddy for the particular holding; beneath these two amounts it lists the rent deducted and the final rent assessed for the year. Dry fields are given the same treatment, as are *yamahata*, or "mountain fields," meager plots carved out of the mountainous areas most likely by slash-and-burn methods; both of these types of fields are assessed a rent in "miscellaneous grains." And so it goes for about twelve meters of scroll, accounting for all of the fields on the estate, tallying up the rents owed, and deducting the amounts allocated for various expenses (such as sake for the annual New Year's banquet for the *hyakushō* and the estate administrator). All of this is typical of such documents, from the ways fields are classified (rice paddy, dry field, mountain field) to the reductions in rent allowed for damaged fields.

Near the end of this prodigious document, though, comes a short segment featuring a slightly different style of notation. At first glance, the accounting seems to follow the form established for the rest of the scroll: one by one, fields are identified, their size listed, and rents attached. On closer examination, the fourteen entries that fall under the heading "accounts relating to the rear gardens of the market dwellings" display certain important differences from the places listed on the rest of the scroll. There is no mention of paddy or dry field; instead, each site is listed simply as a "place." Each of the fourteen places is noted as having a certain amount of "rear garden" and is assessed a rent—in cash, not in rice or other grain. Each also has a certain amount of space labeled "dwelling" attached to it. The dwellings are suspiciously uniform: about twenty meters on a side, minuscule compared to the holdings on other parts of the estate. Hidden away in this rent roll, described in the language of medieval landholding, is a small town: fourteen establishments of uniform size, probably clustered along a road. Other appurtenances of urban space can also be detected. Distinguishing these fourteen "places" from the rest of the estate's lands, the tax they pay is a straightforward cash rent. Finally, a little further on in the roll we find mention of a piece of land set aside for someone described as the "head of the *hō*." This is a unit derived from the grid used in the city of Heian; a *hō* was a subsection of the large blocks defined by the intersections of the city's avenues. And dwellings in the capital were, just like these, assessed a cash rent. Almost despite itself, then, the estate's accounts reveal a tiny market town, a bit of urban space, identified as such by the fact that it follows the practices concerning rents and organization observed in the capital. Yet the general impression left by the estate's accounts is of an overwhelmingly rural place, where agriculture is the way of life. To the estate's distant owners, Niimi must have seemed very much like an agricultural, village community, exactly the sort of place inhabited in later centuries by peasants.

The reality, as we have seen, appears somewhat different from this portrait. Still, living within the system had its effects. *Hyakushō* gained some considerable advantages by conforming to the expectations of landowners. For example, the emphasis on agriculture (rice farming, in particular) and the clumsy way in which proprietors accounted for nonagrarian production meant that *hyakushō* could readily hide such production from the proprietor's gaze. Likewise, observing the form of belonging to a village community lent the voices of *hyakushō* weight: by the thirteenth century it became a matter of course that pleas for rent relief or other forms of protest be launched in the name of the "*hyakushō*" of such-and-such a locale; from the latter thirteenth century it became increasingly common for the *hyakushō* to style themselves the "collected *hyakushō*" (*sōbyakushō*), so as to emphasize the collective nature of their appeals. And from the middle of the fifteenth century, the tight-knit village community seems to have become the norm.

At least certain features of a peasantry seem, then, to have been in place by the late medieval period. But the crucial distinction—the redefinition of *hyakushō* as an occupational category—came later. Only at the close of the sixteenth century did authorities begin to adopt legislation that enforced the separation of warriors from farmers or craftsmen from cultivators. Hideyoshi's sword hunts of 1585 and his Edict on Changing Status (1591) are perhaps the most famous examples of such endeavors, but it would take another century or more for the concept of a peasantry to be firmly established. Only then could one declare truthfully, as one scholar did, that "*hyakushō* means farmer."[5]

Sources and Suggestions for Further Reading

See the bibliography for complete publication data.

Amino Yoshihiko. "Emperor, Rice, and Commoners" (1996).

Conlan, Thomas D. *State of War: The Violent Order of Fourteenth Century Japan* (2003).

Farris, William Wayne. *Japan's Medieval Population: Famine, Fertility, and Warfare in a Transformative Age* (2006).

Gay, Susan. "The Kawashima: Warrior-Peasants of Medieval Japan" (1986).

Keirstead, Thomas E. *The Geography of Power in Medieval Japan* (1992).

Nagahara Keiji. "The Medieval Peasant" (1990).

Souyri, Pierre-François. *The World Turned Upside Down: Medieval Japanese Society* (2001).

Tonomura, Hitomi. *Community and Commerce in Late Medieval Japan: The Corporate Villages of Tokuchin-ho* (1992).
Troost, Kristina. "Peasants, Elites, and Villages in the Fourteenth Century" (1997).

Notes

1. Marx, *The 18th Brumaire of Louis Napoleon*, 317.
2. Marx and Engels, *The Communist Manifesto*, 225.
3. Sanjūniban shokunin utawase e.
4. Souyri, *The World Turned Upside Down*, 189.
5. Itō Tōgai, cited in Amino, *Rekishi o kangaeru hinto*, 85–86.

27

The Medieval Economy

Ethan Segal

In 1393 the Ashikaga Shogunate announced a new tax on moneylenders and sake brewers in greater Kyoto. They would be expected to pay 6,000 *kanmon* (six million coins) in cash each year to help cover government expenses. It was a huge amount—far more than any individual provincial estate (*shōen*) produced in a given year. But the decree was significant for a number of other reasons as well. First, it revealed that money was widely used in the late fourteenth century. Second, it reflected a uniquely Muromachi-period approach to raising revenue, since the earlier Kamakura Shogunate had never directly taxed commoners. Third, it treated those urban moneylenders as a distinct community, which they were starting to become.

Although the decree of 1393 stands out because of the significant size of the tax, in fact it was in keeping with broader changes under way in medieval society and the economy. In the cities, more people were using coins to buy things in markets, and those who needed cash could rely on urban pawnshops to help them out. In the countryside, estates were converting their annual dues (formerly paid in rice, cloth, or other goods) into money, using cash to bribe provincial warriors, and selling surplus produce in local markets. On many roads and waterways, temples set up toll posts to collect fees from travelers and shippers. Perhaps most remarkable of all, the money that these different groups all sought was not even made in Japan; rather, it was copper cash imported from China.

Japan's medieval age is sometimes described in terms of political fragmentation. Certainly the imperial court, the two warrior governments, major religious institutions, and provincial warriors all competed for control of resources, people, and land. But it was also an age of social mobility, economic expansion, and institutional innovation. Urban residents from varied backgrounds came together in neighborhood communities, while provincial villages became more permanent than they had been in earlier times. People relied on talent, ability, or strength of arms to get ahead. The population grew: most estimates are that Japan was home to six or seven million people around the year 1200, but that it had grown to at least twelve and perhaps as many as seventeen million by the year 1600. Few would have described life as easy, but scourges such as famine and disease did not kill as many people as they had in the Heian and earlier periods. Overall, evidence suggests that the medieval economy was expanding and living conditions were slowly improving.

AGRICULTURAL IMPROVEMENTS

Economic changes can be hard to follow because they lack the precise years that we associate with political events such as wars and elections. The spread of markets, the switch to coins, and the formation of autonomous villages were all gradual processes that happened over centuries. The pace of change was not uniform but varied from region to region and depended on many other developments occurring at roughly the same time. Scholars debate the relationship among these changes. For example, did markets lead people to start using money, or did their use of money make possible the creation of markets? Who created the markets and imported the cash that became medieval Japan's currency? Although these questions have not yet been satisfactorily answered, most agree that an increase in agricultural production was a driving force behind the spread of markets and money in medieval Japan.

There were many reasons for the increase in farm and field production. One was the introduction of Champa rice. This grain, originally from Southeast Asia, was probably introduced to the Japanese islands in the twelfth century. It was heartier, matured more quickly, and resisted drought better than varieties of rice native to Japan. Improvements in irrigation techniques also helped peasants to increase their yields. Wet-rice agriculture requires large amounts of water that can be applied to and drained from fields in a controlled manner. In earlier times, most communities relied on natural irrigation, but during the early medieval period, peasants began creating artificial ponds in mountain valleys to serve as reservoirs. By the fourteenth century, they were constructing "saucer ponds" on the plains to collect runoff that could be used during the growing season. Another important change was the wider availability of draft animals such as horses and oxen. The use of these animals by farmers not only allowed them to plow more deeply but also provided a supply of nutrient-rich fertilizer.

These improvements enabled a few estates by the thirteenth century to begin planting more than one crop per year. Double-cropping increased both yields and variety because the second crop was usually a different grain. An estate might grow rice in the summer and wheat or barley in the fall. On some estates, the agricultural communities were able to produce enough to have a surplus that they could sell in local markets. Estate proprietors had difficulty in capturing this extra output because tax rates were fixed. In addition, most proprietors were either major religious institutions based far away from the estate or members of the aristocracy who lived in the capital. As absentee landlords, they found it hard to accurately assess new field development, double-cropping, or yield increases. Finally, the Kamakura Shogunate, eager to see production increase and thereby stave off famine, issued decrees to prevent its warriors from taxing peasant communities' second harvests. Gradually, estate communities began getting involved in newly emerging local markets, where they could sell estate produce, buy goods from others, and use imported Chinese coins to facilitate their transactions.

MARKETS, CASH, AND GUILDS

Metallic coins and local markets were not completely unheard of in earlier times, of course. Back in the Nara period, the imperial court had minted its own copper cash and used it to pay government officials. Although examples of those coins have been unearthed in every region of the country, it does not appear that ordinary people carried out daily transactions in this currency. Furthermore, by the ninth century an inadequate supply of copper led the mints to start debasing coins: they shrank in size and came to contain more lead than copper. By the tenth century few people used them anymore and the government stopped producing new coinage. Instead, people used rice, silk, and other kinds of cloth as money. As for markets, although there are scattered references to local markets in Nara and Heian times, most economic activity was mediated by the central elites. They collected taxes from public lands and private estates in the form of rice, other food products such as fish or vegetables, and a range of commodities from paper and cloth to lumber and metal ore.

The money that started to come into use in the twelfth century, though, was quite different. Most notably, it was foreign cash imported from China. The vast majority were coins of the Northern Song dynasty (960–1127). China's economy was quite advanced during the Song dynasty. Government mints produced huge amounts of copper cash to facilitate commercial activity and pay for the military. After the fall of the Northern Song in 1127, Chinese traders became more willing to exchange cash for other goods, and some of those coins started to make their way to Japan. Documents from as early as the 1150s contain occasional references to coins being used for land purchases and as temple donations. Coin use must have quickly gained in popularity, though, since merely thirty years later, the imperial court tried to ban the use of foreign money in Japan, claiming that it caused price disruptions and should be considered the same as counterfeit currency. Over the course of the thirteenth and early fourteenth centuries, Chinese coins came to displace rice and silk as the primary medium of exchange. Estates started paying their taxes in cash, Buddhist priests and others affiliated with Mt. Hiei became active as moneylenders, and commercial activities began to pick up.

In the countryside, coins were associated particularly with newly emerging local markets. Many of these markets were established near major temples, both because temples attracted visitors and because they might shield the market from intruding warriors or government officials. Often they were located near rivers or highways, which facilitated the transportation of goods. There were still only a few of these markets in the Kamakura period—probably fewer than thirty in the mid-thirteenth century. And they met infrequently—usually only three times per month—leading scholars to refer to them as *sansai-ichi* (three-meeting markets). One of the few visual representations of these markets is an illustrated scroll honoring the life of Ippen, the thirteenth-century founder of the Ji sect of Buddhism. In the scroll's depiction of the Fukuoka market in Bizen province, we can see people putting their wares on display, negotiating prices, and counting coins. Open days may have been few, but when in session these markets appear to have been bustling with lots of activity.

Some of the merchants who kept seats at these markets began to form associations that specialized in the sale of particular goods. These associations, sometimes compared to medieval European trade guilds, were known as *za*. The earliest *za* date to the late Heian period. They provided goods ranging from firewood and lumber to lamp oil and mercury. Later guilds expanded into products including oranges, charcoal, and salt; even Noh actors and *biwa* chanters formed guilds. These *za* would affiliate with a powerful temple or member of the aristocracy, who ensured the guild's monopoly in exchange for goods or services from guild members. In the Muromachi period, as new groups attempted to form *za,* they sometimes came into conflict with older, established *za*, bringing their patrons into conflict as well.

Commercial activities were not limited to the provinces. In Kyoto, "unofficial" market districts began to arise. The areas around Third and Fourth Avenues became business districts, and certain side streets came to be associated with particular commodities, earning names like "Oil Lane" and "Needles Alley." Merchants based in the capital began making rounds in the countryside, facilitating the exchange of goods outside of the state-dominated tax system. The city of Kamakura also grew during the thirteenth century. Although primarily known as the seat of Japan's first warrior government, Kamakura became an important center of commerce in eastern Japan. Warrior officials designated seven districts within the city as commercial zones, including Wagae, an island they constructed to serve as a port.

RESOURCES, COMMERCE, AND THE SHOGUNATE

Commercial districts became a necessity in part because of growing urban populations. Estimates place Kyoto's population at between 100,000 and 200,000 people and Kamakura's population at 60,000 to 100,000 in the second half of the thirteenth century. Other, smaller urban centers could be found at places like Hakata and Ōtsu, both of which prospered in part because of their involvement in trade networks. The overall trend appears to have been positive: Markets were infrequent but slowly spreading, and money was coming to be used more widely.

But not everyone thrived in the new economy. Famine remained a serious concern for most of the thirteenth century. Two particularly bad famines (the Kangi famine of 1229–1232 and the Shōka famine of 1257–1260) devastated many provincial communities. Precipitated by unseasonal weather, these famines left some communities without enough people to cultivate all of their fields even after good weather returned. The amount of land under cultivation did not significantly grow in the Kamakura period, but warriors were taking on new, more secure positions as *jitō* on provincial estates. This meant that more individuals were competing for resources from the same parcels, and estate proprietors could not always count on revenue from their provincial holdings as they had in the past. Even warriors struggled as some borrowed from moneylenders to cover their expenses. Those who could not repay their debts lost their landholdings, leaving them unable to render service to the Kamakura Shogunate.

The warrior government did not take an especially active role in commercial matters, but it was concerned that its retainers were losing their lands. Samurai financial troubles were exacerbated by the costs of defending Japan twice against attempted invasions by the Mongols (see chapter 19). Kamakura attempted to alleviate these problems by issuing proclamations known as *tokusei-rei* (literally, "virtuous government orders") that absolved its retainers of their debts and allowed them to reclaim their lands. The most famous was the Einin *tokusei-rei* of 1297, which also limited moneylending and legal appeals that tied up the courts. As one might expect, these attempts at managing the economy by decree were unsuccessful. There was a great deal of confusion as different parties tried to reclaim land and as retainers found that moneylenders would no longer lend to them. As a result, the government rescinded the Einin *tokusei-rei* less than a year after it was issued.

The Kamakura Shogunate occasionally demanded that its retainers contribute to the costs of ceremonies and building repairs, but it never instituted regular taxes on businesses or individuals. Other authorities, however, were more aggressive in trying to tap into the newly emerging economy. Enryakuji became the patron temple of moneylenders. They paid fees in exchange for affiliation with the temple, which could defend them in times of trouble. Other temples such as Tōdaiji and Tōfukuji received permission from the imperial court to institute toll stations along highways, waterways, and ports. Such fees and tolls increased the costs of borrowing money and transporting goods, but helped traditional institutions like temples recover some of the income that they could no longer rely on from their provincial *shōen.*

NEW ECONOMIC PATTERNS IN THE FOURTEENTH AND FIFTEENTH CENTURIES

Kamakura's successors—Emperor Go-Daigō and the Muromachi Shogunate—also invested considerable effort into raising revenue. Go-Daigō established new imperial taxes on sake brewers and pawnshops, for example. In 1334 he also announced plans to mint new domestic coinage in order to help rebuild the imperial palace. His plans were never enacted, presumably because his administration (1333–1336) did not last long enough for the money to be produced. Nonetheless, his policies set a pattern for future governments. Although the Ashikaga shoguns never attempted to mint money, they eagerly sought it from any and all sources. One reason for locating their headquarters in the Muromachi district of Kyoto was that it facilitated taxing Kyoto-based commercial establishments. As revealed by the example that begins this chapter, they frequently turned to commercial taxes to help fill the shogunate's coffers.

But the Ashikaga rulers did not stop at seeking money in the capital. The third Ashikaga shogun, Yoshimitsu, took steps to reestablish formal relations with China and thereby secure foreign coins from the source. Given that Japan had not sent diplomatic missions to China since the ninth century, this was a bold move. In 1401 Yoshimitsu sent the first of several official missions to the Ming. As a result of these exchanges (described in chapter 28), he accepted investiture as "King of Japan," a title that marked the Japanese ruler as inferior to the Chinese emperor. But these meetings also involved trade and the exchange of gifts, and the Ming presented the Japanese with large quantities of Chinese coins. Yoshimitsu sent more missions, as did his successors Yoshinori (the sixth shogun) and Yoshimasa (the eighth), making the Ashikaga Shogunate the largest official importer of Chinese cash in the fifteenth century.

Most of those exchanges were carried out under a carefully regulated system known as *kangō bōeki* (tally trade) because of the certificates involved for authentication. Ming officials were very concerned about keeping pirates and unauthorized merchants away, so they strictly limited the number of Japanese ships that could visit China. To ensure the legitimacy of trade missions, they required the Japanese to present the matching halves of certificates (or tallies) when they arrived at Chinese ports. The Ming created these certificates, numbering each one and writing the characters for "Nippon" (Japan) on them. They gave half of each tally to the Muromachi Shogunate and retained the other half for authentication. Japanese ships traveling to China had to produce a proper half-certificate before they received permission to conduct trade. Altogether seventeen Japanese embassies went to China using this system between 1404 and 1547. Of course, there was also a significant amount of unofficial trade carried out by pirates and private merchants.

People in the provinces also embraced the newly emerging economy. Although regional markets were few during the Kamakura period, they became more numerous and widespread in the Muromachi period. Some that used to meet only three times per month now came to be held twice as often (known as *rokusai-ichi* or "six-days-per-month markets"). In some cases, these six-day markets allowed competing authorities to utilize the same space on different days. For example, on Niimi Estate in Bizen province, the proprietor (Tōji) sponsored a "days ending in two" market (that is, the market was open on the second, twelfth, and twenty-second of the month), while the local warrior held a "days ending in three" market at the same location. In other instances, the market's sponsor was the same but demand for trade necessitated opening the market on more days.

Another new institution was the bill of exchange (*kawase* or *saifu*). This was a paper certificate that could be redeemed for cash if presented at a specified location. A few temples started using these instruments to send money to their representatives at distant locations, such as monks who represented their temple in the Kamakura courts. By the fifteenth century, rural estate managers were using similar bills to forward rents to central proprietors. Instead of shipping ten thousand coins, which were bulky and might be stolen by bandits, they could ship a bill of exchange that was lighter and more easily hidden in the event of robbery. The use of such bills did not become widespread, but they helped reduce transaction costs for those estates that chose to use them.

COINS, COMMONERS, AND COMMUNITY LANDS

By the mid-Muromachi period, Chinese cash was the dominant medium of exchange and could be used in a wide range of transactions. Korean visitors to Japan in the fifteenth century noted with surprise that coins could be used for everything from buying tea to paying bridge tolls and public bathhouse fees. The increased use and acceptance of money corresponded to the spread of the new agricultural techniques described above and to a reduction in famine and disease from the late Kamakura period. All of these factors led to population growth, particularly after the cessation of hostilities between the Northern and Southern Courts in 1392. William Wayne Farris has labeled the years from 1370 to 1450 the "Muromachi optimum," referring to the rise of commercial activities, the start of long-term population growth, and the creation of permanent cultivator communities that we refer to as villages.

In earlier times, peasant communities appear to have been much less permanent. Archaeological excavations reveal that few communities had histories in the same location that extend back earlier than the fourteenth or fifteenth century. Starting from those years, however, some village sites show evidence of long-term or continuous settlement. In addition, documentary sources reveal that cultivators began using economic power to better look out for their own interests. Estates with access to regional markets began pressing their proprietors to pay taxes in cash rather than in goods. Village communities pooled their resources to bribe local warriors or purchase rights to waterways or forests. Smaller groups of peasants began contributing to collective funds they could draw on for building projects or in times of need. Finally, by late medieval times, some villages began making tax-contracting arrangements whereby they agreed to pay a certain amount to the regional authorities in exchange for being left alone.

As with warriors, some commoners found it necessary to borrow from moneylenders. Interest rates could be quite high, and many found themselves unable to repay loans. Their calls for debt relief led some to march in protest and riot, often in the name of "virtuous government" (*tokusei*), the same term given to Kamakura-period debt relief decrees for warriors. For example, in 1428 commoners from neighboring provinces attacked Kyoto-based sake brewers, pawnshops, and temples engaged in moneylending. They demanded *tokusei*, which for them meant cancelation of their debts. Although the Muromachi Shogunate resisted their calls at that time, a similar uprising occurred in 1441. Provincial commoners laid siege to Kyoto, occupied the grounds of several major temples, and forced the city's markets to close until the Muromachi Shogunate agreed to issue a *tokusei* decree absolving them of their obligations. Similar protests erupted from time to time over the next hundred years, leading urban neighborhoods to transform themselves in order to provide for common defense. As these examples reveal, the expanding economy presented opportunities as well as dangers for late medieval society.

ECONOMIC DEVELOPMENTS OF THE SENGOKU PERIOD

Villages and commoners were not the only groups actively changing in response to the late medieval economy. The most important figures of the period were the regional warlords (daimyo), who operated with little regard for the shogunate, especially after the Ōnin War. Daimyo in this period found that their political and military fortunes depended on access to trade and a strong economic base in their domains, so they devised new ways to assert control over the economy. For example, daimyo began to take an active role in international trade. Although the Muromachi Shogunate sponsored the early tally trade missions to China, from the 1430s onward, major daimyo, temples, and shrines joined in sponsoring boats. By the early sixteenth century, only the daimyo houses of Ōuchi and Hosokawa were able to send missions to China, revealing their power and commitment to overseas trade.

Within their domains, the daimyo took concrete steps to maximize their control of resources and the economy. Some, such as the Hōjō based at Odawara, carried out detailed cadastral surveys so that they could accurately levy and collect the maximum amount possible in taxes. Others, including Oda Nobunaga, ordered the removal of toll barriers that might impede trade and commerce. Nobunaga also commanded that markets in his territories be free (*rakuichi*) and that the exclusive monopolies of guilds were invalid (*rakuza*). Through these measures the daimyo hoped to attract merchants and trade. In addition, Sengoku daimyo sought to control the types of currency used in their domains. By the fifteenth century, markets were encountering difficulties with Chinese cash. One was that cheap Japanese counterfeit currency undermined the value of authentic Chinese copper coins. Another problem was that some regions valued Song coins while other regions valued Ming coins. To address such concerns, daimyo and the shogunate issued coin laws (*erizeni-rei*) that dictated the types of coins (or the mix of different types) that could be used in each domain.

Daimyo also sought to regulate the kinds of goods that left their domains. Recognizing that certain commodities were crucial to their rivals, they attempted to prevent such needed materials from reaching them. For example, warlords based on the seacoast might forbid the export of salt (produced from ocean water) to inland neighbors, while mountain-based rulers might prohibit the export of iron ore to coastal neighbors. These simple embargoes constituted a rudimentary form of economic warfare.

At the same time, their need for weapons, food, and supplies for their troops led daimyo to generally favor commerce rather than restrict it. Some engaged in trade with the Spanish and Portuguese (who first introduced guns to Japan), and in a few cases, daimyo converted to Christianity, in part because they thought it would facilitate trade with the Europeans. Meanwhile, in spite of the prevalence of warfare during this period, the population continued to grow and cities became more common. Some, such as the merchant port of Sakai, were home to 30,000 or more people in the sixteenth century. Other cities emerged from castle towns as large populations of commoners settled around warlords' administrative headquarters.

The military and economic needs of daimyo also led them to employ new mining techniques that dramatically increased Japanese production of silver, copper, and other metals. In the late sixteenth and early seventeenth centuries, Japan became one of the world's great silver exporters, providing one-third or more of the silver sold to China. These kinds of economic policies were crucial to the success of figures such as Oda Nobunaga and Toyotomi Hideyoshi, who unified the country and brought an end to the medieval age.

Sources and Suggestions for Further Reading

See the bibliography for complete publication data.

Farris, William Wayne. *Japan's Medieval Population: Famine, Fertility, and Warfare in a Transformative Age* (2006).

Gay, Suzanne Marie. *The Moneylenders of Late Medieval Kyoto* (2001).

Nagahara Keiji. "Village Communities and Daimyo Power" (1977).

Sasaki Gin'ya with William B. Hauser. "Sengoku Daimyō Rule and Commerce" (1981).

Segal, Ethan Isaac. *Coins, Trade, and the State: Economic Growth in Early Medieval Japan* (2011).

Tanaka Takeo, with Robert Sakai. "Japan's Relations with Overseas Countries" (1977).

Tonomura, Hitomi. *Community and Commerce in Late Medieval Japan: The Corporate Villages of Tokuchin-ho* (1992).

Totman, Conrad. *A History of Japan* (2000).

Troost, Kristina. "Peasants, Elites, and Villages in the Fourteenth Century" (1997).

Yamamura, Kozo. "The Growth of Commerce" (1990).

28

Diplomacy, Piracy, and the Space Between

Japan and East Asia in the Medieval Period

Michael Laver

A study of the "national histories" of East Asia is made difficult for professional historians by the inescapable fact that East Asia has for millennia been tightly intertwined politically, economically, socially, and culturally in what Jurgis Elisonas calls the "inseparable trinity" of China, Korea, and Japan.[1] In the case of Japan, this holds true for almost every facet of premodern society.

It simply is not possible, for example, to glean a real understanding of the development of Kamakura Buddhism without studying the role of Song period Buddhism in Japan, both through Chinese monks coming to Japan and Japanese monks making the "pilgrimage" to China. It is also impossible to understand the strengthening of the Hōjō hegemony in Kyushu without realizing that this was accomplished in the wake of the Mongol attacks of the thirteenth century, with the specter of a third attack in the indeterminate future hanging over Japan. Similarly, we cannot fully understand the decay of Kamakura's power without studying the social, economic, and political pressures that resulted from the prolonged state of heightened vigilance that Kyushu vassals were compelled to undertake combined with the inadequacy of rewards for their service.

In the subsequent Muromachi era, fully comprehending Ashikaga attempts to legitimize the rule of the shogunate requires the realization that Japanese missions to Ming China, as well as Ming envoys to Japan, were an attempt by the regime to enhance its power and prestige. Until the 1390s, the Northern and Southern Courts were vying for power, and envoys from the Ming steadfastly refused to deal with the shogun, Yoshimitsu, opting instead to deal with Prince Kaneyoshi of the Southern Court. Thus it was a great diplomatic victory for the shogun when, in 1401, the Ming acknowledged that the Ashikaga-backed emperor in Kyoto was, indeed, the legitimate ruler of Japan and sent an envoy to confirm this fact.

And, finally, we cannot arrive at a comprehensive understanding of fifteenth-century Japan without recognizing the fluid situation in the China Sea region, where Japanese established settlements in various areas, *wakō* pirates ravaged the coastlines of China, and the kingdom of Ryūkyū emerged as an intermediary among the countries of East Asia. In short, the history of Japan in the medieval period is so intricately entwined with the history of the continent that we would be remiss to ignore these connections.

THE KAMAKURA SHOGUNATE AND THE EAST ASIAN WORLD

It might be tempting to call the thirteenth century a time of isolation for Japan, insofar as there were no official relations between Japan and China or Korea at this time. But while we might be able to speak of diplomatic isolation, we certainly cannot do so in any meaningful way about economic or cultural isolation. In the Heian period, relations between the continent and Japan were conducted by the court at either Dazaifu or the Kōrokan, both in Kyushu and both centers of the China trade since the advent of the imperial state. Even when the Heian court repeatedly turned away official Song attempts to establish diplomatic relations, considerable private trade was still conducted at ports in Kyushu, especially at Hakata, which even saw the establishment of a Chinese community.

This Chinese community in Kyushu played a major role in commerce between the continent and Japan, but it also had significant influence on the cultural life of the region and eventually that of Kamakura as well. The Chinese brought with them their cultural heritage, most notably the Buddhist sect called Chan, or Zen in Japanese. Chinese merchants were instrumental in sponsoring the construction of Zen temples, first in Kyushu, later in eastern Japan, and eventually in Kyoto. Jōtenji, for example, was a Chinese-style Zen temple established in Hakata in 1242, funded by Xie Guoming, a Chinese merchant residing in Kyushu. Similarly, the Shōfukuji was founded at the turn of the thirteenth century by Chinese émigrés in Hakata and represents the oldest Zen temple in Japan. Martin Collcutt notes that between 1246 and 1330, no fewer than twenty Chinese monks came to Japan to take up positions in Japanese monasteries, helping to spread not just religious teachings but also Chinese painting and literary styles throughout Japan, from Kyushu to Kamakura. A number of Japanese monks also made the arduous journey to China. Eighty Japanese priests traveled to the continent between 1168 and 1280, the most notable among them the priest Enni, who returned to found the Tōfukuji temple in 1236.

These monks often traveled aboard the Japanese merchant vessels that were sailing to the Chinese port of Ningbo in increasing numbers in the thirteenth century, laden with gold, sulfur, mercury, and timber and bringing back to Japan mainly Chinese copper coins, which became widely circulated during the Kamakura period. We can obtain a glimpse of the scale of this trade by noting the discovery in 1976 of a sunken ship off the coast of Korea that had been en route to Japan from China. The ship contained several tons of copper coins, over 18,000 pieces of Chinese ceramics, and hundreds of bronze pieces.

In short, it becomes immediately apparent from even a cursory overview of the thirteenth century that while travel across the seas between Japan and China was extremely perilous—despite the relatively short distance in global terms—contacts between the archipelago and the continent were large-scale and frequent.

THE MONGOL INVASIONS

In 1271 Kublai Khan proclaimed the Da Yuan dynasty from his imperial capital, the present-day city of Beijing. This marked the culmination of several decades of battle during which one region after another had fallen to the so-called Mongol hordes. Historians have identified two distinct phases of Mongol interest in Japan, accounting for the two attempted invasions in 1274 and 1281. The first of these was connected to Mongol attempts to destroy the Southern Song, which had been resisting Mongol advances from its capital at Hangzhou. As noted above, the Southern Song had considerable contact with Japan, and the Mongols seem to have been worried that the dynasty might use Japan as a source of supplies. Evidence also suggests that the Mongols viewed Japan as a possible staging area for their own forces in the war against the Southern Song. In the second invasion, it appears that the Mongols' primary motivation was the natural resources of Japan, such as the precious metals beginning to be mined in greater quantities, although the motivation to erase the humiliation of the first failed invasion was surely a factor.

Following precedent, Kamakura deferred to the court for a reply to the Mongol advances, and the court decided to simply ignore them. The shogunate, however, strengthened coastal defense in Kyushu and ordered vassals holding lands there to prepare for an imminent invasion. Between the first and second invasions, Kamakura also constructed fortifications, including a stone wall stretching for nearly ten kilometers around Hakata Bay, and assigned two high-ranking vassals to formulate a plan for a counterinvasion of Koryŏ Korea—although in the end no such invasion took place.

Space here precludes a detailed account of the invasions, but a few points bear emphasis. First, the invasions were truly an East Asian affair. In the first, Koryŏ was ordered to provide the bulk of the ships as well as much of the manpower. In the second, Koryŏ again supplied men and matériel, but the recently conquered territory of the Southern Song was also ordered to supply troops and ships, for a two-pronged attack on Japan.

The second point—the role of the *kamikaze* (divine wind) in each of the two invasions—is well known. On both occasions, in 1274 and 1281, typhoons off the coast of Hakata decimated the invasion fleet with significant loss of life, although, as Thomas Conlan points out, the numbers reported are almost certainly inflated by perhaps a factor of ten. It should be noted, however, that contrary to popular belief, the fortuitous storms did not save Japan from otherwise certain defeat; the Japanese defenders were, in fact, well prepared to meet the invasion force, fighting well and effectively until the storms dispersed the fleets.

The third significant point concerning the Mongol invasions is that they were at once the cause of increased Kamakura control over Kyushu—an area of Japan in which the Hōjō regents had traditionally been rather weak—and a cause of the decline of the shogunate, as it attempted to deal with the continued vigilance necessary after the attacks and with the distribution of rewards for loyal service to its vassals. Kamakura strengthened its position in western Japan by appointing *shugo* who were either related to the Hōjō or closely allied to them, and by establishing a new office, the Chinzei *tandai,* to supervise Kyushu. The ostensible justification for this new post was to coordinate the defenses against a possible third Mongol invasion and also to suppress the bandits preying on local villages and highways in Kyushu. Although these were certainly legitimate reasons to increase security in Kyushu, most scholars recognize that the new office also involved an element of self-serving extension of Hōjō power.

Ironically, just as the Mongol invasions broadened Kamakura's reach, their aftermath served to fundamentally weaken its long-term control. This development stemmed in part from the need to reward warriors for their meritorious service. Such rewards most often took the form of land rights transferred from warriors on the losing side of the conflict, but after the Mongol invasions, there was no land to be confiscated. The shogunate therefore had to find new and creative ways to mollify its vassals as well as the shrines and temples that claimed meritorious services for having marshaled divine intervention on behalf of the realm. One way this was accomplished was through the promulgation of *tokusei* edicts, granting temples and shrines the return of lands that had been previously pawned off under dire financial circumstances. In addition, the shogunate was able to use lands and titles that had been confiscated in the aborted Shimotsuki rebellion of 1285.[2] In the end, however, petitions for remuneration far outstripped available resources, and most of the rewards and offices in Kyushu went to Hōjō supporters. As a result, when courtly intrigue surrounding the figure of the emperor Go-Daigō broke out in the 1330s, significant numbers of warriors were sufficiently disaffected that they joined Go-Daigō's forces in toppling the Kamakura regime.

WAKŌ, PART I: THE SPACE BETWEEN

According to Murai Shōsuke, borders exist in East Asia not as lines drawn neatly on a map, but as boundary regions in which different political entities rub up against one another. Such borders are either relatively peaceful or turbulent, depending on the political and economic circumstances of the various states in the region. For Murai, the era of the first great burst of *wakō* activity represents the breakdown in the mid- to late fourteenth century of the previous international order: the Kamakura Shogunate was overthrown and replaced by the Muromachi regime, thereby instituting sixty years of civil war known as the period of the Northern and Southern Courts (Nanbokuchō); the Yuan dynasty was overthrown by the Ming in 1368; and the Koryŏ kingdom in Korea gave way in 1392 to the Chosŏn state under the Yi dynasty. In the chaos ensuing from all these transitions, the *wakō* arose to conduct illicit trade, facilitate cross-border contacts, and loot and pillage the coastlines of the continent.

Although the high point of the first wave of *wakō* activity in the waters off the Korean peninsula was in the mid-fourteenth century, pirate attacks on Korea had been occurring irregularly for over a century prior to this time. Despite Kamakura's designation of Mutō Sukeyori as governor of Kyushu in the thirteenth century, and despite Mutō's success in capturing and executing dozens of pirates, ultimately Kamakura power was simply not enough to control the pirates. The attacks continued and grew in scale into the 1300s.

Wakō activity during the fourteenth century was a direct result of weakened regional control by the various governments of East Asia. In the case of Japan, the Mutō family, who came to control much of the foreign commerce in Kyushu under the Kamakura regime, severely declined in influence at the same time Yuan China was experiencing internal strife that would lead to that regime's eventual collapse in 1368. At the same time, the Koryŏ dynasty was losing control of Korea, a process more pronounced in the southern regions along the coast. Against this turbulent background *wakō* attacks began to increase in scale and severity. The response of the Koryŏ kings was to ask the newly established Muromachi Shogunate to rein in this piracy. The Ashikaga regime was, however, unable to stop the piracy, largely because it exercised little control in Kyushu owing to the warfare between the Northern and Southern Courts that persisted until 1392.

The solution to the worst of the *wakō* excesses came in the form of a combination of military and diplomatic activity on the part of the Korean kings. The Yi monarchs of the new Chosŏn kingdom, which came to power in 1392, sent military forces, which were occasionally successful, against the *wakō*, but also reached an understanding with the daimyo of western Japan, allowing them to trade peacefully with Korea and even to settle there if they wished, in return for reining in the pirate attacks. The hegemony of the Sō house on the island of Tsushima can, in fact, be traced back to this diplomatic settlement. It was not until the reestablishment of central control in Ming China and Muromachi Japan, however, that a degree of normalcy returned to the waters of East Asia—and, it should be noted, piracy never entirely disappeared.

ASHIKAGA YOSHIMITSU: KING OF JAPAN

In 1402 an embassy from China arrived at the Ashikaga shogun's court in Kyoto bearing a letter from the Ming emperor. This was a return embassy in response to a diplomatic overture to the Ming sent the previous year and bearing gifts and a letter from the third shogun, Yoshimitsu. The tenor of the letter suggested a vassal relationship to the Chinese Son of Heaven. The response took the form of a classic investiture mission in which the Ming emperor bestowed on the shogun the title "King of Japan."

This exchange of letters illustrates most of the major issues involved in Japan's foreign policy under the Muromachi Shogunate: a vassal relationship with the Ming Empire; increased and regular trade with the continent in, among other things, precious metals; and the persistent activity of the *wakō*.

The very fabric of unified governance was destroyed during the era of Northern and Southern Courts. Not until 1392, a full sixty years after the founding of the second shogunate, were the Ashikaga able to broker a deal reuniting the two courts. Although this arrangement quickly fell apart in favor of the erstwhile Northern Court, it effectively ended the simmering civil war that had divided the country for decades. In this context, the Ming envoys were seen as agents of legitimacy for both the Northern and Southern Courts. Although envoys from the Ming Empire had come to Kyoto to announce the advent of the Da Ming, the imperial envoys had refused to negotiate with the Northern Court since Prince Kaneyoshi, the son of the deposed emperor Go-Daigō, was in control of most of Kyushu. The Chinese made it known that, until this issue was resolved, they would not recognize the northern line or, by extension, the Ashikaga. Envoys to the Chinese court in 1374 and again in 1380 were patently rebuffed. The Ming accepted Yoshimitsu's embassy of 1401, only after the settlement with the Southern Court had been reached.

Much ink has been spilled over the meaning of Yoshimitsu's apparent acceptance of vassal status for Japan. Did he have designs on the imperial throne of Japan? Was he simply a practitioner of Machiavellian politics who cynically accepted a meaningless designation in return for lucrative trade with China? These are questions that cannot be answered with any degree of certainty, although the acceptance of the title had everything to do with legitimacy for Ashikaga rule. The Ashikaga were not in as strong a position in Japan as they wished to be, and a long and contentious civil war, one that involved a great deal of ideological banter between the two claimants to the throne, had just ended. An embassy from the Ming Empire recognizing the legitimacy of Ashikaga rule was, therefore, of great significance to Yoshimitsu.

THE BREAKDOWN OF ASHIKAGA RULE AND RELATIONS WITH THE CONTINENT

In many ways trade with the continent under the Ashikaga retained features of earlier trade under the Kamakura regime. Zen monks continued to traverse the East China Sea in both directions, and ships continued to be sent to China for the construction and upkeep of Zen temples in Japan; Japanese and Chinese merchants continued to carry on a brisk international trade from Japanese ports such as Hakata and Sakai; and diplomatic correspondence from both Korea and China continued to flow into Japan, repeatedly asking the shogunate to control the piracy endemic in the waters of East Asia.

In other ways, however, foreign relations took on new dimensions. Most notable among these were the "tally trade" with Ming China, the relatively large overseas Japanese communities in Southeast Asia, and the resurgence of the *wakō* in a new and more international form.

A standout feature of Muromachi trade with the continent was the institution of the *kangō,* or tally trade, with Ming China. In 1403 a Ming envoy arrived in Japan with a gold seal of investiture for Yoshimitsu and one hundred "tallies"—trade passes in two matching halves. One half was kept in China, and the corresponding half was to be carried aboard Japanese ships traveling to China. When that ship arrived at port, usually at Ningbo, a trade official would match up the two halves, thereby determining that the ship was indeed a legitimate trading vessel and not engaged in piracy. The Japanese sent seventeen such trade missions to China from 1404 to 1547, comprising eighty-four ships in total. Although the ships were ostensibly outfitted and sent by the shogunate, by the latter half of the fifteenth century the trade was in reality in the hands of powerful warrior families, such as the Ōuchi and the Hosokawa.

The *kangō* trade was terminated in the mid-sixteenth century for a number of reasons, including Ming unease over competing Japanese tribute ships. This rivalry resulted, in 1523, in Ningbo being severely damaged by fighting between the Ōuchi and Hosokawa ships. Probably more directly related to the collapse of this system, however, was the fact that the Ōuchi family was destroyed in the fighting of the Warring States period, and so was unable to send any more ships to China. At this point other actors stepped in to fill the commercial void, including the newly resurgent *wakō,* as well as merchants from Ryūkyū and Japan.

A Ming ban on overseas trade by its own merchants was enacted in 1371, as an attempt by the Hongwu emperor to monopolize foreign relations under the tribute system, as well as a means to limit the piracy then ravaging the southeastern coast of China. Because of the latter, Japanese merchants were singled out for a discontinuance of trade. The *wakō,* then, can be seen at the confluence of the decline of private trade in China and the decline of Ashikaga power in Japan. The pirates were able to use the various port cities of Kyushu, as well as offshore bases such as Hirado Island and the Gotō Islands, to effect their illegitimate trade with the continent and were often supported by the various daimyo of Kyushu.

A pronounced difference between this and earlier manifestations of *wakō* was that a significant percentage of the "Japanese pirates" were now ethnically Chinese and Korean. This new cosmopolitanism in the ports of East Asia arose from the commercial void created by the Ming ban on private trade and by the cessation of official tally trade between Japan and China.

Another difference in the sixteenth-century *wakō* was that the area of piratical activity shifted decisively to the coast of China, extending even as far south as the island of Hainan. This was largely because Chosŏn Korea had hit upon a more or less effective way of controlling piracy off the Korean coast. Beginning in 1397, the king of Chosŏn opened official relations with the Sō family on the island of Tsushima. The Sō were given a copper seal and allowed to send official trade missions to three ports in Korea, and in exchange the house agreed to help curtail piracy off the Korean coast. While Chosŏn made similar arrangements with other western daimyo, the Sō, throughout the course of the fifteenth century, were effectively able to channel Japanese trade with Korea through Tsushima by the granting of official trade passes to Japanese ships.

As a direct result of the Ming curtailing of private trade, Ryūkyū was able to use its status as a vassal state of the Ming to make the kingdom a flourishing entrepôt for Southeast Asia, Korea, and Japan. In 1423 Shō Hashi unified Ryūkyū, which had been divided into three kingdoms. This new state became a vassal of the Ming dynasty and, as such, was able to send ships to China to pay tribute and to engage in trade. At the same time, Ryūkyūan ships were also making voyages to Satsuma, which was controlled by the Shimazu family, and by the early sixteenth century the Shimazu had an effective monopoly on Ryūkyūan trade in Japan. Ryūkyū merchants were therefore able to act as middlemen in trade between China and Japan and were active in trade with Korea as well.

Unfortunately for the Ryūkyū islanders, this lucrative middleman trade declined severely by the mid-fifteenth century, as merchants from southeastern China routinely flouted the Ming maritime bans and, later, as the Ming lifted its ban on trade with Southeast Asia. Also, the *wakō* came to occupy much of the commercial space that merchants from Ryūkyū once filled, thereby displacing Ryūkyū from the central role that it played for almost a century in facilitating East Asian trade.

The final aspect of late–Muromachi period foreign relations to discuss here is the ambitious attempts by Japanese merchants to travel in great numbers overseas, even establishing Nihonmachi, or Japan towns, in several areas of Southeast Asia. By the latter half of the seventeenth century, significant overseas Japanese populations existed in such Southeast Asian areas as Luzon in the Philippines, Ayutthaya in Siam, Cambodia, and Cochin China. These groups of Japanese carried on a brisk trade with Japan, trading mostly Japanese silver for a variety of luxury goods, including raw silk, deerskins, spices, and sugar. Therefore, in the sixteenth century, a new phenomenon in Japanese relations with East and Southeast Asia developed: the rise of private Japanese merchants traveling in great numbers beyond the islands of Japan and even beyond the relatively traditional boundaries of Japanese overseas activity in China and Korea. As revealed in chapter 31, on early modern Japanese foreign relations, these overseas Japanese played a large role in distributing Japanese silver across the region as well as importing luxury goods into Japan, which were eagerly consumed by an increasingly urban society.

Sources and Suggestions for Further Reading

See the bibliography for complete publication data.

Batten, Bruce. "Cross Border Traffic on the Kyushu Coast, 794–1086" (2007).

———. *Gateway to Japan: Hakata in War and Peace, 500–1300* (2006).

———. *To the Ends of Japan: Premodern Frontiers, Boundaries, and Interactions* (2003).

Borgen, Robert. "Jōjin's Travels from Center to Center" (2007).

Collcutt, Martin. *Five Mountains: The Rinzai Zen Monastic Institution in Medieval Japan* (1981).

———. "Musō Soseki" (1997).

Conlan, Thomas D. *In Little Need of Divine Intervention: Takezaki Suenaga's Scrolls of the Mongol Invasions of Japan* (2001).

Elisonas, Jurgis. "The Inseparable Trinity: Japan's Relations with China and Korea" (1991).

Goble, Andrew Edmund, Kenneth R. Robinson, and Haruko Wakabayashi, eds. *Tools of Culture: Japan's Cultural, Intellectual, Medical, and Technological Contacts in East Asia, 1000s–500s* (2009).
Hazard, Benjamin. "The Formative Years of the Wakō, 1223–1263" (1967).
Ishii Susumu. "The Decline of the Kamakura Bakufu" (1990).
Ishii Yoneo. *The Junk Trade from Southeast Asia* (1998).
Itō, Kōji. "Japan and Ryukyu During the Fifteenth and Sixteenth Centuries" (2008).
Kawazoe, Shōji. "Japan in East Asia" (1990).
Kuno, Yoshi. *Japanese Expansion on the Asiatic Continent* (1937).
Murai Shōsuke. "The Boundaries of Medieval Japan" (2001).
Simkin, C. G. F. *The Traditional Trade of Asia* (1968).
Okamoto, Hiromichi. "Foreign Policy and Maritime Trade in the Early Ming Period: Focusing on the Ryukyu Kingdom" (2008).
Pearson, Richard. "The Place of Okinawa in Japanese Historical Identity" (2001).
So, Kwan-wai. *Japanese Piracy in Ming China During the Sixteenth Century* (1975).
Tanaka, Takeo, with Robert Sakai. "Japan's Relations with Overseas Countries (1977).
Uezato, Takashi. "The Formation of the Port City of Naha in Ryukyu and the World of Maritime Asia from the Perspective of the Japanese Network" (2008).
Von Verschuer, Charlotte. *Across the Perilous Sea: Japanese Trade with China and Korea from the Seventh to the Sixteenth Centuries* (2006).
———. "Ashikaga Yoshimitsu's Foreign Policy, 1398–1408 AD: A Translation from *Zenrin Kokuhōki,* the Cambridge Manuscript" (2007).
———. "Japan's Foreign Relations, 1200–1392 AD: A Translation from *Zenrin Kokuhōki"* (2002).
Yamamura Kozo and Tetsuo Kamiki. "Silver Mines and Sung Coin: A Monetary History of Medieval and Modern Japan in International Perspective" (1983).

Notes

1. Elisonas, "The Inseparable Trinity," 235.

2. The details of this rebellion are unimportant for our purposes, but the confiscated lands were used in part to reward vassals who had still not received compensation from the Mongol invasions.

PART V

Bureaucrats, Burghers, and Bailiwicks in the Early Modern Age

1368–1644	Ming dynasty in China
1392–1897	Chosŏn kingdom in Korea
1543	Arrival of first Portuguese
1549	Arrival of first Jesuit missionaries
1568	Oda Nobunaga enters Kyoto as champion of Ashikaga Yoshiaki
1573	Last Ashikaga shogun deposed
1582	Oda Nobunaga assassinated; Toyotomi Hideyoshi takes power
1585	Toyotomi Hideyashi named imperial regent (*kanpaku*)
1587	Toyotomi Hideyoshi orders Jesuits expelled
1588	Ashikaga Shogunate formally dissolved
1588	Toyotomi Hideyoshi orders first nationwide sword hunts
1592	Toyotomi Hideyoshi orders invasion of Korea
1593	Arrival of first Franciscan missionaries to Japan
1597	Toyotomi Hideyoshi orders second invasion of Korea
1598	Toyotomi Hideyoshi dies
1600	First Dutch ship arrives at Uruga Bay
1600	Battle of Sekigahara
1603	Tokugawa Ieyasu takes title of *seii taishōgun*; beginning of Tokugawa Shogunate
1605	Tokugawa Hidetada becomes second Tokugawa shogun
1609	Shimazu domain invades and conquers Ryūkyū
1612	Shogunate issues first prohibitions of Christianity
1614	First Battle of Osaka Castle
1615	Second Battle of Osaka Castle
1616	Tokugawa Ieyasu dies

1621	Shogunate prohibits Japanese travel overseas
1624	Spanish expelled from Japan
1634	Ban on oceangoing trade
1635	Alternate attendance (*sankin kōtai*) system promulgated
1637–1638	Shimabara rebellion
1639	Portuguese merchants expelled
1641	Removal of Dutch and remaining Europeans to Deshima at Nagasaki
1644–1911	Qing dynasty in China
1651	Yui Shōsetsu rebellion
1657	Tokugawa Mitsukuni begins compilation of *Dainihon shi*
1661	Ōbaku Zen school established at Manpukuji
1682	Ihara Saikaku publishes *Kōshoku ichidai otoko* (*The Life of an Amorous Man*)
1694	Matsuo Bashō, haiku poet, dies
1703	Chikamatsu Monzaemon publishes *Sonezaki no shinjū* (*Love Suicides at Sonezaki*)
1732	Kyōho famine
1733	Jikigyō Miroku fasts to death on Mt. Fuji
1716–1745	Kyōho reforms
1778	Arrival of Russian envoy Adam Laxman
1783–1787	Tenmei famines
1804	Arrival of Russian envoy Nikolai Rezanov
1833–1837	Tenpō famines
1838	Nakayama Miki, first divine possession by Tenri-Ō-no Mikoto
1840–1842	Opium War in China
1853	Arrival of Commodore Matthew Perry
1867–1868	Ee-ja-nai-ka movement
1868	Last Tokugawa shogun resigns

29

The Sixteenth-Century Reunification

Lee Butler

In 1500 Japan was in chaos. Central control was dead, warfare was endemic, and the old verities of status and privilege were defunct. The venerable institutions of the imperial court and the native and Buddhist religions lacked vitality and were under siege. Warfare was taking its toll on them, as it was on the common people, farmers for the most part, who made up the bulk of the population. Local military lords (who numbered some three hundred) held power in most regions, but their reach was limited and most were in fact petty figures, as likely to be overthrown by a neighboring lord or killed by the treachery of a vassal as to survive into the next decade. The economy, which had never been highly developed, remained closely tied to the production of rice and other food crops (which of course suffered as a result of frequent warfare) and lacked a strong commercial foundation.

The Sengoku, or Warring States period, which stretched from the mid-fifteenth to the late sixteenth centuries, had a seeming oneness. The era apparently defied change. And yet by 1600 dramatic change had occurred, and evidence that it would be enduring was abundant. Chaos was replaced by stability, warfare by incipient peace, economic stagnation by growth and vitality—all of which spurred on the process of change such that by 1630 Japan was a much different place than it had been in 1550.

What had happened, and why, and how? Had Japan indeed moved from "medieval" to "early modern" in these few decades? And were the changes as dramatic as outlined above, or is that picture distorted? Answers to these questions are shaped in part by our approach to reunification.

We may focus, for example, on the process or chronology of reunification, beginning in 1568, with the emergence of the first unifier, Oda Nobunaga, and continuing until 1600 or shortly thereafter. This approach tends to emphasize the role of powerful warriors, in particular the "three unifiers" (Oda Nobunaga, 1534–1582; Toyotomi Hideyoshi, 1536–1598; Tokugawa Ieyasu, 1542–1616) and the actions they took as they pacified the country and brought it under their control. Alternatively, we may center our attention on the unifiers' key policies and laws, the reasons behind them, and their meanings and effects; or on the results of unification, intended or otherwise.

A fourth approach, emphasized in this chapter, is to consider reunification not merely as a series of events but as a process built upon underlying structures within fifteenth- and sixteenth-century Japan. An examination of the background to reunification tells us much about what reunification was and why it occurred as it did and when it did. First, however, we need an overview of the era—the events, key figures, policies, and laws that defined it.

In the autumn of 1568 the daimyo Oda Nobunaga marched an army of 50,000 troops to Kyoto and established control of the capital and surrounding regions as he embarked on a path of consolidation. Nobunaga was a powerful lord, one of perhaps twenty or so Sengoku daimyo who stood out as the dominant figures of their age. Nevertheless, it was not obvious at the time that he would be the one to take the first steps toward unification, or that decentralized rule would indeed end rather than continue for decades more.

The fact that reunification began in Kyoto was not a chance occurrence. Kyoto was not only the capital and center of the country but also the seat of authority, the home of the emperor and hereditary nobility as well as the Ashikaga Shogunate. The last named of those, as a military government, would shortly come to an end, but the imperial institution would remain in existence, its position acknowledged and accepted by the new warrior elite. Indeed Nobunaga's entrance into Kyoto in 1568 was predicated upon requests for assistance he received both from the emperor, who desired that he make repairs to the imperial palace and help recover court lands, and Ashikaga Yoshiaki, a claimant to the post of shogun. In this sense, Nobunaga's march to the capital was done to support tradition, and his stated purposes, like those of his two successors, conservative. As in earlier centuries, institutions and practices from the past were not readily discarded, even by the new men of power whose links to that past were thin.

Oda Nobunaga's goal, as reflected in a seal he used to sign documents, was *tenka fubu*, "to extend military control over the realm." And that is what he attempted to do from his extended base of power. It was a difficult task, and he met resistance everywhere he turned: from daimyo, religious institutions, and independent cities like Sakai. An alliance of the shogun Ashikaga Yoshiaki (initially backed by Nobunaga); the daimyo Takeda Shingen, Asakura Yoshikage, and Asai Nagamasa; and the Ikkō Buddhist sectarians was formed in 1573, and although Nobunaga destroyed the Asakura and Asai houses within the year, it took him another two years to subjugate the Takeda and seven years to bring the Ikkō sect to submission.

As the preceding description suggests, resistance from religious bodies was especially fierce. Two institutions in particular presented vigorous challenges to Nobunaga's rule: Enryakuji, the huge temple complex in the mountains north of Kyoto, and the Ikkō sect, headquartered at Ishiyama (now Osaka). Ultimately Nobunaga dealt with them savagely, a step that effectively put an end to the worldly power of medieval Japanese Buddhism.

The two sects were very different. Enryakuji, founded in the eighth century, represented the old schools of Buddhism. It had close ties to the imperial court and was influential not just in spiritual matters but social, political, and economic ones as well, as seen in its numerous monks, vast landholdings, and large armies. Its early resistance to Nobunaga prompted him to send his army against its mountain stronghold in the fall of 1571. Taken by surprise, the temple provided little opposition, and Nobunaga's men razed and burned the whole complex, including temples and residences, and put to death by sword everyone they caught: men, women, and children.

In contrast, the Ikkō sect—formally known as the True Pure Land denomination—was one of the "new" Buddhist religions. Formed in the thirteenth century, it came into its own during the Warring States era through the faith and support of commoners. Although it was headquartered near Kyoto, its real strength lay in the provinces, particularly in Kaga, which it controlled through the political and military efforts of its believers. The term *ikkō* means "single-minded" and was used at the time to describe the sect's adherents, whose unwavering faith and devotion not only sustained them but made them dangerous opponents to warriors like Nobunaga. Historians are correct to note that more than a few Sengoku daimyo breathed a sigh of relief after Nobunaga's subjugation of the True Pure Land sect.

Engaged as he was almost continually in battle, Nobunaga had limited time and opportunity to implement new policies. After all, lasting reform was unlikely to be put into place before stability was attained. Nonetheless, in a few areas, Nobunaga took steps of importance. One that may have had unintended consequences was his decision to support the emperor and court aristocracy. Besides repairing the imperial compound and recovering court lands, Nobunaga regularly offered gifts to the emperor and maintained close ties to courtiers. And from 1575 to 1578 he was the recipient of increasingly lofty court offices and titles. Some historians have made much of the fact that he resigned his offices in 1578, perhaps because he intended to dispense with the imperial institution once and for all. But evidence for that is lacking, inasmuch as his letter of resignation promised he would be "the court's chief support and most loyal minister" and would "again accept high position" once the wars of conquest were over. Four years later, Nobunaga was dead and the matter was closed. In respecting the court and allowing the emperor to remain the ultimate symbol of political legitimacy, however, Nobunaga maintained a posture common to warriors of previous centuries and set a strong precedent for his two successors.

Several of Nobunaga's economic policies had both immediate and lasting significance. One was his abolition of the many toll barriers that daimyo and temples had established along heavily traveled roads, particularly in the region surrounding the capital. The barriers, of course, hindered commerce, and Nobunaga was quick to demand their removal. He likewise encouraged economic growth through policies of "free markets" and "free guilds" (meaning an end to guilds) and by removing taxes on merchants and on the buying and selling of goods. These policies were not unique to Nobunaga, having also been implemented by several other Sengoku daimyo within their domains; and their impact would remain slight until Japan's economy saw greater commercial development. But Nobunaga's decision to push these measures as national policy was clearly significant, and in the long run they would be influential.

Toyotomi Hideyoshi, the second of the unifiers, was one of Nobunaga's generals, having risen from a peasant background to a position of eminence. When Nobunaga was killed in Kyoto in 1582 by a disgruntled vassal, Akechi Mitsuhide, Hideyoshi acted with alacrity to avenge Nobunaga's death and assert control as his successor. He pushed forward with unification (at his death Nobunaga had pacified the central third of the country), subduing enemies and forming alliances. He also established close ties to the imperial court and eagerly sought its offices and titles. In 1585 he managed to be adopted as the son of Konoe Sakihisa, of the Fujiwara line, so that he could accept the post of chancellor, the highest position in the court system except for the emperorship. Thus ostensibly acting as the emperor's servant, and at his decree, Hideyoshi moved to pacify the country. He spoke of "bringing peace to the provinces for fifty years" and offered daimyo the choice of orderly submission or military subjugation. Those who submitted were allowed to maintain their domains and were made his vassals, with obligations to support him and to supply troops and laborers when needed. Those who resisted were destroyed, their domains confiscated and passed on to men loyal to Hideyoshi. The resulting political system kept the structure of the daimyo and their domains intact, ensuring that government would maintain a military character.

In 1590 Hideyoshi sent an army of nearly 200,000 men to destroy the last of his opponents, the Hōjō. With the victory that followed, the land was at peace and Hideyoshi was its master. As head of the new order, Hideyoshi's power lay in a range of rights restricted to him. To begin with, his own holdings spanned a sizable portion of the arable land—approximately 12 percent. Moreover, he directly controlled and administered the capital and all major cities and ports and—closely related to that—regulated foreign affairs and monopolized international trade. He also took control of gold and silver mines, and directed the minting of currency, something that had not been done since the eighth century. Furthermore, as a means of furthering his authority, weakening the influence and wealth of individual daimyo, and putting trusted allies and vassals into strategic positions while rewarding their loyalty, Hideyoshi regularly confiscated domains and transferred daimyo from one domain to another. Among those who lost their domains were daimyo who performed poorly on the battlefield, ruled their lands ineffectively (as evidenced, for example, in peasant uprisings), or failed to produce an heir.

Hideyoshi is generally regarded as the man who established the early modern system, and there is no question of the importance of the policies he enacted. Foremost among these were his sword hunt, the separation of warriors and farmers, and a countrywide land survey.

In the first of these, begun by edict in 1588, Hideyoshi prohibited farmers from keeping weapons of any type: swords, bows and arrows, muskets, and so on. The farmers' swords, he instructed, were to be gathered and melted down for use as "rivets and clamps" for the huge Buddha he was constructing in Kyoto. By this act, he noted, "the farmers will be saved in this life, needless to say, and in the life to come." Armed resistance by villagers to daimyo policy had been a continual concern to warriors during Sengoku times; with this edict Hideyoshi intended to put an end to that. Agriculture, not warfare, was henceforth to be the work of farmers.

Related to the sword hunt was the move to "separate warriors and farmers" or, put differently, to freeze the social order. In an edict of 1591, Hideyoshi gave orders that townsmen and villagers were not to allow warriors to take up residence among them. Likewise farmers were not to abandon their fields for commerce or wage labor, and warriors without masters were to be taken and delivered to their previous masters. In short, social movement and the instability that accompanied it were to be disallowed. Although seemingly innocuous (at least to us today), social movement had characterized the upheaval of the Sengoku era, a time when people did not know their places. At its extreme, it was *gekokujō*, the "low overthrowing the high," a symbol of the loss of order. Of course, it was *gekokujō* that had led to the rise of upstarts like Nobunaga and

Hideyoshi in the first place, but now it had to be stopped. This meant, first and foremost, that warriors were not to carve out land bases in villages from which they could threaten the new state.

This edict of Hideyoshi's lent support to a broad effort by daimyo to restrict their vassals' freedom, and in this sense it was not new. Although loyalty to one's lord would in coming decades be touted as the mark of a samurai, the fact is that the greatest threat to Sengoku daimyo often came from their own vassals. Accordingly, by the 1550s, some daimyo were taking steps to break their vassals' ties to the land by moving them from one parcel to another, keeping them engaged in lengthy military campaigns (the norm at the time), and forcing them to reside in the daimyo's castle town. The process was accelerated during the reunification era and completed in the early decades of the Tokugawa period. The resulting system had clear feudal origins, marked as it was initially by the exchange of land for loyalty, but took on a radically new character, with warriors having been taken off the land and brought into the castle towns of their lords; they now lived not off the land, but off stipends the lords provided in place of land. An unintended consequence was an explosion of urban growth, with castle towns becoming cities overnight, full of warriors and their attendants (as well as merchants and artisans who came to supply the warriors' wants and deplete their incomes).

In the late sixteenth century, land was still at the heart of Japan's economy. As Sengoku daimyo well realized, their armies and administrations depended on effective taxation. But that was difficult because of the complexity of the practices in place—practices that had a long history, predating daimyo political control in nearly all cases. Not only was it common for the ownership and rights to land and income to be divided among various parties, but taxes (and freedom from taxes), and rights to collect them, were often convoluted. Many *sengoku* daimyo had taken steps to overcome this morass, but resistance was strong, particularly among farmers, whose control of land had grown during the Warring States period. Hideyoshi's land surveys were meant to change this. By assessing all of the arable land in the country, the new government could simplify administration and taxation and make them uniform, and it (as well as individual daimyo) would have a basis for enacting effective policies.

The process began with teams of surveyors working their way through Japan's provinces, village by village, surveying each parcel of land and recording its location, size, quality (superior, average, inferior), type (dry field or paddy), and assessed yield, as well as the name of the person to whom it was registered. No longer would there be overlapping rights to income or "ownership." The assessed yield was computed in *koku* of rice, a unit of volume equal to about five bushels or 175 liters, which would become the means both of assessing a domain's value (daimyo, for example, were defined as lords whose lands were assessed at 10,000 *koku* of rice or more) and of assigning tax burdens. The assessed value of the whole country at the time was around 18 million *koku*.

Besides enacting policies that helped transform the country, Hideyoshi also committed vast resources to its physical reconstruction. Foremost among these was the rebuilding of Kyoto. For this, Hideyoshi provided assistance to major monasteries for their repair and expansion, relocated commoners and temples, ordered the construction of a stone and earthen wall about the city, and built the palace Jurakutei, a huge residential complex for himself several blocks west of the imperial palace.

As a symbol of his megalomania, however, Jurakutei would shortly be exceeded by Hideyoshi's decision to invade Korea and subdue China, which, he claimed, he would accomplish during his lifetime. The legacy of the armies Hideyoshi sent to Korea in 1592 was lasting bitterness between the two countries. With the help of the Chinese, the Koreans drove back the Japanese armies in 1593 and again in 1597, after Hideyoshi ordered a second push for power on the continent. The decision to abandon Korea came mid-year in 1598, as the daimyo involved in the invasion took the opportunity to return home upon hearing of Hideyoshi's death.

In the end, Hideyoshi's hopes for an enduring Toyotomi regime rested on shaky ground, depending as they did on a son and heir who was only five years old when Hideyoshi died. For several years after Hideyoshi's death, powerful daimyo jockeyed for position, claiming to support the Toyotomi boy; but in the brief wars of succession in 1600, Tokugawa Ieyasu established himself as the new leader. It was he and his descendants who would dominate the political world of Japan for the next 250 years. And it was they who would be left to deal with the challenges of a peacetime regime, as well as other concerns such as the "southern barbarians" and their religion, Christianity, which were likewise part of Japan's reunification society.

As important as the actions of men like Oda Nobunaga, Toyotomi Hideyoshi, and Tokugawa Ieyasu were, it is naïve to assume that reunification depended primarily on their abilities. The great warriors of the era—and there were many besides these three—did not just appear by chance at this time as an answer to the needs of the age. Various forces drove the country toward unification, and it is probably more correct to say that the unifiers jumped on board the incipient ship of state than to say that they personally built it and launched it. Among the factors that led to reunification, three—one material, one ideological, and one a matter of common practice of the era—stand out: population growth, the idea that Japan had previously been unified and that this was its normative condition, and the formation of communities and confederations.

After reaching a population of 6 million people in 600 CE, the Japanese archipelago entered a lengthy period of demographic stagnation. For the better part of the following seven centuries the population failed to grow measurably; in fact, around the year 950 it may have dipped as low as 4.4 million. The causes of stagnation were varied, but included famine from crop failure, drought, floods, and cool weather; epidemics; high infant mortality and high mortality in general (a major cause being chronic malnutrition); and warfare. Not all of these were continuous problems, and their severity changed over time, but together they combined to make life brutally difficult for the common people and to restrict their numbers. One result was a perpetual shortage of labor, something that suggests that the government's frequent exhortations, and bribes, to reclaim land for planting were often pointless, since there were neither laborers to clear the land nor farmers to plant and tend the fields once they were cleared.

Around 1300 the population at last began to expand, and by 1450 may have reached 10 million. Shortly thereafter, Japan entered the turmoil of the Sengoku era, and while warfare limited population growth somewhat, the period as a whole witnessed a veritable population explosion. By 1600 it had reached somewhere between 15 and 17 million. Important factors in this three-century expansion included fewer epidemics, a more benign climate, and the introduction of new strains of hardier rice (and the double- and triple-cropping of rice). Just as the causes of demographic stagnation had earlier fed one upon another in a vicious cycle, so too did the causes of growth now reinforce and amplify one another. With population growth came a larger labor force, a dramatic increase in land reclamation, surpluses (profits) for new enterprises (such as mining, shipbuilding, and construction), greater work specialization (in areas from pottery and carpentry to cotton ginning and noodle making), and the adoption of new technologies. All of this led to increased trade and commercial activity and ultimately to economic growth and prosperity. Although these developments did not inevitably lead to reunification, there is no question that they made it more likely. For they provided Sengoku daimyo with new economic resources, increased manpower for construction projects, and an abundance of soldiers for their wars. Moreover, increased commercial activity and trade tied together regions that were otherwise politically divided. In short, these changes that were brought about by a significantly increased population advanced the domains of Sengoku daimyo in ways they could not have done merely by dint of effort.

While these material factors were no doubt an impetus to some degree of unification (certainly beyond the chaos of the early decades of the Sengoku period), there remained the very real possibility that the large Sengoku daimyo of the mid-sixteenth century—men like Takeda Shingen, Hōjō Ujimasa, Uesugi Kenshin, Chōsokabe Motochika, Shimazu Tadayoshi, and the three unifiers—

would remain divided, holding strong and independent domains. Instead the country moved rapidly toward unification. The reasons for this are not obvious, but one compelling factor was the broadly held ideal of a single unified state.

In terms of vigor and administrative efficiency, the Chinese-style polity established in Japan during the seventh and eighth centuries was not a resounding success. Its hold over the country, especially distant provinces, was from the first limited, and its governing bureaucracy was hindered by the new state's lack of resources. And yet the economy and authority structure were centralized, the state was unified, governors appointed by the state administered each province, and the army put down those who rebelled against the state. Moreover, many of these conditions persisted in the centuries that followed, even though the structure changed, and even though the ruling body of the state included warriors and their administrations. The ideal of unity, of a well-organized central government that appointed and removed officials as required, endured. Just as significantly, tendencies toward regionalism were weakened by appointments that took officials away from their native environments, that suggested that the location of one's appointment mattered little because the islands and regions of the archipelago were one. Belief in the existence of a unified state did not die easily, as witnessed by warriors defending their actions as "publicly sanctioned," even at the height of the Sengoku era.

Not surprisingly, as the powerful daimyo of the latter half of the sixteenth century moved to expand their authority, they were quick to define the archipelago as a single entity—*tenka*, "the realm"—and themselves as the restorers of peace to the realm. Likewise they spoke of themselves and their authority as "public," suggesting that their motives were high-minded and their purposes singular.

Of course, none of this suggests *why* unification came about as quickly as it did, or why daimyo offered so little coordinated resistance to Nobunaga's, or Hideyoshi's, march to power. Perhaps this can be attributed, at least in Hideyoshi's case, to his invitations to daimyo to join his system, something he offered even to daimyo whom he had defeated in battle. In the process, these lords maintained lands and status while giving up only part of their independence. It is also possible to consider the new warrior-led system as an agreement among the daimyo to seek stability and security in the face of a common threat: the fighting men beneath them.

The third factor that led toward reunification operated at a more practical level. This was the Sengoku custom of forging communities and leagues. At their simplest, these took the form of self-governing villages in central Japan or the religious league of the Ikkō (single-minded) sect of Buddhism. On a broader scale they consisted of groups of villages banding together to provide mutual defense and mutual assistance, or associations of warriors doing likewise. Of course, one might argue that some of these, such as the Ikkō leagues, were ultimately divisive. And so they were, and yet taken as a whole, these groups reveal a clear push toward and desire for greater stability and unity, something that community members were willing to attain at the cost of a portion of their independence.

In short, these underlying factors provided a base upon which a new structure, a new system, could be built. With these in place, late Sengoku era daimyo such as Oda Nobunaga were able to foresee and ultimately realize a reunified and invigorated Japan. That it would be recognized later by historians as "early modern" was obviously beyond their ken, but they may have had an inkling nonetheless that their world was on the cusp of radically new developments.

Sources and Suggestions for Further Reading

See the bibliography for complete publication data.

Asao Naohiro. "The Sixteenth-Century Unification" (1991).

Berry, Mary Elizabeth. *Hideyoshi* (1982).

Butler, Lee. *Emperor and Aristocracy in Japan, 1467–1680: Resilience and Renewal* (2002).

Elison, George. *Deus Destroyed: The Image of Christianity in Early Modern Japan* (1988).

Elison, George, and Bardwell L. Smith, eds. *Warlords, Artists, and Commoners: Japan in the Sixteenth Century* (1981).

Farris, William Wayne. *Japan's Medieval Population: Famine, Fertility, and Warfare in a Transformative Age* (2006).

Ferejohn, John A., and Frances McCall Rosenbluth, eds. *War and State Building in Medieval Japan* (2010).

Hall, John Whitney, Nagahara Keiji, and Kozo Yamamura, eds. *Japan Before Tokugawa: Political Consolidation and Economic Growth, 1500 to 1650* (1981).

Lamers, Jeroen P. *Japonius Tyrannus: The Japanese Warlord Oda Nobunaga Reconsidered* (2000).

McMullin, Neil. *Buddhism and the State in Sixteenth-Century Japan* (1984).

Nagahara Keiji and Kozo Yamamura. "Shaping the Process of Unification: Technological Progress in Sixteenth- and Seventeenth-Century Japan" (1988).

Tsang, Carol Richmond. *War and Faith: Ikkō Ikki in Late Muromachi Japan* (2007).

30

The Political Order

Philip Brown

Although historical overviews of the establishment of the Pax Tokugawa in the late sixteenth and early seventeenth centuries frequently describe a process of national "reunification," and then turn to the development of leadership under the Tokugawa house, Japan's political situation was considerably more complex. On the one hand, the early decades of the Tokugawa order were precarious, marked by the threat of a revival of the Toyotomi or the creation of other anti-Tokugawa factions, especially in the years following Ieyasu's death in 1616. On the other hand, tension frequently characterized relations between domain leaders who sought increasing control over their retainer band and the economic resources of their territory, and their largest retainers. Many of these so-called household confrontations (*oie sōdō*) became violent. Even after the mid-seventeenth century, the level of Tokugawa administrative control at the national level was sufficiently tenuous that some have even questioned whether a Japanese state existed at all at this time, while still others find a state that had a greater bark than bite.

The Tokugawa political order's complexities pose a considerable challenge to any who seek to characterize it. Japanese scholars typically treat the era as "feudal," stressing the importance of pledges of loyalty between daimyo and shogun, and administrative authority broadly dispersed among daimyo. Alternatively, they call it the *baku-han* state, a state comprised of the shogunate (*bakufu*) and daimyo domains (*han*). In the 1960s, American scholars increasingly saw in Tokugawa Japan a greater degree of central control than in the highly decentralized image of feudal European kings, baronial lords, and largely autonomous retainers of medieval Europe. They employed the oxymoron "centralized feudalism" to describe Tokugawa political arrangements. Others have described the order as "federal," evoking images of the relationship between states and the central government in the United States, or as a "compound state."[1]

Despite an arguably fragile administrative structure, the Tokugawa political order has no direct parallel in Western political history, especially if one considers its long, peaceful duration of two and a half centuries. An effective combination of traditional practices marshaled to assure daimyo acquiescence to Tokugawa overlordship and the absence of aggressive foreign challenges created circumstances that obviated the development of a strong, nationally centralized government administration.

No contemporary European or Asian power had this luxury. Invasion and frontier conflict were routine, and those regimes that developed the most effective centralized governments flourished to occupy preeminent status in the international pecking order. The destabilizing impact of Western pressures to gain access to Japan in the mid-nineteenth century is particularly telling evidence. Those pressures aggravated existing social and economic problems and became the focus of anti-Tokugawa sentiments that ultimately brought the shogunate down. Absent such pressures for more than two centuries, Japan did quite well with a far less centralized state.

TIES THAT BIND: POINTS OF CENTRAL CONTROL

Many practices of control employed by the Tokugawa have their origins in the sixteenth century, especially during the regimes of Oda Nobunaga and Toyotomi Hideyoshi. These practices continued largely without change for most of the era.

Shoguns as Liege Lord

In practical terms, the elements of clear shogunal control over the samurai (including daimyo), court aristocracy, and religious orders were grounded in Tokugawa Ieyasu's control of the military coalition that triumphed at Sekigahara and in the Osaka campaigns. As liege lord of that coalition, he had the authority to reorganize his daimyo and direct retainers (*hatamoto*) for military duties, and to regulate family arrangements related to security concerns—such as marriages, which might cement ties among an anti-shogunate coalition. Up through the Osaka campaigns of 1614 and 1615, Tokugawa control faced competing claims from those loyal to the Toyotomi family, and many steps taken after Sekigahara and Osaka were directed at solidifying Tokugawa preeminence.[2] Relations between daimyo and their liege lord were subject to considerable tension and uncertainty in the seventeenth century, but by its end they had become routine and highly ritualized.

Domain Allocation

Right after Sekigahara, Ieyasu allocated domains to daimyo in locations that suited his strategic interests. The largest independent (*tozama*) daimyo were located far from the shogunal base in the Kantō, the distance providing a measure of warning and preparation time should any be so bold as to try to march on the Tokugawa. Lands of one large independent daimyo were, moreover, separated from those of others. Between them, Ieyasu placed domains of hereditary Tokugawa affiliate daimyo (*fudai*) or lands (*tenryō*) directly controlled by the shogun and its direct retainers.

The ability of the Tokugawa to allocate daimyo domains extended beyond the early years of the shogunate. Especially in the early seventeenth century, Ieyasu's successors frequently transferred daimyo to new locations, increased or reduced domain size, or confiscated domains altogether. All of these actions stemmed from shogunal ability to order subordinates to perform military duties of many sorts. Significantly, when large daimyo were the object of transfer or confiscation, it was typically after their defeat in one of the early seventeenth-century battles that established Tokugawa hegemony.

Dispersal of Domain Lands

Nevertheless, the dispersal of domains was even more complicated than the preceding description suggests. Even large domains with contiguous territory participated doubly in a fragmenting of domains that created opportunities to observe military preparations. For example, scattered throughout Kaga domain's primary holdings in three provinces (Kaga, Noto, and Etchū, making Kaga the largest domain after that of the shogun) were small shogunal holdings, as well as lands held by other lords, such as the Hijikata. Conversely, the domain lands included villages in Ōmi, near Kyoto, far away from the domain base and surrounded by the territory of other local lords. To administer these lands, the shogun, daimyo, and direct retainers had to send officials traveling through the domains of others. Such trips were made routinely to assess and collect land taxes, hear suits by villagers, and conduct other ordinary administrative business. While some visits were regularly scheduled and expected, others were not, so that it would have been difficult to hide significant military preparations from observation. In effect, this arrangement created a widespread network of potential observers who could not be trusted by daimyo through whose lands they passed to withhold knowledge of seditious activity from the shogun.

Such a force of observers was more pervasive than the shogun's own inspectors (*junkenshi*), charged with traveling across the land to keep an eye on daimyo activity. It is not clear how effectively this system ever functioned. And even if it had an impact early in the seventeenth century, as shogun-daimyo relations became more settled in the mid- to late seventeenth century, the system operated in a farcical manner.

By the eighteenth century, for example, the daimyo in the Tanabe area (Wakayama prefecture, south of Osaka) was well aware when inspectors were coming. They prepared cheat sheets that were circulated to village officials, indicating questions likely to be asked and providing appropriate replies. One sequence suggests the limits of the Inspectorate's effectiveness. If you were asked, "Is there a castle located here?" you should answer, "It is a residential (not a military) castle and has no storehouse (for weapons)"—a line that suggests the inspectors could not actually go onto the site to examine the facility for themselves!

Alternate Attendance and Military Duties

As liege lord, Ieyasu, drawing on the authority that underlay the obligation of daimyo to perform military service, could also order daimyo to serve guard duty at his castle in Edo under the system of alternate attendance (*sankin kōtai*). In most cases, daimyo spent alternate years on duty in Edo, leaving family members as hostages when they returned to their domains. Although exchanging hostages was a centuries-old practice, the Tokugawa version commenced when Maeda Toshitsune, daimyo of the largest domain (Kaga), sent his mother to Edo as a sign of fealty and loyalty to the Tokugawa shortly after the victory at Sekigahara. Over the first four decades of the shogunate, procedures for Edo residence and hostages were refined and standardized; they remained in effect until the last years of Tokugawa hegemony. Other guard duties, such as Saga's provision of guards for Nagasaki, were assigned to specific daimyo, but did not encompass the heavy expenditures associated with alternate attendance.

The shogun's authority as liege lord also enabled him to order daimyo to contribute to the construction, reconstruction, and maintenance of fortifications. Thus, five years following the destruction of Osaka castle in 1615, Tokugawa Hidetada ordered many daimyo to make contributions to rebuilding it. Late in the era, the shogun ordered daimyo to prepare improved coastal defenses, as Japan confronted an increasing threat from Western powers.

Family Ties

While the shogun did not send hostages to the daimyo domains, he did marry relatives into daimyo families, a practice that put members of the Tokugawa family in the ranks of daimyo and created a sense both of obligation associated with family ties and of social and cultural indebtedness on the part of daimyo, who felt honored to receive a Tokugawa daughter or other relative into their own family. This was part of a broader, elaborate array of marriage alliances—again, a long-standing practice—that drew on the prestigious bloodline of the emperor as well as of the shogun. Additional flexibility in forging these ties came from the common practice of adoption. The shogun might adopt a daughter from the imperial family to marry off to a daimyo, or a son from a daimyo family and then have him adopted into another daimyo family. Over time, these practices created tightly integrated family ties that helped bind the most powerful daimyo to the shogunal family.

Nodal Controls

The shogunate kept under its direct administrative control the imperial capital of Kyoto, the central and critical market of Osaka, key ports like Nagasaki, Japan's largest silver and gold mines, and other areas with important political and military implications.

Shogunal control of Japan's largest commercial centers provided opportunities to manipulate economic activities. Osaka became the major market for daimyo to sell tax rice and other goods to raise cash, and to do so, they had to adopt the weights and measures, use the financial institutions, and observe the ordinances the shogun enforced there. The shogun's officials set the ground rules for anyone who traded there—even those who came from daimyo domains. As the Edo market grew to rival Osaka, it too exerted similar influences.

Control of key ports provided not only commercial regulatory influence but also influence in foreign affairs. At the beginning of the seventeenth century, administration of Nagasaki gave the shogunate control of the port most important to trade with China, as well as the major port for contact with Western shipping. Although there were still remnants of individual daimyo contacts with foreign representatives in the early seventeenth century (the Daté, for example, were negotiating with Mexico), such activities declined as the Tokugawa arranged marriages and adoptions with daimyo families that reinforced formal ties of military allegiance. Control of Nagasaki became more central to overseeing trade with China and the West after the Tokugawa limited officially recognized trade to this one port. Even when not tied to significant foreign trade, the shogun's control of ports like Niigata provided leverage over coastal shipping, a growing segment of the economy.

Finally, control of major gold mines provided significant revenues to finance the shogunate and precious metals for minting the coins that greased Tokugawa-era commerce. The mines also provided the regime with the means to manipulate the value of currency to its own benefit, especially in the eighteenth and nineteenth centuries. Other domains also had gold and silver mines, but none as productive as those held by the shogun.[3]

Control of Kyoto contributed to shogunal commercial influence, but more than that, shogunal authority in the imperial capital gave it leverage over two other important elements of Japanese society: the civilian aristocracy and religious institutions. Kyoto was home to the court aristocracy, and Tokugawa administration of the city assured a high degree of control over a potential rallying point for anti-Tokugawa sentiment and daimyo alliances—supremacy that the shogunate maintained successfully for two centuries.

Occupation of Kyoto also brought control of key religious institutions and networks. Major Shintō shrines were located here, as were the headquarters of Japan's major Buddhist sects. Since the lead temples in Kyoto administered national networks of affiliated temples, control of them gave the Tokugawa leverage even outside its own directly controlled territories. Control of both lead and affiliated temples enabled the shogunate to place restrictions on organizations that had wielded considerable political and even military weight in the past, such as the Ikkō sect, which controlled Kaga province in the sixteenth century.

Diversity Disputes

An additional field in which the shogunate exercised authority lay in the realm of what a legal scholar might call a diversity dispute—rendering judgment on legal conflicts that transcended the boundaries of any one domain—a field through which it could potentially expand its influence. Especially in the seventeenth century, the shogun was called on to negotiate and settle boundary disputes among domains. Again, his supreme military authority—the ability of a superior commander to order the settlement of a dispute between his subordinates—underlay this power. Given the potential for such disputes to erupt in violence and war, this was a critical function. Yet even here, the shogunate could be quite reluctant to impose a settlement that indicated one party was in the right and the other in the wrong. A boundary dispute between Kaga domain and Echizen domain, for example, continued over several decades, with the shogun repeatedly encouraging the parties to reach a settlement on their own. When that proved impossible, the exasperated shogunate finally took direct control of the disputed territory in 1668.

Limited State Growth: Two Instances

Diversity issues provide two examples of efforts to extend shogunal authority during the eighteenth and early nineteenth century. Exercise of the legitimate use of force represents one such effort. Although external aggression was not a challenge for Japan, internal civil disorders could be. In many instances, daimyo dealt with protests and insurrections on their own, but as social unrest mounted over the eighteenth and nineteenth centuries, the scale of popular uprisings expanded, involving disruption of hundreds of villages across multiple domains and, in some cases, involving shogunal arrests of more than 10,000 individuals.

That said, such military activity did not even approach the scale of operations typical of wars among daimyo or foreign invasions; commoners were poorly armed, occupied ill-defended positions, and were not intent on government overthrow. For most of the period, protests were scattered, small, and easily suppressed.

River maintenance and civil engineering of dikes, diversionary channels, and dams represent another realm of increased shogunal activity. By the eighteenth century, the shogunate ordered domain contributions to large hydraulic projects. Some rivers, such as the Tone near Edo, represented flood hazards that threatened not only the shogun's lands but the Edo residences of daimyo as well. In the case of the Tone, like many other urban-area streams, riparian engineering also facilitated transport and water supply. In other cases, construction activities affected streams that crossed domain boundaries. Regardless, the shogunate took an increasingly aggressive role in efforts to limit flood damage.

LIMITATIONS ON CENTRAL CONTROL

Even if we acknowledge areas of state growth, the Tokugawa political order never conceded powers to the shogun comparable to those of the increasingly powerful European states of the late eighteenth and early nineteenth centuries. While the seventeenth-century Tokugawa order may have been on a par with large western European absolutist powers, countries like Great Britain and France created a much stronger central administrative apparatus over the next century and a half. These states had built national armies directly under the control of a state administration. They financed war and other state activities with national systems of taxation. Nationwide, integrated court systems applied nationally applicable laws. Such elements were essentially—often entirely—absent from the Tokugawa order circa 1850.

Taxation

The lack of a national tax must surely represent the most striking weapon missing from the Tokugawa shogunate's administrative arsenal. For regular revenue, the shogun relied solely on income from its own lands, that territory comprising somewhat more than an eighth of Japan's assessed value (*kokudaka*). Thus taxation rights over the vast majority of Japan's villages, towns, and cities resided with the daimyo of Japan, who numbered 260 to 280 at any given time during the era. This situation placed severe constraints on the expansion of shogunal authority—on its ability to develop an expanded army or national police force under its direct financial control, an expanded judiciary to fully engage in nationwide administration of justice, or any administrative structure that could routinely tap the resources outside its own direct control. Consequently, in most regards, daimyo were left alone to determine both policies and administrative structures. Police, court, tax, and civil administration overwhelmingly remained firmly in the hands of daimyo throughout the Tokugawa era.

Domainal Administrative Autonomy

Daimyo exercised considerable administrative initiative in conducting their day-to-day affairs, even in carrying out policies sometimes taken as centrally determined. For example, despite claims of uniform national land surveys undertaken by Hideyoshi, there is considerable evidence of variation in practice, with base survey procedures widely crafted autonomously by daimyo and implemented at their own pace.[4] Similarly, even when daimyo reported population data to the shogun, the figures were not necessarily compiled in the same way for all daimyo. Records of religious affiliation (*shūmon aratame chō*), which were associated with efforts to stamp out Christianity and which have been widely employed by historical demographers, recorded children as young as two (following the Japanese tradition of counting age from conception; by modern counting, these would be one-year-olds). In Kaga domain, however, no one younger than fifteen was counted. Registration of commoners at temples was supposed to take place annually according to a widely accepted interpretation, but there is no evidence of regular registration in the document collections for Kaga domain.

Managing Class Separation

As was true between daimyo and shogun, daimyo relations with their largest retainers, though unstable during much of the seventeenth century, became routine and ritualized by century's end. A critical point of tension concerned the role of samurai within the domain. As a rule, retainers lost administrative rights over their own fiefs and, in effect, became salaried underlings of daimyo.

Within domain administration, daimyo made their own decisions about how completely to remove samurai from farming and village life even in the course of day-to-day administration; and within a single domain, policies could switch back and forth over time. Even when samurai were removed from rural residence, there was interdomain variation in the degree of routine contact between samurai administrators and villagers. For example, in Tokugawa territories, direct oversight of tax collection and other rural administrative oversight of subcounty districts lay in the hands of samurai called *daikan*; in Kaga domain, however, commoners occupied the office equivalent to *daikan* and even key countywide administrative functions were entrusted to wealthy farmers. Important administrative innovations in tax assessment such as replacing annual crop inspections for setting land tax rates (the major source of domain revenue) with fixed tax rates, a major element in the shogunate's early-eighteenth-century Kyōhō Reforms, originated in multiple daimyo domains a century earlier and spread from there as daimyo discussed administrative techniques with one another while residing in Edo on alternate attendance.

The degree to which domains pursued innovative policies and administrative structures appears to have been influenced by their size and distance from Edo. Neither factor was strictly determinative, but as a rule, larger domains commanded greater personnel resources from which to draw ideas, and their larger treasuries may have provided opportunities smaller domains lacked. Rather than innovate, domains with lesser personnel resources may have chosen instead to imitate others, especially the shogunal models. As noted above, large domains were located far from Edo as a rule; but even smaller domains, like those in the Izumo area, show evidence of innovative administrative structures even though situated right next to Tokugawa territories. Domains located in the shadow of the shogunal castle town may have felt less free to pursue courses of action that differed from the Tokugawa models.

The one-castle-per-province order presents a case in point. While the edict was widely interpreted as applying to domains, not provinces (66, far fewer than the 260 to 280 daimyo domains), even large domains maintained more than one castle long after the implementation of this ordinance in 1615. In 1636 Kaga, Japan's largest daimyo domain, comprised three provinces and still maintained six castles. Satsuma maintained many small rural castles throughout the Tokugawa era. This is not to say that the shogun's edict was without impact, but rather to note that domains circumvented the letter of an erstwhile national law.

Village-Level Innovations: Rights in Land

Daimyo were not the only innovators; villagers, too, often crafted local practices to their own needs in realms thought to lie in the hands of daimyo or the shogun. Rights to possess and cultivate land are a case in point. Even within shogunal control, land rights were not structured uniformly. Some regions worked on a system of fee simple land ownership rights that approximates modern conceptions of ownership. In other areas, including shogunal lands in Echigo province, villagers built a system in which rights to cultivate arable land were held and managed jointly by villagers who held superior cultivation rights (as opposed to tenants). In effect, they held shares of village lands. Shareholders held cultivation rights to various amounts of land—rights that they could buy, sell, inherit, or pledge as security on a loan, but not rights to cultivate any specific plots. Access to plots was reallocated by lottery, either periodically or whenever significant land reclamation, floods, or landslides altered the area of cultivated land. These systems were commonly referred to as *warichi* (literally, "dividing the land") and were employed on some 30 percent of Japan's assessed value at some time during the Tokugawa era.

LIMITED ENFORCEMENT

Even when shogunal regulations appeared to apply nationally, efforts at enforcement were limited at best. In 1601, production of saltpeter, the primary ingredient in the manufacture of gunpowder, was prohibited except in designated shogunate-controlled locations. Nonetheless, throughout the Tokugawa era, Kaga domain collected half the annual land taxes from villages in the Gokayama district in saltpeter! The remainder experienced no change.

While in principle the shogun's ability to transfer daimyo and confiscate fiefs provided it with tools for enforcing its orders, examination of the use of these tools from 1601 to 1760, the Tokugawa political order's period of growth and maturation, indicates efforts largely directed at smaller domains and extremely limited use of such tools in enforcing any specific ordinance. This 160-year period was primarily one of peace. The two exceptions are transfers and confiscations associated with the Osaka campaigns and the suppression of the Shimabara Rebellion of 1637–1638 (see chapter 35). Of 551 instances of domain transfer during this time, 357, or 65 percent, involved domains that were less than 100,000 *koku*.[5] Among the other 194, only a handful were really large domains. The data even present an ambiguous picture regarding whether transfer was used as a punishment. Less than half the transfers involved a reduction in domain size, a potential punishment. The largest number, almost half (268), involved receipt of a larger domain (reward).

The records of domain transfers do not identify reasons for transfers, but those for domain confiscations for the same period do. The single greatest reason for confiscation of a domain (and its redistribution to others) was lack of a suitable heir (108 cases out of 235), a problem commonly solved in the 1630s and 1640s by the establishment of branch domains, which provided heirs if a daimyo died without an adult successor. About a quarter of the cases (59) superficially involved efforts at enforcement of shogunal ordinances, but a closer examination of these cases further limits the scope of such use. House disorders (*ōie sōdō*), violation of the *Laws of the Military Houses* (which for the most part controlled daimyo's personal behavior), and maladministration threatening public order within a domain are the primary reasons for confiscation. Of the 59 cases, only 21 seem to be clearly linked to enforcement of laws that were conceivably associated with shogunal efforts to regulate internal domain affairs. Taken together, data on fief transfer and confiscation present poor evidence of shogunal efforts to effect nationwide application of its laws. These data suggest instead that except when civil disorder (by samurai or commoners) threatened, daimyo were practically free to administer their domains as they saw fit.

In the absence of significant foreign pressures, the Tokugawa Shogunate survived for more than two centuries without a strong national administration. It did so by marshaling traditional practices of controlling retainer bands and territory without broadly challenging the autonomy of its landed retainers, the daimyo. Traditional tools included holding hostages and manipulating family linkages. They included rights to command military service, including guard duty in Edo, and order contributions to construction projects, and the associated right to command daimyo service in particular posts in such a way as to enhance security and make it difficult to hide military preparations. In distributing domains, the shogunate retained control of key commercial, aristocratic, and religious centers, which permitted it to exercise influence beyond its directly controlled territories. Settling diversity disputes between subordinates was also a traditional role for liege lords. In combination with military command authority, attention to diversity issues provided some ground for extension of state authority on the national level, but never enough to create institutions of nationwide administrative control, such as a nationwide tax that could fund a national-scale administrative apparatus. All of these arrangements left the traditional rights of daimyo as local administrators largely uncompromised, and even villagers had latitude to create diverse local practices. From the perspective of most commoners, the shogunate was unimportant in their daily lives: daimyo laws, justice, and taxes affected them much more. The Tokugawa political order brought stability to Japan for two and a half centuries, its power as a state expanding over time in subtle ways, but never sufficiently to create a powerful, national administrative apparatus. That development came only with the Meiji Restoration.

Sources and Suggestions for Further Reading

See the bibliography for complete publication data.

Berry, Mary Elizabeth. *Hideyoshi* (1982).

Brown, Philip C. *Central Authority and Local Autonomy in the Formation of Early Modern Japan: The Case of Kaga Domain* (1993).

———. *Cultivating Commons: Joint Ownership of Arable Land in Early Modern Japan* (2011).

Jansen, Marius B. *The Making of Modern Japan* (2000).

Ravina, Mark. *Land and Lordship in Early Modern Japan* (1999).

Reischauer, Edwin O. "Japanese Feudalism" (1956).

Roberts, Luke S. *Mercantilism in a Japanese Domain: The Merchant Origins of Economic Nationalism in 18th-Century Tosa* (1998).

Toby, Ronald P. "Rescuing the Nation from History: The State of the State in Early Modern Japan" (2001).

Notes

1. Berry, *Hideyoshi*, 4; Ravina, *Land and Lordship in Early Modern Japan*, 27.

2. The Tokugawa faced only one more seventeenth-century issue that called for exercise of large-scale military force: suppression of the hodge-podge of discontented farmers, masterless samurai, and others who rebelled over heavy taxation and other issues and made the castle at Shimabara their final stronghold (1637).

3. Although Japan is often thought of as lacking significant natural resources, in fact, Japanese silver production drove down world prices in the seventeenth century, and Japan provided copper for much of Chinese coinage in the eighteenth century.

4. That they reported domain values to Hideyoshi and the Tokugawa was still significant, since the exaction of military duties noted above was based on these reports.

5. *Koku*, a measure of capacity equal to 180 liters, was the standard unit for evaluating land. All agricultural lands, regardless of the crops actually grown on them, were assessed in terms of their annual yield in rice or its equivalent.

31

A Whole New World (Order)

Early Modern Japanese Foreign Relations, 1550–1850

Michael Laver

Historians effectively have debunked the notion that Japan was an isolated or "closed society" (*sakoku*) during its early modern period. While it is true that the Tokugawa government (1603–1868) took decisive measures to expel Europeans from the country, with the exception of a few lonely Dutch merchants in Nagasaki, and while it is true that the government took extraordinary measures to stamp out Christianity at every turn, this does not mean that Japan was somehow disengaged from the outside world. Rather, Japan participated in a great deal of foreign intercourse, mainly with Korea, China, Ryūkyū, and Ezo (present-day Hokkaido), as well as with the Dutch and, in a somewhat disguised form, with Siam (now Thailand). Similarly, through its links with Chinese, Dutch, and Ryukyuan merchants, the shogunate was well informed about events shaping the early modern world.

There is no doubt that Tokugawa foreign relations contrasted greatly with Japanese foreign relations in the last half of the sixteenth century. Japanese merchants, who throughout the sixteenth century had settled in "Japan towns" (Nihonmachi) throughout Southeast Asia, were forbidden to travel abroad from the mid-1630s; Christianity, which had been propagated with such zeal by Iberian missionaries from 1549, was absolutely forbidden in Japan on pain of death; Portuguese merchants, who had brought silk to Japan in such massive quantities for nearly a century, were unceremoniously expelled in 1639; and the Dutch, who enjoyed the relative freedom in the Matsuura domain of Hirado, were transferred to the man-made island of Deshima in Nagasaki. These were startling changes, and the fact that they occurred in a relatively short period of time makes them seem all the more radical.

Nevertheless, a constant theme running through all these changes was the attempt to bolster shogunal domestic power vis-à-vis the daimyo, especially the *tozama* daimyo of western Japan. Japan was transformed politically and economically from a decentralized, relatively open society to one in which Edo became the sole arbiter of foreign relations, even though it "outsourced" those relations to several daimyo outside its direct jurisdiction.

OVERSEAS JAPANESE, SILVER MINES, AND EARLY EUROPEAN CONTACT

Sixteenth-century Japan contrasted greatly with the Tokugawa period in the fluidity of movement throughout maritime Asia. Japanese merchants coped with the Ming ban on direct Chinese-Japanese trade by sailing to various ports in Southeast Asia to trade with the overseas Chinese community as well as with local merchants, using trade contacts back home, along with the increasingly productive silver mines there, to effect profitable trade throughout Asia The two biggest Nihonmachi were on the island of Luzon in the Philippines and in the city of Ayutthaya in Siam, though there were also smaller Japanese communities in Cambodia, Cochin China, and elsewhere. Japanese also became a sizable minority in the European centers of trade, particularly at Batavia, the headquarters of the Dutch East India Company (VOC).

Scholars have estimated that in the sixteenth and early seventeenth centuries, Japan produced fully one-third of the world's silver, even taking into account the Spanish mines of the Americas. Japanese merchants loaded their ships with silver, mined in ever greater quantity thanks to Chinese and European advances in smelting, and headed off to the trading ports of Southeast Asia to obtain luxury goods such as silk and spices. The transfer of Japanese and New World silver to China, which had an insatiable appetite for the metal, must be counted as one of the great engines of the early modern world economy.

Rumors of the richness of Japan's silver mines had, in fact, long set European imaginations ablaze. Marco Polo's account of the island of "Zipangu," combined with early Portuguese rumors of Japanese merchant ships laden with precious metals, made the accidental landing on Japan of two Portuguese merchants aboard a Chinese ship in 1543 all the more significant. These merchants had a considerable effect on Japanese-European relations, completely out of proportion to their time spent on the tiny island of Tanegashima. They not only had discovered a profitable trading destination for Europeans but had also introduced the Portuguese musket to the Japanese.

Almost immediately the daimyo, then competing among themselves for supremacy, recognized the importance of the new weapon and began placing large orders for them. Oda Nobunaga, Toyotomi Hideyoshi, and Tokugawa Ieyasu all used the *teppō*, as the musket was called in Japanese, to great effect in their campaigns of unification. It is telling that on a folding screen depicting the battle of Sekigahara of 1600, a large contingent of Tokugawa troops is armed with muskets, an indication of the importance of the weapon in the Japanese artistic imagination and also in military reality.

The initial visit to Tanegashima was followed by a flood of Portuguese merchants and missionaries to Japan. In Kyushu the daimyo vied with one another to lure the rich Portuguese vessels to ports in their domains, occasionally resorting to mass religious conversions to increase their chances. Eventually, the Portuguese settled at the port of Nagasaki, which was briefly ceded to the Jesuits by the daimyo Ōmura Sumitada. Thus began the extremely lucrative Macao-Nagasaki trade in which the Portuguese became middlemen in the exchange of Chinese silk for Japanese silver.

Jesuit missionaries began their activity in Japan with the visit of Francis Xavier in 1549. Xavier's intention was to travel to Kyoto to convert the emperor to the faith, thereby facilitating the conversion of the entire country. What the venerable priest did not realize, however, was that the imperial court held little more than nominal authority, and the Ashikaga Shogunate was also more or less impotent. In the Warring States period, true power lay in the hands of the daimyo; and so, somewhat dispirited, Xavier headed back to Kyushu and eventually left Japan altogether for China.

His successors, however, enjoyed much better success, so that by the turn of the century, there were an estimated 250,000 converts. The absence of a unified, central authority at the time of the missionaries' arrival in Japan worked, more than anything else, to their advantage and allowed their initial endeavors to prosper. But that situation changed drastically from the 1590s, as Toyotomi Hideyoshi, then Tokugawa Ieyasu, brought to completion the unification of the country that began under Oda Nobunaga.

THE FOREIGN RELATIONS OF THE AZUCHI/MOMOYAMA PERIOD

For all of his ruthlessness in subduing militant Buddhist sects, Nobunaga took a surprisingly tolerant attitude toward the Christians. In fact, many of the more intimate descriptions that we have of Nobunaga have come from Jesuit audiences with him. On several occasions, he personally entertained the fathers and even showed them around his impressive castle at Azuchi. The Jesuits were understandably optimistic about their future success in Japan given their warm welcome, but their hopes were dampened when Nobunaga was assassinated in 1582.

The supremacy of Toyotomi Hideyoshi was at first a boon for the Jesuit missionaries, as Hideyoshi was extremely interested in foreign trade. It seems that

Hideyoshi possessed an enormous appetite for fine Chinese silk and other Southeast Asian luxury goods, going so far as to monopolize the purchase of silk at Nagasaki. After initially tolerating the missionaries, however, in 1587 Hideyoshi suddenly ordered that all priests leave the country immediately.

The reason given was that the Jesuits, or *bateren,* as they were known, had subverted the divinely ordained order of Japan, the "land of the gods"; but Hideyoshi's real motives were probably political. Apparently he had become alarmed at the missionaries' success among the powerful daimyo of western Japan. He had already confiscated the city of Nagasaki from the Ōmura family and placed it under his direct authority, and now, it seems, he began to see Christianity itself, with its allegiance to a foreign clergy and monarchy—the Vatican—as a threat to his rule in Japan.

Most Jesuits ignored the order to leave the country, however, and instead became more circumspect in their missionary activities. Hideyoshi knew about this breach of his orders, of course, but overlooked the Jesuits' defiance as he had more important matters to attend to—including the disastrous invasion of Korea that began in 1592 and ended only with Hideyoshi's death in 1598.

This relatively lax enforcement of the ban on Christianity ended in 1597, when Hideyoshi ordered the execution of twenty-six Christians, including six Europeans, at Nagasaki. It seems that the pilot of a Spanish ship called the *San Felipe,* irked at the confiscation of his cargo when he was wrecked off the coast of Japan, began to boast that Iberian missionary activity was simply a prelude to a European invasion and cited the Philippines as evidence. Hideyoshi appears to have taken this seriously, and acted to stamp out the religion, until his death a year later put an end to the immediate persecution of Christianity. This proved, however, to be more an interlude than a reprieve.

Hideyoshi's son and heir, Hideyori, was only five years old when his father died in 1598. Almost immediately, the five regents designated as caretakers of Hideyori's legacy began to form alliances and fight among themselves. Things came to a head in 1600, at the battle of Sekigahara, in which Tokugawa Ieyasu won a victory over a coalition of his rivals. Lacking sufficient resources to completely vanquish all of the powerful daimyo arrayed against him, however, Ieyasu resorted to a somewhat precarious political balancing act that would have repercussions on Japan's foreign policy as the new shogunate moved to increase its own control throughout the country at the expense of the western daimyo.

TOKUGAWA IEYASU'S FOREIGN POLICY

Among the first tasks confronting Ieyasu was to construct a coherent foreign policy with regard to both other countries and Japanese merchants trading overseas. He instructed the Sō family on the island of Tsushima, the traditional arbiter of relations with Korea, to the relationship between the two countries after the disastrous invasions of the 1590s. The result was a 1604 treaty, under the terms of which Tsushima was permitted a limited amount of trade at the port city of Pusan and state-level letters were exchanged between the two countries. Initially, a certain amount of subterfuge was included in these letters, inasmuch as neither country wanted to be seen as the subordinate partner. The Sō, to facilitate trade and avoid the diplomatic minutia altogether, forged the signatures of Korean and shogunate officials. Interestingly, when the Tokugawa discovered this deception, they meted out a relatively lenient punishment: In a testament to the importance of Korean trade, the Sō were permitted to retain their position as intermediary with only nominal shogunal oversight.

The Koreans and Japanese arrived at a solution to another potential diplomatic impasse when the shogun agreed to use the title "great prince" (*ōkimi*), which carried no sinocentric connotations of status relationship, in interactions with Korea. Over the course of the Tokugawa period, the Koreans sent twelve embassies to Japan, mostly to congratulate new shoguns upon their accession.

Ieyasu also moved to regularize Japan's relations with the Ryūkyū Islands in the west and the island of Ezo in the northeast. Just as the Sō was granted a monopoly over relations with Korea, so the Shimazu family was granted control over the Ryūkyū trade, and the Matsumae family was granted a monopoly on trade and relations with Ezo. In 1609 the Shimazu was given permission to invade Ryūkyū and make it a vassal of Satsuma and, by extension, the Tokugawa—although Ryūkyū also continued to be a Chinese vassal. This intermediate position was, in fact, encouraged by the Shimazu as a way to gain access to the China trade, since Ryūkyū sent regular missions to the continent. The trade in Chinese goods, and later sugarcane cultivation on Ryūkyū, were to play a large role in Satsuma finances throughout the Tokugawa period.

Similarly, the Matsumae were given control over Ezo and its Ainu inhabitants. The Ainu were treated as foreigners, and therefore, trade in exotic goods such as hawks, eagle feathers, sea otter pelts, bear hides, and various medicines constituted a form of foreign trade, although today, of course, Hokkaido is an integral part of the Japanese state.

The Tokugawa welcomed embassies from Ryūkyū, Ezo, and Korea and used spectacles attendant to the reception of these embassies to place itself at the center of a Chinese-style tributary relationship. This political ceremony—in which the "barbarians" paraded from their arrival ports in Kyushu to Edo, the embodiment of civilization, to pay tribute and to recognize their status as vassals to the Tokugawa shogun—enhanced the prestige and the authority of the "center" and lent the shogun a tremendous amount of prestige and legitimacy.

The fact that Chinese foreign relations had for centuries operated through such a tribute system, however, made official relations between Japan and China difficult for the Tokugawa, who were wary about preserving both the prestige of the shogunate *and* the theoretical authority of the imperial court. For that reason, no official relations were ever established, and a type of ad hoc arrangement existed, wherein the shogunate allowed private Chinese vessels to trade at Nagasaki and the question of state-to-state relations was left open.

The Dutch and English came to Japan in the first two decades of the seventeenth century for the same reasons as had the Portuguese: to tap into the lucrative silver trade of the islands. In 1600 the Dutch ship *De Liefde* limped into Uraga Bay with a handful of survivors, perhaps the most famous being Will Adams. The Dutch established a factory at Hirado in 1609, and the English followed suit in 1613, although for a variety of reasons, the English found it difficult to make a profit in Japan and so after a decade closed their factory and left Japan.

Initially, the Dutch also found it hard to make a profit, simply because they did not have access to the Chinese silk market—unlike the Portuguese, who were able to use their position on Macao to tap into the trade in Chinese goods. This changed in 1624 when the Dutch established a factory on the island of Taiwan and began to trade with wealthy Chinese merchant families, such as the Zheng. The most famous member of this house, Zheng Chenggong or, as he was known in Europe, Coxinga, exemplified the cosmopolitan nature of early modern Japan: Born of a Chinese father and a Japanese mother in Hirado, he went on to facilitate trade among the various ports of Asia in a widespread commercial empire based originally at Amoy and later on Taiwan.

THE SAKOKU EDICTS: TOKUGAWA RESTRICTIONS ON TRADE AND RELIGION

The notion that the "closing" of Japan represented a sudden turnabout for the Tokugawa, or that legislation restricting trade and religion was a monolithic piece of xenophobia, is completely mistaken. Rather, the move toward "isolation" began at the very start of Tokugawa rule and continued to its final form in 1641 with the removal of the Dutch to Deshima. These edicts and restrictions were tied up more with Tokugawa domestic control than with the shogunate's concerns about foreign countries.

The first restriction came in the form of the *shuinsen*—literally, "red-seal ships." The *shuin* were formal seals issued by the shogunate, and in this case they represented formal approval for overseas trade. Although this system of controlling foreign trade had been initiated by Hideyoshi, it was expanded by Ieyasu and came to be the only mechanism through which Japanese could trade overseas. It served to control both the piracy that had been rife in East Asian waters for centuries and the movement of people and goods into and out of

Japan. The shogunate issued an average of about ten *shuin* per year for a total of more than 350 ships between 1604 and 1634. The system became more restrictive as the years went by until, in the last few years of this trade, only seven prominent merchant families were allowed to trade overseas, and in 1634, oceangoing trade, save for that with Korea and Ryūkyū, was abandoned altogether on pain of death.

From 1633 to 1639 the new foreign policy came to be finalized in the so-called *sakoku* edicts. These seventeen decrees can be divided into three groups: the prohibition of travel abroad by Japanese; the prohibition of Christianity, embodied in a system of rewards for those who informed on Christians; and the creation of a machinery of foreign trade at Nagasaki that placed the sale and distribution of foreign goods directly into the hands of the shogunate. These edicts brought to an end the relatively free movement of people and goods that had existed during the medieval period. Two further restrictions with far-reaching consequences for foreign trade were the expulsion of the Portuguese in 1639 and the removal of the Dutch to Deshima in 1641.

The decision to expel the Portuguese came about after the Shimabara rebellion of 1637–1638 convinced the shogunate that the Portuguese could never completely divorce trade from religion. The rebellion itself was not a religious uprising—it was a protest over years of heavy taxation in famine conditions—but it did occur in a region that had been a center of Jesuit activity. The Tokugawa regime chose to interpret the rebellion as a Christian challenge to its authority and put it down savagely, with thousands executed in the aftermath. The Portuguese were expelled from Japan shortly afterward, and an embassy sent from Macao in 1640 to reestablish trade was rejected—and all but its thirteen servants were executed as a warning.

The following year, the Dutch factory was shifted from the relative freedom of Hirado to the island of Deshima in Nagasaki. The ostensible reason for the move was the fact that the Dutch had erected a warehouse inscribed with a Christian-style date, which to the Japanese was an unacceptable display of Christianity. But the real reason for the move was so that the shogunate could directly control the trade in Chinese silk. The cartel in charge (the *itowappu*) had control over Portuguese imports of silk, but after their expulsion the Portuguese lobbied heavily for the shogunate to move the Dutch to Nagasaki. In addition, the Tokugawa controlled the city of Nagasaki directly, and so the move placed the Dutch under direct shogunal control, thereby strengthening the regime's position with regard to foreign relations. The Dutch were allowed to stay in Japan, because the shogunate derived a measure of legitimacy from having yearly Dutch embassies present exotic gifts to the shogun, in addition to the fact that the Dutch were a source of intelligence, presenting yearly reports to the shogunate on conditions in Europe and in European colonies in Asia.

With the Dutch removal to Deshima in 1641, the major circumstances of foreign relations were set in place and would not substantially change until the arrival of Commodore Perry in 1853. Henceforth, Nagasaki, Tsushima, Matsumae, and Satsuma represented the four "mouths," or "windows," at which foreign trade was allowed to occur and at which the shogunate was able to gather intelligence about the world beyond Japan's shores.

EPILOGUE: BARBARIANS AT THE GATES

Not until the nineteenth century, when the increasing military and economic might of the Europeans began to encroach on this system, did the shogunate face a real threat to the new international order that it had constructed. Even before Western ships began to call on Japanese ports, the shogunate was relatively well apprised of the situation in Europe and the advances that European countries were making into Asia: The shogunate learned that the British had been steadily encroaching on China and that the Americans had been increasing their merchant shipping in the Pacific. It also seemed to have been aware of American ambitions on the West Coast of the American continent. And finally, it knew of Russian expansion into the Kuril Islands, Sakhalin Island, and even into areas of Ezo. The regime's response to these developments was decidedly reactionary, as the shogun and his councilors moved energetically to address the encroaching Western threat, only to abandon any real reform of the system of foreign relations once the immediate threat had passed.

This cycle of energy and inertia is nowhere more evident than on the island of Ezo. A series of Russian visitors to Japan from the late eighteenth to the early nineteenth centuries convinced the shogunal officials that they must secure Japan's northern borders. They therefore sent inspectors to survey Ezo and the northern islands, conduct interviews with the locals, and assess Matsumae's capacity for defense. The officials concluded that the Matsumae were not able to adequately defend the northern border and had consistently mistreated the natives in their extraction of resources from Ezo. The result was that from 1799 to 1821 Ezo was put under direct Tokugawa control. Characteristically, once the Russian crisis had passed, the island was again returned to Matsumae auspices until the shogunate once again assumed control in 1855.

Nagasaki also experienced a series of crises, as foreign ships tried, by direct negotiation or by the return of castaways, to convince the shogunate to open commercial relations. In 1838 the American ship *Morrison* entered Uraga Bay for just this purpose, but was fired upon by Japanese gun batteries and forced to leave the coast. The reason for this hostile reception was that the shogunate had instituted a policy in 1825 of firing on all ships not authorized to approach the coast—meaning essentially all vessels except those of the Dutch or Chinese. Although the policy resulted in only two incidents of ships being fired upon, it represented the shogunate's harshest measures against foreigners to date and was largely the product of ardently anti-Western thinkers, such as Aizawa Seishisai (1781–1863). The policy was abandoned in 1842 after the shogunate learned of the British victory over the Chinese in the Opium War and the humiliating peace agreement that the Qing dynasty was forced to sign at Nanjing.

The regime's response to foreign encroachment was thereafter adapted to fit the occasion at hand. In the north, for example, it took steps to defend the border against Russian encroachment, including sending survey teams to strengthen its claims to the northern islands. There was also a fair amount of public discourse surrounding Japanese foreign policy in this region. Several scholars, including Honda Toshiyaki, advocated the colonization of Ezo and even dreamed of a substantial Japanese colonial presence on the Asian continent. It is true that pundits had to be careful to avoid the shogunate's ire (they often circulated unpublished manuscripts among themselves), but the point is that, much as with the *sakoku* policy itself, there was no uniformity of opinion concerning the course of action the government should take against the approaching "barbarians." This is perhaps most clearly illustrated by the varied opinions that the daimyo gave to Abe Masahiro's request for advice on what to do about the arrival of Commodore Perry, who so brazenly sailed into Edo Bay in 1853.

In the end, that is perhaps a good way to summarize Japanese foreign policy in the early modern period: there were a few points, such as the bans on Christianity and the Portuguese, that were not open to negotiation, but most aspects of foreign relations were comparatively fluid. Chinese were allowed to trade in Japan in large numbers, despite the lack of any official ties to the Qing dynasty; American ships made several trips to Deshima when the Dutch were unable to maintain contact with their distant outposts during the Napoleonic Wars; Russian merchants made contact with Japanese merchants in the Kurils and Sakhalin; Siamese junks routinely came to Japan under the guise of Chinese vessels; Chinese and Dutch merchants flouted trade restrictions at Nagasaki through the use of "private trade"; and toward the end of the Tokugawa period, Japanese were authorized to supply foreign ships with provisions if they put in along the coast of Japan.

Except for a few years in the nineteenth century, there never was a clear-cut anti-foreign policy, apart from Tokugawa abhorrence of the Portuguese, and even the harsh order to fire on foreign vessels was quickly abandoned. It is no surprise, then, that when the Americans arrived in 1853, and were soon followed by other nations, the Japanese were able to adapt to the new international situation relatively quickly. It is true that the arrival of the foreigners spelled the eventual end of the Tokugawa era, and that a fair amount of anti-foreign violence marked the early years of relations with the West. But it is also true that the Japanese were remarkably adept at quickly conforming to the new international norms of trade and diplomacy, rising within a single generation to join the ranks of the advanced nations of the West. That they were able to adapt so readily to conditions after 1853 and the subsequent Meiji Restoration is surely due, in part, to the relative fluidity of foreign relations under the shogunate, despite the existence of the *sakoku* system.

Sources and Suggestions for Further Reading

See the bibliography for complete publication data.

Boxer, Charles. *The Christian Century in Japan, 1549–1650* (1967).

Cooper, Michael. *They Came to Japan: An Anthology of European Reports on Japan, 1543–1640* (1965).

Corr, William. *Adams the Pilot: The Life and Times of Captain Will Adams, 1564–1620* (1995).

Elison, George. *Deus Destroyed: The Image of Christianity in Early Modern Japan* (1973).

Goodman, Grant. *The Dutch Impact on Japan, 1640–1853* (1967).

Hawley, Samuel. *The Imjin War: Japan's Sixteenth Century Invasion of Korea and Attempt to Conquer China* (2005).

Hellyer, Robert. *Defining Engagement: Japan and Global Contexts, 1640–1868* (2009).

Jansen, Marius. *China in the Tokugawa World* (1992).

Kang, Etsuko Hae-jin. *Diplomacy and Ideology in Japanese-Korean Relations: from the Fifteenth to the Eighteenth Century* (1997).

Keene, Donald. *The Japanese Discovery of Europe, 1720–1830* (1966).

Lensen, George. *The Russian Push Towards Japan: Russo-Japanese Relations, 1697–1875* (1971).

Lewis, James. *Frontier Contact Between Chosŏn Korea and Tokugawa Japan* (2003).

Lidin, Olof. *Tanegashima: The Arrival of Europe in Japan* (2002).

Massarella, Derek. *A World Elsewhere: Europe's Encounter with Japan in the Sixteenth and Seventeenth Centuries* (1990).

Moran, J. F. *The Japanese and the Jesuits: Alessandro Valignano in Sixteenth-Century Japan* (1993).

Shimada, Ryūto. *The Intra-Asian Trade in Japanese Copper by the Dutch East India Company* (2006).

Smits, Gregory. *Visions of Ryukyu: Identity and Ideology in Early-Modern Thought and Politics* (1999).

Tashiro Kazui and Susan Downing Videen. "Foreign Relations During the Edo Period: *Sakoku* Reexamined" (1982).

Toby, Ronald. *State and Diplomacy in Early Modern Japan: Asia in the Development of the Tokugawa Bakufu* (1984).

Walker, Brett. *The Conquest of Ainu Lands: Ecology and Culture in Japanese Expansion, 1590–1800* (2001).

Wakabayashi, Bob Tadashi. *Anti-Foreignism and Western Learning in Early-Modern Japan* (1986).

32

The New Warriors

Samurai in Early Modern Japan

Denis Gainty

Perhaps the most important point in the creation of the samurai legend, and in the codification of the samurai in Japanese history, was the Tokugawa period. The early modern period witnessed a paradoxical shift: As the samurai were codified as an elite and exclusive social class, their role as purveyors of violence—seemingly their raison d'être—was dramatically curtailed by a rebellion-wary shogunate. With these changes came a new flourishing of samurai thought, within which samurai began to question and redefine their social roles in light of shifts in politics, economics, and culture. An increasingly literate and stable nonsamurai population in both cities and countryside engaged even more directly in the creation and consumption of the samurai ideal through literature, drama, images, and other media.

EARLY MODERN SAMURAI: TOKUGAWA TRANSITIONS

These important developments, though dramatic, built on previous transitions in the social and political role of warriors. Following the outbreak of the Ōnin War, the fragile order of the Ashikaga Shogunate fell into further disarray as powerful daimyo assembled and wielded sizable armies and engaged in frequent skirmishes with neighboring lords in order to secure and expand their holdings. This Sengoku, or Warring States, era extended into the late 1500s. It was a time of insecurity and possibility, when political and military fortunes rose and fell. And just as a daimyo's holdings were often in flux, individual warriors themselves enjoyed a fluid identity. Fighting men not infrequently shifted personal allegiances, abandoning or betraying their previous lords to serve their own interests.

At an even more basic level, the very notion of "samurai" was a shifting and poorly defined category. As Michael P. Birt puts it, warriors in the sixteenth century were defined by "the very diversity and ambiguity of what constituted samurai status."[1] Sixteenth-century armies consisted of not just elite hereditary warriors but a wide range of men caught up in a particular domain's mobilization. While those with proven martial ability were prized, military service was a form of tax paid by a particular area under a daimyo's control, and men from all walks of life might be expected to fight in a particular campaign.

As warfare grew more tactically and technologically sophisticated during the 1500s, however, daimyo developed more careful ways to control and use warriors in their domains. The daimyo commissioned more surveys of property and population, and the resulting administrative distinction between regular and occasional samurai helped to lay the foundations for future class distinctions. Similarly, many daimyo began to reorganize their holdings by relocating wealthier vassals in order to discourage local loyalties and possible resistance. Both practices were taken up by Oda Nobunaga, the first great unifier of early modern Japan. His lieutenant and successor, Toyotomi Hideyoshi, took them further by conducting "sword hunts" to disarm village warriors who had, in his view, served their purpose. By the time Tokugawa Ieyasu took control of a loosely unified Japan, the stage had been set for a dramatic refashioning of the social, political, and military significance of the samurai in Japanese history.

THE NEW ORDER

Ieyasu's military dominance marked the beginning of more than two centuries of (virtually complete) peace. Having secured the title of *seii taishōgun* and thus the legitimacy of the court in Kyoto, Ieyasu moved swiftly to forestall the possibility of future challenges to Tokugawa power. Many profound changes in the cultural meaning of the samurai, therefore, stemmed directly or indirectly from Tokugawa efforts to establish and maintain a total monopoly on violence in order to ensure the continuing stability of Tokugawa rule.

An important early move by the Tokugawa regime was a reconfiguration of relationships between daimyo and the shogun. One key strategy was the redistribution of lands. Daimyo who had opposed Ieyasu's forces at the battle of Sekigahara were deprived of their lands, which were then redistributed to Ieyasu's allies. At the same time, those allies were encouraged to move to the new territories they had been granted; by this clever stratagem, Ieyasu deprived even loyal daimyo of their local power bases and a source of military support in any future rebellion against the Tokugawa order. Daimyo were divided into categories according to their relationship to the Tokugawa house: Those who had only recently aligned themselves with the Tokugawa were designated *tozama* (outer) daimyo, while those with histories of allegiance to the Tokugawa were *fudai* (legacy) daimyo. A third category, *hatamoto,* or "bannermen," consisted of wealthy warriors who served the Tokugawa house directly; and *gokenin* were less privileged warriors in the Tokugawa house's employ. Finally, those samurai unlucky enough to have served daimyo who were deprived of land and status (and, in some cases, life) became known as *rōnin*, or "wave men," indicating their free-floating status in the Tokugawa order. In this way, all daimyo and all samurai were defined according to their relationship to the Tokugawa house. When the dust had settled and Tokugawa rule was firmly established, the Tokugawa family personally controlled 15 percent of Japan, with bannermen ruling another 10 percent. The daimyo, numbering 260 to 280 over the course of Tokugawa rule, held three-quarters of the land, and samurai overall constituted about 6 percent of the total population.

In 1615 Ieyasu assembled the daimyo in order to announce a new set of codes regarding daimyo and samurai. These thirteen regulations, the *Buke shohatto* (*Various Laws for Warrior Households*), were revised and expanded to nineteen in 1635 by the third shogun, Iemitsu. The original thirteen items included restrictions on castle building and repair, limitations on interdomainal contact, restrictions on daimyo marriage, and demands that daimyo regularly appear in the Tokugawa capital of Edo. Together, the codes set out the symbolic and literal control of the Tokugawa regime over the actions of subordinate daimyo, including (importantly) regulation of a daimyo's ability to build military power and to form alliances with other daimyo through marriage or treaties. Later revisions included prohibitions against large ships and on Christianity, both seen as potential threats to Tokugawa power.

The Buke shohatto were accompanied by the enforcement of the practice of alternate attendance, or *sankin kōtai,* which demanded that each daimyo maintain residences in both his own domain and the Tokugawa capital and that he move regularly from one to the other. In addition, the daimyo's wives and children were required to live permanently in Edo as guarantees of the continued submission to Tokugawa rule. These policies, standardized in the 1630s, originated in a desire to control daimyo and make rebellious actions difficult or impossible; like many Tokugawa policies aimed at warriors, however, *sankin kōtai* had far-reaching social and economic effects in reshaping the flows of capital and culture through the Japanese population (see chapter 33).

As the Tokugawa regime was instituting these policies toward daimyo, it was also directing careful attention to the place of all warriors in society. The Warring States period had been marked with frequent examples of *gekokujō*, or "those below conquering those above." Warriors—and even some peasants—had historically been able to gain social status and power simply through ambition and martial skills. Unifiers such as Nobunaga, Hideyoshi, and Ieyasu gained power by manipulating the social and political possibilities inherent in those chaotic times; and for that very reason, they were conscious of the need to stabilize society and prevent exactly the kind of social flexibility from which they had benefited. Hideyoshi's efforts to disarm the populace through his "sword hunts" were an early example of this kind of social engineering, and they would be followed by the Tokugawa regime's careful codification and control not only of the samurai class but also of many other aspects of Japanese society.

As already noted, the samurai can be accurately described as a hereditary "class" only after establishment of the measures of the Tokugawa regime to stabilize society. An ancient Confucian system of social order was adopted that divided virtually all of the population into the four classes: *shi* (gentlemen), *nō* (farmers), *kō* (artisans), and *shō* (merchants). Classical Confucian thought placed the highest value on those members of society who interpreted and understood the proper social order. Farmers were valued for their essential role in producing food for the populace, and artisans, though less important, were valued for the work they performed in creating useful or beautiful things. Merchants, at the bottom of the pecking order, created nothing, but simply lived off the blood, sweat, and tears of the rest of the population. Below the Confucian social order were outcastes who dealt with dead bodies, tanned leather, fought fires, or engaged in other taboo professions; above it were members of the imperial court. Importantly, the Tokugawa regime was more rigid than its Chinese model, and it encouraged social stability by creating a hereditary caste system and discouraging mobility.

In the centuries-old bureaucratic structure that formed the backbone of Chinese political life, "gentlemen" were scholars who used their encyclopedic knowledge of Confucian writings to guide the population in right living through proper behavior and correct relationships with one another. In Japan, the title of "gentlemen" was applied to the samurai class, pointing to an interesting contrast between Chinese and Japanese notions of gentility. But as these "gentlemen warriors" became firmly established at the top of the official social order, they were themselves deprived of the ability to move within that order. The Tokugawa regime set forth regulations on the behavior, movement, and political future of samurai, restrictions that varied according to the minute gradations of samurai rank. Samurai were placed on fixed incomes, or stipends, and these varied widely; elite samurai could receive more annual income than some small domains produced, while samurai of lesser rank in the same domain might scarcely earn enough to survive on.

THE COST OF PRIVILEGE: MONEY, WORK, AND PLAY

The fixed stipends that samurai received did more than simply articulate differences in samurai rank. Despite the hierarchy within the samurai class, *all* samurai were expected to conduct themselves as befit the topmost of society's four classes. This involved keeping up appearances for oneself and one's household. In fact, the Tokugawa shogunate issued many lifestyle regulations (called sumptuary laws) during its two and a half centuries of rule, most of them directed at nonsamurai such as merchants, servants, and prostitutes, forbidding them from wearing luxurious clothing or otherwise displaying wealth above their station.

The issuing of sumptuary laws demonstrates a central economic truth in Tokugawa Japan: Despite the establishment of samurai as a class exalted above all others in society, townspeople—especially merchants—were making enormous profits. As a result, merchants enjoyed more material comforts than most samurai, with their fixed stipends, could afford. The result was a sort of cultural *gekokujō,* in which the lower (merchants) were overtaking the higher (samurai) in the social order. The problem was widespread and significant; samurai were forced to borrow from merchants in order to keep up the required appearances of class and rank, and the Tokugawa government at several points was forced to cancel samurai debts to merchants in order to staunch the free flow of capital from the highest to the lowest social class.

The economic woes of many samurai went beyond simply having to keep up appearances. Government posts—fewer than the number of samurai competing for them—were reserved according to rank; thus, while *fudai* daimyo held the highest offices in the shogunal government, and bannermen the middle posts, many lower-ranking samurai had little or no chance at military or government employment and the additional salaries that went with it. In 1705 some 25 percent of shogunal vassals were unemployed and forced to live exclusively on stipends. The situation was similar for those under daimyo; the ranks of administrators in any given domain were drawn from the higher ranks of samurai retainers, leaving many lower-ranking samurai to subsist on dwindling stipends in the midst of a booming merchant economy.

The most common official employment position for samurai was administrator in the government of the shogun or an individual daimyo. Samurai worked as tax collectors and census takers, directors of ritual, managers of households, economic advisers, and in a host of other paper-pushing jobs. The rare samurai working as keepers of the peace would occasionally be called on to function as actual warriors, but for the most part official samurai posts were bureaucratic.

Those samurai lucky enough to find government postings were not free of financial burdens, as such positions usually carried the obligation to wear more expensive clothing, purchase costly gifts for superiors, and generally support an exalted status. Even so high-ranking a bannerman as the early-1700s Master of Court Ceremonies Nagasawa Motochika spent more than he earned in a given year and was forced to borrow more than 75 percent of his yearly income in order to support that year's expenses—of which more than a third went to paying off *previous* debts.[2] There is little indication that Nagasawa was especially imprudent in his spending; instead, it seems clear that for most samurai, even elite positions in government were no guarantee of financial security.

Moreover, because of the scarcity of such jobs relative to the total population of samurai, many samurai were officially unemployed. The plight of samurai in many families became worse over generations. After the Tokugawa regime instituted primogeniture (inheritance by the firstborn) to forestall conflict over succession, second and third sons of samurai families throughout Japan had only their status, wits, and abilities with which to make their way in the world, and the number of official positions did not increase along with the number of samurai who needed work.

The autobiography of one Tokugawa samurai, Katsu Kokichi, reveals much about the day-to-day existence and troubles of samurai in the early 1800s. When the fortunes of his family fell, Katsu joined thousands of other idle warriors who made umbrellas, practiced carpentry, became teachers, or hired themselves out as guards. Samurai women were depended on to manage households as well as take on their own side enterprises, such as weaving, sewing, or gardening.

Despite their exalted status, then, the economic reality for many samurai was grim. In a Kabuki play from the 1700s, a samurai character is chided: "You receive your official stipend, barely enough to cover the palm of your hand, and eke out a living from day to day repapering parasols or making cheap wine. To keep warm you toast your precious person over a lump of dying charcoal, but even in the miserable, stingy existence, you still go on calling yourself a warrior, a samurai?"[3]

Nevertheless, samurai, especially those in large cities, were active consumers of the new urban lifestyle. Since almost all samurai males were literate, they were an important market for the vibrant publishing industry in Tokugawa Japan. According to one estimate, more than a thousand publishers were active in the seventeenth century in the three metropolises of Kyoto, Osaka, and Edo. While most samurai women could not read (due largely to the lack of schooling for girls), other media such as artwork (including erotica) were consumed by both male and female members of the samurai class. Similarly, both samurai men and women played games, viewed cherry blossoms, or joined in festive gatherings.

Theater—which included the formal theater of Noh, the elaborate puppetry of *jōruri* (now often called *bunraku*), and the boisterous and often racy productions of Kabuki—was another important diversion for samurai throughout the period. Kabuki deserves special attention, because throughout the period, it was associated with sex work, and its negative influence on society was lamented by the Tokugawa government even as it was eagerly attended by samurai.

Following the shogunate's attempts to delineate licensed quarters for prostitution and similar activities in 1618, Kabuki that featured women actors was banned in 1629—because it was associated, correctly, with prostitution—and replaced with "youth Kabuki." But given the popularity of male-male sex in Tokugawa Japan, especially among samurai, the shogunate found the young male actors who replaced women in Kabuki as actors and prostitutes equally problematic. The government subsequently decreed that Kabuki actors be older men (playing all roles, female and male), and Kabuki, like prostitution, was relegated to special districts in major cities. Moreover, the shogunate issued multiple injunctions against samurai attendance. Nevertheless, samurai continued to patronize Kabuki. High-ranking samurai would hide their presence in the audience behind special screens, while their low-ranking counterparts seem to have ignored the shogunal injunction against their attendance more or less with impunity.

IF YOU CAN'T FIGHT, THINK: INTELLECTUAL DEVELOPMENTS IN SAMURAI CULTURE

The image of an impoverished, theater-attending bureaucrat hardly fits with the notion of samurai that populates novels, films, video games, and other media today. In fact, many samurai during the Tokugawa period were themselves discontented with their new, pacified roles under Tokugawa rule. To be sure, some elements of samurai life continued to reflect their proud warrior heritage: With very few exceptions, only samurai were allowed the privilege of carrying two swords, and only samurai enjoyed the fabled—albeit rarely exercised—right to kill nonsamurai (*kirisute gomen*; literally, "pardon for cutting and throwing away"). Katsu Kokichi's autobiography describes an encounter between a samurai named Sakurai and a commoner. When Sakurai wounded the commoner, Katsu and an outcaste worked together to disarm the samurai. The samurai was jailed, and the outcaste subsequently rewarded for his bravery, demonstrating the practical reality behind the theoretical right of the samurai. Indeed, most forms of violence by samurai were frowned upon. Private revenge, for example, was generally prohibited, and the exceptions were regulated by an exhaustive legal mechanism designed to discourage independent action.

In practice, then, samurai were only rarely called upon to function as warriors. Paradoxically, however, it was exactly the absence of real fighting and the emphasis on acquiring literacy for bureaucratic roles that generated a new kind of warrior mentality among the Tokugawa samurai. Without the pressing need to learn practical combat techniques, samurai became more introspective about the martial arts. Training in swordsmanship, archery, or any of a dozen other skills became less about warfare and more about personal cultivation and spiritual development. While multigenerational family-based schools of martial arts, or *ryūha,* had existed during the Sengoku period, martial arts instruction became more elaborate and rarefied in the Tokugawa era, focusing less on practical killing techniques and more on moral cultivation and social positioning. By the mid-1600s, martial arts training became a means to explore and embody Confucian, Buddhist, or other intellectual traditions.

The more scholarly approach to martial arts was based on broader transitions in samurai culture and society. With government limitations on violence and with a new command of written language, samurai were able to investigate and appropriate neo-Confucianism and other traditions. These philosophies were not only mobilized to enrich and expand the meaning of swordsmanship or archery, but also reformulated to set forth the basic justification for the continued elite status of samurai in Japanese society. Neo-Confucianism was both emphasized and transformed in the late-seventeenth-century writings of Itō Jinsai and Yamaga Sokō. Exiled for challenging the orthodox Tokugawa Confucianism, Yamaga famously outlined the "way of the gentleman" (*shidō*), claiming that the samurai functioned as the indispensible moral compass of Japanese society. His writings and those of Itō also stressed action over contemplation, a view that flew in the face of Zhu Xi neo-Confucianism but which met with approval from frustrated samurai. Yamaga's teachings are sometimes credited with influencing the dramatic incident in the Akō domain in 1703 when forty-six samurai attacked and killed the daimyo they held responsible for the disgrace and death of their former lord.

Other figures, such as Ogyū Sorai, broke further with Confucian thought, paving the way for scholars like Kamo Mabuchi and Motoori Norinaga in the 1700s. These later figures discarded the Chinese influence of Confucianism in favor of "national learning" (*kokugaku*), which emphasized ancient Japanese texts as the proper source of insights into Japanese society and culture. The emphasis on Japanese history can be linked as well to writings by samurai such as Yamamoto Tsunetomo, whose now famous work *Hagakure* is often heralded as an exposition of the "samurai code." In fact, Yamamoto's writings on proper samurai behavior were not intended for a public audience. Yamamoto's work is best understood not as a coherent code for samurai conduct, but as a bitterly nostalgic critique of the overly philosophized, rationalized, and domesticated role of samurai in Tokugawa Japan, set against Yamamoto's own wistful depiction of the "good old days." Nonetheless, the work is valuable in exposing intellectual trends present among samurai as they strove during the Tokugawa period to come to terms with their confusing social role as an impoverished elite of peacetime warriors.

THE IMAGINARY SAMURAI: COMMONERS AND THE PRODUCTION OF SAMURAI CULTURE

A final important trend in the creation of samurai identity in Tokugawa Japan was the production of stories, images, and other versions of samurai. From well before the Tokugawa period, blind chanters (*biwa hōshi*) and other entertainers recited, sang, or performed famous warrior stories for public consumption. As publishing grew in output and impact during the Tokugawa period and the success of the merchant economy led to an increasingly literate commoner population, works of fiction about samurai heroes from the distant and recent past were produced for an eager audience. These included the stories of Ihara Saikaku, whose works titillated readers and occasionally poked sly fun at the all-too-human shortcomings of samurai. His 1688 *Tales of Samurai Honor* (*Buke giri monogatari*) presented stories of samurai who were ostensibly dedicated single-mindedly to "honor," but whose actions become laughable or ludicrous. Other works present readers with a connoisseur's guidebook to samurai customs; in the case of the famous *Great Mirror of Male Love* (*Nanshoku ōkagami*), Saikaku wrote on sexual practices between older warriors and their young male lovers.

Samurai characters also enthralled theatrical audiences by committing suicide after agonized love affairs, and rousing puppet plays featuring the stories of premodern and ancient warriors excited commoners and samurai alike. Works by famous playwrights—such as Chikamatsu Monzaemon, whose late 1600s–early 1700s career produced insightful and psychologically challenging portraits of Japanese warriors—were important commentaries on the current warrior government (often hidden in distant historical settings). Perhaps more importantly, however, such works also presented a literary and dramatic version of the samurai that would better capture the public imagination than could the everyday reality of bureaucracy and decreasing economic relevance. Audiences responded eagerly to romanticized versions of samurai derring-do; in this way, commoner audiences not only *consumed* but, through their patronage, also *directed the shaping of* samurai images. A prime example of this is the dramatization (and later fictionalization) of the 1703 Akō incident, which thrilled the public with its transgressive version of samurai honor in the face of the shogunate's legal system.

Commoners not only formed an increasingly important part of the audience for literature and theater *about* samurai, but acted as if they *were* samurai as well. Despite attempts by the shogunate to limit contact between the two classes, commoners appropriated the dress, manners, and practices of samurai. As the economic realities of samurai poverty and merchant prosperity became ever more obvious in the eighteenth and nineteenth centuries, many commoners wore at least one sword and, in some cases, won the right to wear the second sword—the coveted sign of samurai status—as well. Commoners educated their children in various kinds of schools and practiced martial arts in significant numbers. They flouted sumptuary laws by dressing like high-ranking warriors. As Saikaku wrote, even commoner wives betrayed inappropriate extravagance: "Although they are not lacking in apparel, they must have another wadded-silk garment of the latest fashion for the New Year. . . . Formerly, even a daimyo's lady would not have dressed in this manner."[4]

THE SAMURAI ARE DEAD: LONG LIVE THE SAMURAI!

Given the trends outlined above, one might predict that the samurai would have descended into irrelevance by the late 1800s. In some ways, this is not inaccurate. Faced with the cost of maintaining stipends and the need for a modern conscript army, the Meiji government dissolved the actual samurai class in the 1870s, encouraging former low-ranking samurai to become homesteaders in the far northern island of Hokkaido. At the same time, several important caveats remind us of the continuing importance of the samurai in modern Japan.

First, it should be remembered that the so-called Meiji Restoration—the dramatic political coup d'état that ended the Tokugawa Shogunate in 1867—was largely engineered and conducted by samurai from outlying domains. Despite the number of peasant uprisings, famines, and other problems that beset Japan in the 1800s, it was among samurai such as those in the Mito School that calls for the recognition of the emperor as political leader and the dissolution of the shogunate emerged. Samurai were thus instrumental in the huge political changes of the 1860s.

Second, even after the samurai were transformed into so-called gentry, or *shizoku,* by Meiji governmental edicts, they continued to claim an overwhelming majority of government positions. Deprived of the formal status of a class, *shizoku* continued to wield (perhaps even more) political power. Ironically, it was (ex-)samurai themselves who advocated and enacted the abolition of the samurai class.

Third, and perhaps most significant, the cultural force wielded by the idea of samurai—the image of Japanese warriors—was actually strengthened by the nation's leap forward into modernity. Freed from the distraction presented by *actual* samurai—those shambling, threadbare, literate bureaucrats with unsupportable social status and fading dreams of martial glory—the imaginary samurai could populate the minds of all Japanese. Japanese military and economic successes in the late 1800s and early 1900s were widely attributed to *bushidō*, the "way of the warrior," and texts like Nitobe Inazō's wildly popular book *Bushidō: The Soul of Japan* offered the intoxicating notion that *all* Japanese were warriors at heart. While the flesh-and-blood reality of the samurai ended with the modernization of the Meiji period, the samurai as a cultural force became even stronger and more influential. Thanks to the complex elevation and domestication of the warrior class during the two and a half centuries of Tokugawa Japan, samurai were transformed from proud, unpredictable warriors to specters haunting the halls of Japan's past and present.

Sources and Suggestions for Further Reading

See the bibliography for complete publication data.

Benedict, Ruth. *The Chrysanthemum and the Sword* (1989).
Birt, M. P. "Samurai in Passage: Transformation of the 16th C. Kanto" (1985).
Friday, Karl. "Bushidō or Bull? A Medieval Historian's Perspective on the Imperial Army and the Japanese Warrior Tradition" (1994).
———. *Legacies of the Sword: The Kashima-Shinryū and Samurai Martial Culture* (1997).
Gerstle, C. Andrew. "Heroic Honor: Chikamatsu and the Samurai Ideal" (1997).
Gunji Masakatsu. "Kabuki and Its Social Background" (1990).
Harootunian, Harry D. "The Progress of Japan and the Samurai Class, 1868–1882" (1959).
Hurst, G. Cameron, III. *Armed Martial Arts of Japan* (1998).
———. "Death, Honor, and Loyalty: The Bushidō Ideal" (1990).
———. *Samurai on Wall Street: Miyamoto Musashi and the Search for Success* (1982).
Ikegami, Eiko. *The Taming of the Samurai: Honorific Individualism and the Making of Modern Japan* (1995).
Katsu Kokichi. *Musui's Story: The Autobiography of a Tokugawa Samurai* (1993).
Maruyama Masao. *Studies in the Intellectual History of Tokugawa Japan* (1974).
Moriya Katsuhisa. "Urban Networks and Information Networks" (1990).
Nitobe Inazō. *Bushidō, the Soul of Japan: An Exposition of Japanese Thought* (1905).
Perez, Louis G. *Daily Life in Early Modern Japan* (2002).
Smith, Henry D., II. "The Capacity of Chūshingura" (2003).

Vaporis, Constantine N. "To Edo and Back: Alternate Attendance and Japanese Culture in the Early Modern Period" (1997).

Yamamura, Kozo. "The Increasing Poverty of the Samurai in Tokugawa Japan, 1600–1868" (1971).

Notes

1. Birt, "Samurai in Passage," 372.

2. Yamamura, "The Increasing Poverty of the Samurai in Tokugawa Japan," 397.

3. Gunji Masakatsu, "Kabuki and Its Social Background," 208.

4. Quoted in Maruyama Masao, *Studies in the Intellectual History of Tokugawa Japan,* 116.

33

Urbanization, Trade, and Merchants

David L. Howell

Japan changed dramatically after the establishment of the Tokugawa shogunate in 1603. Of the many changes, perhaps none had a more profound impact than the growth of cities. The concentration of large numbers of people in urban areas affected the entire society, for urbanization spurred the growth of communications and markets, which in turn provided an environment for cultural developments and even impelled a shared sense of nationhood to spread throughout the archipelago. Although most people continued to live in the countryside, having a critical mass of consumers in urban areas provided the basis for sustained economic growth that benefited town dwellers and villagers alike.

When measured by the standards of the preindustrial world, Tokugawa Japan was one of the most highly urbanized societies on earth. By the middle of the eighteenth century around 10 percent of the country's total population of 30 million lived in cities with populations of 25,000 or more, and there were more than thirty such cities. Edo, with about a million inhabitants, was the biggest city in Japan and probably the world. Osaka and Kyoto were major urban centers as well, with about 400,000 people each, and even regional cities like Nagoya and Kanazawa boasted upwards of 100,000 inhabitants. Although there were comparable urban areas in China, no city in the Western world even came close to Edo in population, and no country approached Japan's level of urbanization. For example, at the end of the seventeenth century, London was a substantial metropolis—with around 575,000 people—but it was the only city in all of England and Wales with a population greater than 30,000.

Cities were nothing new in Japan, of course. Kyoto, founded as Heian-kyō in 794, had had populations as high as 200,000 people at various times in its early history and had grown to about 300,000 by the latter part of the sixteenth century. But the impact of a single large city is just not the same as that of a network of urban areas that function as local centers of consumption and distribution while simultaneously serving as nodes in a national economic network.

CASTLE TOWNS

As with so many Tokugawa institutions, the origins of early modern urbanism lay in the policies of Oda Nobunaga and Toyotomi Hideyoshi, the unifiers who preceded Tokugawa Ieyasu in the sixteenth century. Nobunaga revolutionized castle construction by building fortifications in low-lying areas, near important land and water transportation routes, rather than in easily defended but inaccessible mountain districts. Both he and Hideyoshi encouraged (and eventually required) their retainers to live in the vicinity of their castles. The presence of so many warriors and their families and servants attracted merchants and artisans, and before long the iconic castle town (*jōkamachi*) was born.

Under the Tokugawa regime the vast majority of samurai lived in urban areas, as required by their lords. As a result, whereas samurai constituted only about 6 percent of the national population, they represented half the residents of the typical castle town. This was true of Edo as well, for as the seat of the shogun's government and site of his castle, it was the biggest castle town of all. Edo—now Tokyo—has remained Japan's largest city since the late seventeenth century. Many of contemporary Japan's major urban areas likewise originated as Tokugawa-era castle towns: Nagoya, Hiroshima, Fukuoka, Sendai, and Kanazawa are just a few examples. Indeed, because each of the 260 or so daimyo domains had some sort of urban center (even if they did not have an actual castle), traces of Tokugawa urban policy remain in many small cities around the country.

Kyoto, Osaka, Nagasaki, and a few other important cities were not conventional castle towns. Kyoto was the ancient imperial capital, and it remained the home of the emperor and court nobility throughout the Tokugawa era. Osaka, the "kitchen of Japan," was the center of national markets and commercial life. Most contact with the outside world occurred through Nagasaki, as it was the only port open to authorized trade with Dutch and Chinese merchants. A few samurai lived in each of these cities, but they were far outnumbered by merchants, artisans, and other commoners. A number of other important towns—ports like Shimonoseki, regional trade hubs like Chōshi, and religious centers like Nagano—were born of commerce rather than military institutions.

EDO: THE SHOGUN'S CAPITAL

Nevertheless, the castle town was the iconic urban form. Let us take a brief look at Edo as an example of how castle towns evolved. Edo was a collection of fishing villages surrounding a small, decrepit fortification when Ieyasu made it his headquarters in 1590. In the decades that followed, a series of massive civil engineering projects utterly transformed the landscape of the area. An imposing new castle befitting the station of the shogun who inhabited it took shape in the center of the city. Huge boulders for its outer walls were hauled by boat from quarries in the Izu peninsula. (Imagine the engineering skill required to balance a rock weighing several tons on ropes between two sailboats and carry it across Edo Bay!) Workers leveled a hill, Mt. Kanda, and used its dirt and rock as landfill in Edo Bay. Two rings of moats surrounded Edo Castle, and in time canals connected Edo's rivers in a network that facilitated the movement of commodities. New aqueducts directed drinking water from the Tama River and Inokashira Pond to elite residential districts. No city walls surrounded Edo or other Japanese cities, but the authorities used barriers and checkpoints to control movement into and within the city limits.

A huge population grew up around Edo Castle, which stood on the site now occupied by the imperial palace in central Tokyo. The layout of the city reflected the political and strategic priorities of the time. Samurai occupied the relatively high ground immediately surrounding the castle and to its west, while commoners settled in the lowlands to the east. Samurai did not get the best land simply because they were the elites of society; rather, their residences were supposed to serve as an additional line of defense in case the castle were ever attacked. Commoner districts started out being segregated by trade—lumber dealers here, fish mongers there, blacksmiths over there—but that broke down before long. Nevertheless, the general segregation of warrior from commoner residential areas remained mostly intact throughout the Tokugawa era, despite the occasional destruction of large swaths of the city in fires and earthquakes.

Although samurai and commoners generally lived in different parts of the city, they did interact. In fact, many residents of samurai areas were actually young commoner men and women hired to serve in samurai households. Despite their status, many of the male servants comported themselves as if they were low-ranking samurai; their tendency to swagger about and get into mischief caused the city authorities many headaches. For their part, samurai ventured into commoner neighborhoods on official business and in search of amusement. They routinely ignored prohibitions against frivolous pursuits and visited Kabuki theaters, brothels, and restaurants; as Edo culture matured, some of them participated with commoners in intellectual and cultural salons (see chapter 34).

THE ALTERNATE ATTENDANCE SYSTEM

Many key features of Edo could be found in other castle towns, albeit on a smaller scale: the placement of samurai residential districts around a centrally located castle, the highly engineered landscape, and the tendency to segregate samurai from commoners residentially while allowing for economic and even social interaction. One thing that distinguished Edo, however, was the system of alternate attendance (*sankin kōtai*), which required all daimyo to spend half their time in Edo and half in their home domain and to leave their wives and heirs in Edo at all times. The daimyo did not travel alone, of course. They brought retinues numbering in the dozens or even hundreds on their annual journeys to the shogunal capital and maintained permanent staffs in the city to look after domainal interests. These men occupied the three or more mansions every domain maintained in Edo (some of the "mansions" were actually warehouses; others, lavish compounds with many individual buildings). Because the domains brought very few women to Edo, the city's sex ratio was unnaturally skewed, with an estimated 171 men for every 100 women in 1743.

The alternate attendance system had a number of far-reaching implications for the development of the Tokugawa economy. The very movement of thousands of men to and from Edo each year served to spread wealth and information along the highway routes that joined the shogun's capital to the countryside. It also spurred improvements in communications infrastructure: highways designed in the first instance to support the movement of samurai retinues were opened to use by commoners who traveled for business and pleasure. While staying in Edo, the men were consumers, dependent on the city's economy to support their needs. They absorbed the latest fashions and cultural innovations, which they took back to the countryside when their tours of duty had finished. In short, alternate attendance not only promoted economic change but also helped to foster the development of a truly national culture, as all daimyo and many of their men felt as much at home in Edo as in their ostensible hometowns.

THE "THREE CAPITALS"

Edo was not built in a day. During the first half of the Tokugawa period, Kyoto and Osaka remained dominant in important respects. Edo, Kyoto, and Osaka together were often called the "three capitals," each with its own particular niche—Edo was the political center, of course, while Kyoto retained its position as the cultural capital and Osaka emerged as the economic center of the country. In time, Edo would come to dominate all spheres of national life, but that occurred only after the city's hinterland developed considerably in the late eighteenth and early nineteenth centuries.

In some ways the dispersal of political, economic, and cultural power among the "three capitals" helped to drive both growth and integration during the first half of the Tokugawa period. Having three centers rather than one ensured that Edo would not completely dominate Japan the way London did England. Tax grain and other commodities flowed from the countryside to Osaka, where merchants oversaw their distribution to markets. In the early part of the Tokugawa era, many of those markets were located in the prosperous Kinai plain, which surrounds Osaka and Kyoto, but by the mid-eighteenth century, goods passing through Osaka found their way to every corner of the archipelago. Similarly, Kyoto remained an important center of cultural and intellectual activity throughout the period. The great cultural renaissance of the Genroku era (1688–1704) was driven by the expansion of the publishing industry in Kyoto. Early modern Japan's greatest playwright, Chikamatsu Monzaemon (1653–1725), lived and worked in Kyoto, while his contemporary, the preeminent writer Ihara Saikaku (1642–1693), lived in Osaka but worked with Kyoto publishers. In the decades that followed, Edo came to rival Kyoto as an intellectual center, but the ancient capital's long history and dense concentration of important religious sites ensured its continued relevance.

Cities furthered national cultural integration in other ways as well. The commoner districts of castle towns included many residents who had moved from the countryside to work. Some of these immigrants were desperately poor men and women who hoped to find work as day laborers or servants; others came to take jobs as apprentices in established merchant houses. Although many of them ended up settling permanently in the city, many others returned home after their employment contracts had expired, taking with them vivid memories of the sights, sounds, and attractions of city life, as well as skills such as literacy and numeracy, picked up during their years of work.

MERCHANTS IN TOKUGAWA SOCIETY

A persistent misconception prevails about the place of merchants in early modern Japan. Tokugawa intellectuals sometimes wrote of society as comprising a hierarchy of four classes (samurai, peasants, artisans, and merchants), each with its own particular function. Merchants came last in this taxonomy because, unlike farmers and artisans, they did not produce things but merely bought and sold them. They therefore appeared—in the eyes of some intellectuals—not to contribute much to society. This sort of thinking gave rise to the myth that merchants were *legally* inferior to other social groups, an idea that has, unfortunately, made its way into the historical literature. In fact, no such hierarchy existed: merchants were legally equal to other commoners, and prominent merchants interacted with elite samurai, sometimes at the highest level.

For example, Keishōin, the mother of the fifth shogun, Tsunayoshi (1646–1709; reigned 1680–1709), is often described as a "greengrocer's daughter." This makes it sound as though her father ran a vegetable stand at a farmers' market, but in fact he was a wealthy and well-connected grocery wholesaler. Without wealth, influence, and standing as a respectable member of society he could never have placed his daughter as a concubine of Tsunayoshi's father, the third shogun, Iemitsu.

At the top of the merchant world were a number of elite houses, including some, like the Sumitomo (known for copper smelting) and the Mitsui (leaders in the textile business), whose names remain familiar today. Their enterprises typically combined large-scale trade of some sort with moneylending, often to daimyo domains. As the Tokugawa period progressed, the domains became increasingly beholden to such merchants, not only as sources of financing through loans but also as agents who oversaw the marketing of tax grain and the procurement of all sorts of commodities.

A common theme in narratives of Tokugawa history is the steady descent into chronic debt of the domains and of individual samurai. Most domains did indeed struggle mightily to meet their obligations to merchant creditors, and some found themselves so pressed that they put debt payments ahead of the welfare of their people. A tragic example of this occurred during the depths of a famine in 1734, when the Tosa domain in Shikoku decided to sell more than 20,000 *koku* (equivalent to 3.6 million liters, or around 7 million pounds) of tax rice on the Osaka market to service its debt rather than distribute the grain to starving villagers. "The terrible irony," notes Luke Roberts, "is that the domain could have sold the rice at an even better price in Tosa, but local people could not provide the large advances and financial services of the large Osaka merchant houses."[1]

Early modern thinkers and policy makers considered government debt to be a serious economic and moral issue, and as we have just seen, sometimes it was. Still, it is important not to succumb entirely to the pre-Keynesian logic of eighteenth-century political economists. So long as it is manageable, debt is not necessarily a bad thing (think of mortgages, for example). In fact, domains managed to get by despite their chronic indebtedness. They developed symbiotic relationships with prominent merchants, the two groups depending on each other in many ways. This codependency resulted in policies that were sometimes good for the national economy and sometimes bad, but in any case they bound politics and commerce together in ways that might not have occurred had the domains managed to balance their budgets from year to year.

The authorities did not tax merchants systematically, but they did find ways to tap into their wealth. In addition to taking out regular, interest-bearing loans, domains occasionally pressed merchants for extraordinary contributions to offset the cost of things like ceremonial activities, major construction projects, and levies imposed on them by the shogunate. Although no one enjoyed being touched for a contribution, making irregular donations was generally less burdensome than paying regular taxes, and in any case, merchants who "voluntarily" contributed could expect official favors in the future. Sure enough, favored merchants occasionally won permission to engage in lucrative activities in exchange for a nominal fee; land development was a popular choice in the early Tokugawa period.

TRADE, MARKETS, AND MONOPOLIES

Domains and merchants also helped one another through the authorities' recognition of trade associations, which monopolized regional markets in specific commodities. The associations typically had a fixed number of members who owned shares that allowed them to participate in trade. Membership in an association changed with the buying and selling of shares, thus providing a means for new participants to enter the market while allowing the association to retain its control over pricing and distribution. The price the association paid for control of its market was a regular fee to the shogunate or local domain.

Trade associations formed to control the flow of every conceivable commodity, ranging from everyday goods like rice and cooking oil to items for the rich, such as tortoise shell (used in high-end hair ornaments), and those for the poor, such as used clothing. There was even a pee association: a band of fertilizer wholesalers in Osaka enjoyed the right to buy up the city's residents' urine and sell it to farmers in the hinterland. Solid waste—night soil—was also a valuable commodity, but the urine association's monopoly was strictly limited to "number one."

Monopolistic trade associations were great for wholesalers who possessed the connections and wealth necessary to join them, but otherwise they were unpopular and economically inefficient. Consumers suspected—with good reason—that monopolies led to higher prices, while merchants shut out of the associations resented the privileges enjoyed by their competitors. By the middle of the eighteenth century, some of those resentful merchants began to challenge the entrenched interests by forming their own unofficial associations in the suburbs of Osaka and other big cities. This led to the relative decline of major urban centers and the rise of "country places"—villages that evolved into local centers of commerce and industry.

Few merchant enterprises controlled the far-flung operations and legions of employees of the House of Mitsui or had the grip on regional markets of members of the Osaka rice wholesalers' association. The typical merchant household was a modest affair, consisting of a married couple and at most a few apprentices and family members. In urban areas the wealth and importance of a merchant operation was usually clear from the size of the shop's frontage. The wider the frontage, the higher the rent, particularly if the shop front opened onto a busy street instead of a back alley. Whether wealthy or just getting by, such family businesses lay at the core of urban commoner society. Those few merchants who owned land and buildings were enfranchised by the samurai rulers to exercise considerable autonomous authority over the residents of the townspeople's wards.

Some merchants did not have shops at all, but rather worked as peddlers, hawking their wares—everything from fresh fish to live goldfish—to local residents and passersby. Although many such peddlers were among the poorest urban dwellers, some regions became renowned for their enterprising long-distance salesmen. Drug peddlers from the Toyama region on the Japan Sea coast of central Honshu built networks that have survived to this day. However, the art of long-distance trade was perfected by the merchants of Ōmi province (modern-day Shiga prefecture), just east of Kyoto. They carried local manufactures like mosquito nets to distant markets, where they sold them for local products they could carry home or to another locale for resale. Enterprising peddlers established connections that they then exploited to build sizable businesses. For example, Ōmi merchants were instrumental in developing the trade in marine products such as kelp, salmon, and herring in Ezo (Hokkaido). By the middle of the eighteenth century, nearly all of Ezo's rapidly expanding trade was in the hands of Ōmi merchants.

MERCHANT HOUSE ORGANIZATION

Merchant enterprises, regardless of their size or complexity, drew on the household (*ie*) as their organizational template. This was logical, not merely because businesses were run by families but also because households themselves were corporate units whose continuity over time took precedence over the immediate interests of any individual in them, including even the head. In samurai and farm households and merchant enterprises alike, a son might be passed over for succession if he were deemed not to be old enough, healthy enough, or bright enough to serve as head—even if preserving the line meant adopting an unrelated heir. Moreover, just as households occasionally spun off branches headed by younger sons, merchant enterprises sometimes set up longtime employees (whether related by blood or not) in their own branch shops, which functioned as autonomous subsidiaries that shared the parent enterprise's shop name but were otherwise mostly independent. This practice was called *norenwake*, or "dividing the curtain," referring to the split curtain decorated with the shop name that was hung over the entrance to every business.

The Naraya shop is a wonderful (though not a particularly famous or unusual) example that reveals both the maturation of trade during the first half of the Tokugawa period and the persistence of familial patterns of organization in merchant enterprises. The first-generation head of the shop, Sugimoto Shin'emon, was born the sixth son of a peasant household in Kayumi village in the province of Ise (modern-day Mie prefecture). At the age of fourteen he was sent to work as an apprentice in the Naraya dry goods store in Kyoto. In 1743, after spending a career in the shop, he was allowed, at the age of forty, to "divide the curtain" and set up his own business with the Naraya name. Two decades later, he passed the business onto his nephew, whom he had adopted as his son. The second-generation head kept the main shop in Kyoto, but he also opened a branch in Sawara, a rapidly growing "country place" in Shimōsa province (modern-day Chiba prefecture). He had targeted Sawara, a transportation center on the Tone River east of Edo, as a promising site for a branch during his years as a traveling salesman for his uncle's shop.

The Sawara branch of the Naraya shop survived until the twentieth century. Until the latter part of the nineteenth century, it relied on the same employment system it had implemented at its founding. It recruited its employees—preadolescent boys, typically the younger sons of peasant families—from Kyoto, Ōmi, and particularly the vicinity of the first generation's hometown of Kayumi village, Ise province. Other than maids, it never hired women and it never hired locally. The employees lived in dormitories, had few days off, and little control over their time during the long days of work. They returned home to visit their families less than once a decade, and so long as they remained with the shop, they were unable to marry. As grim as this sounds, employer and employees alike considered the relationship between them to be paternalistic. The shop taught its employees to read and write, supplied them with better food and clothing than they could expect back home, and took responsibility for their health and well-being even when they were unable to work.

Given the conditions, it is not surprising to learn that attrition was high, but those who persevered were eventually rewarded—typically in the Sawara area with adoption (at the age of about forty) into the family of a merchant supplier. Success as a merchant, then, meant a quarter-century of isolation from family, marriage delayed beyond all hope of fatherhood, and a decade or two at the end of life running a supplier's store half a country away from home. Only a small percentage of employees stayed long enough to enjoy such "success," but in fairness, the social standing and economic security they earned left them better off than they otherwise would have been as the second and third sons of poor villagers. The bottom line is that life was rarely easy in the premodern world!

Sources and Suggestions for Further Reading

See the bibliography for complete publication data.

Crawcour, E. S. "Changes in Japanese Commerce in the Tokugawa Period" (1963).

Gramlich-Oka, Bettina, and Gregory Smits, eds. *Economic Thought in Early Modern Japan* (2010).

Hauser, William B. *Economic Institutional Change in Tokugawa Japan: Ōsaka and the Kinai Cotton Trade* (1974).

McClain, James L. *Kanazawa: A Seventeenth-Century Japanese Castle Town* (1982).

McClain, James L., John M. Merriman, and Kaoru Ugawa, eds. *Edo and Paris: Urban Life and the State in the Early Modern Era* (1997).

McClain, James L., and Osamu Wakita, eds. *Osaka: The Merchants' Capital of Early Modern Japan* (1999).

Roberts, Luke S. *Mercantilism in a Japanese Domain: The Merchant Origins of Economic Nationalism in 18th-Century Tosa* (1998).

Sakurai Yuki. "Perpetual Dependency: The Life Course of Male Workers in a Merchant House" (2011).

Smith, Thomas C. *Native Sources of Japanese Industrialization, 1750–1920* (1989).

Vaporis, Constantine N. *Tour of Duty: Samurai, Military Service in Edo, and the Culture of Early Modern Japan* (2008).

Note

1. Roberts, *Mercantilism in a Japanese Domain*, 63.

34

Ukiyo asobi

Urban Arts and Entertainments in Early Modern Japan

Frank Chance

Imagine yourself in a Japanese city in the Genroku era, around the year 1700 on the Western calendar. You are, of course, surrounded by urbanites, people who live and work and play in their town. The city might have as many as a million residents, whose desire for pleasure is nearly as strong as their need for food and clothing. Now imagine all the ways you might enjoy yourself in this sophisticated environment.

Looking about, you see colorful kimonos amid shops selling books, utensils, tea, and food. Your fingers long to touch soft silks, slick lacquer, cool porcelain, and smooth wood. If you are hungry (and have enough cash), you can satisfy your craving at a restaurant, teahouse, or roadside stand. You hear voices raised in song and reciting poetry, the chants of monks, and the shouts of martial artists. Your mind wanders into worlds of poetry and philosophy, Chinese novels, and Japanese stories like those recited on street corners and in amusement houses. For a few coins, you can enjoy a theatrical performance, whether the broad comedy of Kyōgen, the melodrama of the Jōruri puppet theater, or the operatic choreography of Kabuki. And if you are male, your imagination reels at the way all these pleasures come together in the sexually charged atmosphere of the *yūkaku,* restricted zones where all manner of entertainment is available for the right price.

THE CITIES

The culture of each early modern city was both universal and unique, tied to every other center and tuned to the particular locale and the needs of the audience being served. A regional center, such as Nagoya or Kanazawa, might have more of a particular craft item, in part because of the geographic convenience of the stoneware kilns of Seto and Tokoname or the lacquer factories of Noto. Each of the "three capitals" took pride in its accomplishments—Edo (now known as Tokyo) for its military strength, Miyako (today called Kyoto) for its cultural refinement, Naniwa (now Osaka) for its mercantile prowess—and each evolved in a different direction. At the same time, with increasing ease, transportation linked all parts of the country, bringing the products of each area into the others. The exchanges were not always equivalent: *kudarimono* objects that "came down" to Edo from the Kamigata (modern Kansai, the Kyoto-Osaka area) were greatly prized, while local goods were pejoratively called *kudaranai*, meaning both "not come down" and "worthless" or "uninteresting."

Edo was the newest of the three capitals. It began as a set of fishing villages, fortified as early as 1457, where Tokugawa Ieyasu (1543–1616) placed his headquarters in 1593. After the battle of Sekigahara (1600), Ieyasu became shogun (1603) and Edo became the de facto military capital of all Japan. The city grew rapidly, particularly after the institution of *sankin-kōtai* (alternate attendance). By 1700 the population had swelled to nearly a million, and at times some 80 percent of the people in Edo were male—mostly samurai vassals of the warlords, but also carpenters, builders, and other artisans brought in for the construction of the castle, warrior residences, and supporting structures. In corners of this great armed camp, a culture of entertainment and enjoyment also began to thrive, including restaurants, teahouses, theaters, schools of martial or other arts, and of course brothels.

Naniwa, together with Nanba, Sakai, Settsu, and smaller towns of the region, began to be called Ōsaka (or Ōzaka) as early as the late fifteenth century. The city grew to prominence as a grain market, with rice from the southern provinces brought there for transshipment to the interior (specifically to Kyoto) and farther north. In the sixteenth century the Shin sect of Pure Land Buddhism set up headquarters in the heavily fortified Ishiyama Honganji temple, but in 1570, Oda Nobunaga placed it under siege. It held for a decade, but was eventually razed. Nobunaga's successor, Toyotomi Hideyoshi, built a castle on the Honganji ruins, and his heirs remained there after the ascendance of Ieyasu. Finally, in 1614–1615, the Tokugawa forces laid siege to the castle, and Toyotomi Hideyori (1593–1615), the last of Hideyoshi's successors, committed suicide as the castle fell. Osaka became the financial center of early modern Japan, famous for serving the best food and wit "under the sky."

Miyako, founded as Heian-kyō in 794, and residence of the sovereign for more than a thousand years, was the center of high culture in Japan. It took on the modern name of Kyoto in the 1780s. Royal culture had been supported by the production of fine art and superb crafts from its inception, so naturally the top of the artistic pyramid was in the old capital. Ancient arts—*waka* poetry, *gagaku* music, *suibokuga* ink painting, Buddhist sculpture, and the like—were all disseminated through networks centered in Kyoto, and many more modern arts, including Noh, Kyōgen, and Kabuki, as well as tea practice (*chanoyu*), were similarly supported by lineages of masters in the royal capital. Craft artisans of Kyoto, with their long history of supplying the aristocrats of the capital, also created the finest brocades and damasks, lacquer boxes and paper stationery, carved wooden combs and cast metal hairpins, raku tea bowls and polychrome pottery. The publishing industry began there as well, an event that arguably revolutionized Japan more than any other in the seventeenth century. Extravagant textiles were a particular Kyoto specialty—to the extent that the city became famous for *kidaore,* or ruining the family fortune with clothing. By contrast, Osaka was famed for gourmet cuisine resulting sometimes in *kuidaore*—eating oneself into ruin.

In addition to the "three capitals," Japan had smaller urban centers scattered throughout. Nagasaki, in the far south, and Nagoya, just east of the center, were administered directly by the Tokugawa Shogunate—Nagasaki because of the foreign presence tolerated (and strictly controlled) there, and Nagoya as the ancestral home of the Tokugawa family. In addition, each of the daimyo was obliged to maintain a castle (and a castle town) in his primary holding, and the towns were generally proportional to the size of the fief. Kanazawa of the Maeda *han,* Kagoshima of the Shimazu, and Sendai of the Daté grew and prospered through much of the early modern period. Smaller castle towns, including Hiroshima, Akita, and Takamatsu, have become regional centers in modern times. Each developed local specialties of food and crafts and hosted painters and poets, teachers and troupes of entertainers with links in the three capitals. The web of Edo-period culture was produced by the complex interaction of central schools and peripheral practitioners, sometimes impaired by governmental censorship and regulation, but often encouraged by warlord support and merchant patronage.

At the center of virtually every city in early modern Japan stood a castle—symbol of authority and visual reminder of the military dictatorship ruling the land. These were beautiful buildings, towering over the urban landscape, fortified with walls of stone and gates of wood and iron, and topped with tiled roofs leading up to a donjon. Often placed on prominent hills, castle towers of three, five, seven, or more stories afforded a 360-degree view for the martial commanders ensconced in them. More important, the towers were visible from nearly every corner of the surrounding town, so that no merchant or artisan living and working in the city could forget for long the samurai hierarchy he or she served. The gleaming tower of Himeji's stronghold led to the nickname Shirasagijō (White Heron Castle), while the dark paint and charred wood paneling

Figure 34.1. The donjon of Matsue Castle, also known as Plover Castle. Built in 1607–1611 under Horio Yoshiharu, daimyo of Izumo domain. (Photograph by the author.)

of castles in Matsumoto, Okayama, and Matsue led to such monikers as Karasujō (Crow Castle) and Chidorijō (Plover Castle). Roughly a dozen seventeenth-century castles survive in Japan, and all serve today as proud markers of samurai heritage in their towns. By contrast, the main donjons of the castles that once dominated Edo, Kyoto, and Osaka were all lost to fires during the modern period; only that of Osaka has been rebuilt in modern times (both before and after World War II, in fact).

VISUAL ARTS

Nijō-jō, the "second avenue" castle that served as the headquarters for shogunal troops in the royal capital, stands today on the western side of Kyoto, a complex of moats and walls, turrets and palaces and gardens attracting school tours and hordes of tourists. Although the main tower was lost to a lightning strike in 1750, and the inner palace to the great fire of 1788, the outer palace, known as the Ninomaru-goten, remains today. Naturally, the brilliant paintings of its *fusuma* sliding paper panels, *sugido* wooden door panels, fixed walls, and ceilings would have been visible, in early modern times, only to elite members of the warrior class. The paintings, designed by Kano Tan'yū (1604–1672), were completed by the ninth month of 1626, when reigning sovereign Gomizunoo (1596–1680; reigned 1611–1629) stayed there during an official five-day visit to the third Tokugawa shogun, Iemitsu (1604–1651; reigned 1623–1651). Tan'yū's program of decoration embodies a precise hierarchy of power, with fierce images of tigers and hawks in the outer chambers (to intimidate visitors), great pine trees to auspiciously frame the physical presence of the warlord in the audience rooms, and gentle landscapes in the residential quarters.

This visual program and the technical skill required to create it did not spring from Tan'yū's talent alone. He was a sixth-generation master in a lineage begun by the ink painter Kano Masanobu (1434–1530), expanded to include heavily colored Japanese styles by Masanobu's son Motonobu (1476–1559), and fully developed by Motonobu's son Shōei (1519–1592) and grandson Eitoku (1543–1590). Under Eitoku in particular, the grandiose style of Sengoku mural painting reached a peak, decorating the castles of Oda Nobunaga at Azuchi and of Toyotomi Hideyoshi at Fushimi and Osaka. Few panels from these castles survive, but Eitoku's murals at Jukō-in, a subtemple of Daitokuji in Kyoto, create impressions of real space in the sixteen sliding panels painted with ink trees, birds, rocks, and streams on a cloudlike gold background. By contrast, Tan'yū's murals at Nijō-jō are executed mostly in strong mineral color on gold leaf, with bold motifs that frame the spaces of the room hieratically.

The Kano lineage became "official painters" (*goyōeshi*) to the Tokugawa rulers, and until the end of the early modern era, Kano artists not only decorated shogunal buildings but also executed most of the murals for other daimyo structures. This proliferation of patronage allowed the Kano "school" to split into various branches. The Kyoto branch (Kyō-Kano), founded by Tan'yū's adoptive uncle Sanraku (1550–1635) and Sanraku's adoptive son Sansetsu (1589–1651), was known for a gentler, more refined style. Other branches were identified with the locations of their studios in Edo; for example, those at Kobikichō, Kajibashi, and Surugadai.

The mural decorations for castles, palaces, and temples might have been the most magnificent of visual monuments in early modern Japan, but many other graphic forms served a wide variety of audiences. For the royal court (and for those among the samurai with aristocratic pretensions) the Tosa and Sumiyoshi lineages produced works based on Yamatoe, the courtly style developed in the Heian period and characterized by brilliant mineral colors and meticulous designs, often applied to small formats such as hand scrolls or albums illustrating classical texts. The artistic lineage now known collectively as Rinpa included calligrapher Hon'ami Kōetsu (1558–1637); painters Tawaraya Sōtatsu (d. c. 1643), Ogata Kōrin (1658–1716), and Sakai Hōitsu (1781–1828); and the ceramicist Ogata Kenzan (1663–1743); they created a brilliant style applied to larger works and such media as fans, screens, kimono, lacquer boxes, tea bowls, and serving plates. With the loosening of import restrictions in the 1730s, both sinocentric literati styles (Nanga or Bunjinga) and Europhilic realist styles (*shaseiga,* Ranga, and *yōfūga)* flourished, first around Kyoto and later in Edo and elsewhere. The most urban of urban arts, ukiyo-e, developed from paintings of popular entertainments, through portraits of the demimonde and its divas, to woodblock-printed books and pictures.

THE FLOATING WORLD

Ukiyo, roughly translatable as "this sad world," was originally a Buddhist term used to lament the tragic impermanence of human existence. By the middle of the seventeenth century, however, it had come to be written with characters meaning "floating world" and was used to refer to the fleeting pleasures of human life—especially those of plebeian urbanites.

In such stories as *Ukiyo monogatari* by Asai Ryōi (c. 1611–1681), *ukiyo* is defined as a place where "putting everything else aside, we can turn to the moon, the snow, flowers and red maple leaves, sing songs, and drink sake, drifting through life and amusing ourselves."[1] It is the world of the *yūkaku* pleasure quarters, a demimonde of patrons and prostitutes, passion and betrayal, beauty and sadness. This world extended into the fiction of writers and storytellers from Asai and Saikaku, through Fukai Shidōken (c. 1680–1765), to Santō Kyōden (1761–1816), Jippensha Ikku (1765–1831), and Shikitei Sanba (1776–1822). Conceptually, it also plays into the theatrical presentations of Kabuki and the puppet theater called Bunraku, or more properly, *ningyō Jōruri.*

And it is a world familiar today through its depiction in ukiyo-e, woodblock-printed images created to illustrate books of stories from the middle of the seventeenth century on, but growing to independently represent the heroes and heroines of the floating world. The earliest masters of this graphic genre were primarily painters, whose pictures of beautiful women and the sights and sounds of city life are exemplified by the works of Hishikawa Moronobu (1625–1695). By the 1670s, he had also turned to publishing, illustrating a guide to the sights and sounds of Edo's primary pleasure quarters titled *Yoshiwara no tei* (*Pavilions of Yoshiwara*) in 1678. Soon after, single-sheet prints, often embellished with hand coloring, began to appear, including images of Kabuki actors as well as pictures of Yoshiwara women; around the same time, publishers in Osaka, Kyoto, and other cities also began to produce books and, later, prints. By the 1760s the technology was in place to make full-color prints using a dozen or more color blocks to produce *nishikie,* or "brocade prints." Artists explored themes from the erotic (*shunga*) to the theatrical (*yakusha-e* actor portraits), from

Figure 34.2. Example of a *sencha* tea setting, from an album by an unidentified artist using the signature Hōkō. (Private collection, Philadelphia.)

landscapes to sumo matches; printed editions of Nō plays and classic literature (notably *Genji monogatari*) appeared alongside the latest, wittiest *gesaku,* as the stories of the floating world have come to be known.

The world that appears in this literature, and in the prints and paintings illustrating it, pivots around erotic sensibility. It was characterized by a kind of fluid sexuality embracing all forms of pleasure. Male-male relations, valorized in the seventeenth century by works like *Nanshoku ōkagami* (*The Great Mirror of Male Love*"), by Ihara Saikaku (1642–1693), were lionized by some writers, but heterosexuality was primary for most. The culture of the Yoshiwara and other *yūkaku* and the intricacies of relationships between the women of the sex trade and their patrons have been topics of literary and dramatic expression, diaries and poetry, and of course prints and paintings. It was a world where women could be exploited to the utmost, but the image that survives is mostly of fantastic pleasure, and only rarely do we glimpse the depravity at its base. And while few men could afford many nights in Edo's Yoshiwara or Kyoto's Shimabara, nearly anyone could scrape together the cash to buy a theater ticket or a woodblock print and fantasize about the pleasures of the real thing.

One of the overriding notions structuring such social phenomena as the *yūkaku* was that of *tsū*, connoisseurs who knew, through study and experience, reading and "hands-on" practice, collection and commentary, everything there was to know about one topic. Early modern Japan had *tsū* experts for brothels and theater, but also for incense and tea, *gō* and *shōgi* board games, calligraphy and painting, poetry in Chinese and Japanese, fabrics and lacquers, sumo wrestling and archery contests, ancient bronzes and modern clocks. This culture of expertise persists into the contemporary world, as seen in reality shows and championship contests in which contestants are rated, say, on the number of dog breeds they can name in one minute. Another way this culture of the connoisseur survives is through the practice of tea—not only the *chanoyu* of *matcha* (powdered) tea but also, from the mid-eighteenth century onward, of *sencha* (steeped) tea.

ARTS INTERNATIONAL

The boom in *sencha* was just one result of the relaxation of import rules in the Kyōho era (1716–1736), a part of a larger package of reforms enacted under the rule of Tokugawa Yoshimune (1684–1751; reigned 1714–1745). With an eye to frugality, economic and political restrictions were softened, with, for example, a reduction in the frequency of *sankin-kōtai* attendance in Edo by daimyo. For the arts, the important reform was the change in import restrictions, which allowed both books and trade goods from Europe and China to enter Nagasaki. This encouraged fads for European toys, including picture-viewers (*karakuri megane*) and, in turn, the pictures used in them to create the illusion of space through exaggerated perspective (and the distortion of imperfect lenses). Japanese makers of these pictures (*megane-e*) included Maruyama Ōkyo (1733–1795), who went on to become a master of decorative realist painting (*shaseiga*), and Shiba Kōkan (1747–1818), the first Japanese artist to create copperplate etchings; Kōkan also had careers as a woodblock print designer, translator, cartographer, and Western-style painter. Another group of artists centered on the Akita daimyo Satake Shōzan (or Yoshiatsu, 1748–1785), his retainer Odano Naotake (1749–1780), and the translator and anatomist Hiraga Gennai (1729–1779) explored European perspective, chiaroscuro, and other artistic forms in Edo and northern Japan. At the same time, such European products as spectacles, pendulum clocks, and cut glass were first imported and then imitated by Japanese craftsmen.

Asian culture was also disseminated more widely after the Kyōho reforms. Readers and writers of Chinese poetry flourished, and books like Li Yü's *Chajing* (*The Classic of Tea,* reprinted in Japan in 1758) helped spread Chinese culture to a broad audience. Nine visits by Korean envoys between 1607 and 1811 disseminated continental culture, as each was accompanied by painters and poets (writing in classical Chinese) who enjoyed considerable attention in Japan. By the second quarter of the eighteenth century Japanese painters were producing works in Chinese literati style, based in part on the woodblock illustrations of Chinese painting manuals imported through Nagasaki and then reprinted in Japan. This new stylistic trend came to be known as Nanga, a term literally meaning "Southern painting" but based on the Sino-Japanese term *Nanshūga* (Chinese *nanzonghua*), "Southern school painting"; it was also known as *bunjinga,* from the Chinese term *wenrenhua*, "literary men's painting." Literati practitioners included poet Yosa Buson (1716–1783), calligraphers Ike Taiga (1723–1776) and his *waka*-writing wife, Gyokuran (1724–1884), and samurai painter Tani Bunchō (1763–1841).

HAIKU AND OTHER VERSE

Buson is in many ways typical of the multitalented mid-Edo artist. Born in Settsu (now part of Osaka), he moved to Edo around 1736 and studied *haikai* (comic mode poetry), coming to love the style of Matsuo Bashō (1644–1694). Buson retraced Bashō's 1689 journey to northern Japan, recounted in *Oku no hosomichi* and published posthumously in 1702. Buson in fact copied out the whole manuscript of Bashō's text several times and embellished it with illustrations imagining what Bashō and his companion Kawai Sora (1649–1710) looked like on their journey. In his *haikai,* Buson strove to revive the classic style of Bashō, as in, for example:

Furu ike ya
kawazu oiyuku
ochiba kana
Old pond, frogs aging, leaves falling.

This is clearly based on Bashō's famous

Furu ike ya
kawazu tobikomu
mizu no oto
Old pond, frog jumping in, water sounds.

Buson's poems could also be strikingly visual, as in

Nanohana ya
tsuki wa higashi ni
hi wa nishi ni
Yellow flowers, moon in the east, sun in the west.

The yellow flowers, which bear the unfortunate name of "rape" in English, were grown for their oily seeds, which fueled the wicks of most household lamps in early modern Japan. Buson lets us see the blossoms, lit at sunset, midmonth, in late spring, bringing a whole world into his short line, calendar and all.

Just how many of his contemporaries could actually read and understand Buson is impossible to know: many farmers were illiterate, but most city dwellers could read kana and simple characters. Education levels depended on gender, geography, and social class. Samurai males in Edo might have had a literacy rate as high as 80 percent, while fewer than 5 percent of rural farm women could read—and those who did "read" probably could not handle more than simple letters and documents. Merchant and artisan men would have found reading and bookkeeping skills useful, and in many cases their wives and daughters took on some of the record keeping as well. Overall, the populace was sufficiently literate to support numerous groups that met to share poetry of many sorts. There were groups that enjoyed *kanshi* Chinese poetry and others whose members wrote *kyōshi*, "crazy *kanshi*" with a satirical edge. There were clubs that read, wrote, and recited *waka,* the thirty-one syllable Japanese poetic form popular since antiquity, and groups that enjoyed *kyōka,* "crazy *waka*"; others enjoyed linking *waka* verses into *renga*, a diversion tracing its roots to the Heian past. And there were practitioners of the newest form of Japanese poetry, making the first seventeen-syllable verse of a *renga* linkage into an independent *haikai*, or comic, verse they called *hokku;* today we know these poetic gems as haiku. There was even a satirical, often vulgar form of *haikai* called *senryū.* In the higher ranks of the samurai, literacy was ubiquitous: one feudal lord's constant reiteration of the need for both letters (*bun*) and military skill (*bu*) led to a *senryū* describing Matsudaira Sadanobu (1759–1829) as a mosquito buzzing *bunbu bunbu* all the time.

Sadanobu was at the peak of his power, holding the office of senior councilor (*rōju*) during the second major early modern "reform" in the Kansei era (1789–1801). Modeled on Yoshimune's Kyōho reforms, these were a conservative attempt to bring the shogunate back from the rampant commercialism (and corruption) of Tanuma Okitsugu (1710–1788), Sadanobu's predecessor in the shogunal council. Unlike the Kyōho reforms, however, those of the early 1790s increased governmental control over artistic and intellectual pursuits, including a ban on heterodox interpretations of Confucian political philosophy in samurai schools.

Sadanobu's reforms were intended to increase the practice of the military arts as well. By the mid-eighteenth century, Edo had practice halls where samurai could improve their skills in martial arts from archery to swordsmanship and from horsemanship to *naginata-jutsu* (skill with a glaive, a swordlike blade on the end of a pole). There were rumored to be academies of *ninjutsu* where the spies (*shinobi* or, in modern terms, *ninja*) of shogun and daimyo were trained, but of course no one could find them. Public displays of martial prowess occurred as well, developing into one professional sport, sumo. There were even displays of fighting kites, held around the New Year.

THE YEAR IN FESTIVALS

In short, the urban dweller (or visitor) could find entertainment in literally hundreds of forms. From ukiyo-e prints to *ukiyo zōshi* ("books of the floating world"), the pleasures of the floating world of the early modern Japanese city have been preserved. We can trace a whole calendar of seasonal activities, not mere natural events but cultural constructions and performances.

The year began with a shrine visit, kites, battledores, shuttlecocks, and poetry card contests. The second month brought plum blossoms and Chinese poetry, the third the doll festival, and the fourth month parties under the cherry trees—including parades of courtesans in new kimonos, ostentatious gifts from patrons displaying their wealth by proxy. The fifth month witnessed the iris festival, thought to inculcate boys with martial spirit due to the swordlike shape of the leaves, and accompanied by *koinobori,* carp-shaped streamers waving above the walls of houses. Summer in Edo included cooling boat rides on the Sumida and fireworks over the Nihonbashi bridge at the center of the city.

Tanabata, the seventh day of the seventh month, was a festival for star-crossed lovers, based on an old Chinese story of Kengyū, the heavenly herdsman, and Orihime, the weaving princess. Their love was so distracting that cattle roamed about the gods' palaces and the weaving of new clothes was forgotten, until as punishment the lovers were sent to opposite sides of the River of Heaven (our Milky Way), to meet only once a year, on a short summer night when romantics prayed for clear weather on behalf of the celestial pair.

In the eighth month, ancestors were believed to return to their families, so there were folk dances and bonfires to guide the dead, and gruesome stories to chill the blood of the living. Some groups stayed up all night telling the stories of the hundred ghosts, beginning the evening with a hundred candles lighting the room, and each story ending with the extinguishing of one flame, to finish in predawn gloom. Autumn meant excursions to red maple leaves or chrysanthemum blossoms, and winter might bring enough snow to make *yuki-daruma* (snowmen). After sitting through an early-twelfth-month Kabuki performance of *Kanadehon Chūshingura* (*Storehouse of Loyal Retainers,* performed annually since 1748), it was time to prepare for the New Year celebrations again, rounding out the endless cycle of entertainments. The early modern city never rested for long, and the arts always embellished the lives of its residents.

Sources and Suggestions for Further Reading

See the bibliography for complete publication data.

Berry, Mary Elizabeth. *Japan in Print: Information and Nation in the Early Modern Period* (2007).
Crowley, Cheryl A. *Haikai Poet Yosa Buson and the Bashō Revival (*2007).
Davis, Julie Nelson. *Utamaro and the Spectacle of Beauty* (2007).
Gerhart, Karen. *Eyes of Power: Art and Early Tokugawa Authority (*1999).
Graham, Patricia Jane. *Tea of the Sages: The Art of Sencha* (1996).
Guth, Christine. *Art of Edo Japan: The Artist and the City, 1615–1868* (2010).
Johnson, Hiroko. *Western Influences on Japanese Art: The Akita Ranga Art School and Foreign Books* (2006).
Jordan, Brenda, and Victoria Weston, eds. *Copying the Master and Stealing His Secrets: Talent and Training in Japanese Painting* (2002).
Jungmann, Burglind. *Painters as Envoys: Korean Inspiration in Eighteenth-Century Japanese Nanga* (2004).
Kern, Adam. *Manga from the Floating World: Comicbook Culture and the* Kibyōshi *of Edo Japan* (2006).
McCormick, Melissa. *Tosa Mitsunobu and the Small Scroll in Medieval Japan* (2009).
Pflugfelder, Gregory M. *Cartographies of Desire: Male-Male Sexuality in Japanese Discourse, 1600–1950* (1999).
Screech, Timon. *The Lens Within the Heart: The Western Scientific Gaze and Popular Imagery in Later Edo Japan* (2002)
———. *Sex and the Floating World* (1999).
Schalow, Paul Gordon, trans. *The Great Mirror of Male Love* (1990).
Seigle, Cecilia Segawa. *Yoshiwara: The Glittering World of the Japanese Courtesan* (1993).
Shirane, Haruo, ed. *Early Modern Japanese Literature: An Anthology, 1600–1900* (2002).
Shively, Donald H. *The Love Suicide at Amijima: A Study of a Japanese Domestic Tragedy by Chikamatsu Monzaemon* (1953).
Vaporis, Constantine. *Tour of Duty: Samurai, Military Service in Edo, and the Culture of Early Modern Japan* (2008).
Watson, Burton. *Kanshi: The Poetry of Ishikawa Jōzan and Other Edo-Period Poets* (1990).

Note

1. Barber, "Tales of the Floating World," MA thesis, Ohio State University, East Asian Languages and Literatures, 1984, 30.

35

Religion in Early Modern Japan

Barbara Ambros

Scholars of Japanese religions used to discount early modern religion, but the period has now been recognized as tremendously important for the development of Christianity, Confucianism, Buddhism, and Shintō, as well as popular and new religious movements. The maintenance of public order and institutional systemization were important to Tokugawa bureaucrats and religious leaders alike, but various religious traditions and religious travel were marked by devotees' concerns with prosperity, fertility, and healing.

EARLY MODERN CHRISTIANITY

Jesuit missionaries brought Christianity to Japan in 1549, as the Portuguese began trading with daimyo. After less than a half-century of intense missionary activity, Toyotomi Hideyoshi (1537–1598) expelled the missionaries in 1587, but the decree was not strongly enforced. Soon the Jesuits resumed their missionary activities. The arrival of other Catholic orders in the early 1590s led to discord among the various missions and complicated their relationships with Hideyoshi. Tensions escalated in the execution of twenty-six Christians in Nagasaki in 1597. Hideyoshi's successor, Tokugawa Ieyasu, continued the anti-Christian policies, but it was not until the 1630s that Christianity was officially eradicated. The suppression of Christianity was enforced strictly after Japan suspended its trade with Europe (except for the Dutch) through a series of seclusion edicts promulgated between 1633 and 1639.

One major factor behind the Tokugawa persecution of Christians was the Shimabara rebellion (1637–1638). In 1637 a group of masterless samurai joined forces with peasants burdened by heavy taxation and famine. They rose in rebellion in the heavily Christianized Shimabara peninsula and the Amakusa Islands. The rebels eventually occupied Hara Castle and resisted the shogunal forces for months. When Hara Castle fell in the spring of 1638, the shogunal forces executed tens of thousands of rebels who had survived the siege.

Shaken by the rebellion, the shogunate enforced the expulsion of missionaries and the persecution of Japanese Christians with increased vigilance by requiring registration at Buddhist temples and by holding public renunciation rituals, in which the local population had to prove that they were not Christian by stepping on Christian icons (*fumie*). Informants who turned in Christians were promised monetary rewards. From 1687, Christian families were investigated through the fifth generation in order to root out Christians who had gone underground. Violators faced death, torture, and imprisonment.

Nevertheless, some Christian communities in the Nagasaki area and the islands off the coast of western Kyushu managed to persist in underground lay associations. Because of the scarcity of missionaries, Japanese Christians had already been organized during the late sixteenth century into networks of confraternities, which provided the basic structures for underground Christian communities for the rest of the period. Without Catholic priests to administer the sacraments, baptism, the maintenance of a ritual calendar, and the recitation of prayers and confessional formulas derived from Latin became important practices for underground Christians.

Underground Christians also transmitted Christian icons and other religious artifacts. Many objects could pass for Buddhist icons and were recognizable as Christian only because of the incorporation of crosses. Other strategies of concealment were the use of paper crosses, which could be easily destroyed, and the oral transmission of prayer formulas and sacred stories. Only after the persecution measures were relaxed in the late Edo period was an underground retelling of the biblical narrative recorded in writing as *Tenchi hajimaru no koto* (*The Beginnings of Heaven and Earth*), a rich blending of biblical stories, popular Christianity, local folk beliefs, and Buddhism.

Underground Christians reestablished contact with the Catholic Church in 1865, as Christian missionaries returned to Japan to serve the foreign Christian population after the opening of Japan to trade with the West in 1853. As Catholic missionaries strove to reintegrate the underground Christians into the fold, the latter began to renounce their formal ties with Buddhist temples in 1867, eventually leading to further persecution in the early Meiji period. Nevertheless, not all underground Christians were eager to join the Catholic Church, many preferring instead to follow their local practices, which they perceived as more orthodox than Catholicism.

EARLY MODERN BUDDHISM

Whereas scholars used to depict early modern Japanese Buddhism as degenerate and stagnant, more recent scholarship has emphasized sectarian organization and doctrinal systemization. While earlier researchers viewed Buddhism as being co-opted into fulfilling policing duties for the shogunate and turning into funeral Buddhism through the agency of greedy clerics, more recent scholarship has highlighted the vitality of early modern Buddhism as seen in popular pilgrimage and devotional cults, as well as the multifaceted roles of Buddhist clerics in village life.

In the 1570s, the very end of the medieval period, Oda Nobunaga (1534–1582) had curtailed the power of large Buddhist institutions such as Mt. Kōya, Mt. Hiei, and Ishiyama Honganji. During the first few decades of the Tokugawa period, Buddhism was subjected to regulation by the state; regulation, however, also implied legitimization.

Under Tokugawa Ieyasu, the Rinzai cleric Ishin Sūden (1569–1633) compiled regulations for each of the major Buddhist schools, excluding those considered heterodox by the shogunate. Buddhist schools that failed to gain legitimacy faced suppression throughout the period. Sūden consulted the head temples of each of the Buddhist schools in drafting the regulations designed to systematize doctrinal study, the training and duties of clerics, and the relationships between head and branch temples—the last of which was further standardized in the 1630s through the compilation of sectarian head-branch temple registers. From 1635, administration of religious affairs passed from influential Buddhist clerics to daimyo appointed as secular commissioners of temples and shrines. Further regulations that cut across sectarian boundaries continued to be issued in an effort to rein in apparent abuses of the head-branch temple system and the emerging parish system.

Despite their shortcomings, the head-branch temple system and sectarian regulations led to the formation of more highly developed sectarian identities, which manifested themselves in, among other things, a renewed interest in sectarian founders and sectarian doctrine. In the case of the Sōtō Zen school, for example, clerics reformed sectarian lineage transmissions, monastic rules, ordination practices, and the image of Dōgen (1200–1254), the founder of the Sōtō school in Japan.

In their search for sectarian identity, the Sōtō and Rinzai Zen schools, in particular, were spurred not only by sectarian regulations but also by the arrival of the Ōbaku Zen school from China after the fall of the Ming dynasty to the Qing regime in 1644. Ōbaku Zen brought with it a different understanding of monastic discipline, a combination of Pure Land and Zen practices, unique architectural styles, and self-mutilation practices all of which were novelties in the Japanese context and thus demanded responses from Ōbaku's Japanese competitors.

The revival of an interest in monastic precepts was not limited to Zen but also extended to other Buddhist schools, such as the Shingon. Convents, in particular, benefited from the revival of monastic precepts. A reputation for strict adherence to those precepts gave monastics—male or female—greater prestige and thus inspired devotion from followers.

On a local level, most Buddhist clerics interacted with parishioners on a day-to-day basis. The parishioner system grew out of the temple registration system, initially established in the late 1630s to curb the spread of Christianity. By the early eighteenth century, all Japanese households had become affiliated with a Buddhist temple near their residence, which was then responsible for holding funerals and memorial services for them. Buddhist clerics, the majority of whom came from the same background and stock as the populations they served, interacted with villagers in many other ways as well. Temples and their clergy acted as mediators in village disputes, offered career paths to second and third sons who had few prospects of marrying and succeeding to the family line, performed healing rituals, distributed sectarian medicines, and provided special rituals to professional groups in their parish—such as memorial rites for animals killed by fishermen, hunters, or farmers.

There were, of course, also Buddhist temples outside the parish system. Some temples functioned primarily as "prayer temples" and centers of devotional cults for pilgrims. Temples such as Zenkōji in Shinano province and Mt. Kōya in Kii had sizable landholdings and also developed large pilgrimage networks through professional proselytizers. Slightly smaller sacred places—Takaosan, Ōyama, or Daiyūzan in Sagami province, for example—had regional appeal to pilgrims. Temples enshrining particularly sacred icons of divinities, such as Jizō, Kannon, or Fudō Myōō, held public displays of images that were at all other times hidden from view, and thus attracted large numbers of pilgrims. Other temples formed pilgrimage circuits, such as the eighty-eight sacred places of Shikoku, the thirty-three sacred places of Kannon in the Saikoku region, or regional versions of these more famous circuits in other parts of Japan.

Yet other temples were privileged because of the aristocratic family heritage of the successive abbot or abbess. Many of these elite temples wielded considerable power not only through their family connections, which gave them access to the court and the shogunate, but also by having significant landholdings.

Two elite convents in the Kantō region, Tōkeiji and Mantokuji, also served in a special role: just as village temples served as mediators in village disputes, these convents helped broker divorces for women in the region.

Other elite Buddhist temples and convents served as licensing centers for male and female mendicant proselytizers—mendicant monks and Kumano *bikuni*—as well as for members of the two major Shugendō orders. Shugendō, which grew out of mountain asceticism over the course of the medieval period, represents another example of religious orders that stood outside the temple registration system. During the Edo period, two major branches of Shugendō, Honzanha and Tōzanha, developed in affiliation with the Tendai and Shingon schools, respectively. In 1613, by order of the Tokugawa regime, most regional Shugendō networks had to identify themselves with one or the other of these branches.

In the early modern period, Shugendō adepts (*shugenja*) settled in villages and were treated as peasant cultivators in official census documents until the late eighteenth century. Once settled in villages, many *shugenja* served as priests at village shrines and officiated during cyclical village rituals to ensure adequate rainfall and protection from agricultural pests. They also conducted life-cycle rituals for children; provided cures for illnesses through spells, incantations, exorcisms, and divination; performed various rituals for this-worldly benefits; and acted as pilgrimage guides for villagers.

Unlike Buddhist clerics, whose parishioners were required by law to register with a local temple, *shugenja* depended entirely on voluntary affiliations with their patron households. *Shugenja* further differed from their Buddhist counterparts in that most were not celibate and relied on hereditary succession. Women in *shugenja* households often served as shamanistic mediums during exorcisms. Some were licensed religious professionals in their own right, such as Kumano *bikuni* and female shamans (*miko*).

EARLY MODERN SHINTŌ

As previous chapters show, Shintō and Buddhism were not distinct entities during the medieval period, and the use of the term "Shintō" in the context of premodern religion is anachronistic. Cultic centers, even those linked to hereditary Shintō lineages, operated within a combinative paradigm that was strongly indebted to esoteric Buddhism. During the early modern period, however, a more independent Shintō identity was gradually formulated, although it was not fully implemented until the Meiji era.

As in the case of the Buddhist clergy, the Tokugawa Shogunate was eager to create authorized agencies for shrine priests, diviners, and shamans that were ultimately responsible to the government. During the Edo period, sacerdotal Shintō lineages linked to the imperial Council of Worship (Jingikan), such as the Yoshida house and the Shirakawa house, came to grant ranks to Shintō priests, while the aristocratic Tsuchimikado house licensed yin-yang diviners, and Tamura Hachidayū in Edo controlled female shamans and male dance masters. Encouraged by the shogunate's demands for social order, the licensing of religious professionals became a common phenomenon in the status-conscious early modern society.

Yoshida Shintō, systematized by Yoshida Kanetomo (1435–1511), became a major force in the early modern period. In 1665 the shogunate issued comprehensive regulations for Shintō priests that gave the Yoshida house the authority to control priestly ranks through its leadership role in the imperial Council of Worship. Thereafter, Shintō clerics seeking advancement had to obtain permission from the Yoshida. Conversely, affiliation with the Yoshida allowed Shintō priests to gain leverage in disputes with Buddhist temples, which often served as supervisors of local shrines. Nevertheless, many small village shrines remained unaffiliated with the Yoshida: Some wanted to maintain their own autonomy, and others found the Yoshida teaching problematic; some were administered collectively by villagers, and others were run by Shugendō adepts or Buddhist clerics. From the mid-eighteenth century, the Yoshida also had to compete with the Shirakawa, an aristocratic sacerdotal house also linked to the imperial Council of Worship. The Shirakawa began issuing their own licenses to shrine priests and artisans such as carpenters and others craftsmen linked to shrines.

Yoshida Shintō also influenced Yoshikawa Shintō, developed by Yoshikawa Koretari (1616–1694). Born in Edo, Koretari was of humble origins, but he moved to Kyoto, where he was eventually initiated into the secret traditions of the Yoshida house. In 1682 he returned to Edo to become a Shintō liaison for the shogunate.[1] While Yoshikawa Shintō resembled Yoshida Shintō in its claim that Shintō was superior to Buddhism and Confucianism and in its incorporation of yin-yang and five-phases correlative theory,[2] it also stressed ethical principles, such as reverence.

Just as Buddhism in earlier eras had developed various theories of Shintō, Confucian interpretations of Shintō appeared in the early Edo period, when Neo-Confucian scholars, such as Hayashi Razan (1583–1657) and Yamazaki Ansai (1618–1682), seeking political influence, began to explain key Confucian concepts in terms of Shintō ideas and deities with which shogunate figures were already familiar. Hayashi, for example, rejected the combinative Buddhist-Shintō heritage of the medieval period and argued that the *kami* corresponded to the Neo-Confucian concepts of "principle" (*ri*), "material substance" (*ki*), and the "Great Ultimate" (*taikyoku*).

Yamazaki had been initiated into esoteric purification rituals by the head priest of the Ise Shrines and into Yoshida Shintō by Yoshikawa Koretari. He eventually developed Suika (Revelation and Blessing) Shintō, which recast *kami* worship through the lens of Zhu Xi's ethics and metaphysics. Through its emphasis on reverence, Suika Shintō would become an influential force among loyalists seeking imperial restoration in the mid-eighteenth century. Suika Shintō also influenced the Shirakawa house, which was beginning to compete with the Yoshida for control over provincial shrine priests, and the Tsuchimikado house, which expanded its control over yin-yang diviners in the late eighteenth century.

Nevertheless, it was nativism that was to have the strongest impact on the eventual imperial restoration in 1868. During the eighteenth century, national learning (*kokugaku*) grew out of a revival of interest in Japan's antiquity and a new textual studies method called evidential learning. National learning scholars from Keichū (1640–1701) to Motoori Norinaga (1730–1801) rejected medieval esoteric exegetical traditions and reexamined classical Japanese texts—such as the *Manyōshū* and the *Kojiki*—from a new philological perspective. In this endeavor, these scholars attempted to uncover the purely indigenous traditions of Japan that had (in their eyes) been diluted by foreign ideas. Eventually this effort developed into a search for a new way of life.

Motoori rejected Neo-Confucian moralism and instead emphasized emotions and aesthetics. He also asserted that the meaning of the myths could not be grasped through rationalism or doctrinal study, but that they appealed intuitively to the natural temperament of the Japanese. He also dismissed the idea of posthumous judgment based on one's moral conduct, as commonly taught in Buddhism, and instead considered the realm of the dead a polluted and gloomy world.

Through Hirata Atsutane (1776–1843), national learning developed fully into nativism. Even though Hirata considered himself Motoori's intellectual heir, he differed significantly in thought and methodology from the earlier scholars of national learning, in that he was convinced that all other religions, even Christianity, were ultimately corruptions derived from the truths of Shintō. Hirata was also deeply interested in the posthumous fate of the soul. He rejected Motoori's gloomy concept of the underworld and instead asserted that while the body putrefies, the spirit migrates to the realm of the *kami* Ōkuninushi.

Hirata did not rely exclusively on textual studies but also resorted to ethnographic methods. To study the world of the *kami*, he interviewed a young boy who claimed to have been abducted by mountain goblins (*tengu*), whom Hirata promptly recast as immortals residing in the world of the *kami*. He was able to spread his teachings through a wide network of students. Hirata also developed a relationship with the Shirakawa network. Through this network, his views found favor with many shrine priests for whom these beliefs seemed to offer a justification for making Shintō completely independent of Buddhism institutionally as well as intellectually.

Not all Shintō activity in the early modern period was, however, limited to scholarly learning and intellectual debates. On a local level, small shrines dedicated to divinities of good fortune and fertility, such as Benten and Inari, were the focus of fervent devotion. Major Shintō shrines such as the Ise Shrines in central Honshu and the Konpira Shrine in Shikoku were highly popular pilgrimage destinations sustained by networks and associations. The pilgrimage to Ise was particularly significant as it represented the largest movement of people in the entire period, involving millions of people. While such pilgrimages, often undertaken without permission from village authorities or employers, have sometimes been cast as instances of protest again the authorities—and as such, akin to peasant uprisings—most did not have any particular political agenda. They were usually tolerated by the authorities without negative repercussions for the pilgrims, who were reintegrated into village society after their return.

Mass pilgrimages may, in fact, have functioned like carnivals, releasing pent-up energy and forestalling more serious conflict. The carnival-like nature of the Ise cult is particularly evident in the *ee ja nai ka,* or "ain't it grand," movement of the late 1860s. When Ise Shrine amulets were rumored to be raining from the sky in certain neighborhoods, costumed revelers would gather for wild dance parties that disregarded everyday strictures of gender and decorum.

EARLY MODERN FOLK RELIGION AND NEW RELIGIOUS MOVEMENTS

The Edo period was rife with popular religious movements, many of which escape precise classification as Buddhist, Shintō, or Confucian. For example, Wang Yang-ming Neo-Confucianism influenced popular thinkers Ishida Baigan (1685–1744), who founded the Shingaku (Study of the Mind) movement. But with its focus on self-cultivation and contemplation, Shingaku also incorporated Daoist, Buddhist, and Shintō elements. Baigan, a Kyoto townsman of peasant stock, started as a popular Shintō street preacher and eventually founded a school in his own home, where he taught a practical morality that stressed frugality, benevolence, and knowledge of human nature. Baigan's teachings appealed first and foremost to townspeople but also found a following among peasants and warriors. Baigan held that human desires and selfishness had to be overcome through meditation, self-restraint, and dedication to one's vocation and social responsibilities. After Baigan's death, Shingaku spread throughout Japan through the efforts of his disciples.

Figure 35.1. "Keiō yon hōnen odori no zu," by Kawanabe Kyōsai (1831–1889). The image depicts the *ee ja nai ka* dances of 1868 as an illustrated calendar. A divinity in the upper left-hand corner showers the ecstatic dancers with gold coins and amulets. Beginning in the lower right-hand corner and moving counterclockwise, the thirteen dancers each represent one month—including the intercalary fourth month depicted by a boy led by his mother, the fourth month. Each dancer is flanked by a corresponding animal of the Chinese zodiac linked to the first day of the respective month. Months with thirty days are represented by men and months with twenty-nine days by women or children. A fox representing the second month alludes to the Inari festival, celebrated on the day of the first horse during that month. A woman representing the sixth month on the lower left is waving a fan bearing the image of Mt. Fuji to mark the beginning of the climbing season that month. The tenth month is presented by the god Ebisu, and the twelfth month by a woman carrying New Year's decorations.

Several popular religious movements that arose in the Edo period were also influenced by mountain asceticism. For instance, Mt. Fuji, believed to be inhabited by the bodhisattva Sengen, had been an active Shugendō site in the medieval period but turned, in the Edo period, from a place of practice for *shugenja* into a popular pilgrimage destination. This shift was facilitated in part by the activities of the Fuji *oshi*, who served as innkeepers and proselytizers, and in part by pilgrimage associations (*kō*) inspired by charismatic ascetics who practiced on Mt. Fuji. The first of the Mt. Fuji pilgrimage association networks is attributed to the ascetic Kakugyō (1541–1646).

The Fuji cult gained widespread popularity due to another ascetic, Jikigyō Miroku (1671–1733), who taught a simple ethical doctrine that emphasized

Figure 35.2. "Shonin tozan" from *Thirty-Six Views of Mt. Fuji* (*Fugaku sanjūrokkei*), a series by Katsushika Hokusai (1760–1849). The image shows pilgrims ascending the volcanic slopes of Mt. Fuji around sunrise. A group of pilgrims is resting in a cave.

righteousness, benevolence, compassion, and frugality, as well as yin-yang–related fertility practices. Eventually his followers came to consider him a savior who would usher in an age of plenty. In response to a famine in the early 1730s, Jikigyō climbed Mt. Fuji and fasted to death in 1733 in an effort to bring salvation to others.[3] His teachings, disseminated by his closest disciple, spread widely throughout Edo and the Kantō region. Devotees even constructed miniature replicas of Mt. Fuji that functioned as accessible proxy pilgrimage places. Many Fuji devotees were women, even though they were officially barred from the summit. Toward the end of the period, this prohibition was lifted during certain years to allow women to participate more fully. In the early nineteenth century, Jikigyō's descendants founded a subgroup out of Fuji pilgrimage associations that became known as Fujidō (The Way of Fuji). The movement stressed the idea of world renewal (*yonaori*; also *yonaoshi*) millenarianism that emerged as an important component of most popular and new religious movements in the late Edo period.[4]

New religious movements were particularly accommodating of women, as their religious leaders questioned traditional notions of female impurity and inferiority, promoted fertility and healing, and allowed women to take leadership roles as shamanistic mediums. One of the first new religious movements was Nyoraikyō, founded in Nagoya by a woman called Kino (1756–1826), the daughter of a peasant-turned–mountain ascetic. Kino lived with another mountain ascetic, Kakuzen, and his son. In 1802 she claimed to have been possessed by a succession of various divinities, the most important of which was Konpira Daigongen, a deity associated with Mt. Konpira, in Shikoku. Kino served as Konpira's spirit medium until her death two decades later. Through Konpira Daigongen, she cured illness and helped her followers with various this- and other-worldly problems. Kino's teachings went beyond ordinary Konpira devotion, however; her Konpira divinity claimed to be the messenger of a universal divinity called Nyorai (the "Thus Come One," a common epithet for the Buddha) who wanted to bring salvation to mankind and who provided teachings about the origins of humanity and the world.

Because of their lack of legitimacy and their unorthodox teachings, Nyoraikyō and other popular religious movements often faced persecution. Kino's teachings, for example, raised the suspicions of the authorities, who investigated her in 1820. Under her adoptive daughter and successor, Kiku (1791–1874), the group faced further persecution and was eventually accused of propagating Christianity because they used water in healing rites. In the end, Nyoraikyō was integrated into the Sōtō Zen school.

Tenrikyō, founded in 1838 by another peasant woman, Nakayama Miki (1798–1887), faced similar difficulties before it gained recognition as a sectarian Shintō group in the Meiji period. Nakayama Miki was the wife of a wealthy peasant. At age forty, she claimed to be possessed by the divinity Tenri Ō no Mikoto while serving as a spirit medium for a *shugenja* who was trying to cure her son of a pain in his foot. Miki's state of possession continued for three days, until her family acquiesced to the divinity's demand that Miki—her physical person—become his permanent shrine. Tenri Ō no Mikoto made continuous revelations to Miki, recorded by Miki in the *Ofudesaki,* from 1869. Miki attracted followers through her healing abilities, especially in ensuring safe childbirth, and through her teachings, which promised a happy life through sacred labor, thereby shedding dust accumulated through one's past lives. Miki also propagated idiosyncratic teachings about the origins of humanity. Together with her faith-healing activities, these would later cause friction with the orthodox ideology of Meiji Shintō, leading to more than a dozen arrests.

There were also several popular new religious movements initiated by men, including Kurozumikyō, founded in 1814 by Kurozumi Munetada (1780–1850); Konkōkyō, founded in 1859 by Kawate Bunjirō (1814–1883); and Honmon Butsuryūshū, founded in 1857 by Nagamatsu Nissen (1817–1890). This last was a Nichiren Buddhist lay movement, whereas the first two movements attracted devoted followers through their healing practices and accessible teachings that incorporated simplified Neo-Confucian ethics stressing frugality and diligence, and were eventually (during the Meiji period) recognized as sectarian Shintō groups.

During the Edo period, shogunal religious policies were established to preserve the social order and suppress heterodox movements. That does not mean that religion during this period was stagnant. To the contrary, strong sectarian identities formed among Buddhist schools, and Shintō began to develop the beginnings of an independent identity. Furthermore, while official policies sought to maintain public order and social stability, religious pilgrimage and devotional cults provided room for spatial mobility. Confucian ethics such as frugality, benevolence, and sincerity were first propagated among the ruling elite but eventually penetrated various popular religious movements. Yet at the same time, millenarianism, concerns with fertility, and belief in spirit possession were equally important forces. These were particularly pronounced in popular and new religious movements. It was especially here that women found ways to participate fully in religious practices and take on roles as religious leaders despite the patriarchal norms of the period.

Sources and Suggestions for Further Reading

See the bibliography for complete publication data.

Ambros, Barbara. *Emplacing a Pilgrimage: The Ōyama Cult and Regional Religion in Early Modern Japan* (2008).

Ambros, Barbara, and Duncan Williams, eds. *Local Religion in Tokugawa History* (2001).

Baroni, Helen. *Ōbaku Zen: The Emergence of the Third Sect of Zen in Tokugawa Japan* (2000).

Elison, George. *Deus Destroyed: The Image of Christianity in Early Modern Japan* (1973).

Endō, Jun. "The Early Modern Period: In Search of a Shintō Identity" (2003).

Hansen, Wilburn. *When Tengu Talk: Hirata Atsutane's Ethnography of the Other World* (2008).

Hardacre, Helen. *Kurozumikyō and the New Religions of Japan* (1989).

———. *Religion and Society in Nineteenth-Century Japan: A Study of the Southern Kanto Region, Using Late Edo and Early Meiji Gazetteers* (2002).

Hur, Nam-lin. *Prayer and Play in Late Tokugawa Japan: Asakusa Sensōji and Edo Society* (2000).

———. *Death and Social Order in Tokugawa Japan: Buddhism, Anti-Christianity, and the Danka System* (2007).

McNally, Mark. *Proving the Way: Conflict and Practice in the History of Japanese Nativism* (2005).
Miyake, Hitoshi. *Shugendō: Essays on the Structure of Japanese Folk Religion* (2001).
Ng, Wai-ming. *The I Ching in Tokugawa Thought and Culture* (2000).
Nosco, Peter, ed. *Confucianism and Tokugawa Culture.* (1984).
———. *Remembering Paradise: Nativism and Nostalgia in Eighteenth-Century Japan* (1990).
Ooms, Herman. *Tokugawa Ideology: Early Constructs, 1570–1680* (1985).
Ruch, Barbara, ed. *Engendering Faith: Women and Buddhism in Premodern Japan* (2002).
Sawada, Janine. *Confucian Values and Popular Zen: Sekimon Shingaku in Eighteenth-Century Japan* (1993).
———. "Tokugawa Religious History: Studies in Western Languages" (2002).
Thal, Sarah. *Rearranging the Landscape of the Gods: The Politics of a Pilgrimage Site in Japan, 1573–1912* (2005).
Turnbull, Stephen R. *The Kakure Kirishitan of Japan: A Study of Their Development, Beliefs, and Rituals to the Present Day* (1998).
Whelan, Christal. *The Beginning of Heaven and Earth: The Sacred Book of Japan's Hidden Christians* (1996).
Williams, Duncan. *The Other Side of Zen: A Social History of Sōtō Zen Buddhism in Tokugawa Japan* (2005).

Notes

1. The various Buddhist schools and Shugendō had similar liaisons (*furegashira*), who served as intermediaries between the schools and the shogunate.

2. Five-phases theory originated in China and related the five phases, or elements (Chinese *wu xing*, Japanese *gogyō*) of the universe—wood, fire, earth, metal, and water—in a complex system for describing interactions and relationships between phenomena.

3. Self-mummification was also practiced by mountain ascetics in northern Japan and by one Fuji devotee after Jikigyō. This ritual, which involved slowly starving oneself through a diet of nuts, seeds, pine needles, bark, and other unusual substances in order to prevent the body from decomposing after death, was thought to turn the practitioner into a Buddha. There were only just over a dozen cases of successful mummification during the Edo period.

4. The nuances distinguishing *yonaori* and *yonaoshi* are subtle, in some cases differing only by regional preference. *Yonaoshi,* however, often implies a more radical, forceful, even violent transformation, accompanied by natural disaster and social unrest, than *yonaori*, which connotes more gradual, cyclical changes.

36

Peace Dividend

Agrarian Developments in Tokugawa Japan

Anne Walthall

Peasants are like sesame seeds: the more you squeeze them, the more you get.

—KAN'O HARUHIDE, FINANCE MAGISTRATE IN 1749

Following the final battle at the end of the film *Seven Samurai,* the samurai leader turns to his henchman and says, "The peasants won, not us." In the distance, the peasants are planting rice paddies, happy in the knowledge that having defeated the brigands, this year they will reap the harvest. As the strife that marked the closing years of the Warring States period faded away, farmers all over Japan poured their energies into increasing agricultural production, aided and encouraged by their daimyo overlords, who demanded taxes to feed their coffers.

Ever since Thomas C. Smith wrote *The Agrarian Origins of Modern Japan* in 1959, historians in the English-speaking world have known what their Japanese colleagues already knew: The Tokugawa period saw remarkable developments in agriculture that fueled economic growth. While some have lauded an agrarian regime in which 85 percent of the population worked the land for having laid the foundation for industrialization, others deplore the growing gap between a wealthy few and the impoverished many. Recently historians have also pointed to the ecological costs of expanding agricultural production, from deforestation and floods to soil erosion and famines caused by reliance on monoculture.

More than one factor contributed to agricultural development, which in any case did not progress smoothly from 1600 to 1868. This chapter highlights general trends, starting with the conditions that first made economic growth possible in the seventeenth century. The vicissitudes of the eighteenth century led to innovations in a number of areas from crop specialization to banking. The early nineteenth century saw renewed growth in some regions; stasis or decline in others. At the same time, rural depopulation and the spread of social ills associated with vagrancy and gambling led village leaders and their superiors to fear that the social order was crumbling.

SEVENTEENTH-CENTURY GROWTH

Once the cessation of warfare removed that opportunity for warlords to increase the size of their domains, boosting agricultural productivity became the chief way for them to enhance their incomes. In this agrarian regime, which celebrated the virtues of hard manual labor by ranking farmers second in importance only to the ruling class, taxes were assessed on harvests and made the collective responsibility of the village as a whole. In a happy coincidence of interests, cultivators too sought higher yields, and the first agronomy experts started recommending the innovations that led to an approximate doubling of productive capacity. Although the population rose, it did not keep pace with this growth in production, leading to higher overall levels of prosperity than Japan had ever experienced before. Nonetheless, ecological limitations meant that the yields obtained by the Genroku era of 1688 to 1703 proved unsustainable.

Factors favoring growth first took the form of expanding the arable—the amount of land under cultivation. Easiest and first tried was to bring back into production land that had previously been abandoned or to convert low-yielding dry fields to rice paddies. Thereafter farmers painstakingly leveled paddies that followed the contours of hillsides; they also built paddies on flatland in river basins. On steeper slopes they carved out dry fields to plant wheat, millet, and barley. To irrigate the new fields, they built canals; in northern Japan they hollowed out ponds where icy water from snowmelt could warm in the sun before dousing tender seedlings. In many cases the capital for large-scale reclamation and irrigation projects came from domain coffers, samurai officials supervised planning and construction, and farmers provided labor.

Improving seeds made incremental contributions to raising agricultural productivity that over the long term made it possible to raise more rice on less land. Japan received new rice varieties from Vietnam through Korea; adapted to local conditions, these matured so quickly that they permitted double-cropping much more extensively than before. In addition, village elites with some knowledge of Chinese agricultural treatises carefully monitored rice yields under different conditions, holding back seed rice from the most abundant plants. Over time their efforts led to infinite variations in rice, each adapted to a specific ecological niche.

While most village leaders stuck close to home, a few agronomy specialists traveled widely in search of the best agricultural techniques. The most famous was Miyazaki Yasusada (1623–1697); born the second son of a Hiroshima domain retainer, Miyazaki turned to farming as an adult. In addition to accumulating practical experience, he spent forty years amassing information on best farming techniques from local experts, which he published the year before he died in the ten-volume *Nōgyō zensho* (*Compendium on Agriculture*). Modeled on a Ming dynasty agronomy encyclopedia but based on empirical research in the style advocated by Kaibara Ekiken (1630–1714), *Nōgyō zensho* aimed at teaching its readers tried-and-true ways to increase productivity. Having witnessed the stunning yields achieved by farmers in the Osaka region through the liberal application of fertilizers, Miyazaki advocated the collection and application of soil amendments ranging from grasses to commercial fertilizer to night soil.

Although domain rulers competed with each other in devising measures designed to raise economic productivity and tried to protect industrial secrets, the spread of social networks across domain boundaries ensured that best agricultural practices diffused from one region to another. In many cases merchants in cities, castle towns, or rural areas constituted crucial nodes in the dissemination of technology and skills. Rural elites in the northern domain of Akita recognized that their short, relatively cool summers limited the extent to which they could apply Miyazaki's teachings, designed for the long, hot summers of western Japan, but they applied his principles of observation and learning from experts to their own locality. Throughout the Tokugawa period, peripatetic agronomy experts and their writings found a welcome audience in villages whose leaders made multigenerational efforts to find and refine ways to increase yields.

Technological innovations also contributed to raising productivity. Developed in the Genroku period, the multitoothed thresher (*senba koki*) was a simple device consisting of a series of iron sticks placed next to each other on a stand akin to a sawhorse. By drawing rice plants through the sticks so as to catch the ears, the user could separate grain from the stalks. This was primitive technology, to be sure, but it was still more efficient than holding two sticks in one hand while pulling plants through with the other. In some regions the thresher was accused of being the ruination of widows because it eliminated the need to hire extra labor after the harvest. Once rice had been dried, it then had to be flailed to break open the husks. A winnower (*tōmi*) introduced from

Figure 36.1. A winnower from Kakunodate in northern Japan. (Photograph by the author.)

China in the late seventeenth century made use of the suction produced by hand-cranked fan blades rotating in a barrel to separate grains from chaff (see figure 36.1). Modifications to plows, hoes, and other farm implements adapted each to local soils. Rather than replacing human power with machines, improvements in tools made labor more efficient.

Changes in village social structure contributed to increasing productivity. In the early seventeenth century, kinship, pseudokin ties, and hereditary bonds of servitude meant that most villagers worked directly for a single family, sometimes the village founder, sometimes a rusticated samurai. Over time and with the encouragement of daimyo who wished to discourage the formation of local power blocks, village leaders allowed their dependents autonomy in farming small parcels of land in return for subservience to their authority. Once free to work their own plots, smallholders were much more willing to exploit their own labor. Praise for their diligence turned necessity into virtue.

Increasing yields in food while reducing the amount of labor needed to produce it left Japanese farmers with more energy and land to devote to nonsubsistence, commercial crops at the same time that their rulers were encouraging (demanding) products to which value could be added. Chief among these was cotton. The importation of seeds suitable to Japan in the sixteenth century introduced a textile that came to dominate the clothing market. Less expensive or luxurious than silk, but not as rough as hemp or ramie, cotton cloth could be produced in greater quantity than either. While acknowledging that the region around Osaka grew the best cotton, seventeenth-century agronomists in central and northern Japan noted that farmers in their localities grew it as well. Harvested in fall, cotton could be spun and woven over the long winter months, thus keeping women occupied in moneymaking endeavors.

Although Japan had long maintained a silk industry—again, in the Kyoto-Osaka region—only after the shogunate banned silk imports from China in 1685 did sericulture spread more widely. In the Ina valley of central Japan, raising silkworms and spinning silk remained a niche industry concentrated in villages near castle towns until the opening of Yokohama to foreign trade in 1859, when it became Japan's leading export. At the same time, the demands of silk production fostered regional specialization, with villages in northern Japan producing silkworm eggs while villages in milder climates hatched and fed the worms, tending them assiduously until they spun cocoons. Then women hurried to spin the silk before the pupa turned into moths. Once spun, silk floss could easily be transported long distances to weaving centers in western and eastern Japan.

Textiles were just two of the by-employments that encouraged farmers to make more industrious use of time not otherwise spent tilling fields. Transforming rice stalks into straw mats, raincoats, horseshoes, and other products kept men busy during long winter nights. Lacquer and paper derived from trees or shrubs that could be grown in otherwise nonproductive soil. Dishes, bowls, and combs made of wood and fashioned into distinctive shapes became regional specialties. In mountainous areas farmers collected wood to make charcoal for sale in cities. Acquiring these raw materials put pressure on forests.

The spate of urban construction in the early seventeenth century soon robbed Japan's forests of their largest trees. Following the great Meireki fire (named after the calendar era) of 1657, timber was so scarce that temples, daimyo compounds, and even the shogun's castle had to be rebuilt to a more modest scale. The combination of elite demands for timber and farmers' demands for raw materials led to acute deforestation. The loss of cover led in turn to erosion and the silting of rivers.

From the mid-seventeenth to the mid-eighteenth centuries, governments launched initiatives to rectify the damage. Some measures simply restricted access to forests and their products; in the eighteenth century, agronomists and officials started promoting afforestation. As early as 1642, farmers were encouraged or obliged to plant trees. In the nineteenth century, plantation forestry spread so widely that few if any of Japan's forests can be considered virgin. In the meantime, however, farmers living downstream from denuded mountains watched helplessly as floods destroyed rice paddies painstakingly constructed too close to rivers.

EIGHTEENTH-CENTURY VICISSITUDES

Historians of rural Japan often point to the 1750s as a turning point. By that time, the ubiquity of by-employments brought increased differentiation between the wealthy and the poor in villages, the rise of rural entrepreneurs, the spread of tenant farming, and the development of new banking systems through mutual credit associations predicated on trust. Other historians see the eighteenth century as a period of stasis because the productivity gains of the seventeenth century proved unsustainable, the population stagnated, and famines increased in frequency and severity. Conflicts between farmers and the ruling authorities sparked large-scale protests and limited the taxes that could be extracted from villages. At the end of the century, commoners in town and country started to blame merchants for their problems by attacking them in food riots.

Eighteenth-century famines owed much to vagaries of the weather, exacerbated by human error. The Kyōhō famine of 1832–1833 in southwestern Japan spread after a decade of poor harvests and the refusal of officials to lower taxes. Some areas suffered from cold rains during prime growing season; others from an infestation of insects that ate crops, grasses, and leaves. More than 10,000 people died and millions suffered from hunger. Periodic lesser famines afflicted specific localities thereafter. The most devastating famine occurred after the eruption of Mt. Asama in 1783, which killed thousands directly while leaving ash piled in fields and dust blanketing the sky. Deprived of sunlight, crops failed. Even in the best of times, the growing season in northeastern Japan was barely long enough to grow rice; in 1783, winter came early. Nonetheless, the daimyo of Hirosaki insisted on shipping every grain of rice to Osaka to reduce domain debts. More than 80,000 people there died. Morioka domain had decided that having farmers grow nothing but soybeans, used in a host of products from sauce to tofu, would solve its financial problems. There too tens of thousands died when the crop failed. Farmers who had replaced food crops with cotton or tobacco in the Osaka region discovered that their reduced harvests left them with no means to buy food. Many people died; others blamed greedy merchants for hoarding rice. The year 1787 saw the largest, most widespread riots in Japanese history.

Farmers had few channels through which to express their grievances. The ruling authorities deemed collective action to be "conspiracy" and threatened its leaders with death. Individuals who protested on behalf of their villages ran the risk of overstepping the line between legitimate remonstrance and illegal direct appeal. Criticizing the authorities also courted execution. Eighteenth-century farmers tried to get around these injunctions by signing petitions in a circle to obscure the ringleaders; they marched en masse to castle gates to present their demands. In 1754 more than 150,000 farmers marched in Kyushu's Kurume domain. When some 100,000 marched on Edo in 1764 to protest new demands for corvée labor at post stations, the shogunate armed its retainers with guns and authorized their use. Because grievances were always local and specific, farmers never launched rebellions against the political system. Few regions saw more than one large-scale uprising; many did not even experience that. Yet the fear that unrest would expose a domain's administrative failings to outsiders had to be figured in the calculus of the tax burden to be assessed on villages.

By 1720 even the shogunate could no longer afford to pay all its retainers, and few daimyo escaped falling into debt to moneylenders; yet tax revenues remained flat or declined. Despite efforts to tighten administrative procedures, find new products to tax, and supplement taxes with forced loans, income did not match expenditures. In part the cause was ecological—the number of fields under production shrank as the environment degraded. In part the cause was also political. Seventeenth-century officials had assessed taxes by viewing the harvest, a time-consuming process fraught with the potential for corruption. One consequence of the 1720s reforms in many areas was a fixed tax system (*jōmen*) that guaranteed governments a stable income except under extraordinary circumstances. Historians credit this system with contributing to the farmers' retention of surpluses accruing from rural economic development.

A crucial institution that proliferated in the late eighteenth century was the mutual assistance society, or *kō*. These had a number of names and purposes, from village-based organizations that saved a portion of the yield against crop failures, to religiously based societies in which participants contributed funds to support pilgrimages by the group's representatives or insured themselves against misfortune, to institutions that functioned more like credit unions or banks. In all cases each member contributed a sum annually with the expectation that at some point he or she would receive a defined payout. To function effectively, each such organization had to be based on trust, and to build trust, it had to maintain accurate records showing precise calculations of principal and interest.

Crucial to rural economic development was the appearance of rural entrepreneurs. They grew crops (in the case of one individual, his mother and wife weeded the fields); they rented land to tenant farmers; they acted as middlemen in arranging deliveries of raw materials to be processed, such as silk cocoons to be spun into thread; they bought and sold finished goods at market; they owned small-scale factories that produced soy sauce or sake; they served as village officials; and they lent money at rates of 10 to 20 percent a year. Although urban merchants fostered their rural counterparts' rise and developed enterprises on much larger scales, they never sucked all the capital out of the countryside.

Enough remained to make some farmers extremely wealthy and to support the growth of rural businesses, a trend that accelerated in the nineteenth century.

NINETEENTH-CENTURY RECOVERY, GROWTH, AND TURMOIL

The first decades of the nineteenth century showed clear signs that in many rural areas, conditions were improving. Although tax rates remained flat, members of the ruling class complained that the villages were becoming too prosperous. Despite stagnation of the overall population, declines in regions suffering depopulation were balanced by increases in others. Proof that growth could still easily be derailed appeared in the third devastating famine of this period, in 1833–1837. Of longer-term concern were divisions within villages between youths and their elders, laborers and landlords, newly wealthy farmers and descendants of village founders.

Both domain administrations and rural entrepreneurs promoted by-employments to generate income that accrued more to the promoter than the worker. Cotton and tobacco crops in the fields around Osaka required so much fertilizer that they stimulated new methods for catching herring off the coast of Hokkaido. Developed by commercial fisheries, these enterprises competed with individual fishermen, eventually turning the latter into contract laborers. In Tosa, castle town merchants urged the domain to export to Osaka paper produced by farmers living high in the mountains. In cotton- and silk-producing regions, men who through luck or skill amassed capital and land challenged the village's hereditary leadership. In some cases even ordinary farmers challenged hereditary privileges and accused the leadership of corruption and arrogance. Village disputes exploded across the landscape, leading to reforms of local administration and new principles for the selection of village headmen, sometimes on a rotating basis, sometimes by ballot.

Village youth groups comprising men between the ages of fifteen and forty provided the structure for collective activities, not always in ways approved by local leadership. Sometimes they demanded more holidays than their elders thought prudent; sometimes they used their funds to put on plays or to hire traveling Kabuki troupes to perform for them. Nearly every village in the lower Ina valley built Kabuki stages in the early nineteenth century, some with revolving stages, an indication of rural prosperity found in other parts of the country as well. Festivals too became more elaborate and more boisterous except when suppressed by officials.

Village leaders deplored gambling, and regulations for youth groups forbade it, yet it spread throughout regions well integrated into a monetary economy. In the Kantō hinterland to Edo, professional gamblers were accused of seducing young men from their hereditary occupation with the promise of an easy, adventurous life. Gambling threatened families with financial ruin; it also corrupted morals. At the beginning of the nineteenth century the shogunate instituted patrols to suppress undesirables. Recognizing the scale of the problem, villages took to organizing themselves into leagues to drive vagrants away. Some officials hired sword fighters to train militias for self-defense. These militias signaled the farmers' realization that they could no longer rely on the government for protection. But did they represent the village's resilience in face of change, or a desperate response to a crumbling social order?

Written in 1816 by Buyō Inshi, *Seiji kenbunroku* (*Record of Observations on Current Affairs*) contains a chapter on farmers that describes an expansion in luxury, competition for profit, and growing polarization between rich and poor brought about by the circulation of goods and money in a commercial economy. This circulation promotes the development of by-employments, but it distracts farmers from their fundamental occupation, to till the soil. It spurs the spread of usurious and deceitful lending practices; it encourages the flow of goods, including food, from the countryside to cities; and eventually it leads to depopulation. In short, it benefits people who learn how to profit from trade; it disadvantages those who do not.

The increased circulation of goods leads to increased circulation of people. In Buyō's eyes, two types of people leave harsh conditions in the countryside for the city—those who want an easier life and those forced out by destitution. The former have already been corrupted by urban morals; rather than try to earn an honest living, they become gangsters and turn to a life of crime. What distinguishes gangsters is their ability to travel in complete freedom, a term of disapprobation in a world in which farmers were supposed to remain in place, as restricted as much by community mores as by government fiat.

If the reason for going to the city was to flee destitution, Buyō was more sympathetic. He waxes indignant over the plight of the good, honest, dull-witted farmer exploited by the wealthy, by village officials, and by the government. Leaving family behind, the worthy farmer travels to the city, hoping to earn enough by contract labor and side jobs to supplement his family's income back in the village. Alas he is never able get ahead, and often never returns home at all. Out of desperation parents may commit infanticide; widowers, widows, orphans, and people without children are left to die alone; and provinces suffer depopulation.

The issues identified by Buyō resonated with village leaders and the rural elite. Some tried to help their fellows by educating them in temple schools that taught both girls and boys, in contrast to domain schools open to men only, and samurai men at that. Others found inspiration in the teachings and example of Ninomiya Sontoku (1787–1856), who organized regional leagues of villages into Hōtokusha (Return of Virtue Associations) to revive depopulated areas devastated by the Tenpō famine of 1833–1837. Based on the same microfinance practice and ethical principles of accountability and trust that informed mutual aid confraternities (*kō*), Hōtoku associations aimed at rescuing farmers by having them save money that would over time generate a surplus to be held in reserve for emergencies. Detailed regulations told each household how much to set aside for taxes, how much to keep as an emergency fund, how much to spend on household needs, and how much to contribute to the Hōtoku savings and loan fund that also provided support for others. Sontoku gained such fame for his achievements in revitalizing villages that he was made the shogun's retainer and received invitations from numerous domains to put his ideas into practice. Although the modern state used his name to promote capitalism in the countryside, historian Tetsuo Najita emphasizes that the ethical component to Sontoku's teachings fitted ill with the state's goal of profit in place of charity.

The results of two and a half centuries of change in rural Japan contributed substantially to the process of building a strong state and an industrial economy in the latter half of the nineteenth century. Local schools had raised literacy rates, though more for boys than for girls. Starting with Thomas C. Smith, historians have tracked the ways that rural entrepreneurs amassed capital and protoindustrialization generated labor. Although many by-employments produced the type of handicrafts made obsolete by machine-made goods, the practice of supplementing work in the fields with nonagricultural labor provided a useful model for modern farm family economies. More important, the values of diligence and industriousness instilled in generations of hardworking farmers offered employers the prospect of a potentially disciplined workforce. The mutual aid confraternities and the return of virtue societies also offered a combination of practice and ethical training that resembled banking and thrift.

But the legacy was not unmixed for capital, labor, or morality. The capital reserves amassed by rural entrepreneurs in the first half of the nineteenth century often proved too small to pay for modern factories. In the Ina valley, tiny silk-spinning factories employing six to twelve women could not compete in quality with larger outfits using more modern equipment. Although mutual aid societies had taught people to trust others with their money, they had not accustomed people to the scale and risk associated with late-nineteenth-century banks that, undercapitalized and overextended, went bankrupt during the government-mandated deflation of the 1880s. Before surplus men started finding jobs in heavy industry in the late nineteenth to early twentieth century, rural women had been recruited to work in textile factories starting in the 1870s. Because they were not considered independent householders, they were not paid a living wage; because their earnings went to their families, landlords took their wages into account in setting rents. Squeezed by property taxes and rents that had to be paid regardless of the harvest, smallholders and tenant farmers continued doing the same work their ancestors had done. Not until the 1950s did mechanization start to save farmers from backbreaking drudgery.

Sources and Suggestions for Further Reading

See the bibliography for complete publication data.

Cornell, Laurel L. "Infanticide in Early Modern Japan: Demography, Culture, and Population Growth" (1996).

Furushima Toshio. "The Village and Agriculture During the Edo Period" (1991).

Hauser, William B. *Economic Institutional Change in Tokugawa Japan: Osaka and the Kinai Cotton Trade* (1974).

Howell, David L. *Capitalism from Within: Economy, Society, and the State in a Japanese Fishery* (1995).

Morris-Suzuki, Tessa. *The Technological Transformation of Japan from the Seventeenth to the Twenty-First Century* (1994).

Najita, Tetsuo. *Ordinary Economies in Japan: A Historical Perspective, 1750–1950* (2009).

Ooms, Herman. *Tokugawa Village Practice: Class, Status, Power, Law* (1996).

Pratt, Edward E. *Japan's Proto-industrial Elite: The Economic Foundations of the Gōnō* (1999).

Roberts, Luke S. *Mercantilism in a Japanese Domain: The Merchant Origins of Economic Nationalism in 18th-Century Tosa* (1998).

Smith, Thomas C. *Native Sources of Japanese Industrialization, 1750–1920* (1988).

Totman, Conrad. *Early Modern Japan* (1993).

———. *The Green Archipelago: Forestry in Preindustrial Japan* (1989).

White, James W. *Ikki: Social Conflict and Political Protest in Early Modern Japan* (1995).

Wigen, Kären. *The Making of a Japanese Periphery, 1750–1920* (1995).

37

Family, Gender, and Sex in Early Modern Japan

Denis Gainty

Historical studies of the government, economy, foreign policy, philosophy, art, and other aspects of the Tokugawa period have for decades provided us with an increasingly clear picture not only of Japan's past, but also of how developments during those two and a half centuries help us to understand the so-called Meiji Restoration, Japan's role in the twentieth century, and Japan today. Studies in political, economic, intellectual, and art history have also been complemented in recent years by a focus on day-to-day life, recognizing that what humans eat and wear, whom they love, and how they define and relate to their families is as revealing—and as significant—as the so-called big issues of politics, economics, and so on. Daily life, in all its seemingly mundane detail, has become an important lens through which to understand power structures, resource allocation, intellectual trends, and how people establish and maintain identities in history.

Perhaps one of the most basic and immediate social units experienced by individuals in societies across time and place is that of the family. In Tokugawa Japan, the idea of family or kinship network was most powerfully represented by the *ie*, or household. While *ie* were significantly different from what anthropologists analyze as kinship networks or families, they contained and represented the elements of kinship, descent, and corporate identity usually associated with families. Through *ie*, Tokugawa Japanese established, maintained, and challenged their respective positions in the larger society. Moreover, the definition of *ie* was established both by government edict and various local practices, showing again how daily life is a useful medium for understanding large-scale history. From early Tokugawa village life and questions of daimyo inheritance to the rise of *ie*-based commercial enterprise and the rise of the "family state," the changing meanings and uses of *ie* reveal a great deal about larger shifts in Tokugawa history.

Along with family, the theme of gender has become increasingly important in histories of Japan and elsewhere. Historians have in recent decades begun to acknowledge that the understanding and practice of gender-based identities constitute an important and overlooked sphere within which humans experience, interact with, and help to create their societies. Gender—the collection of meanings and expectations assigned to "male" and "female" roles in society—was a basic way in which Tokugawa Japanese at all levels defined themselves and each other. The expectation for samurai male behavior toward other males or females, the possibilities for economic or political power for merchant women, the legal codes regarding divorce and adultery, and the different educational opportunities for women and men were all ways in which ideas about gender both shaped and reflected Tokugawa history.

Sexuality is a third aspect of daily life that has recently caught the attention of historians as an important field of human activity and historical inquiry. The question of who is having sex with whom is increasingly viewed as central to how human societies are constructed. Like family and gender, sexuality changed under the new social order and stability of the Tokugawa period. And as with both family and gender, changes in how sex was practiced and understood during the Tokugawa period reveal shifts in government attempts at social control, public interest in sexual connoisseurship, class-based social relationships, population pressures, and other important historical questions.

FAMILY AND SOCIETY IN EARLY MODERN JAPAN: THE *IE* SYSTEM

The idea of family is at once universal and specific. While some idea of family or kinship is found in virtually every human society, family in Tokugawa Japan united and defined its members in ways unique to that time and place. In fact, it may be misleading to use the term "family"; as mentioned, the rough analog in Tokugawa Japan is the *ie*. The *ie* did not depend *solely* on either blood or marriage relationships; instead, as anthropologists and historians have pointed out, the *ie* was a means by which political and economic control over a certain area could be ensured for a specific multigenerational group. Nevertheless, its similarity to family structures—including its use of inheritance, marriage, and other family relationships and its fundamental role as a social unit—allows us to think of *ie* as loosely connected to the ideas of relationship and loyalty that we commonly associate with contemporary Western families.

While *ie* was an important idea among warriors seeking to control territory before and during the Sengoku period, it gained importance as a social unit for all members of society during the Tokugawa era. Economist Murakami Yasusuke calls the Tokugawa social order itself a "meta-*ie*" under which the ideas of *ie* became a sort of governing ideology for the entire country. The establishment of Tokugawa rule, including both careful control of the new samurai class and the ordering of village life, effectively spread *ie* as an organizational scheme throughout the populace.

For samurai, who constituted a newly codified elite social stratum, the idea of *ie* was not new. Nevertheless, when Ieyasu orchestrated the succession of his grandson Iemitsu to the position of shogun, he formalized the practice of primogeniture among all samurai families. Although this solved the problem of family holdings spreading too thin among exponentially larger numbers of descendants, it also created a vast underclass of second and third sons who were essentially forced to fend for themselves. At the same time, the Tokugawa regime claimed the right to confirm or deny heirs. Without an heir, an *ie* was dissolved and its property reverted to the government; this meant that a samurai *ie* needed to be carefully documented in order to avoid catastrophe and dissolution. It also meant that adoption became increasingly important as a means of continuing the *ie*.

Because of its success in monitoring and regulating samurai, and its value as a central organizing logic for all of society, the *ie* system was extended to commoner families as well. This does not mean that the samurai *ie* was replicated exactly among commoners, but many elements of the *ie* model carried over to structure the lives of commoners as well. Before the new Tokugawa social order removed samurai from their agricultural lands, the *ie* had functioned as a means of protecting that group's control of its territory. Under the Tokugawa regime, a similar logic was applied to commoners, especially farmers. Farmers made up some 80 percent of the total population, of whom some owned land (*hon-byakushō*) and others were tenants (*mizunomi-byakushō*, or "water-drinking farmers"). While the landowning group clearly had more assets to protect, it is noteworthy that both sorts were granted *ie* status. In this way, we can see the migration of the *ie* model across boundaries of class and economic status.

In both samurai and commoner *ie*, the basic structure consisted of a married couple and their natural or adopted son. Other children (either daughters or subsequent sons) were encouraged to leave the household when they became adults. In the case of commoner *ie* with surplus resources, such as merchant and landowning farmer households, such sons might establish a branch household with the support of the main *ie*. The more common practice, however, was for them to enter into another *ie* through marriage or adoption. The third and least attractive option for unlucky children was to find marginal employment. A daughter was occasionally able to stay in her birth family, but usually only because her husband—the *ie* couple's son-in-law—was adopted as the official heir of the *ie*.

Any property, status, or advantage claimed through the *ie* was the property of the *ie* and not of any individual member. The male head of the *ie* made decisions regarding the dispensation of that property, but only as a representative and steward of the *ie* itself. In this way, Tokugawa society emphasized continuity and the relationship of individuals to their corporate interest, the *ie*. The fact that more and more *ie* were established and endured in rural areas shows that the Tokugawa period was—despite high taxation and other abuses—a time of relative success and stability for many Japanese farmers. At the same time, an increasing number of second and third sons disenfranchised through the *ie* system naturally gravitated toward cities and towns, where they were more likely to find opportunities for employment and, ideally, be adopted into a merchant or artisan *ie*. In this way, the *ie* system also contributed to the growth of urban society and economy in the Tokugawa period.

Among the artisans and merchants living in towns and cities, the *ie* functioned in much the same way as it did for farmers or samurai. Artisan and merchant families established *ie* to safeguard their assets, and both artisan and merchant *ie* frequently adopted heirs so they could select the best and most capable successor. In fact, adoption sometimes happened even in the presence of a male child. In such cases, the firstborn son of the head of a merchant or artisan *ie* might be apprenticed to another *ie*, while a competent male adult was adopted as heir to the original *ie* in order to guarantee its continuity.

Such practices show clearly the corporate nature of the *ie* and how it differs from the notion of family as a purely kinship-based arrangement. At the same time, it is clear that relationships within the *ie* involved the kind of intimacy and interdependence usually associated with kinship and family in other cultures. Moreover, as the *ie* was established as a central feature of social order throughout the Tokugawa period, it also gained symbolic importance. The Japanese character for *kokka*, used before and during the Tokugawa era to indicate a collective governing structure, consists of the individual characters for "country" and "*ie*." While *kokka* initially referred either to the Tokugawa polity or to the government of a particular domain, proponents of national learning (*kokugaku)* and imperial restoration in the nineteenth century began to apply the term specifically to the *kokka* of Japan as a whole, casting the imperial family as the core of the national *ie*. In this way, the *ie* became not only the building block or even governing logic of social organization, but also the household to which all Japanese belonged.

CHANGING GENDER ROLES IN EARLY MODERN JAPAN

Before discussing gender in Tokugawa Japan, it may be useful to offer both caution and clarification. Despite some intriguing developments in cognitive science and other disciplines that straddle natural and social sciences, it is fairly well accepted that gender—how identity is understood and performed through (and beyond!) the broad categories of male and female—is a social construction. That is, while biological sex is understood to be a *relatively* clear physical marker of physical capabilities to reproduce, gender is seen by most historians as a way in which people in a given historical context tend to justify certain kinds of behavior, beliefs, possibilities, and limitations through the ideas of masculinity and femininity. Gender is a broad and often contested set of ideas that link sex with society in a given place and time.

Early Modern Japanese Women

There is no doubt that many histories of Japan feature men in prominent roles. With very few exceptions, sovereigns have been men; male warlords, shoguns, politicians, and thinkers dominate the landscape of early modern Japanese history. This is due in part to the bias of historians, who have only recently begun to focus on questions of gender. At the same time, the masculine cast of early modern Japanese history also reflects trends in early modern Japanese society at large. Women were not, on average, educated as frequently or as well as men; women did not have the access that men had to formal public roles such as administrators, policemen, bureaucrats, merchants, or village leaders; and women tended to be the subject of harsher legal penalties for sexual indiscretions.

Historians have previously argued that the Tokugawa period, with its emphasis on social order and its comparative conservatism, helped to produce new limitations on the roles of women in society. Part of this argument rested on the idea that the Tokugawa ideology of Neo-Confucianism emphasized hierarchical familial relationships. The establishment and articulation of such a Confucian conceptualization of women's roles are found in popular literature of the Tokugawa period, exemplified by the famous *Great Learning for Women* (*Onna daigaku*), attributed to Kaibara Ekken and published in the early eighteenth century. *Great Learning* enjoined women to stay at home, take care of children, and obey their husbands as their masters.

At the same time, the Tokugawa government paid careful attention to the reproductive activity of samurai households; managing inheritance and accumulating resources to put down potential rebellions were, after all, basic concerns for the Tokugawa Shogunate. As we have seen, the *ie* model of the household, though originally formulated within the samurai class, was appropriated by commoner families as well. The role of women within the *ie* structure, therefore, spread beyond the samurai to affect the lives of commoner women. And beyond the *ie*, the Tokugawa tried repeatedly to control the wilder forms of urban entertainment including theater, dance, and prostitution by enclosing them in carefully designated areas. As a result, those women not safely confined within the *ie* structure were subjected to a different set of spatial and social restrictions.

The general attitude toward women exemplified by *Great Learning*—the emphasis on women for their reproductive work in the *ie* and fear of their dangerous sexuality in the pleasure districts—was collectively cast as "traditional." This stood in contrast to what many historians viewed as the "modern" reality of higher status for women in the Meiji and later periods. Recent work, however, has shown that this picture is simplistic. Women enjoyed greater freedom and more diverse social and economic opportunities during the Tokugawa period than was previously thought, and women living in modern, industrialized Japan did not necessarily enjoy dramatic improvements in their lives.

The ease with which men could obtain a divorce, for example, was thought to indicate the low status of Tokugawa women and their insecurity in society. But more careful research has shown that the consequences of divorce were not necessarily dire or even negative for many women, as divorcées tended to remarry quickly and easily with relatively little hardship to themselves or their children. Comparison studies show, in fact, that late-twentieth-century women suffered more, in material and social terms, from divorce than did their Tokugawa counterparts.

The economic role of Tokugawa women is another area that deserves a closer look. *Great Learning*, with its stark emphasis on propriety and hierarchy, was only one of many books about women in Tokugawa Japan; other texts, like the late-seventeenth-century *Important Treasures for Women* (*Onna chōhōki*) and *One Hundred Women of Japan* (*Wakoku hyakujo*), present more diverse views of women and their occupations and pastimes. Women in samurai households frequently undertook weaving or sewing for money, and were an indispensable component of the household's financial well-being. For rural commoners, the situation was even more egalitarian. Women in rural families toiled alongside their husbands, performing many of the same tasks. An early-eighteenth-century text on women's occupations describes the cooperative nature of maritime work: "The husband controls the boat and the woman dives to the bottom of the sea."[1] In short, both women and men practiced both *productive* and *reproductive* labor.

Among urban merchant households, the division between male and female roles was even more flexible. A small but significant number of businesses were run by women, and numerous extant accounts reveal women managing business operations in large merchant *ie* or even functioning as heads of those households. Overall, then, women performed important economic functions in almost every stratum of Tokugawa society; while written records generally tend to downplay or ignore the contributions of women, the available sources indicate that women wielded considerable economic power in Tokugawa Japan.

On the other hand, not all women's work was equalizing. While prostitution may also be one of the ways in which women contributed to the Tokugawa economy, it was also a locus of abuse and oppression. Institutionally, prostitutes were subjected to sometimes harsh regulatory action; personally, the girls and women who became prostitutes were deprived of security, liberty, social recognition, and sometimes life. Beginning during the rule of Toyotomi Hideyoshi in the late 1500s, brothels in Kyoto were relocated and concentrated in a confined area of the city, and the creation of pleasure districts in Osaka and Edo followed in the early 1600s. All three districts were surrounded by moats, showing a seemingly clear spatial delineation between where prostitutes could and could not live and work. Within the pleasure quarters, the prostitutes were typically girls sold by poor families to brothel owners. The younger girls (sometimes as young as seven or eight) would serve older prostitutes until deemed ready to be trained as prostitutes themselves.

Outside the pleasure quarters, informally regulated prostitution existed under the guise of "serving girls" at tea shops and other establishments on the roads to and from Edo. Other forms of prostitution were more strictly prohibited, but still flourished in Edo and elsewhere. Despite the lack of government oversight, however, the limitations imposed on these women were no less harsh. One account describes a prostitute in 1800 who contracted syphilis (a common disease in her profession) and fled. Her pimp retrieved her and beat her to death. The threat of syphilis was real, and many prostitutes suffered from the disease (and passed it on to clients).

Women in Tokugawa Japan, then, faced a range of prospects and problems. Women in many social classes seem to have wielded more power and have had a greater impact on the economy than previous historians thought; at the same time, both structural and interpersonal interactions surrounding prostitution emphasized the vulnerable position of many women in Tokugawa Japan.

Men in Tokugawa Japan: A Reevaluation

Because men and male activities have been the de facto subject of traditional historiographies, the study of gender has in many cases led to an emphasis on women's history: in this way, "traditional" scholarship has been counterbalanced and complemented by histories that include women. Another important trend in the focus on gender, however, is to reexamine the assumptions about men and masculinity that have informed previous studies. A focus on gender offers historians of Japan a way to rethink rather than simply add to previous interpretations by asking not only how women's roles have been ignored but how men's roles may also deserve a closer look.

As noted above, women were shopkeepers, managers, and even heads of households, fulfilling roles previously thought exclusively male. Men, too, often fulfilled roles previously thought to be part of the "female" sphere. When women in rural households, especially the young wife of the male household heir, were busy with productive work such as sewing, weaving, or other labor, older men would frequently care for children so that younger women could perform more lucrative labor. Even heads of households would often care for children; an early 1800s account of urban family life shows a doting father with obvious expertise in child care who arrives at the bathhouse with a little boy and girl. He undresses and bathes them skillfully, distracting them from the hot water, and promising: "Mommy's waiting for us, and she'll probably have something nice for you if you're good."[2] Other accounts of merchant families indicate that commoner men would engage frequently and without stigma in housework and shopping as well as child care and education.

At the same time, men were in some cases discouraged from participating in "female" labor. The transition from hemp to cotton clothing in the sixteenth and seventeenth centuries, for example, led to a more sophisticated manufacturing economy that depended on specifically female labor, and Ihara Saikaku's late-seventeenth and early-eighteenth-century writings portray men who were mocked for doing "women's work."[3]

Toward the end of the Tokugawa period, masculinity became increasingly intertwined with the political trends that contributed to and moved beyond the so-called Meiji Restoration. Representations of male figures in literature and other media were appropriated by anti-shogunal forces, as pre-Meiji representations of samurai "served as a model of defiant, aggressive masculinity for a community of militarized, anti-government political activists."[4] These activists would eventually overthrow the Tokugawa regime. With the subsequent need to stabilize the newly reconfigured Japanese society, however, came new images of male warriors who were both fierce and controllable, the "ideal masculine icon for an age of imperial expansion."[5] In short, while men undeniably held privileged positions in political, social, and economic realms throughout the Tokugawa period, norms for male behavior could have the effect of limiting and controlling Japanese men as well as privileging them.

Finally, it must be mentioned that many examples of gender-bending exist in Tokugawa history. Kabuki actors, exclusively male from the early 1600s, highlight the normalization of feminine roles performed by men. Such gender shifts were not always welcome, however. In the 1830s a woman named Take took on the identity of "Takejirō" and passed for a man. Her employer raped her on discovering her secret, and she was subsequently arrested and exiled for her continued attempts to assume a masculine identity. Gender throughout Tokugawa Japan, then, was at turns flexible and fixed; while both male and female gender roles could be manipulable in surprising and even advantageous ways, social expectations of gender were also formidable limitations, and transgressing them could carry significant risk.

GETTING IT ON: SEXUALITY IN TOKUGAWA JAPAN

While norms of gendered behavior were assigned to the professional and family realms, another marker of gender—especially masculinity—was found in sexual activity. While sexual activity among various partners was practiced and celebrated, recent scholarship has focused on how male-male sex, especially between an older, experienced man and a younger partner, constituted an important cultural phenomenon in the Tokugawa period. Such sex and the attendant romantic relationships went by a number of terms, the most common of which were *nanshoku* (male love) and *shudō* (shortened from *wakashudō*, or the "way of youths"). Publications like Ihara Saikaku's 1687 *Great Mirror of Male Love* (*Nanshoku ōkagami*), a compendium of stories about male-male romance and sex, indicate great public interest in sexual practices as a key component of male identity. *Great Mirror* became famous both as entertainment and as a sort of connoisseur's guide to the traditional samurai practice of male-male sex.

Both the Tokugawa and various domain governments issued multiple proclamations concerning *shudō* or *nanshoku*, although in most cases these were directed toward controlling rather than eliminating the practice. As historian Greg Pflugfelder argues, the practice of male-male sex and the attendant romantic bonds did not infringe on or relate to the parent-child or husband-wife relationships so key to the legal definition of the *ie*. Authorities had little reason, therefore, to limit sexual contact between men. Instead, authorities tended to focus on the more threatening adulterous male-female sexual contacts, which could produce illegitimate heirs and trouble society. When authorities did attend to male-male sexuality, it was to control the context of such liaisons in the interests of social stability. It is perhaps indicative of the same government priorities that almost no regulatory attention was devoted to female-female sexuality.

This is not of course to ignore the importance of male-female sex in Tokugawa culture. Not only was male-female sex at least potentially reproductive and therefore linked to the political and economic issues of *ie*, but it was also—like other forms of sexual activity—the subject of public interest. Several of Saikaku's works present both women and men who are sexually active with partners of the opposite sex. In his 1682 *Life of an Amorous Man* (*Kōshoku ichidai otoko*), the protagonist Yonosuke (literally, "man of the world") is supposed to have slept with a total of 3,742 women before departing for the "Island of Women" at the age of sixty. Female protagonists in other works are similarly if not quite so spectacularly active with male (and, less often, female) partners. Along with such written representations of sexuality and the careful control of female prostitutes mentioned above, further evidence of what we might now call the "sex industry" in Tokugawa Japan was the production and consumption of erotic art. Chiefly in the form of drawings or woodblock prints, erotic art—sometimes known as *shunga,* or "spring pictures"—circulated widely thanks to the rapid expansion of the publishing industry and a growth in readership with disposable income. The purpose of such erotic art is debated; while some may have been used for sexual stimulation, other examples may be better understood as advertisements for Kabuki actors or sex workers. In any case, the production of sexually explicit pictures, like both prostitution and literary works by authors such as Saikaku, indicated the importance of sexuality in the economy of Tokugawa Japan. Moreover, the range of sexual practices between male, female, and nonhuman partners depicted presents the varied and lively nature of sexuality during the Tokugawa period.

The realms of household, gender, and sex constitute some of the most intimate experiences of Tokugawa Japanese. Moreover, all three areas were subject to the explicit attention of Tokugawa and domainal governments, as well as less formal social expectations and definitions. Finally, economic concerns such as inheritance, shared property, and direct control of wealth were all mediated significantly within these three areas. In this way, household, gender, and sex can be understood as cultural spheres within which the most personal constructions of self and society came into contact with the broadest social, political, and economic structures of Tokugawa Japan.

Sources and Suggestions for Further Reading

See the bibliography for complete publication data.

Ariga Kizaemon. "The Family in Japan." *Marriage and Family Living* (1954).

Cornell, Laura L. "Peasant Women and Divorce in Preindustrial Japan" (1990).

Karlin, Jason G. "The Gender of Nationalism: Competing Masculinities in Meiji Japan" (2002).

Nakane, Chie. "Tokugawa Society" (1990).

Perez, Louis G. *Daily Life in Early Modern Japan* (2002).

Pflugfelder, Gregory. *Cartographies of Desire: Male-Male Sexuality in Japanese Discourse, 1600–1950* (1999).

Reichert, James. "'Samurai' Fantasies in Late-Nineteenth-Century Japan" (2000).

Roberson, James E., and Noboe Suzuki, eds. *Men and Masculinities in Contemporary Japan: Dislocating the Salaryman Doxa* (2003).

Robertson, Jennifer. "The Shingaku Woman: Straight from the Heart" (1991).

Rubinger, Richard. *Popular Literacy in Early Modern Japan* (2007).
Shimizu, Akitoshi. "Ie and Dozoku: Family and Descent in Japan" (1987).
Uno, Kathleen S. "The Household Division of Labor" (1991).
Yamamura, Kozo, and Murakami Yasusuke. "Ie Society as a Pattern of Civilization: Introduction" (1984).
Yokota Fuyuhiko. "Imagining Working Women in Early Modern Japan" (1999).

Notes

1. Yokota, "Imagining Working Women in Early Modern Japan" 160.

2. From Shikitei Sanba's *Ukiyo buro* (*Bathhouse of the Floating World*), quoted in Kathleen S. Uno, "The Household Division of Labor," 32.

3. Quoted in Yokota, "Imagining Working Women in Early Modern Japan," 163.

4. Reichert, "'Samurai' Fantasies in Late-Nineteenth-Century Japan," 194.

5. Ibid., 202.

38

Thought, Education, and Popular Literacies in Early Modern Japan

Richard Rubinger

Just as the political configuration of Japan changed dramatically in the late sixteenth and early seventeenth centuries through the efforts of the three great unifiers—Oda Nobunaga, Toyotomi Hideyoshi, and Tokugawa Ieyasu—so did the intellectual discourse. Whereas the predominant concerns of the medieval world had been the Buddhist themes of suffering and the quest for personal salvation, the main concern of the early Tokugawa world became the maintenance of a stable and harmonious society, with the responsibility of achieving social order falling on man, not supernatural forces. Ronald Dore once remarked that thought in Tokugawa Japan (1603–1868) came in "country packets"—Chinese, Japanese, and Western (Dutch)—and his point remains a convenient way to summarize the varieties of influences on early Tokugawa thought.[1]

LEGACIES OF NEO-CONFUCIANISM

Chinese thought arrived very early in Japan, at least as early as the sixth century BCE, with a fully equipped philosophy, ethics, and view of history. The foremost contributors to the traditional Chinese Confucian canon were Confucius (551–479 BCE), the originator and the one who drew together the first set of texts, and Mencius (373–288 BCE). But it was the twelfth-century interpretation of

Zhu Xi (1130–1200 CE), the main stream of what is called Neo-Confucianism, that made the deepest inroads into Japan in the early modern period. Concerned that many people in his native China had become more interested in the superstitious aspects of Confucian rites than its moral and ethical foundations, Zhu Xi sought to reinvigorate Confucianism as an intellectual discipline. He stressed the importance of study of the Way of the Sages expressed in the basic Confucian canon—the Four Books—*Analects*, *Mencius*, *Great Learning*, and *Doctrine of the Mean*. He also added a metaphysical system that interpreted all reality in terms of a single cosmic principle (*ri*). It saw the universe characterized by order, regularity, and harmony and suggested that it was possible to understand the moral laws that underlay reality by an "investigation of things." This was to be done by careful study of the Confucian classics to clarify the values of the ideal society of the ancient past, values that the Neo-Confucians believed could restore stability in the contemporary world. In its rationality, historical-mindedness, emphasis on social hierarchy, and desire to restore an ancient moral framework, the Zhu Xi system contained elements attractive to the new Japanese regime, which was eager to establish a permanent and lasting order.

There is no question but that Neo-Confucian ideas spread quickly in seventeenth-century Japan, primarily among the leadership class. By the eighteenth century, Neo-Confucian ideas had spread to merchants, penetrated the popular culture in towns and cities, and gained adherents among the upper reaches of the provincial farming class. The seventeenth-century impact of Neo-Confucian ideas had much to do with early recognition by the Tokugawa when Ieyasu summoned Hayashi Razan (1583–1657) to his castle at Sunpu and ordered him to take the tonsure in the manner of Zen-Confucian advisers of an earlier era. Thus began Razan's long service to the shogunate as a Confucian adviser.

It is possible that too much has been made of this event, for in recent years scholars have called into question the view that Neo-Confucianism rapidly became an orthodox ideology used by the Tokugawa to justify the regime. According to Herman Ooms the "fiction" that Hayashi Razan helped establish a Neo-Confucian, shogunate-supported orthodoxy still governs much of today's scholarship. Even the famous "Maruyama thesis," arguing that modern thought in Japan emanated from the strong reactions to the dominance of Neo-Confucianism, has been adjusted in view of the evidence that early Tokugawa ideology was complex, that Buddhist and Shintō concerns were not set aside, and that the regime had many other ways besides Neo-Confucianism to justify itself. Furthermore, the emphasis on learning and books stimulated scholarship in many fields some of which competed openly with the Neo-Confucian tradition.

The most forceful challenge came from the so-called Ancient Learning (Kogaku) school, which argued that to understand Confucian ideas, one had to read and study the ancient Confucian texts, not the later interpretations of Zhu

Xi. Yamaga Sokō (1622–1685), believed, for example, that the society of the ancients was a more appropriate model for a military-dominated state like Japan than later China. Itō Jinsai (1627–1705) insisted that everything in the world could not be explained with one principle, undermining the Neo-Confucian notion of *ri*. Ogyū Sorai (1666–1724), a major advocate of Ancient Learning and a proponent of all things Chinese, argued that it was necessary to go back to texts that predated even the Confucian classics; he led a movement to study ancient Chinese civilization directly through ancient texts. Other thinkers, such as the independent scholar Nakae Tōju (1608–1648), suggested, based on the thought of Chinese philosopher Wang Yangming (1472–1529) and in contrast to Zhu Xi, that the principle of *ri* was not an objective and timeless supreme ultimate but existed in the mind a priori and was known intuitively. Nakae's thought added to the heterodox mix of Neo-Confucian interpretations in the seventeenth and eighteenth centuries.

Neo-Confucianism in all its variety appears to have left a mark on Japan with its concern for hierarchical relations and harmony in the home as the basis for harmony in the state. But scholars continue to debate whether Confucianism created these tendencies or merely reinforced and justified social practices that preceded the advent of Neo-Confucianism in Japan. The problem of Chinese influence also concerned some early Tokugawa thinkers.

NATIONAL STUDIES

The focus on China as the repository of value and morality, and the fact that none of the Neo-Confucian schools seemed able to solve satisfactorily the problems in the political economy of eighteenth-century Japan, inevitably led to a reaction to the Chinese model in the form of the National Studies (Kokugaku) school. National Studies began with classical literary study in the seventeenth century, but by the early nineteenth century it carried a powerful political message as well. The term "Nativism" is now used by scholars to refer to the later, more distinctly xenophobic manifestations of Kokugaku. In both the eighteenth and nineteenth centuries this school was also responsible for carrying serious scholarly study of Japanese literature to the leadership of the provincial countryside.

The greatest of the early modern scholars of National Studies, Motoori Norinaga (1730–1801), agreed with Sorai's Confucian fundamentalism that universal truths could be gleaned only from ancient texts, but Norinaga asked why those texts had to be Chinese and not Japanese. Motoori and other Kokugaku scholars believed that Japanese classics such as *Kojiki* (*Records of Ancient Matters*; 712), Japan's most ancient text, and the eleventh-century classic *Genji monogatari* (*The Tale of Genji*) were more appropriate models than any Chinese text for Japanese seeking to behave according to the way of the gods.

Unlike the Confucianists, Motoori was more concerned with individuals and human sentiment than politics and moral exhortation. The goal of literary study, in his view, should be *mono no aware,* or a sympathetic awareness of the sadness of things. Trying to control or conceal one's emotions through samurai rigidity or Chinese rationalism was dishonest, in this view. Great emphasis was therefore placed on native poetry as the best expression of human sentiment and of Japanese "spirit" overall. *Waka*, or Japanese poems, were often written in Japanese phonetic script (*hiragana*) rather than Chinese characters and therefore attracted the interests of those not formally trained in Chinese, such as women and provincial leaders.

Under the influence of Hirata Atsutane (1776–1843) Kokugaku ideas became strongly associated with Shintō and spread throughout the countryside. Whereas Neo-Confucianism had been primarily directed at the leadership class in the seventeenth and eighteenth centuries, Nativism appealed not only to warriors but also, by the eighteenth century, to a rising class of town merchants and provincial village leaders. By the nineteenth century it had taken on a strong patriotic focus and promoted the superiority of Japan through Hirata Atsutane's revival of primitive ideas of the emperor and his descent from gods. This mythological strain became part of the dubious contributions of the Nativist revival to the imperial restoration of 1868 and to the Meiji state. But this should not cloud the fact that the scholarly study of Japanese classical literature and language was an intimate part of the rich intellectual ferment of the eighteenth century.

DUTCH STUDIES

Part of the pre–nineteenth century intellectual legacy was a growing interest in science. Investigations of the material world had roots growing out of Confucianism itself, no less than did the heterodox challenges to Neo-Confucianism. The Zhu Xi Confucianist Kaibara Ekken(1630–1714), for example, was also trained in medicine and did empirical studies of herbal remedies, botany, and the flora and fauna of his native Fukuoka domain. Indeed, the early modern Japanese study of the natural world was driven by a Neo-Confucian understanding of the cosmos. Progress in science was further enhanced by Western learning that filtered in through the tiny Dutch trading post on Dejima in Nagasaki harbor. The early work in Western studies was in medicine; then the work moved to studies of Dutch language and the translations of texts; and eventually by the nineteenth century a small coterie of specialists were reading works in natural science and Western civilization as a whole. Empirical science not only began without official sanction but often operated in opposition to official policy.

As part of a series of edicts that culminated in 1639 in the expulsion from Japan of all Europeans except the Dutch, the shogunate placed severe restrictions on information from the West (particularly Christianity) and on contacts with foreigners. After 1641 only the Dutch and Chinese were permitted limited trade through Nagasaki. A prohibition on the importation of Western books—and Chinese translations of them—limited knowledge of the West in the seventeenth century to official Nagasaki interpreters. In 1720, however, the eighth shogun, Yoshimune (ruled 1716–1745), convinced that certain aspects of Western knowledge, such as astronomy and military tactics, could be useful in governing, lifted the ban on Western books (with the exception of books on Christianity).

This initial step led to the first serious study of Dutch by a small group of domain and shogunate physicians, who laboriously produced the first translations of Dutch medical texts. The most important of these was a Dutch book on anatomy (Johann Adam Kulmus's *Tafel Anatomia*; 1731) translated in 1774 by a group led by Sugita Genpaku (1733–1817) and titled *Kaitai shinsho* (*New Treatise on Dissection*).

Early Dutch studies was characterized by the intellectual curiosity and interest of physicians working in official service in Edo. The early career of Ōtsuki Gentaku (1757–1827) suggests both the limits and the possibilities of Dutch studies at the end of the eighteenth century. He was the son of a domain physician who was apprenticed to Sugita Genpaku in Edo, then sent to Nagasaki for study of the Dutch language with Nagasaki interpreters. Gentaku returned to Edo a year later to set up a practice and do research. He wrote and translated in a variety of fields from language studies to the natural sciences, considerably broadening Dutch studies beyond its narrow medical beginnings. In a popular book titled *Rangaku kaitei* that he published in 1788, he championed Dutch studies, as opposed to Chinese studies, in the phonetic Japanese syllabary rather than Chinese characters.

Dutch studies certainly did not replace other intellectual traditions. But this new school of thought focused less on morality than on practicality and empirical study—quite different from the focus of classical learning in the China-centered world. It became an important part of the rich amalgam of ideas and scholarly traditions that characterized seventeenth- and eighteenth-century Japan, and it had profound implications for the future.

EDUCATION

The richness and variety of intellectual life during the first two centuries of Tokugawa rule were further reflected in the institutional supports used to sustain and encourage learning. While the specific legacies of Neo-Confucian thought in early modern Japan are complex and hotly debated, there is no question that official support for a system of thought that focused on the importance of learning and on books vastly expanded the constituencies for literacy and learning in Japan.

Indeed, the extension of learning beyond the narrow and limited confines of the court nobility, the clergy, and the upper reaches of the leadership samurai class (the medieval inheritance) to townspeople, the upper reaches of the peasantry, and eventually to ordinary landowning farmers is one of the most important social phenomena of the Tokugawa period and, indeed, of the entire premodern epoch of Japanese history.

The initial impetus for education in Tokugawa Japan came from the shogunate. In 1630 it provided a plot of land and funds for the Hayashi family to expand their private school into a center for the Zhu Xi brand of Neo-Confucianism. In 1790 the Hayashi school was upgraded as a shogunal college for the training of Tokugawa retainers. Called Shōheikō, it became the leading institution of Neo-Confucian studies. That year's so-called Ban on Heresy, instituted as part of a larger economic and political reform, restricted learning among Tokugawa retainers to Zhu Xi thought. Ironically, although the policy was intended to limit the curriculum, the heightened shogunal concern about education stimulated similar developments in domains all around the country. The domains were under no compulsion to follow shogunal leads in education, but many of them did. By the end of the eighteenth century more than half had domain schools for their own samurai retainers. By the end of the Tokugawa period most domains had at least one official school, and some had more than one.

These schools undoubtedly helped transform the samurai from a largely illiterate warrior order at the beginning of the seventeenth century to an educated and disciplined class of loyal bureaucrats with a shared intellectual culture by the nineteenth century. The constituency of these schools, however, with minor exceptions, remained restricted to the upper ranks of the samurai within the geographical borders of the domain. The official schools tended to resist teaching outside the Zhu Xi tradition and were slow to introduce practical knowledge and Western studies.

It was in the many and various private academies, outside official control, where innovative and practical subjects were taught. These institutions, which existed as early as the original Hayashi school, ran the gamut from small intimate tutorial types to huge centers with elaborate administrative machinery, from writing schools to advanced research institutes. By definition they were privately run usually in the home of an independent scholar who attracted students by his scholarship or his views on politics or philosophy. His personality and style determined the school's atmosphere. The curriculum, unlike that of the official schools, was free from official control and dependent solely on the interests and training of the headmaster.

The private academies thus could, and did, offer various specialized studies such as Dutch Learning, Nativism, military studies, medicine, and any of the heterodox varieties of Confucianism. In this way, the educational world fully represented the diversity of thought of the early Tokugawa years. The constituency of the private academies imposed no geographical or class barriers to entrance. Unlike the official schools, they could attract a truly national constituency from the various classes and from all parts of the country. In 1789, just at the time when official schools were narrowing their courses of study in a vain attempt to strengthen feudal discipline, Ōtsuki Gentaku opened the first Dutch studies academy, the Shirandō. Open to all, with promotion based on principles of merit and competition, Gentaku's academy set the standard for the larger nineteenth-century schools that trained competent specialists in fields relating to Western science and civilization.

Outside the few domains that imposed compulsory attendance on their higher-level samurai, education in Tokugawa Japan remained almost entirely a family or individual matter. It is important to remember that for all of the teachers, textbooks, and writing paraphernalia on hand in these schools, this was not a modern system. There was no central authority, no standards beyond those set by individual teachers, no established texts, and no compulsory attendance. Today it is hard to imagine the degree of freedom of educational choice open to the privileged few in premodern Japan. Beginning in the eighteenth century, it was possible for ambitious boys, and sometimes girls, to put together individualized sequences of their own making that could take them from one end of the country to another and could include Confucian, Dutch, or Nativist learning in a highly sophisticated sequence of studies. At the end of the Tokugawa period, when many of the coastal domains were looking for well-educated young people to advise them in coastal defense and Western science, they did not go to the official schools but recruited graduates of the large and famous private academies in the big cities, like Ogata Kōan's Dutch academy, Teki Juku, in Osaka.

The private academies were not for everyone, because they imposed fees and usually had rigorous courses of study. The National Studies schools, however, went out of their way to appeal to the provincial population and did so with some success. Motoori Norinaga's Suzu no ya created correspondence courses to enable farmers who lived far away to correspond with the master, and Hirata Atsutane's school included a large constituency of farm women. What about the premodern educational opportunities for others, those who lacked the status, the financial ability, or the scholarly ambition to attend either official schools or private academies?

LITERACIES AND POPULAR LEARNING

Traditionally, attempts to estimate the spread of basic literacy in Tokugawa Japan—that is, the ability to read or write to some extent—have been based on the proliferation of popular writing schools most often called *terakoya*, "temple schools," although this is a misnomer. They are more properly referred to as *tenaraisho* (writing schools), because by the seventeenth century they were no longer primarily associated with temples. More recent studies, however, have cast doubt on the reliability of writing school data in assessing popular literacy in the early modern period and have drawn instead on a wide array of other materials, such as signatures, diaries, agricultural manuals, encyclopedias of general knowledge, rural poetry contests, village literacy surveys, election ballots, and family account books to describe not only the quantitative rise of literacy among those who were not part of the elite but some of the qualitative aspects as well.

Recent work does not call into question the expansion of literacy but points to some of the dynamics of the process and emphasizes qualitative aspects. Literacy is seen now not as a simple phenomenon, reducible to a single, simple national average figure—as tempting as that might be for national comparisons. It is seen rather as an indicator of changing social and historical contexts and the needs and aspirations of specific segments of the population—small farmers, village heads, shop employees, men and women.

Contributing to the difficulty of setting a single standard for literacy in premodern Japan is the nature of the Japanese script. The written language of scholarship and government was a version of classical Chinese, somewhat analogous to Latin in Medieval Europe. This was out of the reach of all but the well-educated classes. The existence of the phonetic kana scripts, however, provided a simplified method of written communication for those who needed only the rudiments of literacy. The entirely phonetic Japanese kana probably made vernacular Japanese more accessible in written form than the alphabet did for any Western language. The popularity of kana script suggests a broad range of intermediary skills between total illiteracy and full literacy in Sino-Japanese. Hence the difficulty of setting a single standard and the wisdom of looking at specific literacies as they evolved according to time, place, and circumstance in the premodern world.

The key event in the history of popular literacy in Japan was probably the late-sixteenth-century separation of warriors and peasants (*heinō bunri*) implemented by the hegemon Toyotomi Hideyoshi (1537–1598). Warriors were brought into the castle towns—stimulating a huge wave of urbanization—where they developed over time into urban bureaucrats more skilled with the pen than the sword. Peasants were left behind in the countryside, entirely responsible for tax collecting as well as dealing with the profusion of edicts and regulations that characterized administration under Tokugawa rule. The need to read and write created an elite class within the peasantry that combined administrative authority with extraordinary literacy and numeracy skills, far beyond the rudimentary level, and not very different from their samurai betters.

During the seventeenth century, the literacy attainments of the village leadership class pertained primarily to administration, tax collecting, representing peasants to higher authority, and other requirements of their position. By the eighteenth century, however, following the rise of urban culture in the major cities, village leaders became mediators between city and country, and their literacy skills in many cases developed into scholarly interests in Confucianism, Buddhism, Shintō, poetry, and science. Interestingly, they tended at first not to share their skills with ordinary peasants. Literacy was one of the hallmarks of leadership and tended not to be shared widely in the seventeenth and early eighteenth centuries. It was passed on for the most part from father to son within families.

Written documents from the early seventeenth century show that in the larger cities like Kyoto, not only ward heads but most male household heads of merchant families had advanced literacy of the type required for tax computation and administration. In these cities, there is evidence that literacy had spread to sons of household heads, male employees, fathers, nephews, uncles, and in some cases to adult women. In provincial towns like Nagasaki, the evidence suggests that advanced literacy did not spread much beyond male household heads. In farming villages, as early as the seventeenth century, two cultures had begun to appear—a small elite who were highly literate and the overwhelming illiterate majority.

In the eighteenth century the members of this elite group did not expand dramatically, but the quality of their literacy was enhanced. During the period known as Genroku (1688–1704) the vigorous popular culture of the cities attracted the interest of village leaders, who extended their reading and writing capabilities beyond village administration into scholarly areas such as Confucianism, Buddhism, Chinese and Japanese poetry, medicine, and science. Some became serious contributors to these fields by networking with urban intellectuals, samurai officials, and other like-minded provincial literati. Some amassed respectable libraries by traveling to the cities to buy books. They then traded and borrowed among their peers in the suburbs of Osaka, Kyoto, and Edo.

By the nineteenth century both quantitative and qualitative changes had occurred. There is evidence that women, especially in commercial families, were using their literacy skills to enhance their roles in the family (they were often the record keepers) and in business (often as stand-ins for traveling husbands). Some were making a mark in the arts. Kikuchi Sodeko, for example, gained a provincial reputation as a poet. It was in the nineteenth century, particularly during such periods of economic strife as the Tenpō period (1830–1844), that writing schools began to increase dramatically, suggesting that the rudiments of reading and writing were extending to the broader population of rural children. With popular ire often directed at them, village leaders no doubt saw it in their interest to train village children in Confucian morality, and so actively supported popular writing schools.

In terms of access to writing schools, geography clearly mattered. Proximity to urban areas, access to roads, available means of communication, and a family's commercial activity could stimulate interest in sending a child to school. Gender mattered, as well as class. Extant Tokugawa-period enrollment data show far fewer opportunities for women, particularly in rural areas. But in merchant-dominated areas of big cities, women enrolled at writing schools at a far higher rate than their rural sisters, higher even than rural males, on a par with males of the merchant class.

The case of a young woman named Hatsu, who worked as a maidservant in a post town of what is now Gunma prefecture, suggests the benefits of literacy for the otherwise powerless. The daughter of a poor farmer, she left home in 1840 to seek employment in a faraway post town. She secured a contract to work for eight years at a roadside inn. After two years things became so unbearable for her that in desperation she wrote a letter to the daimyo explaining her situation and asking to be allowed to cancel her contract. She explained that she had become sick but had been forced to work anyway. When she asked for rest, she was physically abused. She had run away, but her employer found her and returned her to the inn. The letter was clearly in her own hand, written mostly in kana and full of mistakes but understandable. It was sufficient for Hatsu to explain her unfortunate situation and to appeal to an official in writing. The outcome of the appeal is unknown, but the letter is an indicator of how rudimentary literacy could be put to use to improve the circumstances of lower-level farming women by the mid-nineteenth century.

Popular literacy in Japan began early in the seventeenth century in every village with a privileged few who showed extraordinarily high levels of skill. Not until the nineteenth century, however, did the needs of ordinary farmers and the interests of village leaders coalesce into widespread support for writing schools for ordinary farmer children. The complex tapestry of individual skills revealed in literacy records should alert us to the fact that at the level of individual skills, populations exhibit more differences than similarities. Disparities in literacy by region, gender, and class, clearly evident in the seventeenth and eighteenth centuries, persisted. When the modern school system was inaugurated in 1872, the Japanese population was nowhere near homogeneity with respect to its ability to take advantage of the opportunities the system made available.

Sources and Suggestions for Further Reading

See the bibliography for complete publication data.

Dore, R. P. *Education in Tokugawa Japan* (1984).
Jansen, Marius B. *The Making of Modern Japan* (2000).
Najita, Tetsuo. *Visions of Virtue in Tokugawa Japan* (1987).
Nivison, David S., and Arthur F. Wright. *Confucianism in Action* (1959).
Nosco, Peter, ed. *Confucianism and Tokugawa Culture* (1984).
Ooms, Herman. *Tokugawa Ideology: Early Constructs, 1570–1680* (1985).
Platt, Brian. "Elegance, Prosperity, and Crisis: Three Generations of Tokugawa Village Elites" (2000).
Rubinger, Richard. *Popular Literacy in Early Modern Japan* (2007).
———. *Private Academies of Tokugawa Japan* (1982).
Walthall, Anne. "The Family Ideology of Rural Entrepreneurs in Nineteenth-Century Japan" (1990).

Note

1. Dore, *Education in Tokugawa Japan*, 160.

Bibliography

Abé, Ryūichi. *Weaving the Mantra: Kukai and the Construction of Buddhist Esoteric Discourse.* New York: Columbia University Press, 2000.

Adolphson, Mikael S. *The Gates of Power: Monks, Courtiers, and Warriors in Premodern Japan.* Honolulu: University of Hawai'i Press, 2000.

———. "Social Change and Contained Transformations: Warriors and Merchants in Japan, 1000–1300." In Johann P. Arnason and Björn Wittrock, eds. *Eurasian Transformations, Tenth to Thirteenth Centuries,* 309–337. Leiden, The Netherlands: E. J. Brill, 2004.

———. *The Teeth and Claws of the Buddha: Monastic Warriors and Sōhei in Japanese History.* Honolulu: University of Hawai'i Press, 2007.

Adolphson, Mikael, Edward Kamens, and Stacie Matsumoto, eds. *Heian Japan: Centers and Peripheries.* Honolulu: University of Hawai'i Press, 2007.

Addiss, Stephen, ed. *Tokaido: Adventures on the Road in Old Japan.* Lawrence: University of Kansas Press, 1980.

Aikens, C. Melvin, Irina S. Zhushchikhovskaya, and Song Nai Rhee. "Environment, Adaptation, and Interaction in Japan, Korea, and the Russian Far East: The Millennial History of a Japan Sea Oikumene." *Asian Perspectives* 48.2 (2009): 207–248.

Aikens, C. Melvin, and Takeru Akazawa. "The Pleistocene/Holocene Transition in Japan and Adjacent Northeast Asia: Climate and Biotic Change, Broad-Spectrum Diet, Pottery, and Sedentism." In Lawrence Guy Straus, Berit Valentin Eriksen, Jon M. Erlandson, and David R. Yesner, eds., *Humans at the End of the Ice Age: The Archaeology of the Pleistocene-Holocene Transition,* 215–227. New York: Plenum Press, 1996.

Ambros, Barbara. *Bones of Contention: Animals and Religion in Contemporary Japan.* Honolulu: University of Hawai'i Press, 2012.

———. *Emplacing a Pilgrimage: The Ōyama Cult and Regional Religion in Early Modern Japan.* Cambridge, MA: Harvard University Asia Center, 2008.

Ambros, Barbara, and Duncan Williams, eds. *Local Religion in Tokugawa History* (Special Issue of the *Japanese Journal of Religious Studies*). Nagoya: Nanzan Institute of Religion and Culture, 2001.

Amino Yoshihiko. "Commerce and Finance in the Middle Ages: the Beginnings of 'Capitalism.'" *Acta Asiatica* 81 (September 2001): 1–19.

———. "Emperor, Rice, and Commoners." In Donald Denoon, Mark Hudson, Gavan McCormack, and Tessa Morris-Suzuki, eds., *Multicultural Japan: Palaeolithic to Postmodern,* 235–245. Cambridge: Cambridge University Press, 1996.

———. *Rekishi o kangaeru hinto.* Tokyo: Shinchōsha, 2001.

Anazawa, W., and J. Manome. "Two Inscribed Swords from Japanese Tumuli: Discoveries and Research on Finds from the Sakitama-Inariyama and Eta-Funayama Tumuli." In R. J. Pearson et al., eds., *Windows on the Japanese Past: Studies in Archaeology and Prehistory,* 375–396. Ann Arbor: Center for Japanese Studies, University of Michigan, 1986.

Ariga Kizaemon. "The Family in Japan." *Marriage and Family Living* 16.4 (1954): 362–368.

Arnesen, Peter J. *The Medieval Japanese Daimyo: The Ōuchi Family's Rule of Suō and Nagato.* New Haven: Yale University Press, 1979.

———. "The Provincial Vassals of the Muromachi Shoguns." In Jeffrey P. Mass and William Hauser, eds., *The Bakufu in Japanese History,* 99–129. Stanford, CA: Stanford University Press, 1985.

———. "The Struggle for Lordship in Late Heian Japan: The Case of Aki." *Journal of Japanese Studies* 10.1 (1984): 101–141.

———. "Suo Province in the Age of Kamakura." In Jeffrey Mass, ed., *Court and Bakufu in Japan: Essays in Kamakura History,* 92–120. New Haven: Yale University Press, 1982.

Arntzen, Sonja. *Ikkyū and the Crazy Cloud Anthology: A Zen Priest of Medieval Japan.* Tokyo: Tokyo University Press, 1986.

Asakawa Kan'ichi. *The Documents of Iriki.* Westport, CT: Greenwood Press, 1974.

———. *Land and Society in Medieval Japan.* Edited by Committee for the Publication of Dr. K. Asakawa's Works. Tokyo: Japan Society for the Promotion of Science, 1965.

Asao Naohiro. "The Sixteenth-Century Unification." In John Whitney Hall, ed., *The Cambridge History of Japan,* Vol. 4: *Early Modern Japan,* 40–95. Cambridge: Cambridge University Press, 1991.

Aston, W. G., trans. *Nihongi: Chronicles of Japan from the Earliest Times to A. D. 697.* Rutland, VT: Tuttle, 1972.

Atkins, Paul S. *Revealed Identity: The Noh Plays of Komparu Zenchiku.* Michigan Monograph Series in Japanese Studies, 55. Ann Arbor: Center for Japanese Studies, University of Michigan, 2006.

Barber, Daniel Lewis. "Tales of the Floating World." MA thesis, Ohio State University, East Asian Languages and Literatures, 1984.

Barnes, Gina L. *China, Korea, and Japan: The Rise of Civilization in East Asia.* London: Thames & Hudson, 1993. Reissued as *The Rise of Civilization in East Asia: Archaeology of China, Korea, and Japan.* London: Thames & Hudson, 1999.

———. "Landscape and Subsistence in Japanese History." In I. Peter Martini and Ward Chesworth, eds., *Landscapes and Societies—Selected Cases,* 321–340. London: Springer, 2010.

———. "Earthquake Archaeology in Japan: An Overview." In M. Sintubin, I. S. Stewart, T. M. Niemi, and E. Altunel, eds., *Ancient Earthquakes*, 81–84. Special Paper 471. Boulder, CO: Geological Society of America, 2010.

———. "The Making of the Japan Sea and the Japanese Mountains: Understanding Japan's Volcanism in Structural Context." *Japan Review* 20 (2008): 3–52.

———. *The Rise of Civilization in East Asia: the Archaeology of China, Korea and Japan.* London: Thames & Hudson, 1999.

———. "The Role of the *Be* in the Formation of the Yamato State." In E. Brumfiel and T. Earle, eds., *Specialization, Exchange, and Complex Societies*, 86–101. Cambridge: Cambridge University Press, 1987.

———. *State Formation in Japan: Emergence of a 4th-Century Ruling Elite*. London: Routledge, 2006.

———. *State Formation in Korea: Emerging Elites*. London: Routledge, 2000.

Baroni, Helen. *Ōbaku Zen: The Emergence of the Third Sect of Zen in Tokugawa Japan.* Honolulu: University of Hawai'i Press, 2000.

Batten, Bruce. "Cross Border Traffic on the Kyushu Coast, 794–1086." In Mikael Adolphson, Edward Kamens, and Stacie Matsumoto, eds., *Japan: Centers and Peripheries*, 357–383. Honolulu: University of Hawai'i Press, 2007.

———. "Climatic Change in the Japanese Islands: A Comparative Overview." Reischauer Institute of Japanese Studies Online Archive, Harvard University, 2008. http://www.fas.harvard.edu/~rijs/pdfs/batten.pdf (accessed Sept. 12, 2011).

———. "Foreign Threat and Domestic Reform: The Emergence of the Ritsuryō State." *Monumenta Nipponica* 41.2 (1986): 199–219.

———. *Gateway to Japan: Hakata in War and Peace, 500–1300*. Honolulu: University of Hawai'i Press, 2006.

———. "Provincial Administration in Early Japan: From Ritsuryō kokka to Ōchō kokka." *Harvard Journal of Asiatic Studies*, 53.1 (June 1993): 103–134.

———. *To the Ends of Japan: Premodern Frontiers, Boundaries, and Interactions*. Honolulu: University of Hawai'i Press, 2003.

Bender, Ross. "Changing the Calendar: Royal Political Theology and the Suppression of the Tachibana Naramaro Conspiracy, 757." *Japanese Journal of Religious Studies* 37.2 (2010): 223–245.

———. "The Hachiman Cult and the Dōkyō Incident." *Monumenta Nipponica* 34.2 (1979): 125–153.

———. "Performative Loci of the Imperial Edicts in Nara Japan, 749–70." *Oral Tradition* 24.1 (2009): 249–268.

Benedict, Ruth. *The Chrysanthemum and the Sword.* Boston: Houghton Mifflin, 1989.

Bentley, Jerry H. "Cross-Cultural Interaction and Periodization in World History." *American Historical Review* 101.3 (1996): 749–770.

Berger, Gordon, Andrew Edmund Goble, Lorraine Harrington, and G. Cameron Hurst, III, eds. *Currents in Medieval Japanese History: Essays in Honor of Jeffrey P. Mass*. Los Angeles: Figueroa Press, 2009.

Berry, Mary Elizabeth. *The Culture of Civil War in Kyoto*. Berkeley: University of California Press, 1994.

———. *Hideyoshi*. Cambridge, MA: Harvard University Press, 1982.

———. *Japan in Print: Information and Nation in the Early Modern Period*. Berkeley: University of California Press, 2007.

Bird, Winifred. "In Japan's Managed Landscape, a Struggle to Save the Bears." *Yale Environment 360* (Yale School of Forestry and Environmental Studies) 29 (2009), http://e360.yale.edu/content/feature.msp?id=2204 (accessed Aug. 23, 2010).

Birt, M. P. "Samurai in Passage: Transformation of the 16th C. Kanto." *Journal of Japanese Studies* 11.2 (1985): 369–400.

Bix, Herbert. *Peasant Protest in Japan, 1590–1884*. New Haven: Yale University Press, 1985.

Bialock, David T. *Eccentric Spaces, Hidden Histories: Narrative, Ritual, and Royal Anthologies from* The Chronicles of Japan *to* The Tale of the Heike. Asian Religions and Cultures. Stanford, CA: Stanford University Press, 2007.

Blum, Mark L. *The Origins and Development of Pure Land Buddhism: A Study and Translation of Gyōnen's* Jōdo Hōmon Genrushō. New York: Oxford University Press, 2002.

Bock, Felicia, trans. *Engi-shiki: Procedures of the Engi Era Books I–IV*. Tokyo: Monumenta Nipponica Monograph, 1970.

Bodiford, William, M. "The Medieval Period: Eleventh to Sixteenth Centuries." In Paul L. Swanson and Clark Chilson, eds., *The Nanzan Guide to Japanese Religions*, 163–183. Honolulu: University of Hawai'i Press, 2006.

———. *Sōtō Zen in Medieval Japan*. Honolulu: University of Hawai'i Press, 1993.

Borgen, Robert. "The Japanese Mission to China, 801–806." *Monumenta Nipponica* 37.1 (1982): 1–28.

———. "Jōjin's Travels from Center to Center (with Some Periphery in Between)." In Mikael S. Adolphson, Edward Kamens, and Stacie Matsumoto, eds., *Heian Japan: Centers and Peripheries*, 384–413. Honolulu: University of Hawai'i Press, 2007.

———. *Sugawara no Michizane and the Early Heian Court*. Revised edition. Honolulu: University of Hawai'i Press, 1994.

Bolitho, Harold. *Treasures Among Men: The Fudai Daimyo in Tokugawa Japan*. New Haven: Yale University Press, 1974.

Boscaro, Adriana. *101 Letters of Hideyoshi*. Tokyo: Sophia University Press, 1975.

Bowring, Richard. *The Religious Traditions of Japan, 500–1600*. Cambridge: Cambridge University Press, 2005.

———, trans. *The Diary of Murasaki Shikibu*. New York: Penguin, 1993.

Boxer, Charles. *The Christian Century in Japan, 1549–1650*. Berkeley: University of California Press, 1967.

Brazell, Karen, trans. *The Confessions of Lady Nijō*. Stanford, CA: Stanford University Press, 1973.

Breen, John, and Mark Teeuwen. *A New History of Shinto*. New York: Wiley-Blackwell, 2010.

Brewster, Jennifer, trans. *Fujiwara no Nageko: The Emperor Horikawa Diary (Sanuki no Suke Nikki)*. Honolulu: University of Hawai'i Press, 1978.

Brower, Robert H., trans. *Conversations with Shōtetsu (Shōtetsu Monogatari)*. With an Introduction and Notes by Steven D. Carter. Michigan Monograph Series in Japanese Studies, 7. Ann Arbor: Center for Japanese Studies, University of Michigan, 1992.

Brown, Delmer M., ed. *The Cambridge History of Japan*, Vol. 1: *Ancient Japan*. New York: Cambridge University Press, 1993.

Brown, Delmer, and Ishida Ichirō, trans. and eds. *The Future and the Past: A Translation and Study of the Gukansho, an Interpretive History of Japan Written in 1219*. Berkeley: University of California Press, 1979.

Brown, Philip C. *Central Authority and Local Autonomy in the Formation of Early Modern Japan: The Case of Kaga Domain*. Stanford, CA: Stanford University Press, 1993.

———. *Cultivating Commons: Joint Ownership of Arable Land in Early Modern Japan*. Honolulu: University of Hawai'i Press, 2011.

Brown, Steven T. *Theatricalities of Power: The Cultural Politics of Noh*. Stanford, CA: Stanford University Press, 2001.

Brownlee, John S. "Crisis as Reinforcement of the Imperial Institution—The Case of the Jōkyū Incident of 1221." *Monumenta Nipponica* 30.2 (1975): 193–201.

———. "Shōkyū War and the Political Rise of Warriors." *Monumenta Nipponica* 1.2 (1969): 59–77.

Bruschke-Johnson, Lee. *Dismissed as Elegant Fossils: Konoe Nobutada and the Role of Aristocrats in Early Modern Japan*. Japonica Neerlandica, 9. Amsterdam: Hotei, 2004.

Burke, Peter. *New Perspectives on Historical Writing*. University Park: Penn State Press, 1992.

Buyō Inshi. *Seji kenbunroku*. Edited by Honjō Eijirō and Naramoto Tatsuya. Tokyo: Iwanami Shoten, 1994.

Butler, Lee. *Emperor and Aristocracy in Japan, 1467–1680: Resilience and Renewal*. Cambridge, MA: Harvard University Asia Center, 2002.

———. "Patronage and the Building Arts in Tokugawa Japan." *Early Modern Japan* 12.2 (2004): 39–52.

———. "'Washing Off the Dust': Baths and Bathing in Late Medieval Japan." *Monumenta Nipponica* 60.1 (2005): 1–41.

Cahill, Suzanne. *Transcendence and Divine Passion*. Stanford, CA: Stanford University Press, 1993.

Carter, Steven D. *Regent Redux: A Life of the Statesman-Scholar Ichijō Kaneyoshi*. Ann Arbor: Center for Japanese Studies, University of Michigan, 1996.

———. *Householders: The Reizei Family in Japanese History*. Harvard-Yenching Institute Monograph Series, 61. Cambridge, MA: Harvard University Asia Center, 2007.

———. *The Road to Komatsubara: A Classical Reading of the Renga Hyakuin*. Harvard East Asian Monographs, 124. Cambridge, MA: Harvard University Press, 1987.

———. *Traditional Japanese Poetry: An Anthology*. Stanford, CA: Stanford University Press, 1991.

———, trans. *Waiting for the Wind: Thirty-Six Poets of Japan's Late Medieval Age*. New York: Columbia University Press, 1989.

Chance, Frank, and Julie Davis. *Modern Impressions: Theatre Prints from the Gilbert and Shirley Luber Collection*. Philadelphia: University of Pennsylvania Press, 2007.

Chance, Linda H. *Formless in Form: Kenkō, Tsurezuregusa, and the Rhetoric of Japanese Fragmentary Prose*. Stanford, CA: Stanford University Press, 1997.

Childs, Margaret Helen. *Rethinking Sorrow: Revelatory Tales of Late Medieval Japan*. Michigan Monograph Series in Japanese Studies 6. Ann Arbor: Center for Japanese Studies, University of Michigan, 1991.

Collcutt, Martin. *Five Mountains: The Rinzai Zen Monastic Institution in Medieval Japan*. Cambridge, MA: Harvard University Press, 1981.

———. "Musō Soseki." In Jeffrey P. Mass, ed., *The Origins of Japan's Medieval World: Courtiers, Clerics, Warriors, and Peasants in the Fourteenth Century*, 261–294. Stanford, CA: Stanford University Press, 1997.

———. "Nun Shogun: Politics and Religion in the Life of Hōjō Masako (1157–1225)." In Barbara Ruch, ed. *Engendering Faith: Women and Buddhism in Premodern Japan*, 165–177. Ann Arbor: Center for Japanese Studies, University of Michigan, 2002.

Como, Michael. "Horses, Dragons, and Disease in Nara Japan." *Japanese Journal of Religious Studies* 34.2 (2007): 393–415.

———. *Shōtoku: Ethnicity, Ritual, and Violence in the Japanese Buddhist Tradition*. Oxford: Oxford University Press, 2008.

———. *Weaving and Binding: Immigrant Gods and Female Immortals in Ancient Japan*. Honolulu: University of Hawai'i Press, 2009.

Conlan, Thomas D. *From Sovereign to Symbol: An Age of Ritual Determinism*. Oxford and New York: Oxford University Press, 2011.

———. "Instruments of Change." In John Ferejohn and Frances Rosenbluth, eds., *War and State Building in Medieval Japan*, 124–158. Stanford, CA: Stanford University Press, 2010.

———. *In Little Need of Divine Intervention: Takezaki Suenaga's Scrolls of the Mongol Invasions of Japan*. Cornell East Asia Series, 113. Ithaca, NY: East Asia Program, Cornell University, 2001.

———. *State of War: The Violent Order of Fourteenth Century Japan*. Ann Arbor: Center for Japanese Studies, University of Michigan, 2003.

———. "Traces of the Past: Documents, Literacy, and Liturgy in Medieval Japan." In Gordon Berger, Andrew Goble, Lorraine Harrington, and G. Cameron Hurst III, eds., *Currents in Medieval Japanese History: Essays in Honor of Jeffrey P. Mass*, 19–50. Los Angeles: University of Southern California East Asian Studies Center; Figueroa Press, 2009.

———. *Weapons and Fighting Techniques of the Samurai Warrior*. London: Amber Press, 2008.

Cooper, Michael, ed. *They Came to Japan: An Anthology of European Reports on Japan, 1543–1640*. Berkeley: University of California Press, 1965. Reprint, Ann Arbor: Center for Japanese Studies, University of Michigan, 1995.

Cornell, Laurel L. "Infanticide in Early Modern Japan: Demography, Culture, and Population Growth." *Journal of Asian Studies* 55.1 (1996): 22–50.

———. "Peasant Women and Divorce in Preindustrial Japan." *Signs* 15.4 (1990): 710–732.

Corr, William. *Adams the Pilot: The Life and Times of Captain Will Adams, 1564–1620*. Folkstone, Kent, UK: Japan Library, 1995.
Crawcour, E. S. "Changes in Japanese Commerce in the Tokugawa Period." *Journal of Asian Studies* 22.4 (1963): 387–400.
Crowley, Cheryl A. *Haikai Poet Yosa Buson and the Bashō Revival.* Leiden, The Netherlands: E. J. Brill, 2007.
Davis, Julie Nelson. *Utamaro and the Spectacle of Beauty*. Honolulu: University of Hawai'i Press, 2007.
Deal, William. *Handbook to Life in Medieval and Early Modern Japan*. New York: Facts on File, 2006.
De Bary, Wm. Theodore, Donald Keene, George Tanabe, and Paul Varley, eds. *Sources of Japanese Tradition,* Vol. 1: *From Earliest Times to 1600*. 2nd Ed. Introduction to Asian Civilizations. New York: Columbia University Press, 2001.
Denoon, Donald, Mark Hudson, Gavan McCormack, and Tessa Morris-Suzuki, eds. *Multicultural Japan: Palaeolithic to Postmodern*. Cambridge: Cambridge University Press, 1996.
Dobbins, James C. *Jōdo Shinshū: Shin Buddhism in Medieval Japan*. 1989. Reprinted, Honolulu: University of Hawai'i Press, 2002.
———. *Letters of the Nun Eshinni: Images of Pure Land Buddhism in Medieval Japan*. Honolulu: University of Hawai'i Press, 2004.
Dore, R. P. *Education in Tokugawa Japan*. London: Althone Press, 1984.
Dunn, Charles J. *Everyday Life in Imperial Japan*. New York: Putnam, 1969.
———. *Everyday Life in Traditional Japan*. New York: Putnam, 1969.
Duus, Peter. *Feudalism in Japan*. 3rd ed. New York: McGraw-Hill, 1993.
Ebersole, Gary L. "The Buddhist Ritual Use of Linked Poetry in Medieval Japan." *Eastern Buddhist* 16.2 (Autumn 1983): 50–71.
Edwards, Walter. "Event and Process in the Founding of Japan." *Journal of Japanese Studies* 9.2 (1983): 265–295.
Egami, Namio. "The Formation of the People and the Origin of the State in Japan." *Memoirs of the Research Department of the Toyo Bunko* 23 (1964): 35–70.
Elison, George. *Deus Destroyed: The Image of Christianity in Early Modern Japan*. Cambridge, MA: Harvard University Press, 1973.
Elison, George, and Bardwell L. Smith, eds. *Warlords, Artists, and Commoners: Japan in the Sixteenth Century*. Honolulu: University of Hawai'i Press, 1981.
Elisonas, Jurgis. "The Inseparable Trinity: Japan's Relations with China and Korea." In John Hall, ed., *The Cambridge History of Japan,* Vol. 4: *Early Modern Japan*, 235–300. Cambridge: Cambridge University Press, 1991.
Elisonas, Jurgis S. A., and Jeroen P. Lamers, trans. and eds. *The Chronicle of Lord Nobunaga*. Leiden: Brill, 2011.
Endō, Jun. "The Early Modern Period: In Search of a Shintō Identity." In Inoue Nobutaka, ed., *Shintō: A Short History,* 108–158. London: Routledge Curzon, 2003.
Eubanks, Charlotte. *Miracles of Book and Body: Buddhist Textual Culture and Medieval Japan*. Berkeley: University of California Press, 2011.

Farris, William Wayne. *Heavenly Warriors: The Evolution of Japan's Military, 500–1300.* Cambridge, MA: Council on East Asian Studies, Harvard University, 1995.

———. *Japan's Medieval Population: Famine, Fertility, and Warfare in a Transformative Age.* Honolulu: University of Hawai'i Press, 2006.

———. *Japan to 1600: A Social and Economic History.* Honolulu: University of Hawai'i Press, 2009.

———. *Population, Disease, and Land in Early Japan, 645–900.* Cambridge, MA: Harvard University Press, 1985.

———. *Sacred Texts and Buried Treasures: Issues in the Historical Archaeology of Ancient Japan.* Honolulu: University of Hawai'i Press, 1998.

———. "Trade, Money, and Merchants in Nara Japan." *Monumenta Nipponica* 53.3 (1998): 303–334.

Faure, Bernard. *Visions of Power: Imagining Medieval Japanese Buddhism.* Princeton, NJ: Princeton University Press, 1996.

Fogel, Joshua. *Articulating the Sinosphere: Sino-Japanese Relations in Space and Time.* Cambridge, MA: Harvard University Press, 2009.

Ferejohn, John A., and Frances McCall Rosenbluth, eds. *War and State Building in Medieval Japan.* Stanford, CA: Stanford University Press, 2010.

Friday, Karl F. "Bushidō or Bull? A Medieval Historian's Perspective on the Imperial Army and the Japanese Warrior Tradition." *The History Teacher* 27.3 (1994): 339–349.

———. "The Futile Paradigm: The Quest for Feudalism in Early Medieval Japan." *History Compass* 8.2 (2010): 179–196.

———. *The First Samurai: The Life and Legend of the Warrior Rebel Taira Masakado.* New York: John Wiley & Sons, 2008.

———. *Hired Swords: The Rise of Private Warrior Power in Early Japan.* Stanford, CA: Stanford University Press, 1992.

———. *Legacies of the Sword: The Kashima-Shinryū and Samurai Martial Culture.* Honolulu: University of Hawai'i Press, 1997.

———. "Pushing Beyond the Pale: The Yamato Conquest of the Emishi and Northern Japan." *Journal of Japanese Studies* 23.1 (1997): 1–24.

———. *Samurai, Warfare and the State in Early Medieval Japan.* New York: Routledge, 2004.

Fröhlich, Judith. *Rulers, Peasants, and the Use of the Written Word in Medieval Japan: Ategawa no sho, 1004–1304.* New York: Peter Lang, 2007.

Fujiki Hisashi. *Kiga to sensō no sengoku o iku.* Tokyo: Asahi shinbunsha, 2001.

———. *Sengokushi o miru me.* Tokyo: Azekura shobō, 1995.

Fukutō Sanae. *Rekishi no naka no kō jotachi.* Tokyo: Shōgakkan, 2002.

Fukutō Sanae, with Takeshi Watanabe. "From Female Sovereign to Mother of the Nation: Women and Government in the Heian Period." In Mikael S. Adolphson, Edward Kamens, and Stacie Matsumoto, eds., *Heian Japan, Centers and Peripheries,* 15–34. Honolulu: University of Hawai'i Press, 2007.

Furuse Natsuko. *Nihon kodai ōken to gishiki.* Tokyo: Yoshikawa kōbunkan, 1998.

Furushima Toshio. "The Village and Agriculture During the Edo Period." Translated by James L. McClain. In John Whitney Hall, ed., *The Cambridge History of Japan,*

Vol. 4: *Early Modern Japan,* 478–518. Cambridge: Cambridge University Press, 1991.

Gay, Suzanne Marie. "The Kawashima: Warrior-Peasants of Medieval Japan." *Harvard Journal of Asiatic Studies* 46.1 (1986): 81–119.

———. *The Moneylenders of Late Medieval Kyoto.* Honolulu: University of Hawai'i Press, 2001.

Geertz, Clifford. *Negara: The Theatre-State in Nineteenth Century Bali.* Princeton, NJ: Princeton University Press, 1981.

Gerhart, Karen. *Eyes of Power: Art and Early Tokugawa Authority.* Honolulu: University of Hawai'i Press, 1999.

Gerstle, C. Andrew. "Heroic Honor: Chikamatsu and the Samurai Ideal." *Harvard Journal of Asiatic Studies* 57.2 (1997): 307–381.

Goble, Andrew Edmund. *Confluences of Medicine in Medieval Japan: Buddhist Healing, Chinese Knowledge, Islamic Formulas, and Wounds of War.* Honolulu: University of Hawai'i Press, 2011.

———. "Images of Illness: Interpreting the Medieval *Scrolls of Afflictions.*" In Andrew Edmund Goble, Kenneth R. Robinson, and Haruko Wakabayashi, eds., *Tools of Culture: Japan's Cultural, Intellectual, Medical, and Technological Contacts in East Asia, 1000s–1500s,* 163–216. Ann Arbor: Association for Asian Studies, University of Michigan, 2009.

———. "The Kamakura *Bakufu* and Its Officials." In Jeffrey P. Mass and William B. Hauser, eds., *The* Bakufu *in Japanese History,* 31–48. Stanford, CA: Stanford University Press, 1985.

———. *Kenmu: GoDaigo's Revolution.* Cambridge, MA: Council on East Asian Studies, Harvard University, 1996.

———. "Medieval Japan." In William M. Tsutsui, ed. *A Companion to Japanese History,* 47–66. Chichester, West Sussex, UK: Wiley-Blackwell, 2009.

———. "Rhythms of Medicine and Community in Late Sixteenth Century Japan: Yamashina Tokitsune (1543–1611) and His Patients." *East Asian Science, Technology, and Medicine* 29 (2008): 13–62.

———. "War and Injury: The Emergence of Wound Medicine in Medieval Japan." *Monumenta Nipponica* 60.31 (2005): 297–338.

Goble, Andrew Edmund, Kenneth R. Robinson, and Haruko Nishioka Wakabayashi, eds. *Tools of Culture: Japan's Cultural, Intellectual, Medical, and Technological Contacts in East Asia, 1000s–1500s.* Ann Arbor: Association for Asian Studies, University of Michigan, 2009.

Goodman, Grant. *The Dutch Impact on Japan, 1640–1853.* Leiden, The Netherlands: E. J. Brill, 1967.

Goodwin, Janet. *Selling Songs and Smiles: The Sex Trade in Heian and Kamakura Japan.* Honolulu: University of Hawai'i Press, 2007.

Gotō Michiko. *Sengoku o ikita kuge no tsumatachi.* Tokyo: Yoshikawa kōbunkan, 2009.

Graham, Patricia Jane. *Tea of the Sages: The Art of Sencha.* Honolulu: University of Hawai'i Press, 1996.

Gramlich-Oka, Bettina, and Gregory Smits, eds. *Economic Thought in Early Modern Japan.* Leiden, The Netherlands: E. J. Brill, 2010.

Grapard, Allan G. *The Protocol of the Gods: A Study of the Kasuga Cult in Japanese History*. Berkeley: University of California Press, 1992.

Groner, Paul. *Saicho: The Establishment of the Japanese Tendai School.* Honolulu: University of Hawai'i Press, 2000.

———. *Ryōgen and Mt. Hiei: Japanese Tendai in the Tenth Century*. Honolulu: University of Hawai'i Press, 2002.

———. *Ryōgen: The Restoration and Transformation of the Tendai School.* Honolulu: University of Hawai'i Press, 2000.

Grossberg, Kenneth A. *Japan's Renaissance: Politics of the Muromachi Bakufu*. Cambridge, MA: Harvard University Press, 1981.

———. *The Laws of the Muromachi Bakufu*. Tokyo: Monumenta Nipponica Monograph, 1981.

Gunji Masakatsu. "Kabuki and Its Social Background." In Nakane Chie and Ōishi Shinzaburō, eds., *Tokugawa Japan: The Social and Economic Antecedents of Modern Japan,* 192–212. Tokyo: University of Tokyo Press, 1990.

Guth, Christine. *Art of Edo Japan: The Artist and the City, 1615–1868*. New York: Abrams, 1996. Reprint, New Haven: Yale University Press, 2010.

Habu, Junko. *Ancient Jōmon of Japan*. Cambridge: Cambridge University Press, 2004.

———. *Subsistence-Settlement Systems and Intersite Variability in the Moroiso Phase of the Early Jōmon Period of Japan*. Ann Arbor: International Monographs in Prehistory, 2001.

Hall, John W., ed. *The Cambridge History of Japan,* Vol. 4: *Early Modern Japan*. Cambridge: Cambridge University Press, 1991.

———. "Foundations of the Modern Japanese Daimyō." In John W. Hall and Marius B. Jansen, eds., *Studies in the Institutional History of Early Modern Japan,* 65–79. Princeton, NJ: Princeton University Press, 1968.

———. *Government and Local Power in Japan, 500 to 1700: A Study Based on Bizen Province*. Princeton, NJ: Princeton University Press, 1966.

———. *Japan, from Prehistory to Modern Times.* New York: Dell, 1970.

Hall, John W., and Marius B. Jansen, eds. *Studies in the Institutional History of Early Modern Japan*. Princeton, NJ: Princeton University Press, 1968.

Hall, John Whitney, Nagahara Keiji, and Kozo Yamamura, eds. *Japan Before Tokugawa: Political Consolidation and Economic Growth, 1500 to 1650*. Princeton, NJ: Princeton University Press, 1981.

Hall, John W., and Toyoda Takeshi, eds. *Japan in the Muromachi Age*. Berkeley: University of California Press, 1977.

Hansen, Wilburn. *When Tengu Talk: Hirata Atsutane's Ethnography of the Other World.* Honolulu: University of Hawai'i Press, 2008.

Hardacre, Helen. *Kurozumikyō and the New Religions of Japan*. Princeton, NJ: Princeton University Press, 1989.

———. *Religion and Society in Nineteenth-Century Japan: A Study of the Southern Kanto Region, Using Late Edo and Early Meiji Gazetteers.* Ann Arbor: Center for Japanese Studies, University of Michigan, 2002.

Hare, Thomas Blenman. *Zeami's Style: The Noh Plays of Zeami Motokiyo*. Stanford, CA: Stanford University Press, 1986.

Harootunian, Harry D. "The Progress of Japan and the Samurai Class, 1868–1882." *Pacific Historical Review* 28.3 (1959): 255–266.

Harrington, Lorraine. "Social Control and the Significance of the Akutō." In Jeffrey P. Mass, ed., *Court and Bakufu in Japan: Essays in Kamakura History*, 221–250. Stanford, CA: Stanford University Press, 1988.

Hauser, William B. *Economic Institutional Change in Tokugawa Japan: Ōsaka and the Kinai Cotton Trade*. Cambridge: Cambridge University Press, 1974.

Hawley, Samuel. *The Imjin War: Japan's Sixteenth Century Invasion of Korea and Attempt to Conquer China*. Berkeley: Institute of East Asian Studies, University of California, 2005.

Hayami Akira, Osamu Saito, and Ronald Toby. *The Economic History of Japan*, Vol. 1: *Emergence of Economic Society in Japan, 1600–1859*. Oxford: Oxford University Press, 2004.

Hazard, Benjamin. "The Formative Years of the Wakō, 1223–1263." *Monumenta Nipponica* 22 (1967): 260–277.

Hellyer, Robert. *Defining Engagement: Japan and Global Contexts, 1640–1868*. Cambridge, MA: Harvard University Press, 2009.

Hempel, Rose. *The Golden Age of Japan, 794–1192*. New York: Rizzoli, 1983.

Holcombe, Charles. *The Genesis of East Asia: 221 B.C.–A.D. 907*. Asian Interactions and Comparisons. Honolulu: Association for Asian Studies; University of Hawai'i Press, 2001.

Hōnen Jōnin Eden. Komatsu Shigemi, ed. Vols. 1–3, Zoku Nihon no emaki. Tokyo: Chūō kōronsha, 1990.

Hong, Wontack. *Paekche of Korea and the Origin of Yamato Japan*. Seoul: Kudara International, 1994.

Hori, Kyotsu. "The Economic and Political Effects of the Mongol Wars." In John W. Hall and Jeffrey P. Mass, eds., *Medieval Japan: Essays in Institutional History*, 184–198. 1974. Reprint, Stanford, CA: Stanford University Press, 1988.

Horton, H. Mack. *Song in an Age of Discord: The Journal of Sōchō and Poetic Life in Late Medieval Japan*. Stanford, CA: Stanford University Press, 2002.

Howell, David L. *Capitalism from Within: Economy, Society, and the State in a Japanese Fishery*. Berkeley: University of California Press, 1995.

Huey, Robert N. *The Making of Shinkokinshū*. Harvard East Asia Monographs, 208. Cambridge, MA: Harvard University Asia Center, 2002.

Hur, Nam-lin. *Prayer and Play in Late Tokugawa Japan: Asakusa Sensōji and Edo Society*. Cambridge, MA: Harvard University Asia Center, 2000.

———. *Death and Social Order in Tokugawa Japan: Buddhism, Anti-Christianity, and the Danka System*. Cambridge, MA: Harvard University Asia, 2007.

Hurst, G. Cameron, III. *Armed Martial Arts of Japan*. New Haven: Yale University Press, 1998.

———. "Death, Honor, and Loyalty: The Bushidō Ideal." *Philosophy East and West* 4.4 (1990): 511–527.

———. *Insei: Abdicated Sovereigns in the Politics of Late Heian Japan, 1086–1185.* New York: Columbia University Press, 1973.

———. "The Kobu Polity: Court-Bakufu Relations in Kamakura Japan." In Jeffrey P. Mass, ed. *Court and Bakufu in Japan: Essays in Kamakura History*, 3–28. New Haven: Yale University Press, 1982. Reprint, Stanford, CA: Stanford University Press, 1995.

———. "*Kugyo* and *Zuryo*: Center and Periphery in the Era of Fujiwara no Michinaga." In Mikael Adolphson, Edward Kamens, and Stacie Matsumoto, eds., *Heian Japan: Centers and Peripheries*, 66–101. Honolulu: University of Hawai'i Press, 2007.

———. "The Reign of Go-Sanjo and the Revival of Imperial Power." *Monumenta Nipponica*, 27.1 (Spring 1972): 65–83.

———. *Samurai on Wall Street: Miyamoto Musashi and the Search for Success.* UFSI Report. 44, "Asia" 1982.

———. "The Warrior as Ideal for a New Age." In Jeffrey P. Mass, ed., *The Origins of Japan's Medieval World: Courtiers, Clerics, Warriors, and Peasants in the Fourteenth Century*, 203–236. Stanford, CA: Stanford University Press, 1997.

Ikawa-Smith, Fumiko. "Humans Along the Pacific Margin of Northeast Asia Before the Last Glacial Maximum: Evidence for Their Presence and Adaptations." In D. B. Madsen, ed., *Entering America: Northeast Asia and Beringia Before the Last Glacial Maximum*, 285–309. Salt Lake City: University of Utah Press, 2004.

Ikegami, Eiko. *The Taming of the Samurai: Honorific Individualism and the Making of Modern Japan*. Cambridge, MA: Harvard University Press, 1995.

Imamura, Keiji. *Prehistoric Japan: New Perspectives on Insular East Asia*. London: University College London Press, 1996.

Inoue Mitsusada. "The Century of Reform." In Delmer Brown, ed., *Cambridge History of Japan,* Vol. 1: *Ancient Japan,* 163–220. Cambridge: Cambridge University Press, 1993.

Inoue Shōichi. *Nihon ni kodai ha atta no ka?* Tokyo: Kadokawa, 2010.

Inoue Tatsuo and Michiko Aoki. "The Hitachi Fudoki and the Fujiwara." In Joan R. Piggott, ed. *Capital and Countryside in Japan, 300–1180: Japanese Historians in English*, 103–207. Cornell East Asia Series, 129. Ithaca, NY: East Asia Program, Cornell University, 2006.

Ippen. *No Abode: The Record of Ippen*. Translated by Dennis Hirota. Honolulu: University of Hawai'i Press, 1997.

Irumada Nobuo and Murai Shōsuke. "Atarashii chūsei kokka zō wo saguru." *Rekishi hyōron* 437 (1986): 11–33.

Ishii Susumu. "The Decline of the Kamakura Bakufu." In Kozo Yamamura, ed., *The Cambridge History of Japan,* Vol. 3: *Medieval Japan*, 128–174. Cambridge: Cambridge University Press, 1990.

Ishii Susumu, Ishimoda Shō, Kasamatsu Hiroshi, Katsumata Shizuo, and Satō Shin'ichi, eds. *Chūsei seiji shakai shisō 1.* Tokyo: Iwanami shoten, 1972.

Ishii Yoneo. *The Junk Trade from Southeast Asia*. Singapore: Institute of Southeast Asian Studies, 1998.

Ishimoda Shō. *Kodai makki seijishi josetsu.* Tokyo: Miraisha, 1964.

Itō, Kōji. "Japan and Ryukyu During the Fifteenth and Sixteenth Centuries." *Acta Asiatica* 95 (2008): 79–99.

Jansen, Marius B. *China in the Tokugawa World.* Cambridge, MA: Harvard University Press, 1992.

———. *The Making of Modern Japan.* Cambridge, MA: Belknap Press, Harvard University Press, 2000.

———, ed. *The Cambridge History of Japan,* Vol. 5: *The Nineteenth Century.* New York: Cambridge University Press 1989.

Johnson, Hiroko. *Western Influences on Japanese Art: The Akita Ranga Art School and Foreign Books.* Leiden, The Netherlands: Hotei, 2006.

Jordan, Brenda, and Victoria Weston, eds. *Copying the Master and Stealing His Secrets: Talent and Training in Japanese Painting.* Honolulu: University of Hawai'i Press, 2002.

Jungmann, Burglind. *Painters as Envoys: Korean Inspiration in Eighteenth-Century Japanese Nanga.* Princeton, NJ: Princeton University Press, 2004.

Kamens, Edward. *Three Jewels: A Study and Translation of Minamoto Tamenori's* Sanboe. Ann Arbor: Center for Japanese Studies, University of Michigan, 1988.

Kaminishi, Ikumi. *Explaining Pictures: Buddhist Propaganda and* Etoki *Storytelling in Japan.* Honolulu: University of Hawai'i Press, 2006.

Kanda James. "Methods of Land Transfer in Medieval Japan." *Monumenta Nipponica* 23.4 (1978): 379–405.

Kang, Etsuko Hae-jin. *Diplomacy and Ideology in Japanese-Korean Relations: From the Fifteenth to the Eighteenth Century.* New York: Saint Martin's Press, 1997.

Karlin, Jason G. "The Gender of Nationalism: Competing Masculinities in Meiji Japan." *Journal of Japanese Studies* 28.1 (2002): 41–77.

Katsu Kokichi. *Musui's Story: The Autobiography of a Tokugawa Samurai.* Translated by Teruko Craig. Tucson: University of Arizona Press, 1993.

Kawaoka Tsutomu. *Muromachi bakufu to shugo kenryoku.* Tokyo: Yoshikawa kōbunkan, 2002.

Kawashima, Terry. *Writing Margins: The Textual Construction of Gender in Heian and Kamakura Japan.* Harvard East Asian Monographs 201. Cambridge, MA: Harvard University Press, 2001.

Kawazoe, Shōji. "Japan in East Asia." In Kozo Yamamura, ed., *The Cambridge History of Japan,* Vol. 3: *Medieval Japan,* 396–446. Cambridge: Cambridge University Press, 1990.

Keene, Donald. *The Japanese Discovery of Europe, 1720–1830.* Stanford, CA: Stanford University Press, 1966.

———. *Seeds in the Heart.* New York: Henry Holt, 1993.

———. *Yoshimasa and the Silver Pavilion: The Creation of the Soul of Japan.* Asia Perspectives Series. New York: Columbia University Press, 2003.

Keirstead, Thomas. "Fragmented Estates: The Break-up of the Myo and the Decline of the Shoen System." *Monumenta Nipponica,* 40.3 (Autumn 1985): 311–330.

———. "Gardens and Estates: Medievality and Space." *Positions* 1.2 (1993): 289–320.

———. *The Geography of Power in Medieval Japan*. Princeton, NJ: Princeton University Press, 1992.

———. "Inventing Medieval Japan: The History and Politics of National Identity." *Medieval History Journal* 1.1 (1998): 45–71.

———. "Outcastes Before the Law: Pollution and Purification in Medieval Japan." In Gordon Berger, Andrew Edmund Goble, Lorraine Harrington, and G. Cameron Hurst, III, eds. *Currents in Medieval Japanese History: Essays in Honor of Jeffrey P. Mass*. Los Angeles: Figueroa Press, 2009.

Kern, Adam. *Manga from the Floating World: Comicbook Culture and the* Kibyōshi *of Edo Japan*. Cambridge, MA: Harvard University Asia Center, 2006.

Kidder, J. Edward. *The Lucky Seventh: Early Horyu-ji and Its Time*. Mitaka, Japan: ICU Hachiro Yuasa Memorial Museum, 1999.

———. *Prehistoric Japanese Arts: Jōmon Pottery*. Tokyo: Kodansha, 1968.

Kiley, Cornelius J. "Estate and Property in the Late Heian Age." In J. W. Hall and J. P. Mass, eds. *Medieval Japan: Essays in Institutional History*, 109–126. New Haven: Yale University Press, 1974.

———. "State and Dynasty in Archaic Yamato." *Journal of Japanese Studies* 3.1 (1973): 25–49.

Kim, Young-Hee. *Songs to Make the Dust Dance*. Berkeley: University of California Press, 1994.

Kimbrough, R. Keller. *Preachers, Poets, Women, and the Way: Izumi Shikibu and the Buddhist Literature of Medieval Japan*. Ann Arbor: Center for Japanese Studies, University of Michigan, 2008.

Kimura Shigemitsu. *Kokufū bunka no jidai*. Tokyo: Aoki shoten, 1997.

Kitagawa, Hiroshi, and Bruce T. Tsuchida, trans. *The Tale of the Heike*. Tokyo: University of Tokyo Press, 1975.

Kleeman, Terry. *Great Perfection*. Honolulu: University of Hawai'i Press, 1998.

Klein, Susan Blakeley. *Allegories of Desire: Esoteric Literary Commentaries of Medieval Japan*. Harvard–Yenching Institute Monograph Series 55. Cambridge, MA: Harvard University Asia Center, 2002.

Koike, Hiroko. "Prehistoric Hunting Pressure and Paleobiomass: An Environmental Reconstruction and Archaeozoological Analysis of a Jōmon Shellmound Area." In Takeru Akazawa and C. Melvin Aikens, eds., *Prehistoric Hunter-Gatherers in Japan: New Research Methods*, 27–53. University of Tokyo Bulletin 27. Tokyo: University Museum, 1986.

Komine Kazuaki. *Setsuwa no gensetsu: Chūsei no hyōgen to rekishi jojutsu*. Tokyo: Shinwasha, 2002.

Kominz, Laurence R. *Avatars of Vengeance: Japanese Drama and the Soga Literary Tradition*. Ann Arbor: Center for Japanese Studies, University of Michigan, 1995.

Kondo Shigekazu. "1247 as a Turning Point for the Kamakura Bakufu." In Bert Edström, ed., *Turning Points in Japanese History*, 25–33. Richmond, UK: Japan Library, 2002.

Kōnoshi Takamitsu. "Constructing Imperial Mythology: Kojiki and Nihon shoki." In Haruo Shirane and Tomi Suzuki, eds., *Inventing the Classics: Modernity, Na-*

tional Identity, and Japanese Literature, 51–67. Stanford, CA: Stanford University Press, 2000.

Kubota Jun and Kawamura Teruo, eds. *Gappon Hachidaishū*. Tokyo: Miyai Shoten, 1986.

Kudō Keiichi. "Shōen." *Acta Asiatica* 44 (1983): 1–27.

Kuno, Yoshi. *Japanese Expansion on the Asiatic Continent*, Vol. 1. Berkeley: University of California Press, 1937.

Kuroda Toshio. "Chūsei no kokka to tennō." In *Iwanami kōza Nihon rekishi*, Chūsei 2, 261–301. Tokyo: Iwanami shoten, 1963.

Kurushima Noriko. "Marriage and Female Inheritance in Medieval Japan." *International Journal of Asian Studies* 1.2 (2004): 223–245.

LaFeber, Walter. *The Clash: US-Japanese Relations through History*. New York: W. W. Norton, 1997.

LaFleur, William R. *Awesome Nightfall: The Life, Times, and Poetry of Saigyō*. Boston: Wisdom, 2003.

———. *The Karma of Words: Buddhism and the Literary Arts in Medieval Japan*. Berkeley: University of California Press, 1983.

Lamers, Jeroen P. *Japonius Tyrannus: The Japanese Warlord Oda Nobunaga Reconsidered.* Leiden, The Netherlands: Hotei, 2000.

Laver, Michael. *Japan's Economy by Proxy in the Seventeenth Century: China, the Netherlands and the Bakufu*. London: Cambria Press, 2008.

———. *The Sakoku Edicts and the Politics of Tokugawa Hegemony*. London: Cambria Press, 2011.

Li, Michelle. *Ambiguous Bodies: Narrating the Grotesque in Japanese* Setsuwa *Tales*. Stanford, CA: Stanford University Press, 2009.

Lieberman, Victor. *Beyond Binary History: Reimagining Eurasia to c. 1830*. Ann Arbor: University of Michigan Press, 1997.

———. *Strange Parallels: Southeast Asia in Global Context, c. 800–1830*. 2 vols. Cambridge: Cambridge University Press, 2009.

Lensen, George. *The Russian Push Towards Japan: Russo-Japanese Relations, 1697–1875*. New York: Octagon Books, 1971.

Levy, Ian Hideo, trans. *The Ten Thousand Leaves: A Translation of the Man'yoshu, Japan's Premier Anthology of Classical Poetry, Volume One*. New York: Columbia University Press, 1981.

Lewis, Archibald. *Knights and Samurai: Feudalism in Northern France and Japan*. London: Temple Smith, 1979.

Lewis, James. *Frontier Contact Between Chosŏn Korea and Tokugawa Japan*. London: Routledge Curzon, 2003.

Lidin, Olof. *Tanegashima: The Arrival of Europe in Japan*. Copenhagen: NIAS Press, 2002.

Loewe, Michael. *Ways to Paradise: The Chinese Quest for Immortality.* London: George Allen & Unwin, 1979.

Manyoshū. Tokyo: Nippon Gakujutsu Shinkokai, 1940. Reprinted, New York: Columbia University Press, 1965; New York: Dover, 2005.

Marra, Michele. *The Aesthetics of Discontent: Politics and Reclusion in Medieval Japanese Literature*. Honolulu: University of Hawai'i Press, 1991.

———. "*Mumyōzōshi*: Introduction and Translation." *Monumenta Nipponica* 39.2 (1984): 115–45; "*Mumyōzōshi*, Part 2," *Monumenta Nipponica* 39.3 (1984): 281–305; "*Mumyōzōshi*, Part 3," *Monumenta Nipponica* 39.4 (1984): 409–434.

———. *Representations of Power: The Literary Politics of Medieval Japan*. Honolulu: University of Hawai'i Press, 1993.

Maruyama Masao. *Studies in the Intellectual History of Tokugawa Japan*. Princeton, NJ: Princeton University Press, 1974.

Marx, Karl. *The Eighteenth Brumaire of Louis Napoleon*. In David McLellan, ed., *Karl Marx: Selected Writings*. Oxford: Oxford University Press, 1977.

Marx, Karl, and Friedrich Engels. *The Communist Manifesto*. In David McLellan, ed., *Karl Marx: Selected Writings*. Oxford: Oxford University Press, 1977.

Mason, Penelope. *History of Japanese Art*. New York: Harry N. Abrams, 1993.

Mass, Jeffrey P. *Antiquity and Anachronism in Japanese History*. Stanford, CA: Stanford University Press, 1992.

———, ed. *Court and Bakufu in Japan: Essays in Kamakura History*. New Haven: Yale University Press, 1982.

———. *The Development of Kamakura Rule 1180–1250: A History with Documents*. Stanford, CA: Stanford University Press, 1979.

———. *Family, Law, and Property in Japan, 1200–1350*. Occasional Papers in Japanese Studies. Boston: Edwin O. Reischauer Institute of Japanese Studies, 2000.

———. "Formative Period of Kamakura Justice." *Transactions of the International Conference of Orientalists in Japan* 21 (1976): 148–150.

———. "Jitō Land Possession in the Thirteenth Century: The Case of Shitaji Chūbun." In John W. Hall and Jeffrey P. Mass, eds., *Medieval Japan: Essays in Institutional History*, 157–183. 1974. Reprint, Stanford, CA: Stanford University Press, 1988.

———. *The Kamakura Bakufu: A Study in Documents*. Stanford, CA: Stanford University Press, 1976.

———. "The Kamakura Bakufu." In Kozo Yamamura, ed., *The Cambridge History of Japan*, Vol. 3: *Medieval Japan*, 46–88. Cambridge: Cambridge University Press, 1990.

———. *Lordship and Inheritance in Early Medieval Japan: A Study of the Kamakura Soryo System*. Stanford, CA: Stanford University Press, 1989.

———. "The Missing Minamoto in the Twelfth-Century Kanto." *Journal of Japanese Studies* 19.1 (Winter 1993): 121–145.

———. "Of Hierarchy and Authority at the End of Kamakura." In Jeffrey P. Mass, ed., *The Origins of Japan's Medieval World: Courtiers, Clerics, Warriors, and Peasants in the Fourteenth Century*, 17–38. Stanford, CA: Stanford University Press, 1997.

———, ed. *The Origins of Japan's Medieval World: Courtiers, Clerics, Warriors, and Peasants in the Fourteenth Century*. Stanford, CA: Stanford University Press, 1997.

———. "Origins of Kamakura Justice." *Journal of Japanese Studies* 3.2 (1977): 299–322.

———. "Patterns of Provincial Inheritance in Late Heian Japan." *Journal of Japanese Studies* 9.1 (1983): 67–96.

———. "Translation and Pre-1600 History." *Journal of Japanese Studies* 6.1 (1980): 61–88.

———. *Warrior Government in Medieval Japan: A Study of the Kamakura Bakufu, Shugo and Jitō*. New Haven: Yale University Press, 1974.

———. *Yoritomo and the Founding of the First Bakufu*. Stanford, CA: Stanford University Press, 1999.

Massarella, Derek. *A World Elsewhere: Europe's Encounter with Japan in the Sixteenth and Seventeenth Centuries*. New Haven: Yale University Press, 1990.

Matisoff, Susan. *The Legend of Semimaru: Blind Musician of Japan*. Studies in Oriental Culture, 14. New York: Columbia University Press, 1978.

McCallum, Donald F. *Zenkōji and Its Icon: A Study in Medieval Japanese Religious Art*. Princeton, NJ: Princeton University Press, 1994.

McClain, James L. "Castle Towns and Daimyo Authority: Kanazawa in the Years 1583–1630." *Journal of Japanese Studies* 6.2 (1980): 267–300.

———. *Kanazawa: A Seventeenth-Century Japanese Castle Town*. New Haven: Yale University Press, 1982.

McClain, James L., John M. Merriman, and Kaoru Ugawa, eds. *Edo and Paris: Urban Life and the State in the Early Modern Era*. Ithaca, NY: Cornell University Press, 1997.

McClain, James L., and Osamu Wakita, eds. *Osaka: The Merchants' Capital of Early Modern Japan*. Ithaca, NY: Cornell University Press, 1999.

McCormick, Melissa. *Tosa Mitsunobu and the Small Scroll in Medieval Japan*. Seattle: University of Washington Press, 2009.

McCullough, Helen C. *Classical Japanese Prose: An Anthology*. Stanford, CA: Stanford University Press, 1990.

———, trans. *Kokin Wakashū: The First Imperial Anthology of Japanese Poetry; with Tosa Nikki and Shinsen Waka*. Stanford, CA: Stanford University Press, 1985.

———, trans. *The Taiheiki: A Chronicle of Medieval Japan*. New York: Columbia University Press, 1959.

———, trans. *The Tale of the Heike*. Stanford, CA: Stanford University Press, 1988.

———. "A Tale of Mutsu." *Harvard Journal of Asiatic Studies* 25 (1964): 178–211.

———, trans. *Yoshitsune: A Fifteenth-Century Japanese Chronicle*. Stanford, CA: Stanford University Press, 1966.

McCullough, William. "The Heian Court, 794–1070." In Donald H. Shively and William H. McCullough, eds., *Cambridge History of Japan*, Vol. 2: *Heian Japan*, 20–96. Cambridge: Cambridge University Press, 1999.

———. "Japanese Marriage Institutions in the Heian Period." *Harvard Journal of Asiatic Studies* 27 (1967): 103–167.

McKelway, Matthew Philip. *Capitalscapes: Folding Screens and Political Imagination in Late Medieval Kyoto*. Honolulu: University of Hawai'i Press, 2006.

McKinney, Meredith, trans. *The Pillow Book*. New York: Penguin, 2007.

McMullin, Neil. *Buddhism and the State in Sixteenth-Century Japan*. Princeton, NJ: Princeton University Press, 1984.

———. "Historical and Historiographical Issues in the Study of Pre-modern Japanese Religions." *Japanese Journal of Religious Studies* 16.1 (1989): 3–40.

McNally, Mark. *Proving the Way: Conflict and Practice in the History of Japanese Nativism*. Cambridge, MA: Harvard University Asia Center, 2005.

Miller, Richard J. *Ancient Japanese Nobility: The Kabane Ranking System*. Berkeley: University of California Press, 1973.

Minato, Masao. *Japan and Its Nature*. Tokyo: Heibonsha, 1977.

Miyake, Hitoshi. *Shugendō: Essays on the Structure of Japanese Folk Religion*. Ann Arbor: Center for Japanese Studies, University of Michigan, 2001.

Mizubayashi Takeshi, Ōtsu Tōru, Nitta Ichirō, and Ōtō Osamu, eds. *Shintaikei Nihonshi 2—hōshakaishi*. Tokyo: Yamakawade shuppan, 2001.

Morrell, Robert E., trans. *Sand and Pebbles (Shasekishū): The Tales of Mujū Ichien; A Voice for Pluralism in Kamakura Buddhism*. Albany: State University of New York Press, 1985.

Moran, J. F. *The Japanese and the Jesuits: Alessandro Valignano in Sixteenth-Century Japan*. New York: Routledge, 1993.

Morrell, Robert E. *Sand and Pebbles (Shasekishū)*. Albany: State University of New York Press, 1985.

Moriya Katsuhisa. "Urban Networks and Information Networks." In Nakane Chie and Ōishi Shinsaburō, eds., *Tokugawa Japan: The Social and Economic Antecedents of Modern Japan*, 97–123. Tokyo: University of Tokyo Press, 1990.

Morris, Dana Robert. "Land and Society." In Donald H. Shively and William McCullough, eds., *The Cambridge History of Japan*, Vol. 2: *Heian Japan*, 183–235. Cambridge: Cambridge University Press, 1999.

Morris-Suzuki, Tessa. *The Technological Transformation of Japan from the Seventeenth to the Twenty-First Century.* Cambridge: Cambridge University Press, 1994.

Mulhern, Chieko Irie. *Heroic with Grace: Legendary Women of Japan*. Armonk, NY: M. E. Sharpe, 1991.

Murai Shōsuke. "The Boundaries of Medieval Japan." *Acta Asiatica* 81 (2001): 72–91.

Murai Yūki, ed. *Sengoku ibun: Sasaki Rokkaku-shi hen*. Tokyo: Tōkyōdō shuppan, 2009.

Nagahara Keiji. "Landownership under the Shōen-Kokugaryō System." *Journal of Japanese Studies* 1.2 (Spring 1975): 269–296.

———. "The Lord-Vassal System and Public Authority (Kōgi): The Case of the Sengoku Daimyō." *Acta Asiatica* 49 (1985): 34–45.

———. "The Medieval Origins of the Eta-Hinin." *Journal of Japanese Studies* 5.2 (1979): 385–405.

———. "The Medieval Peasant." In Kozo Yamamura, ed., *The Cambridge History of Japan*, Vol. 3: *Medieval Japan*, 306–310. Cambridge: Cambridge University Press, 1990.

———. "The Social Structure of Early Medieval Japan." *Hitotsubashi Journal of Economics* 1.1 (1960): 90–97.

———. "Village Communities and Daimyo Power." In John Whitney Hall and Toyoda Takeshi, eds., *Japan in the Muromachi Age*, 107–123. Berkeley: University of California Press, 1977.

Nagahara Keiji and Kozo Yamamura. "Shaping the Process of Unification: Technological Progress in Sixteenth- and Seventeenth-Century Japan." *Journal of Japanese Studies* 14.1 (1988): 77–109.

Najita, Tetsuo. *Ordinary Economies in Japan: A Historical Perspective, 1750–1950.* Berkeley: University of California Press, 2009.

———. *Visions of Virtue in Tokugawa Japan.* Chicago: University of Chicago Press, 1987.

Nakane, Chie. "Tokugawa Society." In Nakane Chie and Ōishi Shinsaburō, eds., *Tokugawa Japan: The Social and Economic Antecedents of Modern Japan,* 213–231. Tokyo: University of Tokyo Press, 1990.

Nakane Chie, Shinzaburō Ōishi, and Conrad Totman, eds. *Tokugawa Japan.* Tokyo: University of Tokyo Press, 1990.

Nakashima Minehiro. *Nihon no tanada: hozen e no torikumi.* Tokyo: Kokin Shoin, 1999.

Naumann, Nelly. *Die Mythen des Alten Japan.* Munich: C. H. Beck, 1996.

Ng, Wai-ming. *The I Ching in Tokugawa Thought and Culture.* Honolulu: University of Hawai'i Press, 2000.

Nickerson, Peter. "The Meaning of Matrilocality: Kinship, Property, and Politics in Mid-Heian." *Monumenta Nipponica* 1993: 429–468.

Nitobe Inazō. *Bushidō, the Soul of Japan: An Exposition of Japanese Thought.* New York: G. P. Putnam's Sons, 1905.

Nitta Ichirō. *Chūsei ni kokka ha atta ka?* Tokyo: Yamakawa shuppansha, 2004, 16–22.

Nivison, David S., and Arthur F. Wright. *Confucianism in Action.* Stanford, CA: Stanford University Press, 1959.

Nosco, Peter, ed. *Confucianism and Tokugawa Culture.* Princeton, NJ: Princeton University Press, 1984.

———. *Remembering Paradise: Nativism and Nostalgia in Eighteenth-Century Japan.* Cambridge, MA: Harvard University Asia Center, 1990.

Okamoto, Hiromichi. "Foreign Policy and Maritime Trade in the Early Ming Period: Focusing on the Ryukyu Kingdom." *Acta Asiatica* 95 (2008): 35–55.

Okuno Takahiro and Iwasawa Yasuhiko, comps. *Shinchō kōki.* Tokyo: Kadokawa shoten, 1969.

Omoto, Keiichi, and Naruya Saitou. "Genetic Origins of the Japanese: A Partial Support for the Dual Structure Hypothesis." *American Journal of Physical Anthropology* 102 (1997): 437–446.

Onoyama Setsu. "The Sumptuary Restrictions on Tomb Mounds in the 5th Century AD." *Kōkogaku Kenkyū* 16.3 (1970): 73–83.

Ooms, Herman. *Charismatic Bureaucrat: A Political Biography of Matsudaira Sadnobu, 1758–1829.* Chicago: University of Chicago Press, 1975.

———. *Imperial Politics and Symbolics in Ancient Japan: The Tenmu Dynasty.* Honolulu: University of Hawai'i Press, 2008.

———. *Tokugawa Ideology: Early Constructs, 1570–1680.* Princeton, NJ: Princeton University Press, 1985.

———. *Tokugawa Village Practice: Class, Status, Power, Law.* Berkeley: University of California Press, 1996.

Oyler, Elizabeth. *Swords, Oaths, and Prophetic Visions: Authoring Warrior Rule in Medieval Japan*. Honolulu: University of Hawai'i Press, 2006.

Ozawa Tomio. *Buke kakun, ikun shūsei*. Tokyo: Perikansha, 2003.

Pandey, Rajyashree. *Writing and Renunciation in Medieval Japan: The Works of the Poet-Priest Kamo no Chōmei*. Ann Arbor: Center for Japanese Studies, University of Michigan, 1998.

Parker, Joseph D. *Zen Buddhist Landscape Arts of Early Muromachi Japan (1336–1573)*. Albany: State University of New York Press, 1999.

Parker, Kenneth. "Okyōsama: Documentation of the Founding of the Nyorai-kyō, Japan's First 'New Religion.'" Ph.D. dissertation, University of Pennsylvania, 1983.

Pearson, Richard. "The Place of Okinawa in Japanese Historical Identity." In Donald Denoon et al., eds., *Multicultural Japan*, 95–116. Cambridge: Cambridge University Press, 2001.

Pearson, Richard J., Gina Lee Barnes, and Karl L. Hutterer, eds. *Windows on the Japanese Past: Studies in Archaeology and Prehistory*. Ann Arbor: Center for Japanese Studies, University of Michigan, 1986.

Perez, Louis G. *Daily Life in Early Modern Japan*. Westport, CT: Greenwood Press, 2002.

Pflugfelder, Gregory M. *Cartographies of Desire: Male-Male Sexuality in Japanese Discourse, 1600–1950*. Berkeley: University of California Press, 1999

Philippi, Donald L., trans. *Kojiki*. Tokyo: University of Tokyo Press, 1969.

Piggott, Joan R., ed. *Capital and Countryside in Japan, 300–1180: Japanese Historians in English*. Cornell East Asia Series, 129. Ithaca, NY: East Asia Program, Cornell University, 2006.

———. "Chieftain Pairs and Co-rulers." In Hitomi Tonomura, ed., *Women and Class in Japanese History*, 17–52. Ann Arbor: Center for Japanese Studies, University of Michigan, 1999.

———. *The Emergence of Japanese Kingship*. Stanford, CA: Stanford University Press, 1997.

———. "The Last Classical Female Sovereign: Kōken-Shōtoku Tennō." In Dorothy Ko, JaHyun Kim Haboush, and Joan R. Piggott, eds., *Women and Confucian Cultures in Premodern China, Korea, and Japan*, 47–44. Berkeley: University of California Press, 2003.

———. "Mokkan: Wooden Documents from the Nara Period." *Monumenta Nipponica* 45.4 (1990): 449–470.

———. "Review of Barnes, *State Formation in Japan*." *Journal of Japanese Studies* 35.2 (2009): 413–419.

Piggott, Joan R., et al., eds. *Dictionary of Sources of Classical Japan*. Paris: Collège de France, Diffusion De Boccard, 2006.

Piggott, Joan R., and Sanae Yoshida, eds. *Teishinkoki: The Year 939 in the Journal of Regent Fujiwara no Tadahira*. Ithaca, NY: East Asia Program, Cornell University Press 2008.

Platt, Brian. "Elegance, Prosperity, and Crisis: Three Generations of Tokugawa Village Elites," *Monumenta Nipponica* 55.1 (2000): 45–81.

Plutschow, Herbert. *Chaos and Cosmos: Ritual in Early and Medieval Japanese Literature*. Leiden, The Netherlands: E. J. Brill, 1990.

Pollack, David. *The Fracture of Meaning: The Japanese Synthesis of China from the Eighth through the Eighteenth Centuries*. Princeton, NJ: Princeton University Press, 1986.

———. *Zen Poems of the Five Mountains*. American Academy of Religion Studies in Religion, 37. New York: Crossroad Publishing Company & Scholars Press, 1985.

Pratt, Edward E. *Japan's Proto-industrial Elite: The Economic Foundations of the Gōnō*. Cambridge, MA: Harvard University East Asia Center, 1999.

Quinn, Shelley Fenno. *Developing Zeami: The Noh Actor's Attunement in Practice*. Honolulu: University of Hawai'i Press, 2005.

Rabinovitch, Judith N. *Shōmonki: The Story of Masakado's Rebellion*. Tokyo: Monumenta Nipponica Monograph, 1986.

Rabinovitch, Judith N., and Timothy R. Bradstock. *Dance of the Butterflies*. Ithaca, NY: East Asia Program, Cornell University, 2006.

Rambelli, Fabio, and Mark Teeuwen, eds. *Buddhas and Kami in Japan: Honji Suijaku as a Combinatory Paradigm*. New York: Routledge, 2003.

Ramirez-Christensen, Esperanza. *Heart's Flower: The Life and Poetry of Shinkei*. Stanford, CA: Stanford University Press, 1994.

———, trans. *Murmured Conversations: A Treatise on Poetry and Buddhism by the Poet-Monk Shinkei*. Stanford, CA: Stanford University Press, 1998.

Rath, Eric C. *The Ethos of Noh: Actors and Their Art*. Harvard East Asian Monographs, 232. Cambridge, MA: Harvard University Asia Center, 2004.

Ravina, Mark. *Land and Lordship in Early Modern Japan*. Stanford, CA: Stanford University Press, 1999.

Reichert, James. "'Samurai' Fantasies in Late-Nineteenth-Century Japan." *Issues of Canonicity and Canon Formation in Japanese Literary Studies. Proceedings of the Association for Japanese Literary Studies* 1 (2000): 193–206.

Reischauer, Edwin O. *The Japanese Today: Change and Continuity*. Cambridge, MA: Belknap Press, Harvard University Press, 1980.

———. "Japanese Feudalism." In Rushton Coulborn, ed., *Feudalism in History*, 26–48. Princeton, NJ: Princeton University Press, 1956.

Revel, Jacques, and Lynn Hunt, eds. "Braudel's Emphasis on the Long Term." In *Histories: French Constructions of the Past*, 115–145. New York: New Press, 1995.

Rhee, Song Nai, C. Melvin Aikens, Sung Rak Choi, and Hyuk-jin Ro. "Korean Contributions to Agriculture, Technology, and State Formation in Japan: Archaeology and History of an Epochal Thousand Years, 400 BCE–600 CE." *Asian Perspectives* 46.2 (2007): 404–459.

Roberson, James E., and Noboe Suzuki, eds. *Men and Masculinities in Contemporary Japan: Dislocating the Salaryman Doxa*. London: Routledge, 2003.

Roberts, Luke S. *Mercantilism in a Japanese Domain: The Merchant Origins of Economic Nationalism in 18th-Century Tosa*. Cambridge: Cambridge University Press, 1998.

Robertson, Jennifer. "The Shingaku Woman: Straight from the Heart." In Gail Lee Bernstein, ed., *Recreating Japanese Women, 1600–1945*, 88–107. Berkeley: University of California Press, 1991.

Rodd, Laurel Rasplica, and Mary Catherine Henkenius, trans. *Kokinshū: A Collection of Poems Ancient and Modern*. Princeton, NJ: Princeton University Press, 1984.

Rothery, David A. *Volcanoes, Earthquakes and Tsunamis*. London: Hodder Education, 2007.

Rubinger, Richard. *Popular Literacy in Early Modern Japan*. Honolulu: University of Hawai'i Press, 2007.

———. *Private Academies of Tokugawa Japan*. Princeton, NJ: Princeton University Press, 1982.

Ruppert, Brian. *Jewel in the Ashes: Buddha Relics and Power in Early Medieval Japan*. Cambridge, MA: Harvard University Asia Center, 2000.

Ruch, Barbara, ed. *Engendering Faith: Women and Buddhism in Premodern Japan*. Ann Arbor: Center for Japanese Studies, University of Michigan, 2002.

———. *Mō hitotsu no chūsei zō: Bikuni, otogi zōshi, raise*. Kyoto: Shibunkaku, 1991.

Ruijū sandaikyaku. 2 vols., Shintei zōho kokushi taikei. Tokyo: Yoshikawa kōbunkan, 1983.

Ryō no gige. Shintei zōho kokushi taikei. Tokyo: Yoshikawa kōbunkan, 1985.

Sakurai Yuki. "Perpetual Dependency: The Life Course of Male Workers in a Merchant House." In Sabine Frühstück and Anne Walthall, eds., *Recreating Japanese Men*, 115–134. Berkeley: University of California Press, 2011.

Sanford, James H. *Zen Man Ikkyū*. Studies in World Religions, 2. Chico, CA: Scholars Press, 1981.

Sanjūniban shokunin utawase e. In Mori Tōru, ed., *Shinshū Nihon emakimono zenshū*, vol. 28. Tokyo: Kadokawa shoten, 1979.

Sansom, George. *A History of Japan*. 3 vols. Stanford, CA: Stanford University Press, 1958.

Sasaki Gin'ya, with William B. Hauser. "Sengoku Daimyō Rule and Commerce." In John W. Hall, Nagahara Keiji, and Kozo Yamamura, eds., *Japan Before Tokugawa: Political Consolidation and Economic Growth, 1500 to 1650*, 125–148. Princeton, NJ: Princeton University Press, 1981.

Sasaki Muneo. "The Court-Centered Polity." In Joan R. Piggott, ed., *Capital and Countryside: Japanese Historians in English*, 227–244. Cornell East Asia Series, 129. Ithaca, NY: East Asia Program, Cornell University, 2006.

Sato, Elizabeth. "The Early Development of the Shoen." In John W. Hall and Jeffrey P. Mass, eds., *Medieval Japan: Essays in Institutional History*, 91–108. 1974. Reprint, Stanford, CA: Stanford University Press, 1988.

Satō Shin'ichi, Ikeuchi Yoshisuke, and Momose Kesao, eds. *Chūsei hōsei shiryō-shū*. 6 vols. Tokyo: Iwanami shoten, 1965–2001.

Sawada, Janine. *Confucian Values and Popular Zen: Sekimon Shingaku in Eighteenth-Century Japan*. Honolulu: University of Hawai'i Press, 1993.

———. "Tokugawa Religious History: Studies in Western Languages." *Early Modern Japan* 10.1 (2002): 39–85.

Schalow, Paul Gordon, trans. *The Great Mirror of Male Love*. Stanford, CA: Stanford University Press, 1990.

Screech, Timon. *The Lens Within the Heart: The Western Scientific Gaze and Popular Imagery in Later Edo Japan*. Honolulu: University of Hawai'i Press, 2002.

———. *Sex and the Floating World*. Honolulu: University of Hawai'i Press, 1999.

Seeley, Christopher. *A History of Writing in Japan*. Honolulu: University of Hawai'i Press, 2000.

Segal, Ethan Isaac. "Awash in Coins: The Spread of Money in Early Medieval Japan." In Gordon M. Berger, Andrew Edmund Goble, Lorraine F. Harrington, and G. Cameron Hurst III, eds., *Currents in Medieval Japanese History: Essays in Honor of Jeffrey P. Mass*, 331–361. Los Angeles: Figueroa Press, 2009.

———. *Coins, Trade, and the State: Economic Growth in Early Medieval Japan*. Cambridge, MA: Harvard University Asia Center, 2011.

Seidensticker, Edward G., trans. *The Gossamer Years*. Routledge, VT: Tuttle, 1989.

———, trans. *The Tale of Genji*. New York: Knopf 1978.

Seigle, Cecilia Segawa. *Yoshiwara: The Glittering World of the Japanese Courtesan*. Honolulu: University of Hawai'i Press, 1993.

Sen Sōshitsu XV. *The Japanese Way of Tea: From Its Origins in China to Sen Rikyū*. Translated by V. Dixon Morris. Honolulu: University of Hawai'i Press, 1998.

Shimada, Ryūto. *The Intra-Asian Trade in Japanese Copper by the Dutch East India Company*. Leiden, The Netherlands: E. J. Brill, 2006.

Shimizu, Akitoshi. "Ie and Dozoku: Family and Descent in Japan." *Current Anthropology* 28.4 (1987): S85–S90.

Shinoda, Minoru. *The Founding of the Kamakura Shogunate, 1180–1185: With Selected Translations from the* Azuma Kagami. New York: Columbia University Press, 1960.

"Shin sarugakki." In *Kodai seiji shakai shisō*. Tokyo: Iwanami shoten, 1986.

Shirane, Haruo, ed. *Traditional Japanese Literature: An Anthology; Beginnings to 1600*. New York: Columbia University Press, 2007.

———. *Early Modern Japanese Literature: An Anthology, 1600–1900*. New York: Columbia University Press, 2002.

Shively, Donald H. *The Love Suicide at Amijima: A Study of a Japanese Domestic Tragedy by Chikamatsu Monzaemon*. Ann Arbor: University of Michigan Press, 1953. Reprint, 1991.

Shively, Donald H., and William H. McCullough, eds. *The Cambridge History of Japan*, Vol. 2: *Heian Japan*. New York: Cambridge University Press, 1999.

Shoku Nihongi. 2 vols. Shintei zōho kokushi taikei. Tokyo: Yoshikawa kōbunkan, 1986.

Simkin, C. G. F. *The Traditional Trade of Asia*. London: Oxford University Press, 1968.

Skord, Virginia, trans. *Tales of Tears and Laughter: Short Fiction of Medieval Japan*. Honolulu: University of Hawai'i Press, 1991.

Smith, Henry D., II. "The Capacity of Chūshingura." *Monumenta Nipponica* 58.1 (2003): 1–42.

Smith, Thomas C. *The Agrarian Origins of Modern Japan*. Stanford, CA: Stanford University Press, 1959.

———. *Native Sources of Japanese Industrialization, 1750–1920*. Berkeley: University of California Press, 1989.

Smits, Gregory. *Visions of Ryukyu: Identity and Ideology in Early-Modern Thought and Politics*. Honolulu: University of Hawai'i Press, 1999.

So, Kwan-wai. *Japanese Piracy in Ming China During the Sixteenth Century*. East Lansing: Michigan State University Press, 1975.

Souyri, Pierre Francois. *The World Turned Upside Down: Medieval Japanese Society*. Translated by Käthe Roth. New York: Columbia University Press, 2001.

Statler, Oliver. *Japanese Inn*. New York: Secker & Warburg, 1961.

Steenstrup, Carl. "The Gokurakuji Letter: Hojo Shigetoki's Compendium of Political and Religious Ideas of 13th Century Japan." *Monumenta Nipponica* 32.1 (1977): 1–34.

———. *Hojo Shigetoki (1198–1261) and His Role in the History of Political and Ethical Ideas in Japan*. London: Curzon Press, 1979.

———. "Hojo Shigetoki's Letter of Instruction to His Son, Naga-toki: A Guide to Success in 13th Century Japan." *Acta Asiatica* 36 (1974): 417–438.

———. "The Imagawa Letter: A Muromachi Warrior's Code of Conduct Which Became a Tokugawa Schoolbook." *Monumenta Nipponica* 28.3 (1973): 295–316.

———. "The Origins of the Houselaws (Kakun) of the Warriors of Medieval Japan." *Proceedings of the International Association of Historians of Asia, 7th Conference Bankok 2* (1977): 868–909.

———. "Sata Mirensho: A 14th Century Law Primer." *Monumenta Nipponica* 35.4 (1980): 405–436.

Stone, Jacqueline. *Original Enlightenment and the Transformation of Medieval Japanese Buddhism*. Honolulu: University of Hawai'i Press, 1999.

Tabata Yasuko. *Nihon chūsei joseishiron*. Tokyo: Chikuma shobō, 1994.

Takahashi Tomio and Karl Friday. "The Classical Polity and Its Frontier." In Joan R. Piggott, ed. *Capital and Countryside in Japan, 300–1180: Japanese Historians in English*, 130–145. Cornell East Asia Series, 129. Ithaca, NY: East Asia Program, Cornell University, 2006.

Tanabe, George J., Jr. *Myōe the Dreamkeeper: Fantasy and Knowledge in Early Kamakura Buddhism*. Cambridge, MA: Harvard University Press, 1992.

Tanaka Takeo, with Robert Sakai. "Japan's Relations with Overseas Countries." In John Whitney Hall and Toyoda Takeshi, eds., *Japan in the Muromachi Age*, 159–178. Berkeley: University of California Press, 1977.

Tashiro Kazui and Susan Downing Videen. "Foreign Relations During the Edo Period: *Sakoku* Reexamined." *Journal of Japanese Studies* 8.2 (1982): 283–306.

Teeuwen, Mark. "Comparative Perspectives on the Emergence of Jindō and Shinto." *Bulletin of SOAS* 70.2 (2007): 373–402.

Teeuwen, Mark, and John Breen. *A New History of Shinto*. New York: Wiley-Blackwell, 2010.

Teeuwen, Mark, and Bernhard Scheid. *The Culture of Secrecy in Japanese Religion*. London: Routledge, 2006.

———. "Tracing Shinto in the History of Kami Worship." *Journal of Japanese Studies* 29.3–4 (2002): 195–207.

Teeuwen, Mark, and Fabio Rambelli. *Buddhas and Kami in Japan: Honji Suijaku as a Combinatory Paradigm*. London: Routledge, 2002.

Thal, Sarah. *Rearranging the Landscape of the Gods: The Politics of a Pilgrimage Site in Japan, 1573–1912*. Chicago: University of Chicago Press, 2005.

Toby, Ronald P. "Carnival of the Aliens: Korean Embassies in Edo-Period Art and Popular Culture." *Monumenta Nipponica* 41.4 (1986): 415–456.

———. *Japan and Its Worlds: Marius Jansen and the Internationalization of Japanese History*. Tokyo: I-House Press, 2007.

———. "Rescuing the Nation from History: The State of the State in Early Modern Japan." *Monumenta Nipponica* 56.2 (2001): 197–237.

———. *Sakoku to iu gaikō*. Tokyo: Shogakukan, 2008.

———. *State and Diplomacy in Early Modern Japan: Asia in the Development of the Tokugawa Bakufu*. Princeton, NJ: Princeton University Press, 1984.

———. "Why Leave Nara? Kammu and the Transfer of the Capital." *Monumenta Nipponica* 40.3 (1985): 330–347.

Toby, Ronald P., with Kuroda Hideo. *Gyoretsu to misemono*. Tokyo: Asahi Newspaper Company Publishing, 1994.

Tonomura, Hitomi. *Community and Commerce in Late Medieval Japan: The Corporate Villages of Tokuchin-ho*. Stanford, CA: Stanford University Press, 1992.

———. "Re-envisioning Women in the Post-Kamakura Age." In Jeffrey P. Mass, ed., *The Origins of Japan's Medieval World: Courtiers, Clerics, Warriors, and Peasants in the Fourteenth Century*, 138–169. Stanford, CA: Stanford University Press, 1997.

———. "Women and Inheritance in Japan's Early Warrior Society." *Comparative Studies in Society and History* 32.3 (July 1990): 592–623.

———. "Women and Sexuality in Premodern Japan." In William A. Tsutsui, ed., *A Companion to Japanese History*, 351–371. Malden, MA: Blackwell, 2007.

Tonomura, Hitomi, Anne Walthall, and Wakita Haruko, eds. *Women and Class in Japanese History.* Ann Arbor: Center for Japanese Studies, University of Michigan, 1999.

Totman, Conrad. *The Collapse of the Tokugawa Bakufu, 1862–1868*. Honolulu: University of Hawai'i Press, 1980.

———. *Early Modern Japan*. Berkeley: University of California Press, 1995.

———. *The Green Archipelago: Forestry in Preindustrial Japan*. Berkeley: University of California Press, 1989.

———. *A History of Japan*. Oxford: Blackwell, 2000.

———. *The Origins of Japan's Modern Forests: The Case of Akita*. Honolulu: University of Hawai'i Press, 1984.

———. *Politics in the Tokugawa Bakufu*. Cambridge, MA: Harvard University Press, 1967.

———. *Tokugawa Ieyasu: Shogun*. Tokyo: Heian International, 1983.

Toyoda Takeshi. *A History of Pre-Meiji Commerce in Japan*. Tokyo: Kokusai bunka shinkokai, 1959.

Trewartha, Glenn T. *Japan: a Geography*. Madison: University of Wisconsin Press, 1978.

Troost, Kristina. "Peasants, Elites, and Villages in the Fourteenth Century." In Jeffrey P. Mass, ed., *The Origins of Japan's Medieval World: Courtiers, Clerics, Warriors, and Peasants in the Fourteenth Century*, 91–109. Stanford, CA: Stanford University Press, 1997.

Tsang, Carol Richmond. *War and Faith: Ikkō Ikki in Late Muromachi Japan*. Cambridge, MA: Harvard University Asia Center, 2007.

Tsude Hiroshi. "Chiefly Lineages in Kofun-Period Japan: Political Relations Between Centre and Region." *Antiquity* 64 (1990): 923–931.

Tsude Hiroshi and Walter Edwards. "Early State Formation in Japan." In Joan R. Piggott, ed. *Capital and Countryside in Japan, 300–1180: Japanese Historians in English*, 13–53. Cornell East Asia Series, 129. Ithaca, NY: East Asia Program, Cornell University, 2006.

Tsukada, Matsuo. "Vegetation in Prehistoric Japan: The Last 20,000 Years." In R. Pearson et al., eds., *Windows on the Japanese Past: Studies in Archaeology and Prehistory*, 11–56. Ann Arbor: Center for Japanese Studies, University of Michigan, 1986.

Tsunoda Ryūsaku and L. Carrington Goodrich. *Japan in the Chinese Dynastic Histories: Later Han through Ming Dynasties*. South Pasadena, CA: P. D. and Ione Perkins, 1952.

Tsutsui, William M., ed. *A Companion to Japanese History*. Chichester, West Sussex, UK: Wiley-Blackwell, 2007.

Tuge, Hideomi. *Historical Development of Science and Technology in Japan*. Tokyo: Kokusai bunka shinkokai, 1968.

Turnbull, Stephen R. *The Kakure Kirishitan of Japan: A Study of Their Development, Beliefs and Rituals to the Present Day*. Richmond, UK: Japan Library, Curzon Books, 1998.

Tyler, Royall, trans. and ed. *Japanese Nō Dramas*. New York: Penguin Books, 1992.

———, trans. *The Tale of Genji*. New York: Viking 2001.

Uezato, Takashi. "The Formation of the Port City of Naha in Ryukyu and the World of Maritime Asia from the Perspective of the Japanese Network." *Acta Asiatica* 95 (2008): 57–77.

Uno, Kathleen S. "The Household Division of Labor." In Gail Lee Bernstein, ed., *Recreating Japanese Women, 1600–1945*, 17–41. Berkeley: University of California Press, 1991.

Ury, Marian. *Poems of the Five Mountains: An Introduction to the Literature of the Zen Monasteries*. 2nd ed., revised. Michigan Monograph Series in Japanese Studies, 10. Ann Arbor: Center for Japanese Studies, University of Michigan, 1992.

Van Goethem, Ellen. *Nagaoka: Japan's Forgotten Capital*. Leiden, The Netherlands: E. J. Brill, 1990.

Vaporis, Constantine N. "Post Station and Assisting Villages: Corvee Labor and Peasant Contention." *Monumenta Nipponica* 41.4 (1986): 377–414.

———. "To Edo and Back: Alternate Attendance and Japanese Culture in the Early Modern Period." *Journal of Japanese Studies* 23.1 (1997): 25–67.

———. *Tour of Duty: Samurai, Military Service in Edo, and the Culture of Early Modern Japan*. Honolulu: University of Hawai'i Press, 2008.

Varley, H. Paul, trans. *A Chronicle of Gods and Sovereigns: Jinnō Shōtōki of Kitabatake Chikafusa*. New York: Columbia University Press, 1980.

———. "The Hōjō Family and Succession to Power." In Jeffrey P. Mass, ed., *Court and Bakufu in Japan: Essays in Kamakura History*, 143–167. New Haven: Yale University Press, 1982.

———. *Imperial Restoration in Medieval Japan*. New York: Columbia University Press, 1971.

———. *The Onin War: History of Its Origins and Background, with a Selective Translation of the Chronicles of Onin*. New York: Columbia University Press, 1967.

———. "The Place of Gukansho in Japanese Intellectual History." *Monumenta Nipponica* 34.4 (1979): 479–488.

———. *Warriors of Japan As Portrayed in the War Tales*. Honolulu: University of Hawai'i Press, 1994.

Verschuer, Charlotte von. *Across the Perilous Sea: Japanese Trade with China and Korea from the Seventh to the Sixteenth Centuries*. Translated by Kristen Lee Hunter. Cornell East Asia Series, 133. Ithaca, NY: East Asia Program, Cornell University, 2006.

———. "Ashikaga Yoshimitsu's Foreign Policy, 1398–1408 AD: A Translation from *Zenrin Kokuhōki*, the Cambridge Manuscript." *Monumenta Nipponica* 62.3 (2007): 261–297.

———. "Demographic Estimates and the Issue of Staple Food in Early Japan." *Monumenta Nipponica* 64.2 (2009): 337–362.

———. "Japan's Foreign Relations, 1200–1392 AD: A Translation from *Zenrin Kokuhōki*." *Monumenta Nipponica* 57.4 (2002): 413–445.

———. *Le riz dans la culture de Heian: Mythe et réalité*. Paris: Collège de France; distributed by De Boccard, 2003.

———. *Les relations officielles du Japon avec la Chine aux VIIIe et IXe siècles*. Geneva: Librairie Droz, 1985.

———. "Life of Commoners in the Provinces: The Owari no gebumi of 988." In Mikael Adolphson, Edward Kamens, and Stacie Matsumoto, eds. *Heian Japan: Centers and Peripheries*, 305–328. Honolulu: University of Hawai'i Press, 2007.

———. "Looking from Within and Without: Ancient and Medieval External Relations." *Monumenta Nipponica* 55.4 (2000): 537–566.

Vovin, Alexander, trans. *Man'yōshū: Book 15*. Folkestone, UK: Global Oriental, 2009.

Wakabayashi, Bob Tadashi. *Anti-foreignism and Western Learning in Early-Modern Japan*. Cambridge, MA: Council of East Asian Studies, Harvard University, 1986.

Waida Manabu. "Sacred Kingship in Early Japan." *History of Religions* 15.4 (1976) 319–342.

Wakita Haruko. "Cities in Medieval Japan." *Acta Asiatica* 44 (1983): 28–52.

———. "Marriage and Property in Premodern Japan from the Perspective of Women's History." *Journal of Japanese Studies* 1.2 (1984): 321–345.

———. *Women in Medieval Japan: Motherhood, Household, Management, and Sexuality*. Translated by Alison Tokita. Tokyo: University of Tokyo Press, 2006.

Wakita Osamu. "The Emergence of the State in 16th Century Japan from Oda to Tokugawa." *Journal of Japanese Studies* 8.2 (1982): 343–369.

———. "Kokudaka System: Device for Unification." *Journal of Japanese Studies* 1.2 (1975): 297–320.

Walker, Brett. *The Conquest of Ainu Lands: Ecology and Culture in Japanese Expansion, 1590–1800*. Berkeley: University of California Press, 2001.

Walthall, Anne. "The Family Ideology of Rural Entrepreneurs in Nineteenth-Century Japan." *Journal of Social History* 23.3 (1990): 463–483.

———. *The Weak Body of a Useless Women: Matsuo Taseko and the Meiji Restoration*. Chicago: University of Chicago Press, 1998.

———, ed. *Servants of the Dynasty: Palace Women in World History*. Berkeley: University of California Press, 2008.

Walthall, Anne, Patricia Ebrey, and James Palais. *East Asia: A Cultural, Social, and Political History*. Florence, KY: Wadsworth, 2008.

Wang Zhenping. *Ambassadors from the Islands of the Immortals: China-Japan Relations in the Han-Tang Period.* Honolulu: University of Hawai'i Press, 2005.

Watsky, Andrew M. *Chikubushima: Deploying the Sacred Arts in Momoyama Japan*. Seattle: University of Washington Press, 2004.

Watson, Burton, trans. *The Demon at Agi Bridge and Other Japanese Tales*. Edited, with an Introduction, by Haruo Shirane. New York: Columbia University Press, 2011.

———. *Kanshi: The Poetry of Ishikawa Jōzan and Other Edo-Period Poets*. New York: North Point Press, 1990.

Whelan, Christal. *The Beginning of Heaven and Earth: The Sacred Book of Japan's Hidden Christians*. Honolulu: The University of Hawai'i Press, 1996.

White, James W. *Ikki: Social Conflict and Political Protest in Early Modern Japan*. Ithaca, NY: Cornell University Press, 1995.

Wigen, Kären. *The Making of a Japanese Periphery, 1750–1920*. Berkeley: University of California Press, 1995.

Wickham, Chris. "Historical Transitions: A Comparative Approach." *Medieval History Journal* 13.1 (2010): 1–21.

Wiley, Peter Booth. *Yankees in the Land of the Gods: Commodore Perry and the Opening of Japan*. New York: Viking, 1990.

Williams, Duncan. *The Other Side of Zen: A Social History of Sōtō Zen Buddhism in Tokugawa Japan*. Princeton, NJ: Princeton University Press, 2005.

Wilson, William R. "The Way of the Bow and Arrow: The Japanese Warrior in the Kojaku Monogatari." *Monumenta Nipponica* 28.1–4 (1973): 177–233.

Wintersteen, Prescott. "The Muromachi Shugo and Hanzei." In John W. Hall and Jeffrey P. Mass, eds., *Medieval Japan: Essays in Institutional History*, 210–220. 1974. Reprint, Stanford, CA: Stanford University Press, 1988.

Yamada, Shōji. *Shots in the Dark: Japan, Zen, and the West (Buddhism and Modernity)*. Translated by Earl Hartman. Nichibunken Monograph Series, 9. Chicago: University of Chicago Press; Kyoto: International Research Center for Japanese Studies, 2009.

Yamamura, Kozo. "The Growth of Commerce." In Kozo Yamamura, ed., *The Cambridge History of Japan*, Vol. 3: *Medieval Japan*, 344–395. Cambridge: Cambridge University Press, 1990.

———. "The Increasing Poverty of the Samurai in Tokugawa Japan, 1600–1868." *Journal of Economic History* 31.2 (1971): 378–406.

———, ed. *The Cambridge History of Japan*, Vol. 3: *Medieval Japan*. Cambridge: Cambridge University Press, 1990.

Yamamura, Kozo, and Murakami Yasusuke. "Ie Society as a Pattern of Civilization: Introduction." *Journal of Japanese Studies* 10.2 (1984): 279–363.

Yamamura, Kozo, and Tetsuo Kamiki. "Silver Mines and Sung Coin: A Monetary History of Medieval and Modern Japan in International Perspective." In J. F.

Richards, ed., *Precious Metals in the Early Medieval and Early Modern Worlds*, 329–362. Durham, NC: Carolina Academic Press, 1983.
Yanase Kazuo. *Hōjōki kaishaku taisei*. Tokyo: Taishūkan Shoten, 1972.
Yasuraoka Kōsaku. *Tsurezuregusa zenchūshaku*. 2 vols. Tokyo: Kadokawa Shoten, 1967.
Yokota Fuyuhiko. "Imagining Working Women in Early Modern Japan." In Hitomi Tonomura, Anne Walthall, and Wakita Haruko, eds., *Women and Class in Japanese History*, 153–168. Ann Arbor: University of Michigan Press, 1999.
Yonehara Masayoshi. *Sengoku bushi to bungei no kenkyū*. Tokyo: Ōfūsha, 1976.
Yonekura, N., et al. *Nihon no chikei 1: sosetsu*. Tokyo: Tokyo University Press, 2001.
Yoshida Kenkō. *Essays in Idleness: The Tsurezuregusa of Kenkō*. Translated by Donald Keene. New York: Columbia University Press, 1967.
Yoshie, Akiko. "Gender in Early Classical Japan: Marriage, Leadership, and Political Status in Village and Palace." *Monumenta Nipponica* 60.4 (2005): 437–479.
Yoshikawa Torao, Kaizuka Sohei, and Ota Yoko. *The Landforms of Japan*. Tokyo: University of Tokyo Press, 1981.
Zhushchikhovskaya, Irina S. *Prehistoric Pottery-Making of the Russian Far East*. BAR International Series 1434. Oxford: Archaeo Press, 2005.

About the Authors

Mikael S. Adolphson is Professor of Japanese Cultural Studies in the Department of East Asian Studies at the University of Alberta. He is the author of *The Gates of Power: Monks, Courtiers, and Warriors in Premodern Japan* and *The Teeth and Claws of the Buddha: Monastic Warriors and* Sōhei *in Japanese History*, as well as the coeditor (with Edward Kamens and Stacie Matsumoto) of *Heian Japan: Centers and Peripheries.*

C. Melvin Aikens was born in Ogden, Utah, in 1938. He holds a B.A. in anthropology from the University of Utah (1960), and M.A. and Ph.D. degrees in anthropology from the University of Chicago (1962 and 1966). He has studied cultural history and human ecology in western North America since the late 1950s and, since 1971, also in Japan, with collateral interests in Korea, China, and Northeast Asia. His early academic appointments were at the University of Utah and the University of Nevada–Reno, with most of his career spent at the University of Oregon, where he is now Professor Emeritus.

Barbara Ambros earned her Ph.D. in East Asian languages and civilizations from Harvard University. She is Associate Professor of Religious Studies at the University of North Carolina, Chapel Hill. Her research interests include topics in early modern and contemporary Japanese religions such as pilgrimage and sacred space, religion and ethnicity in Asian diaspora communities, human-animal relationships, and religion and the environment. She is the author of *Emplacing a Pilgrimage: The Ōyama Cult and Regional Religion in Early Modern Japan* and *Bones of Contention: Animals and Religion in Contemporary Japan.*

Gina L. Barnes is Professor Emeritus at Durham University and Professorial Research Associate at the School of Oriental and African Studies, University of London. She taught East Asian archaeology at Cambridge University for fifteen years (1981–1995) before becoming Professor of Japanese Studies in the Department of East Asian Studies at Durham (1996–2006). Her work focuses on early state formation in Japan and Korea, with a strong interest in geoarchaeology as well. Her books include *The Rise* *of Civilization in East Asia: The Archaeology of China; Korea and Japan; State Formation in Korea*; and *State Formation in Japan*.

Bruce L. Batten (Ph.D., Stanford, 1989) is Professor of Japanese History and Vice President for International Affairs at J. F. Oberlin University, Tokyo. A specialist on ancient and medieval Japan, he is the author of *To the Ends of Japan: Premodern Frontiers, Boundaries, and Interactions* and *Gateway to Japan: Hakata in War and Peace, 500–1300*. His current research focuses on climate change in Japanese history.

Ross Bender received his Ph.D. in premodern Japanese history and religion from Columbia University in 1980. He is an independent scholar specializing in the Nara period. In addition to his early work on the Hachiman cult, Bender has more recently published articles on the imperial edicts and royal political theology in Nara. His book reviews, occasional research notes, and translations may be found in *PMJS Papers* and Academia.edu.

Mary Elizabeth Berry is Class of 1944 Professor of History at the University of California, Berkeley. She is the author of *Hideyoshi, The Culture of Civil War in Kyoto*, and *Japan in Print: Information and Nation in the Early Modern Period*. She is an elected member of the American Academy of Arts and Sciences and a former president of the Association for Asian Studies.

William M. Bodiford is a professor in the Department of Asian Languages and Cultures at the University of California, Los Angeles, where he teaches courses on religion in the cultures of Japan and East Asia, and Buddhist studies. He received his Ph.D. from Yale University. He also studied in Japan at Tsukuba University and Komazawa University. His research spans the medieval, early modern, and contemporary periods of Japanese history. Currently he is investigating religion during the Tokugawa period, especially those aspects of Japanese culture associated with manuscripts, printing, secrecy, education, and proselytizing. Although many of his publications focus on Zen Buddhism (especially Soto Zen), he also researches Tendai and Vinaya Buddhist traditions, Shintō, folklore, and popular religions, as well as Japanese martial arts and traditional approaches to health and physical culture.

Robert Borgen is Professor Emeritus of Japanese Literature and History at the University of California, Davis. His research focuses on Heian court culture and early Sino-Japanese relations. His publications include *Sugawara no Michizane and the Early Heian Court* and various articles, notably on Tenjin worship and on the pilgrimage to China by the monk Jōjin in 1072–1073.

Philip Brown is Professor of Japanese History at The Ohio State University. He is author of *Cultivating Commons: Joint Ownership of Arable Land in Early Modern Japan*; *Central Authority and Local Autonomy in Early Modern Japan: The Case of Kaga*

Domain; and numerous articles appearing in the *Journal of Asian Studies, Social Science History, Historical Geography,* the *Journal of Japanese Studies,* and other English- and Japanese-language journals, essay collections, and reference works.

Lee Butler is an independent scholar of the late medieval and early modern eras. His work extends from cultural and social history to art history and linguistics. His publications include *Emperor and Aristocracy in Japan, 1467–1680: Resilience and Renewal*; "Patronage and the Building Arts in Tokugawa Japan"; and "'Washing Off the Dust': Baths and Bathing in Late Medieval Japan." A forthcoming study examines the political and social history of southern Izumi during the opening years of the sixteenth century, based on the diary of Kujō Masamoto.

Frank Chance is Associate Director of the Center for East Asian Studies, University of Pennsylvania. A scholar of East Asian art born and raised in Kansas City, Kansas, he received bachelor's and master's degrees in Asian art history from the University of Kansas, and his Ph.D. from the University of Washington. He has served as Director of Shofuso, a Japanese house and garden in Fairmount Park, Philadelphia; curated exhibitions of Japanese prints at the University of Pennsylvania Museum, Haverford College, and Ursinus College; and served for three years as Far Eastern Bibliographer for the Marquand Library of Art and Archaeology at Princeton University. Though his primary research has been in Japanese art, he has also studied the arts of China and Korea extensively. His most recent publication, *Modern Impressions: Theatre Prints from the Gilbert and Shirley Luber Collection*, was co-authored with Julie Nelson Davis of the University of Pennsylvania.

Linda H. Chance is Associate Professor of Japanese Language and Literature in the Department of East Asian Languages and Civilizations at the University of Pennsylvania. Her specialization is nonfiction prose of the medieval era. She would never have gone into the field without the encouragement Professor Hurst gave her at the University of Kansas in 1977. Her book, *Formless in Form: Kenkō, Tsurezuregusa, and the Rhetoric of Japanese Fragmentary Prose,* is not his fault, however.

Thomas D. Conlan, Professor of Japanese history at Bowdoin College, graduated from the University of Michigan (B.A.) and Stanford University (M.A., Ph.D.). He is the author of *In Little Need of Divine Intervention*, *State of War: The Violent Order of Fourteenth Century Japan*, *Weapons and Fighting Techniques of the Samurai*, and *From Sovereign to Symbol: An Age of Ritual Determinism in Fourteenth-Century Japan*, which explores how ritual mimesis determined political legitimacy in fourteenth-century Japan.

David Eason is Assistant Professor of Japanese in the Department of East Asian Studies at the University at Albany, State University of New York. His main area of research concerns late medieval and early modern legal and cultural history, with a focus on conflict and dispute resolution. He received his doctorate in history from the University of California, Los Angeles, in 2009. He has regularly participated in a series of recent workshops and conferences organized around the theme of "Japan's Long Sixteenth Century" and is currently at work on a larger study that examines the interplay among legal codes, violence, and emotional rhetoric in late-sixteenth- and early-seventeenth-century Japan.

Karl F. Friday (Ph.D., Stanford University, 1989) is the Director of the IES Abroad Tokyo Center. A specialist in the Heian and Kamakura periods, his publications include *Hired Swords: The Rise of Private Warrior Power in Early Japan*; *Legacies of the Sword: The Kashima Shinryu and Samurai Martial Culture*; *Samurai, Warfare, and the State in Early Medieval Japan*; *The First Samurai: The Life and Legend of the Warrior Rebel Taira Masakado*, and numerous shorter works.

Douglas Fuqua is Professor and Vice Chancellor at Hawai'i Tokai International College. He received his M.A. in archaeology from Meiji University (1995) and his Ph.D. in history from the University of Hawai'i at Manoa (2004). His doctoral dissertation is titled "The Japanese Missions to Tang China and Maritime Exchange in East Asia, 7th–9th Centuries."

Denis Gainty is Assistant Professor of History at Georgia State University, where he teaches courses in World and Asian history. His work investigates how social and biological bodies are envisioned and experienced in the context of modern collectives. He is the author of the forthcoming book *Martial Arts and the Body Politic in Meiji Japan.*

Andrew Edmund Goble is Associate Professor of Japanese History and of Religious Studies at the University of Oregon. A specialist on medieval Japan, his interdisciplinary research spans a wide range of topics. Earlier research focused on institutional, social, and intellectual history: the government of the Kamakura shogunate, the fourteenth-century Kenmu revolution, and the intellectual profile of Emperor Hanazono. His recent research has focused on premodern medical history. Recent publications include *Confluences of Medicine in Medieval Japan: Buddhist Healing, Chinese Knowledge, Islamic Formulas, and Wounds of War*; "Images of Illness: Interpreting the Medieval *Scrolls of Afflictions*"; and "Rhythms of Medicine and Community in Late Sixteenth Century Japan: Yamashina Tokitsune (1543–1611) and His Patients." He is coeditor of *Tools of Culture: Japan's Cultural, Intellectual, Medical, and Technological Contacts in East Asia, 1000s–1500s* and *Currents in Medieval Japanese History: Essays in Honor of Jeffrey P. Mass.*

David L. Howell is Professor of Japanese History at Harvard University. He is the author of two books—*Capitalism from Within: Economy, Society, and the State in a Japanese Fishery* (1995) and *Geographies of Identity in Nineteenth-Century Japan* (2005)—and numerous articles on Tokugawa and Meiji social history, including "The Social Life of Firearms in Tokugawa Japan" (2009) and "The Girl with the Horse-

Dung Hairdo," in *Looking Modern: East Asian Visual Culture from the Treaty Ports to World War II* (2010). Howell's current research is on the fear of social disorder in the decades preceding the Meiji Restoration.

Thomas Keirstead is Chair of the Department of East Asian Studies at the University of Toronto. His major publications include *The Geography of Power in Medieval Japan*; "Gardens and Estates: Medievality and Space"; "Inventing Medieval Japan: The History and Politics of National Identity"; and "Outcastes Before the Law: Pollution and Purification in Medieval Japan."

Michael Laver received his doctorate in East Asian languages and civilizations from the University of Pennsylvania, where he studied under Cappy Hurst. He is Assistant Professor of History at the Rochester Institute of Technology in Rochester, New York, and is the author of *Japan's Economy by Proxy in the Seventeenth Century* and *The Sakoku Edicts and the Politics of Tokugawa Hegemony*. In the few moments in which he is not consumed with getting tenure, Professor Laver enjoys spending time with his wife, Annie, and two boys, Bennie and Ham.

Joan R. Piggott is Gordon L. MacDonald Professor of History and Director of the Project for Premodern Japan Studies at the University of Southern California in Los Angeles. She is the author of *The Emergence of Japanese Kingship* and coeditor of *Dictionary of Sources of Classical Japan* (with Ivo Smits, Michel Viellard-Baron, Ineke Van Put, and Charlotte von Verschuer); *Capital and Countryside in Japan 300–1180*; and *Teishinkoki: The Year 939 in the Journal of Regent Fujiwara no Tadahira* (with Sanae Yoshida). She is currently finishing a translation and research on Fujiwara Akihira's *New Monkey Music* (*Shinsarugakuki*), which portrays the urban world of the Heian capital in the mid-eleventh century, as the Fujiwara regency faded and the leadership of retired monarchs was emerging.

Richard Rubinger received his Ph.D. from Columbia University in 1979. He has taught Japanese language and history at Vanderbilt University, University of Hawai'i, and now Indiana University. He specializes in Tokugawa and Meiji educational history and the history of literacy. He is the author of *Private Academies of Tokugawa Japan*, *Popular Literacy in Early Modern Japan,* and numerous articles and chapters in books. He has been a visiting professor at Columbia University (1984–1986), the Jinbun Kagaku Kenkyūjo at Kyoto University (1994–1995), Nichibunken (2000–2001) in Kyoto, and the University of Paris (2003). He was Chair of the Department of East Asian Languages and Culture at Indiana University in 1990–1993 and 1998–2002.

Ethan Segal is Associate Professor of East Asian History at Michigan State University. He earned his Ph.D. at Stanford University and was a Fulbright Scholar at the University of Tokyo. Topics of Segal's research include money and trade, women and gender, history education, and depictions of Japan in Hollywood film. He has published articles in a variety of journals, and his first book, *Coins, Trade, and the State:*

Economic Growth in Early Medieval Japan, was published by Harvard University Press in 2011.

Joseph T. Sorensen is an Assistant Professor of Japanese at the University of California, Davis. His forthcoming book, *Optical Allusions: Screens, Painting, and Poetry in Classical Japan*, is about screen poetry of the Heian and Kamakura periods. His research focuses on the social and literary contexts of *waka* composition.

Mark Teeuwen is Professor of Japanese Studies at Oslo University, Norway. He has published extensively on the history of *kami* cults and Shintō. His main publications are *A New History of Shinto* (with John Breen); *The Culture of Secrecy in Japanese Religion* (with Bernhard Scheid); *Buddhas and Kami in Japan* (with Fabio Rambelli); and "Tracing Shinto in the History of Kami Worship" (special issue of *Japanese Journal of Religious Studies*; with Bernhard Scheid). He is currently working on a history of the Ise Shrines (with John Breen).

Hitomi Tonomura is Professor of History and Women's Studies at the University of Michigan. Her areas of study include commerce and merchants, war and violence, and gender and sexuality. Her next book will examine the gendered meanings associated with warfare and the war-prone society of medieval Japan. Her publications include *Community and Commerce in Late Medieval Japan: Sō Villages of Tokuchin-ho* and *Women and Class in Japanese History*.

Charlotte von Verschuer holds a Ph.D. in Oriental studies from Institut National des Langues Orientales (INALCO), in Paris, and a Ph.D. in history from Ecole Pratique des Hautes Etudes (EPHE), in Paris. She has also studied at Bonn University, International Christian University in Tokyo, and the University of Tokyo. Currently Professor of Ancient and Medieval History at EPHE, her main fields are East Asian relations from the seventh to sixteenth centuries, the economy of classical Japan, and the material culture of ancient and medieval Japan. Her publications include translations from *Zenrin kokuhōki* (1470) in *Monumenta Nipponica*; *Les relations officielles du Japon avec la Chine aux VIIIe et IXe siècles*; *Le riz dans la culture de Heian–mythe et réalité*; *Dictionnaire des sources du Japon classique* (*Dictionary of Sources of Classical Japan*) (with Joan Piggott, Ineke Van Put, Ivo Smits, and Michel Viellard-Baron); and *Across the Perilous Sea: Japanese Trade with China and Korea from the Seventh to Sixteenth Centuries*.

Anne Walthall is Professor of Japanese History at the University of California, Irvine. Among her publications are *The Weak Body of a Useless Women: Matsuo Taseko and the Meiji Restoration*; *Servants of the Dynasty: Palace Women in World History* (edited); and *East Asia: A Cultural, Social, and Political History* (coauthored with Patricia Ebrey and James Palais). She is currently researching the biographies of Hirata Atsutane and his descendants from the perspectives of faith and family.

Index